# Smoldering E

## Long and Unnending Wait for Justice for the Dissappeared in Panjab
### (Volume 2)

Voices for Freedom

Booksurge
2007

First published, January 2007

© Voices For Freedom
www.voicesforfreedom.org

Published by: BOOKSURGE.

Printed by: BOOKSURGE.

Cover Design: Allegra Print and Imaging

Address of Publisher: Charleston, South Carolina.

Visit www.booksurge.com to order additional copies.

# Smoldering Embers

# Contents

# Acknowledgments

Voices For Freedom wishes to acknowledge all those who have contributed directly and indirectly in making this report a reality. This report has its genesis in the extensive field work of Mr. Amrik Singh and Mr. Harshinder Singh and other unknown Human Right activists, without whose painstaking efforts this large amount of data would never have seen the light of day.

The data reproduced in chapter "Those Lost Forever" is based on the work of Mr. Amrik Singh and other volunteers who undertook the task on behalf of Voices For Freedom and collected the data of victims who belonged to the other parts of Panjab besides District Amritsar,which is already being enquired into and dealt by the National Human Rights Commission New Delhi for granting compensation to the next of kin of those people who were illegally killed and cremated in the three cremation grounds of District Amritsar.

We would also like to acknowledge the courage of the families of the victims who have come out and given the details of disappearances inspite of an atmosphere of fear and repression.

Though it is not possible to name all those who have been a part of the preparation of this report there are some organizations that we would like to acknowledge, Committee for Coordination of Disappearances in Punjab (CCDP),Association of Families of Disappeared in Punjab (AFDP)and Lawyers for Human Rights International.

Finally though not the least were the members of the Voices For Freedom team who compiled this data and prepared this report. Navkiran Singh (Advocate),Mrs. Paramjeet Kaur Khalra, Sukhinderpal Singh, Advocate, Dalveer Kaur human rights field activist, Meerat Kaur and Sudip Minhas; our team of volunteers Jasdev Singh and Tuvrayn Kaur.

# CONSEQUENCES

## THOSE LEFT BEHIND

As the legal fight to get justice for the disappeared persists, it is increasingly important to remember the effect the disappearances have had and continue to have on those left behind. More than twenty years have passed and the uncertainties surrounding those who have disappeared have left their mark on the everyday life of their children, spouses and parents. The wider community and other children frequently ostracize children of the disappeared. Deemed 'children of militants' they find it difficult to make friends and integrate into the mainstream community. Consequently, the events of 1984 and beyond still haunt them. They survive in the shadows of society unable to live the lives of other young children their age.

The wives, husbands and parents left behind fair no better. The police still take an acute interest in their daily lives, visiting them at regular intervals and especially after they have been visited by international visitors or those working in the human rights or media sectors. Aging parents are now passing away without ever finding out what happened to their children and without anybody accepting responsibility. Spouses struggle to move on, psychologically scarred from what they have witnessed and experienced. They must continue to raise their children, provide for their dependents, and live in a society, which still views them as troublemakers at best and a breed of terrorists at worst.

People simply forget to ask whether it is ever justified for those who are in charge of maintaining law and order to arbitrarily take the lives of people without any attempt of due process of law. As the plight of the families continues to demonstrate, those who have disappeared are increasingly forgotten and the extra judicial killings and forced disappearances are continually dismissed as the only solution that was available to solve the 'militancy' in Panjab. Yet, as persons left behind reiterate, many of those who were disappeared were not involved in the 'militancy movement'.

Such is the case of Paramjeet Kaur and Gurdev Kaur. Paramjeet Kaur is the wife of prominent human rights activist Jaswant Singh Khalra. Gurdev Kaur is the mother of the unfamiliar and unknown Bhupinder Singh Bhinda, an 18-year-old who disappeared in 1993. The two disappeared were strangers to each other, the only connection being the circumstances of their disappearance—picked up by the Panjab police and disappeared in unknown circumstances.

The lives of Paramjeet Kaur and Gurdev Kaur highlight how the plight of the families of the disappeared continues to vary depending on the social and financial status of the family and the level of education of the next of kin. It shows how some families are determined to continue the fight for justice, while other families due to meager social and financial circumstances have little time to worry about family members who are no longer around. Those who continue the fight for justice—to find out what happened to their loved ones and to make the police and other officials accountable for their actions—are those who can afford to do it. As Gurdev Kaur stated, they would rather not have the added burden of another fight. "We have no hope that Bhupinder will return, so it is best to forget the incident ever happened."

Paramjeet Kaur Khalra lives in a very convenient part of Amritsar in a quiet, quaint and clean housing complex with neat gardens and plenty of non-resident Indians. As she led the way down the curved path to her modest dwelling, we paused at the driveway where she told me "this is the spot from which they took Khalra Sahib."

There was no need to explain who "they" were—Paramjeet Kaur is probably the most famous surviving family member of the countless people who have been disappeared by the police in Panjab. Her husband was Jaswant Singh Khalra, a man still held in high regard by Panjabis and the international community for his role in bringing global acceptance and recognition to the mass disappearances in Panjab from 1984 until his own disappearance in 1995. His tireless and unrelenting determination successfully led to the acknowledgement of "the cases of Panjabi Sikhs who were disappeared under the banner of militancy and then tortured, killed and cremated so they could not be identified."[1]

The rainy season was finally ending in Panjab and it was a rather pleasant Wednesday 6 September 1995. Jaswant Singh was washing his car outside his home in Amritsar, Panjab. Paramjeet Kaur was as usual getting ready for work. Her job as an assistant librarian at the well-respected local University was very important to her. Just before leaving, Jaswant Singh told his wife that he was going out that day to continue work on the cases of disappearances in Panjab. This was the last conversation they had.

"As I turned the corner of the street, I saw two police cars standing with a number of officers inside. One of the policemen had his head down but peered at me from above his glasses in a manner, which gave me quite a fright. I thought it was strange to see the police cars, but since many people in the neighborhood were friends with police officers, I thought an officer might have been visiting a friend.

I continued to walk, as I had to arrive at work by 9 a.m. I had just arrived at work and had not even had chance to put my bags down when the phone rang telling me the police had picked up Khalra ji. All the neighbors and everyone in the area had witnessed the event as the police had come in broad daylight. One of the neighbors wrote down the car registration number. The next day, the police arrest of Khalra Sahib was all over the papers and we thought this would compel them to release him. On September 8, when they had still not released him, we made our way to Delhi to file a writ petition.

All this time, the police kept saying they would release Khalra Sahib and then they started saying they would find Khalra Sahib. The police were asked countless times to produce Jaswant Singh Khalra and in November, they gave the answer saying we can't find the man."[2]

The events surrounding the day that Jaswant Singh Khalra disappeared have been recounted many times. Paramjeet Kaur herself states that she has been interviewed many times by researchers, journalists, academics and many others from around the world[3], begging the question, how many times can you retell the same story and yet be only questionably further on the path of justice. Yet, Paramjeet Kaur is a high profile person in the cases of the disappeared in Panjab, making her one of the lucky ones. As she herself states, "it is because of the international support we received from outside India that the police are afraid of us." Gurdev Kaur is not so lucky.

Gurdev Kaur[4] lives in Rangian village, in the Ropar district of Panjab, a picturesque area of the arid state. The family converted the front section of the house into a Gurdwara and lived in the back of the house. Using the more anonymous back entrance to the house means they are further away from the main road and as Gurdev Kaur's frail and sick husband said, "it is safer this way."[5]

The stress caused by the disappearance of her son is visible in Gurdev Kaur. She is suspicious of visitors and their intentions, perhaps fearful of further and continuing repercussions if she speaks to the 'wrong' people. As the visitor slowly gains her trust Gurdev Kaur begins to narrate the incidents surrounding her son's disappearance. She recants the long period of turmoil and torture that the family had experienced and lets the tears flow uninterrupted.

"Bhupinder Singh was not associated with any movement or any militant activity," reiterates Gurdev Kaur. She is fully aware this is often the excuse given for the disappearances, and wants to clarify that her son was an innocent victim. Then she narrates the incidents she would rather forget:

On 29 September 1993, at 4 a.m., a group of police officers from Morinda Police Station came to our house in three vehicles led by SHO[6] Jaswinder Singh Mangat and inquired about Bhupinder Singh. I told them that he and his wife were sleeping in their room and I went to wake up Bhupinder. The police arrested him. We asked them why they were taking our son and where he would be kept. SHO Mangat replied that they wanted him for questioning and we should come in the morning with the Panchayat[7] to Morinda Police Station. At 8 A.M. the next morning, we did as suggested and made our way to the police station where the SHO called Bhupinder's father inside and told him that they would release his son after five days. Yet, Bhupinder was not released so his father and brother-in-law went back to the police station where they spotted him and saw he was in good health. After fifteen days, his father was told that Bhupinder Singh had been sent to Ropar's Central Investigation Agency Staff and had been handed over to DSP[8] Mahinder Singh. However, DSP Mahinder Singh denied having taken Bhupinder Singh into his custody. His father then met with Ropar's Senior Superintendent of Police, Ajit Singh Sandhu, who told him that he would find out where Bhupinder Singh was within eight days. After eight days, his father returned to see Sandhu and was told his son was not in his custody. Since then, we have had no idea of his whereabouts.[9]

Unlike Paramjeet Kaur, Gurdev Kaur would rather forget the incidents surrounding the disappearance of her son than fight for justice. She has no awareness of the campaign for justice, does not understand legal proceedings, and has never heard of the financial compensation that other families have been offered. She is uneducated and struggles to maintain her household as Bhupinder Singh was the sole breadwinner; after his disappearance, they had to lease their land to maintain an income. She has little time to think about justice she may never receive. Indeed, "the disappearance left such an indelible mark on our psyche that we did not make any reports against the police. We still fear the police and we do hope for strict and stringent action against the guilty officers but know to expect little."[10]

The lack of involvement by Gurdev Kaur in the campaign to attain justice for victims like her son is understandable when you realize that she has not received support from any organization involved in the cases of disappearances in Panjab. "We are neither aware of any such organizations, nor of any ruling of the Supreme Court or the National Human Rights Commission and do not even expect any help from these."[11] Her response further highlights the need to provide resources to the organizations working in the area of disappearances in Panjab so that they can extend their arms to all the families, and provide essential and well-placed support and increase awareness of the current campaign. As Paramjeet Kaur maintained, "some people's parents have gone mad. They have had no moral support, and keep wondering over and again what has happened to their child."[12]

Gurdev Kaur and her husband sent Bhupinder's wife back to her parents. They had been married shortly before his disappearance, so his family hoped she would be able to continue her life instead of becoming a lifelong widow. Bhupinder's wife did indeed remarry. In this respect, Bhupinder's wife was lucky. It is becoming increasingly apparent that many families of the disappeared are scared to allow the wives of the disappeared to return to their parents, fearing any future justice or compensation would solely be in the wife's control. Consequently, there are unknown numbers of wives of the disappeared unable to return to their parents' home, and unable to carry on with their lives.

Paramjeet Kaur is carrying on with her life by making her husband's work her life's mission:

"Khalra Sahib gave his life for [the disappearances work] so my mission is to get the unidentified identified. It is my moral duty because although Khalra Sahib and I only spent fifteen years together (since our marriage in 1980) and I learned a lot from him and value our time together. My parents made us study when we were younger and that is why I am still here fighting this fight. They gave me the ability to do that.

I cope because of the dedication I have to complete my mission. I am fighting for others. People need me and that role has helped me a lot. God sends you what you need."[13]

Essentially, Paramjeet Kaur's role in the community has given her the strength that many others do not have. She is often a first point of call for all that are interested in the cases, with mothers and wives of the disappeared regularly seeking her advice, support and knowledge. One elderly mother, whose son disappeared in Patiala, now lives in Amritsar and often comes to visit Paramjeet Kaur. She frequently asks about the hearing events and Paramjeet Kaur provides the latest information, even though the mother does not completely understand the process. This role provides Paramjeet Kaur with a community of support many of the other families do not have and helps her maintain her strength to continue the fight. This support extends to that given by the international community, something about which many other relatives of the disappeared would not even dream.

This international support has been instrumental, as it has prevented Paramjeet Kaur and her family facing the same level of harassment from the police as many other families of the disappeared have. As she herself states:

"It is because of the support we have received from outside India that the police are afraid of us. It is only because of such support that things have not become worse for us. Even then, the children were scared whenever they saw the police, knowing what they were capable of. The police would harass my father-in-law and I, and even my children. They would take us aside and keep pestering us, telling us to drop the case. But, we have had it easier than many."14

When the police harass families like that of Gurdev Kaur, without the same level of fame and international support as Paramjeet Kaur Khalra, they can do so because they have destroyed and dramatically changed the power dynamics of the families. The police manage to create fear by abducting and disappearing either a dominant family member who had an active role in providing income or support to the family, and/or a family member who was the most physically capable. The disappearance of such central individuals creates fear for surviving family members. Since the person that disappears is often the most likely to fight back, the family's own fighting spirit disappears. As the legal system continues to delay any form of justice, and simply prolongs proceedings which few families of the disappear understand, the family's fighting spirit is shattered.

Families without international support consequently have no avenue of resolve when they become victims of police harassment so harassment becomes an effective tool for silencing them. Gurdev Kaur and her family are exemplary of the families of the disappeared, who since they are poor or have limited access to education, would be unlikely to report the disappearance or any further harassment by the police to the authorities or concerned organizations. This is particularly true of families who live in small villages. We cannot force these families who would rather forget the disappearances to join the campaign for justice, especially when no provisions and protections are offered to them. These families know that they could face further police harassment and particularly fear for the safety of younger family members, if the family were to 'cause trouble' for the local law enforcement officials. However, if we can offer support and protections these families may well be inclined to join the campaign rather than forget the events they have experienced.

Although in this chapter, we only interviewed one mother and one wife it reveals how polarized the families of the disappeared can be. In addition it shows that some families still possess little knowledge of the current campaign for justice, while others have such resolute determination that they avow "[the police] can take us in, arrest us, disappear us, but we will keep on fighting."[15] Much more help needs to be given to these families, especially the poorer mothers and wives whose stories are rarely heard and often not repeated. Safe avenues to voice their stories may be a crucial source of empowerment, helping them not only to deal with the psychological and social consequences of the disappearances, but also to enable them to feel powerful enough to join the campaign themselves. Yet, the faith in the Indian justice system is also waning among families and activists alike. The Indian government has promised much , but little has been delivered by the domestic justice system, encouraging few families who have not already shared their stories to highlight the plight of their loved ones. The patriotism, pride and potency which the people of Panjab were once so famous for, is being systematically destroyed, along with their faith in the republic of India:

"In India, you cannot get justice. You can get it outside where people know of their rights, but here people do not know. We fought the fight with our brains using our knowledge of our rights, but not everybody in India can do that. The issues cannot be forgotten and people should publicize it widely—too many people lost their lives for us to simply forget.

I was not afraid of [Jaswant Singh Khalra's] disappearance because I thought India is *our* nation, *our* land and it has a constitution to protect us. Now I do not feel this is our country. Therefore, when my son says he wants to leave the country, I will never attempt to stop him." 16

# NATIONAL HUMAN RIGHTS COMMISSION: WHAT NEXT

**By Navkiran Singh**
Advocate,
Panjab and Haryana High Court

S tate of Panjab underwent a period of turmoil from 1984 to 1994. After the attack on the Holiest Shrine of the Sikhs the Harmandar Sahib at Amritsar, also known as the Golden Temple, a reign of terror was let loose against innocent Sikh youth of Panjab. Special instructions[17] were issued to the Army which attacked Harmandar Sahib on June 4, 1984, that after cleansing the Gurudwara of the armed political activists who had gathered in the Gurudwara under the leadership of Sant Jarnail Singh Bhindranwale, they should look for young Sikhs who were baptised (Amritdhari). The "orders" said that the army should look out for young boys with flowing beards and wearing kirpans, as they were the people who could be the trouble makers in the making. Young Sikhs were hounded by the army as well as the police. Thousands were killed in the days that followed and many out of fear of being humiliated / tortured and then killed left the country.

The attack on the Harmandar Sahib, which is also called "Operation Blue Star" at Amritsar, left a deep scar on the psyche of the Sikhs. The religious sentiments of the Sikhs were deeply hurt as the army action took place at Amritsar on the eve of Martyrdom day of Guru Arjan Dev Jee, the Fifth Guru of the Sikhs and hundreds of innocent devotees, who had come to pay their obeisance at Harmandar Sahib, also lost their lives in the army action. Not only this, the army conducted such actions at scores of other Gurudwaras in whole of India[18], which was seen as an act of aggression by the state in order to demoralise the Sikhs.

Mrs. Indira Gandhi the then Prime Minister of India, was shot dead by her Sikh body guards. This was followed by a massacre of the Sikhs in the whole of India. The unofficial figures[19] reveal that around seven to ten thousand Sikhs were killed within 3 days in the first week of November 1984. To make matters worse the attitude of the State and their perusal of discriminatory policies towards the minorities and in particular towards the Sikhs worsened the situation. The movement of Khalistan, which was initially a social reformist movement was very popular with the people, however with the deep infiltration of Intelligence Agencies into the rank and file of the political activists, the situation worsened and the State took a decision to use force in order to snub the movement of Khalistan and then the era of killing people in "false encounters" and "Involuntary Disappearances" started and from the year 1980 to 1994 armed political activists and their sympathisers including Human Rights Activists, Lawyers, Journalists and Writers were abducted and killed by the State. The State not only targeted the people who were carrying the gun, but also the people who carried the idea of a separate nation for the Sikhs. The people who opposed the oppressive policies of the State were also killed. The worst part was that the dead bodies of those who were abducted and killed, were never handed over to their relatives. The State was apprehensive that by handing over the dead bodies, the killers would be identified and could be brought to the book.

Out of the list of Human Rights Activists, Journalists, Lawyers and Writers who were killed by the State, the name of Mr. Jaswant Singh Khalra a Human Rights Activist who was then working as General Secretary of the Human Rights Wing of Shiromani Akali Dal is on the top. He was instrumental in collecting evidence which disclosed that thousands of young Sikh boys had been killed by the State in Amritsar District and he was able to collect the records of three crematoria in the Amritsar district. In his report, he released a list of around 2500 (twenty five hundred) people who were cremated as unclaimed dead bodies in District Amritsar and Mr. Khalra gave a rough estimate that if this would be the extent of violations in one district, one could easily conclude that in the State of Panjab around 25000 (Twenty five thousand) were eliminated. His report rang the warning bells for the police. The then S.S.P. of Tarn Taran (part of Amritsar district) Mr. Ajit Singh Sandhu who was accused of eliminating maximum number of Sikh youth in Amritsar district, started threatening Mr. Khalra. In those messages he clearly conveyed his intentions. Mr. Khalra used to encourage the victims of the State repression for approaching the court of law for redress of their grievances. Such activities earned him the wrath of the police and on September 6, 1995 he was abducted by Panjab policemen. When his whereabouts could not be known, a telegram was sent to the Supreme Court of India by late Mr. Gurcharan Singh Tohra, the then President of Shiromani Gurudwara Prabandhak Committee and later the wife of Mr. Khalra, Paramjeet Kaur filed writ petition[20] (Criminal) No. 497 of 1995 in the Honorable Supreme Court giving the details of the incident of abduction of her husband at the hands of the police officials in these words as quoted in the judgement :-

"It is alleged in the petition that on September 6, 1995 at about 9.20 A.M. while petitioner's husband J.S. Khalra was washing his car outside the gate of House No. 8, Kabir Park, Amritsar, a Maruti Van, sky blue colour bearing Registration No. BBN-5969 came and stopped close to the place where Mr. Khalra was working. Four uniformed Policemen, with black head dresses (Patkas), and armed with automatic weapons, jumped out of the Van. They had walky-talky instruments with them. They pointed the weapons at Khalra, mishandled him despite his protests and pushed him into the Van from the rear. It is further alleged that the policemen informed through walky-talky to some-one presumably their superior that Khalra had been taken into custody and the job/mission was a success. The Van was followed by an open police Gypsy wherein 4/5 policemen, fully armed were standing and an officer was sitting in the front seat. The Gypsy gave cover to the Maruti Van. It is, thus, alleged in the petition that Khalra was kidnapped by some persons in police uniforms at 9.20 a.m. from a busy residential area of Amritsar".

In the same petition the Honorable Court also dealt with the matter relating to the report released by Mr. Jaswant Singh Khalra pertaining to the cremation of dead bodies in District Amritsar and the court while dealing with the matter reproduced a press note dated January 16, 1995 which was released under the signature of Mr. Khalra and Mr. J.S. Dhillon, both office bearers of the Human Rights Wing of Shiromani Akali Dal. The said paragraph reads as under:-

"The investigation team decided to work in the Amritsar area and its neighbouring police districts. It was learnt that the police regularly bring bodies to the municipality cremation grounds for cremation, declaring them as unclaimed. The team found that 400 unclaimed bodies had been brought for cremation to grounds. Bodies brought to the Patti municipality committees cremation grounds came from as far as Khalra 40 Kms., Kairon 10 Kms, Harika 15 Kms. Valtoha 30 Kms, Bhiki 25 Kms 700 unclaimed bodies to the Tarn Taran municipality cremation grounds. The only record of these unclaimed bodies is available from the receipt book through which firewood was issued for the disposal of the bodies. The receipt book has the date and number of bodies brought recorded on it.

In Amritsar district the maximum unclaimed bodies brought for cremation was to the cremation grounds near the Durgiana Mandir.

From 1st June 1984 to the end of 1994 about 2000 bodies have been cremated as unclaimed. The officials of the Durgiana Mandir cremation grounds expressed their inability to show any records, but suggested that details will be available with the Amritsar Registrar of Births and Deaths. The details which could be gathered at the Registrar's office are given below.

During the 1st year of the govt. of Mr. Beant Singh 300 unclaimed bodies were brought to the Durgiana Mandir cremation grounds by the police department. Out of these 300 bodies names of 112 have been given and the rest were declared as unidentified. 41 persons have been recorded to have died of bullet injuries or police encounters. No reason has been recorded for the cause of the death of 259 persons. Post-mortems were conducted only on 24 bodies by the Amritsar Medical College. No post-mortem was conducted on 276 bodies. 5 bodies of females, as per the record, out of which names of 3 have been recorded. The details of the 3 female bodies are: Harpal Kaur village, Dhulka dated 25.12.1992. Achint Kaur & companion dated 30.9.92.

Two bodies are of those of Kashmiris of Sopore, cause of death, "encounter". One unclaimed body is from, near Chamkaur Sahib, in Ropar District.

Bhagel Singh alias Gurdarshan Singh of village Deriwal was nabbed by the Panjab police in Bihar. Various organisations in Panjab suspected that he was eliminated in a fake encounter. This was around the last week of Nov. or the first week of Dec. /91. On 19.1.1992 the police knowing fully well the identity of Bhagel Singh and his village, brought him to the cremation grounds as an unidentified and unclaimed body.

Mr. Piara Singh S/o Shingara Singh, Director of Central Cooperative Bank in Amritsar, Paternal uncle of Harminder Singh Sultanvind (Militant). Mr. Piara Singh had gone to a relatives' farm in Pilibhit in Uttar Pradesh. One morning a jeep drove up to the farm house, a team of doctors in white coats, sporting stethoscopes approached the residents of the farm requesting them that a VIP was coming to the neighbouring village to inaugurate a govt. medical clinic and some respectable citizens should also grace the occasion. They requested (sic) Mr. Piara Singh to attend the function but he ended up at the Durgiana Mandir cremation ground on 16.12.92.

Mr. Pargat Singh 'Bullet' was undergoing treatment at Guru Nanak Hospital, Amritsar. He was abducted by Raja Sansi police and his "unidentified" body was bought to the Durgiana Mandir cremation grounds on 5.11.92."

Mr. Jaswant Singh Khalra could not be traced and the Honorable

Supreme Court of India in the said writ petition passed the orders on November 15, 1995 and directed the C.B.I. to investigate the matter relating to the abduction of Mr. Khalra as well as the cremation of unidentified dead bodies in the below terms:-

"Mr. M.L. Sareen, learned Advocate-General, Panjab has very fairly stated that keeping in view the serious allegations leveled by the petitioner against the officers/officials of the Panjab Police, it would be in the interest of justice that the investigation in this matter be handed over to an independent authority. Even otherwise, in order to instill confidence in the public-mind and to do justice to the petitioner and his family it would be proper to withdraw the investigation from Panjab Police in this case. We, therefore, direct the Director, Central Bureau of Investigation to appoint an investigation team headed by a responsible officer to hold investigation in the kidnapping and whereabouts of Khalra. We further direct the Director General of Police, Panjab, all concerned Panjab Police Officers, Home Secretary and Chief Secretary, Panjab to render all assistance and help to the CBI in the investigation.

The second issue highlighted in this petition is equally important. This Court cannot close its eyes to the contents of the Press Note dated January 16, 1995 states to be investigated by Khalra and Dhillon. In case it is found that the facts stated in the Press Note are correct—even partially—it would be a gory tale of Human Rights violations. It is horrifying to visualize that dead bodies of large number of persons—allegedly thousands—could be cremated by the police unceremoniously with a label "unidentified". Our faith in democracy and rule of law assures us that nothing of the type can ever happen in this country but the allegations in the Press Note—horrendous as they are—need thorough investigation. We, therefore, direct the Director, Central Bureau of Investigation to investigate into the facts contained in the Press Note dated January 16, 1995. We direct all the concerned authorities of the State of Panjab including the Director General of Police, Panjab to render all assistance to the CBI in the investigation. All authorities of the Panjab Government shall render all help and assistance to the CBI team as and when asked by any member of the said team. We give liberty to the CBI to seek any further directions from this Court from time to time as may be necessary during the investigation.

The CBI shall complete the investigation regarding kidnapping of Khalra within three months of the receipt of this order. So far as the second investigation is concerned we do not fix any time limit but direct the CBI to file interim reports regarding the investigation in this Court after three months."

The CBI, the premier investigation Agency of India filed a charge sheet against certain Panjab Police officials including Mr. Ajit Singh Sandhu (who, during the impending trial, while on bail committed suicide by jumping before a running train) and after a prolonged trial in 2006 certain Panjab police men were convicted of the crime of abduction /killing of Mr. Khalra.

In the meantime the enquiry relating to the cremation of dead bodies as unclaimed in the District of Amritsar was also investigated by the C.B.I. Further the Supreme Court directed the National Human Rights Commission (NHRC) to examine the matter "in accordance with law and determine all the issue which are raised before the commission by the learned counsel for the parties."[21] The Supreme Court had in its order observed that, "Needless to say that the report discloses flagrant violation of human rights on a mass scale."[22] The NHRC started the process of identifying the persons who had been cremated in the cremation grounds of District Amritsar as unclaimed dead bodies.

The NHRC was constituted by the government of India as a response to the international pressure to improve its human rights track record. It came into effect through an act of Parliament in 1993. This act was known as the Protection of Human Rights Act, 1993. It came into effect from September 28, 1993. The functions and powers of the Commission are;

12. Functions of the Commission

The Commission shall perform all or any of the following functions, namely :

(a) inquire, suo motu or on a petition presented to it by a victim or any person on his behalf, into complaint of

(i) violation of human rights or abetment thereof or

(ii) negligence in the prevention of such violation, by a public servant;

(b) intervene in any proceeding involving any allegation of violation of human rights pending before a court with the approval of such court;

(c) visit, under intimation to the State Government, any jail or any other institution under the control of the State Government, where persons are detained or lodged for purposes of treatment, reformation or protection to study the living conditions of the inmates and make recommendations thereon;

(d) review the safeguards provided by or under the Constitution or any law for the time being in force for the protection of human rights and recommend measures for their effective implementation;

(e) review the factors, including acts of terrorism that inhibit the enjoyment of human rights and recommend appropriate remedial measures;

(f) study treaties and other international instruments on human rights and make recommendations for their effective implementation;

(g) undertake and promote research in the field of human rights;

(h) spread human rights literacy among various sections of society and promote awareness of the safeguards available for the protection of these rights through publications, the media, seminars and other available means;

(i) encourage the efforts of non-governmental organisations and institutions working in the field of human rights;

(j) such other functions as it may consider necessary for the protection of human rights.

13. Powers relating to inquiries

(1) The Commission shall, while inquiring into complaints under this Act, have all the powers of a civil court trying a suit under the Code of Civil Procedure, 1908, and in particular in respect of the following matters, namely:

(a) summoning and enforcing the attendance of witnesses and examine them on oath;

(b) discovery and production of any document;

(c) receiving evidence on affidavits;

(d) requisitioning any public record or copy thereof from any court or office;

(e) issuing commissions for the examination of witnesses or documents;

(f) any other matter which may be prescribed.

(2) The Commission shall have power to require any person, subject to any privilege which may be claimed by that person under any law for the time being in force, to furnish information on such points or matters as, in the opinion of the Commission, may be useful for, or relevant to, the subject matter of the inquiry and any person so required shall be deemed to be legally bound to furnish such information within the meaning of section 176 and section 177 of the Indian Penal Code.

(3) The Commission or any other officer, not below the rank of a Gazetted Officer, specially authorised in this behalf by the Commission may enter any building or place where the Commission has reason to believe that any document relating to the subject matter of the inquiry may be found, and may seize any such document or take extracts or

copies therefrom subject to the provisions of section 100 of the Code of Criminal Procedure, 1973, in so far as it may be applicable.

(4) The Commission shall be deemed to be a civil court and when any offence as is described in section 175, section 178, section 179, section 180 or section 228 of the Indian Penal Code is committed in the view or presence of the Commission, the Commission may, after recording the facts constituting the offence and the statement of the accused as provided for in the Code of Criminal Procedure, 1973, forward the case to a Magistrate having jurisdiction to try the same and the Magistrate to whom any such case is forwarded shall proceed to hear the complaint against the accused as if the case has been forwarded to him under section 346 of the Code of Criminal Procedure, 1973.

(5) Every proceeding before the Commission shall be deemed to be a judicial proceeding within the meaning of sections 193 and 228, and for the purposes of section 196, of the Indian Penal Code, and the Commission shall be deemed to be a civil court for all the purposes of section 195 and Chapter XXVI of the Code of Criminal Procedure, 1973.

14. Investigation

(1) The Commission may, for the purpose of conducting any investigation pertaining to the inquiry, utilise the services of any officer or investigation agency of the Central Government or any State Government with the concurrence of the Central Government or the State Government, as the case may be.

(2) For the purpose of investigating into any matter pertaining to the inquiry, any officer or agency whose services are utilised under sub-section (1 ) may, subject to the direction and control of the Commission.

(a) summon and enforce the attendance of any person and examine him;

(b) require the discovery and production of any document; and

(c) requisition any public record or copy thereof from any office.

(3) The provisions of section 15 shall apply in relation to any statement made by a person before any officer or agency whose services are utilised under sub-section (1 ) as they apply in relation to any statement made by a person in the course of giving evidence before the Commission.

(4) The officer or agency whose services are utilised under sub-section (1 ) shall investigate into any matter pertaining to the inquiry and submit a report thereon to the Commission within such period as may be specified by the Commission in this behalf.

(5) The Commission shall satisfy itself about the correctness of the facts stated and the conclusion, if any, arrived at in the report subbed to it under sub-section (4) and for this purpose the Commission may make such inquiry (including the examination of the person or persons who conducted or assisted in the investigation) as it thinks fit.[23]

The Commission vide its proceedings dated 28th January 1997, desired to know from the parties and their learned counsel their views "as to the scope and ambit of the subject-matter before the Commission... and the capacity in which the Commission was to function: whether under within the pale of the Protection of Human Rights Act, 1993 ('Act' for short) on the premise that the mandate of Supreme Court has had the effect of removing the bar of limitation under section 36(2)[24] of the Act or whether the NHRC is designated sui-generis to perform certain functions and adjudicate certain issues entrusted and referred to it by the Supreme Court". The counsels were asked to "clarify what according to them is the concept and content of the idea of compensation referred for determination by the Commission."[25]

In taking up the matter the NHRC limited its scope to compensations and left out a major aspect of holding the guilty police officers/ agencies accountable for the disappearances. This was further limited to the three crematoria of Amritsar district. Repeated pleas and petitions to widen the scope of the enquiry were rejected by the Supreme Court and the NHRC. It stated that the, "the Commission considers it fair to say that the scope of the inquiry under the Supreme Court's direction, is limited only to those illegal killings / disappearances that culminated in the cremation of 2097 bodies (585 bodies fully identified, 274 bodies partially identified and 1238 bodies unidentified) in the crematoria located at Durgyana Mandir, Patti Municipal Committee Crematorium and Tarn Taran Crematorium located in the Police districts of Amritsar, Majitha and Tarn Taran, which were also the subject matter of inquiry by the CBI in pursuance of the Order of Supreme Court dated 15th November 1995. The contention of the Petitioners to the contrary that the Commission should undertake an investigation of all the alleged Police killings in the State of Punjab, apart from being extremely expansive in nature, does not seem to square or be reconcilable with the express terms of the Court's remit".[26]

The NHRC was seized of the matter regarding 2097 dead bodies since 1997 out of which after seeking claims from the general public, it came to light that 1245 bodies were identified and that the actual total figures were 2059 instead of 2097. The NHRC vide its order dated October 10, 2006 granted compensation of Rs. 175,000 to the next of the kin of 1051 persons who were cremated as unidentified dead bodies, but now have been identified. These cases were other than those in which compensation of Rs. 250,000 was awarded by the NHRC vide its order dated November 11, 2004, initially to 109 claimants, but which arose to a figure of 194 till date, as in these cases the State of Panjab admitted that these 194 persons were admittedly in custody of the Panjab police, before their being cremated as unclaimed dead bodies. The NHRC vide its latest order dated October 10, 2006 had referred the case of 814 dead bodies which could not be identified by the State, to special Commissioner retired High Court Justice K.S. Bhalla, who has been directed by the NHRC to complete the enquiry of identification of dead bodies within a period of 8 months.

The latest order of NHRC dated October 10, 2006 has shattered the hopes of families of the victims of the State repression who had faced the wrath of the Panjab police during period 1984 to 1994. On the one hand the families lost their near and dear ones, while on the other hand due to loss of the earning hand the families were forced into conditions of sheer penury. The children of the victims had to remain without schooling, many widows were turned out of the matrimonial homes, young girls could not be married at the right age, young boys were stigmatized and were further harassed by the police being off springs of slain armed political activists. The old parents of the victims had to live under the suspense as to whether their young children were dead or alive. The trauma through which the people of Panjab went through cannot be described in words.

The NHRC at the initial stages moved in the right directions when it had called for claims from individuals through public notices and the activists of CCDP and other organisations and individuals worked hard in assisting the NHRC in procuring the claims from individuals and the activists personally filled up forms, which were supplied by the NHRC. But through its order dated October 10, 2006 it has exhibited total insensitivity and non seriousness towards the Human Rights of the people of the Panjab. The NHRC has abandoned the line of action being pursued by it on the basis of which 194 claims of people who were admittedly in custody of the police and were later on cremated as unclaimed dead bodies, as it has now made a u-turn and has now only confined itself to the issue of cremation of dead bodies as unclaimed and granted compensation to the tune of Rs. 175,000 to the next of the kin of 1051 identified dead persons and has remitted the remaining 814 cases to the Special Commissioner.

The Commission also decided in favour of the CBI's plea to keep their findings secret. It reasoned that the, "their objection is that the access to the contents of the documents to the claimants / complainants / Public Police officials would hamper smooth investigation."[27] The NHRC was under a moral obligation to address the issue of holding an enquiry by asking the people to lead evidence to the effect as to whether the 1051 identified plus 814 still to be identified were ever in custody before their being cremated as unclaimed dead bodies. The NHRC has failed to appreciate the arguments placed before it in the shape of written submissions by the counsels for Mrs. Paramjit Kaur Khalra and CCDP. The reasoning given by the NHRC that it does not need to go into this aspect also does not appeal to logic, as it itself had granted compensation to the tune of Rs. 250,000 to the next of the kin of 194 people who were admitted by the State of being in their custody , but closing the case on the face of the claimants by not giving the Special Commissioner powers to hold an enquiry into this aspect, gives us a reason to believe that the NHRC changed its mind to even wipe the tears of the victim families at this belated stage. The decision of the NHRC has sealed the fate of the victim families and is a betrayal of the confidence which was reposed by the people of Panjab in NHRC during its prolonged 10 years sittings.

There are Human rights groups that are committed and are determined to ensure that justice is delivered to the people of Panjab who have already been discriminated by the Akali Government as well as the Congress Government, as these governments have failed to help the families in rehabilitation, whereas the civilians as well as the employees of the State who lost their life during the turmoil period in Panjab have been suitably compensated by giving ex-gratia grants, job reservations, pensions and other benefits, whereas the people who were involved in the political movement in the State of Panjab and lost their lives at the hands of the State functionaries have been totally ignored by the successive governments of the Akalis and the Congress

These Human Rights groups have resolved to stand by the families of the Amritsar district who have now to lead evidence in order to prove that the 814 dead bodies belong to their near ones, so that the families can be compensated. In this regard "Lawyers For Human Rights International" and "Association For Families Of Disappeared Persons" have resolved to provide free legal aid to the families who have to stake their claims before the Special Commission and to also extend moral support to them. An office has been opened at Amritsar, where Lawyers and activists are helping the families to identify their near ones, so that they could be compensated.

Panjab as a whole has undergone a period of turmoil from 1984 to 2004, but how can the courts entertain claims for compensation only to the people who were illegally cremated in the Cremation grounds of Amritsar District only. The Honorable Supreme Court of India refused to enlarge the scope of the reference made to the National Human Rights Commission and restricted the enquiry only to the 3 cremation grounds of the Amritsar District. There are still questions that remain to be answered.

- What about those people who were abducted from Amritsar and killed in false encounters in other Districts?
- What about those people who have undergone similar violations in other Districts?
- What about the people who were abducted from whole of Panjab and their whereabouts are not known till date?
- If the guilty elsewhere can be sentenced to death for similar crimes why not the security agencies and the police officers? Why should they be granted impunity?

The Indian Courts have failed to respond and address these important issues, the people of Panjab now only see hope either in the international law or international pressure upon the Governments of New Delhi and Panjab .

# ACKNOWLEDGING THE PAST: ESTABLISHING A TRUTH COMMISSION

No healing takes place on the buried sands of the past. For healing to become a corrective process, we have to admit and rectify the mistakes of the past and that depends on how our systems of justice bring the culprits and perpetrators of crimes against humanity to face the consequences of their misdeeds. No forgiveness depends on obliteration of the past, as time can never be severed from its chains. "True reconciliation might depend on a clear end to the threat of further violence; a reparations program for those injured; attention to structure inequalities and basic material needs of victimized communities; the existence of natural linkages in society that bring formerly opposing parties together..."[28] History remains an essential part of our cultural existence, our sense of who we are and what we are made of. To take us away from our roots is to take us away from our identity. To ask a community to move on without acknowledging its painful past is to take its existence out of context. Half-truths, misunderstandings and myths abound when we and all those who feel the large-scale responsibility of seeking justice on behalf of others relinquish their efforts in seeking truth. In an effort to serve the purpose of justice, it is essential that those responsible for large-scale violence against the Sikhs, a religious minority in India, be tried according to the law of the land. Truth Commissions have been appointed around the world to investigate human rights violations; such a Commission must be created in India. The States have a duty and they are obligated to prosecute and punish those who commit the crime. A duty made more so important as a large number of those who abused the power of the State remain unpunished. The weight of the number of disappeared in Panjab and other states should serve as persuasion to the NHRC to make amendments in its terms of reference.

"The world now seems to be confronting questions of justice and accountability at every turn...it has become clear, however, that there are a whole range of needs arising out of these circumstances that cannot be satisfied by actions in the court—even if the courts function well and there are no limits placed on prosecuting the wrongdoers. Many alternative and complementary approaches to accountability have thus slowly taken shape. The concrete needs of victims and communities damaged by the violence will not be addressed through such prosecutions, except of course in providing some solace if the perpetrators are successfully prosecuted. The institutional or societal conditions that allowed the massive abuses to take place—the structures of the armed forces, the judiciary, or the laws that should constrain actions of officials, for example—may remain unchanged even as a more democratic and less abusive government comes into place. Many questions may remain open about exactly what took place during the years of repression, and tensions between communities may continue to fester, or deepen, if these are left unaddressed."[29]

**Why a Truth Commission?**

One painfully clear aspect of the situation in India is the glaring inability of the judicial system and the political will either to investigate crimes or to enforce the law, especially when it comes to crimes committed with the direct or indirect support of the State. It is because of these shortcomings that the demand to create an instrument such as a Truth Commission is needed to perform tasks, which should normally have been undertaken by the bodies responsible for the administration of justice. Had the judiciary functioned satisfactorily, the violations would never have taken place or had violations occurred the judiciary would have imposed penalties on the erring officials. The inability of the courts to apply the law to acts of violence committed under the direct or indirect cover of the public authorities is the cause célèbre and the reason for outside intervention. It is not always within such Truth Commissions' powers to directly impose penalties on those responsible because most of the times these commissions do not have judicial functions and therefore do not have the ability to impose a particular penalty on a person found liable for the crimes. That is a function, which by its nature, properly belongs to the courts, a question which raises serious problems for any commission. It is through such complexities that the victims and their families will have to tackle a way forward.

The reason demand for Truth Commissions in areas of conflict has risen and more and more commissions are being established is to get to the truth and nothing but the truth. As one of the Truth Commissions said, "Learning the truth and strengthening and tempering the determination to find it out; putting an end to impunity and cover-up; settling political and social differences by means of agreement instead of violent action: these are the creative consequences of an analytical search for the truth."[30]

**Some Truth Commissions**
**Chile**

It would not be out of place to look into the commissioning of other Truth Commissions and their success in tracking and bringing into public consciousness the crimes against humanity which otherwise remain in anonymity. The Chilean *National Commission on Truth and Reconciliation* is one such example of unearthing the truth bringing about reconciliation. It was set up after the return of popular democratic government in Chile. The country had suffered for a long time under the repressive rule of its military dictator Augusto Pinochet Ugarte. The Commission had a clear mandate to:

- To establish as complete a picture as possible of those grave events, as well as their antecedents and circumstances;
- To gather evidence that might make it possible to identify the victims by name and determine their fate or whereabouts;
- To recommend such measures of reparation and the restoration of people's good name as it regarded as just; and
- To recommend the legal and administrative measures, which in its judgment should be adopted in order to prevent further grave human rights violations from being committed.[31]

The findings of the report, which came to be known as the Rettig Report recorded damaging findings against the Pinochet administration. It brought to light the many disappearances inflicted upon political opponents of the Pinochet administration. The DINA (National Intelligence Directorate)[32] was to gather information from around the nation for the purpose of planning a national security policy.. It was mainly manned by the armed forces personnel and occasionally by civilians. Headed by Pinochet it had almost limitless powers. In the period from 1974 to 1977, the Junta progressively repressed any political group that had any existence in Chile. Successive constitutional acts eradicated any political resistance. Later the DINA was dissolved and in its place, another organization called CNI[33] (National Center for Information) was instituted with even greater authority. The period from 1978 to 1990 marked an increase in Human Rights violations and forced disappearances of political opponents.

The Truth Commission set out to document these violations in a systematic manner. It looked into various factors leading to these violations and it examined every aspect of the Government in its attempt to realize the extent of the violations and the impunity, which the institutions enjoyed. In one of its observations the Commission had this to say of the Judiciary "This Commission believes it must deal with the posture of the judicial branch toward the most serious human rights violations; otherwise, it would be impossible to present an overall picture of what took place in this regard as its founding supreme decree requires it to do.

During the period in question the judicial branch did not respond vigorously enough to human rights violations. That fact combined with other factors such as the conditions of that period, restrictions imposed by an array of special laws and the general lack of resources, particularly with help from the police, prevented the judicial branch from truly working to protect the essential rights of persons when those rights were jeopardized, threatened or crushed by government officials, or by private citizens operating with the complicity or tolerance of those officials...After a very rigorous examination, this Commission concluded that more than two thousand people were killed as a result of human rights violations attributable to government agents during this period, most of them as a result of political repression. It can be said that, a few exceptional cases apart, the courts did not investigate these events, which were violations of human rights, nor were guilty parties punished."[34] Such incisive and damaging findings ultimately led to the world's recognition and acknowledgement of the gross violations that had taken place. The realization of truth leads to the reparation that each victim demands. The loss of a loved one is irreparable but those responsible for this loss must be brought to justice and this is the primary function of a Truth Commission as envisioned by the various Commissions currently working and those that have submitted their recommendations.

The Commission made certain recommendations about social welfare and politics suggesting administrative reforms. It also recommended restoration of dignity and the "good name" of the victims and their families. As part of the "most urgent recommendations", it recommended prevention of Human Rights abuses, which it believed could be achieved through a culture that respects human rights and the strengthening of the public law system. Finally, the Commission created the Public Law Foundation, designed to continue the Commission's unfinished business. The Commission maintained that the "functions of the proposed foundation should be to keep searching. To that end it should be authorized to become a plaintiff in judicial investigations that may be carried out for that purpose, and it should have access to the initial summary investigation, and in general it should enjoy such faculties as may facilitate its work."[35] The most commendable outcome of this commission was that Mr. Pinochet was arrested in London, England on one of his foreign tours for the crimes committed during and under his rule. This arrest was largely a result of a growing feeling among democratic nations that a human rights violator could be arrested no matter which nation he was in, his absence from the country of crime did not make him immune to justice and prosecution. Human Rights Watch hailed his arrest and José Miguel Vivanco, executive director of Human Rights Watch's Americas division commented that "This arrest is a great victory for Pinochet's thousands of victims. It does credit to Chilean democracy and to its legal system. Judge Guzman has conducted a very thorough and careful investigation."[36]

**Argentina and the Dirty War**

Following the coup against Isabel Perón, the Argentinean armed forces formally exercised power through a junta led consecutively by Videla, Viola, Galtieri and Bignone until December 10, 1983. These *de facto* leaders termed their government program "National Reorganization Process." Based on this program, the ruling junta attempted to start an economic recovery by favoring some pro-market reforms and deregulation, but it was mainly employed as a disguise for the ongoing disappearance, torture and murder of thousands of suspected political dissidents and leftists.

The expression "national reorganization process" was used to imply orderliness and control of the critical sociopolitical situation of Argentina at the time, but the dictatorial regime soon showed its true aim. Forced disappearances on ideological grounds and illegal arrests, often based on unsubstantiated accusations, became common. Armed soldiers arrived at randomly selected people's houses to rob them. The police would pull over cars for no reason, beat the occupants senseless, and leave without explanation, as part of a program to intimidate the populace and decrease its willingness to protest against the government. Government spies were dispatched to infiltrate the universities; students who openly professed even slightly leftist political opinions would simply disappear. Official investigations undertaken after the end of the Dirty War documented the "disappearance" of about nine thousand persons, noting nevertheless that the correct number is bound to be higher, since many cases were not reported and the records were destroyed by the military authority; unofficial estimates by most human rights organizations place the number closer to 30,000[37]. Among the "disappeared" were pregnant mothers whose babies were then illegally adopted by military families. SIDE secret service also cooperated with

DINA and other South American intelligence agencies in Operation Condor.[38]

Using the terrorist tactics adopted by the Montoneros (left-wing Peronists) and Trotskyist Ejército Revolucionario del Pueblo (Revolutionary Army of the People or ERP) as justification, the armed forces, among them the *Batallón de Inteligencia 601* and SIDE the infamous equivalent of the DINA, used inhuman measures against all who opposed or were suspected of opposing the dictatorship. The "ideological war" doctrine of the Argentine military focused on eliminating the social base of insurgency. In practice that meant liquidating many middle class students, intellectuals and labor organizers, most of whom had few ties to the guerrillas they were suspected of supporting. By the end of the 1970s, such tactics had suppressed the insurgents, but Argentina had suffered terribly.

The costs of the "Dirty War" were high in terms of lives lost and the violation of basic human rights. About 1,500 deaths were attributed to various guerrilla attacks and assassinations. The 1984 Commission on the Disappeared[39] documented the disappearance and probable death at the hands of the military regime at about 11,000 people. Human rights groups estimate that over 30,000 persons "disappeared" during the 1976–1983 period; and many others may have gone into exile. Few dared speak out, except for the very few like an organization Mothers of the Plaza de Mayo[40], mothers of the dead and disappeared, who began holding vigils in April 1977, demanding (unsuccessfully) an accounting for these crimes.

Following the humiliating defeat of Argentina at the hands of the UK in the Falklands War, serious economic problems, mounting charges of corruption and mounting public revulsion in the face of human rights abuses, the Argentine military regime was discredited. Under strong public pressure, the junta lifted bans on political parties and gradually restored basic political liberties.

On October 30, 1983, Argentines went to the polls in elections considered by international observers to be fair and honest. Raúl Alfonsín created the National Commission on the Disappearance of Persons (CONADEP), led by Argentine writer Ernesto Sábato. However, in a very controversial decision he granted amnesty to all acts committed before December 10, 1983. It would not be until June 2005 after the Supreme Court's decision to overturn all amnesty laws that investigations could once again move forward.

"The Commission staff inspected detention centers, clandestine cemeteries, and public facilities; exiles returned from abroad to testify;

and statements were taken in Embassies and Consulates of Argentina around the world. The Commission also worked closely with families of the disappeared to locate persons who might still be alive, but it found none. The Commission took over 7,000 statements over nine months' time, documenting 8,960 persons who had disappeared. Among those interviewed were over 1,500 people who had survived the military's detention camps, who gave detailed descriptions of conditions in the camps and the kinds of torture used. The Commission's primary investigations focused on identifying detention and torture camps, often visiting former camps with survivors to assist in confirming their locations. A list of 365 former torture centers is included in the commission's final report, with accompanying photographs of a number of them. After nine months the Commission submitted its full report, Nunca Mas (Never Again), to the President."[41]

## El Salvador: The Civil War and the Reconciliation:

In the 1980s, El Salvador was ravaged by a bitter civil war. This was a result of gross inequality between a small and wealthy elite, which dominated the government and the economy, and the overwhelming majority of the population, who continue to live in abject squalor and poverty. The United States was actively supporting the government throughout these years supplying them with money and military equipment fearing infiltration into the Americas of outside terrorists. Reagan's policies were criticized by his own congress and internationally. The war left around 70,000 people dead and caused damage worth $2 billion.

The Truth Commission was established as a part of the UN brokered peace accord. The Chilean truth commission served as the reference point for establishing this commission. The UN accord had agreed to set up a Commission in April 1991 just a year after the Chilean Truth Commission had presented its report. This commission was funded by the contributing countries of the UN the US being its largest contributor. "The signatories to the accord considered specifying exactly which cases should be investigated by the commission, but they were unable to come to an agreement on key cases, and thus left its mandate open, indicating only that it should investigate "serious acts of violence" that occurred since 1980 whose 'impact on society urgently demands that the public should know the truth.'"[42]

The Commissioners appointed for the job were Belisario Betancur as Chairman and Reinaldo Figueredo Planchart and Thomas Buergenthal as member commissioners.

The Commission upon its introduction summed up the violence that had engulfed this nation:

"Violence was a fire which swept over the fields of El Salvador; it burst into villages, cut off roads and destroyed highways and bridges, energy sources and transmission lines; it reached the cities and entered families, sacred areas and educational centers; it struck at justice and filled the public administration with victims; and it singled out as an enemy anyone who was not on the list of friends. Violence turned everything to death and destruction, for such is the senselessness of that breach of the calm plenitude which accompanies the rule of law, the essential nature of violence being suddenly or gradually to alter the certainty which the law nurtures in human beings when this change does not take place through the normal mechanisms of the rule of law. The victims were Salvadorians and the foreigners of all backgrounds and all social and economic classes, for in its blind cruelty violence leaves everyone equally defenseless."[43]

The commission interviewed and took testimony from over two thousand victims and witnesses. It recorded tortures, disappearances, abductions and killings. "The Commission on the Truth registered more than 22,000 complaints of serious acts of violence that occurred in El Salvador between January 1980 and July 1991. Over 7,000 were received directly at the Commission's offices in various locations. The remainder were received through governmental and non-governmental institutions.

Over sixty per cent of all complaints concerned extrajudicial executions, over twenty-five per cent concerned enforced disappearances, and over twenty per cent included complaints of torture.

Those giving testimony attributed almost eighty-five per cent of cases to agents of the State or paramilitary groups allied either to the State or death squads.

Armed forces personnel were accused in almost sixty per cent of complaints, members of the security forces in approximately twenty-five per cent, members of military escorts and civil defence units in approximately twenty per cent and members of the death squads in more than ten per cent of cases...Despite their large number, these complaints do not cover every act of violence. The Commission was able to receive only a significant sample in its three months of gathering testimony."[44]

For the purpose of making a systematic understanding of the whole period of violence, the Commission divided the years 1980-1991 into four periods, 1980-83, 1983-87, 1987-89 and 1989-91. "Each of these periods corresponds to political changes in the country, developments in the war and the systematic nature or frequency of certain practices that violated human rights and international humanitarian law."[45] It also performed some case studies to highlight the atrocities and the manner in which the Human Rights of these victims were violated. The report makes a clear mention of where International Human Rights were applicable and the approach necessary for the redress of the victims' grievances through its application. In their illustrative examples it took cases under the heading of the murder of the Political Opponents of the ruling party, Jesuit priests, Extra Judicial Killings, Enforced Disappearances, killing of the Judges and the Massacre of the Peasants. The report in its conclusion gave a hard-hitting indictment of the Armed Forces naming many top-level officials. The Commission recommended that these high level officials be dismissed from the Armed Forces, Civil Service jobs and disqualified from holding public office. In a serious indictment of their acts the Commission observed that "The findings on the cases investigated by the Commission on the Truth and published in this report give the names of officers of the Salvadorian Armed Forces who are personally implicated in the perpetration or cover-up of serious acts of violence, or who did not fulfill their professional obligation to initiate or cooperate in the investigation and punishment of such acts."[46] The controversial Amnesty took the momentum out of the process of getting these people punished but the most important achievement from the Commission's report were the many judicial reforms that were initiated after it was released. As part of the peace process, it suggested new procedures for the selection of Supreme Court Judges. The establishment of a National Council of the Judiciary completely independent of interference from the Supreme Court and their members can only be dismissed for strictly legal reasons by the Legislative Assembly.

### Greensboro Truth Commission

Another very relevant truth commission from our perspective was the Greensboro Truth and Reconciliation Commission constituted to bring out the facts of the infamous massacre of five anti-clan demonstrators on November 3, 1979 in Greensboro, North Carolina, USA. This commission was a result of insufficient steps taken by the administration to heal the wounds of the victims with integrity and honesty. Three trials before the present truth commission was instituted had acquitted the shooters of any racial hostility. This resulted in a public outcry but nothing came of it. The commission members termed it as "Injustice in the justice system." The all white jury had obviously been biased in their judgment. The Commission also mentioned that the under-representation of the minorities and the poor on the jury panel was a major reason for such lop-sided judgments.

The Greensboro massacre occurred on November 3, 1979 in Greensboro, North Carolina. It was the culmination of attempts by the Maoist Communist Workers Party (CWP) to organize industrial workers, predominantly black, in the area. The Ku Klux Klan members killed five CWP marchers. They were: Sandy Smith, a nurse and a civil rights activist; Dr. James Waller, president of a local textile workers union who gave up his medical practice to defend workers; Bill Sampson, a Harvard University graduate in the school of divinity; Cesar Cause, an immigrant from Cuba who graduated magna cum laude from Duke University; and Dr. Michael Nathan, chief of pediatrics at Lincoln Community Health Center in Durham, NC, a clinic that helped children from low-income families. It began as a peaceful rally and a lawful one as well when the protestors agreed to abide by the orders of the police not to carry firearms. According to accounts on that day Klansmen and members of the American Nazi Party opened fire on the demonstrators injuring several and killing five. This massacre was filmed by local journalists and remains strong evidence of the unprovoked firing.

The mandate of the commission as laid out below had peace and reconciliation as major factors for its function.

The Greensboro Truth and Community Reconciliation Project, including the signers of its Declaration, calls for the examination of the context, causes, sequence and consequence of the events of November 3, 1979.

We affirm that the intention of this examination shall be:

a)  Healing and reconciliation of the community through discovering and disseminating the truth of what happened and its consequences in the lives of individuals and institutions, both locally and beyond Greensboro.

b)  Clarifying the confusion and reconciling the fragmentation that has been caused by these events and their aftermath, in part by educating the public through its findings.

c)  Acknowledging and recognizing people's feelings, including feelings of loss, guilt, shame, anger and fear.

d)  Helping facilitate changes in social consciousness and in the institutions that were consciously or unconsciously complicit in these events, thus aiding in the prevention of similar events in the future.

This examination is not for the purpose of exacting revenge or recrimination.[47]

In their conclusion, they indicted the judicial system, which had let to the acquittal of the police officers. They found that the process of jury selection was biased and the roots of injustice lay in the way the people were commissioned for the jury. Had the jury selection been fair the police would not have been exonerated. The Commission said: "We find a problematic jury selection process led to producing panels unrepresentative of the community due to many factors including the following:

- Until 1986, it was entirely legal to strike a potential juror from the panel based on his or her race;
- Sources of jury pools under-represent the poor and people of color.

We believe that the unrepresentative juries undoubtedly contributed significantly to the verdicts."[48]

Like many other truth commissions, this commission also decided to make positive suggestions rather than intrude in the judicial process and proclaim punishments on the guilty. In the same essence they asked the " Individuals who were responsible for any part of the tragedy of November 3, 1979, should reflect on their role and apologize—publicly and/or privately—to those harmed."[49] This responsibility was also fixed on the city of Greensboro as it was asked to tender an apology to the family of the victims and especially to the Communist Workers Party demonstrators, Morningside Homes residents, media representatives and others present at the shooting. This apology was a way of asking the authorities to acknowledge the wrong that had been committed on that fateful day. Many individuals did in fact apologize during the course of the investigation.

One factor which makes this Commission's findings and the sequence of events of the judicial process adopted by the Greensboro administration similar to the National Human Rights Commissions (NHRC) continued judgments in the Panjab Cremations case is the financial settlement of the issue. For instance, the civil trial in Greensboro (which incidentally had one black jury member) resulted in the US police along with the white supremacists being found guilty of wrongful death and liable for monetary damages. The city agreed to pay "$400,000 in settlement to all defendants, including the Klan and Nazi defendants, in exchange for plaintiff's release of all defendants from future civil action."[50] This action reflected on the city as condoning the acts of the Klan and the Nazis.

The NHRC's judgments in the Panjab Cremations case have a similar trajectory in their interpretation turning down of the plea to extend the purview of its findings to other districts of Panjab. It decided to make the compensation to victims of Human Rights abuse or more appropriately to the family of the disappeared in the form of monetary allowance reasoning thus: "that monetary or pecuniary compensation is an appropriate and indeed an effective and sometimes perhaps the only suitable remedy for redressal of the established infringement of the fundamental right of life of a citizen by the public servants and the State is vicariously liable for their acts."[51]

The Greensboro Commission concluded that the Greensboro incident had several negative effects that the people directly and indirectly suffered. According to the report there was apart from the psychological trauma, strained relationship, separations, economic and social isolation, which included loss of employment and economic hardships and race and class tensions. The same analogy can be extended to the sufferings of the people in Panjab. The families of the disappeared in Panjab and adjoining areas continue to suffer ignominy as they are tainted as the "terrorists" just because the police or the armed forces arbitrarily eliminated or killed their family members. The Greensboro Commission remains a landmark in the US for bringing to fore the failure of the judicial system and the partisan police. The Commission believed that the first step towards reconstructive reparation is admission of wrong-doing. It believed "Nothing can restore a loved one's life that has been taken, or fully restore the health and well-being of those battered by the events, but we believe that some meaningful gestures toward acknowledgment and redress can help those most harmed see a better future ahead. We believe that facing the truth about the past is an important first step toward repair."[52] It suggested that the city of Greensboro should formally acknowledge the events of November 3, 1979 as tragic and those directly or indirectly responsible for the incident should apologize publicly for the incident and reflect on their role. The police and the City officials were asked to tender apologies to the public. Others who either publicly or privately regretted their role should offer restitution to the funds being raised for the victims. It also suggested that the religious community of Greensboro should plan and facilitate healing workshops and camps for the children of the victims.

Another important recommendation of the Commission was to make institutional reforms in the administrative set up. Most important was the proposition to include anti-racism training for all city employees and for the state justice systems; the lack of conviction of the guilty and the limits of retributive justice led to the Commission making the suggestion that there should be a community justice center for Greensboro. The extensive suggestions by the Commission point towards an important element of social interaction and that is progress of a community is based on acknowledgement and learning form past experiences.

### Guatemala

In another very relevant Truth Commission the counterinsurgency operations of the extreme right wing in Guatemala employed extremely brutal strategies to assassinate students, villagers, political opponents or anyone suspected of having sympathy for the left. The extreme right-wing groups of self-appointed vigilantes, including the Secret Anti-Communist Army (ESA) and the White Hand (La Mano Blanca), tortured and murdered students, professionals, and peasants suspected of involvement in leftist activities. It was during the autocratic rule of General Ydígoras Fuentes that many junior officers of his army revolted and formed what later became the guerilla forces. They became the nucleus of the forces that were in armed insurrection against the government for the next thirty-six years. The civil war continued until the late eighties, but low-level conflict continued well into the nineties when the UN brokered the peace. Ríos Montt's brief presidency was probably the most violent period of the thirty-six year internal conflict. It resulted in thousands of deaths of mostly unarmed indigenous civilians. Although leftist guerrillas and right-wing death squads also engaged in summary executions, forced disappearances, and torture of noncombatants, the vast majority of human rights violations were carried out by the Guatemalan military and the PACs (civilian defense patrols) they controlled. Another aspect of the government's interference was the way that people were recruited for the PACs, participation was in theory voluntary, but in practice, many rural Guatemalan men (including young boys and the elderly) had no choice but to either join the PACs or be labeled as guerrillas.

"Among the most controversial issues on the table during the negotiations was the question of how past human rights abuses would be addressed during the transition to peace...Most significant was that the Guatemalan armed forces leadership insisted that the Salvadoran model of naming perpetrators would not be repeated in Guatemala."[53]

After considerable discussions amongst various civil groups and victims groups and their interests, the final commission was set up with many restrictions that these groups vehemently opposed. Among the many provisions was the following, which the victims groups were not expecting to be the direction of the investigation, "The Commission shall not attribute responsibility to any individual in its work, recommendations and report nor shall these have any judicial aim or effect."[54] However, the integrity and the earnestness of the Commissioners appointed with a non-Guatemalan as the chair of the Commission, finally brought these groups back into the fold with their confidence restored.

Facing an uphill task in getting to the victims in many remote villages in order to get the information the Commission members "requested the declassification of files from the U.S. government, with the assistance of a nongovernmental organization in Washington, D.C., the National Security Archive. This resulted in the successful declassification of thousands of documents, including detailed information sufficient for the National Security Archive to build a database outlining the structure and personnel of the armed forces in Guatemala over many years' time."[55] Far less information was available from the Guatemalan armed forces. Many other nongovernmental organizations such as the Catholic Church's Project for the Recovery of Historical Memory (REMHI) came forward to help sharing their data with the Commission. This organization published a report from hundreds of testimonies they had collected over time. Another organization which helped the Commission was *Centro Internacional para Investigaciones en Derechos Humanos* (CIIDH), which also collected thousands of testimonies. The data collected from both of these organizations was used by the commission to ascertain the number of killed, disappeared and to "confirm overall patterns."[56]

Arriving at the conclusion, "in the documentation of human rights violations and acts of violence connected with the armed confrontation, the Commission for Historical Clarification (CEH) registered a total of 42,275 victims, including men, women and children. Of these, 23,671 were victims of arbitrary execution and 6,159 were victims of forced disappearance. Eighty-three percent of fully identified victims were Mayan and seventeen percent were Ladino."[57] In its findings despite the fact that the Commission was hindered by the terms of reference which had placed restrictions on it in naming the perpetrators, it stated that the government committed acts of "genocide" against the Mayans. "In consequence, the CEH concludes that agents of the State of Guatemala, within the framework of counterinsurgency operations carried out between 1981 and 1983, committed acts of genocide against groups of Mayan people which lived in the four regions analyzed."[58] Finally, the most relevant act the Commission was to make was to fix the responsibility of genocide on the government of Guatemala, "crimes in the acts of genocide committed in Guatemala, the State is also responsible, because the majority of these acts were the product of a policy pre-established by a command superior to the material perpetrators."[59]

### NHRC Judgment the Raison d'être for a Truth Commission in Panjab

The above mentioned Truth Commissions have been taken as an example of the many commissions set up for the redress of many human rights violations committed in other parts of the world, and the way the world organizations such as the United Nations have responded to the questions of providing justice to the survivors and the families of the victims. The study of these commissions have revealed some very relevant questions especially since the violations that they were dealing with were similar to the ones inflicted on the victims as (seen in chapter three volume I) in the State of Panjab. For a long time the onus of responsibility had been fixed on the national institution of human rights, the National Human Rights Commission. However, the latest judgment delivered by the Commission on October 9, 2006 dealt a blow to the hopes that the families of the victims had in the institution. The NHRC had believed "that human rights of 109 persons, who were admittedly in the custody of the police immediately prior to their death, stood invaded and infringed when they lost their lives, while in custody of the police thereby rendering the state vicariously liable. There was a very great responsibility on the part of the police and other authorities to take reasonable care so that citizens in their custody were 'safe' and not deprived of their right to life as in such cases "the duty of care on the part of the State is strict and admits of no exception." The State of Panjab is, therefore, accountable and vicariously responsible for the infringement of the indefeasible right to life of those 109 deceased persons as it failed to "safeguard their lives and persons against the risk of avoidable harm."[60] Despite such unequivocal judgment about the culpability of the State and its agencies mainly the Police, its decision to leave alone the other disappearances in districts other than Amritsar appears not only short of justice but in a way a travesty of the judicial system. If people had been believed by the NHRC to have been killed by the police in the district of Amritsar what forces them to shut out the other districts? This argument is detailed in greater length in the chapter on NHRC though the ramifications of this denial of justice is a valid reason for a demand for a Truth Commission set up on the lines of the ones discussed above and many more in operation worldwide.

Every region is unique and therefore it would be best left to the people of Panjab, the nongovernmental organizations who have been collecting testimonies and data, International organizations with an experience in situations like these and an external judicial body along with the NHRC to conduct a fact finding truth commission is the way forward in Panjab. A Truth Commission would ensure, punishment to the guilty, more money/funds for the families of the victims, benefits equal to those paid to the families of the police personnel lost during the period and for the people of Panjab be given a chance to decide their own future vis-à-vis the systems of governance and policing.

# THE DISAPPEARED

VFF/0500

Jasvir Singh alias Jagsir(23) son of Gurdev Singh and Chotti Kaur a resident of Kakara, Dist Sangrur was a labourer* by profession. He was married to Rajinder Kaur (25) and they had a daughter Ramandeep Kaur.

Jasvir went missing on 27<sup>th</sup> march 1992.

He was abducted in a white Maruti Van by uniformed policemen.

That was the last time that he was seen by anybody.

VFF/0501

Amar Singh (28) son of Harchand Singh and Bachan Kaur was a resident of village Aloa rakh, Dist Sangrur. He worked in the Punjab State Electircity Board earning Rs.2000 per month.

He was not married.

Amar Singh was had been jailed earlier along with Bhai Piara Singh and also subjected to brutal torture by the police. They were later released on bail.

On 27<sup>th</sup> October 1991, he consumed Cyanide after he was surrounded by Police at village Baghraul

The Police statements regarding his having committed suicide were published in some daily newspapers like The Tribune and Ajj Di Awaj.

VFF/0502

Malkeet Singh (19) son of Bhinder Singh and Kuldeep Kaur was a resident of Rajo majra, Dist Sangrur. He lived with his mother who was dependent on him.

Malkeet Singh's father Late Sardar Bhinder Singh had retired from the Indian Army as a Naik and had joined the food and Supplies Department as a Peon. He had three sons and Malkeet Singh was the middle one. He (Malkeet Singh) was not much interested in studies. As such, he had abandoned his studies in class IX and started helping his brothers in farming. Like other youth of his Village, Malkeet Singh also had got himself baptised under the influence of Sant Chand Singh Rajo Majra who had his headquarters at the Village Gurdwara. However, he (Malkeet Singh) was not involved in any sort of political activities. According to his mother Kuldeep Kaur, the Police had never arrested him earlier. They were not aware of any of his activities from which they could have got some hint about his links with militant youth who were active in those days.

On 2 February 1993 at 8 A.M., Malkeet Singh had gone to pay his obeisance at the Village Gurdwara. He was arrested from there by plainclothes Policemen while he was taking bath in the 'Sarovar' (Holy Tank). The Police pushed him forcibly into a Maruti Van and sped away. The Villagers who witnessed this operation informed his family members immediately.

According to his mother Kuldeep Kaur, they met Shamsher Singh, SHO Dhuri and Surjit Singh, DSP Dhuri several times. They had received (unofficial) information also that Malkeet Singh had been detained inside Dhuri Police Station. Their man namely Joga Singh, was a resident of Dumal had served him tea inside the Police Station. At that time (10-12 days after his arrest), his condition was critical. 3-4 days after the arrest of Malkeet Singh, Dhuri Police had brought Malkeet Singh to the Village. A search of his house and field was conducted. The Police had seated Malkeet Singh inside the four wheeler. All this was witnessed by several residents of the village. The family members continued to receive information through their own sources that he was detained at Dhuri Police Station for 15 days and thereafter he was detained at Samundgarh Police Post, C.I.A. Staff Bahadur Singh Wala and Sangrur. Thereafter, the newspapers of 5 March carried a news item about his escape from Police custody. The Police had got a news item published in the newspapers that when a Police party were taking a militant namely Malkeet Singh for the recovery of arms, they were attacked by militants near Village Ghanauri. At that time Malkeet Singh escaped from Police custody and an unidentified militant was killed. After the publication of the news item, the family members tried to get some information from the Police about this episode, but, instead of giving them any information, the Police advised them to perform 'Bhog' (religious last rites) of their son.

On 6th November 1995, Malkeet Singh's father Ex-Naik Bhinder Singh filed a Writ Petition (No. 1264/1995) in the High Court through his Advocate Ranjan Lakhanpal. His family members are in possession of a copy of the Petition bearing the next date of hearing as 4th March 1997, but Bhinder Singh expired on 24th August 1997. Thereafter,

Malkeet Singh's brother Jagjit Singh met Advocate Ranjan lakhanpal who said that the case was still sub-judice. However, he did not tell him anything about the outcome of the case. Jagjit Singh had last met Ranjan Lakhanpal on 25 February 2000. But, the family members don't know anything about the legal status of the case.

**VFF/0503**

Sukhjit Singh alias Mintu(26) son of Harpal Singh and Ajmer Kaur a resident of village Rajo Majra, Dist Sangrur was a farmer.

He was married to Gurmeet Kaur and they had a son Karamjit Singh (8).

Sukhjit Singh, aged 26-27 years was an ordinary farmer youth. He was not associated with any sort of political activities whatsoever. He was the middle one among three brothers. His younger brother was serving in the Army and the elder one was a farmer like him. During the period of militancy, he was neither arrested anytime on the basis of suspicion nor was any case registered against him ever. According to his father Harpal Singh, his son had never visited the Gurdwara even. He was not bothered about anything other than his own business. He further told that even though the Police used to raid various houses in their village in view of it being the hotbed of militancy, yet, the Police had never raided their house; not even on the basis of suspicion.

On 4th February 1993 at about 9.30 P.M., Sukhjit Singh was asleep in his house along with his wife and small child. The Police entered the house after scaling the walls and directed him to come along with them. They made him to sit in their vehicle and departed. This Police party had come from C.I.A. Staff Bahadur Singh Wala. During the same night, the same Police party had arrested Master Kirpal Singh also,was a resident of Village Rajo Majra. He was released 15-18 days later from C.I.A. Bhawanigarh. He had been lodged at C.I.A. Bahadur Singh Wala and C.I.A. Bhawanigarh along with Sukhjit Singh.

On the day following the arrest of Sukhjit Singh, his father Harpal Singh along with the Sarpanch (Head of Village Council) Jeet Singh and other eminent persons went to C.I.A. Staff Bahadur Singh Wala. They told them to contact the DSP or the SSP. Harpal Singh and the Panchayat met SSP Jasminder Singh at his office on the same day. He directed them to see DSP Pannu. The Panchayat met the DSP on the same day who told that if directed by the SSP, he would release him. He also assured them that he himself would talk to the SSP. Harpal Singh told that like this the Police kept on passing the buck for 22 days. Fed up with all this, they approached Comrade Chand Singh Chopra, a political leader. He told the Panchayat that the SSP was not available there and that he would talk to the SP (Operations). The SP (IOps.) called Sub Inspector (S.I.) Sardara Singh of his office who showed some papers to the SP (Ops.). SP (Ops.) told that his (Harpal Singh's) son was lodged at Sadar Police Station . However, when Harpal Singh and the Panchayat went to Sadar Police Station , they said, "There is no one with the name of Sukhjit Singh here."

On the following day, Harpal Singh along with the Panchayat met the SSP at Sangrur. He asked them to see him at 2 P.M. the next day and promised to give them complete information. On reaching there the following day, the panchayat* got to know that the SSP* had gone away to attend some function. However, the newspaper of that day had carried a news item that a militant namely Sukhjit Singh Mintu had escaped from Police custody. According to Harpal Singh, the news item had not mentioned the name of the Village of Sukhjit Singh. They met Chand Singh Chopra and requested him to get them the information about the identity of Sukhjit Singh. He rang up and told them that according to the Police, Sukhjit Singh Mintu belongs to Village Rajo Majra only. On being asked by the Investigation Team as to how he understood that Sukhjit Singh had been killed when the Police had declared him as having escaped only, Harpal Singh replied that in those days, such a news item was understood to mean that only. On being asked by the Investigation Team whether he tried to obtain the copies of the Police papers regarding Sukhjit Singh's arrest and subsequent escape from Police custody, Harpal Singh said, "Our son had been killed anyway, what use it were for us to obtain those copies."

His parents are mentally upset. At times, they are fine, but they always miss him. He was their only son. They always keep crying. Our family has been ruined. I wonder what will happen.

**VFF/0504**

Gurcharan Singh (27) son of Mukhtiar Singh and Surjit Kaur a resident of village Dhanaula, Dist Sangrur was a mason by profession and was married to Gurdeep Kaur (30).

They had a son Gurpinder Singh (7) staying with them and Gurcharan Singh's sister who was 18years of age, also stayed with them.

In the past the police used to raid their house several times, but in October 1991, he was picked up from his residence by men in plain clothes. Nothing is known about him since then.

**VFF/0505**

Nahar Singh alias Nahara(24) son of Atma Singh and Gurdev Kaur was a resident of village Alipur khalsa, Dist Sangrur .

He studied up to his 3rd grade .He was not married and thus stayed with his father.

The Handiaya Staff (C.I.A.) raided Nahar Singh's house many times for three months. Once, they picked up somebody else in lieu of Nahar Singh. He was got released by Joginder Singh Sarpanch* and Ex-Sarpanch Mukhtiar Singh. The Panchayat had promised also to produce Nahar Singh.

On 4th or 5th June 1993 at 11 A.M., at the house of Surjit Singh son of Natha Singh, Mazhabi Sikh in village Kuthala, two motor cycle borne youth dressed as Sikhs came and took Nahar Singh along by making him to sit in between them on the motorcycle. They took him to the house of aunt ('Maasi') of a SPO who belonged to village Alipur, at village Jhalur. There, they got him arrested by uniformed police. At the house of the 'Maasi'* of above mentioned SPO*, Nahar Singh was given drug tablets and made to sleep. Then the Barnala Sadar police arrested him. Later the Police sent a message to Alipur for identification of the dead bodies. His father along with Ex-Sarpanch Mukhtiar Singh and Chowkidar Muhammad Shah went to Sadar Police Station Barnala and identified the dead body (of Nahar Singh). There were bullet injury marks on the right temple and ribs on right side. His hair was loose and blood soaked. He was stark naked except for an underwear. Blood channels had been formed on the right side of his body, throughout.

His grand mother Bhagi Kaur became insane. And the death of Nahar Singh was confirmed by the pictures that the family got from the police.

### VFF/0506

Surinder Singh alias Sinder (32) son of Nachattar Singh and Gurbachan Kaur a resident of village Wajipur Badesha, Dist Sangrur was a farmer earning 8000 Rs per month.

In the year 1990, Surinder Singh ran away from home due to the looming threat of the police as the police were raiding his house too frequently. After that he never returned home, but the police continued to enquire at his house.

Surinder Singh's mother Gurbachan Kaur has been seriously affected due to unending torture and use of abusive language by the police. She has lost her mental balance and is always sick.

An electric motor held in partnership with another person was forcibly handed over to the other party in full, by obtaining Gurbachan Kaur's signatures on a blank stamp paper, by the Police.

### VFF/0507

Harbans Singh alias Bansa (22) son of Taru Singh and Gurnam Kaur was a resident of village Wajipur Badesha, Dist Sangrur was a farmer earning Rs.300 per month.

He was arrested from Sri Harmandir Sahib during Operation Blue Star and sent to Bahadar Singh Wala (Wada Graon) Police Station in Dist Sangrur. Later he was shifted to Sherpur Police Station afterwards; Sherpur Police dropped him at his home and informed the Panchayat accordingly. He used to perform Puja-Path (reciting Gurbani). Whenever, he would go outside for performing 'Path', the Police would intercept him.

On 14 January 1991 at 6 A.M., he was shot dead by Police of Malerkotla at the Bus Stand of village Shergarh Cheema (Dist Sangrur). On 16 January 1991, the village Panchayat collected his last remains from the Police Station of Malerkotla.

A truck load of the 'Sangat' (congregation of people) accompanied his last remains to Kiratpur Sahib, where, the same were immersed.

**VFF/0508**

Gulzar Singh (35) son of Mahinder Singh and Chand Kaur a resident of village Dhandran, Dist Sangrur was a farmer by profession.

He was married to Charanjit Kaur and they had a daughter Inderpal Kaur and a son Amritpal Singh.

The Police of Bahadar Singh Wala and Dhuri used to pick him up often and then let him off. There was a continuous harassment by the police. He was an 'Amritdhari' (Baptised) Sikh. He had held the post of President of Sikh Students Federation, Dhuri Circle. One year before this incident, he had absconded and joined the 'Kharku' (Militant) Movement. Main reason for his absconding was repeated arrests and torturing by Police, due to his association with Sikh Students Federation.

NOTE:-

His news came in a daily newspaper Ajit dated 14th December 1991. In Ajj Di Awaj dated 17th December 1991, there was an article exposing the treacherous game of the Punjab Police of killing militants in fake encounters. Prior to this, he was not in the news. The true translation of the report by a Staff Reporter of 'Ajj Di Awaj' regarding this case is appended below:-

*BHAI DHANDRA WAS KILLED IN A FAKE ENCOUNTER AT LASOI*

*Malerkotla, 15 December (Staff Reporter) — In Punjab, hardly there will be any Canal, Nullah, or Road where the Police have not shown a Fake encounter (to have taken place). The reality of everyday killing of unidentified militants is something else. Nobody dares to expose or speak against, that in the lap of darkness of the night, , how the Punjab Police is snatching away brothers from sisters, husbands from wives, and sons from their mothers.*

*On 14 December 1991, all newspapers carried a news item regarding the killing of two unidentified militants by the Police. It was claimed that one AK-47, one 12 Bore Rifle, and 33 Cartridges were recovered from them. This is an absolutely concocted story of the Police. When this correspondent visited the concerned village, the villagers told him that they themselves also have come to know of this police encounter from the newspapers only that day. Gunshots were heard a day before at about 10 or 11 P.M. Neither the villagers were shown the dead bodies nor got the dead bodies identified. When the journalists asked ASP Malerkotla about the details of this encounter he put them off by saying that the said encounter took place between the C.I.A. Staff and the militants and not between Malerkotla Police and militants. They (C.I.A. Staff) only had a clue and they only had laid a Naka. The surprising thing about it is that so far C.I.A. Staff has never laid any Naka anywhere. If at all C.I.A. had laid a Naka, how come the ASP Malerkotla did not know about it, as the said area falls under his jurisdiction. Why did the C.I.A. lay a Naka without the police of the concerned Police Station ? All these things raise a doubt (about the genuineness of the encounter). ASP Malerkotla was here (village Lasoi) to attend a Medical Camp organised jointly by the Military and Civil authorities. The SDM Malerkotla, while chatting informally, tried to find out the reason for the low turnout of the people at the Medical Camp. On being told that it is due to the scare created among the people by the killing of youth in a police encounter last night; he was astonished to hear that an encounter had taken place there the previous night. Even after the lapse of 36 hours after the encounter, the seniormost Officer of the Sub Division did not know about a police encounter having taken place in his area.*

*The family members have come to know from reliable sources that in this so called encounter, former President of All India Sikh Students Federation and Ex-President of Circle Dhuri, Bhai Gulzar* Singh *Dhandra were killed. Nothing is known about the other youth so far. Bhai Gulzar* Singh *Dhandra was arrested on 7 December 1991 from village Dhadewali (Malerkotla) at 2.30 P.M. One AK-47, one scooter, and some cash were recovered from him. He was waylaid near village Dhadewali by police by dashing their Allwyn Nissan vehicle against his scooter. Bhai Dhandra had escaped from there but due to a bullet injury, he dropped down about 200 meters away. His attempt to consume cyanide was foiled by the police. According to people who were standing by, he told them his name and that of his village. But the police carried him away in their Allwyn Nissan vehicle.*

*The arrest of Bhai Gulzar* Singh *was confirmed by Khalistan Liberation Force on 12 December 1991 through Ajit newspaper. Same day,* Dist *Sangrur Secretary of Punjab Human Rights Organisation, sent telegrams to Chief Justice of High Court, Governor Punjab, DC Sangrur, and Amnesty International demanding his production in a court of law. General Secretary of Punjab Human*

*Rights Organisation has, through a statement in the newspapers, demanded that Bhai Gulzar* Singh *Dhandra should be produced in a court of law. But the Police without observing the legal procedures liquidated them during the same night between 10 and 11 P.M. near village Lasoi. And next day, without getting the dead bodies identified, got their post mortem done at Malerkotla Hospital, and declaring the dead bodies as unclaimed, cremated them at cremation ground of Jamalpura by pouring oil on them in a surreptitious manner. It is worth mentioning that about three and a half months ago, Maghar* Singh *Ladewala, and Preetam* Singh *Rabbo were killed in a fake encounter by the Police.*

*General Secretary of Punjab Human Rights Organisation, Malwinder* Singh *Mali, Disrict President Ranjit* Singh *Toor, Vice President of Bhartiya Kisan Union S. Narang* Singh *Guara, Press Secreatry Preetam* Singh *Naudharni, Major* Singh *Matran, President of Desh Punjab Students Union Gurmeet* Singh *and General Secreatry Kuldeep* Singh *Bittu have condemned the murder of Bhai Gulzar* Singh *Dhandra by C.I.A. Staff Bahadar* Singh *Wala (Ladda Kothi) in a so called encounter and demanded an independent enquiry into this case.*

*His dead body was declared to be unidentified and unclaimed and cremated at Jamalpur (Malerkotla) by the Police.*

## VFF/0509

Kulwinder Singh (30) son of Balvir Singh and Surjit Singhwas a resident of village Dhuri, Dist Sangrur worked as a labourer*.

He was married to Kuldeep Kaur and they had 1daughter Kulbir Kaur and 1 son Kulpreet Singh. Other than them, his parents were also dependent on him.

The Dhuri Police used to pick him up often and release him after some time. At that time, SHO at Dhuri Police Station was Gurbakhsh Singh.

On 3rd June 1994, at about 3.30 A.M., he was again picked up by SHO* Gurbaksh Singh and his party consisting of 4-5 men.

His father and mother both are suffering from blood pressure. His sister and wife have become mental patients. They all are under treatment continuously. His father is suffering from Reuhmatism (especially the right leg) also.

Written representations were submitted twice personally to the then Chief Minister, Beant Singh, but, all in vain. The whole incident was witnessed by Surjit Kaur.

Even though there is no proof of the disappeared person having been killed, yet, the abduction and subsequent disappearance of his personal friend Sukhpal Singh Pali, Journalist, shows that Kulwinder Singh also has been killed.

**VFF/0510**

Pala Singh alias Bhola(19) son of Taru Singh and Gurnam Kaur was a resident of village Wajipur Badesha, Dist Sangrur.

He was married to Baljit Kaur (19) and they had a daughter Saranjit Kaur.

His parents were totally dependent on him for a living.

He served as a gunman to Smt. Bimal Khalsa M.P*. After the death of Smt. Bimal Khalsa, he visited the residence of Balwant Singh Tohra at Chandigarh. He was picked up by police from there. S. Tohra got him released after 21 days. To his dismay, he was again picked up by ASI* Darshan Singh of Sandaur police chowki from Malerkotla. Sandaur police chowki was surrounded by the whole village. He was got released by Sh. Raj Singh Kheri, M.L.A*. On his return, Pala Singh said that he had been kept at Police Chowki Manwan (Sangrur).

In Jan-Feb 92, Pala Singh had gone to his in-laws house at Bhullarheri. He was shot dead there at the house of a Zamidar by Dhuri Police.

His family came to know about his death on the following day from a report in the newspapers regarding his having been killed in an encounter with the Police. It is believed that the Police must have cremated his dead body.

**VFF/0511**

Santokh Singh (27) son of Sher Singh and Jaswant Kaur was a resident of village Saron, Dist Sangrur. He was married to Avtar Kaur and they had 3 children.

Santokh Singh was a Registered.Medical.Practitioner and was running a clinic at Mandi Kalan in Dist Bathinda. Especially since 1989, the Police used to pick him up often, question him and let him off. Sometimes, they used to take him along and the Panchayat and other persons used to get him released. Most of the time, he used to be picked up by the police of Balian Wali. Apart from that, police of Rampura Phool also picked him up once or twice. Once, he was picked up by the C.I.A. Staff Bathinda also and released at the intervention of Sarpanch* and Panchayat of Mandi Kalan.

On 4th July, 1991, at about 11.30 A.M., five persons came in civil dress and in an un-numbered Maruti Van to Santokh Singh's clinic at Mandi Kalan. Four of them came out while the fifth kept the engine of the vehicle running. They asked Santokh Singh to examine a patient. Santokh Singh ran towards inside of the room as those persons had grappled with him and started dragging him towards the vehicle. Ultimately, they put him in the vehicle and sped away. This incident was witnessed by Sukhdev Singh, Ajaib Singh Fauji and Dhanna Singh.

The news of this incident came in Ajit (Punjabi) on 5<sup>th</sup> July 1991. Before that, he was never in the news.

His elder brother Gurjant Singh, who is a Havaldar in the Army, submitted an application to his Officers regarding abduction and subsequent disappearance of his brother Santokh Singh. Army authorities enquired from the Sarpanch and other people. The outcome of that enquiry is not known to the family till today.

### VFF/0512

Labh Singh alias Swarna(25) son of Chotta Singh and Gurmel Kaur was a resident of Rajo majra, Dist Sangrur was a farmer earning 4000 Rs per month. He was unmarried but had family to fend for which included his parents.

Labh Singh's mother Gurmel Kaur , aged 60 years, was a resident of Village Rajo Majra, is the wife of a poor farmer namely Sukhdev Singh. She had three sons and four daughters. Her eldest son had died due to illness and her youngest son Labh Singh (victim) was arrested by the Punjab Police and killed in a fake encounter. After passing his Matriculation, Labh Singh had got a job as welder in Thermal Plant Bathinda. After some time, he quit that job and joined a private factory at Dera Bassi. In those days, an incident involving militants took place at Dera Bassi. The Police arrested all the youth who were employed in the above mentioned factory. He was interrogated for several days in custody. After this incident, his family members called Labh Singh back home and he started helping his brother Maghar Singh in agricultural farming. At the Village, he started frequenting the Village Gurdwara. He was influenced by Sant Chand Singh rajo majra who used to manage the affairs of the local Gurdwara and got himself baptized. He used to take active part in religious programmes organized at the local Gurdwara. Once, Labh Singh had gone to Dhuri for some job where he was arrested by the SHO Bharat Kumar on the basis of suspicion. However, the Village Panchayat (Council) reached the Police Station promptly and got him released. According to his family members, he used to visit Sant Chand Singh, often and the Sant was active politically. At that time, Sant Chand Singh Rajo Majra was the President of the District unit of Akali Dal. Later on, the Police had abducted Sant Chand Singh also and disappeared him.

In those days, once, the Moonak Police raided his house with a view to arrest Labh Singh. Labh Singh made a run, due to fear. But the Police picked up his father Sukhdev Singh and took him away. However, he was released after 3-4 days. Thereafter, the Police started raiding their hoiuse very frequently. They used to pick up his brother and father. His brother Maghar Singh appeared before the Deputy Inspector General (D.I.G) Patiala Range in a 'Khula Darbar' (Open House) organized by the said DIG and complained against the highhandedness of the Police. Later, he produced himself before the Police. They questioned him for few days and released him on the condition that he would not leave the Village. However, the Police continued to visit his house.

In the meantime, on 22nd March 1992, Labh Singh was arrested along with one of his associates namely Amritpal DSingh alias Ambi son of Avtar Singhwas a resident of Rajo Majra from the Gurdwara at Village Thullewal. The villagers informed his family members at his Village that Labh Singh and Amritpal Singh had been arrested by a Police party led by Bakhshish Singh, SHO of Barnala (Sadar) Police Station .

On the following day, their family members along with the Panchayat met SHO Bakhshish Singh. However, he flatly denied having arrested them. The family members continued to pursue their case. During this period, Avtar Singh (Father of Amritpal Singh), Sukhdev Singh (father of Labh Singh) and Labh Singh (brother-in-law of Labh Singh) along with the Village Panchayat met the SSP Barnala Mr. Ishwar Chander, DSP Joginder Singh Kutiwal and SHO Bakhshish Singh. The SSP and the SHO flatly denied their custody, but DSP Joginder Singh Kutiwal admitted their custody once and demanded Rs. 50,000/- in return for recording their arrest formally. Avtar Singh and Labh Singh promised to pay him the money. They said, "As and when you send them to jail, we will pay you the money." The DSP agreed. Avtar Singh even mortgaged 13 bighas of his land for Rs.50,000/- for this purpose. However, the DSP did not record their arrest formally. He continued to make false promises for a few days.

On the intervening night of 1 and 2 April (1992), Amritpal Singh and Labh Singh were killed in a fake encounter near the brick Kiln at Village Sanghera. They were shown as unidentified. After reading this news, their family members met DSP Joginder Singh Kutiwal who told them that their sons had been taken away from him by SP (D) Gurdev Singh Sahota. Unofficially, some of the Policemen told both the families that the unidentified militants killed near Sanghera were their sons only. On getting this confirmation, the family members of Labh Singh performed his 'Bhog' (religious last rites).

His parents are mentally upset. They miss him very much. Economic condition of the household is miserable.

**VFF/0513**

Harpal Singh (42) son of Bhagwan Singh and Gobind Kaur was a resident of village Bhindran, Dist Sangrur worked as an elecetrician earning Rs. 1200 per month.

He was married to Gurmit Kaur (40) and they had 2 sons Kuldeep and Jagdeep.

On 22<sup>nd</sup> December 1992 at 6 A.M., Harpal Singh was called by Inspector* Gurmel Singh, SHO* Bhawanigarh through one Jeeta Singh. At about 8 A.M., Jeeta Singh informed the wife of Harpal Singh that Harpal Singh had been detained by Inspector Gurmel Singh at Bhawanigarh Police Station and asked her to make some arrangement (to get him released). But the Bhawanigarh Police did not give any information about Harpal Singh.

His wife was the only witness to the entire incident and since that day on his mother Gobind Kaur has become a heart patient.

### VFF/0514

Kishan Singh alias Krishan Kumar (27) son of Lajjia ram and Hukma deviwas a resident of village Rajo majra, Dist Sangrur was a milk vendor by profession and earned 4500 rupeees per month.

He was unmarried but his brother Jaswinder pal (20) stayed with him.

Lajjia Ram, aged 66 years was a Hindu Brahman,was a resident of Village Rajo Majra. He had five sons and two daughters. Kishan Singh was the youngest. After passing his Middle exam, Kishan Singh was engaged in agricultural farming for one year and thereafter he started the business of milk-vending. He was doing well in his business.

Kishan was a Brahman boy and had the habit of using intoxicants also. But, in 1989, he came under the influence of Sant Chand Singh and converted himself to Sikhism and became an "Amritdhari" (Baptized) Sikh. Once, DSP Sukhdev Singh Brar had assembled the whole Village at the School and directed Lajjia Ram to produce his son Kishan. One of the relatives of Lajjia Ram (son-in-law's brother) was a body guard to Darshan Singh, SHO of Dehlon Police Station . Lajjia Ram went to Dehlon and talked to his relative who was a Havaldar (Head Constable). The SHO (Darshan Singh) told Lajjia Ram to bring his son to him. Lajjia Ram produced Kishan Singh before Darshan Singh at Dehlon. Darshan Singh kept Kishan Singh at Dehlon for a few days and on 22<sup>nd</sup> August 1992, he along with Lajjia Ram and his relative Havaldar produced Kishan Singh before DSP Sukhdev Singh Brar at Malerkotla. Sukhdev Singh Brar questioned Kishan Singh for a few minutes in front of the Panchayat itself and told Lajjia Ram that his son was not guilty. He also advised Lajjia Ram to send his son abroad.

On 25<sup>th</sup> September 1992, Kishan Singh and his father Lajjia Ram had gone to Dhuri for purchasing oil and cattle feed. They purchased these items and loaded them onto their 'Rehra' (horse-cart). Kishan

Singh told his father to go along with the Rehra and that he himself would come by bus. Just then, Jagdev Singh son of Preetam Singh was a resident of Dhuri arrived there and told Kishan Singh that if he was going to the Village, then he could come along with him on scooter. Jagdev Singh belonged to Village Rajo Majra but in those days he used to reside at Dhuri. In the evening, a resident of his Village told Lajjia Ram that his son had been arrested by Darbara Singh, SHO of Dhuri Police Station from the house of Preetam Singh Goldsmith. Nothing could be done at night. In the morning, Lajjia Ram went to Dehlon to see SHO Darshan Singh. But, Darshan Singh had been transferred to Police Station Raikot. However, Lajjia Ram could not meet him at Raikot Police Station also. According to Lajjia Ram, he continued to meet SHO Dehlon, Darshan Singh and SHO Dhuri Darbara Singh for six months but he did not get any information about the whereabouts of Kishan. Darshan Singh continued to make false promises of helping him, Lajjia Ram said. SHO Darbara Singh flatly denied that he had arrested Kishan Singh. Even Preetam Singh Goldsmith and his family members denied that Kishan Singh had been arrested from their house. Lajjia ram told that the abovementioned family (that of Preetam Singh) had got his son arrested, by deceit.

Lajjia Ram told that for more than one year he continued to meet various police officers. He submitted written representations also to several higher authorities including Chief Minister, Beant Singh. But nobody listened to him.

In 1997, Lajjia Ram filed a Habeas Corpus Petition in the High Court through his advocate Ranjan lakhanpal. The High Court dismissed the Petition on 17th February 1999 on the basis of delay in filing the same and advised the Petitioner to file a complaint in a lower Court. A copy of the Petition and High Court Order (hand written) are attached herewith.

His mother and brother are mentally depressed. His brother keeps shouting 'police', 'police'. They had five sons, out of them only one is left. He too is mentally disturbed. Their family is in great distress.

**VFF/0515**

Mehma Singh son of Gulzar Singh and Basant Kaur was a resident of village Dhilwan, (Locality Nabha Bard), Dist. Sangrur. He was a farmer by profession with a stable monthly income of about 3500 rupees.

He was picked up from his residence on 14th December 1992 by a Police Party consisting of DSP Sher Singh, One Inspector and other Police personnel of Rampura Phool.

He was last seen on 15th December 1992 at the CIA Staff, Rampura Phool, (Dist. Bhatinda) by Jarnail Singh, Narain Singh and Gokal Singh.

Mehma Singh was shown to have been killed in an 'encounter' on 17th December 1992. His dead body was not handed over to the family. News of his being killed in an 'encounter' was published in all the newspapers.

His mother Basant Kaur is mentally upset since then. She has four daughters and he was the only son. After this incident, his father Gulzar Singh died. He used to keep on uttering 'Mehma', 'Mehma' always.

Mehma Singh left behind 3 dependents, who include his mother Santi Kaur (50), and Sisters Sukhjeet Kaur (4), Samanjeet Kaur (8)

### VFF/0516

Gurjant Singh alias Janta son of Dhanna Singh and Malkeet Kaur, resident of village Rureke Kalan (locality Ladha Patti), Dist. Sangrur.

He was a mason by profession. This being the only source of income to him, he managed to scrap around 3200 rupees a month.

He was picked up on 05th April 1992 at 7 a.m. by a police party from Sunam P.S., led by SHO Baldev Singh, resident of village Kala Ugo Wala. He assured the family that since he belonged to a neighbouring village, he would see to it that no harm came to Gurjant Singh. (Baldev Singh is now posted as DSP Barnala)

He was last seen on the same day by his family members and Darshan Singh and Raj Singh of Rurke Kalan

Gurjant Singh has left behind his mother Malkeet Kaur (55) as his only dependent. His mother is mentally upset since then. She misses him a lot.

### VFF/0517

Gurlal Singh alias Leela, son of Jaginder Singh and Bhan Kaur was a resident of village Kaleke (locality Salima Patti), Dist.Sangrur. (DATE OF BIRTH provided by sources is 20th April1972.). He was a farmer by profession with a monthly income of 2500 rupees.

Before this incident, the Police or any member of Security Forces had no enmity with him. However, the family of Roop Singh of the same village was inimical towards his family. One of the sons of Roop Singh namely Avtar Singh, was a policeman. These people were not bothered about the honour of Gurlal's family. They used to get Gurlal Singh's elder brother namely Balwant Singh picked up, and beaten by the Police. .

They did not spare Gurlal Singh as well. On 7th day of 'Sawan' (around 21 July) in the year 1992, he was abducted at the instance of Avtar Singh son of Roop Singh of the same village, by a Police party headed by Inspector Sant Kumar, C.I.A. Staff, (Handiaya) and including Havaldar Avtar Singh, Havaldar Joginder Singh and 20 other men.. They then approached Inspector Sant Kumar for his release. But Sant Kumar abused them and told them to produce Balwant Singh and take him back. But they could not produce Balwant Singh. Later on, it was learnt that Balwant Singh had been killed in an 'encounter'. Even then, Sant Kumar did not release Gurlal Singh.

This incident was witnessed by Baldev Singh and Gurmel Singh of village Kaleke.

Gurlal was last seen on the 21st July'92 by the witnesses and his family members at his residence.

His only dependent is Babu Singh (60) who is his uncle (Chacha), and is mentally depressed since the time of his abduction.

**VFF/0518**

Hardev Singh son of Garib Singh and Bant Kaur, resident of village Rurke Kalan (loc. Ladha Patti), Dist. Sangrur. His DATE OF BIRTH is 08th October 1955. He was a labourer by profession and was married to Angrej Kaur (35) resident of village Sanghera. They had two kids (both boys) namely Gurpreet Singh (13) and Harpreet Singh (11).

On 13th April 1992, Baldev Singh, SHO of Police Station Sunam went to the house of Hardev Singh and inquired about him. On being told that he had gone for a holy dip at Talwandi Sabo (Damdama Sahib) on the occasion of Baisakhi festival, he picked up Baldev Singh alias Janta and taking him along, went to that place. He picked up Hardev Singh as well as Gurjant Singh son of Dhanna Singh from there and took them to Jorki Police Station . The family members of Hardev then went to the Jorki Police Station and enquired about him .But officials on duty did not disclose his whereabouts. Since then, there is no trace of him.

Since that day on, his parents are mentally upset and are awaiting his return. He has left behind 5 dependents in the family , namely Garib Singh(70)Father , Bant Kaur(65)Mother, Angrej Kaur(35)Wife ,Gurpreet Singh(13)Son , Harpreet Singh(11)Son.

**VFF/0519**

Case off Suleman Khan Alias Sullu (41) son of Jora Khan and Rajji Begum of village Sehna (locality Gill Dahoori Patti), Dist. Sangrur.

(DATE OF BIRTH-20th May 1948).

He was a potter by profession and also dealt in cattle. He could scrape rupees 4500 in all from the two jobs that he carried out in order to run his family. He was married to Chhoto (48) and they had 5 children. The first 3 were girls, Moorti (22)        , Sinder (19), Binder (17) and two boys Badh Khan (15)     and Veera Khan (13).

He was coming from Pakhoke, towards Sehna on a Bi-cycle. On the bridge of Pakhoke Water Channel, on 14th December 1990, between 6 to 7 P.M. He was shot dead by a police party headed by Inspector Harjap Singh, SHO* of Sehna. Another person namely Mohinder Singh who was with him at that time, ran away and escaped. The police did not hand over the dead body to the Panchayat* and other villagers. On this, the villagers gheraoed the Police Station and then the police had to hand over the dead body to the villagers after getting the post mortem conducted at Barnala .

There was a lot of hue and cry in the media about the incident and as per the details given in a newspaper called "AJIT "on 20th December 1990, the incident was described as follows,

*(NOTE: Before this, there was no news item about him in any newspaper. The true translation of the news item published in the Punjabi daily Ajit dated 20 December 1990 is appended below:-*

*BUFFALO TRADER KILLED AND SHOWN AS KILLED IN POLICE ENCOUNTER*

*Barnala, 19 December-(Correspondent)*

*F.I.R. has been registered at Police Station Sehna, against the SHO of the same Police Station and three other policemen, under public pressure, in connection with the murder of 40 year old Sulu Khan @ Suleman, who was killed on Friday night, near Basti Gill Kothe on Barnala-Bazkhana road.*

*According to Mohinder Singh son of Sh. Preetam Singh, aged 20 years, resident of village Shehna itself, he and Sulu Khan were coming to Shehna from Pakhoke on bicycle between 6 to 7 P.M. Sulu Khan was pedalling the bicycle and he was sitting on the rear seat. They had gone a little distance past the Pakhoke-Rajwaha Bridge when a Police Tempo passed them at great speed. It stopped at a distance of one furlong; the Police got down and fired at them with an intention to kill. He got down from the bicycle and hid behind the embankment on the left side and thus saved himself. He came to the village and narrated the whole story to Gulzar Khan, brother of Sulu Khan and the village Panchayat.*

*Sarpanch Gurcharanjit Singh told that he along with other villagers enquired about Gulu Khan at Police Station Shehna and Police Post Pakhoke, but, they said that they did not know anything. However, the Police called for reinforcements and recorded this murder as a police encounter and sent the dead body to Barnala during the night itself for a post mortem.*

*On the following day, on Saturday, the people again went to the Police Station . They surrounded the blood stained Police Jeep and deflated its tyres. They sat on a Dharna in front of the Police Station . The City closed down, in protest. Panches and Sarpanches from the neighbouring villages also arrived and a crowd of more than five thousand people including some women, assembled there. Former Minister Giani Kundan Singh Patang, Jathedar Kartar Singh Joshila (Longowal Akali Dal), Pandit Som Dutt (Congress), Sant Chand Singh Rajomajra, Sh. Ajmer Singh Lohatbaddi (Panthic Akali Dal), Naginder Singh (Sikh Students Federation), Nirmal Singh Nimma (BSP), Jameel Rehman and Abdul Wahid from Malerkotla, also reached there.*

*Succumbing to public pressure, DSP Sukhdev Singh Chheena from Sangrur reached there. He told that the Police were ready to register whatever complaint they had to make. At this, the above mentioned report was registered at the instance of Mohinder Singh.*

*It is said that Gulu Khan belonged to the Kumhar caste of Muslim community and was a resident of village Sehna itself. He used to deal in the sale and purchase of buffaloes.*

*Rs 16,000/- which Suleman Khan had on his person and one Bi-cycle worth Rs 1,200/- The money and Bi-cycle were not returned by police. The following Punjab Police personnel are responsible for this, Harjap Singh SI & three other policemen.*

*He has left behind his wife and their five children as his dependents.*
**VFF/0520**

### A CASE OF DISAPPEARANCE

Baldev Singh (41) son of Prem Singh and Jasmel Kaur. He was the resident of village Meemsan, Dist. Sangrur. (DATE OF BIRTH-20th April 1952).

He had completed his middle school and was now into farming which yielded him an income of 4500 rupees.

He was married to Preetam Kaur (42). They had two kids, a girl named Manjit Kaur(20) and a boy Ranjit Singh(18).

Baldev Singh was produced in front of SHO Police Station Dhuri Mr. Shamsher Singh on 18th April 1993 by Gurmel Singh Sarpanch (Head of Village Council) of the victim's village, Tarlok Singh Sarpanch of Bangawali, Dharam Pal Sarpanch of village Rajindra Puri. His whereabouts are known since then.

The witnesses to the incident are Najar Singh, Jagdev Singh, Lal Singh.

Victim's mother and sister are mentally upset. They miss him a lot.
**VFF/0521**

The case of Ranjit Singh alias Reeta(38) son of Gurdev Singh and Kartar Kaur, resident of Meemsa, Tehsil Dhuri, Dist. Sangrur. (DATE OF BIRTH- 01st June1956). He had compeleted his middle school and was now into farming and with a monthly income of 5000 rupees. They had three children, two girls Namandeep Kaur (16), Premdeep Kaur (15) and boy Satbir Singh (10).

Ranjit Singh was not associated with any sort of political activities before 1984. According to his brother Ram Singh, their family had leftist leanings and their father had been an active member of the Communist Party (Marxist) since his youth. Ranjit Singh had 5 brothers. One of them is settled in the USA. Ram Singh is a Govt. School Teacher. Three others are farmers.

Ranjit Singh was arrested for the fisrt time in January 1991 before the Republic Day. He was released after two days of illegal detention. However, he was not tortured. Thereafter, a number of raids were carried out by Dhuri and Malerkotla Police with a view to arrest him, but each time, he slipped through the net. But then the Police used to pick up his elder brother Ram Singh and detain him in illegal custody for a day or two and they used to release him only at the intervention of the Panchayat. It happened 5-6 times.

In January 1994, a Police party led by SHO Inspector Gurbaksh Singh of Police Station Dhuri raided their house and took Ram Singh and Sarwan Singh (another brother) into his custody and took them to Police Station Dhuri. They were released five days later but only after Ranjit Singh had been produced before the Police. Ranjit Singh was detained for two days at Police Station Dhuri and thereafter he was shifted to C.I.A. Staff Bhawanigarh where he was detained illegally for 24 days. There, he was tortured brutally using third degree methods for about 15 days. He was released by the efforts of his family members after 24 days through the good offices of DSP Gurdeep Singh Pannu. At that time, he was in a very bad shape due to torture, so much so thathe was incapacitated. He was unable to stand on his feet and had lost about 35 Kgs weight. At Bhawanigarh, he had been tortured under the supervision of SSP Jasminder Singh and DSP Jagjit Singh Gill. He was bed-ridden for a period of about 4 months. However, he could move around after about 20 days. It is said that Inspector Balwinder Singh, incharge of C.I.A. Staff at Bhawanigarh, used to torture the detenues there brutally and in an inhuman manner.

On 31 July 1994, Ranjit Singh, along with one of his brothers namely Malkiat Singh and 40 other residents of their village, had gone to Malerkotla riding in a truck, to watch the evening show of a Circus. It was past 10 PM when the show ended. Just then, three plainclothesmen abducted Ranjit Singh in a white un-numbered Maruti Van. However, Malkiat Singh (brother) identified those three men as ASI Surinderpal Singh Ghora, Malkiat Singh and Bahadar Singh, both Head Constables.

The very next morning, his father Gurdev Singh started pursuing the matter. He approached all Police officers of the district, right from the SSP, Jasminder Singh, to the SHOs of various Police Station s, but all in vain. He tried to meet the incharge of C.I.A. Staff Malerkotla but was not allowed to enter the building. He submitted written representations to the SSP Sangrur and DSP Malerkotla. Ram Singh (brother) approached Capt. Amarinder Singh, who is presently the President of Congress Party in Punjab, and requested him to visit Sangrur and help in getting his brother released from Police custody. Accordingly, Capt. Amarinder Singh visited Sangrur and met the SSP who denied Ranjit Singh having been taken into custody by any official of his Police district. At Police Station Malerkotla, Gurdev Singh (father) was made to sign an entry in a register telling him that the same was regarding Ranjit Singh's abduction. However, later on, during the course of an inquiry conducted by a DIG on the orders of the High Court, the family members wanted to produce that register as evidence of having got their FIR registered. But, the Police said that they had not obtained Gurdev Singh's signatures against any entry. As such, there was no question of a FIR having been registered at that time. The family members of Ranjit Singh suspect that the Police had obtained Gurdev Singh's signatures on some dummy register. Unfortunately, the family members had not sent any telegrams or written representations to any other higher authorities.

The family members of Ranjit Singh believe that he is no more. This belief is based on unofficial information received from their sources in the Police department, according to which, Ranjit Singh had been killed by the Police and his dead body had been thrown into the Bhakra canal.

Ranjit Singh's mother suffered a tremendous shock due to this incident and she has become hard of hearing now. His wife has lost her mental euilibrium. She has become short tempered and abuses her children in a fit of anger, very often. His elder brother Ram Singh has suffered an attack of paralysis recently, in March, 2001. Tears flowed from his eyes a number of times during the course of this interview. He stated that after the disappearance of Ranjit Singh, he had to shoulder the responsibilty of Ranjit Singh's family also in addition to that of his own. As a consequence, he suffered from depression, often.

**VFF/0522**

The case of Sukhwinder Singh alias Bhola Singh(21) son of Ram Dhan Singh and Chand Kaur resident of village Wajidpur Badesha, Dist. Sangrur.

He had completed his primary education (i.e. upto his fifth

standard) and was now working a labourer. As a side job, he also had his tailoring business which in total gave him an income of 4000 rupees. He was married to Baljit Kaur(26) and had no kids.

He was abducted from his residence on 8th July 1993 by a police party headed by DSP (Deputy Superintendent of Police) Sukhdev Singh Brar in vehicle no. PB-67-9517. The police party was in plain clothes.

The whole incident was witnessed by

Chand Kaur resident of Wajidpur Badeshan

Sarbjit Kaur resident of Khatar Hakimpura

Satpal Singh resident of Wajidpur Badeshan.

According to them, the main accused for it were Sukhdev Singh Brar (50) DSP, Amrik Singh Grewal (45) ASI, Bahadur Singh Kutban (45) Constable.

His father Ram Dhan Singh died after his abduction. DSP Sukhdev Singh Brar had demanded Rs. 1,50,000/- from Ram Dhan Singh for the release of Sukhwinder Singh alias Bhola. He could not arrange such a huge amount. As a result of mental depression, because of this, he died. His mother is mentally upset, since his abduction. Her nephew (Bhanja) who used to live with her has also died.

### VFF/0523

The case of Ram Singh Billing alias Midda Singh son of Himmat Singh and Jaswant Kaur, Resident of village Dhadogal, Dist. Sangrur. He was an educated man and had completed his formal education unto High School. He now worked as a journalist and earned 4000 rupees monthly. He wass married to Rajinder Kaur (33) and had 2 kids

Libtar Singh (10-Male) and Pavittar Pal Kaur (7-Female).

He had clean past with no cases to his name and no anti-social contacts as well.

He was picked up from his residence on 3rd January 1992 by a Police party headed by SHO of Lohat Baddi P.S., S. Tarlochan Singh.

Ram Singh Biling left his house in the early morning of 3rd January 1992 at about 6 AM. He departed for Jalandhar regarding his press work. After his having reported about the false Police encounter he apprehended that the Police might pick him up from outside his village or house as he had information that the Police were keeping tab on him and were always on the look-out to nab him at some place where there could be no witnesses. For this reason, he never used to board the bus from the same place and particularly from the village. He was dropped by one Bharpur Singh of his own village on his bicycle at the bus stand of village Amargarh. In the presence of Bharpur, he boarded a bus for Malerkotla Town and reached Malerkotla. after alighting at Malerkotla he met one Mr. Gian Chand Sharma (Vice President of the Malerkotla news-reporters Union) who had his office at the bus stand. It is pertinent to mention that it was through Mr. Sharma that Mr. Ram Singh Billing had met the then ASP Iqbalpreet Singh at Malerkotla and pleaded before him that the Police should stop harassing him. The ASP had told them that if he stopped writing against the Police then the Police shall stop harassing him. Later on, Mr. Sharma was killed by the militants on the suspicion that Mr. Billing was picked up by the Police on the basis of information provided by Mr. Sharma.

After meeting Sharma, Mr. Billing boarded the bus for Jalandhar. As the bus reached near village Bhogiwal, it was stopped by the Police at the Police 'Naka' (barrier). Ram Singh Billing was made to alight from the bus and taken into custody by the Police of Lohat Baddi Police Post. The family came to know about this incident at around 3 PM from one Pappu (Commission Agent dealing in fruits), resident of Dhuri Vegetable Market, who was informed by one of the passengers in the bus namely Gurcharan Singh resident of village Palasour. However, later on, he refused to testify during the court proceedings. It may also be mentioned that Pappu was also picked up by the Police and killed after fifteen days of Billing's abduction. Ranjodh Singh and his father were not present in the house when the news was received by the family. The female family members who were present in the house at that time immediately informed Billing's uncle ('chacha') Sant Singh who lived next door. Sant Singh immediately approached Sarpanch (Head of Village Council) Satwant Singh of the village. Thereafter, Sant Singh, Sarpanch Satwant Singh, Panch (Member Panchayat i.e. Village Council) Hakam Singh, Sakinder Singh and Bharpur Singh, all from the same village went to Police Post Lohat Baddi and reached there at about 4.30 PM. As the main gate of the Police Post was open, they had no difficulty in going inside the Police Post. The Incharge of the Police Post Tarlochan Singh was not present there at that time. The Policemen present at the said Police Post at that time were Head Constable (HC) Teja Singh and HC Amrik Singh. After entering the Police Post, the delegation members started lodging a protest with the Police officials present there in a loud and shrill voice. The Police officials present there refused having taken Ram Singh into their custody. But Ram Singh Billing, who had been locked up in one of the rooms at the Police Post heard the uproar outside. He climbed the door and stood behind the glass pane of the ventilator on top of the door. The delegation members saw him standing there. They showed Ram Singh Billing standing in front of the ventilator to the Policemen who had been denying his custody so far. At this, they admitted his custody but they told the Panchayat that they must talk to ASI Tarlochan Singh, Incharge of the said Police Post about his release because only he could take a decision in this matter. The delegation members waited for ASI Tarlochan Singh till 7 PM but he did not turn up. They requested the Police officials present there to let them meet Ram Singh Billing but they said that they were not authorized to do so in the absence of their Incharge. So, the delegation returned to the village.

On the following day at about 7 AM, the same delegation again visited Lohat Baddi Police Post. On that day also they saw Ram Singh Billing standing behind the ventilator. ASI Tarlochan Singh, Incharge of the Police Post, admitted his custody but said that he had been detained under the instructions of SSP Sangrur, Narinderpal Singh and that he only could order his release from their custody. He advised them to meet the SSP. The delegation reached Sangrur around noon time and met the SSP there. The SSP feigned ignorance but promised to look into the matter and make enquiries and that thereafter he would inform the delegation accordingly. At 4 or 5 PM, they again met the SSP who told them that he had enquired from various places but he had been unable to trace the whereabouts of Ram Singh Billing. At this, the Sarpanch and other members of the delegation told the SSP that they had seen with their own eyes Ram Singh Billing in custody at Police Post Lohat Baddi. On hearing this, he relented a bit and asked the delegation to come on the following day.

On the following day, the delegation which met the SSP Sangrur consisted of about 35 persons including Gurcharan Singh Tohra, all the above mentioned members, Ram Singh's brother Ranjodh Singh, his father Himmat Singh and a number of press reporters from Sangrur district. Throughout their meeting, the SSP maintained that the Police of his Police district had not picked up Ram Singh Billing. However, when his statement was challenged by the Sarpanch who told him that he had seen Ram Singh Biling detained at Police Post Lohat Baddi, the SSP made a ridiculously lame excuse that he might have been lodged there by the Police of some other Police district and those Police personnel might have made a halt at the said Police Post for rest and refreshment. With a view to avoid further embarassment, he assured the delegation members that he would enquire from other Police districts also about Ram Singh Billing.

The family members of Ram Singh Billing had been meeting the SSP often along with various political leaders including those belonging to the Congress Party, but he did not budge an inch from his earlier stand.

*The family members believe that Ram Singh Billing has been killed by the Police and he is no more. They have come to such a conclusion after making enquiries from ASI Tarlochan Singh through somebody who was close to him. ASI Tarlochan Singh informed the said person unofficially that Ram Singh Billing had been done away with.*

*Ranjodh Singh stated that as Ram Singh Biling was eldest in the family and was the first in the whole family to have obtained graduation degree, the progress and social and economic upliftment was totally dependent on him. His disappearance shattered the whole family not only economically but mentally also. The family has still not been able to mentally overcome his loss.*

*The greatest tragedy for the family is that Billing's uncle ('chacha') Sant Singh, who was a prime witness and had been helping them throughout, refused to testify in the Court.*

*Ram Singh Billing's father owned just 3 acres of land only. The family incurred an expenditure of about Rs. 70,000/- in pursuing his case and had to sell off 3/5 acres of their land holding in order to meet these expenses. Ranjodh Singh said that their's is not a rich or well-off family and are undergoing economic hardships as the whole family are dependent on this meagre land holding.*

*Livtar Singh, son of Ram Singh Billing, who was a student of Nursery at Baru Sahib Academy at the time of this incident, had to be withdrawn from the said school in class I as the family could not afford his fees. The family approached the school authorities for concession, but it was refused. Now both the children are studying in a school at a nearby town Amargarh.*

### VFF/0524

Kuldip Singh son of Kartar Singh and Tej Kaur resident of village Kuthala, Tehsil Malerkotla, Dist. Sangrur. DATE OF BIRTH- 15th July 1954

He had completed his primary education and discontinued his studies at the sixth grade for following into his father's footsteps and getting into farming. This yielded him a total of 5500 Rs*.

He was married to Gurmit Kaur (42) and had 2 boys named Jasvir Singh (22) and

Gurbaj Singh (19).

Hhe had no past linking him to anti social activities.

He was picked up from his residence on 17th October 1992 by a police party headed by DSP Sherpur, Mr. Hadeep Singh and including Darshan Singh SHO Dehlon P.S., Bakshish Singh SHO Sherpur Police Station and other police personnel. Subsequently, on 15th May 1994, his wife Gurmit Kaur was also taken to Police Station Bhadaur by SHO Police Station Sherpur, S. Bakshish Singh. There she was interrogated and tortured brutally so that she may not file any report/case against the police. After that she was taken to C.I.A. Staff Handiaya by Inspector Sant Kumar who threatened to kill her if she filed any report/case against the police.]

Victim's wife Gurmit Kaur became frightened after this incident and her torture subsequently. Her parents as well as the victim's parents have become mentally depressed after the incident.

### VFF/0525

Karnail Singh alias happy (19), son of Sukhdev Singh and Nirmal Kaur resident of village tibba, Dist. Sangrur.

DATE OF BIRTH-20th April 971

He had his primary education and stated working after that, as he had failed to clear his 7th grade. He worked as a carpenter and managed to gather 5000 rs per month.

At midnight on 8th April 1991, a police party headed by Bharat Kumar, SHO of Police Station Sherpur came and enquired the whereabouts of Karnail Singh, from S. Sukhdev Singh, father of Karnail Singh. He told them that he was at his furniture shop at village Ganda Singh Wala, Gurbakhshpura. Kuldeep Singh alias Keepa was also there in the police vehicle. Sukhdev Singh recognised Kuldeep Singh and uttered that Keepa is there in the vehicle. On this, Gurcharan Singh alighted from the vehicle, hit him (Sukhdev Singh) with a Rifle Butt and said "We are Kharkus (militants)". However, Sukhdev Singh had recognised the police personnel. They were SHO of Police Station Sherpur Mr. Bharat Kumar, Constable Gurcharan Singh, Constable Darshan Singh, and SPO Devinder Singh. Two of them were in uniform and the other two were in civil clothes.

Kuldeep Singh was a resident of village Tibba, Tehsil Dhuri, district Sangrur was a 25 years old youth. He had learnt the trade of an electrician after passing his Matriculation and he was engaged in the business of repairing electric motors at his village. He used to help his father Mukand Singh and brother Lakhbir Singh in agricultural farming also. He got married to Charanjit Kaur in 1989 and a child (son) was born out of this wedlock in 1990. He was an 'Amritdhari' (baptised) Sikh youth and a member of the Gurdwara Management Committee of his village. He was a religious minded youth, but, he was not involved in any sort of political activities. His brother Karnail Singh told the Investigation Team that in those days, a youth namely Devinder Singh Rashin who was a Police "Cat" used to live in their village. According to him, Devinder Singh, on one hand, used to pose as a militant among the militant ranks and on the other he used to inform the Police about the activities of the militants and get them arrested. He was notorious for committing robberies and extortion also, under this (Police) cover. Once, Devinder Singh demanded ten thousand rupees from Kuldeep Singh who was a member of the Gurdwara Management Committee, but he refused. Kuldeep Singh was a courageous youth and he was not afraid of anyone. He was also aware of immoral activities of Devinder Singh. Devinder Singh had got Kuldeep Singh arrested also, once or twice, by the Police of Malerkotla and Sherpur, on the basis of suspicion.

On 8 April 1991 at about 11 P.M., a Police party of Sherpur Police Station consisting of a few Policemen in civil clothes and a few others in uniform, raided the house of Kuldeep Singh. He was asleep in the 'Baithak' (drawing room) of his house. His wife had gone to her parents' house. His father, uncle ('Chacha'), brother and mother were also present in the house. The Police had entered the house after scaling the walls of the house. The Policemen woke up Kuldeep Singh and said that they wanted to enquire about somebody's house from him. They did not allow him to put on his clothes. At such a behaviour by the Police, his family members got suspicious about the intentiion of the Police and it was evident to them that the talk of enquiring about somebody's house was an excuse only (for taking him away). The family members informed the people in their neighbourhood about this incident.

The Police party went away towards the house of Karnail Singh Happy son of Sukhdev Singh, resident of the same village. At Karnail Singh's house, they enquired from the family members about Karnail Singh. Sukhdev Singh told that his son was at his shop at village Gandewal (Gurbakhshpura) at that time. To a query by his wife as to who were enquiring about Karnail Singh, Sukhdev Singh replied, "These are Policemen." At this, the members of the raiding party hit Sukhdev Singh with rifle butts and said, "We are Singhs (Militanta)." Some time later, Mukand Singh (Kuldeep Singh's father) saw three persons riding a Hero Honda motor cycle coming from the side of village Gandewala. Mukand Singh was on his way back from the house of an aquaintance, after informing him about the arrest of Kuldeep Singh. Just a few minutes later, Mukand Singh and other family members heard the sound of gunshots. The sound of gunshots seemed to be coming from the drain side. According to Mukand Singh, he immediately ran towards that side and saw that a large number of people were going towards that side. He saw that two dead bodies were lying on the track of the drain. Blood was flowing. Mukand Singh recognised Kuldeep Singh by touching him. As it was a moon-lit night, Mukand Singh could recognise Kuldeep Singh. However, he did not know anything about the other dead youth. Mukand Singh came back and informed his family members and those neighboiurs who had woken up by now, that Kuldeep Singh had been killed.

In the morning, Mukand Singh and his family members came to know that the other killed youth was Karnail Singh Happy about whom the raiding party had enquiured from his family members and later on had arrested him from his shop at village Gandewal and broughgt him to that place. Karnail Singh's neighbour had come to know about his abduction. Karnail Singh's family members went to Gandewal at 4 A.M. and came to know about this (Karnail Singh's abduction). Thereafter, they went to the site of the incident and recognised the body of Karnail Singh.

At about 6.30 or 7 A.M., fathers of both the youth and eminent persons of the village, in a tractor trolley, reached Police Station Sherpur. The SHO Bharat Kumar was present at the Police Station . They informed him about the incident which had occured at their village. The SHO asked them to return to the village and said that he would follow them. The villagers had just reached the village when the SHO along with a Police party reached directly at the site of the incident. Some of the villagers were already standing at the incident site. Those people who had returned from the Police Station also reached at the site of the incident. Karnail Singh Happy's father Sukhdev Singh recognised two of the Policemen namely Darshan Singh (Constable) and Gurcharan Singh (Constable) as members of the party which had raided his house on the previous night. Sukhdev Singh told all those present there about this fact. The family members and the villagers got alerted and told the SHO clearly that it was their own handiwork. The villagers told that the said Policemen were there along with the party which had killed them (those two youth). But, the SHO flatly denied the allegation. At this, there was a heated argument between the villagers and the Police party. The SHO and the accused Policemen said, "OK. We have killed them. Do whatever you wish to." Seeing such an attitude of the Police, the villagers made an announcement that they wpould not allow the dead bodies of both the youth to be taken away. They demanded that the Deputy Commissioner (DC) of the district should come there. Gradually, the tractor trollies full of people of the villages around the site of the incident reached the site. By noon, thousands of people had assembled there. In view of the public pressure, senior officers like SDM Malerkotla and DSP Chheena (Malerkotla) reached the site of the incident. A very large Police force also arrived there. The situation was very critical. At times, it seemed that the Police would use force and disperse the people. The SSP of the district, Mr. Bhullar ordered the people several times, to disperse and threatened them, but the people stuck to their guns.

Ultimately, the district administration had to bow before the public opinion. In the presence of thousands of people, the accused Policemen namely Darshan Singh and Gurcharan Singh were ordered to remove their uniforms and they were hand-cuffed. The F.I.R. was recorded and postmortem got conducted, on the spot. The name of the third accused namely Devinder Singh Rashin (Police Cat) was also mentioned in the F.I.R. In those days, he used to be with the Police only. According to the villagers, he was a SPO (Special Police Officer). Later on, he also was arrested. Only Devinder Singh Rashin was jailed. Darshan Singh (Constable) and Gurcharan Singh (Constable) were not prosecuted. In the meantime, SDM Malerkotla strated investigation into this incident. Whenever the family members used to go for deposing before the SDM, Gurcharan Singh and Darshan Singh used to threaten them not to depose against them. The family members complained about it to the SDM. However, the SDM did not take any action whatsoever. Meanwhile, the case remained sub judice in a Court at Dhuri. They (the Police) continued to produce Devinder Singh in the Court for about a year. According to the information received by the family members, the Police withdrew the case after some time, as Devinder Singh Rashin (Police Cat) had threatened them that if they did not withdraw the case against him, he would implicate all of them. The family members suspect that the case was hushed up, either on the basis of the inquiry by the SDM or in some other way. They are not aware of the exact status of the case. On seeing that nothing happened in the case, the family members had filed a case in the High Court through their advocate Navkiran Singh. The documents of the case are not with the family. However, according to the information available with the family, about a year ago, the High Court had issued orders to proceed on the basis of the original F.I.R. in this case. Both the families don't know whether any follow-up action was taken on the said order or not.

*Investigation Team of VFF (Amrik Singh Muktsar and others) are of the opinion that the legal position of this case can be found out by going through the documents of the case including the High Court orders. The family members, being illiterate, are not in a position to tell anything about the legal position of the case.*

*He has been killed by police. All the witnesses and other evidence are there. Dead body was handed over by the SSP Sangrur, to the family members after getting a postmortem conducted on the spot. The cremation was carried out by the family members and other villagers.*

*The news was published in all the newspapers. On 15th April 1991, it was published in the Punjabi daily newspaper 'Ajj Di Awaz' (published from Jalandhar). This incident continued to make headlines and it was a hot topic of discussion in all the newspapers, for several days.*

### VFF/0526

Kuldeep Singh alias Keepa(25), son of Mukand Singh and Mukhtiar Kaur, resident of village Tibba, Dist. Sangrur. DATE OF BIRTH- 15th March1966

He was a matriculate* and later discontinued school to get into farming. He managed to earn 5500 Rs per month.

He was married to Charanjit Kaur (30) and they had an 11 year old son Kiranjit Singh.

Before this incident also, he was taken to Malerkotla Police Station and Sangrur (Sadar) Police Station . After that he was being harassed unnecessarily by the police of Police Station Sherpur. Then he appeared before the DSP and told him the names of police personnel who were harassing him. That is why, perhaps, those police personnel abducted him from his residence and killed him.

He was abducted from his residence by a police party headed by Mr. Bharat Kumar, SHO Police Station Sherpur and including other police personnel of the same Police Station like Constable Darshan Singh, Constable Gurcharan Singh, and SPO Devinder Singh. Later at about 12.30 A.M. on 9th April 1991, he along with Karnail Singh was shot dead by the abovementioned police party. The dead body was handed over to the family and cremated at the same village. A FIR was got registered at Police Station Sherpur by a Havaldar (Head Constable) on the instructions of SHO Bharat Kumar.

Kuldeep Singh son of Mukand Singh, resident of village Tibba, Tehsil Dhuri, district Sangrur was a 25 years old youth. He had learnt the trade of an electrician after passing his Matriculation and he was engaged in the business of repairing electric motors at his village. He used to help his father Mukand Singh and brother Lakhbir Singh in agricultural farming also. He got married to Charanjit Kaur in 1989 and a child (son) was born out of this wedlock in 1990. He was an 'Amritdhari' (baptised) Sikh youth and a member of the Gurdwara Management

Committee of his village. He was a religious minded youth, but, he was not involved in any sort of political activities. His brother Karnail Singh told the Investigation Team that in those days, a youth namely Devinder Singh Rashin who was a Police "Cat" used to live in their village. According to him, Devinder Singh, on one hand, used to pose as a militant among the militant ranks and on the other he used to inform the Police about the activities of the militants and get them arrested. He was notorious for committing robberies and extortion also, under this (Police) cover. Once, Devinder Singh demanded ten thousand rupees from Kuldeep Singh who was a member of the Gurdwara Management Committee, but he refused. Kuldeep Singh was a courageous youth and he was not afraid of anyone. He was also aware of immoral activities of Devinder Singh. Devinder Singh had got Kuldeep Singh arrested also, once or twice, by the Police of Malerkotla and Sherpur, on the basis of suspicion.

On 8 April 1991 at about 11 P.M., a Police party of Sherpur Police Station consisting of a few Policemen in civil clothes and a few others in uniform, raided the house of Kuldeep Singh. He was asleep in the 'Baithak' (drawing room) of his house. His wife had gone to her parents' house. His father, uncle ('Chacha'), brother and mother were also present in the house. The Police had entered the house after scaling the walls of the house. The Policemen woke up Kuldeep Singh and said that they wanted to enquire about somebody's house from him. They did not allow him to put on his clothes. At such a behaviour by the Police, his family members got suspicious about the intentiion of the Police and it was evident to them that the talk of enquiring about somebody's house was an excuse only (for taking him away). The family members informed the people in their neighbourhood about this incident.

The Police party went away towards the house of Karnail Singh Happy son of Sukhdev Singh, resident of the same village. At Karnail Singh's house, they enquired from the family members about Karnail Singh. Sukhdev Singh told that his son was at his shop at village Gandewal (Gurbakhshpura) at that time. To a query by his wife as to who were enquiring about Karnail Singh, Sukhdev Singh replied, "These are Policemen." At this, the members of the raiding party hit Sukhdev Singh with rifle butts and said, "We are Singhs (Militanta)." Some time later, Mukand Singh (Kuldeep Singh's father) saw three persons riding a Hero Honda motor cycle coming from the side of village Gandewala. Mukand Singh was on his way back from the house of an acquaintance, after informing him about the arrest of Kuldeep Singh. Just a few minutes later, Mukand Singh and other family members heard the sound of gunshots. The sound of gunshots seemed to be coming from the drain side. According to Mukand Singh, he immediately ran towards that side and saw that a large number of people were going towards that side. He saw that two dead bodies were lying on the track of the drain. Blood was flowing. Mukand Singh recognised Kuldeep Singh by touching him. As it was a moon-lit night, Mukand Singh could recognise Kuldeep Singh. However, he did not know anything about the other dead youth. Mukand Singh came back and informed his family members and those neighbours who had woken up by now, that Kuldeep Singh had been killed.

In the morning, Mukand Singh and his family members came to know that the other killed youth was Karnail Singh Happy about whom the raiding party had enquiured from his family members and later on had arrested him from his shop at village Gandewal and brought him to that place. Karnail Singh's neighbour had come to know about his abduction. Karnail Singh's family members went to Gandewal at 4 A.M. and came to know about this (Karnail Singh's abduction). Thereafter, they went to the site of the incident and recognised the body of Karnail Singh.

At about 6.30 or 7 A.M., fathers of both the youth and eminent persons of the village, in a tractor trolley, reached Police Station Sherpur. The SHO Bharat Kumar was present at the Police Station . They informed him about the incident which had occured at their village. The SHO asked them to return to the village and said that he would follow them. The villagers had just reached the village when the SHO along with a Police party reached directly at the site of the incident. Some of the villagers were already standing at the incident site. Those people who had returned from the Police Station also reached at the site of the incident. Karnail Singh Happy's father Sukhdev Singh recognised two of the Policemen namely Darshan Singh (Constable) and Gurcharan Singh (Constable) as members of the party which had raided his house on the previous night. Sukhdev Singh told all those present there about this fact. The family members and the villagers got alerted and told the SHO clearly that it was their own handiwork. The villagers told that the said Policemen were there along with the party which had killed them (those two youth). But, the SHO flatly denied the allegation. At this, there was a heated argument between the villagers and the Police party. The SHO and the accused Policemen said, "OK. We have killed them. Do whatever you wish to." Seeing such an attitude of the Police, the villagers made an announcement that they would not allow the dead bodies of both the youth to be taken away. They demanded that the Deputy Commissioner (DC) of the district should come there.

Gradually, the tractor trollies full of people of the villages around the site of the incident reached the site. By noon, thousands of people had assembled there. In view of the public pressure, senior officers like SDM Malerkotla and DSP Chheema (Malerkotla) reached the site of the incident. A very large Police force also arrived there. The situation was very critical. At times, it seemed that the Police would use force and disperse the people. The SSP of the district, Mr. Bhullar ordered the people several times, to disperse and threatened them, but the people stuck to their guns.

Ultimately, the district administration had to bow before the public opinion. In the presence of thousands of people, the accused Policemen namely Darshan Singh and Gurcharan Singh were ordered to remove their uniforms and they were hand-cuffed. The F.I.R. was recorded and postmortem got conducted, on the spot. The name of the third accused namely Devinder Singh Rashin (Police Cat) was also mentioned in the F.I.R. In those days, he used to be with the Police only. According to the villagers, he was a SPO (Special Police Officer). Later on, he also was arrested. Only Devinder Singh Rashin was jailed. Darshan Singh (Constable) and Gurcharan Singh (Constable) were not prosecuted. In the meantime, SDM Malerkotla started investigation into this incident. Whenever the family members used to go for deposing before the SDM, Gurcharan Singh and Darshan Singh used to threaten them not to depose against them. The family members complained about it to the SDM. However, the SDM did not take any action whatsoever. Meanwhile, the case remained sub judice in a Court at Dhuri. They (the Police) continued to produce Devinder Singh in the Court for about a year. According to the information received by the family members, the Police withdrew the case after some time, as Devinder Singh Rashin (Police Cat) had threatened them that if they did not withdraw the case against him, he would implicate all of them. The family members suspect that the case was hushed up, either on the basis of the inquiry by the SDM or in some other way. They are not aware of the exact status of the case. On seeing that nothing happened in the case, the family members had filed a case in the High Court through their advocate Navkiran Singh. The documents of the case are not with the family. However, according to the information available with the family, about a year ago, the High Court had issued orders to proceed on the basis of the original F.I.R. in this case. Both the families don't know whether any follow-up action was taken on the said order or not.

*Investigation Team of VFF (Amrik Singh Muktsar and others) are of the opinion that the legal position of this case can be found out by going through the documents of the case including the High Court orders. The family members, being illiterate, are not in a position to tell anything about the legal position of the case.*

*He has been shot dead. The dead body was seen by his father. Cremation was carried out by his family members and other villagers at their village.*

*All the newspapers. In 'Ajj Di Awaz' on 15th April 1991. This incident continued to make headlines and it was a hot topic of discussion in all the newspapers, for several days.*

### VFF/0527

Sarabjit Singh alias Lovely, son of Balbir Singh and Sukhdev Kaur, resident of village Bhadarvad, tehsil Dhuri, Dist. Sangrur. DATE OF BIRTH- 06th October 1966.

He was an M.A. (Master's in Arts), and was at the time pursuing his M.Phil.

There was no known source of his income.

He went missing on 10th July from Dhanaula. The records do not show his being involved in any anti-social activities.

Before this incident, since 1989, the Police used to call his cousin Iqbal Singh to the Police Station. His father Balbir Singh was also called to the Police Station several times. They were unnecessarily harassed by the police. On 10th July 1993, police came to the house of Sarbjit Singh and enquired about him. His family members told them that he had gone to his maternal uncle's house at Dhanaula. Iqbal Singh was already in their custody. Then they went to Dhanaula and picked up Sarbjit Singh and his father Balbir Singh. Balbir Singh was dropped at Sangrur by-pass and was told that they were taking Sarbjit Singh to Police Station He was asked to come to Dhuri Police Station next day. Next day, Iqbal Singh was sent home with Balbir Singh but Sarbjit was not released. On the same day i.e. 11th July 1993, Balbir Singh and Ranjit Singh saw Sarbjit at Police Station Dhuri. Balbir Singh was asked to contact SSP Sangrur for the release of Sarbjit. When he approached SSP Sangrur, he refused to release him saying that he was with them and would not be released yet. His whereabouts are not known till date.

The family members believe that he may be still alive even though there is no solid basis for this belief. They also believe that his body had not been creamated or disposed of in some other manner.

The witnesses to this incident are Balbir Singh , Iqbal Singh, Ranjit Singh and Surjit. His grandmother (Naani) expired after this incident. She used to utter 'Lovely', 'Lovely' till the time of her death. She felt that he had been snatched from her own hands. His parents are mentally upset since that time.

**VFF/0528**

Bikkar Singh alias Driver (36), son of Prithi Singh and Surjit Kaur resident of village Tibba, tehsil Dhuri, Dist. Sangrur . DATE OF BIRTH- 15th June 1957. He was Truck driver by profession and earned 4000Rs. per month

Bikkar Singh was an illiterate truck driver. He was not associated with any sort of political or militant activities whatsoever. His brother Mall Singh was involved in militant activities. That is why the Police used to pick him up often and torture him. Ultimately he died due to internal injuries caused by Police torture.

He was picked up from Ludhiana along with truck No. PAT-8362. The truck belonged to his brother Baldev Singh and was enlisted at Truck Union Dhuri. On that day he had brought some cargo from Rajasthan and it was to be delivered at Ludhiana.

Victim Bikkar Singh's brother Mall Singh was a truck driver. He had three brothers and three sisters. His father had expired when the children were still young. On being grown up, Mall Singh started learning the trade of a truck driver. His family did not own any land. Mall Singh was also influenced by the political and militant movement which had erupted in Punjab in the aftermath of Army attack on Sri Darbar Sahib at Amritsar in 1984. He was a sentimental youth and he had got himself baptised after the Operation Blue Star in 1984. His family members told that he was doing well in his business and that they did not know what influenced him, he sold out his truck and joined the ranks of the militants. Once, Mall Singh had been arrested also by the Police and he had been jailed also. However, the family members did not know the details about the same.

Due to the activities of Mall Singh, the Police of Sherpur Police Station and that of Handiaya C.I.A. Staff started raiding his house. The family members told that they did not have any knowledge about the activities of Mall Singh. They came to know about it only when the Police raided their house with a view to arrest him. The Police enquired about Mall Singh whereas the family members did not know anything about his whereabouts. The Police used to pick up his brothers namely Bikkar Singh, Darshan Singh and Baldev Singh and torture them. Gradually, the Police started raiding their house daily. Later on, it became difficult for the family members to keep track of the Police raids as to from which Police Station they had come. Whosoever male member of the family they could lay their hands on, the Police used to pick him up and take him away. So much so that the Police started raiding the houses of their relatives also like the in-laws of his brothers and sisters and arresting them. The Police used to torture the brothers of Mall Singh more and ask them about the whereabouts of Mall Singh. Whereas, the family members did not know anything at all about him.

When the Investigation Team visited his house, no male member of the family was present at home. Nasib Kaur and Malkeet Kaur, wives of Mall Singh's brothers namely Darshan Singh and Baldev Singh were present at home. According to them, this process continued till the time of Mall Singh's arrest. Both the women and all other family members also are illiterate. They do not know about the dates, not even the years, of incidents which occured in their family. According to Nasib Kaur and Malkeet Kaur, the memory of those terrible days sends shivers down their spine. The Police used to pick up and take away male membrers of their family. It became difficult to bring up the children even, they said.

According to Nasib Kaur, about one and a half or two years prior to the arrest of Mall Singh, the Sherpur Police had raided their house, picked up Bikkar Singh and took him away. He was tortured brutally in illegal custody for 7-8 days. He received grievous internal injuries near his neck due to this inhuman torture. With the passage of time, water started accumulating in those wounds. He was completely bed-ridden after his release. Despite medical treatment, his physical condition deteriorated day by day. About one year after this torture, in January (on Lohri day) he breathed his last. During the same year, in the month of September, Nachhatter Singh, SHO of Mehal Kalan Police Station arrested Mall Singh and another person namely Sukhdev Singh Mahant resident of village Nihaluwal, at Calcutta and brought them (to Punjab). The family members told that at the time when the Police had arrested and brought Mall Singh, his brother Baldev Singh was in the custody of Sherpur Police. He had heard the shrieks of Mall Singh as the Police were torturing him in the other room but Baldev Singh was released the very next day. Mall Singh was detained in illegal custody for about a month and thereafter, he and Sukhdev Singh, who was brought along with him, were shot dead in a fake encounter near village Kurar. According to Naisb Kaur, once, the Police had brought Mall Singh to the village also while he was in their custody. Several villagers had seen him in Police custody and they had informed his family members about it. On being asked by the Investigation Team as to whether they pursued Mall Singh's case while he was in Police custody, Nasib Kaur said, "Veera (Brother), what to talk of pursuing his case, on the contrary we heaved a sigh of relief that now that he had been arrested the Police won't harass us. However, we never thought that the Police will kill him."

Nasib Kaur further told that the movement (militancy) which rocked Punjab, had claimed two lives of their family. Economically they have suffered so much that now-a-days they were making both ends meet by working as daily wagers. She told that after the Police had killed Mall Singh, even though they stopped harassing them, yet, whenever a new officer is posted at their Police Station , he visits their house to make enquiries about Mall Singh and notes down the details about the other family members.

The office-bearers of the Akali Dal (Amritsar) of district Sangrur told the Investigation Team that after Mall Singh's arrest, a habeas corpus petition was filed by the party in the High Court. But, the record of the same is available neither with the said party nor with the family members. According to his family members, this incident seemed to have taken place in the year 1994.

He died at home itself, as a result of injuries caused by brutal and inhuman torture inflicted upon him by the Police. Cremation was carried out by the family members and other villagers at his native village.

**VFF/0529**

Mall Singh (35), son of Late Prithi Singh and Late Surjit Kaur, resident of village Tibba, tehsil Dhuri, Dist. Sangrur. DATE OF BIRTH- 20th May1959.

He was a school drop-out and worked as a Truck driver and earned 4000Rs. per month.

He was abducted on 10th January 1994 by a police party headed by DSP Harbhajan Singh and including Nachhatter Singh SHO Mehal Kalan, ASI Gurcharan Singh and some other policemen. He was tortured so brutally that he died because of that. Later, the police fabricated the story of an encounter.

Mall Singh was a truck driver. He had three brothers and three sisters. His father had expired when the children were still young. On being grown up, Mall Singh started learning the trade of a truck driver. His family did not own any land. Mall Singh was also influenced by the political and militant movement which had erupted in Punjab in the aftermath of Army attack on Sri Darbar Sahib at Amritsar in 1984. He was a sentimental youth and he had got himself baptised after the Operation Blue Star in 1984. His family members told that he was doing well in his business and that they did not know what influenced him and he sold out his truck and joined the ranks of the militants. Once, Mall Singh had been arrested also by the Police and he had been jailed also. However, the family members did not know the details about the same.

Due to the activities of Mall Singh, the Police of Sherpur Police Station and that of Handiaya C.I.A. Staff started raiding his house. The family members told that they did not have any knowledge about the activities of Mall Singh. They came to know about it only when the Police raided their house with a view to arrest him. The Police enquired about Mall Singh whereas the family members did not know anything about his whereabouts. The Police used to pick up his brothers namely Bikkar Singh, Darshan Singh and Baldev Singh and torture them. Gradually, the Police started raiding their house daily. Later on, it became difficult for the family members to keep track of the Police raids as to from which Police Station they had come. Whosoever male member of the family they could lay their hands on, the Police used to pick him up and take him away. So much so that the Police started raiding the houses of their relatives also like the in-laws of his brothers and sisters and arresting them. The Police used to torture the brothers of Mall Singh more and ask them about the whereabouts of Mall Singh. Whereas, the family members did not know anything at all about him.

When the Investigation Team visited his house, no male member of the family was present at home. Nasib Kaur and Malkeet Kaur, wives of Mall Singh's brothers namely Darshan Singh and Baldev Singh were present at home. According to them, this process continued till the time of Mall Singh's arrest. Both the women and all other family members also are illiterate. They do not know about the dates, not even the years, of incidents which occured in their family. According to Nasib Kaur and Malkeet Kaur, the memory of those terrible days sends shivers down their spine. The Police used to pick up and take away male membrers of their family. It became difficult to bring up the children even, they said.

According to Nasib Kaur, about one and a half or two years prior to the arrest of Mall Singh, the Sherpur Police had raided their house, picked up Bikkar Singh and took him away. He was tortured brutally in illegal custody for 7-8 days. He received grievous internal injuries near his neck due to this inhuman torture. With the passage of time, water started accumulating in those wounds. He was completely bed-ridden after his release. Treatment continued. However, his physical condition deteriorated day by day. About one year after this torture, in January (on Lohri day) he breathed his last. During the same year, in the month of September, Nachhatter Singh, SHO of Mehal Kalan Police Station arrested Mall Singh and another person namely Sukhdev Singh Mahant resident of village Nihaluwal, at Calcutta and brought them (to Punjab). The family members told that at the time when the Police had arrested and brought Mall Singh, his brother Baldev Singh was in the custody of Sherpur Police. He had heard the shrieks of Mall Singh as the Police were torturing him in the other room. Next day itself, Baldev Singh was released. Mall Singh was detained in illegal custody for about a month and thereafter, he and Sukhdev Singh, who was brought along with him, were shot dead in a fake encounter near village Kurar. According to Naisb Kaur, once, the Police had brought Mall Singh to the village also while he was in their custody. Several villagers had seen him in Police custody and they had informed his family members about it. On being asked by the Investigation Team as to whether they pursued Mall Singh's contrary we heaved a sigh of relief that now that he had been arrested the Police won't harass us. However, we never thought that the Police will kill him."

Nasib Kaur further told that the movement (militancy) which rocked Punjab, had claimed two lives of their family. Economically they have suffered so much that now-a-days they were making both ends meet by working as daily wagers. She told that after the Police had killed Mall Singh, even though they stopped harassing them, yet, whenever a new officer is posted at their Police Station , he visits their house to make enquiries about Mall Singh and notes down the details about the other family members.

The office-bearers of the Akali Dal (Amritsar) of district Sangrur told the Investigation Team that after Mall Singh's arrest, a habeas corpus petition was filed by the party in the High Court. But, the record of the same is available neither with the said party nor with the family members. According to his family members, this incident seemed to have taken place in the year 1994.

He was shown by the Police as having been killed in an "encounter" with them. However, it is suspected that the Police had beaten him to death and later on, concocted the story of an "encounter".

His brother Bikkar Singh was tortured brutally by the Police in their illegal custody and he received grievous internal injuries near his neck. His condition deteriorated day by day and he remained bed-ridden for about a year but never recovered despite medical treatment. He succumbed to the same injuries which he had received during inhuman torture inflicted upon him by the Police.

This incident has left an imprint of terror on his family members who are till date terrified of the police.

**VFF/0530**

Case of Bhagwan Singh alias Bhana (45), son of Chitan Singh and Dalip Kaur resident of village Kumbharwal, Dist. Sangrur.

He was a school drop-out and had started his career as a truck driver. He also tilled his ancestral land which fetched him a total of 1000Rs a month. He was married to Harbans Kaur (40). They had no kids.

Bhagwan Singh had been a victim of police harassment since a long time. Once, his brother Kartar Singh paid Rs. 40,000/- to DSP Pawar through Sarpanch Nachhatter Singh to get Bhagwan Singh released.

However on 20th December 1993, Head Constable Nirmal Singh went over to his place and asked Kartar Singh to accompany him because he wanted to arrest Bhagwan Singh. Bhagwan Singh had gone to his aunt's house in village Gurman. So Kartar Singh took HC Nirmal Singh to village Gurman. There he left Kartar Singh and took Bhagwan Singh into custody and asked Kartar Singh to come to Police Station Bhawanigarh to get Bhagwan Singh released. Kartar Singh went to the said Police Station many times but he could not meet Bhagwan Singh.

The incident was witnessed by Kartar Singh and Naranjan Singh. His mother is mentally upset since that day and is awaiting his return.

**VFF/0531**

Kirpal Singh son of Gurdial Singh and Jangir Kaur resident of village Benra, Dist. Sangrur. He was a matriculate and was working as a Constable in B.S.F.*.

He earned Rs.3500 per month. He was married to Harjit Kaur (32) and they had a 5 year old girl child, Navdeep Kaur.

Police party came to his house on the intervening night of 19th/20th February 1993 looking for Kirpal Singh. Next morning, he was produced by the village Panchayat in front of the Police personnel namely SI Harpreet Singh, ASI Sardara Singh and ASI Gurmeet Singh. His whereabouts are not known since then.

Representations were sent. Proof of the same would be presented on the spot, (at the time of Enquiry).

His is a case of pure inhumane and atrocious activities carried out on the people of Punjab by the police.

**VFF/0532**

Veer Singh alias Fauji Dharmi son of Sundar Singh and Bahgwan Kaur resident of village Kaheru, Dist. Sangrur was working as a laborer earning about 1500Rs. per month.

He was married to Manjit Kaur (38_) and had three children namely, Sandeep Kaur (14), Jaspal Kaur (7) and Sukhwinder Singh (6).

He was abducted from Gurdwara Fatehgarh Sahib on 10<sup>th</sup> February 1993 by a police party consisting of Sardara Singh and Gurmel Singh of Police Station Bhawanigarh. His whereabouts are not known since then.

*(NOTE:-Not much information has been provided in the case because a lack of evidence as per the absence of the witnesses whose names will be disclosed at an appropriate time.)*

### VFF/0533

Bhagat Singh alias Bhagata son of Uttam Singh and karKartar Kaur resident of village Ghanauri Kalan, Dist. Sangrur. DATE OF BIRTH- 15<sup>th</sup> May1949

He had studied uptil the 4<sup>th</sup> grade and was now into farming. He earned 3000Rs. per month.

He was married to Balwant Kaur 45 and had 5 children Sapinder Kaur(21) Swarn Kaur(13) Harbans Singh(19) Surjan Singh(17) Jaswinder Singh(15).

Sardar Bhagat Singh was a resident of Village Salempur in District Sangrur belonged to a well-to-do farmer family. They were three brothers who used to live separately. Bhagat Singh had studied upto third or fourth standard only and had taken up agricultural farming when he grew up.

According to his family members, Bhagat Singh was a healthy youth who was interested in weight lifting. He had no political affiliations whatsoever. However, he used to take active interest in factionalism in the Village which is usually the outcome of the Panchayat (Village Council) electoral politics. He was an 'Amritdhari' (baptised) Sikh and a religious minded person. During the period of militancy, neither he was arrested ever on the basis of suspicion nor any case was registered against him ever.

On 11 June 1993 at about 4 A.M., a Police party raided Bhagat Singh's house and enquired about Bhagat Singh. But, Bhagat Singh was not available at home at that time as he had gone to a relative's place. The same Police party entered his brother Sant Singh's house by scaling the walls. Sant Singh took notice of the Police action and protested, saying that if they intended raiding his house then at least they should have brought the Village Sarpanch (Head of Village Council) along with them. Even as this argument was going on, the Village Sarpanch, Sardar Gurbachan Singh also arrived on the scene. At that time, Sant Singh was being put in the vehicle by the the Police. An ASI who was leading the Police party told the Sarpanch that they had arrested Sant Singh in compliance with the orders of the SSP Sangrur, Mr. Jasminder Singh. He directed the Sarpanch also to produce Bhagat Singh. According to Sant Singh, as the Police made him to sit in the Canter (four wheeler) vehicle, he saw that his brother-in-law (wife'e brother) Raghubir Singh son of Ajaib Singh resident of Village Katron was already seated in the said vehicle. However, they could not talk to each other inside the vehicle. The said Police party took them to C.I.A. Staff Bhawanigarh. On the following day, Sant Singh and Raghubir Singh were tortured brutally by the Police. The Police alleged that they gave shelter to the militants. SSP Jasminder Singh, SP (D) Pritpal Singh Virk and Inspector Ram Kumar of C.I.A. Staff used to be present at the time of torturing them (Sant Singh and Raghubir Singh). The Police continued to torture them for 4-5 days. In the meantime, DSP Sukhdev Singh Brar of Malerkotla Police raided the house of Sant Singh on the intervening night of 12-13 June (1993) and abducted his younger brother Kunda Singh and Vaid Singh (brother-in-law—sister's husband). The Malerkotla Police directed their family to produce Bhagat Singh and told that then they would releasse them. The Malerkotla Police released Vaid Singh one or two days later with a direction that he produce Bhagat Singh before them.

On 17th June1993, Bhagat Singh was produced before DSP Sukhdev Singh Brar in his office at Malerkotla, by a delegation consisting of the Village Sarpanch Gurbachan Singh, Amar Singh Sarpanch of Village Natt, Gurdev Singh Dhuri (Akali Leader) and Vaid Singh. The DSP assured all those eminent persons that they would release Bhagat Singh after interrogation for a day or two. Bhagat Singh was detained at Himmatiana Police Post under Malerkotla Police Station and tortured brutally. Megh Singh, resident of Village Sangali, who happened to visit the said Police Post for some job, saw Bhagat Singh in a very bad shape due to Police torture. Megh Singh infortmed Jathedar Jagdhir Singh Katron about it. Meanwhile, the eminent persons who had produced Bhagat Singh before DSP Sukhdev Singh, continued to meet the said DSP, but, he continued to make false promises of releasing him.

On 26 or 27 June 1993, the Police took Bhagat Singh to C.I.A. Staff Bhawanigarh where his brother Sant Singh and Sant Singh brother-in-law were already in the illegal custody of the Police. Even though Bhagat Singh was kept in a separate room, yet, Sant Singh and Raghubir Singh saw him from a distance. He was unable to walk or eat his food. On 28 or 29 June 1993, the Police released Raghubir Singh and on 30th June1993 they released Sant Singh also. Sant Singh was brought home by the Village Sarpanch Gurbachan Singh, Vaid Singh and Ajaib Singh

Katron (father-in-law). Sant Singh was in a very bad shape physically. Bhagat Singh was still in the custody of C.I.A. Staff when Sant Singh was released. The SSP Sangrur and DSP Malerkotla continued to make false promises about the release of Bhagat Singh.

For about one year, Bhagat Singh's family members, relatives, eminent persons of the area and the Village Panchayat ran from pillar to post, to get him released. For some time, the Police officers continued to make false promises of releasing him, but later on, they began to avoid these people. Ultimately, the family members also lost all hope of Bhagat Singh being alive. According to his brother Sant Singh, as per their capacity, they left no stone unturned to get Bhagat Singh released, but they were helpless.

A Criminal Writ Petition No. 183 of 1997 was filed by Sant Singh, brother of victim Bhagat Singh through Advocate Ranjan Lakhanpal.

During the hearing of this case, an affidavit was filed by one Jagjit Singh Gill, Deputy Superintendent of Police in which he averred that Bhagat Singh had escaped from police custdoy by breaking the buckle of the belt of the Constable to which he had been attached, with a jerk, while the Police were taking him for the recoveruy of arms. However, Justice S.C. MALTE of Punjab & Haryana High Court did not agree with this story of the Police. As such, he ordered an enquiry into this case to be conducted by the Sessions Judge Sangrur himself or by a subordinate officer to be appointed by him and the report submitted to the        High        Court within six months. The Order signed by the Judge S.C. Malte is dated 2nd September 1997. The Sessions Judge (Sangrur) detailed Additional Sessions Judge to enquire into this case. The inquiry into this case continued for about one year in the Court at Sangrur. At the time of recording of statements of the witnesses, Sukhdev Singh Brar who was DSP Malerkjotla at the time of this incident, issued threats of dire consequences to the family members of Bhagat Singh. However, the family members and other witnesses were not cowed down by those threats and they deposed boldly in this case. In the meantime, DSP Sukhdev Singh Brar offered to pay Rs. 10 Lakhs (Ten Lakhs only) to the family of Bhagat Singh in return for the withdrawal of the case, through Surjit Singh Barkandi who was sent by him to meet Jagdhir Singh Katron (brother of the President of Akali Dal (Badal) district Muktsar unit). However, he refused to accept this offer. During the course of inquiry by Additional Sessions Judge, the family members and their Lawyer felt that the attitude of the said Judge was extremely biased. For example, in order to prove their version of Bhagat Singh's escape from their custody to be true, the Police produced ASI NIrmal Singh before the Judge. In his statement, twice the said ASI said that Bhagat Singh escaped by breaking the handcuffs and once he said that he broke the belt of the

Constable to whom he had been strapped and ran away. On being requested by the Advocate

of Bhagat Singh's family to record this discrepancy in the statement of the said ASI, the Judge refused to record the same in the proceedings of the Court. Apart from that, the family members, through their own efforts, succeeded in getting a confessional statement from one Constable namely Satnam Singh to the effect that DSP Sukhdev Singh had killed Bhagat Singh. The Police, in their concocted story, had shown Constable Satnam Singh also as a member of the Police party from the custdoy of which Bhagat Singh had allegedly escaped. The family members produced the tape recording of the said confessional statement in the Court and requested the Judge to record the same in the proceedings of the case. However, the Judge did not accept the tape as a part of the proceedings of the Court and recorded only the statements of the persons namely Jagdhir Singh and Amrik Singh son of Amar Singh who had participated in the interview at the time of said tape recording, in the Court proceedings. During the course of the inquiry, the Judge was transferred and a new Judge was posted in. According to the family members, the attitude of the new Judge seemed to be somewhat OK. However, the family members are not fully satisfied with the Inquiry Report as they believe that despite clear evidence, the Inquiry Report was vague and biased.On the basis of the said Inquiry, the High Court, on 14-7-2000, directed that a F.I.R. be registered in the said case. However, the Order has not been  written yet. In fact, the decision of the High Court would be known only after a  copy of the said Order is received. His brother is mentally disturbed and has become physically weak and his mother who missed him a lot has recently died.

VFF/0534

Nirbhai Singh son of Dharam Singh and Labh Kaur resident of village Alal, Dist. Sangrur. DATE OF BIRTH- 15th January 1969

He was a matriculate* and had got a job in the Police. He was a Constable* in the Punjab Police (NOTE- his income is not mentioned)

Nirbhai Singh was an intelligent and well behaved boy. He had completed his Commando training in the Punjab Police and was a loyal member of the force. He had never absented himself from his duty and his superiors did not have any complaint regarding his performance on duty.

Nirbhai Singh's cousin (Maasi's son) Avtar Singh Tari son of Sadhu Singh resident of village Tur Vanjara had joined the militant ranks. He was killed in an encounter with the Police of Division No. 6 Ludhiana, on 2nd September 1991 at Ludhiana. The Police got suspicious of Nirbhai Singh on somebody's complaint. Nirbhai Singh had come home on leave on 5<sup>th</sup> October 1991. On 9<sup>th</sup> October 1991, the Ludhiana Police came to their house and told hid family members to send Nirbhai Singh to Ludhiana. But, Nirbhai Singh was not at home. Thereafter, on 12<sup>th</sup> October 1991, Patiala Police raided the house. They picked up their other son Avtar Singh saying that he would be released after Nirbhai Singh was produced before the Police.

On 14<sup>th</sup> October 1991, Nirbhai Singh was produced before Jasvir Singh Sandhu SP (Operations) at Sangrur by his father along with Comrade Chand Singh Chopra Ex-MLA and in the presence of Sukhwinder Singh Bhola Comrade Sarpanch of Ladda, Major Singh Punawal Tehsil Secretary CPM, Bhagwant Singh Dhandra, Sahib Singh, President Kisan Union Dhandra, Ajaib Singh Jakhlan, and his brotherr Gurmel Singh. After that he was handed over to Inspector Sant Kumar C.I.A. Staff Patiala. He talked to his brother Avtar Singh at C.I.A. Staff Patiala. When the family contacted Sant Kumar, he said that he had handed him over to Sumedh Singh Saini of Chandigarh. He was kept at Chandigarh for four days. When his father contacted DSP Surjit Singh Grewal at Patiala, he told him that his son was innocent and further said that they had sent him to Narinder Kumar Bhargo at Ludhiana Focal Point No. 6 (Sadar) Police Station . He was detained there for 17-18 days. Thereafter, he came to know that Inspector Sant Kumar had taken him to Patiala.

Later, his father saw Nirbhai Singh with Inspector Sant Kumar at the fair at Sirhind on 12-13 Poh (month of December). He then along with some respectable persons requested Sant Kumar to either release him or send him to Jail. However, Sant Kumar flatly denied having Nirbhai Singh in his custody.

Thereafter, Inspector Sant Kumar was transferred to Patiala (Sadar) Police Station and he took Nirbhai Singh along with him there. In the month of May, his father went to Patiala (Sadar) Police Station to meet Inspector Sant Kumar. At that time, Nirbhai Singh was there in the lock-up. He noticed him and came near the bars and wept. He consoled him by signalling him with his hand because he was afraid that if the Police came to know that he had seen his son in their custody, they may eliminiate him. He met Inspector Sant Kumar and cried in front of him begging him to send his son to Jail. But, Inspector Sant Kumar was hesitant to disclose the whereabouts of Nirbhai Singh. In response to the poor father's pleadings, he asked him to see him 4-5 later saying that in the meantime he would find out and if he could locate him. When he met him after 4-5 days, he flatly refused having Nirbhai Singh in his custody and also said that he could not locate him. Since then, the whereabouts of Nirbhai Singh are not known.

DETAILS OF THE WITNESSES:-

Dharam Singh of Vill. Alal Teh Dhuri Dist. Sangrur ; Ajaib Singh of Vill. Jakhlan Teh. Dhuri Dist. Sangrur ; Sahib Singh **President Kisan Union** * Dhandra Teh.Dhuri Dist.Sangrur ; Bhagwant Singh of Vill. Dhandra Teh.Dhuri Dist. Sangrur.

He was last seen in May 1992 by his father. That was the last that anyone had ever known or heard of him.

### VFF/0535

Gurcharan Singh alias Charna 25 son of Jeet Singh and Surjeet Kaur resident of village Rajo majra, Dist. Sangrur. DATE OF BIRTH-20th February 1961.

He was a matriculate* and was now into agriculture. He would make a living by tilling his own family land and running a Dairy farm in his village.

He was married to Baldev Kaur (35) and they had a girl Gurpreet Kaur (14) and boy Prem Singh (12).

Gurcharan Singh was a religious minded and an "Amritdhari" (Baptised) Sikh youth. He had one brother and two sisters. He was the eldest. After passing his 10+2 exam, he got busy in agricultural farming. He got married in 1982. Shortly after the attack on Sri Darbar Sahib and Akal Takht at Amritsar in June 1984, Gurcharan Singh was arrested and sent to jail. He was in jail for about five months. Gurcharan Singh was very close to Sant Chand Singh who was a religious and political leader. The Police viewed Gurcharan Singh with suspicion due to his proximity to him (Sant Chand Singh) as also due to he being an "Amritdhari". Thereafter, Dhuri Police used to arrest him often whenever the militants used to carry out any operation. The Police accused him of having links with militants. He was tortured several times, in Police custody. Whenever the Police used to pick him up, eminent persons of the village used to get him released on their responsibility.

On 12th November 1987 at 5 A.M., the Police raided Gurcharan Singh's house. On seeing the Police, Gurcharan Singh slipped away. The Police party was led by SP Paramjit Singh, DSP Malerkotla Hardev Singh Bedi and SHO Dhuri Rajinder Singh Sodha. The above mentioned Police officers called Sarpanch (Head of village Council) Ajit Singh and other eminent persons of the village there. About 200 villagers had assembled there. The Police officer urged the Panchayat to produce Gurcharan Singh before them and promised that they would release him after interrogation. The Panchayat fell into the trap of Police officers and they advised Gurcharan Singh to produce himself before the Police. Initially he did not agree but ultimately he agreed and he was produced before the Police. The Police arrested Gurcharan Singh formally and obtained his remand upto 17th November 1987. On the third day, his brother Pargat Singh was also produced before the Police as the Police had directed (the village Panchayat) to produce him also. The Police sent Pargat Singh in judicial custody to Patiala.

However, on 17th November 1987, instead of producing Gurcharan Singh in the Court, a Police party led by Rajinderpal Singh Sodha (SHO Dhuri) raided his house in the morning and told his family members that Gurcharan Singh had escaped from their custody near village Kaul Sheri. The Police searched the house. The family members suspected that the Police had killed Gurcharan Singh, but the Police was busy in enacting a drama that Gurcharan Singh had escaped. The Police used to raid his house daily.

His younger brother Pargat Singh was released on bail after 8 months. But still, the Police used to pick him up often. His mother told that the Police killed one of her sons and extensively damaged the body of her other son Pargat Singh by thrashing him repeatedly over a number of years. According to Surjit Kaur (mother), they have gone bankrupt while pursuing the cases of her sons. "We used to sit in front of the Police Station s daily along with the Panchayat", she said. She further told that just two years have elapsed since the Police left them alone.

The whole incident was witnessed by Jeet Singh of Rajo Majra and Whole Panchayat of Village Rajo Majra.

It is suspected that the Police had killed him and to cover up their crime they enacted a drama of his escape from their custody.

**VFF/0536**

Budh Singh 17 son of Babu Singh and Nachattar Kaur resident of village Mangewal PO Kurad, Tehsil Barnala, Dist. Sangrur was an agriculturist and ran his own business of Dairy farming. He earned an amount of Rs. 1000 per month for his upkeep of the 5 dependents i.e. Babu Singh (60) Father, Nachhattar Kaur (55) Mother, Amarjit Kaur (35) and Gurjit Kaur (32) Sisters, Ajmer Singh (25) Brother.

He had a clean past with no political or anti-social contacts.

The following is a true account of what this correspondent had been told by Babu Singh, the father of the deceased.

*On 26th July 1992 morning, our house was raided by a Police party from CIA Staff Handiaya, headed by Inspector Bharpur Singh. They wanted to arrest my son Budh Singh, but he was not available at home at that time. So, they took me (Babu Singh) in their custody and before departing, warned the family members to produce Budh Singh at the CIA Staff Handiaya, otherwise, the consequences would be disastrous.*

*That on 27-7-92, my other son Gurmel Singh along with Harbans Singh son of Kaku Singh resident of Mangewal, Jit Singh son of Piara Singh resident of Mangewal, and Lal Singh son of Shri Mukand Singh resident of Handiaya, produced my son Budh Singh in front of DSP Joginder Singh Kutiwala, and Inspector Bharpur Singh at CIA Staff Handiaya. They detained Budh Singh there and sent all others back. We met Budh Singh at the CIA Staff 7-8 times thereafter and for the last time on 8-8-92.*

*That when we went to meet Budh Singh on 9-8-92, we came to know that Inspector Bharpur Singh had been transferred from there to Police Station Shaina and Inspector Baj Singh had taken over the charge of CIA Staff Handiaya. We met Inspector Baj Singh. He told us that Budh Singh had been taken by Inspector Bharpur Singh along with him to Police Station Shaina. Then we went to Police Station Shaina and enquired about the whereabouts of Budh Singh from Inspector Bharpur Singh. He shouted at us and said that he had not brought Budh Singh by putting in his pocket to that place. He shunted us out of the Police Station .*

*That a SPO who had been posted at Police Chowki Jagjitpura at the time of this incident, disclosed that Budh Singh, Sudagar Singh resident of Mangewal, and Bala Singh resident of Manal had been killed by Inspector Bharpur Singh near Kairewala bridge of Canal in his presence. The said SPO is now in District Jail Sangrur and he will be produced in the Court in due course.*

*That we approached Govt. Officials at each and every level to enquire about the whereabouts of my son Budh Singh, but in vain.*

*This incident was witnessed by Harbans Singh son of Kaku Singh & Jit Singh son of Piara Singh Vill. Mangewal, Tehsil Barnala, Dist. Sangrur.*

*His father fell ill as a result of this incident. Rs. 60,000/- has been spent on his treatment. That a SPO who had been posted at Police Chowki Jagjitpura at the time of this incident, disclosed that Budh Singh, Sudagar Singh resident of Mangewal, and Bala Singh resident of Manal had been killed by Inspector Bharpur Singh near Kairewala bridge of Canal in his presence. The said SPO is now in District Jail Sangrur and he will be produced in the Court in due course.*

*His family was not allowed to cultivate their 6 acres of land for one year, resulting in a loss of Rs. 30,000/- . Their household items like Aluminium Boxes, Beddings, Utensils, Refrigerator, Cooler, Ceiling and Engine Fans were taken away by the Police, resulting in a further loss of Rs. 50,000/-.*

**VFF/0537**

Sukhdev Singh (60) son of Santa Singh and Isar Kaur resident of village Moom, Dist. Sangrur, was a farmer by profession and earned Rs4000 per month to keep up his family's needs.

He was married to Surjeet Kaur (53) and had 3 daughters Binder Kaur (30), Raj Kaur (26), Amarjit Kaur (22) and a son Pargat Singh (28).

He was abducted from his residence, by the Police. His abduction was witnessed by Jeet Singh and Surjeet Kaur of village Mooma. The reason for his abduction is not known.

Family does not believe that he has been killed and cremated or his body disposed off in any other manner.His family is being harassed by the Police.

**VFF/0538**

Gurpal Singh alias Teetu son of Babu Singh (61) and Bachan Kaur (58) was a resident of village Mangwal, Locality Mann Patti (near Guru Ghar), Dist. Sangrur. He was a graduate pursuing a course in law. He had no record of any criminal activity. About 15 days **prior to his abduction**, SHO Tarlochan Singh of Police Station Sangrur (Sadar) visited the village on a Motorcycle and knocked at the door of Gurpal Singh's house. The inmates opened the door. On entering, the SHO saw Gurpal Singh whose leg was plastered. He ordered him to get up. Gurpal Singh stood up with the help of crutches. (There are no details provided of the incident)

Then at 9 P.M. on 30<sup>th</sup> November 1992 the police entered the house after scaling the boundary wall and abducted Gurpal Singh. Police party consisted of SHO of Police Station Sangrur (Sadar) , Tarlochan Singh, DSP Sangrur, Mr. Bhullar and SSP Dist. Sangrur, Narinderpal Singh. They were in the Khaki Police uniform with red turban. They had wrapped their bodies with blankets. That was the last time that anyone had ever seen Gurpal.

Gurpal's parents are mentally upset.. His brother Palwinder's son and daughter also miss him a lot. Gurpal's brother Palwinder Singh fell sick after his disappearance as he could not bear the sight of whole family always crying for Gurpal Singh. And he died later.

Gurpal had 5 dependents in his family that he had to look after. They include:-

His father Babu Singh(61), mother Bachan Kaur(58), sister-in-laxxw Paramjit Kaur(33), niece Preetinder Kaur(6) and nephew Kulbir Singh(3).

**VFF/0539**

Maghar Singh (50) son of Labh Singh and Gurdial Kaur , resident of village Dhuliwal.

He was educated up to primary level* and was a farmer by profession. He earned Rs.5500 per month. He was married to Nasib Kaur(48) and they had four children. 3 sons Jagtar Singh(28), Resham Singh(24), Paramjit Singh(22) and a daughter Sukhwinder Kaur(26).

On the day of the abduction (i.e. 18th October 1992), he got down from a bus along with his wife, Nasib Kaur and another person named as Jangan Singh resident of Jhordan village. He was taken into custody by a police party led by DSP Barnala Surinder Singh Pawar. Thereafter, his whereabouts are not known, so far.

The police party consisting of DSP Surinder Singh Pawar, Parmatma Singh, Pooran Singh and Gurdit Singh had taken away 4 Buffaloes, 2 Bullocks, and one cow from the house. They also ploughed 4.25 acres of land illegally without paying anything to the victim for a period of three years, thus causing a loss of Rs. 1,50,000/- to the victim.

### VFF/0540

Darshan Singh alias Kaka(22) son of Amar Singh and Surjit Kaur resident of village Barnala, tehsil Barnala , Dist Sangrur. His date of birth provided is15th april 1970 .

He studied up to his middle* school and now used to deal in cattle (mainly buffaloes) and earned Rs. 2500 per month. He was an unmarried youth and used to live with his parents.

Prior to this also, police used to harass the victim unnecessarily. In 1992, he had been to Jail also once. On 18th March 1993, the police along with another victim Gurmeet Singh alias Geeta came to the victim's house and enquired who 'Kaka' was. He told them that he himself was 'Kaka'. On this ASI Gurcharan Singh said 'come, you are wanted'. In the meantime other policemen came inside the house, caught hold of Darshan Singh, put him in the vehicle and drove away. The police party was led by DSP Barnala Surinder Singh Pawar and included Inspector Sant Kumar of C.I.A. Staff Handiaya, Bakhshish Singh SHO Kotwali Barnala and ASI Gurcharan Singh of Police Station Chowk Barnala.

### VFF/0541

Satgur Singh (23) son of Kaku Singh and Jal Kaur resident of Palasaur PO* Bhalwan Dist Sangrur earned a living as a labourer* earning 3000 rupees per month. He was married to Baljit Kaur(30) and they had a son Gurdeep Singh (7).

He has been missing since 20th July 1990 from his residence. There were no anti-social activities and nothing abnormal that was known about him in the past. Around 20 July1990, he was abducted by SI Dalbara Singh of Dhuri Police Station , from near the Brick Kiln at village Bhullarheri while he was going on a Bicycle. Since then, his whereabouts are not known.

Initially Satgur Singh had been lodged in Jail at Chandigarh for a period of four months.

He along with three other detainees was sent to Amritsar Jail on 23rd June 1995.

Satgur Singh had called his parents to meet him at Nabha Court on the day of his appearance there i.e. on 11th August 1995.

The following points have been taken from a letter dated 22nd Sep 96, written by Kaku Singh, father of the victim Satgur Singh, to the Incharge of Security Jail at Amritsar:-

1.    That policemen from Dhuri Police Station had visited the house of Kaku Singh, father of the victim Satgur Singh, before the receipt of Satgur Singh's letter, and told him to perform 'Bhog' ceremony for Satgur Singh, but, directed him not to gather people on that occasion.

2.    That he (Kaku Singh) had gone to Nabha Court on 11-9-95, but Satgur Singh did not appear in the Court there on that day.

3.    He had pleaded with the Superintendent (incharge) of Security Jail Amritsar to let him meet his son Satgur Singh and also to let him know in which case he had been lodged there.

After all his unending strife for meeting his son, Kaku Singh was still unable to make any contacts and today he still lies there waiting for him. Both Satgur's parents are mentally upset.

**VFF/0542**

Sukh Sagar Singh alias Chabila(21), son of Jatinder Singh and Mahinder Kaur, resident of village Beehla, Dist Sangrur. He was a matriculate* and was still a studying. He was not married.

He had a clean past and was not attached to any anti-social activities .

On 18th August 1993 at mid-night, he was abducted from his residence, by uniformed policemen including commandoes.

NOTE-no witnesses whatsoever have come forward till now and there is no clue as to what happened to him.

**VFF/0543**

Jasbant Singh alias Khalsa (27) son of Maghar Singh and Dalip Kaur, resident of Kaul chheli PO Bhullar Heri, Dist Sangrur.

He was a graduate* and now pursued farming as a profession. He earned 5500 rupees per month. He was married to Dharmjit Kaur and they had two sons; Amritpal Singh(8) and Aminder Singh (6).

The Police or any other agency was not inimical towards Jasbant

Singh before he was appointed President of the Kisan Union Dhuri. After that, the police started harassing him.

On 22nd June 1992, he was picked up from his sister's house at Dhuri City by a police party headed by DSP Malerkotla, Sukhdev Singh Brar including SHO Dhuri, Darshan Singh. He was produced in a Court at Dhuri on 5th August 1992 and the next appearance was scheduled for 10th August 1992. However, the Police showed him as having escaped from their custody, on 9th August 1992. Thereafter, nothing is known about his whereabouts.

He was last seen by his brother-in-law and mother before 08th May 1992 at the Malerkotla Police Station *.

His parents are mentally upset. They miss him too much.

### VFF/0544

Bikkar Singh alias Chiri (23), son of Jagroop Singh and Balwant Kaur resident of village Ghunsan, Dist Sangrur was a farmer by occupation and earned Rs.5000 per month. He was unmarried with his parents as his only dependents.

Prior to this incident, the police or any other agency was not inimical towards Bikkar Singh. Nobody in the village had any grudge against him. When the men folk used to go to their fields, the police used to harass the residents. Fed up with this, a deputation from the village met the SSP and apprised him of the situation. At this, the police got furious. They came to his house and asked Bikkar Singh to show them the house of Dhanna Singh. They threatened to shoot him if he refused to accompany them to Dhanna Singh's house. Bikkar Singh led them to Dhanna Singh's house. There, they picked up Dhanna Singh as well as Bikkar Singh.

On 12th November 1992 at 6 A.M., a police party headed by Inspector Sant Kumar of C.I.A. Staff Handiaya and including ASI Mohinder Singh and Head Constable Gurcharan Singh and 10 more police personnel again picked up Bikkar Singh from his residence. Dhanna Singh also had been picked up by them. They told the family that they wanted to enquire something from them and after that they would release them. However, their whereabouts are not known since then.

His parents are mentally upset since the time of his disappearance. They miss him.

### VFF/0545

Mukhtiar Singh alias Khalsa (53), son of Mahala Singh and Harnam Kaur, resident of Dist Sangrur was a pathi* at a Gurdwara, earning 3500 rupees per month.

He was married to Baldev Kaur (60) and they had 7 kids. There were 3 daughters Harvinder Kaur(38); Sukhvinder Kaur (36) Tejvinder Kaur(34) and 4 sons Balvinder Singh(32) ; Jasvinder Singh(30) ; Surinder Singh(28) ; Harjinder Singh(26).

His past was very peaceful. A police party headed by Pargat Singh SHO* and Rabbi Singh ASI* visited his house on 11<sup>th</sup> March 1993, and took him to Police Station Sehna. He was not allowed to meet his family. This whole incident was witnessed by his son Jaswinder who was not told the cause of his father's abduction. He was last seen by his son Jaswinder Singh at the Police Station * Sehna on 13<sup>th</sup> march 1993.

There was also a news item in this regard about the police having declared him to have escaped from police custody.

There has been no trace of him since then and his family is mentally upset, especially his wife Baldev Kaur.

## VFF/0546

Gurdev Singh son of Santa Singh and Isar Kaur resident of village Moom, Dist Sangrur was 55 years of age and a farmer by profession. He was unmarried and the only possible information that has been provided is that he has been missing without any further information.

## VFF/0547

Paramjit Singh alias Pammi(36) son of Joginder Singh and Dalip Kaur resident of Gehla Bagha Patti Dist Sangrur had completed his matriculation * and was pursuing the job of an electrician earning 2000 rupees per month. He was married to Sarbjit Kaur (34) and they had a son Manpreet Singh(13) who was studying in primary school.

On 15<sup>th</sup> October 1992, Paramjit Singh was picked up by Police and produced before DSP Gurdip Singh. He was released after being tortured for ten days.

On 19<sup>th</sup> May 1993 at 12 noon, Joginder Singh was picked up by a police party consisting of ASI Sampuran Singh and Inspector Sarup Singh and taken to C.I.A. Bhawanigarh. Then he was presented before SSP Jaswinder Singh and DSP (D) Gurdeep Singh Punnu. They enquired about Paramjit Singh from him. He told them that he had gone to his sister's house at village Hasanpur. Same day, police party along with Joginder Singh went to Hasanpur and brought Parmjit Singh and Joginder Singh to C.I.A. Bhawanigarh and produced them in front of DSP (D) Gurdeep Singh. DSP (D) Gurdeep Singh presented them before SSP Jaswinder Singh who ordered the detention of Joginder Singh and torture of Paramjit Singh. Since then, there is no trace of Paramjit Singh.

This whole incident was witnessed by Sadhu Singh and Amarjit Singh of village Hassanpur.

NOTE- The true translation of the news item published in the Punjabi daily Ajit, on 24<sup>th</sup> May 1993, is appended below:-

*MILITANT ESCAPES: Last night, a police party was taking a militant Paramjit Singh for recovery of arms, at his instance. Some militants who were lying in ambush attacked the police party near village Channo of Sangrur district. Paramjit Singh escaped from police custody during the attack.*

Joginder Singh kept on meeting SSP Jaswinder Singh and DSP (D) Gurdeep Singh. They assured him that his son was OK and only a case of possessing a pistol will be registered against him.

Victim's father, mother, wife and son are mentally disturbed. Father and mother have become patients of Sugar and high blood pressure and his wife's mental state is not balanced. Victim's uncle and Father-in-law have expired after his disappearance.

### VFF/0548

Hardeep Singh alias Deepa (20) son of Darshan Singh and Kuldeep Kaur resident of village Rajo Majra, Dist Sangrur was a matriculate* but had given up studies to help his family with their farming. His monthly income was roughly 900 rupees. He was unmarried.

He has been missing since 25<sup>th</sup> February 1994. The only witness to this is his father Darshan Singh according to whom, the culprits are Sardara Singh SHO; Vidya Sagar SHO; Gurdeep Singh Pannu DSP ; Jaswinder Singh SSP.

He was last seen on 03<sup>rd</sup> January 1994 by his father at Police Station * Bhawanigarh.

### VFF/0549

Nirmal Singh alias Kanda (27), son of Sukhdev Singh and Surjit Kaur, resident of Rajo majra , Dist Sangrur was a matriculate* but was now a farmer by profession. He earned about 1000 rupees a month. He has been missing since 12<sup>th</sup> February 1993 from village Meemsa, at 12:30 AM.

Sukhdev Singh (victim Nirmal Singh's father) who has become a mental wreck, as two of his sons have been killed at the hands of the Police, had five sons and two daughters. His eldest son is a farmer and two younger ones are serving in the Army. The youngest one Jaswinder Singh had studied up to primary level and thereafter he had started helping his father and brother in agricultural farming. Sukhdev Singh is an old Akali worker and an "Amritdhari" (Baptised) Sikh. His father Jagdeep Singh had taken part in the Gurdwara Reform Movement.

Sukhdev Singh's youngest son (victim Nirmal Singh's brother Jaswinder Singh) was an "Amritdhari" (Baptised) Sikh youth. In 1990, he was arrested by the Dhuri Police and sent to jail at Sangrur. The Police of different Police Station s had registered several cases against Jaswinder

Singh. About one year later, the militants kidnapped one of the nephews of a Congress leader and in return for his release they got Jaswinder Singh and some other militants released. Thereafter, Jaswinder Singh did not return home. In the month of Baisakh (Apr-May) 1991, he was killed by the Sangrur Police at Village Chooga under Malerkotla Police Station , after a fierce encounter.

During the period Jaswinder Singh was absconding, the Police used to pick up his father and brothers and detain them in illegal custody. This process continued even after Jaswinder Singh had been killed in an encounter with the Police. In August-September 1991, the Moonak Police raided the house of Nirmal Singh Kanda (brother of Jaswinder Singh) in order to arrest him. However, Kanda was not available at home. A few days later, the family members produced him before the Sangrur Police through one of their relatives. Nirmal Singh was detained for 15 days at the Kotwali Police Station at Sangrur and released thereafter. Thereafter, Nirmal Singh used to stay at home only. But, the Police of Sanaur, Dhuri and Sangrur (Sadar) Police Station s used to raid his house often and pick up Nirmal Singh. However, the Panchayat used to get him released after a few days.

On 2nd February 1993 at 9 P.M., the Police of C.I.A. Staff Sangrur (Bahadur Singh Wala) raided his (Nirmal Singh's) house. Shamsher Singh, SHO of Dhuri Police Station also was there along with the Police party. At that time all the family members including his father Sukhdev Singh, Surjit Kaur (mother) and Balwinder Singh (brother) were present in the house. The Police enquired about Nirmal Singh, made him sit in the vehicle and took him away. On being asked by his family members the reason for his arrest, the police replied, "You come to Sangrur in the morning."

The following day, family members along with the Panchayat went to the C.I.A. Staff Bahadur Singh Wala. The Police said that DSP Sahib was not available and asked them to come on the following day. The Panchayat and family members continued to go to the Police Station for several days but the Police continued to dodge them by making vague and false statements.

On 10 February 1993, SSP Sangrur, Jasminder Singh got a news item published in the newspapers that the Police had arrested a militant Nirmal Singh Kanda, who was wanted by the Police in connection with several cases. The family members came to know that the Police had produced him in a Court and obtained Police remand for three days. He was to be produced in the Court again on 13th Feb 1993. The same day his family members, Sukhdev Singh (father), Balwinder Singh

(brother), relatives and other important persons reached the Court and
waited. However, the Police did not produce him in the Court. Finally,
at 5 P.M., the Magistrate issued a copy of a F.I.R. No. 31 dated 12$^{th}$ Feb
1993 registered at Dhuri Police Station u/s 301/34/224/225 IPC, 25/54/59
of Arms Act and 3,4 and 5 of TDA (P) Act. According to the said FIR,
a Police party of Dhuri Police Station were taking Nirmal Singh for
the recovery of arms when they were attacked by some unidentified
militants lying in ambush near Village Meemsa. Nirmal Singh escaped
taking advantage of the fog and an unidentified militant was killed in
the encounter which ensued. The family members and the villagers
understood that the Police had killed Nirmal Singh and had concocted a
story of escape and encounter. According to Balwinder Singh (brother),
though, according to the F.I.R. the Police had shown Nirmal Singh as
having escaped from their custody, yet, in those days, it was common for
the Police to concoct such stories in order to cover up their misdeeds.
Balwinder Singh further told that on the day when the Police produced
Nirmal Singh in the Court for the first time and obtained a remand, he
was unable to walk, according to eyewitnesses. The Police had lifted him
physically and brought him down from the vehicle. His hands had been
covered and it seemed that there were injuries on his hands. Balwinder
Singh told that they accepted it as the Will of God and performed his
'Bhog' (religious last rites).

His brother Jaswinder Singh was killed in an encounter with the
Sangrur Police at Village Chooga, in Apr-May, 1991.

**VFF/0550**

Saudagar Singh son of Kartar Singh and Tej Kaur, resident of
Mangewal PO Khurd ,tehsil Barnala, Dist Sangrur was a farmer by
profession and earned 5500 rupees per month, and was not married. He
had, apart from his parents, one Brother Bahadur Singh (35) and Sister
Rajdeep Kaur (17) who were dependent on him.

No body was inimical towards Saudagar Singh earlier. There was a
dispute in the village but a compromise had been reached. The police
used to patrol the village and would get angry with the villagers when
they were not offered tea and food etc. by the villagers. The Police
ordered the villagers to produce three village youth in front of them.

On 26$^{th}$ July 1990, Saudagar Singh was produced before Inspector
Bharpur Singh C.I.A. Staff Handiaya by his father Kartar Singh along
with Sarpanch Nachhattar Singh and some other villagers. They were
assured that he would be released soon, but, so far, his whereabouts are
not known.

A written representation was submitted to the SSP Barnala, on 10<sup>th</sup> October 1994. But, to no avail.

A Criminal Writ Petition No. 1163/97 was filed through Advocate Ranjan Lakhanpal.

The Writ was dismissed by Justice M.L. Koul vide order dated 01<sup>st</sup> August 1997. The said Order read as follows:-

"It is a belated matter of 1992 and does not require any consideration. Hence rejected."

His parents are mentally upset since the time of his disappearance.

**VFF/0551**

Balraj Singh alias Balla (15), son of Sawarn Singh and Sukhbant Kaur, resident of village Manal Dist Sangrur was studying in grade 8<sup>th</sup> at the time of his disappearance. He was a farmer by profession and earned 4500 rupees per month. He had 2 sisters, Rajwinder Kaur(15) and Narinder Kaur(26) and a brother Gurjeet Singh(20).

Balraj Singh was a student of class VIII at Govt. High School Thulliwal, Tehsil Barnala, and District Sangrur. Swaran Singh's wife Sukhwant Kaur's brother Daya Singh Lahoria was a renowned militant leader who is detained at Tihar Jail at present. Daya Singh had become active in the Sikh Students Federation in February 1984. Since then, the Police had been harassing his family members and relatives, due to his activities. As Sukhwant Kaur is sister of Daya Singh Lahoria, the Police used to pick up her family members also, often. The Police used to pick up her husband Swaran Singh and her elder son Gurjit Singh. In those days, the Police of different Police Station s used to raid their house and used to pick up whosoever family members they could lay their hands on. Most of the time, it was the Police of Barnala (Sadar), C.I.A. Staff Handiaya and C.I.A. Staff Patiala (Mai Di Saran) who used to pick them up. Often, the Police used to inflict inhuman torture on Sukhwant Kaur, Swaran Singh and Gurjit Singh. According to Sukhwant Kaur, in 1992, the Baghapurana Police tortured her brutally. When the Investigation Team members tried to find out more details about the torture inflicted by the Police on her family members, Sukhwant Kaur said, "Brother, We were tortured so many times that we ourselves have lost count of it."

On 27<sup>th</sup> July 1992, a Police party led by Inspector Bharpur Singh of C.I.A. Staff Handiaya raided their house. Only Sukhwant Kaur was at home at that time. Inspector Bharpur Singh inquired about her sons Gurjit Singh and Balraj Singh. She said, "My elder son Gurjit Singh is a bus conductor and younger Balraj Singh has gone to the fields with his father." The Police party went to their fields. On seeing the Police, Balraj Singh slipped away. The Police picked up Swaran Singh and took him away. While departing, the Police directed her to produce her sons before them. The family members produced Balraj Singh at C.I.A. Staff Handiaya through a Police officer hailing from their area namely Hardeep Singh Bhau, a DSP. On 5th Aug 1992, Sukhwant Kaur along with her father Sardar Kirpal Singh resident of Bhagal Town (Sangrur) and son Balraj Singh went to DSP Hardeep Singh Bhau at Sherpur. They had already talked to Hardeep Singh that they would produce Balraj Singh at the C.I.A. Staff Handiaya, through him. DSP Hardeep Singh detailed three Policemen to accompany them for producing Balraj Singh at C.I.A. Staff Handiaya, in his own vehicle.

Inspector Bharpur Singh made Balraj Singh sit near him. His father Swaran Singh was released with a direction to take Balraj Singh back after one or two days as they had to interrogate him. On the following day, Kirpal Singh (Balraj Singh's maternal grandfather) met DSP Joginder Singh Kutiwal at C.I.A. Staff Handiaya. He told him to take Balraj Singh back on the following day. On 10th August 1992, Kirpal Singh and Joginder Singh, Sarpanch (Head of Village Council) of Village Lohgarh went there, Bharpur Singh (Insp.) told them that he had been taken away to some other place. Also he told them that he had dropped him at Police Station Sehna. Sukhwant Kaur told that the Police flatly refused to release him. They used to give some excuse or the other. She further told that when they approached DSP Hardeep Singh, he also said, "What can I do?" As they approached DSP Hardeep Singh time and again, he began threatening them that he would put them behind bars. They ran from pillar to post for one or one and a half month, got his case recommended but they were helpless, she said.

Sukhwant Kaur told that some time later, her husband Swaran Singh and son Gurjit Singh came to know that Balraj Singh had been killed by the Police but they did not disclose the same to her. However, she had suspected such a thing judging from the attitude of the Police. Sukhwant Kaur told that after exhausting all other means, ultimately, in 1995, they filed a case in the High Court through their Advocate Ranjan Lakhanpal. The High Court ordered the Police to inquire into this case. In 1994, SP (Operations) Sangrur (Mr. Vichak, she did not remember the full name) conducted an inquiry. Sukhwant Kaur was ignorant as regards the outcome of the case or the current legal status of the case. She remembers the last date of hearing of their case as 24th November 1998. She doesn't know anything about further dates. However, she is constantly in touch with her Lawyer who had told her that the case was in limelight. But, it was evident to the Investigation Team that due to lack of legal knowledge, the family members were in the dark about the real status of their case and they were lagging in pursuing their case.

His parents are still mentally upset.

**VFF/0552**

Surjit Singh alias Seeta(23), son of Amar Singh and Preetam Kaur resident of village Kattu , Dist Sangrur was a farmer earning 5500 rupees per month and was not married.

He had 3 brothers Jarnail Singh (24), Meg Singh (37) and Sarbjit Singh(35).

Before Surjit Singh's abduction, his elder brother had been abducted on 12th February 1991 by C.I.A. Staff Bahadargarh, tortured and released. There was no case against Surjit Singh.

On the Baisakhi day (14th April) in 1992, Surjit Singh had gone to the fair at Damdama Sahib. From there, he went to Barnala to see an Akali leader namely Paramjit Singh who was also his relative. Paramjit Singh was not at home. Surjit Singh boarded a bus at Barnala for his village. However, he got down on the way at village Bhaini with a view to meet one of his acquaintances Poohla Singh. He had just reached Poohla Singh's house and was having tea when women of the house told that the Police were coming as they had seen the Police coming. As such, Surjit Singh started walking towards a house nearby. He entered a house where a woman was cutting fodder, nearby. The Police followed him as they suspected that he had gone towards that side and arrested him. The residents of Bhaini village informed Nambardar Dhann Singh of Kattu village who happened to visit village Bhaini on that day that Surjit Singh of his village had been arrested and taken away by the Police.

On the following day, his brother Megh Singh visited the place of the incident. The woman from whose house Surjit Singh had been arrested told him that Surjit Singh had hid himself in their house but the Police followed him. They conducted a search of the house and arrested him.

After this incident, his family members along with the village Panchayat visited various Police Station s of Barnala Police District and enquired about Surjit Singh. This process (of enquiring at various Police Station s) continued for 4-5 months. Ultimately, the family members got frustrated and sat at home quietly. During this period they had enquired about Surjit Singh at Badbad, Sherpur, C.I.A Staff Handiaya, Barnala, Dhanaula Police Station s and at Police Post Dunne Ka Kote. They, along with the village Panchayat comprising Sarpanch Jaswant Singh, Panch Joginder Singh Bhullar, Panch Joginder Singh Siddhu,

Panch Ranjit Singh and many other eminent persons, had also enquired at the office of the SSP, Shri Ishwar Chand. They met the SHOs of concerned Police Station s several times. But, none of them gave them any clue about the whereabouts of Surjit Singh.

His father Amar Singh and mother Preetam Kaur are mentally upset since the time of his disappearance. They miss him too much. representations were submitted to the following authorities, IG Punjab Police Deputy Commissioner, Sangrur and Chief Minister, Punjab. But there was no reply from any of them.

### VFF/0553

Gurjant Singh alias Lalli(25) son of Gurnam Singh and Karnail Kaur resident of village Dhilwan , Dist Sangrur had completed his primary* school education and was now a farmer earning 4500 rupees per month. He was not married and had a sister Manjit Kaur (20) who lived with him.

Gurnam Singh (victim Gurjant Singh's father) is a Sikh farmer, resident of village Dhilwan. He had four sons and two daughters. Gurjant Singh was his youngest son who had studied up to third standard only and was engaged in agricultural farming since his childhood. Like other Sikh youth, Gurjant Singh was also deeply hurt by the Army attack on Sri Darbar Sahib at Amritsar. In 1985-86, when the militancy erupted in Punjab, Gurjant Singh got himself baptised. Whenever any of the pro-militant political or religious organization used to organize any program, he used to participate in it. In view of his activities, the Police used to arrest him often, on the basis of suspicion. The Panchayat (village council) and other eminent persons used to get him released. This process of arrest and release continued for several years. Whenever Gurjant Singh used to be not available at home, the Police used to arrest whosoever family member they could lay their hands on. The Police used to beat up Gurjant Singh severely whenever they used to take him into their custody. In 1990, he was arrested, several cases were registered against him and he was sent to jail. He was in jail for about two years. His family members bailed him out in February 1992 and he started living at home.

On 2nd April 1992, Gurjant Singh went away from home saying that he was going to village Burj Dhilwan in district Bathinda to see one of his friends Gurdev Singh. According to his father, in those days, they had organized 'Paath' (recitation of Gurbani) of Sri Guru Granth Sahib at their home. Gurjant Singh had gone to deliver the invitation card for the same to his friend. On 3rd April 1992 at 10 A.M. a woman from village Burj Dhilwan came to their house and delivered a message that their son Gurjant Singh had been picked up and taken away by Dharam Singh,

SHO (Station House Officer) of Rampura Police Station . According to his father Gurnam Singh, he along with 5-6 tractor trolleys full of people from his village reached Rampura Police Station , immediately. Several eminent persons of village Burj Dhilwan along with large number of other villagers had also reached Rampura Police Station . A large crowd had assembled there and they surrounded the Police Station so that the Police may not smuggle Gurjant Singh out of the Police Station . Gurnam Singh (father) along with Sarpanch (Head of village Council) Manjit Singh and several other eminent persons of the village talked to the SHO Dharam Singh about the release of Gurjant Singh. Dharam Singh admitted in front of the whole Panchayat that he had picked up Gurjant Singh and promised to release him a few days later. However, his father and the Panchayat told the SHO that 'Bhog' (Closing Ceremony) of 'Paath' of Sri Guru Granth Sahib was scheduled to be held at his house on 5th April, 1992. At this, the SHO said that he would release him by that date. The Panchayat talked to the DSP (Deputy Superintendent of Police) Rampura also who also assured them that they would release him. On being reassured by the Police, they returned to the village. According to his father Gurnam Singh, they used to meet the SHO and the DSP daily. On 4th April also they assured them that they would release him. However, on 5th April, the Police told that they had recovered a letter head from his (Gurjant Singh's) pocket in which responsibility for some incident (militancy related) had been owned. Even then, they promised to release him. Gurnam Singh told that they took a senior leader of the area namely Sukhdev Singh Rampura (Ex-MLA) also along with them. The Police continued to assure them that they would release him. But, on the intervening night of 7-8 April, 1992, they showed him as having been killed in an encounter with the Police between the villages Gillan and Chakk Bakhtu under Balian Wali Police Station . On getting the information, Gurnam Singh along with eminent persons went to Rampura Police Station . The SHO told that he had been sent away for interrogation and would be back soon. At this Gurnam Singh got furious and told the SHO that he was telling a lie and that they had already killed his son. On hearing this, the SHO kept mum. Even some Policemen of Rampura Police Station also told Gurnam Singh that Gurjant Singh had been killed in an "encounter" during the night. On the following day, a news item about the "encounter" was published in the newspapers. After reading the news, Gurnam Singh and other villagers went to cremation ground at Bathinda and collected his ashes.

According to Gurnam Singh (father), a few months after the killing of Gurjant Singh, Faridkot Police picked up Karnail Kaur (Gurjant's mother) alleging that they were in possession of militants' money. Karnail Kaur was released after 40 days of illegal detention. Even as Karnail Kaur was in illegal custody of the Police, C.I.A. Staff Faridkot picked up Gurjant's father Gurnam Singh also. He was released after 20 days of illegal detention that too, after he had paid Rs. 45,000 /- as bribe to the SHO Jhilmil Singh. He had raised that amount by mortgaging his land. According to Gurnam Singh, the Police visited their house to made enquiries and they also noted down the names of their family members and relatives. Gurnam Singh lamented that on the one hand the Police killed his son illegally (fake encounter) and on the other they continued harassing the family.

There was a news item in The Punjabi Tribune about this but to no effect.

His parents are under mental stress. As the family planned to file a case against the Police, the Police began to harass women of the house. Two of his brother's children had died. The Police threatened his mother that in case they filed a case, the whole family would be liquidated.

### VFF/0554

Mohinder Singh alias Bhilla, son of Ram Rakha Singh and Gurdev Kaur resident of village Balian, Dist Sangrur was a matriculate* and was working as a Registered Medical Practitioner earning 3800 rupees per month. He was married to Daljit Kaur (32) and they had a daughter Kirandeep Kaur and 2 sons Mandeep and Gurdeep.

Earlier, the village Sarpanch* had been murdered by someone. Due to the friction between the two, he was named as one of the suspects by some village people. He was behind bars for two months after which he was released on bail. Since the police used to harass him, he joined the police as SPO and was appointed a gunman to one wholesale Contractor Prem Kumar of Sherpur.

On 6th March 1993, he was picked up from Sherpur by Pargat Singh, SHO of Sehna Police Station . The next day, his father Ram Rakha Singh, Gurdial Singh Sekha and Jagir Singh Mallowal went to the Sehna Police Station and met Mohinder Singh. He told them that nothing had been found against him but they still beat him.

His parents are mentally upset and are still waiting for his return.

### VFF/0555

Narain Singh alias Gokal Singh, son of Bant Singh and Krishna devi, resident of village Dhilwan, Dist Sangrur worked as a helper at a flour mill and earned Rs.2000 per month.

He was unmarried and had a younger sister Amandeep Kaur(11) to fend for.

There is nothing abnormal that is known of this poor laborer that could be reason for any enmity. On 14th December 1992, he was abducted by uniformed policemen of Rampura Phool Police Station in district Bathinda. Since then, his whereabouts are not known.

His elder brother died due to the shock of his disappearance. Now, his (elder brother's) children also are starving. His mother Krishna Devi is mentally upset and waits for him.

**VFF/0556**

Dhanna Singh alias Giani son of Mehar Singh and Mukhtiar Kaur resident of village Ghunsan, Dist Sangrur was educated up to middle* school and was now a farmer earning 5000 rupees per month. He was married to Sukhwinder Kaur (32) and they had 3 daughters, Simarjit Kaur, Harpreet Kaur and Jaspreet Kaur.

Before this incident, the police or any other agency had no enmity towards Dhanna Singh. The police used to harass the residents when the men used to be away to their fields. So, a deputation from the village had met the SSP and apprised him of the situation. At this, the police got furious.

The Police party led by Inspector Sant Kumar of C.I.A. Staff Handiaya in Police District Barnala, came to the house of Dhanna Singh. Bikkar Singh of the same village had also been picked up earlier. ASI Mohinder Singh and HC Gurcharan Singh Thulewal were also there along with another 10 policemen. They took away Dhanna Singh and Bikkar Singh saying that they had to enquire something from them and after that they would release them. However, they did not release them and their whereabouts are not known since then.

His brother-in-law died due to shock and his parents are mentally upset .

**VFF/0557**

Amarjit Singh alias Giani (35) son of (late) Inder Singh and Tej Kaur resident of village Dhadiala Natt, Dist Sangrur was a matriculate and was now a farmer earning 2500 rupees per month. He was married to Manjit Kaur (38) and they had a son Balbir Singh (15).

His family was deeply religious and he got himself baptised at a young age. Amarjit Singh was a youth with a religious bent of mind who used to recite the Gurbani and visit the Gurdwara, daily. He got married in 1980. His two brothers used to live separately. His mother had expired in 1982-83.

After the Shiromani Akali Dal (a political party) launched their 'Dharam Yudh Morcha' (political agitation) in 1982, Amarjit Singh started taking active interest in politics. He was deeply hurt at the Army attack on Sri Darbar Sahib in 1984. Thereafter, he started participating in the religious and political activities organized by Sikh Students Federation and Akali Dal. His wife Manjit Kaur told that she did not know much about his political activities. She told that two youth of their village Sarbjit Singh and Harpal Singh had joined the ranks of the militants. Eventually, Sarbjit Singh was arrested by the Police. On getting this information, Amarjit Singh collected a large number of people from the surrounding villages and held a demonstration to demand his legal arrest. Since then he had become an eyesore for the Police. Because, due to public pressure, Sarbjit Singh had escaped death in a fake encounter and the Police was forced to record his arrest formally. In July 1992, the other youth of his village Harpal Singh was killed at the hands of the Police. Amarjit Singh played an active role in organizing his 'Bhog' (religious last rites) and immersing his ashes.

In view of his above mentioned activities, he was arrested once, by Malerkotla Police and tortured brutally for 7-8 days in illegal custody. He was released at the intervention of the Village Panchayat (Council) and eminent persons of the Village. Mr. Brar was the DSP at Malerkotla at that time.

On 9th November 1992 at about 9 P.M., Amarjit Singh, his wife Manjit Kaur, his father Inder Singh (handicapped), his brother-in-law Labh Singh and his son Balbir Singh had not retired to bed yet, when the Police entered their house after scaling the walls. The Police party was led by Bakhshish Singh, SHO of Sherpur and Inspector Sant Kumar of C.I.A. Staff Handiaya. Amarjit Singh was tying his dog at the gate at that time. The Policemen who had entered inside pounced upon him. They caught hold of him and brought him inside the room. They searched the room. The Police directed him to put on his clothes. According to Manjit Kaur, the Policemen were 15-20 in number and they were holding torches in their hands. The Police searched both the rooms. Nothing (incriminating) was recovered from the house. The Police directed Amarjit Singh to come along with them. On being asked by his wife Manjit Kaur as to where they were taking him, they replied that they were taking him to Sherpur Police Station. The Police entered the neighboring house also, that of Amarjit Singh's brother Kulwant Singh, and searched it. As the Police party departed along with Amarjit Singh, his wife, brother and sister-in-law came up to the gate but they did not follow the Police, due to fear. The Police had parked their vehicles at a little distance. They boarded their vehicles and went away towards Sherpur. His wife Manjit Kaur and other family members intimated the Sarpanch (Head of Village Council) and other villagers immediately.

According to Manjit Kaur, the situation was very bad in those days. The Police used to act very tough. As such, there was no question of going to the Police Station during the night.

On the following day, Preetam Singh (Amarjit Singh's father-in-law), Sarpanch Gurdev Singh, members of the Panchayat and other eminent persons of the village went to Sherpur and met the SHO Bakhshish Singh. Bakhshish Singh flatly denied that he had arrested Amarjit Singh and brought him there. He used filthy language against the Panchayat. Nobody had the temerity to speak out that he was with the Police party at the time of Amarjit Singh's arrest last night.

Manjit Kaur told that she did not know much. But, her father Preetam Singh played an active role in pursuing his case. He along with eminent political leaders of the area, continued to approach senior officers of the district Police, Police officers of Sherpur Police Station and C.I.A. Staff Handiaya for about one year. But, none of the Police officers admitted that they had arrested and brought Amarjit Singh. Manjit Kaur said that after running from pillar to post for one year, they reconciled themselves to their fate. She further told that they have not been even informed whether Amarjit Singh was alive or he had been killed. According to her, even though, by seeing the attitude of the Police, they could make out that the Police must have killed him, yet, they were not willing to believe it in the absence of any proof. That is why the family members have not performed his last rites even.

According to Manjit Kaur, they submitted written representations to senior officers, Chief Minister and the Governor. Nobody listened to them. The village Panchayat made lot of efforts to know about the whereabouts of Amarjit Singh by meeting senior officers and political leaders, but the Police had not disclosed anything, so far. The family kept in constant touch with the Police authorities, but to no avail.

**VFF/0558**

Gurmit Singh alias Geeta son of Jagroop Singh and Nachattar Kaur resident of village Barnala, Dist Sangrur had completed his education up till middle school. He was unmarried and his parents were his only dependents.

He had a clean past with nothing abnormal and nobody inimical towards him.

On 17th March 1993, Gurmit Singh was picked up by a Police party headed by DSP Barnala , Surinder Singh Pawar, Inspector Sant Kumar C.I.A. Staff Handiaya, Bakhshish Singh SHO, Gurcharan Singh ASI and other police personnel.

Writ petition was filed in the Punjab & Haryana High Court

through Advocate Lalit Mohan Gulati **(File No. is 555.)** the Case was dismissed.

### VFF/0559

Jaswinder Singh alias Kaka (20) son of Ajaib Singh and Baldev Kaur resident of village Jahangir, Dist Sangrur had completed his primary education and was now a farmer earning 6500 rupees per month. He was married to Harjit Kaur(25) and they had a son Hardeep Singh (5).

The Police or any other State Agency had nothing against him till 1992.

On 30th January 1993, a Police party from C.I.A. Staff Bahadar Singh Wala led by SHO Gurmel Singh including ASI Sardara Singh, HC Nirmal Singh, and other policemen raided his house. Jaswinder Singh alias Kaka was watering the fields at that time. They picked up and detained his parents at CIA Staff Bahadar Singh Wala at 10 P.M. His father was a mental patient, even then, he was beaten up, thrown into the vehicle and taken away.

On 1st February 1993, Jaswinder Singh along with some persons from his village met DSP Hardeep Singh Pannu and told him that they had come to enquire about his parents who had been taken to an unknown destination by the Police. DSP Hardeep Singh Pannu told them to find out from Bahadar Singh Wala. On reaching Bahadar Singh Wala , they met SHO Gurmel Singh, ASI Sardara Singh and HC Nirmal Singh who were present there. Although his parents were released, but Jaswinder Singh was detained saying that they had to ask him some questions. His parents pursued his case consistently from 1st February 1993 to 17th February 1993. On 17th February 1993 they came to know that he had been produced in front of the Magistrate at Sangrur and remand obtained for 24 hours. Thereafter, the whereabouts of Jaswinder Singh are not known.

The main accused in this case are SHO Gurmel Singh, ASI Sardara Singh, HC Nirmal Singh, DSP Hardeep Singh Pannu, and SSP Jaswinder Singh. After his disappearance, whenever hi family used to approach these Officers for his release, they used to abuse and shunt them out of the Police Station saying that if they went there again, they would also be killed. Thereafter, they did not initiate any action, due to fear.

A news item appeared in the newspapers saying that Jaswinder Singh had been declared as having escaped from police custody. His parents are mentally upset since the time of his disappearance.

### VFF/0560

Budh Singh alias Darshan Singh ,son of Kandal Singh alias Kahn Singh and Jagir Kaur ,resident of Jagjit Pura, Dist Sangrur studied up till the 9<sup>th</sup> grade and was now into farming earning Rs.4500 per month. He was married to Ranjit Kaur (25) and they had a son Gurjant Singh (7).

Prior to his abduction, the Police used to harass him because his brother Pooran Singh had been declared as having escaped from police custody. No family member was allowed to come home. That is why he used to live at his sister's house.

On 15<sup>th</sup> March 1993, he was abducted from his sister's house at Bhadaur by a police party led by DSP Surinder Singh Pawar including Inspector Sant Kumar CIA Staff Handiaya among other police personnel. Since then, his whereabouts are not known.

Everything was looted by police party led by DSP Surinder Singh Pawar and Inspector Sant Kumar.

His parents are mentally upset because one of their only two siblings was killed in a fake encounter and another had been abducted.

**VFF/0561**

Kuldeep Singh alias keepa(24) son of Jaginder Singh and Gulab Kaur r/ovillage Bhularheri ,thsil Dhuri ,DistSangrur.

His date of birth given is 19<sup>th</sup> October 1968.

He was a graduate* with a BA in hand. He worked as a farmer earning 6000 rupees per month.

He lived with his parents and worked to fend for the whole family.

Prior to this incident, police used to pick him up on the basis of suspicion and release him later. On two occasions, he was picked up by Dhuri police and let off later. Police personnel involved were Baldev Singh Ugoke SHO Dhuri (later C.I.A Staff Patiala), Inspector Sant Kumar and Surjit Grewal DSP.

He was picked up on 31<sup>st</sup> May 1993 by SHO Dhuri, Gurbakhsh Singh who had come in a Maruti van and Havaldar Malkiat Singh of Police Post Samandgarh . There are two eye witnesses, but their names will be disclosed as and when necessary, on the spot.

The family wanted to register an FIR but the police personnel did not register it despite all their efforts.

The then Chief Minister of Punjab, Mr. Beant Singh was approached ,but to no avail.

They met the SSP Sangrur, Sh. Jaswinder Singh. He advised them to find out from Police Post Bhullarheri (Patiala). They went there, but, could not get any information about his whereabouts. Apart from that, the family met several Police Officers at different times, but, all in vain.

His parents are mentally upset and have developed many physical ailments also.

### VFF/0562

Amarjit Singh alias Amra(23) son of Hajura Singh and Parsann Kaur resident of village Dhilwan tehsil Barnala , Dist Sangrur.

His Date of birth given is 20$^{th}$ april 1968.

He was educated up to his middle* school and worked as an electrician earning 4500 rupees per month. .He was married to Rajinder Kaur(28) and they had 2 daughters Gurpreet and Manpreet and one son Jagsir .

Amarjit Singh was asked by Teja Singh, SHO of Police Station Sehna to accompany him as he had been called by DSP of Tappa Police Station . On being asked by Rajinder Kaur, wife of Amarjit Singh, Teja Singh replied that he did not know (the reason) but he had been called by the DSP. Amarjit Singh was got released by Sarpanch Manjit Singh. Rajinder Kaur enquired from the Sarpanch as to what the charge against him was, he told that there was no charge against him and that hereafter the Police would not arrest him.

On 10the October 1991 at about 2 P.M., 4 persons including Amarjit Singh were picked up by a Police party consisting of 6 uniformed policemen and one person in civil dress who had come in a Canter Van. Two of them alighted from the Van and asked the names. After the other three had told their names they asked Amarjit Singh as to what his name was. After he disclosed his name, he was made to sit in the Van. Rajinder Kaur told that they were proceeding to attend a marriage and asked why they were taking him away but they did not reply. He was taken to an unknown destination. His family along with the Sarpanch and the Panchayat enquired at the Police Station , but neither they gave them any information nor registered any report regarding Amarjit Singh.

On this ,they sent a letter to DGP* Dogra and one letter each to the former DGP and Sh. Badal, Chief Minister of Punjab. They received the acknowledgement of their letter which was sent to the Chief Minister, Punjab from a Deputy Secretary. However nothing else was disclosed. DGP sent a reply to them and another to the Senior Officer i.e. DSP of Sherpur. The said Senior Officer conducted an enquiry at Mehal Khurd. Later, he enquired at Amarjit Singh's Village, Dhilwan also. Thereafter the family did not receive any communication either from the DGP or the said Senior Officer.

His wife is mentally upset. She has two daughters and one son (who was born after his abduction) to look after. She is facing financial difficulties also.

The loss of assets that family calculated was enough to give them a hard time financially as the material used by him for winding motors and repairing other electrical gadgets including items like Fans, Churners (Madhani) were taken away by police.

### VFF/0563

Gurmeet Singh alias Jeeta(22) son of Ravinder Singh (Ghari wala) and Mukhtiar Kaur resident of Rajo majra ,tehsil Dhuri ,Dist Sangrur .

He was a matriculate * and a farmer by profession earning 5000 rupees per month.

He was unmarried but his brother Amarjit Singh and his family of 3 used to stay with Gurmeet .

He was not inimical towards anyone and there was nothing against him ever.

On 15th May 1991, he was abducted from his residence by C.I.A. Staff Bahadar Singh Wala and the police officers responsible for the same are:-

Jagga Singh, Inspector, Bahadar Singh Wala , Shamsher Singh, SHO Dhuri Police Station and Dilbagh Singh, SI Dhuri Police Station

There were witnesses in this case whose names will be disclosed later.

### VFF/0564

Hakam Singh (22)son of Jagdev Singh and Labh Kaur resident of Bhaini Kalan PO. Himmatana ,tehsil Dhuri ,Dist Sangrur .

He was a matriculate* now into farming earning 3000 rupees.

On 23rd October 1992, he had gone along with his mother to buy some clothes from Ludhiana. After buying the clothes, he was waiting for a bus along with his mother at Ludhiana Bus Stand. Just then, SSP Jagraon, Swaran Singh 'Ghotna' came there along with other policemen. They (police) told his mother that they had to question him on the grounds of suspicion. They also told her to come to Jagraon to collect her son after he had been interrogated by the police. The following Police Officers are responsible for his abduction and subsequent disappearance:-

Swaran Singh 'Ghotna', SSP* Jagraon and Darshan Singh, SHO
And other members of police party.

His father Jagdev Singh along with respectable persons of the Village met the SSP Swaran Singh alias 'Ghotna' twice (on 25the October 1992 and 27th October 1992) and requested him to release Hakam Singh. They saw Hakam Singh in the custody of C.I.A. Staff Jagraon on both the occasions. But the SSP dodged them by saying that they would releasse Hakam Singh that day or the day after. However, when they met him for the third time, the SSP was evasive and told that Hakam Singh would reach home by himself and that there was no need for them to come to Jagraon. He further told them that Hakam Singh was in the custody of SHO of Dehlon Police Station , Darshan Singh. But, when Jagdev Singh along with other people of the Village met the SHO Dehlon, he did not tell them anything and flatly denied having taken Hakam Singh in his custody. Later, Jagdev Singh submitted written representations to several authorities, but in vain. Whereabouts of Hakam Singh are not known till today. It is suspected that he had been killed by the Police of C.I.A. Staff Jagraon while he was in the custody of SSP Swaran Singh alias Ghotna there.

Uncertainity has creeped into their lives after his disappearance . both his parents are mentally disturbed and miss him a lot.

### VFF/0565

Gurjit Singh alias Guri (24)son of Surjit Kaur and Jasvir Kaur ,resident of Bhaini kalan ,tehsil huri ,Dist Sangrur . DOB-25$^{th}$ april 1967. He was a graduate* with a BA* in hand.

He was a farmer earning 10,000rupees per month. He was married to Ranjit Kaur (30) and they had 2 sons Jagatbir (10) and Diabir(8).

He had a clean past with nobody against him. On 15$^{th}$ August 1992 at 7.45 P.M., he was picked up from his residence at H.No. 106, 13B, Mohalla Rahi Basti, Near S.D. College, Railway Fatak by a police party led by DSP Surinderpal Singh Parmar and his gunmen, and SI Ashutosh, SHO City Barnala.

Since the time of his abduction , his Father is mentally upset. His wife feels that her life is incomplete without her husband.

*NOTE_ A memorandumin this regard was submitted by Sh. Simranjit Mann to the Governor Punjab in August 1992.*

### VFF/0566

Jagseer sing halias Kaka(20) son of Arjan Singh and Harnam Kaur resident of village SSurjitpura ,tehsil Barnala ,Dist Sangrur .

He finished his primary school* to join farming and earned 4500 rupees per month.

He was not married and stayed with his parents.

Jagseer Singh alias Kaka was an 'Amritdhari' (Baptised) Sikh youth. He was sympathetic towards the militant movement going on in the Punjab at that time. He used to give shelter to absconding militants. He was the eldest son of Arjan Singh (70 years) and he was a hard working farmer. Jagseer Singh's family owned 2-3 acres of land only, but, he used to cultivate other people's land on contract basis.

On 17$^{th}$ April 1991 , the Police of Barnala (Sadar) Police Station raided his house at the time when Phoola Singh Sanghera (Barnala), a renowned militant, had taken shelter in his house. On seeing the Police, Phoola Singh tried to escape through the rear door. But the Police had surrounded the house from all sides. As such, Phoola Singh committed suicide by consuming cyanide. Jagseer Singh ran away from home as he was scared of the Police. The Police began harassing his family members. A case was registered against his father Arjan Singh and he was sent to jail where he was detained for three and a half months. Apart from that, his brother Malkeet Singh was picked up by the Police and detained in their illegal custody for a month.

On 15th October 1991, his family members received information that the youth killed by the Police near village Deewana was Jagseer Singh. As such, his father Arjan Singh reached Civil Hospital Barnala where the Bhadaur Police had brought the body for a post mortem. Arjan Singh identified the body of Jagseer Singh. The village Panchayat also reached the place and demanded the dead body. But the Police did not hand over the body and did not allow them to collect his ashes even. The Police had declared Jagseer Singh to be an unidentified militant in the newspapers even though his father Arjan Singh had identified the body at the Civil Hospital at the time of post mortem. According to the family members, this attitude of the Police was illegal . However, the family members do not know as to what had happened to Jagseer Singh; whether he was arrested and killed or he was killed in an encounter with the Police as claimed by the Police. Later on, they heard several rumours.

The news reagrding his killing was published in all newspapers, but as an unidentified militant. The police confiscated all the copies of newspapers that were available with his family.

His father and mother are not keeping well. His father has been crippled as a result of police beating and his mother is sick and bed-ridden. Economic condition of the family is miserable.

### VFF/0567

Sukhdev Singh alias Kana (38)s/ Hari Singh and Karam Kaur (late) resident of village Dhilwan ,tehsil Barnala ,Dist Sangrur.

He was married to Ranjit Kaur(40) and they had 1 song and 2 daughters.

Sukhdev Singh was a young labourer and belonged to a Mazhabi Sikh family. He was one of the *emotional victims* of the attack on Sri Darbar Sahib,* Amritsar. He became an 'Amritdhari' (baptised) Sikh and became active in Akali Dal politics. He used to participate in the religious programmes organized in his area. He was arrested by the

Police in 1987 on the basis of suspected links with the militants. A case was registered against him on the allegation of giving shelter to militants and he was sent to jail where he was incarcerated for two and a half years. After his release from jail he was appointed body guard of Rajdev Singh, Member Parliament and he remained active politically also. Meanwhile, his wife and children used to live at his in-laws' place.

Later due to the fear of police raids ,his wife went to her parents house along with her children.nobody from her family even dared to pursue her husband's case and therefore his own father and brother used to pursue his case.

According to Ranjit Kaur, wife of Sukhdev Singh, in February, 1992, some persons from village Dhilwan came to her parents' house at village Bhadaur and told that Sukhdev Singh had been killed at the hands of the Police. On hearing this news, she and her parents reached Dhilwan. The villagers of Dhilwan had received Sukhdev Singh's dead body from the Police and brought it to the village, before their arrival, she said. The family members and other villagers carried out the cremation. Ranjit Kaur told that according to the Police, Sukhdev Singh had been killed along with one of his associates who was a resident of village Kahne Ke at a drain on the Dhilwan—Ghunnas road. The family members of Sukhdev Singh said that they were not sure whether the Police were telling the truth as they suspected that Sukhdev Singh had been arrested by the Police and then killed.

*The news item giving details of his having been killed in an encounter with the Police, was published in all the newspapers on the day following the alleged encounter.*

*The family members of Sukhdev are still terrified of the police.*

## VFF/0568

Gulab Singh alias Gulabi(30) son of late. Bakhshish Singh and late. Gurnam Kaur ,resident of village Dhilwan ,tehsil Barnala , Dist Sangrur .

He was married to Paramjit Kaur and had 2 children.

Gulab Singh, a farmer by profession, was an 'Amritdhari' (baptised) Sikh youth. However, he was not politically active. According to his family members, in 1992, he had gone along with other villagers to attend the 'Bhog' (a religious ceremony symbolising the closing of last rites ceremony) of a militant namely Sukhpal Singh Babbar. There, he was influenced (by the speeches made by various speakers) so deeply that soon after his return, he joined the ranks of the militants. But, before this, Gulab Singh was not involved in any sort of (unlawful) activities.

Just two months after Gulab Singh had absconded, the Police got a scent of his activities. The Police started raiding his house. The Police used to pick up his brother Tarsem Singh and his father also. All the family members deserted home, due to fear and began living at the headquarters of Namdhari sect at Bhaini village of district Ludhiana. All his family members were followers of Namdhari sect.

After all his family members had left home, the Police of C.I.A. Staff Handiaya used to pick up their relatives and subject them to brutal torture. The Police used to pressurise the relatives to either produce Gulab Singh or get him arrested. According to the family members, in Jun-Jul, 1994, somebody gave information to the Police that the family members of Gulab Singh were living at the headquarters of Namdhari sect at Bhaini village. A Police party of C.I.A. Staff Handiaya led by DSP (D) Sant Kumar raided Bhaini Sahib. Just then, Gulab Singh happened to come there to meet his family members. A Policeman who hailed from village Dhilwan recognised Gulab Singh. The Police arrested him and took him to C.I.A. Staff Handiaya. Before raiding Bhaini Sahib, the Police had picked up Gulab Singh's sister Beet Kaur, wife Paramjit Kaur and brother-in-law (sister's husband) Jeet Singh and had detained them at C.I.A. Staff Handiaya. On the second or third day after Gulab Singh's arrest, three other youth of Dhilwan village namely Sukhdev Singh son of Gurnam Singh, Nachhatter Singh son of Channan Singh and Gurjant Singh (cousin) son of Mohinder Singh were also arrested by C.I.A. Staff Handiaya. All the three of them saw Gulab Singh in Police custody. They told that Gulab Singh had been subjected to brutal and inhuman torture, so much so, that hot iron rods were pierced through various parts of his body. One of his legs had been fractured. On the fourth or fifth day of his arrest, the Police showed him as having been killed in an encounter with them at the drain near village Nangal near Barnala city. His family members and other villagers came to know about this encounter after reading the newspapers. Even then, the family did not return home due to the shock of Gulab Singh's death and Police terror. Two years after this incident, his father died at Bhaini Sahib itself and one year thereafter, his mother also expired.

*A news item giving details of the "encounter" with the Police was published in all the newspapers.*

**VFF/0569**

Surjit Singh (50)son of late. Gurdial Singh and late. Jeevan Kaur resident of village Sanghera ,tehsil Barnala , Dist Sangrur. He was matriculate * and a farmer by profession earning 10,000 rupees per month.

He was married to Ranjit Kaur (60) and they had 3 children with whom they lived.

Surjit Singh, was an 'Amritdhari' (Baptised) Gursikh. The religious influence on his life was due to his father Gurdial Singh's religious way of life. Surjit Singh used to take a leading part in the religious and social activities in his village and he was an office-bearer of the Gurdwara Management Committee of his village also.

In October-November, 1984, after Indira Gandhi was assassinated, there occured massacre of Sikhs in Delhi. A few months later, a Sikh family who claimed themselves to be riot-affected, came to village Sanghera. The Gurdwara Management Committee of the village provided all help to the said family and helped them to settle down in the village. Surjit Singh was in the forefront in helping the said family by virtue of his being a office-bearer of the Gurdwara Management Committee. However, two youth of this family were involved in militant activities. The family members of Surjit Singh told that they don't know whether Surjit Singh was aware of the involvement of those youth of the abovementioned family in the militant activities or not. In those days, a murder took place at Barnala and youth of the abovementioned family were suspected to be responsible for the same. The Barnala Police arrested Surjit Singh and six other persons of village Sanghera, registered a case against them on the allegation of giving shelter to militants and sent them to Sangrur jail. Ten months later, Surjit Singh and his companions came out on bail. But, two months later, the Barnala Police arrested Surjit Singh again and sent him to jail under N.S.A. However, some time later, the charge under NSA was dismissed. But, thereafter, it became a routine for the Police to arrest Surjit Singh on the basis of suspicion. After his release from jail, Surjit Singh again got busy in religious activities. Surjit Singh was close to Damdami Taksal and former Jathedar of Akal Takht, Singh Sahib Bhai Gurdev Singh Kaonke. That was one of the reasons why the Police used to harass him too much. Whenever Surjit Singh used to be not available at home, the Police used to harass his family members and used to arrest them and take them away. Due to frequent Police raids, Surjit Singh began to stay away from home and used to visit his home rarely. He stopped visiting his home altogether, after 1990. He used to be busy in religious activities only during this period. His family members told that Surjit Singh was a supporter and sympathiser of the militant movement alright, but, he had not taken up arms himself. The Police used to harass Surjit Singh merely on the basis of suspicion that he had links with the militants.

On 4th or 5th April, 1993, the Barnala Police had brought dead bodies of two militants for postmortem to Civil Hospital at Barnala. A few people of Sanghera village recognised one of the bodies as that of Surjit Singh and informed his family members accordingly. His family members went to Barnala immediately and enquired from the doctors who had conducted the postmortem. The doctors, on seeing his photograph told that he was one of the two dead militants. The family members went to Ram Bagh at Barnala (cremation ground) and collected his ashes as pointed out by the employees there. While collecting his ashes, his family members recognised the 'Karra' (A Steel Bangle worn by Punjabis in general and baptised Sikhs in particular) of Surjit Singh. Thus, they were certain that the deceased was indeed Surjit Singh. Later on, his family members came to know that the Police of C.I.A. Staff Handiaya had shown Surjit Singh and another person as having been killed in an encounter with them at a bridge in between the villages Mangewal and Khiali yet, they were certain that the Police had arrested Surjit Singh and killed him in a fake encounter. They said that various rumours were afloat about Surjit Singh's arrest, but they were not sure so far, as to from where Surjit Singh had been arrested. They further told that each and every person of the area and each and every Police officer knew Surjit Singh. Even the doctors at the Hospital had recognised his body. The basis of their suspicion was the fact that the Police had declared him as unidentified. The family members said that declaring a person whom several (Police) employees of Barnala Police district and C.I.A. Staff knew very well, as unidentified, illustrated one thing only that the Police wanted to hush up the matter. They said that had the villagers not recognised his dead body at the Hospital, they would have never come to know as to what happened to Surjit Singh. They further said that if an independent inquiry is held into this incident, then it would be proved that Surjit Singh and another militant killed along with him were arrested and then killed.

**VFF/0570**

Narinder Singh alias Nindi, son of Baldev Singh and Karanajit Kaur r/o

Village Dangarh, tehsil Barnala , Dist Sangrur.

He was an educated youth who had passed his middle school and was still studying. His monthly income is stated to be around 8000 rupees. He was not married and was living with his family which included Parsinn Kaur (85) Grandmother ; Baldev Singh (42) Father ; Karanjit Kaur (39) Mother Gurvinder Kaur (17) Sister ; Lakhwinder Singh (15) and Bikramjit Singh (13) Brothers.

On 16th July 1992, SHO Dhanaula S. Darshan Singh picked up

Narinder Singh. On 18th July 1992, his father Baldev Singh was also picked up by the same SHO. They were detained at Police Station Dhanaula for one month after which Baldev Singh was released. Baldev Singh used to take food for Narinder Singh daily to Police Station Dhanaula. On 20th September 1992, when, as usual, Baldev Singh went to the Police Station with food for his son, he was informed by the SHO that his son had been taken away by DSP Hardip Singh alias Bhau of Sherpur. After that, Baldev Singh along with Narinder's grandfather (Nana) of vill. Dhanauri Kalan met Hardip Singh and enquired about Narinder. He did not give them any information.

His father met SSP Ishwar Chand and Inspector C.I.A. Staff Sant Kumar. But so far there is no information about him.

He has left behind his family of 6 which are waiting for his return.

**VFF/0571**

Amritpal Singh alias Ambi(20), son of Avtar Singhh and Gurcharan Kaur, resident of village Rajo majra, tehsil Dhuri, Dist Sangrur .

He was a matriculate* and was now into farming for earning his living. He earned about 800 rupees per month.

Sardar Avtar Singh aged 55 years had two sons and one daughter. Amritpal Singh alias Ambi was his elder son. After passing his Matriculation, he joined his father in agricultural farming. Avtar Singh himself was an "Amritdhari" (Baptised) Sikh and it had its impact on his children also. Amritpal Singh had got himself baptised at a young age and he was a religious minded youth. By virtue of being religious minded , he had come in contact with Sant Chand Singh Rajo Majra who was busy in getting the people baptised with a view to propagate Sikh religion, in those days. Amritpal Singh used to spend most of his time in the company of Sant Ji and he used to be one of the 'Panj Pyaras' (Five beloved Ones) who used to offer 'Amrit' to those being baptised.

In September 1991, the Lehragaga Police raided the house of Amritpal Singh with a view to arrest him, but, he had gone to Dhuri for selling paddy. The Police party picked up Avtar Singh (father) and took him away. Same day, the above mentioned Police party, had raided the houses of ChamKaur Singh son of Nachhatter Singh, Labh Singh son of Chhota Singh, Nirmal Singh Kanda son of Sukhdev Singh also. The Police picked up Bhag Singh (Grandfather of ChamKaur Singh), Chhota Singh (father of Labh Singh), Balwinder Singh (Kanda's brother) and took them also to Lehragaga. They were detained at Lehragaga Police Station for one night and for three nights at Daska Police Post. On the fourth day, they were got released by the Panchayat (Village Council). Thereafter, the Police harassed Amritpal Singh's family, regularly.

On 22 March 1992 at about 5 A.M., Bakhshish Singh, SHO of Barnala (Sadar) Police Station arrested Amritpal Singh along with one of his associates Labh Singh son of Sukhdev Singh from the Gurdwara at Village Thullewal (under Police Station Barnala). The family members of Amritpal Singh and Labh Singh got the news of this incident on the same day. On the following day, their family members along with the Panchayat met SHO Bakhshish Singh. However, he flatly denied having arrested them. The family members continued to pursue their case. During this period, Avtar Singh (Father of Amritpal Singh), Sukhdev Singh (father of Labh Singh) and Labh Singh (brother-in-law of Labh Singh) along with the Village Panchayat met the SSP Barnala Mr. Ishwar Chander, DSP Joginder Singh Kutiwal and SHO Bakhshish Singh. The SSP and the SHO flatly denied their custody, but DSP Joginder Singh Kutiwal admitted their custody once and demanded Rs. 50,000/- in return for recording their arrest formally. Avtar Singh and Labh Singh promised to pay him the money. They said, "As and when you send them to jail, we will pay you the money." The DSP agreed. Avtar Singh even mortgaged 13 bighas of his land for Rs. 50,000/- for this purpose. However, the DSP did not record their arrest formally. He continued to make false promises for a few days.

On the intervening night of 1 and 2 April (1992), Amritpal Singh and Labh Singh were killed in a fake encounter near the brick Kiln at Village Sanghera. They were shown as unidentified. After reading this news, Avtar Singh met DSP Joginder Singh Kutiwal who told him that their sons had been taken away from him by SP (D) Gurdev Singh Sahota. Unofficially, some of the Policemen told both the families that the unidentified militants killed near Sanghera were their sons only. On getting this confirmation, the family members of Amritpal Singh performed his 'Bhog' (religious last rites).

He was last seen by Avtar Singh (father) at the CIA* Handiaya on 27th March1992.

**VFF/0572**

Darshan Singh alias Chamku (21), son of Tarlok Singh and Sukhdev Kaur resident of village Longowal , tehsil Longowal, Dist Sangrur. He was educated up to middle school.

He was a farmer by profession earning rupees 5000 per month.

Tarlok Singh (father of vicitim Darshan Singh), aged about 65 years, resident of Village Longowal, is the head of a well-to-do Sikh family. He had four sons and two daughters. Darshan Singh, his youngest son, had taken up agricultural farming after passing grade VI. Darshan Singh was an "Amritdhari" (Baptised) Sikh youth. However, he was not active politically. Tarlok Singh told that his son might have been close to some militant youth but he had no direct link whatsoever with the then ongoing militant and political movement in Punjab. He was never arrested on the basis of suspicion, either.

On 28ᵗʰ June 1992 at 11:30 P.M., a large Police force raided his house. The Police scaled the walls and entered the house from the roof. At that time, his brother Amarjit Singh was at home. The Police enquired from him about Darshan Singh. He told them that Darshan Singh had gone to water the fields. The Police took Amarjit Singh along and went to the fields. His father Tarlok Singh was also available there at that time. They woke him up and enquired about Darshan Singh. Tarlok Singh replied that Darshan Singh was on the roof. The Police climbed onto the roof and brought Darshan Singh down. There were several officers in the Police party like SSP Bhullar, DSP Baldev Singh (Sunam), SI Rampal Singh etc. According to Tarlok Singh, the Police had come in 10-15 vehicles on that day. The Police made Amarjit Singh and Darshan Singh to sit in different vehicles and took them away. They carried away one Jeep also bearing registration no.(RSK-5697). The same Police party arrested Sher Singh alias Shera also from Village Singhpura.

On the following day, Tarlok Singh, along with Chand Singh, Mahant of the Gurdwara, Nambardar Preetam Singh Dhillon and other eminent persons reached Police Station Longowal. The SHO Tarlochan Singh told that he did not know anything about Darshan Singh and Amarjit Singh. Tarlok Singh told that he along with the Panchayat members, met various Police officers like SSP Sangrur, DSP Sangrur, SP (D) and DSP (D) several times. In the beginning, all the Police officers assured him that Amarjit Singh and Darshan Singh would be released.

On the 16th day, Amarjit Singh was released from Sunam Police Station . He told that he was kept at Bhawanigarh, Sangrur and Sunam Police Station s. However, according to him, Darshan Singh was kept separately from him and he did not know anything about his whereabouts. On the other hand, his family members were getting information regularly that Darshan Singh had been detained at C.I.A. Staff (Sangrur) Bahadur Singh Wala. They got another information also that Darshan Singh had been taken away on the 13th day.

SSP Bhullar assured Tarlok Singh (father) and other eminent persons that they would release Darshan Singh some time later. He gave the reason for this delay that Darshan Singh had been thrashed (by the Police) excessively. As such, as and when he recovered, they would release him. However, later on, the SSP also started making false promises.

Tarlok Singh told that they had been to each and every Police Station in district Sangrur, but they did not get any clue about his whereabouts. The Police did not return their Jeep also. Once, Tarlok Singh and several other persons saw the same Jeep in the possession of the SHO of Dibra Police Station . According to Tarlok Singh, they ran from pillar to post for several years, but in vain. They met the newly posted SSP Jasminder Singh and other officers also. Every officer either made false promises to them or used to pass the buck on to somebody else.

After the formation of Akali Government in Punjab, Tarlok Singh met Chief Minister Parkash Singh Badal at Chandigarh, twice. He received his application and told him that he would get his case inquired into. Tarlok Singh received an acknowledgement also from the Chief Minister's office, with respect to his application that his case had been marked for an inquiry. According to Tarlok Singh, once an ASI had come and recorded his statement and at another time, DSP Sangrur had called him and recorded his statement. But nothing came out of the said inquiry. He further told that last year SP (D) also had recorded his statement. He (SP (D)) was hesitant to record the details of SSP Bhullar's role in his statement. However nothing has come out of these inquiries, Tarlok Singh said.

Note: Tarlok Singh still believes that Darshan Singh was alive. He told that some people had delivered his (Darshan Singh's) messages to them. This is not the first case of its kind in Punjab. Numerous parents still hope, like Tarlok Singh, that their sons were alive and the Police were holding them in their custody.

His parents are mentally upset. They miss him so much. His father is bed-ridden since his disappearance, due to shock.

### VFF/0573

Amrik Singh , son of Fakir Singh and Gurdev Kaur, resident of village Amargarh , tehsil Malerkotla, Dist Sangrur. Date Of Birth- 11th December 1957.

He was an educated youth of the village and one of the very few who had completed their primary studies. He had also done a PTI* course which helped him get the job of a Ground keeper at the Dist Sports. He earned a total of 2800 rupees per month . He was married to Harminder Kaur(32) and they had a daughter Kiranpreet Kaur(7).

Amrik Singh was a peace loving citizen. He was not associated with any sort of political or Militant Organisation. He used to go for duty to his Office at Dist Sports Officer's Office at Patiala and come back home in the evening. He never stayed overnight at Patiala or any other place.

He is missing since 01ˢᵗ October 1992 from a bus stop near village Dheengi. On 1ˢᵗ October 1992 at 6.30 P.M., he was coming from Patiala to Amargarh in a bus when he was abducted by a police party of 4-5 men in civil clothes, headed by Gurmel Singh SHO Amargarh and including Bir Atma Ram SHO Sadar Police Station Nabha. His family came to know about this incident at 7.30 P.M. At 9 P.M. same night, they met Bir Atma Ram, SHO Nabha (Sadar). He expressed ignorance about this incident.

On 2ⁿᵈ October 1992, they again met Bir Atma Ram, SHO Nabha (Sadar). He told that there is a possibility of Amrik Singh having been picked up by C.I.A. Staff Patiala. Then they met Satpal Singh, incharge of C.I.A. Staff Patiala (Mai Ki Saran). But, no clue could be found regarding the whereabouts of Amrik Singh.

On 3ʳᵈ October 1992, we met Bir Atma Ram, SHO Nabha (Sadar). He said,"Don't worry, your son is with the Police only. You come tomorrow and take him back." Apart from Fakir Singh, Mukhtiar Singh retired SP of Nabha, Iqbal Singh Khanna, and Manpal Singh Raipur were present there when he uttered these words.

On 4ᵗʰ October 1992, they met DSP Gurmeet Singh at Nabha. He asked the SHO about the boy. The SHO denied any knowledge about the whereabouts of the boy. On being reminded about his words of the previous day, he denied having spoken those words also. We enquired at other Police Station s around Nabha, like Bhawanigarh, Chheenta etc, but no clue was found anywhere.

On 5ᵗʰ October 1992, a delegation of the Panchayat of Amargarh met the SHO and DSP of Nabha again. But, to no avail. When requested to register the FIR, SHO Nabha evaded doing so till the evening. Ultimately, in the evening, SHO Nabha registered a DDR No. 21 dated 5ᵗʰ October 1992, with great hesitation.

On 6ᵗʰ October 1992, they met the then Taxation and Excise Minister, Punjab, Sh. Shamsher Singh Doolo. He gave a letter addressed to SSP Sangrur Narinder Pal Singh. They met the SSP with that letter. He enquired from all Police Station s in Sangrur District on the Wireless, but no clue was found.

On 7ᵗʰ October 1992, they met Karam Singh, the then Minister for Industry, Punjab. He gave a letter addressed to SSP Patiala, Sh. Suresh Arora. They then went to the SSP's Office at Patiala with that letter. The SSP was not present, but, the SP (D) was present there. He enquired over the Wireless from all Police Station s in Patiala District, but no clue was found.

On 10th October 1992, Chief Minister of Punjab, Sh. Beant Singh had come to Khanna to attend a wedding. They along with Amrik Singh, Sarpanch of village Rauni (Ludhiana) met him and narrated the incident to him. He put the application in his pocket and asked them to meet him at Chandigarh.

Then they met Sh. Beant Singh, Chief Minister Punjab at Chandigarh. He directed his political advisor Gurmeet Singh to inquire into the matter. On meeting Gurmeet Singh after 3-4 days. He said that there was no information about Amrik Singh.

On 13th October 1992, registered written representations were sent to DGP Punjab, Governor Punjab, Chief Minister Punjab, and SSP Patiala. Representatives of various newspapers also came to their home and enquired about this incident. A news item about his disappearance was published in various newspapers.

On 15th October 1992, a delegation of the village Panchayat met the IG Punjab Sh. Sube Singh. But, after 3-4 days, he also sent a mesage that no information was available regarding the whereabouts of Amrik Singh.

On 16th October 1992, a delegation of the village Panchayat met the SSP Patiala, Sh. Suresh Arora. He told them that they had come late; thereby implying that the boy had been arrested by the Police, but had now disappeared. Same day, a delegation of Shere Punjab Club Amargarh met the MLA of the area, Sh. Dhanwant Singh (Dhuri). The MLA rang up DIG Sh. Rajan Gupta. The DIG replied that Amrik Singh had indeed been arrested and had been kept underground in a Cellar along with some other boys. He said that they would release them after a few days. 4-5 days later, the MLA again rang up the DIG. Then he denied his earlier statement saying that he had mistaken some other boy for Amrik Singh.

On 21st October 1992, DIG Patiala came to village Amargarh to listen to the people's complaints against Police excesses. First of all, the Panchayat of village Amargarh put forth the serious complaint of the disappearance of Amrik Singh. They also told the DIG that in case the boy was found to be guilty i.e. he may be a militant, then he may be shot dead in front of all of them. But, if he was innocent, then why was he picked up without informing about his crime to his parents.

4-5 days later, the family members again met the DIG. He expressed his ignorance again. Thereafter, for two three months, residents of the village, friends, relatives and other sympathisers made every effort to locate him. Whosoever had an approach in any Police Station , he enquired from there, but, all in vain.

So far, they do not know as to what his fault was. Whether he had any connection with any militant Organisation. Or which Police had arrested him, where he was taken and what they did to him. It is still a mystery.

### VFF/0574

Palwinder Singh (36)son of Gurbachan Singh and Ranjit Kaur ,resident of village Gehlan, tehsil Bhawanigarh, Dist Sangrur.

He was a graduate* and was working as a Cashier in Central Co-op Bank. He earned a total of 6500 rupees per month. He was married to Baldev Kaur(35) and they had three daughters Arminder Kaur(15) ; Rajvir Kaur(12) and Karamvir Kaur(7).

There is nothing that conforms of him having a malign past. He has been missing since 19th May1993 from the Sangrur Police Station *. Police used to visit Central Co-op. Bank Sangrur for him. Doubting the antecedents of the people who visited the Bank (his father had been abducted and killed by Black Cat (Kalian Billian) Commandoes earlier), he appeared voluntarily before SP Sangrur S. Jaswinder Singh. He was arrested by Sangrur Police and never returned home after that. The incident was witnessed by Avtar Singh   (Employee of Central Co-op. Bank Sangrur ) and Gurdev Singh (Vill. Gehlan PO. Mehsampur Teh. Bhawanigarh Dist Sangrur).

Palwinder Singh was a Bank employee and was doing his duty and looking after his family. He never committed any crime and was never involved in any case. He was held just because of his brother Mahesh Inder Singh. His mother met SP Sangrur, S. Jaswinder Singh , along with Panchayats of many neighbouring villages. Jathedar Jagdev Singh Talwandi also rang up the SP personally for getting him released. But all this proved to be an abortive attempt.

His mother Ranjit Kaur has suffered a heart attack once and has become a heart patient. She can't move about and is bed-ridden.

### VFF/0575

Jagdish Singh alias Babbu 19 son of Piara Singh and Charan Kaur was a resident of Leel Kalan in Gurdaspur. Jagdish Singh's father Piara Singh had died while he was about 7 years old. Late Piara Singh was a resident of village Leel Kalan. Jagdish Singh had one brother and two sisters. He was the youngest. After the death of his father, his maternal uncle Jathedar Charan Singh brought his (Jagdish Singh's) whole family to his house at village Nangali Kalan (Amritsar). Jagdish Singh and his elder brother Sarabjit Singh started helping their maternal uncle in agricultural farming.

Jagdish Singh was an "Amritdhari" (baptised) Sikh youth who was deeply influenced by the militant and political movement, going on in Punjab. The Police used to arrest him often. Once, the Qadian Police had arrested him, registered a case against him under TADA and sent him to jail. He was in jail for about one year. As the Police came to know about the return of Jagdish Singh to village Nangali, the Mehta Police began arresting him on the basis of suspicion. At times, Jagdish Singh used to be away from home for days together, due to the fear of the Police. On 12ᵗʰ July1991 at about 8 PM, Jagdish Singh and one of his friends, Baljit Singh, were having their meals at his (Charan Singh's) house at village Nangali Kalan. A Police party barged into the house and rest of the Policemen surrounded the house. Immediately on their arrival, the Policemen, without asking them anything, pounced upon both the youth, tied their hands at their backs and put them in their vehicle. The family members did not know which Police Station did they belong to?

The following morning, Jathedar Charan Singh, Gurditt Singh, father of the other boy, Baljit Singh and some other villagers went to Police Station Mehta and enquired about the arrested boys. The SHO replied that neither had they arrested them nor do they know as to who had arrested and taken them away. The attitude of the SHO was non-cooperative according to the family. The family members ran from pillar to post for a few days trying to find out as to from where the Police had come. They enquired at Qadian also. However they did not get any clue about their whereabouts.

In the meantime, a news item was published in the newspapers on 16ᵗʰ July1991 that a Police party who were taking three arrested militants, Jagdish Singh Babbu, Baljit Singh and Narinder Singh Nindi, resident of Bham (Gurdaspur) for the recovery of weapons, in the area of Majitha Police district, were attacked by a group of militants. The Police returned the fire. All the three militants, in custody, were killed in the cross-firing.

After reading the news item, the family members enquired at Police Station Mehta where the police told them that they did not know anything and advised them to find out from Amritsar. On the following day, Gurditt Singh, father of the other boy, Baljit Singh, along with some other villagers, collected the ashes of both of them from the cremation ground at Durgiana Mandir at Amritsar. According to the employees of the cremation ground, the Mehta Police had carried out the cremation of the bodies of three youth, on 15ᵗʰ July 1991.

The news that appeared in a Punjabi daily newspaper, *Ajit*, published from Jalandhar, dated 16 July 1991 is appended below:

*A Police party which was taking three militants, Baljit Singh, Narinder Singh Nindi, resident of Bham (Gurdaspur) and Jagdish Singh Babbu, resident of Leel Kalan, who had been arrested earlier, for the recovery of weapons, were attacked by a group of militants near village Mehta of Majitha Police district. The Police returned the fire. Consequently, all the three militants, in custody, were killed.*

### VFF/0576

Ram Singh (18) son of Gurmail Singh and Harbans Kaur of Patiala was a farmer who lived with his parents and Sister Bhagwant Kaur (22). He had been to Amritsar and met the Sant (Jarnail Singh Bhindranwale) before 1984. He took the vows of Sikhi (to follow the Sikh code of conduct) after his return from Amritsar. He was a member of the Akali Dal Amritsar (Mann Dal). He was once in Jail for one and a half years.

He was killed in the firing at Nabha Jail.

### VFF/0577

Mahinder Singh 20 son of Karam Singh and Jaginder Kaur of Bhappal, Patiala worked as an Apprentice Salesman at a shop Kisan Sewa Centre. He lived with his mother, brother Hardeep Singh 30, sisters Manjit Kaur 33 and Rajwinder Kaur 20.

According to Mahinder Singh's father Karam Singh when on 12th Feb 1993, he had gone to Rajpura Town along with his wife to get some medicines for her he had visited their son at his workplace. Co-incidentally, in their presence, some persons (suspected to be policemen) in civil dress came in a Maruti car No. PCS-3635, and forced their son Mahinder Singh into the car and fled away. He (Mahinder Singh's father) shouted for help but nobody came forward to help him. According to Karam Singh, most of the people who witnessed this incident and who knew the Policemen involved, belong to the Hindu community in the Mandi and none of them would come forward to testify in their favor. Many people including local shopkeepers and some persons from their village were present there, but nobody is willing to depose against the Police. He (Mahinder Singh's father) followed the car and found that it had gone into the C.I.A. Staff Headquarters, Rajpura. From a distance, he saw the car of the colour and registration number described by the people, rushing into the CIA building. But, he was not allowed to go inside the building by the security guards posted at the gate.

Thereafter, Karam Singh returned to the Grain Market and in the evening, he, along with his brother-in-law Gurcharan Singh and one Dharam Singh of his village, went to the C.I.A Staff. They were not allowed to enter the premises of the C.I.A Staff and had to return. However, it is pertinent to mention that a raid had been conducted on the house of one Gursewak Singh s/o Joga Singh, nephew of above mentioned Dharam Singh. Gursewak Singh was produced by his family members before the C.I.A Staff, Rajpura and they were able to secure his release two days later. Later on, Gursewak Singh disclosed to Karam Singh that he and Mahinder Singh had been detained together at the C.I.A Staff. He has, however, refused to testify in their favor against the Police officials.

On the following day, Karam Singh, along with other people met the then DSP Rajpura as well as the SHO Sub-Inspector Balwinder Singh, who refused to admit to the custody of Mahinder Singh. Next day, Karam Singh, who happened to be the Sarpanch of his village at that time, was accompanied by Panchayats of about 20 villages when he met the then SSP of Patiala, Mr. CSR Reddy. The SSP refused to admit to the custody of his son. Thereafter, he approached Gurcharan Singh Tohra who met the SSP on their behalf. The SSP again refused to admit that his son was in his custody before Mr. Tohra. Karam Singh continued his efforts to get his son released. It was after about 12 days of his son's abduction that Karam Singh, along with his brother-in-law, was able to see his son Mahinder Singh in the custody of the C.I.A. Staff. The Policeman who allowed him to see his son from a distance, did not allow him to go near him or talk to him. Now that he was sure that his son was still alive in the custody of C.I.A Staff, Rajpura, Karam Singh stepped up his efforts to get his son released. Along with the various Panchayats and eminent persons of the area, he continued to meet the SSP Patiala and he met the DGP, Punjab, Mr. KPS Gill also twice. On the last occasion, Mr. KPS Gill assured him that his son would return home and that he should not worry about it. But, each time, the SSP maintained that Mahinder Singh was not in the custody of his district Police. It was during these efforts that Karam Singh met the then DSP (D), Gurnam Singh Mehra of Patiala who admitted to his son's custody and promised to release him in return for a payment of Rs. 70,000/- (Seventy Thousand only). Karam Singh paid the said amount to him. But, the said DSP (D) backtracked from his promise and said that he was not in a position to release Mahinder Singh as he had to hand him over to the then DSP Rajpura, Tejinderjit Singh Aulakh. Karam Singh had great difficulty in recovering his money from DSP (D) Gurnam Singh Mehra.

Karam Singh had submitted written representations to the SSP and DGP. The copies of the same are attached with the petition.

Karam Singh stated that he spent about Rs. 1,50,000/- in pursuing the case of his son in order to get him released from Police custody.

Mahinder Singh's mother, Jatinder Kaur, is suffering from depression due to the shock of this incident. Her eyesight also has deteriorated. Karam Singh said that they were able to cope up with this tragedy as both of them were "Amritdharis" (baptised) and they practiced meditation.

A Cr writ petition was filed in the Punjab & Haryana High Court Chandigarh on 12th Aug 1996 through Advocate Harjit Singh Minhas. The Writ was disposed off by Judge R.L. Anand of Punjab & Haryana High Court, Chandigarh vide his order dated 9th Nov 1998 with the observation that:-

"Let the petitioner may file a criminal complaint in the competent court of jurisdiction as the relief as prayed for by the petitioner cannot be granted after a lapse of 5 years. Extra ordinary powers on the question of fact are not supposed to be invoked in the High Court after a considerable delay. The petitioner will be permitted to take all the pleas which have been taken up in the present petition before the competent court of jurisdiction."

Written representations were also submitted to the following authorities:-

1.  SSP Patiala. (Dated 17th Feb 1993)
2.  Mr. KPS Gill, DGP Punjab (dated 3rd May 1993, counter-signed by Panchayat Members of their and village neighboring villages).
3.  IGP (Crime), Punjab (dated 19th Mar 1993, counter-signed by Panchayat Members of their village and neighboring villages).

## VFF/0578

Balwinder Singh alias Binder 35, son of Sadha Singh and Prakash Kaur; resident of village Mulowali; Dist Gurdaspur

In 1985, he was detained illegally by Police of Dera Baba Nanak for three days and tortured. In May 1988, during Operation Black Thunder, he was arrested and tortured. 19 cases were fabricated against him and he was sent to Jail where he was acquitted in 17 cases and was released on bail in April 1991 in the remaining two cases. He was arrested at the Jail Gate, kept in detention for a few days and let off. On 22nd March 1993, at about 12 Noon, he was picked up from his residence by a Police party of Police Station Dera Baba Nanak led by SHO Baldev Singh and including Gunmen Nirmal Singh, Tarlok Singh, and Sulakhan Singh etc. Same day in the afternoon at 2 P.M., he was shot dead along with two other youth in a fake encounter. The other two youth were Balwinder Singh resident of Vill. Lalpura under Dera Baba Nanak Police Station and Baljinder Singh Latu resident of village Kalanaur under Police Station Kalanaur. This whole action was carried out under the supervision of Madan Gopal, DSP Dera Baba Nanak.

### VFF/0579

Gurmej Singh alias Geja 22, son of Jaswant Singh and Gurbachan Kaur was a resident of village Dharamkot Randhawa. Dist Gurdaspur

In 1987, one day at 3 A.M., he was abducted from home by Police, was detained illegally and tortured for 20 days at Beeco Interrogation Centre, Batala, Malmandi Amritsar, and Sadar Police Station Gurdaspur. At last he was implicated in a case in connection with a Bomb blast at Courts Complex and sent to Jail. He was released on bail from there after 9 months. On 31st January 1991, Gurmej had been to his sister Ranjit Kaur's place at village Udhowal and after meeting her, he had gone to his cousin sister (Bhua's daughter) Kans Kaur's house at village Dialgarh under Police Station Sadar Batala, to meet her. After meeting her, when he came out of the village, he was surrounded by a Police party which was waiting for him and was led by SSP Sita Ram. The Police tried to catch him and he tried his level best to escape. When he lost all hope of escape, he took out his Kirpan from Gatra, sharpened it at the dais of a tubewell, wrote 'Khalistan Zindabad' over there. Before the Police could lay their hands on him, he poked his Kirpan into his stomach and attained martyrdom. ASI Kashmir Singh from Police Station Batala and resident of Bhakthana Boharwala pumped bullets into the dead body of Gurmej Singh.

Note: According to the affidavit submitted by Gurbachan Kaur, mother of the victim Gurmej Singh, to Amrik Singh Muktsar, Kanso is said to be the real sister of Gurmej Singh, whereas, in this proforma, she is shown as his cousin sister (Bhua's daughter). In the said affidavit it is stated that the Police had surrounded Kanso's house and arrested Gurmej Singh in front of Kanso and her husband Lakhwinder Singh. Also as per the said affidavit, Gurmej Singh was shot dead by the Police just outside the house in the fields. Whereas, in this proforma it is mentioned that Gurmej Singh was surrounded by the Police after he came out of the Village. And that he tried to escape, but, since he could not escape, he committed suicide with his Kirpan and the Police fired at him when he had already died. The said affidavit is appended below for cross reference.

AFFIDAVIT

I, Gurbachan Kaur w/o S. Jaswant Singh resident of Village Dharamkot Randhawa, PS & Tehsil Dera Baba Nanak, Dist Gurdaspur, do hereby affirm and declare as under:-

1) That I have four, sons and one daughter. My, son namely Gurmej Singh who has been killed by the Police was my youngest, son aged 20 years and a Matriculate.

2) That the Police used to harass our family as we belong to the family of Bhai Satwant Singh who was involved in Indira Gandhi assassination case. My, son Gurmej Singh had been subjected to torture in illegal custody several times without any reason whatsoever, for days together.

3) That my son had served in the SGPC from 1987 to 1988. On 13th July1988 at 7 A.M., Rambagh (Amritsar) Police took him into custody in front of me and other members of my family. He was implicated in a case and sent to Amritsar Jail from where he was released on bail on 17th October 1988.

4) That after his release from Jail, Gurmej Singh remained at home for 3-4 months. However, during this period also, the Police used to raid our house and Gurmej Singh used to remain in hiding. Thereafter, fed up with continuous Police harassment, he absconded.

5) That after Gurmej Singh had absconded, Dera Baba Nanak Police used to pick up my husband Jaswant Singh and also torture him. Once, Kundan Singh, SHO of Dera Baba Nanak Police Station arrested my husband and detained him in illegal custody at different Police Station s for two months. This cycle of Police repression against our family continued for two years. The Police used to raid our house often.

6) That Gurmej Singh had gone to his sister KansoÆs house at Dialgarh. On 31 January 1991 at 8 P.M. the Police surrounded the house of his sister Kanso and Sub-Inspector Kashmir Singh of Police Station Sadar Batala arrested him in front of my daughter Kanso and, son-in-law Lakhwinder Singh. The Police party shot him dead then and there outside the house in the fields and carried away his dead body in a Vehicle.

7) That on the next day, Bapu Tarlok Singh, Akali leader (cousin) went to Cremation Ground at Batala and collected his ashes. Thereafter, we did not take any action due to the fear of the Police.

DEPONENT

VERIFICATION

I, Deponent, do hereby solemnly affirm and declare that the contents of the above affidavit are true and correct to my knowledge and no part of it is false. Nothing material has been concealed. The same have been read over to me in Punjabi and after understanding it, I have affixed my Signature/Thumb Impression on this affidavit.

Place:

Date:23/12/98
DEPONENT

**VFF/0580**

Dalbir Singh alias Pappu 26, son of Channan Singh and Swaran Kaur; resident of village Talwandi Goraya; dist Gurdaspur

In April 1986, he was taken into illegal custody in the Police action ordered by Chief Minister Surjit Singh Barnala, when he had gone to Amritsar to pay obeisance at the Darbar Sahib. He was implicated in a case and sent to Jail. And was released after 5-6 months, on bail.

*As per affidavit submitted to Amrik Singh Muktsar by the family of the Victim Dalbir Singh, the date of his arrest during Police Action at Darbar Sahib is 30th November 1986. (Refer PC-0520). On 27th March 1989, Dalbir Singh alias Pappu had gone to his sister Jasbir Kaur's house at Village Sarafkot under Police Station Fatehgarh Churian to attend Bhog of Shri Akhand Path in connection with birthday celebrations of his nephew (Bhanja). He was picked up from there by a Police party led by SHO Police Station Sadar Batala at 8 A.M. in front of hundreds of people gathered there for the Bhog ceremony. Same day at about 8.30 P.M. he was shot dead at Village Bhullar (on Bhullar—Batala Road) in a fake encounter. This operation was carried out on the orders of Gobind Ram, SSP Batala.*

Note: In the affidavit submitted to Amrik Singh Muktsar by the mother of the victim Dalbir Singh, the name of his sister has been mentioned as Narinder Kaur whose house is situated at Sarafkot. (Refer PC-0520).

**VFF/0581**

Avtar Singh alias Taru 31,son of Banta Singh and Amar Kaur ; resident of village Thetherke ; dist Gurdaspur

In 1987 Avtar Singh was kept in illegal detention and tortured brutally for several days. He was released only after the intervention of respectable persons of the village. On 3rd June 1989 at about 9 A.M. he was picked up from his home by a party of BSF Battalion No. 15 or 18 belonging to BSF Chowki village Kamalpur under Police Station Ramdas Dist Amritsar saying that they had to get somebody identified from him and after that they would send him back. Earlier also, they had taken him like that once or twice and deposited him back. However, at about 11 P.M.on that day, he was shot dead at Kamalpur BSF Chowki under Police Station Ramdas Dist Amritsar.

### VFF/0582

Balwinder Singh alias Keeri, son of Shangara Singh and Joginder Kaur; resident of village Nikko Saran; Dist Gurdaspur

On 30 April 1988 Balwinder Singh had gone to Darbar Singh to pay obeisance. He was arrested under the Police action ordered by Chief Minister Barnala, implicated in a case and sent to Gurdaspur Jail. He was released from Jail after one month on bail. After that also, till the time of his martyrdom, he was taken into illegal custody several times by Police, and tortured at Police Station Dera Baba Nanak. On 30th April 1992 he was abducted from Village Mustrapur at midnight by a Police party led by Makhan Singh SHO of Police Station Dhariwal. Later on 2nd April 1992, during night, he was killed in a fake encounter at a little distance from Mustrapur on the bridge at Village Mughal Narwana.

### VFF/0583

Balwinder Singh alias Binda, son of Bawa Singh and Joginder Kaur; resident of village Thetherke; Dist Gurdaspur

On 12th October 1986 Balwinder Singh had gone to the house of Rachhpal Singh at village Pakhoke, stayed there for the night and was sleeping at the 'Bambi' (tubewell bore). He was arrested from there by a combined patrol of Police and BSF led by Inspector Mehta of BSF and Harmel Singh SHO of Police Station Dera Baba Nanak along with, son of Rachhpal Singh also named Balwinder Singh. The victim resisted his arrest. At this, Inspector Mehta of BSF shot him dead.

### VFF/0584

Tara Singh 80, son of Wasawa Singh and Harnam Kaur; resident of village Sagarpura ; dist Gurdaspur

On 24th December 1987 at night time, the house of Tara Singh was surrounded by a Police party led by Kirpal Singh SHO of Police Station Sadar Batala and SI Ajaib Singh of Police Station Sadar Batala. They woke up Tara Singh and his grandson Avtar Singh Roopowali PO.Bholeke DistGurdaspur and shot them dead.

### VFF/0585

Avtar Singh alias Tola 23, son of Veer Singh and Gurmeet Kaur; resident of village Roopowali, Dist Gurdaspur

In November 1984, Avtar Singh had gone to his maternal (Nanake) village Sagarpur under Police Station Sadar DistGurdaspur to meet his relatives there. He was picked up from there by Police of Police Station Sadar Batala, kept in illegal custody for some days, implicated in a case and sent to Jail. He was released from Jail after about 8 months, on bail. On 24ᵗʰ December 1987, Avtar Singh had gone to his maternal (Nanake) village Sagarpur under Police Station Sadar Batala DistGurdaspur along with his wife Kanwaljit Kaur to meet his relatives there. He and his 'Nana' Tara Singh were woken up by a Police party from Sadar Police Station Batala led by SI Kirpal Singh and SI Ajaib Singh and shot dead. Later, the police concocted the story of an encounter. His wife Kanwaljit Kaur, 'Mami' Sawinder Kaur (Jasbir Kaur) were arrested, implicated in a case and sent to Jail, from where they were released after one year, on bail.

### VFF/0586

Ranjit Singh alias Rana 28, son of Kirpal Singh and Simarjit Kaur; resident of Thetharke Dist Gurdaspur.

In December 1986, Ranjit Singh had gone to Ferozepur for some domestic work. He was arrested and kept for 8 days there, 18 days at Batala Sadar P.S., 4 days at Majitha Police Station in illegal custody and tortured, due to which, his right leg was damaged. Ultimately, he was implicated in a case and sent to Amritsar Jail. He was in Jail for about 8 months. In July 1987, Ranjit Singh was picked up from Patiala City by CRPF and killed in a fake encounter. This information was given by Munshi of Police Station Manoot Chhatwali, Amrik Singh resident of village Rattar Chhattar under Police Station Dera Baba Nanak, DistGurdaspur.

Note: There is a contradiction between the information given in this Proforma and that given in the affidavit submitted by Kirpal Singh, father of victim Ranjit Singh @ Rana. It is as follows:-

* As per the affidavit, Ranjit Singh was arrested and shot dead at Banur by CRPF whereas in this Proforma it is mentioned that he was picked up from Patiala City by CRPF and killed in a fake encounter. In the affidavit, there is no mention of the per , son who informed the family of Ranjit Singh about his killing, namely Amrik Singh resident of Vill. Rattar Chhattar, a Munshi at Police Station Manoot Chhatwali. As per the affidavit, Kirpal Singh (father) came to know about killing of Ranjit Singh through TV news on 25 July 1987.

The said affidavit is appended below for ready reference.

AFFIDAVIT

I, Kirpal Singh s/o Late Sh. Fateh Singh, aged 60 years, resident of Vill. Thetharke, PO. Dera Baba Nanak, PS & Tehsil Dera Baba Nanak, Dist Gurdaspur, do hereby solemnly affirm and declare as under:-

1. That my , son Ranjit Singh @ Rana, aged 28 years had passed 10+2. Ranjit Singh @ Rana was my elder son.

2. That my son Ranjit Singh and my whole family are æAmritdhariÆ (Baptised). Army attack on Sri Darbar Sahib Amritsar had a deep impact on him. After 1984, Ranjit Singh had started taking part in the political activities of Sikh Students Federation. The Police had started harassing him due to his political activities. That is why Ranjit Singh remained away from home most of the time after 1984.

3. That after June 1986, Dera Baba Nanak Police started raiding our house regularly for arresting Ranjit Singh. The Police used to pick up family members viz. Kirpal Singh (father), Simarjit Kaur (mother), Sukhjit Kaur (sister), Gurmeet Singh (brother), Major Singh (brother) and relatives Dalip Singh (Phuphar), Jaswant Singh (maternal uncle), and their family members, often. The Police used to detain the family members in illegal custody for days together and pressurise them for producing Ranjit Singh. I, along with my sons Gurmeet Singh and Major Singh was tortured by the Police several times.

4. That in 1986 (date and month not known), Ranjit Singh was arrested by Ferozepur Police. They kept him in illegal custody for 4-5 days, registered several cases against him and produced him in Court. During the Police remand itself, Ranjit Singh was brought by Batala Police and implicated in several cases. Ranjit Singh was detained at Amritsar Jail for about 6 months.

5. That in 1987 (date and month not known), when Ranjit Singh had come to appear in Court at Amritsar under Judicial remand, his associates got him released from Police custody forcibly. After this incident, Gobind Ram, SSP Batala, Kundan Singh, SHO of Dera Baba Nanak Police Station began to harass the family. The Police started raiding our house daily. They used to pick up members of the family including women and used to torture also after keeping us in custody for days together. This attitude of the Police continued even after the killing of Ranjit Singh till the time militancy was alive.

6. That on 25 July 1987, I saw a news item on TV which stated that Ranjit Singh Rana resident of Thetharke had been killed in an encounter near Banur Bus Stand. Same night, the BSF raided our house and picked up my, son Gurmeet Singh. On the following day morning, the family members who had gone to get Gurmeet Singh released was told by the Commanding

Officer of BSF Dera Baba Nanak Post, Mr. Mehta, to collect the dead body of Rana from Banur.

7. That after hearing this news, I along with my relative Jasbir Singh resident of Thetharke and Swaran Singh Thetharke went to Patiala and met the SSP there (I don Æt remember the name). The SSP told us to find out from Sadar Police Station and we went to Sadar Police Station There we were told to go and find out at Banur. We reached Banur at 6 P.M. and met the SHO there. He told that the said encounter had taken place with the CRPF at 10 A.M. that day. The CRPF had brought Ranjit Singh Æs dead body only, to them. He told that they had carried out Ranjit Singh Æs cremation at Rajpura. After knowing this, Jasbir Singh and Swaran Singh started for the Village and I spent that night at Banur Police Station itself.

8. That on the following day morning, Banur Police told me that in case I wanted to collect the ashes of Ranjit Singh, then, I should reach the Office of the DSP Rajpura by 10 A.M. and that they would send their employee Amrik Singh Havaldar (Munshi) there. I boarded a bus from Banur at 8 A.M. and first went to the site of the Police encounter on the main road. I introduced myself to the people (shopkeepers) as the father of the killed boy and asked them about the details of the Police encounter. The shopkeepers present there told me that the deceased youth was riding a Motor Cycle. He was signalled by a plainclothes man and he stopped. Immediately he was surrounded by Police and CRPF men, arrested and forcibly taken to the ground of a College nearby. Thereafter, after few minutes, they heard the sound of gunshots. After hearing this, I was convinced that my son was arrested and killed.

9. That after coming to know of this fact, I boarded a bus and reached the DSP Æs Office at Rajpura. Policemen from Banur Police Station had already reached there. They produced me in front of the DSP and the DSP granted the permission for collecting the ashes of Ranjit Singh. He sent two Constables with me to the Cremation Ground. There I collected the ashes of Ranjit Singh from his pyre (as told by Policemen). I returned to my Village.

10. That Jagbani of 26 July 1987 carried a news item which stated that a dreaded militant Ranjit Singh Rana had been killed in an encounter with a patrolling party of CRPF led by DSP Sh.

J.S. Rawat near Banur Bus Stand. As per the news item, SP (HQ) Patiala Sh. Baldev Singh told newsmen that Ranjit Singh Rana was riding on the pillion seat of the Motor Cycle with a companion. They were signalled to stop by a patrolling party of CRP, but, they accelerated the Motor Cycle and tried to escape and fired at the Police party. CRPF returned the fire as a result of which Ranjit Singh Rana was killed whereas his accomplice succeeded in escaping.

11. That after this incident, Kundan Singh, SHO of Dera Baba Nanak used to pick up myself and my family members and subject us to inhuman torture. He accused us of giving shelter to militants whereas no militant was ever arrested from our house. This cycle of Police repression continued till the end of militancy.

12. That justice may be meted out to me in the case of killing of my son Ranjit Singh after arresting him. I and my family members had not taken any legal action against this action of the Police due to the terror of the Police.

DEPONENT

VERIFICATION

I, Deponent, do hereby solemnly affirm and declare that the contents of the above affidavit are true and correct to my knowledge and no part of it is false. Nothing material has been concealed. The same have been read over to me in Punjabi and after understanding it, I have affixed my Signature/Thumb Impression on this affidavit.

Place:     Batala

Date:23/12/98

DEPONENT

**VFF/0587**

Inderjit Singh (24) lived with his father Bachan Singh (65), mother Kartar Kaur (58) and brother Balvir Singh (24) at PO. Bela, Chamkaur Sahib in Ropar. He was a high school graduate and tilled his land earning about Rs. 2000 a month.

In 1984, he was detained under N.S.A.* in Patiala Jail. He was brutally tortured by the Military. He had deserted home 11 months prior to this imprisonment.

On 10th June 1988, he was killed in an encounter with the Security forces at Kalesar near village Sarnana. A month before this incident, Chamkaur Sahib Police registered a case against his brother Balbir

Singh of allegedly giving shelter to the militants and sent him to Jail. Chamkaur Sahib Police came to Inderjit Singh's house on the day when this news item was published, and took his father Bachan Singh to Chamkaur Sahib Police Station and from there to Jalandhar. There they showed him a photograph of the dead body of Inderjit Singh. After he had identified it as that of his son Inderjit Singh, he was sent back. Six months after this incident, a person hailing from Gurdaspur had told Inderjit Singh's sister, Jaswant Kaur (since deceased), that Inderjit Singh had been made to get down from a bus and arrested along with him from village Kala Bakkra (Jalandhar) by Jalandhar (Sadar) Police. He further told that he had been released on the day following Inderjit Singh's death in an alleged police encounter.

The news regarding his having been killed in an encounter with the Security Forces was published along with his photograph, in Punjabi Daily Jagbani dated 10th June 1988.

In the Jagbani on 10-6-88 along with his photograph stating that a militant Inderjit Singh was killed in an encounter with the Security Forces, near village Sarnana near Jalandhar.

### VFF/0588

Kulwant Singh son of Darbara Singh and Mohinder Kaur lived in village Talwandi Nepalan, District Ferozepur. Darbara Singh, was a poor farmer and had had three sons and four daughters. One of the sons of Darbara Singh, named Kala Singh was a Kabaddi player and had died as a result of an injury which he got while playing Kabaddi. Kulwant Singh was his second son who was an illiterate farmer.

In 1990, Kulwant Singh was arrested on the basis of suspicion of involvement in a murder case. This murder was a result of personal enmity. According to the family members, Kulwant Singh was not involved in this murder. Still, he was implicated in this case. Kulwant Singh was sentenced to 20 years imprisonment in this case.

In July 1992, he had come home on parole from jail. The family members sent him to his Bhua's (father's sister's) house at village Sabhrawan (District Patiala), where the police arrested him. According to the police, when he was arrested at village Pippal Theh under Police Station Ghanauri Mandi (Patiala), another youth namely Jassa Singh resident of Talwandi Nepalan was also with him. As per the police, the said youth consumed cyanide on the spot due to which he died. Darbara Singh suspects that his son was got arrested by his (Darbara Singh's) sister.

The information about Kulwant Singh's arrest was given to his family by another female relative of Darbara Singh namely Bir Kaur, resident of Sabhrawan, on the same day. Darbara Singh told that they did not go there due to fear.

Few days later, Darbara Singh came to know that the Makhu police had brought Kulwant Singh from Patiala police. However, the Makhu police did not allow the family members or the Panchayat to meet Kulwant Singh. The family members do not know whether the Makhu police had recorded Kulwant Singh's arrest legally or they had brought him from Patiala police unofficially. Meanwhile, one day (date not known), the family members came to know that the police had killed Kulwant Singh in an encounter near village Varpal. The family members along with prominent persons approached Makhu police for getting the dead body. They were told that the police had taken the dead body to Zira for cremation. The police had already cremated the dead body before the arrival of family members and prominent persons. On the next day, the family members collected his ashes from the cremation ground.

The news of Kulwant Singh was published in the Newspaper(Ajit published from Jalandhar, dated 9-8-1992). It was published that last night, a police party which was taking a militant Kulwant Singh for the recovery of weapons, was ambushed by militants near village Varpal of District Ferozepur. Militant Kulwant Singh was killed in the cross firing when he tried to escape from police custody. His mother is in a state of shock. She often starts crying while talking about her son.

### VFF/0589

Gurpal Singh alias Titu s/o Babu Singh and Bachan Kaur had completed his Bachelor's degree and was pursuing an LLB course in Law. His family tilled the ancestral land in Village Mangewal Mohalla in Mann Patti, in Dist. Sangrur. About 15 days prior to his abduction, SHO of PS Sadar Tarlochan Singh visited the village on a motorcycle and knocked at the door of Gurpal Singh's house. He was let in by the family and he saw that Gurpal's leg was in a cast and he(Tarlochan Singh) still insisted on his standing up.

Later on 30th Nov 1992 at 9PM Tarlochan Singh accompanied by DSP Sangrur, Mr. Bhullar and SSP Sangrur, Mr. Narinderpal Singh all in police uniforms scaled the walls of Gurpal Singh's house and abducted him(Gurpal Singh). The incident was witnessed by Gurpal's family and some other people whose names shall be disclosed at an appropriate time. Gurpal never came back home again. Gurpal's elder brother Parminder Singh died after a few years afetr falling ill due to the impact of the incident. His parents, his sister-in-law Paramjit Kaur(33 yrs), his nephew Kulbir Singh (3 yrs) and his niece Preetinder Kaur (6yrs) are all in a miserable state and miss him a lot. The family reported the details of the incident to us on 17th Jan 1998.

**VFF/0590**

Mehma Singh 14 years of age s/o Gulzar Singh and Basant Kaur belonged to Village Dhilwan, Tehsil Barnala, Dist Sangrur. He was his parents' only son and had four sisters. He was picked up from his residence on 14th Dec 1992 by DSP Sher Singh who was accompanied by an Inspector and other police officials. The members of the raiding police team were all posted at the CIA staff, Rampura Phul. Mehma Singh was last seen on 15th Dec. 1992 by Jarnail Singh, Narain Singh and Gokul Singh. Two days later it was reported in the newspapers that he (Mehma Singh) had been allegedly killed in an "encounter". His body was never handed over to the family members. His mother is mentally upset over the incident and his father died due to his son's killing.

**VFF/0591**

Gurjant Singh 17 alias Janta s/o Dhanna Singh and a resident of village Rureke Kalan, Ladha Patti, Tehsil Barnala, dist Sangrur was picked up by a police party from Police Station Sunam led by SHO Baldev Singh on 4th May 1992. Janta was a mason earning around Rs. 3200 a month. He was abducted by the police from his residence on 4th May 1992 at 7 in the morning. SHO Baldev Singh had assured the family that he would see to it no harm came to Gurjant Singh as he belonged to a neighbouring village. But Janta never came back home again. His family, Darshan Singh and Raj Singh were witness to the abduction by the Police Party led by SHO Baldev Singh. Baldev Singh is currently posted as DSP Barnala.

**VFF/0592**

Harpal Singh alias Bhala 18 of Zafarwal in Gurdaspur went missing on April 26, 1989. He was arrested by SSP Gobind Ram from Batala, kept in police custody for 19 days, and later killed in a fake encounter on 16-5-89. His family members were harassed afterwards.

**VFF/0593**

Baldev Singh alias Debu 22 of Batala in Gurdaspur went missing on October 23, 1989. On 23 October 1989, Baldev Singh was going to work in his fields as usual along with his brother Harjit Singh. They had hardly gone a little distance away from home when they were surrounded by the Police. An SI got down from the police Gypsy and started questioning them. Baldev Singh told him that they were going for work in their fields, but he did not listen to him. The SI put Baldev Singh in the Gypsy. His brother Harjit Singh pleaded with him repeatedly to release him but he did not oblige him. The SI told him that they were taking him to Batala for interrogation and after that they would release him. But so far, the whereabouts of Baldev Singh are not known to the family.

### VFF/0594

Gurdev Singh alias Sona 16 of Batala in Gurdaspur went missing on July 17, 1989. On 17-7-89, he was transplanting paddy in his fields at his 'Bambi' (small tubewell). A police party consisting of Sub Inspector Ajaib Singh, Inspector Gurpal Singh, and Santa Singh of Beeco came to village and he (Gurdev Singh) alongwith his father Lakha Singh was produced by the villagers in front of the Police party. He was taken away by the Police party in front of all the villagers. Telegrams were sent. His father alongwith the village Panchayat met SSP Gobind Ram, SI Ajaib Singh, Insp. Gurpal Singh and other Police officials. A habeas corpus was filed in Punjab & Haryana High Court Chandigarh through Advocate Rajvinder Singh Bains, H.No. 22, Sector 2, Chandigarh.

### VFF/0595

Bhan Singh 50 of Batala in Gurdaspur on August 29, 1992. On the intervening night of 29-30 August 1992, at 11 P.M., two armed persons entered our house after scaling the side wall. They woke up Bhan Singh who was sleeping in the courtyard and asked him to accompany them. On hearing the sound, his wife also woke up. She questioned those persons in protest. They replied that they wanted to take him upto the road only and that he would be back within 5 minutes. But, his whereabouts are not known till today.

This incident is described in somewhat more detail in the application submitted by Bachan Kaur w/o Bhan Singh, to the People's Commission. The true translation of the same is appended below:

To

The Secretary,
People's Commission,
H.No. 742, Sector 8-B,
Chandigarh.

Sir,

It is submitted humbly that I, Bachan Kaur w/o Bhan Singh, am a resident of village Ranghar Nangal (Nawan), Tehsil Batala, District Gurdaspur. My husband was abducted by some armed men who were in Police uniform, on the intervening night of 29-30 August, 1992. In response to my pleadings, they said that they would send him back soon. I have five daughters and one son who was 9 years old only at that time. There was no other male member in the house.

I did not initiate any action during the night due to fear and because of my young daughters. Next day i.e. on 30 August 1992, in the morning, I along with some eminent persons of the village went to the Police Station Ranghar Nangal in order to lodge a complaint. The then SHO, Mr. Jarnail Singh, told us that he had written the report and asked us to go back. No case was ever registered by the Police against my husband. (One of the nephews of my husband namely Jaswinder Singh s/o Mohan Singh, resident of village Chachowali in Amritsar district was, according to the Police, a militant who was killed in an encounter with the Police, later on). Apart from this, he did not have any enmity or ill will towards anyone.

Thereafter, according to my capability, I tried my level best to locate him, but, his whereabouts could not be known. I own about one and a half acres of land. With no other source of income, I have brought up my children with great difficulty. After the situation had normalized, we began to enquire again in the hope that may be at least now somebody might listen to us. However, we came to know at the Police Station that even our FIR had not been registered. Then I personally handed over an application (copy enclosed) to the Chief Minister, Sh. Parkash Singh Badal, and demanded justice. As a consequence, I was called to the Ranghar Nangal Police Station and they sent me to the SP's office where I was questioned. They told me that they had sent the reply. But, no details were given to me about the same. On my consistent queries, they gave me despatch Nos. only, which are 3217 SO/DGP/ dated 26.11.97 and 2444 P.C. dated 23.12.97. Due to financial constraints, I could not pursue the matter further. It was about one year ago. There has been no response so far

Later on, I wrote a letter addressed to the Chief Minister through a newspaper namely "Desh Sewak" in order to draw his attention to my plight, which was published in the issue dated 26 February 1998 (copy enclosed), but even then nobody bothered. We came to know about the People's Commission set up by you through the newspaper dated 3 November. It is requested that my application may be given a serious consideration and I may be helped in this matter. I shall remain indebted to you for ever.

Thanking you,

> Yours Sincerely,
> Bachan Kaur w/o Bhan Singh,
> Vill. Ranghar Nangal (Nawan),
> Tehsil Batala, Distt. Gurdaspur.

### VFF/0596

Harbans Singh 29 of Batala in Gurdaspur went missing March 21, 1993. On 21 march 1993 at 10 AM, a Police party of Kathu Nangal Police Station, led by SHO Dilbagh Singh, came to Harbans Singh's house and enquired about him. The family members told the Police that he had gone to attend 'Bhog' (closing ceremony) of Sri Akhand Paath at somebody's house in the village. The Police took his wife along and went to the house of Dalbir Singh where Harbans Singh had gone to attend the said function. The Police arrested Harbans Singh and made him to sit in their vehicle.

On the following day, his family members including his uncle ('chacha'), Milkha Singh (brother) and Preetam Singh (brother) met the SHO at Police Station Kathu Nangal. The said SHO assured them that they would release him after interrogation. The family members continued to visit Harbans Singh at the Police Station daily and they used to serve him tea and meals there. Apart from that, his employer (owner of Ball Service Station) also met Harbans Singh in Police custody, 2-3 times. The SHO assured him also that they would release him soon.

But on 30 March, 1993, the newspapers published a news item that the militants namely Harbans Singh, Mangal Singh, Jagtar Singh and Balwinder Singh were killed in an encounter with the Police near village Sehania Wali. Neither did the Police hand over the body of Harbans Singh to his family nor were they invited to attend his funeral.

### VFF/0597

Kuldeep Singh of Dera Baba Nanak in Gurdaspur went missing on 25-3-91. Kuldeep Singh was coming to Kohali along with one of his freinds in his Ambassador car whicvh was being driven by a resident of Kot Maulvi. As they reached near Vill. Kotli Soorat at about 6-7 P.M., they were killed in a false encounter and after declaring them unidentified their dead bodies were cremated at Batala. It is a fact that Kuldeep Singh was having the identity card issued by the Punjab State Electricity Board on his person at that time. Moreover, Kuldeep Singh or any of the boys accompanying him were not involved in any anti-social activities. They were not wanted also by the Police in any case.

The affidavit submitted by Sharanjit Kaur, mother of the victim Kuldeep Singh and recorded in PC-0055 (Word Document) is also appended below for reference.

AFFIDAVIT

I, Sharanjit Kaur w/o Late Sh. Kartar Singh, aged 70 years, r/o Chakkari Mohalla, Kalanaur, C/O Gurcharan Singh Kahlon Tent Wala,

Kalanaur, P.S. Kalanaur, Tehsil & Distt. Gurdaspur, do hereby solemnly affirm and decalre as under:-

1. That my husband had expired in 1988. At that time I was living with my family at Village Kuhali, PO. Rai Chakk, Tehsil Dera Baba Nanak, Distt. Gurdaspur. I had two sons and five daughters. Both of my sons Baljit Singh and Kuldeep Singh have been killed at the hands of the Punjab Police. All the five of my daughters are married. Now I have been burdened with the responsibility of bringing up my two grand sons namely Sher Ranjit Singh (9 years), Sukhnander Singh (7 years), sons of Kuldeep Singh and looking after my daughter-in-law Sukhwant Kaur. I am an aged lady and don't have any source of liveliohood. All the four members of our family are pulling on with the help of our relatives.

2. That both of my sons namely Baljit Singh and Kuldeep Singh were 'Amritdhari' (Baptised) youth. Baljit Singh was an active member of Sikh Students Federation. That is why, after 1984, the Punjab Police used to pick him up often and torture him in custody for days together. The Punjab Police of Police Stations Batala and Dera Baba Nanak used to pick him up from his residence. In 1987, Baljit Singh was arrested by the Police of Batala (City). A case was registered against him and he was sent to Central Jail Gurdaspur where he was incarcerated for 11 months. During the detention of Baljit Singh, his younger brother Kuldeep Singh was picked up by a party of the BSF Headquarters Dhianpur, detained in illegal custody and tortured brutally for nine days. Kuldeep Singh was an employee of Punjab State Electricity Board and used to attend his duties regularly. He continued to attend his duties after the release of Baljit Singh. After the release, the Police began to harass both the brothers. The Police used to pick them up from their residence often, beat them up and releasae them on the responsibility of the Panchayat. The Police accused Baljit Singh and Kuldeep Singh of having links with militants. Sometimes, Baljit Singh and Kuldeep Singh used to live at their relatives' places in hiding due to the fear of the Police.

3. That in October 1990, Baljit Singh had gone to the house of his maternal uncle Joginder Singh at Kalanaur, due to the fear of the Police. On 9-10-1990 at 6 P.M. he started for his Village

Kuhali on Bicycle but did not reach home at his Village Kuhali that night.

4.   That on 10-10-1990 at about 7 A.M. Prakash Singh alongwith another youth from Village Dhesian came to the house of Baljit Singh at Village Kuhali and told that Baljit Singh had been shot dead at Village Dhesian last night. According to them this incident occured at 7 P.M. The residents of Village Dhesian heard the sound of gunshots at 7 P.M. and the people went indoors due to fear. Immediately after receiving this news, I alongwith my son Kuldeep Singh and other Villagers reached the site of the incident. The bullet riddled dead body of Baljit Singh was lying at the 'Phirni' (a track at the periphery of the Village) of Village Dhesian. Till that time, the Police had not arrived even though there is a Police Post at Village Dhesian close to the site of the incident. After half an hour, ASI Bachan Singh from Police Station Dera Baba Nanak reached there alongwith a Police party. The Police took the dead body to Batala for a post mortem and after the post mortem handed it over to the family members. We tried to find out from the Police as to what had happened to Baljit Singh, but, they did not tell us anything.

5.   That after this incident, the Police began to harass his younger brother Kuldeep Singh, even more. They used to pick him up often, detain him in illegal custody and torture him brutally for days together. Fed up with Police harassment, Kuldeep Singh started living at Fatehgarh Churian alongwith his wife Sukhwant Kaur and son Sher Ranjit Singh (1 year). Then Kuldeep Singh was transferred to Fatehgarh Churian. Thereafter also, the Police used to raid our house and ask about Kuldeep Singh.

6.   That on 25-3-1991 at 7 A.M., Kuldeep Singh told his wife Sukhwant Kaur that he was going for some job and would be back by evening. But Kuldeep Singh did not return home in the evening. On the third day, I came to know from the people of Village Dhesian that Kuldeep Singh had been killed in an encounter by Dera Baba Nanak Police (SHO Kundan Singh) near Village Kotli, alongwith two other youth. After getting this news, I reached Fatehgarh Churian but my daughter-in-law was not there. She had received this news already.

7.   That she had gone to her Village Kuhali. Not finding Sukhwant

Kaur at home, I went to Dera Baba Nanak Police Station and tried to find out from the Sentry on duty at the gate of the Police Station as to who were the three youth killed at Village Kotli on 25-3-1991. He did not tell me anything and I returned home. We did not try to meet any Police Officer to enquire as to what happened to Kuldeep Singh, after all, due to fear of the Police.

8. That even after the killing of Kuldeep Singh, the Police used to raid our house at Village Kuhali and search the house. After this incident, Punjab State Electricity Board did not pay the service dues of Kuldeep Singh to us. We have no source of livelihood at present. I am getting my two grand sons educated by getting assistance from Mata Gujari Trust. Justice should be meted out to us.

DEPONENT

VERIFICATION:

I, Deponent, do hereby solemnly affirm and declare that the contents of the above affidavit are true and correct to my knowledge and no part of it is false. Nothing material has been concealed. The same have been read over to me in Punjabi and after understanding it, I have affixed my Signature/Thumb Impression on this affidavit.

Place:     Kalanaur

Date: 19/11/98

DEPONENT

**VFF/0598**

Ajit Singh alias Jeeta of Dera Baba Nanak in Gurdaspur went missing on April 10, 1992. In 1987, once he was arrested due to ill-will. A false case was registered against him and he was sent to jail. He got released on bail after 6 months. Later on, he was acquitted in the said case. Ajit Singh was arrested and taken away from the house of his father-in-law, S. Preetam Singh, on 2.10.1992. News was published in two leading Punjabi daily newspapers, Ajit & Jagbani, both published from Jalandhar.

**VFF/0599**

Jasvir Singh 15 of Hoshiarpur went missing on April 1, 1993. On 4 January, 93, he was called by village people who were on 'Thikri Pehra' (Patrolling by village folk for security purposes) at the first floor of the house of Patwari Sarwan Singh, who is our neighbour. When he did not return even by 9 A.M. next day, his wife went to the house of Patwari

Sarwan Singh to enquire about his whereabouts. His wife did not give any satisfactory reply to them regarding his whereabouts. The persons responsible for his death include SP (D) Hoshiarpur Lok Nath Agra, i/c of Mehndiana Police Chowki Chhaju Ram, i/c of Rajpur Police Chowki Mr. Kahko, and members of 'Thikri Pehra' team.

### VFF/0600

Malkit Singh 26 alias Babbu of Hoshiarpur went missing on August 3, 1993. Malkeet Singh had gone to Anandpur Sahib to witness the Holla Mohalla celebrations. He was picked up by C.I.A. Staff Jalandhar on 08-3-93 from there but the family was never informed about it. The family came to know about his arrest by Jalandhar C.I.A after about one month from a third person who declined to identify himself. His father Saroop Singh went to Jalandhar C.I.A alongwith relatives and respectable persons of the village. The Officer on duty told them that Malkeet Singh is in fact there but they have orders from above not to let him meet anybody. Thereafter, his father tried to meet his son by using political influence, but, to no avail. Later, the C.I.A. Staff Jalandhar told that he was not with them and had been taken to some other place. He submitted written representations to Chief Minister Punjab, DGP Punjab, DC Hoshiarpur, and SSP Hoshiarpur. Still, so far, the whereabouts of his son are not known.

### VFF/0601

Kuldeep Singh 17 of Usman Shaheed, Dasuya, Hoshiarpur was killed in a "false encounter" by the police on September 3, 1991. In the words of his father Tarlok Singh, "at 8.30 or 9 P.M., a party of 6-7 policemen of Dasuya police, in a Gypsy, raided our house. However, I could not recognize any of them as my eyesight is weak. They had entered the house by scaling the wall and pushed open the drawing room where I and other members of my family viz. wife Surjit Kaur, brother Karnail Singh, sons Kuldeep Singh, Jasjit Singh, Jaswinder Singh and daughter Ravinderjit Kaur were watching TV. They asked us our names and took myself, my brother Karnail Singh, and my three sons into custody. All of us were taken to Dasuya police station in two Gypsies. At the police station, each of us was subjected to inhuman torture for 15-20 minutes. Rollers were rolled on our thighs and we were beaten up with rubber belts. After that, they locked all of us in the lock-up. Kuldeep Singh was put in a Gypsy and taken away somewhere, in front of all of us. I could not identify the police officers at that time. They had searched my house but nothing (incriminating) was recovered. Next day morning, at about 10 A.M., we were got released from the police station by Nishan Singh

Nambardar, Karnail Singh s/o Hazara Singh (brother of the applicant), and the village Panchayat. After coming out of the police station at a distance of about one Km, the villagers informed me that they suspected that Kuldeep Singh had been killed in a false encounter by the police. We tried a lot to collect the dead body, but it was not handed over by the police. The police cremated his dead body themselves, declaring it as an unidentified. Later, on 14-9-1991, after I had identified Kuldeep Singh from the photograph of the dead body, Mohan Singh, SHO of Dasuya Police Station, attested under his signature, that the young man killed in the encounter on the morning of 4-9-91 at village Mehar Bhatoli, was Kuldeep Singh s/o Tarlok Singh and that this incident is recorded at police station Dasuya, Distt. Hoshiarpur vide F.I.R No. 99 dated 4-9-91."

Appended below is a copy of an Affidavit dated 17-11-1998, submitted by Tarlok Singh, father of the victim Kuldeep Singh, to the People's Commission:-

AFFIDAVIT

I, Tarlok Singh s/o Sh. Hajara Singh r/o Vill. Usman Shaheed, Tehsil Dasuya, Distt. Hoshiarpur do solemnly affirm and decalre as under:-

1.   That the Dasuya police raided my house on 15-16 August 1991. The policemen were six in number and they had come in Mahindra Mini Bus. They asked me about my youngest son Kuldeep Singh. When I told them that he had gone to attend the marriages of his cousin brother and cousin sister at village Ethal situated in Hardwar (Distt.) U.P. they took me to Dasuya police station. It was about 8 or 8.30 P.M. After half an hour, the police party took me along and departed for the house of my sister Amarjit Kaur. We reached the house of Amarjit Kaur in the afternoon next day and came to know that Kuldeep Singh had not reached there. So the police party brought me and my nephew (brother's son) Harmeet Singh, who was present there, back to Dasuya P.S. We reached Dasuya P.S. late at night on the next day. Immediately, on reaching the police station, the above mentioned police party began torturing me. Rollers were rolled over my body and I was lashed with rubber belts. This torture continued for 10 minutes. Next day, at the intervention of the whole Panchayat, I and my nephew Harmeet Singh were released on the condition that I would produce Kuldeep Singh at the P.S. at the earliest.

2.   That on 3-9-1991, the Dasuya police raided my house again,

but I could not recognise anybody due to weak eyesight. All the policemen were in uniform and they were 6-7 in number. They had come in two Gypsies. They entered the house after scaling the wall and banged the door of the room facing the courtyard and opened it. I and my family members including my wife Surjit Kaur, brother Karnail Singh, and sons Kuldeep Singh, Jasjit Singh, and Jaswinder Singh, daughter Ravinderjit Kaur were watching the T.V. They enquired our names, put myself, my brother, and my three sons into two Gypsies and took us away (to the P.S.)

3.    That on reaching the police station, myself, my brother, and my three sons, each one of us was subjected to inhuman torture for 15-20 minutes. After that, all of us were locked up in the lock up. And they took Kuldeep Singh out of the police station in a Gypsy in front of us.

4.    That next day on 4-9-91 between 10 and 11 A.M., all of us were released at the intervention of all the respectable persons of the village and went home. On reaching home, I came to know that the police had killed a youth in the area of village Mehar Bhatoli. We thought over this matter and reached village Mehar Bhatoli in order to verify this information. We came to know that one youth had indeed been killed in an 'encounter' with the police. Thereafter we reached Civil Hospital Dasuya. There we were told this much only that the post mortem of one dead body had indeed been conducted and that it had been sent to the Cremation Ground. The dead body had been already cremated before we reached there. The description of the dead body given by the workers at the Cremation Ground, resembled that of Kuldeep Singh. Next day on 5-9-91 we received his ashes after signing in the receipt book, performed his last rites and then approached the police station.

5.    That on 14-9-91 we approached SHO Mohan at P.S. Dasuya. Sarpanch Iqbal Singh was with me at that time. The SHO showed us the colour photograph of the dead body of Kuldeep Singh. I could recognise Kuldeep Singh clearly from that photograph. Large marks of pools of blood were clearly visible on his chest on the side of the heart. One of the eyes had an injury mark. His hair were flowing. On our identifying the dead body from the photograph, SHO Mohan Singh gave us a report attesting that the young man who was cremated

on 4-9-91 was Kuldeep Singh s/o Tarlok Singh. A copy of that report is attached.

6.  That the names of the police officials, responsible for killing Kuldeep Singh in a false encounter are as follows:- SI SHO Mohan Singh police station Dasuya, ASI Karnail Singh P.S. Dasuya, ASI Salwinder Singh P.S. Dasuya, Constable Harpal Singh No. 1551 P.S. Dasuya, Constable Harjit Singh 1429 P.S. Dasuya, Constable Malkeet Singh 1375 P.S. Dasuya, Constable Gian Chand 1373 P.S. Dasuya, Constable Vikramjit Singh 1354 P.S. Dasuya, and DSP Jaimal Singh, Dasuya and his gunmen Constable Vinod Kumar 897, Constable Daljit Singh 1406, Constable Iqbal Singh 362, Constable Balwinder Singh 1560, Constable Surinder Pal 1354, Constable Daljit Singh 1414, Constable Hans Raj 1402, Driver Constable Kewal Singh 1414, Driver Constable Surinder Kumar, Driver Constable Kulwant Singh 1053. The names of all the above mentioned police officials have been mentioned in the F.I.R No. 99 dated 4-9-91 registered at police station Dasuya in connection with this so called encounter. A copy of the same is enclosed herewith.

7.  That I did not approach anybody else due to fear of the police. The police used to raid our house daily. There was a fear psychosis in our family due to that.

8.  That on 14-9-91 at the time of identification of the dead body from the photograph, the police obtained our signatures on some blank papers under duress.

DEPONENT

VERIFICATION

I, Deponent, do hereby solemnly affirm and declare that the contents of the above affidavit are true and correct to my knowledge and no part of it is false. Nothing material has been concealed. The same have been read over to me in Punjabi and after understanding it, I have affixed my Signature/Thumb Impression on this affidavit.

Place:    Dasuya
Date:     17-11-98

DEPONENT

True translated copy of attestation of the identification of the dead body by Mohan Singh, SHO Dasuya, Distt. Hoshiarpur.

PS

Distt. HPR

Case F.I.R No. 99/91 dt. 4-9-91 u/s 307/34 IPC, 25 AA, 3/4/5 T.D. Act
IDENTIFICATION OF DEAD BODY
Sir,

It is requested that in the above mentioned case the cremation of an unidentified dead body was got done by you. The same has been identified from the photograph of the dead body by Sh. Iqbal Singh Sarpanch of village Usman Shaheed as that of Kuldeep Singh s/o Tarlok Singh Jat r/o Usman Shaheed. The same has been identified by Tarlok Singh also, the father of the accused Kuldeep Singh. Kindly issue the death certificate of the accused Kuldeep Singh after making the necessary entries.

Sd/-
(Mohan Singh)
SHO, P.S. Dasuya
dt. 14/9/91

Some additional information was collected by Amrik Singh Muktsar and submitted on 28th February, 2000 and accordingly this proforma was updated on 1st March, 2000 as under:-

Victim Kuldeep Singh's father Tarlok Singh aged about 56 years is a R.M.P. and he owns 2 acres of agricultural land also. He had three sons and one daughter. Kuldeep Singh was his youngest son. He had discontinued his studies while he was studying in class VIII and began to help the family members in agricultural farming.

Note:- Despite the sanction accorded by the Court for issuing the post mortem report, the S.M.O. Dasuya did not issue the post mortem report of his son to Tarlok Singh. The S.M.O. asked him to get the Police Report first. According to Tarlok Singh, he did not approach the Police due to fear. As such, he could not obtain the post mortem report.

Note: According to Tarlok Singh, when he approached the Tehsildar for getting his affidavit to be submitted before the People's Commission, attested, he attested it only after he had approached him three times along with eminent persons. First time the Tehsildar refused to attest the affidavit of Tarlok Singh saying that it was 'against the Police'. It is a clear tell tale sign of Police terror.

**VFF/0602**

Nachhatter Singh 22 of Lohian Khas, Nakodar in Jalandhar He was performing his duty at Gurdwara Sahib at (Village) Lakhu Dian Chhanna and living within the Gurdwara premises with his family. The Police came at 4 A.M., woke him up, asked his name, held him by the arm and made him to sit in the Gypsy. One policeman held his wife Gurbakhsh

Kaur by the arms so that she should not go out and make a hue and cry. The Police were standing outside the Gurdwara also, in strength. There were 10-11 policemen and they had come in a Gypsy and a Canter. After the abduction of Nachhatter Singh, his wife Gurbakhsh Kaur came to her in-laws place at Raiwal Bet and informed them. The Panchayats of Raiwal Bet and Lakhu Dian Chhanna reached police station Lohian. They said that he had been taken to Sultanpur. At Sultanpur they told that he had been taken to Kapurthala. At Kapurthala they said he had been taken to Amritsar. There they said he had been taken to Patti. At Patti they said that he had been taken to Ferozepur. At Ferozepur they kept the family waiting for an interview till 3 P.M. Then they took his wife Gurbakhsh Kaur and his father Kartar Singh inside, showed some Sikhs and asked to see if he was there but they could not see Nachhatter Singh anywhere. Then the Ferozepur Police told them to go back to Amritsar and enquire there only. This continued for a while and then the family with meager means just gave up the struggle to find him.

**VFF/0603**

Gurdev Singh alias Debu of Dhirpur, Kartarpur in Jalandhar. This case was invsetigated by Amrik Singh Muktsar, personally. The true translation of the details of the incident, as narrated to him by Gian Kaur, mother of the victim Gurdev Singh, are as given below:-

After 1984, Gurdev Singh absconded. The Police began to raid his house often. The Kartarpur Police (Jalandhar) used to pick up his family members—his mother, wife, and father, often, keep them in illegal custody for a few days and then release them. During this period, his father Gurbachan Singh was tortured so brutally that his intestines were ruptured and ulcerated. Rollers were rolled over his body several times. His legs were pulled apart in opposite directions. He was hung upside down from the ceiling and they used to pull and give jerks to his body from below. The family could not cultivate their land and the land continued to lay barren.

On 01 July 1987, Gurdev Singh was abducted from village Mithapur, near Hoshiarpur and subjected to barbaric torture for three days. He was boiled in water, burnt with press, and his eyes were taken out. His teeth had been broken. Ultimately, he was killed on 03 July 1987.

In May 1988, C.I.A. Staff Kapurthala picked up myself (Gian Kaur), my son Sardul Singh, and my daughter Narinder Kaur and kept us in illegal custody for 22-23 days. Sardul Singh was tortured brutally. His hair were long. The Police used to tie his hair with his ankles and put a wooden roller across. They used to beat him with leather belts also. The Police used to do all this in front of my own eyes and used to say that they would kill my this son also as they had killed my other son (Gurdev Singh).

Narinder Kaur (23 years) used to be given electric shocks on her temples and they used to beat her mercilessly with fists, also.

I (Gian Kaur) used to be hung upside down after tying my arms at my back. They used to give electric shocks to my feet from below. I used to faint. They continued to torture me like this for five days.

We were released after 22 days, at the intervention of eminent persons of the area.

Whenever any incident used to occur, the Police used to come to our house or call us to the Police Station and release us after questioning. Three months ago, a murder had been committed in our area. The Police picked up my son from my residence and released him in the evening. They repeated the same act for two three days.

### VFF/0604

Rajinder Singh 38 of Adampur in Jalandhar went missing on January 19, 1993. Sarbjit Kaur, aged 32 years, wife of vicitm Rajinder Singh, had got married to him in 1983. Rajinder Singh was an "Amritdhari" (Baptised) Sikh youth and a farmer. In 1984, he along with his wife went to Delhi and used to make a living by plying a three wheeler Auto Rickshaw there. In 1985, they returned to their village. In 1986-87, the Jalandhar Police started picking up Rajinder Singh, often, on the basis of suspicion of his links with the militants. This process of arrest and release continued for a long time. According to his wife Sarbjit Kaur, she did not remember the date and other details of his abduction by the Police. However, she told that no case was ever registered by the Police against Rajinder Singh on the basis of suspicion of his links with militants. But, the Police used to pick him up often and detain him in illegal custody for days together. Mostly, the Village Panchayat used to get him released.

According to Mehnga Singh, father of vicitm Rajinder Singh, his son was picked up by Inspector Mangal Singh, Sub Inspector Didar Singh and Amarjit Singh, a Police tout, resident of Daroli Kalan. Lok Nath was the SP (D) Hoshiarpur at that time. Details are available in the Civil Writ Petition No. 11816/1995 filed by Mehnaga Singh in the High Court of Punjab & Haryana. However, he did not remember the details about his arrest and other details or the name of the lawyer. He did not know as to what happened to Rajinder Singh after his abduction by the Police.

Note: In the copy of Order of Addl. Sessions Judge, Jalandhar, dated 6-8-1994 in proceedings under section 446 Cr.P.C. it hass been mentioned that the Police took away the accused (Rajinder Singh) on 19/20.1.1993 and his whereabouts were not known since then.

Amrik Singh Muktsar who investigated this case, adds :-

Mehanga Singh, father of vicitim Rajinder Singh said, "As Darshan Singh, father of Paramjit Singh of our village had reached a compromise with accused Police officers regarding the disappearance of his son, Ranjit Singh, Sarpanch of our village (now a member of SGPC) contacted me and advised me that I should also reach a compromise with the Police officers. This approach was made on behalf of SSP Hoshiarpur, Lok Nath who was accused in our case. Lok Nath had approached through SP (D) Jalandhar, Balkar Singh as he (Balkar Singh) had already succeeded in reaching a compromise in his own case. initially, I rejected his offer of compromise.

"Ultimately, under the influence of the Sarpanch, I agreed to meet SP (D) Balkar Singh at Jalandhar. Sarpanch Ranjit Singh took me to the house of SP (D) Balkar Singh at Jalandhar. Balkar Singh said, "Bapu Ji, your son has been killed by the Police. Now, nothing (useful) will come out of it (litigation). You stand to gain only if you reach a compromise by accepting something (money) in lieu of it." I also had got exhausted due to the legal battle and judging from my experience so far, I realised that I won't be able to win this battle in the end, because the accused Police officers were stronger financially as compared to me and they could hire best possible laywers. Finallty, I agreed to reach a compromise if they paid me Rs. 3,00,000/- (Three Lakh only)."

"This money was paid to me after I had filed an Affidavit in the High Court of Punjab & Haryana at Chandigarh."

### VFF/0605

Avtar Singh 23 of Bir Pind, Nakodar in Jalandhar May 5, 1989. Victim Avtar Singh alias Tari's father Gurnam Singh aged about 60 years is a poor farmer who owns just two acres of land. Gurnam Singh is a resident of village Bir Pind in Tehsil Nakodar. He retired from service in JCT Mills Phagwara after serving for 32 years and now lives in his native village. He had two sons and one daughter. Avtar Singh was his elder son. Avtar Singh's sister Baljinder Kaur who is elder to him had got married when he was studying in class VIII. Avtar Singh's father used to go on bicycle for duty at Phagwara and return home in the evening.

After passing his Matriculation examination, Avtar Singh also took up a job at JCT Mills Phagwara, along with his father. He was serving at Phagwara itself at the time of Army attack on Sri Darbar Sahib in June, 1984. He had got himself baptised during those days only. According to his mother Bhajan Kaur, he had become religious minded alright, but they never suspected that he might be involved in some militant activities. But, two boys from their village namely Amarjit Singh and Paramjit Singh Pamma were involved in militant activities.

In 1987, one day (date not known), Avtar Singh went from home as usual but did not return home. His family members got worried. On the following day, the people of their village informed them that Avtar Singh had been arrested from village Badal Khan De Kot. On the day folowing the incident, the Noormahal Police came to their house and conducted a search of the house. But, nothing incriminating was found. The Police registered a case against Avtar Singh and sent him to Central Jail Jalandhar where he was detained for two years. His family members did not get him bailed out as the situation was bad outside. However, in the beginning of 1989, they came to know that Avtar Singh had managed bail on his own and had come out of jail. But, he did not come home. Meanwhile, the Police started raiding his house.

On 7 May, 1989, his family members read a news item in newspapers that Avtar Singh had been killed in an encounter with the Police. According to the newspaper, the Director General of Police, Punjab had informed that in the encounter which had taken place on the night of 5 May at village Dhakk Aujla, Avtar Singh Tari, resident of Bir Pind and Sohan Singh resident of Thalla had been killed whereas Paramjit Singh alias Pamma had escaped. But, members of the Investigation Team were informed by the family members of both Paramjit Singh and Avtar Singh that they came to know about this incident from the newspapers of 7 May, 1989 only. The Police neither contacted the families of both of them nor handed over their dead bodies to them.

Both the families told that later on, they had received information from the people of the area that Paramjit Singh, Avtar Singh and Sohan Singh had been arrested from somebody's house at village Masanian, Tehsil Phillaur. This news had spread among the people of village Masanian and those of the area. However, later on, the Police enacted the drama of killing these three youth in separate encounters.

On being asked by the Investigation Team as to whether they could produce any evidence of the arrest of these three youth by the Police, both the families said, "So far, we (next-of-kin) could not muster courage to state the truth, then why somebody else (stranger) will take this risk." But, his family members claimed that if the people are freed from the fear of the Police, then solid proof of their arrest from village Masanian can be obtained.

Note: In the prevailing circumstances, the family members are not at all willing to fight a legal battle against this illegal act (of the Police). So much so that the family members refused to sign this proforma even.

### VFF/0606

Narinder Singh alias Ninder 20 Dawali, Jandiala in Jalandhar went missing December 28, 1994. On 28-12-94 morning, Narinder Singh was picked up by Bathinda Police from his residence at Village Dawali. The Police personnel involved are Sukhdev Singh, S.P. Bathinda, and A.S.I. Om Parkash who was posted at P.S. Nathana at that time.

### VFF/0607

Rupinder Singh Deol alias Rupi 22 of Haripur, Adampur in Jalandhar. Victim Rupinder Singh's father Mohinder Singh had retired from the Air Force in 1973 and took up agricultural farming at his Village Haripur under Adampur Police Station in Jalandhar district. Mohinder Singh had two children the elder one being a daughter and younger being Rupinder Singh. Rupinder Singh stood first in the Village School by securing 83% marks in his Matric exam in 1984. After June 1984, Rupinder Singh became religious minded. After Matriculation, Rupinder Singh got admission in the Ludhiana Agriculture University and he used to stay there only in the hostel.

According to Mohinder Singh, he was not aware whether his son had any link with any sort of political or militant activities because he used to live in the hostel. However, neither was he ever arrested by the Police on the basis of suspicion nor their family questioned any time, about the activities of Rupinder Singh. However he had realised since 1990 that the life style of his son had undergone a change and his way of living had become like that of a Gursikh. He used to visit home, often. He had visited home on 24 February 1991 for the last time. Till that time his father Mohinder Singh was not aware of his activities of any sort.

Approximately in the second week of March, 1991 the Police of Focal Point in district Ludhiana raided Mohinder Singh's house at Village Haripur at 11 P.M. The Police abused Rupinder Singh's family members and pushed them around. The Police picked up Mohinder Singh, Harbans Singh (elder brother) and one of their servants and took them to Focal Point Police Station. Harbans Singh was detained at some other Police Station. They were released 14 days later at the intervention of relatives and eminent persons.

Thereafter, the Police of local Police Station started visiting their house. On 18 May, 1991 morning, Mohinder Singh received a message that Rupinder Singh along with four of his accomplices had been killed in an encounter with the Police at Village Hans Kalan in Police district Jagraon. The people of the area had blocked the traffic and obtained the bodies of all the five youth from the Police. This encounter had taken place on 17 May, 1991. Mohinder Singh was informed by the people of Jagraon area on 18 May, 1991. Mohinder Singh along with eminent persons of his VIllage received the dead body of his son from the Civil hospital Jagraon.

Thereafter, in 1993 the Villagers nominated Mohinder Singh for the post of Sarpanch during the elections to the Panchayats. The local Police (Adampur Police Station) picked up Mohinder Singh and took him to the Police Station. They pressurised Mohinder Singh not to fight the election for the post of Sarpanch. Mohinder Singh promised them that he would not fight the election, due to fear of the Police. Thereafter, the Police never harassed Mohinder Singh.

On being asked by the Investigation Team whether he suspected that his son was arrested by the Police and then killed in a fake encounter, Mohinder Singh replied, "No. my son attained martyrdom after he was surrounded along with four of his accomplices." Mohinder Singh told that according to the people of Jagraon area these youth consumed cyanide when their ammunitiion was exhausted during the said encounter.

According to Mohinder Singh, the names of the other youth who were killed in this encounter are as follows :-

1.　Dr. Darshpreet Singh resident of Village Roopi (Jagraon)
2.　Hardip Singh Hipi resident of Village Posa (Ludhiana)
3.　Mohan Singh resident of Village Shekhupura (Ludhiana)
4.　Sukhwinder Singh resident of Village Kala Jhande

**VFF/0608**

Paramjit Singh alias Pamma 23 of Lidhar Khurd, Phagwara in Jalandhar went missing on June 5, 1989. Victim Paramjit Singh's mother Joginder Kaur, widow of Kabal Singh, had three sons and three daughters. Joginder Kaur's in-laws' lived in village Lidhar Kalan in district Nawanshahr, but her family used to cultivate the land of her brothers also who had gone abroad (Canada). Paramjit Singh was her youngest child. One of the brothers of Paramjit Singh used to live at village Nawan Pind and used to cultivate the land of his maternal uncles. Later on, Paramjit Singh also started living at his maternal uncles' house along with his brother.

Before the Army attack on Sri Darbar Sahib in June, 1984, Paramjit

Singh was influenced by "Dharam Yudh Morcha" (political agitation launched by the Akali Dal in 1982) and he had got himself baptised. He was studying at that time. After 1984, he abandoned his studies and began helping his brother agricultural farming. according to his family members, at that time they did not have any knowledge of Paramjit Singh's political activities or of his links with the militants. He used to perform domestic duties and used to go out rarely only.

In 1989, one day, a Police party raided his house and enquired about Paramjit Singh. He was not at home. The Police directed the family members to produce him before them. But, Paramjit Singh did not return home after this incident and joined the ranks of the militants once for all. The Police started picking up his family members. Mostly, the Police used to pick up his brothers and father. They used to detain them in illegal custody for days together and torture them. The Police used to pick up their relatives also repeatedly. The Police prevented his family members from cultivating their land. The village Panchayats (Councils) of the area used to get them released but after fews days again the Police used to pick them up. This process continued till the time Paramjit Singh was not killed. According to his sister-in-law ('Bhabi') Rachhpal Kaur, the Police used to raid their house almost daily and they had made their life miserable. According to Gurmeet Kaur, "In those days, none of their relatives dared to visit their house due to the fear of the Police."

On 7 May, 1989, a news item was published in the newspapers that Paramjit Singh had been killed in an encounter with the Police, on 6 May morning at village Apran, Tehsil Phillaur in Jalandhar district. According to the newspaper, the Director General of Police, Punjab had informed that in the encounter which had taken place on the night of 5 May at village Dhakk Aujla, Avtar Singh Tari, resident of Bir Pind and Sohan Singh resident of Thalla had been killed whereas Paramjit Singh @ Pamma had escaped. But, members of the Investigation Team were informed by the family members of both Paramjit Singh and Avtar Singh that they came to know about this incident from the newspapers of 7 May, 1989 only. The Police neither contacted the families of both of them nor handed over their dead bodies to them.

Both the families told that later on, they had received information from the people of the area that Paramjit Singh, Avtar Singh and Sohan Singh had been arrested from somebody's house at village Masanian, Tehsil Phillaur. This news had spread among the people of village Masanian and those of the area. However, later on, the Police enacted the drama of killing these three youth in separate encounters.

On being asked by the Investigation Team as to whether they could produce any evidence of the arrest of these three youth by the Police, both the families said, "So far, we (next-of-kin) could not muster courage to state the truth, then why somebody else (stranger) will take this risk." But, his family members claimed that if the people are freed from the fear of the Police, then solid proof of their arrest from village Masanian can be obtained.

### VFF/0609

Balraj Singh alias Raji of Noor Mahal, Phillaur of Jalandhar went missing on March 29, 1989. Balraj Singh Raji was first arrested from home. Later, he was produced at the P.S. by respectable persons of the village. His father and brother Gurdish Singh were the last persons to see Raji at the Noormahal P.S. At Nakodar Cremation Ground, one of the workers told the family members that one of the pyres which were burning, was that of Raji. Pointing towards his brother Gurdish Singh, he said that his face resembled that of him. Also, they came to know about it through the news on the Radio and newspapers.

In daily newspaper Jagbani, published in Punjabi from Jalandhar, dated 19 April, 1989. True translated excerpts are as follows:-

'The Police conducted raids and arrested three terrorists from Sarhali village under Noormahal P.S. of Jalandhar Distt., last night. One LMG, 250 Cartridges, and one Remote Control were recovered from them. According to Police sources, the arrested terrorists included Kahan Singh, Joga Singh, and Raji...............................

According to the information gathered by K.P. Singh, from Noormahal...................

Remember that one suspected terrorist Balraj Singh r/o Sarhali had committed suicide by consuming some poisonous substance in the police cordon itself while they (police) were trying to recover a Bomb which can be exploded with a Remote Control.

### VFF/0610

Bhupinder Singh alias Pappu of Dhuni Ki Patti, Phillaur of Jalandhar was a student in a college.

The details of occurance are not given in this Proforma. However, the same are available in the written representation dated 17/05/93, submitted by Dr. Dalbir Singh Sidhu, father of the victim Bhupinder Singh, to S. Beant Singh, Chief Minister of Punjab. The true translation of the same is appended below:-

To
S. Beant Singh,
Chief Minister, Punjab,

Chandigarh.

Sub: Regarding whereabouts of Bhupinder Singh son of Dr. Dalbir Singh Sidhu, Jandiala, Jalandhar.

Sir,

It is humbly submitted that my son Bhupinder Singh s/o Dr. Dalbir Singh, VPO. Jandiala, P.S. Noormahal, Distt. Jalandhar, had gone to Yamuna Nagar for a few days on 20/11/92. On somebody's complaint and on the basis of suspicion, Yamuna Nagar Police picked him up on 22/11/92 at 5 A.M. while he was asleep. After questioning, the Haryana Police called Chandigarh Police and handed him over to them. The Chandigarh Police, after interrogating him, took him to various places under Police Stations Noormahal, Goraya, Phillaur, and Jalandhar Cantt. and handed him over to the SHO of one of the abovementioned Police Stations.

It is not known for what crime, but, two and a half years ago, Noormahal Police and Goraya Police had slapped one case each under section 382 and 325 of IPC respectively against him. Bhupinder Singh was on bail in those cases and he used to attend Court regularly, on scheduled dates, in connection with his cases, which were being heard.

The next date of hearing and arguments, in the case registered by P.S. Goraya u/s 325 IPC had been fixed on 27/11/92. He went from home to Yamuna Nagar on 20/11/92. He was picked up from home by Haryana Police on 22/11/92. When he did not attend Court on the scheduled date i.e. 27/11/92, we started a search for him. 15 days later, we came to know that Bhupinder Singh was in the custody of Punjab Police. For the last 6 months, I have been making enquiries from all the Officers/SHOs of Police. He is neither a militant nor he has any link with any militant Organization. So far, his whereabouts are not known.

Five years ago, I became disabled from both of my legs due to an accident. Neither I can walk nor I can do any work. Bhupinder Singh is my only son and my only support for the rest of my life. I have no source of income.

You are requested to get my only son located and intimate his whereabouts. I shall be highly grateful to you.

Yours faithfully,

Sd/-

Dr. Dalbir Singh Sidhu,

VPO. Jandiala, Distt. Jalandhar.

**VFF/0611**

Balwinder Singh alias Binder 30 of Chukhiara, Adampur in Jalandhar. Victim Balwinder Singh's mother Daljit Kaur, wife of

Darshan Singh (Ex-Havaldar of Indian Army) had three sons. Her elder son Balwinder Singh had abandoned his studies while he was studying for Pre-University and had gone to Dubai for employment. He returned home in 1983 after staying there for one and a half years. Some time later, he obtained a loan and opened a Dairy Farm in his Village.

According to Daljit Kaur, Balwinder Singh was like any ordinary youth and he used to drink also. One day, in 1986, two youth who were militants and were known to him came and stayed at our house. After they were arrested, the Police raided our house and picked up Balwinder Singh, his father Darshan Singh and brother Jagjit Singh (since expired). Darshan Singh and Jagjit Singh were released on the following day at the intervention of the Village Panchayat. Balwinder Singh was taken away by Jalandhar Police where he was tortured brutally. After keeping him in their illegal custody for 22 days, the Police registered a case of giving shelter to the persons accused of murderous attack on Shri Ribiero, against him and sent him to jail. He was released on bail after one month and three weeks. He got busy in his job at home. The family members sent him to Jalandhar for the job of a Driver.

In May-June 1987 the Police began raiding their house repeatedly and compel the family members to produce Balwinder Singh. He was produced before Adampur Police through eminent persons of the Village. The Police continued to make vague promises for his release for several days. Then the family members came to know that C.I.A Staff Jalandhar had taken him away. Several cases were registered against him including under N.S.A and he was sent to Sangrur jail. In the meantime, the family members got Balwinder Singh's brother Jagjit Singh enrolled in the C.R.P.F.

According to his mother Daljit Kaur, this time, his incarceration in jail brought about a change in the life of Balwinder Singh. In the jail he came in contact with Jathedar of Sri Akal Takht, Bhai Gurdev Singh Kaonke and he became religious minded.

"One day, the Hoshiarpur Police raided our house. On seeing the Police, Balwinder Singh slipped away. The Police picked up his father and relatives. The family members produced him before the Police on the following day. The Police registered several cases against him and sent him to Sangrur jail. The family members decided not to get Balwinder Singh released on bail this time, because they thought that Balwinder Singh was safer inside the jail. However, Balwinder Singh arranged for his bail on his own and came out. The family members do not know as to how he succeeded in coming out on bail. He came home and started the business of Commission Agent at Village Nawin Daroli (Focal Point).

He worked there for one season. One day the Police raided our house. Balwinder Singh slipped away on his scooter. It was in 1992.

Thereafter, the Police used to pick up his family members like his father, uncle ('Taya'), maternal uncles and brother-in-law. They used to keep them in their (illegal) custody for days together and sometimes for months together. This process continued till the time of publication of news item about the killing of Balwinder Singh. Once, Balwinder Singh's father was detained illegally for nine months at a stretch.

On 8 July, 1993 a news item was published in a Punjabi daily newspaper Ajit that one of the unidentified Punjab militants who had been killed on 6 June in an encounter at Badgaon in Sunder Nagar district of Orissa has been identified as Balwinder Singh son of Darshan Singh, resident of Village Chukhiara under Adampur Police Station."

**VFF/0612**

Rajvinder Singh alias Baba 22 of Sanghe Jagir, Noormahal in Jalandhar. Victim Rajvinder Singh's father Joga Singh who was a resident of village Sanghe Jagir, Tehsil Phillaur in district Jalandhar was a teacher by profession and he owned agricultural land also. Joga Singh had two sons only. Rajvinder Singh was his younger son. Rajvinder Singh passed his B.A. from Guru Nanak National College, Nakodar and six months later he joined the Punjab Police as a Constable. He was an "Amritdhari" (baptised) and a religious minded youth. However, neither was he associated with any sort of political activities nor was he ever arrested by the Police on the basis of suspicion during the zenith of militancy in the Punjab.

He was posted in Jalandhar district and after some time he was transferred to Kartarpur Police Station. During his tenure at Kartarpur Police Station, he was detailed for Commando training at Police Centre (Sangrur). During that period, Rajvinder Singh was arrested and brought by a Police party of C.I.A. Staff Jalandhar along with another youth namely Baljit Singh (Gurdaspur). His family members were informed about his arrest by his colleagues on the same day.

Note:     Further details about this case are available in the case papers filed by his family members in the High Court. Advocate was Navkiran Singh. This case was sent by the High Court to Jalandhar for inquiry. Rajvinder Singh's parents and brother have gone to America. The case papers and other details can be had from them.

According to Rajvinder Singh's uncle ('Chacha') Avtar Singh, after the High Court had ordered an inquiry, the family was offered money for a compromise but they declined the same. The case had been filed by Rajvinder Singh's family and that of the other youth namely Baljit

Singh. Both these youth along with two other youth were shown as having been killed in an encounter with the Police at village Chitti under Police Station Labra. According to Avtar Singh, the family members of Baljit Singh and those of another youth have accepted money from the Police (accused officers) and reached a compromise with them. More details about this case may be obtained from the case file which may be available at the Coordination Committee's office.

## VFF/0613

Amarjit Singh alias Jeeta 25 of Bir Pind, Jalandhar. Victim Amarjit Singh's mother Prakash Kaur, widow of Channan Singh, had four sons and one daughter. Channan Singh had expired about 20 years ago. Her family owned very little land and their economic condition was not good. Her youngest son Amarjit Singh abandoned his studies while he was studying in class VII and started working as a labourer in the Yarn Mill at Nakodar. Amarjit Singh was a bachelor. All of his brothers were married and lived separately. Prakash Kaur used to live with her son Amarjit Singh. Now-a-days, Prakash Kaur is paralysed and lying unconscious on the bed. As it was not possible for the Investigation Team to extract any information from her about Amarjit Singh, the same was obtained from his elder brother Gurmeet Singh, who looks after his mother now-a-days.

According to Gurmeet Singh :-

In those days, he (Gurmeet Singh) had gone abroad (Bahrein) in search of livelihood. It was in 1988-89 when Amarjit Singh used to work in the Yarn Mill. One day, the Nakodar Police raided Amarjit Singh's house. Amarjit Singh was not at home at that time. Thereafter, due to fear, Amarjit Singh deserted home. A few days later, the Police started harassing his family members. His family members also had come to know that Amarjit Singh had joined the ranks of the militants. The Police used to pick up Surjit Singh (brother) and Baljit Singh (nephew) and torture them brutally in illegal custody for days together. This process of harassment of his family members at the hands of the Police continued intermittently till the time the Kapurthala Police arrested Amarjit Singh from Chandigarh.

He was arrested from Chandigarh on the basis of information extracted from a boy of their area who had been arrested by the Police on the basis of suspicion. This operation was carried out by Kapurthala Police. Gurmeet Singh did not remember the full name of the youth on whose instance the Police had arrested Amarjit Singh, but, he was called 'Kanda'. He had been arrested by the Police a few days earlier from Dussehra Ground, on Dussehra Day. Amarjit Singh was arrested on the basis of information provided by 'Kanda'. Later on, the Police killed 'Kanda' also in an "encounter".

Gurmeet Singh further told that at that time, he had returned home from Bahrein as his family was too terrorised due to harassment at the hands of the Police and that he could not stay back after hearing all this. Even though his family members had advised Gurmeet Singh not to come back as the Police could arrest him also. Gurmeet Singh was in doubt about the year of occurance of this incident but he tried hard to remember and he told that this incident occured in the year 1991. However he did not have any doubt about the date and the month because he had come back on 1 October and the news item about Amarjit Singh's killing had appeared on 10 October. In the newspapers, the Police had shown this encounter as having taken place near village Ranipur under Phagwara Police Station in Kapurthala District. His name and that of the village had been published in the newspapers. The news was telecast on Television also.

In those days, their family was terrified by the Police to such an extent that after reading the news item they did not approach the Police to get his dead body nor the Police contacted the family about this incident. After this incident, even though the Police continued to visit their house for a long time, yet, they used to go back after questioning them.

*       This incident had a deep adverse impact on his mother Prakash Kaur. She became chronically ill and is bed ridden since long.

Note: Amarjit Singh's grandfather Sardar Bhola Singh had attained martyrdom in the Jaito Morcha during the Gurdwara Reform Movement. Even though Bhola Singh had died at home, but he had succumbed to the injuries inflicted on him by the Police, four days after his release from Police custdoy.

### VFF/0614

Amrik Singh 24 of Damunda, Adampur in Jalandhar. Victim Amrik Singh's mother Surinder Kaur wife of Ajit Singh (Retired from GREF—Indian Army's Road construction Wing) is a resident of Village Damunda. They are Ramgarhia Sikh family. She had two sons and two daughters. Amrik Singh was her elder son. After completing his education he got trained as a Motor Mechanic and opened a workshop at Adampur in partnership with somebody. According to Surinder Kaur, her son was a Gursikh alright, but, he had no link whatsoever with any sort of political or militant activities. He used to go from home to his workshop in the morning daily and return home in the evening. One of the youth of Amrik Singh's Village namely Kulwinder Singh Pinki was a renowned militant. Pinki and Amrik Singh had undergone the training of Motor Mechanic together and since then they had been friends. However, after Pinki had absconded, Amrik Singh did not have any link whatsoever with the activities of Pinki.

On 6 January, 1993 Amrik Singh had gone from home to his workshop as usual at about 8 A.M. At about 10 A.M. his family members received a message that Amrik Singh had been abducted from his workshop by a Police party which had come from Hoshiarpur. On reaching Adampur, the family members came to know that a Police party of C.I.A Staff Hoshiarpur led by Inspector Mangal Singh and Sub Inspector Makhan Singh had abducted Amrik Singh and his partner Onkar Singh. They also came to know that the same Police party had abducted another youth also of Adampur namely Komal Singh.

According to Surinder Kaur, her husband was serving in Assam at that time. She along with the eminent persons of the Village went to C.I.A Staff Hoshiarpur and met the Police Officers present there. They assured them that they would release him after interrogation. Other boys namely Onkar Singh and Komal Singh were released. Their family members had approached the Police on their own and got them released. But, Amrik Singh was not released. Once, she along with some other persons of her Village had approached the SP (D) Lok Nath who had assured her that Amrik Singh would be released. A few days later, the Police officials did not even allow them to meet him. She used to visit Hoshiarpur daily but nobody listened to her pleas there.

On 29 March, 1993 a news item was published in the newspapers that Amrik Singh along with two other militants had been killed in an "encounter" in the area of Mukerian Police Station of Hoshiarpur district. According to Surinder Kaur, after reading the news in the newspaper they visited Hoshiarpur, Dasuya and Mukerian Police Stations but the Police officers did not hand over any of the items of Amrik Singh to them. The only proof with them of Amrik Singh having been killed is the news item in the newspaper. Or it is the unofficial admission by the Police officials that they had killed Amrik Singh in an "encounter".

\* Surinder Kaur said, "A grave injustice has been done to our family. My son was innocent. The Police abducted him in braod day light, detained him illegally for a long time and then killed him in a fake encounter. I don't know about the mothers of the other two youth killed along with Amrik Singh. They also must be wailing like me. Those brutes should have shown us his dead body at least so that we could have reconciled ourselves."

### VFF/0615

Darshan Singh (Nambardar) 70 of Dhirpur, Kartarpur in Jalandhar. Darshan Singh was Nambardar of the Village and a prominent person. He had no link whatsoever with the militant movement in the Punjab and he had no political affiliations at all. His nephew (sister's son) Avtar Singh, resident of Village Vishrampur had absconded. That is why the Police used to arrest him.

In December 1988, Kartar Pur Police picked up Darshan Singh and tortured him brutally (in illegal custody). He was in a very bad shape, physically, due to Police beating. His family members got him treated first at Sacred Heart Hospital at Maqsooda and later at a Hospital at Patel Chowk at Jalandhar. But, he did not recover. Blood had started oozing out from his mouth due to internal injuries he had suffered. Ultimately, on 8/9 January 1988, he breathed his last at the Patel Chowk Hospital at Jalandhar.

### VFF/0616

Bahadar Singh 27 of Helar in Jalandhar. Bahadar Singh had taken up agricultural farming after passing his Matriculation. He passed his Matric in 1982 and had joined the Punjab Police as a Constable in 1984. He was an "Amritdhari" (Baptised) Sikh youth and religious minded. He got married to Darshan Kaur in March 1988. In March, 1989, he was dismissed from service in the Punjab Police on the charge of his links with the militants. At that time, Bahadar Singh had been posted as a gunman with a senior Akali leader Kabal Singh in district Hoshiarpur. Before his dismissal, Bahadar Singh was arrested while he was on duty at Akali leader Kabal Singh's village, Thida. He was tortured brutally in illegal custody for about 20 days at Police Station Mahilpur and C.I.A Staff Hoshiarpur. However, he was let off after 20 days without registering any case against him. He began to cultivate his land at home. During this period, he was arrested twice, once by Kartarpur Police and at another time by Kapurthala Police. However, he was released after detaining him in custody for one or two days, on both these occasions.

On 22 March, 1991, at about 12 Noon, two uniformed policemen from C.I.A Staff Jalandhar came to his house. Bahadar Singh was not at home at that time. His parents and his wife were at home. Those policemen told that they had come from CIA Staff Jalandhar and that the SSP had summoned Bahadar Singh. The family members told them that Bahadar Singh had gone to Hoshiarpur and that they would send him as and when he returned from there.

At about 3.30 PM, Bahadar Singh returned from Hoshiarpur and the family members informed him about the visit of the policemen. At about 4 PM, Bahadar Singh along with the Sarpanch of his village namely Dev Raj, went to the CIA Staff Jalandhar. Dev Raj came to his house in the evening and told the family members that he had accompanied Bahadar Singh to the CIA Staff Jalandhar. He further told that Bahadar Singh asked him to wait outside and he himself went inside. When he did not return for one or one and a half hours, he (Dev Raj) came back to the village.

On the following day and thereafter, his family members continued to meet Gajjan Singh, Inspector In-charge of CIA Staff Jalandhar, SP (D) Raj Kishan Bedi and the SSP. These Police officers maintained that they had indeed called Bahadar Singh but he had gone back after meeting them. They did not take him into their custody. However, the family members were firmly convinced that the Police were telling a lie. Bahadar Singh's family members and those of his in-laws' family along with prominent persons, continued to approach the Police officers in order to know his whereabouts, but, so far, the Police have not given any hint as to what happened to Bahadar Singh, after all.

The shock of this incident was unbearable for the young wife of Bahadar Singh. She has two daughters. Bahadar Singh's younger daughter Sardeep was born on 18 August 1991 after his disappearance. It was like a bolt from the blue for Darshan Kaur, when, about two years after the disappearance of Bahadar Singh, her in-laws turned her out of their house. All this while, the family members used to quarrel with her, daily. They were three brothers including Bahadar Singh. Amarjit Singh is the eldest and Jarnail Singh is the youngest. The family owns about 12 acres of land. But, Darshan Kaur's in-laws neither gave her any share in the property nor are they paying her any maintenance allowance so that she could make both ends meet. Darshan Kaur is staying with her parents at village Kahalwan and is doing a job in a shoe manufacturing factory at a salary of Rs. 700/– 800/- per month. On the one hand, Darshan Kaur is worried about the upbringing and future of her children and on the other she is forced to fight a legal battle for claiming her due share in her in-laws' property. She is spending money on this legal battle also. Her paternal family are helping her to some extent in this. According to Darshan Kaur, "My world is ruined. A few years hence, my daughters will be of marriageable age. I see my future to be dark."

**VFF/0617**

Jagdev Singh 21 of Jalla Singh, Kartarpur in Jalandhar. Jagdev Singh had three brothers and two sisters. Jagdev Singh was the youngest. After passing his Middle examination, Jagdev Singh went to his brother-in-law (sister's husband) in Gujarat and started working there. During the anti-Sikh riots (Genocide of the Sikhs) in November 1984, Jagdev Singh had to abandon his job and along with his relatives was forced to return to the Punjab. This incident proved to be a turning point in his life. He became religious minded. He got himself baptised and became active in the Sikh Students Federation. He was staying at the Sri Darbar Sahib, Amritsar. Jagdev Singh got arrested for the first time in 1986 along with Singh Sahib Bhai Gurdev Singh Kaonke at the time of Police entry into Sri Darbar Sahib at Amritsar and was jailed for several months. After his release, Jagdev Singh did not return home and joined the ranks of the militants. In May 1988, Jagdev Singh was arrested again from Sri Darbar Sahib, Amritsar during Operation Black Thunder.

Due to the activities of Jagdev Singh, the Police used to harass his family members too much and used to pick up his brothers. The Police registered cases under T.A.D.A against elder brothers of Jagdev Singh namely Gurdev Singh and Sukhdev Singh and they were jailed for several months. The Police used to torture the family members and pressurise them to produce Jagdev Singh. His family remained the victim of Police repression till Jagdev Singh had not been killed.

On 6 April, 1989, Jagdev Singh was surrounded by the Police in between the villages Salempur and Sadaipur, after one of the Police "Cats" had identified him. Finding himself surrounded by the Police, Jagdev Singh consumed cyanide and died. According to the eye witnesses, Jagdev Singh was talking to one of his acquaintances when a Police Gypsy passed nearby. After going a little further the Police Gypsy turned back. On seeing this, Jagdev Singh fled towards the fields. But, the Police surrounded him from all sides and called for reinforcements through wireless. On seeing himself surrounded by the Police, Jagdev Singh consumed cyanide. Next day, this news was published in the newspapers. The Police neither handed over his dead body to his family nor informed his family about this incident. Two of the brothers of Jagdev Singh were detained in jail at the time of this incident.

Even after Jagdev Singh had died, the Police repression against his family intensified. The Kartarpur and Jalandhar Police arrested two of his brothers namely Gurdev Singh and Sukhdev Singh several times, tortured them and sent them to jail after registering cases against them. They remained in jail for several months. This routine continued till 1993.

### VFF/0618

Avtar Singh 32 of Vishrampur, Kartarpur in Jalandhar. Victim Avtar Singh's mother Harbans Kaur, a widow, has two daughters and he was her only son. Avtar Singh had to discontinue his studies to look after the household while he was studying in B.A. I, due to the death of his father. He got married in 1978. In 1983, he partook of "Amrit" i.e. he got himself baptised and his religious fervor increased. Due to his religious devotion only, he came into contact with Damdami Taksal. Though Avtar Singh was not active politically, yet, due to his religious leanings, he often used to attend religious programs. He had never been arrested on the basis of suspicion during the militant movement which had erupted in the Punjab after 1984.

In the year 1987, one day (date not known), while Avtar Singh was away to the headquarters of Damdami Taksal at Chowk Mehta, Jalandhar Police raided his house at the instance of a militant who had been arrested by the Police. A certain amount of money which had been looted from a Bank during a dacoity at Ludhiana was recovered from his house. The Police directed the family members to produce Avtar Singh. When Avtar Singh learnt about this incident, he did not return home, due to the fear of the Police.

Thereafter, the Police of Kartar Pur and Jalandhar Police Stations started raiding his house. Often, the Police used to arrest his mother Harbans Kaur and wife Jasvir Kaur. Jasvir Kaur was tortured brutally in custody at Police Station Kartar Pur, by male policemen and later, a case was registered against her under T.A.D.A and she was sent to jail. She got released on bail after a few days. In the meantime, the Police used to pick up the relatives of Avtar Singh like brother-in-law (sister's husband), maternal uncles, in-laws and other relatives, often. The Police used to torture the family members, brutally. Avtar Singh's maternal uncle, Darshan Singh Nambardar, resident of Dhirpur, also became a victim of this Police repression. In December, 1987, the Kartar Pur Police arrested Darshan Singh and tortured him brutally in illegal custody. He was released after a few days at the intervention of the village Panchayat. He was in a very bad shape physically at that time. Even though Darshan Singh could move around, yet, blood was oozing out from his mouth as the Police beatings had caused grievous internal injuries in his abdomen. Immediately after his release, Darshan Singh was got admitted to Sacred Heart Hospital at Maqsooda by his family members. A week later, he was shifted to a Hospital at Patel Chowk at Jalandhar where he remained under treatment for one or one and a half week. Around 7/8 January 1988, he died at Patel Chowk Hospital at Jalandhar. Neither the family members maintained any record of his medical treatment nor they initiated any legal action (against the Police) about this incident.

According to Harbans Kaur, "We dare not think of taking any legal action against the Police, because, in those days, the Police used to raid our house and those of our relatives, every day. All our family members had become homeless. The Police used to carry away our household items. They had taken away the Engine and the Motor."

On 27 May 1988, a news item was published in the newspapers that Avtar Singh had been killed in an encounter with the Kapurthala Police near Village Bihari Pur. After reading this news item, the family members along with the Panchayat went to Kapurthala. On reaching there, they came to know that the Police had cremated his dead body themselves.

Later on, the family members came to know that Avtar Singh had been arrested by the Kapurthala Police, on 25 May, 1988, afternoon, from the fields of Village Pattar. At that time, one of the accomplices of Avtar Singh, namely Balbir Singh, resident of Village Khassan was also with him (who was arrested a month later and killed, by the Police). However, he started working like a farm worker and thus succeeded in dodging the Police. According to Harbans Kaur, several people had witnessed the arrest of Avtar Singh. But, she did not know whether someone would depose in their favour or not. According to her, even though they had come to know that Avtar Singh had been arrested and killed, yet, keeping in view the situation prevailing at that time, they were helpless in taking any action. And that they never even considered taking any legal action about the death of these two members of their family. The Police used to raid their house often, till 1993-94.

### VFF/0619

Joginder Singh alias Joga Singh 32 of Folariwal in Jalandhar. He was an 'Amritdhari' (baptised) Sikh. He remained in Central Jail Jalandhar from 1987 to 1989. The Police taken his remand till 24 March 1992. On 28 March 1992, they told that he had escaped from their custody. He was last seen by Advocate Amarjit Singh Shergil and Balwinder Kaur (Wife) on March 24, 1992 in a Jalandhar court.

### VFF/0620

Paramjit Singh alias Buggu of Model House number 10-L, Jalandhar. On 05-9-95 in the morning, Paramjit Singh had gone to Guru Nanak Dev University to deposit his form for admission to M.Sc part I (Human genetics). It is suspected that he had been picked by police for interrogation. After the assassination of Punjab Chief Minister Beant Singh on 31 August 1995, the police and the C.B.I had rounded up hundreds of youth on the basis of suspicion. It is suspected that,

Paramjit Singh fell a prey to mistaken identity. All efforts to trace him since then, have proved futile.

**VFF/0621**

Manmohan Singh alias Mohani 28 of 110, Nawi Dana Mandi, Jalandhar. On 5 August 1987 at 7 P.M., he was picked up by the Police from village Ladhewali under Police Station Sadar, Jalandhar. The persons responsible are:-

1.  S. Ranbir Singh
2.  Sarpanch of a village, little ahead of Adampur
3.  Jathedar Arjan Singh
4.  Jathedar Kuldeep Singh Bhatia
5.  Jathedar Rajinder Singh Bhatia
6.  Gulzar Singh

**VFF/0622**

Manjit Singh alias Billa 31 of Lohara in Jalandhar. On 12-8-1992 at about 7.30 P.M., he was picked up from a Chemist shop near Hotel Preet, Jalandhar City by some unknown Policemen. "We (the family) came to know about it from Paramjit Singh s/o Jaswant Singh, H.No. E.S. 203 Mohalla Maqdoompura, Jalandhar. Paramjit Singh was let off near BSF Chowk, because, his brother Mahinder Singh Teetu is a Police helper." The basis of the belief that he has been killed is that since the time he was picked up, there is no clue regarding his whereabouts so far. The Police Officers also whomsoever we contacted said this only that he was untraceable.

An affidavit was submitted to the Secretary Punjab Human Rights Organization, Amritsar and an application was submitted to the Chairman, Human Rights Organization Delhi. But, to no avail.

**VFF/0623**

Harjon Singh alias Jona 20 of Helar in Jalandhar. Harjon Singh, aged 20 years, was influenced by the political activities of his father Jathedar Gian Singh. Jathedar Gian Singh has been active in Akali Dal politics since his youth and he had taken an active part in all the political programmes of the Akali Dal from "Punjabi Suba" agitation to the "Dharam Yudh Morcha". He had gone to jail several times during the Akali campaigns. The whole family are "Amritdharis" (Baptised Sikhs). Jathedar Gian Singh had two sons and a daughter. Manjit Singh is his eldest son and Harjon Singh was his youngest child. After June 1984, thanks to the political activities of Jathedar Gian Singh, his sons also began to show their interest in politics. Manjit Singh and Harjon Singh became active in the Sikh Students Federation.

In 1986, Harjon Singh was arrested u/s 107/151 IPC for the first time during a demonstration organised against the arrest of former Jathedar of Akal Takht, Darshan Singh Ragi at D.M.C Chowk at Jalandhar. The family became suspect in the eyes of the Police, due to their political activities. In those days, whenever any militancy related incident used to take place in the area, the Police used to raid their house and pick up either Manjit Singh or Harjon Singh or their father Jathedar Gian Singh and detain them in custody for days together.

On 9 June 1987, Jalandhar (Sadar) Police raided their house and arrested Manjit Singh. They registered several cases against him under T.A.D.A and sent him to jail. In October 1987, Jathedar Gian Singh was arrested from his residence and sent to jail in several cases. The Police tortured both Manjit Singh and Gian Singh brutally using third degree methods during their detention. In the meanwhile, Harjon Singh went underground fearing his arrest by the Police.

In March 1988, Harjon Singh was arrested near Dharam Singh Market at Amritsar while he was proceeding towards Sri Darbar Sahib for paying his obeisance there. At that time, Manjit Singh was still in jail while Jathedar Gian Singh had come out of jail in Decemebr 1987, on bail. Harjon Singh was subjected to brutal torture at Mall Mandi Interrogation Centre for seven days during which one of his legs was fractured. The Amritsar Police registered several cases against him u/s 25/54/59 (of Arms Act) and T.A.D.A and produced him in the Court. From there, the Jalandhar Police brought him on remand. The Jalandhar Police registered several cases against him and sent Harjon Singh to Sangrur jail where his brother Manjit Singh was already incarcerated. He was shifted out of that jail after 15-20 days. A few days later, NSA (National Security Act) was invoked against Harjon Singh.

Manjit Singh was released from Sangrur jail in January 1990. Thereafter, the Jalandhar Police started arresting him again. In April 1990, Harjon Singh got released on bail from Nabha jail. The Police started arresting Harjon Singh also on the basis of suspicion. During this period, the Police used to torture both the brothers. The village Panchayat and prominent citizens used to get them released. In view of the cycle of Police repression, Jathedar Gian Singh sent his elder son Manjit Singh to Germany. Thereafter, the Police began to harass Harjon Singh even more.

Fed up with beatings by the Police, Harjon Singh deserted home once for all and joined the ranks of the militants. In the meanwhile, the Police used to pick up his father Jathedar Gian Singh, often. According to Jathedar Gian Singh, in those days, if he used to spend two days out of the Police Station then the next days used to be spent in detention at the Police Station. This routine continued till the time Harjon Singh was not arrested.

The newspapers of 20 March, 1992 carried a news item that a militant namely Harjon Singh was killed in an encounter with the Police along with one of his accomplices namely Amarjit Singh Khera at village Sunra under Police Station Phagwara. It was also mentioned in the said news item that during the said encounter another accomplice of the above mentioned militants escaped. Jathedar Gian Singh read the said news item at night only on that day and that too after being informed about it by somebody else. On the following day, Jathedar Gian Singh went to Phagwara and met DSP Preetam Singh there. The DSP told him that his son had been killed in an encounter along with another militant and that they had cremated his dead body already. The DSP did not even tell him where he had been cremated. However, Jathedar Gian Singh, on his own, found out that the Police had cremated the above mentioned two youth at Cremation Grounds at Phagwara.

A few days after this incident, Jathedar Gian Singh got information that Harjon Singh, Amarjit Singh and another youth were arrested from somewhere by the "Cats" of Phagwara Police one or two days prior to the incident of the encounter and that he was detained at the Phagwara Police Station. The source of this information, an Akali leader of Jalandhar district and a former General Secretary of Shiromani Committee, Bir Singh Jalandhar, told Jathedar Gian Singh that before Harjon Singh was killed in the said encounter, Darshan Singh, resident of village Phulahi Wala (Distt. Jalandhar) had told him two days prior to the publication of the news item about the killing of Harjon Singh in an encounter that his son Joginder Singh (who was in judicial custody at that time and later on was killed by the Police) had told Darshan Singh during his appearance in the Court that Harjon Singh had been arrested and was detained in Phagwara Police Station at that time. Joginder Singh had also told his father Darshan Singh that the Police had brought him (Joginder Singh) in front of Harjon Singh in connectiion with some case. Darshan Singh could not deliver this message at the house of Harjon Singh, but, he told about it to Bir Singh (Akali leader) on the same day. However, Bir Singh could not convey this message to Jathedar Gian Singh. But, Bir Singh told Jathedar Gian Singh about it after the news item about the encounter had been published.

According to Jathedar Gian Singh, in those days, he received several tips about the arrest of Harjon Singh, but, he did not pursue them further because he did not hope to get justice from anywhere.

\*       According to Jathedar Gian Singh, when he visited the Cremation Ground at Phagwara for collecting the ashes, the Pandit there had told him that the Police had brought three bodies for cremation on that day. Two of them were cremated on a single pyre and the third one was cremated on a separate pyre. Jathedar Gian Singh said that he had collected the ashes from all those three pyres. Prominent residents of his village had accompanied Jathedar Gian Singh on that day.

### VFF/0624

Paramjit Singh alias Dhunn 30 of Dhirowal Patti, Adampur in Jalandhar. Victim Paramjit Singh's father Darshan Singh is a 70 years old Rajput Sikh, a small farmer, resident of Daroli Kalan in district Jalandhar. Darshan Singh had three sons and three daughters. Paramjit Singh was his eldest son. Darshan Singh is a farmer who has been associated with the political activities of the Akali Dal. He is an "Amritdhari" Sikh who had spent one year in jail also during the "Dharam Yudh Morcha" (political agitation) launched by the Akali Dal in 1982.

According to Darshan Singh, his son Paramjit Singh was religious minded since childhood and he had passed his Matriculation examination. When Paramjit Singh was studying in class VIII, his right arm had been chopped off from the elbow down. After his studies, Paramjit Singh took up agricultural farming. He was a hard working youth and apart from agricultural farming he used to pursue one or the other ancillary occupation also. He had been married before June, 1984 itself.

After the Army attack on Sri Darbar Sahib in June, 1984, a political and militant movement had begun in Punjab. However, neither Paramjit Singh was associated with any sort of political activities in the beginning of this movement nor he had been arrested by the Police any time. According to Darshan Singh, the Jalandhar Police began arresting him since 1987-88 on the basis of suspicion of his links with militants. The process of arrests by the Police continued till the time he was killed at the hands of the Police. He used to be arrested mostly by the C.I.A. Staff Jalandhar, Adampur Police and C.I.A. Staff Hoshiarpur. He had been tortured brutally several times in illegal custody for days together. According to Darshan Singh, as he is an eminent person and a member of the Panchayat of the Village, he used to pursue his (Paramjit's) case and get him released.

Further details of this case are contained in an Affidavit dated

21/10/97, submitted by Darshan Singh (father), the relevant portion of which is reproduced below :-

1.  That my son namely Paramjit Singh was picked up by the Police party headed by S. Balkar Singh, DSP, then posted as DSP Nawanshahr at about 8 p.m. from my residence in the presence of Balbir Kaur w/o Paramjit Singh and myself. Since then Paramjit Singh has not returned. I had informed S. Ranji Singh Sarpanch of our village about this incident on next day i.e. 8/11/1992.

2.  That one Subhash Chander s/o Sh. Mehnga Ram, Clerk in BDO office Aur, Teh. Nawanshahr and a resident of our village Daroli Kalan told me in the month of January 1993 that he (Subhash Chander) while posted at BDO office at Aur had seen Paramjit Singh in the custody of Police Post Aur and had also personally talked to Paramjit Singh twice during that period.

3.  That on this information, I had approached S. Balkar Singh DSP Nawanshahr who initially promised to do something but had backed out later on.

4.  That one Giano, widow of S. Karam Singh, cousin of petitioner and resident of our village aged about 40 years is a loose character and ASI Didar Singh then posted at Police Station Adampur was a regular visitor to her. The village Panchayat at the instance of Paramjit Singh, my son, and myself had objected to this activity and the Panchayat had caught ASI Didar Singh in the house of Giano while he was under the influence of liquor through a DSP of CRPF posted at Focal Point Daroli Kalan. The Panchayat had passed many resolutions against Mrs. Giano and ASI Didar Singh about their illicit relations. Litigations arising out of this were pending before different authorities between Mrs. Giano and petitioner's family during these days.

5.  That one Mohinder Singh Patwari, resident of our village was a Police informer and tout. He was also attacked by the militants in year 1992 and he was seriously injured because of his associations with the Police. I being a member Panchayat belonged to opposite group of Mohinder Singh Patwari and opposed each other in different cases.

6.  That both Mohinder Singh and Giano wanted my son Paramjit Singh to be implicated in some false cases and got him eliminated through Police i.e. ASI Didar Singh etc.

7.  That upon the above circumstances I have filed criminal Writ petition No. 1170 of 1995 in the honorable High Court of Punjab & Haryana. The WRIT petition vide order dated 9/8/1996 was marked to C.J.M. Jalandhar by honourable Justice H.S. Bedi for inquiry. The C.J.M. vide order dated 4/3/1997 has not believed my version and accordingly the High Court dismissed my petitions.

8.  That new developments have taken place since the finding in the enquiry was given by C.J.M. which are enumerated as below :-

That two inland letters anonymous cards by same writer were received by the petitioner wherein the writer had disclosed that my son had been killed by the Police encounter on the night 20-21/1/1993 and case FIR No. 9 dated 21/01/1993 under section 307 IPC P.S. Banga had been registered. The identity of my son had also been given in the letters. The Police party which allegedly killed my son during the false encounter was headed by Insp. Rajinder Singh. That on the basis of this information, I got the post mortem report of my son which has further proved the identity of my son.

That I had also received a letter from my son Paramjit Singh while he was in custody of Police Post Banga regarding his whereabouts, but I had not disclosed this information to anybody because it was written in that letter that information be not disclosed to anybody fearing death of my son.

That the above factors further establish my view point that the Police has eliminated my son in the false encounter and has proved my earlier version.

Sd/-

Deponent

Verification.

Verified that the above contents stated in the afidavit are true and correct to the best of my knowledge and belief.

Deponent

Sd/-

Note:     According to Darshan Singh, as the High Court had ordered an inquiry into this case and the same was in progress, one day, Jalandhar Police picked up Darshan Singh and Sukhjit Singh, took them to Jalandhar and questioned them about the case which he (Darshan Singh) had filed in the High Court. Later on, Balkar Singh, then SP (D) approached him through the Sarpanch of his Village for a compromise.

However, it was less of an offer for compromise and more of pressure tactics using Police authority.

Darshan Singh said, "I also had got exhausted due to running from pillar to post for three four years. Moreover the Police terror was always hanging on my head like domiciles' sword. My family members and other villagers also advised me not to confront the Police. Under such circumstances, I reached a compromise with SP (D) Balkar Singh through the Sarpanch. Under this compromise Balkar Singh SP (D) called me to his house at Jalandhar and paid me Rs. 2,00,000/- (Two Lakhs only). Thereafter I stopped pursuing my case and I don't know as to what happened in my case thereafter.

**VFF/0625**

Gurmit Singh alias Geeta 25 of Khassan, Bhullath in Jalandhar. On 5 August 1992 at 9 A.M., Gurmit Singh was forcibly lifted and pushed into their vehicle by a party of four policemen in civil clothes led by ASI Dilbagh Singh incharge of Police Post of Kishangarh under Kartarpur police station. His neighbouring shopkeepers and owners of a Petrol Pump were present at that time. Before raiding the shop, the police party had gone to his house and inquired about Gurmit Singh. I told them that he was at his shop. However I got suspicious that they might be policemen. I informed my father-in-law about it and he immediately started for Nadala. On reaching there, he came to know that the police had forcibly put Gurmit Singh into their vehicle and took him away. Karnail Singh had gone on Cycle. As such, he reached half an hour late. Karnail Singh returned home and informed his family members about this incident.

Same day, Karnail Singh along with the Panchayat (village council) met the SSP Kapurthala who told that he would find out and inform them.

From 6 August 92 to 9 August 92, the family members along with the Panchayat enquired at various police stations, but, the whereabouts of Gurmit Singh could not be known.

On 9 August 1992, photograph of the dead body of Gurmit Singh was published in the newspaper along with a news item saying that the above unidentified militant had been killed in an encounter with the police at village Ghudowal under Kartarpur police station.

On 11 August 1992, a Punjabi daily newspaper Jagbani carried a news item saying that the militant killed in an encounter with the police at village Ghudowal under Kartarpur police station had been identified as Gurmit Singh Mita @ Patwari resident of village Khassan, PO. Bhullath. Earlier he was the President of Kapurthala unit of S.S.F. But now-a-days, he was involved in militant incidents

After reading this news, I along with the village Panchayat consisting of Channan Singh (Panch), Darshan Singh (Sarpanch) reached Kartarpur police station and met SHO Gurdip Singh Bakra. The SHO denied any knowledge of this incident and said that he had not arrested Gurmit Singh. However, I recognised ASI Dilbagh Singh there and came to know from the policemen that he was incharge of Police Post Kishangarh at that time. We had not known earlier that Gurmit Singh had been lifted by Kartarpur police. We got this information only from the newspaper. Later, I recognised also ASI Dilbagh Singh at the Kartarpur police station.

After the publication of the news of the killing of Gurmit Singh, on 13 August 1992, Gurdip Singh Bakra, SHO of Kartarpur police station picked up Channan Singh (Gurmit Singh's uncle). And on 15 August 1992, he picked up Gurmit Singh s/o Balwant Sinvgh (since gone abroad), Pappu s/o Hazara Singh. Channan Singh was detained at Rawalpindi Police Post whereas Gurmit Singh s/o Balwant Singh and Pappu were detained at Kishangarh Police Post. ASI Dilbagh Singh used to interrogate them about Gurmit Singh Patwari only. These three boys were also subjected to brutal torture. They were released after 15 days when the panchayat vouched for their good character.

On 24-9-92 registered written representations regarding this incident were sent to the Deputy Commissioner and the Chief Minister of Punjab, from Kartarpur. Receipt of the same was acknowledged by both the offices.

**VFF/0626**

Surjit Singh Sandhu 24 of Bhullath in Kapurthala. The story, as narrated by Sarbjit Kaur, sister of the victim Surjit Singh Sandhu, to Amrik Singh Muktsar, in June 1999, is as follows:-

On 9 July, 1990 at about 2.30 P.M., my husband Mehanga Singh and my son Sukhwinder Singh went to my parents' house at village Littan, because we had received a message from my brother Surjit Singh that he needed our Three-Wheeler for ferrying doors and windows for his newy constructed house. My husband reached my parents' house which is situated outside village Littan, along with his Three-Wheeler. Hardly 10-15 minutes had passed that the sound of gun shots being fired outside was heard. My both the brothers used to live separately, their houses being separated by a wall. My husband and my son were sitting in the house of my elder brother (Balbir Singh).

Just then, Surjit Singh called out and said, "The police have surrounded the house. I am slipping away. You people also slip away if you can." But, my brother, my husband, my sister-in-law (brother's wife Jasvir Kaur), Gurwinder Singh (9 years) s/o Balbir Singh stayed put inside the house itself as firing was on, outside. My parents used to live with Surjit Singh in the house adjacent to that of Balbir Singh with a wall separating the courtyards.

Actually, on that day, an absconding militant Balwinder Singh of my parental village had come to my brother Surjit Singh. He was sitting on the first floor of Surjit Singh's house. The police had got the scent of it and that is why they had laid a seige to the house. Balwinder Singh fired from the first floor, killing a Sub-Inspector of police. Balwinder Singh also jumped out from the first floor, and got killed by police firing in the nearby fields. Surjit Singh suceeded in slipping away despite the police cordon and reached a nearby village Surkhan. The police followed him and killed him in a house, there.

The firing continued from 2.45 P.M. to 5.30 P.M. By the time the firing stopped, the SSP and a large police force had arrived on the spot.

At 5.30 P.M., the police entered our house and took out my father Darbara Singh, mother Gurmej Kaur, my husband Mehanga Singh, my son Sukhwinder Singh, my brother Balbir Singh, my sister-in-law Jasvir Kaur, Bachan Singh r/o Ramgarh, who used to till Surjit Singh's land on crop-sharing basis, and my nephew Gurwindrer Singh (9 years). My sister-in-law dodged the police and saved her life by saying that she was the wife of Bachan Singh and that they used to till our land on crop-sharing basis. The police segregated Bachan Singh, Jasvir Kaur and Gurwinder Singh from others and made all others to stand in a line outside the house and shot them dead. The SSP H.S. Kahlon and several other police officers were present on this occasion. This incident was witnessed by my sister-in-law Jasvir Kaur, Bachan Singh, and my cousin (maternal uncle's son) Jagdish Singh r/o Bhullath. Jagdish Singh had saved his life by hiding in the Motor room (Tubewell) and telling the police that he was our servant who had come for transplanting paddy. Jagdish Singh was clean-shaven, so, the police did not suspect his statement.

I came to know about this incident at 7 P.M. However, my family members did not inform me about the death of my husband, brothers, parents, and son. They told me this much only that Surjit Singh had been wounded. I, along with my mother-in-law reached my parents' house at village Littan at 10 A.M. on 10 July. I came to know about the whole incident on reaching there. On 10 July, the police brought all the bodies (those of six family members and one that of Balwinder Singh) at 4 P.M. and got them cremated at the Village Cremation Ground under their supervision.

The police concocted a story that all these people had been killed in the encounter and got the same published in the newspapers. Whereas the fact is that the police killed six members of our family in revenge against the killing of one of their Sub-Inspectors at the hands of militant Balwinder Singh.

That all political parties of Punjab raised their voice against this episode. Representatives of all political parties of Punjab and prominent Akali leaders attended the 'Bhog' ceremony (religious service) of the killed persons. The newspapers also raised their voice against this episode and for several days, this episode remained in the news headlines. But, the Govt. neither got any inquiry conducted into this incident nor any of the policemen involved was punished.

All of my family members and those of my parents' family were 'Amritdharis' (Baptised).

All of our relatives were terrorised due to the killing of six members of our family. In my parents' house only my sister-in-law and her son are alive. We sent Gurwinder Singh s/o Late Balbir Singh to a foreign country, due to fear, as only one male member was left alive in my parents' family.

After the killing of my husband and son, no male member is left in my family. I had four daughters. My in-laws did not give my husband's share of land to me. I am pulling on with the income from the land of my brother Surjit Singh Sandhu and my husband's pension.

My sister-in-law Jasvir Kaur is terrified due to this incident, till today. She does not wish to initiate any action against this incident.

**VFF/0627**

Avtar Singh alias Tari 21 of Kalru, Sultanpur in Kapurthala. On 3-5-1990 at 10 A.M., Avtar Singh hired a tractor trolley and went to the Mandi (market) at Sultanpur Lodhi for selling wheat. Same day I also hired another tractor trolley and went to Mandi Sultanpur Lodhi for selling wheat. By the time I reached the Mandi, first trolley (that of Avtar Singh) had been unloaded. I sent Avtar Singh back. I reached home on bicycle at 4/5 A.M. on 4-5-1990 after selling my wheat. On reaching home I came to know that Avtar Singh had not reached home. I got worried and suspicious that Avtar Singh might have been arrested by the police because he never went anywhere without informing us.

On the following day morning, I enquired at my in-laws' place at village Bhanipur and came to know that Avtar Singh had not gone there. Then I enquired at Sultanpur Lodhi police station. The policeman present there told me that they had not arrested him. Thereafter I enquired at C.I.A Staff Kapurthala and Talwandi Chaudhary police stations, but, could not get any clue about his whereabouts.

On 5-5-1990 I enquired at several other police stations but did not get any information from anywhere. Same day evening, I heard the news on the Radio that a militant namely Avtar Singh had been killed in an encounter near village Kassochahal under Kapurthala police station. The newspapers of 6-5-1990 also carried a news item that the militant Avtar Singh had been killed along with one of his unidentified accomplices near village Kassochahal under Kapurthala (Sadar) police station. Later on, it became known that the other boy who had been killed was Sukhwinder Singh resident of Noormahal Dalla in district Jalandhar. He was picked up and killed in this fake encounter. He had been picked up from his fields, on 3-5-1990, by Pooran Singh Kubba, SHO of Kapurthala (Sadar).

Note:    According to Amrik Singh Muktsar, who investigated this case, the victim's father has become a drunkard and was unable to give complete details of the incident. However, an inquiry was conducted by SDM Kapurthala into this case. As per Advocate Harjit Singh Sandhu, he (Sandhu) has handed over the inquiry report by SDM to Advocate Navkiran Singh in connection with a case which is sub judice at Punjab Human Rights Commission, Chandigarh.

### VFF/0628

Jagir Singh 24 of Gillan Diwana, Sultanpur Lodhi in Kapurthala. According to his father Charan Singh, "On 2 Asharh (Around 14 June) 1993 at about 7 P.M., a police party of Sultanpur Lodhi police station led by the SHO Surinder Singh Saini picked up Jagir Singh from his shop. The neighbouring shopkeepers saw this. We got this news one hour later through a worker who was working at the shop at the time of Jagir Singh's arrest.

I along with Charan Singh (member panchayat), Bhupinder Singh Cheema (Poultry farm owner), Amar Singh (Sarpanch) reached Sultanpur Lodhi police station at about 9 P.M. The SHO was not present at the police station at that time. The Munshi told us that there was no one there with the name of Jagir Singh in the police station. We returned home.

On the next day again I along with the Panchayat went to the police station but the police did not give us any clue about the whereabouts of Jagir Singh. In the meantime, we had met the Senior Officers including the SSP.

The police produced him at the house of a Magistrate on 20th June and obtained remand upto 25th June.

The police showed him as having been killed along with another militant in cross firing between the police and militants when the police were taking them for the recovery of arms and the militants attacked the police party.

His body was brought for postmortem on the day of expiry of his remand."

### VFF/0629

Darbara Singh 75 of Littan, Bhullath in Kapurthala. The story, as narrated by Sarbjit Kaur, d/o the victim Darbara Singh, to Amrik Singh Muktsar, in June 1999, is as follows:-

"On 9 July, 1990 at about 2.30 P.M., my husband Mehanga Singh and my son Sukhwinder Singh went to my parents' house at village Littan, because we had received a message from my brother Surjit Singh that he needed our Three-Wheeler for ferrying doors and windows for his newy constructed house. My husband reached my parents' house which is situated outside village Littan, along with his Three-Wheeler. Hardly 10-15 minutes had passed that the sound of gun shots being fired outside was heard. My both the brothers used to live separately, their houses being separated by a wall. My husband and my son were sitting in the house of my elder brother (Balbir Singh).

Just then, Surjit Singh called out and said, "The police have surrounded the house. I am slipping away. You people also slip away if you can." But, my brother, my husband, my sister-in-law (brother's wife Jasvir Kaur), Gurwinder Singh (9 years) s/o Balbir Singh stayed put inside the house itself as firing was on, outside. My parents used to live with Surjit Singh in the house adjacent to that of Balbir Singh with a wall separating the courtyards.

Actually, on that day, an absconding militant Balwinder Singh of my parental village had come to my brother Surjit Singh. He was sitting on the first floor of Surjit Singh's house. The police had got the scent of it and that is why they had laid a seige to the house. Balwinder Singh fired from the first floor, killing a Sub-Inspector of police. Balwinder Singh also jumped out from the first floor, and got killed by police firing in the nearby fields. Surjit Singh suceeded in slipping away despite the police cordon and reached a nearby village Surkhan. The police followed him and killed him in a house, there.

The firing continued from 2.45 P.M. to 5.30 P.M. By the time the firing stopped, the SSP and a large police force had arrived on the spot.

At 5.30 P.M., the police entered our house and took out my father Darbara Singh, mother Gurmej Kaur, my husband Mehanga Singh, my son Sukhwinder Singh, my brother Balbir Singh, my sister-in-law Jasvir Kaur, Bachan Singh r/o Ramgarh, who used to till Surjit Singh's land on crop-sharing basis, and my nephew Gurwindrer Singh (9 years). My sister-in-law dodged the police and saved her life by saying that she was the wife of Bachan Singh and that they used to till our land on crop-sharing basis. The police segregated Bachan Singh, Jasvir Kaur and Gurwinder Singh from others and made all others to stand in a line outside the house and shot them dead. The SSP H.S. Kahlon and several other police officers were present on this occasion. This incident was witnessed by my sister-in-law Jasvir Kaur, Bachan Singh, and my cousin (maternal uncle's son) Jagdish Singh r/o Bhullath. Jagdish Singh had saved his life by hiding in the Motor room (Tubewell) and telling the police that he was our servant who had come for transplanting paddy. Jagdish Singh was clean-shaven, so, the police did not suspect his statement.

I came to know about this incident at 7 P.M. However, my family members did not inform me about the death of my husband, brothers, parents, and son. They told me this much only that Surjit Singh had been wounded. I, along with my mother-in-law reached my parents' house at village Littan at 10 A.M. on 10 July. I came to know about the whole incident on reaching there. On 10 July, the police brought all the bodies (those of six family members and one that of Balwinder Singh) at 4 P.M. and got them cremated at the Village Cremation Ground under their supervision.

The police concocted a story that all these people had been killed in the encounter and got the same published in the newspapers. Whereas the fact is that the police killed six members of our family in revenge against the killing of one of their Sub-Inspectors at the hands of militant Balwinder Singh.

That all political parties of Punjab raised their voice against this episode. Representatives of all political parties of Punjab and prominent Akali leaders attended the 'Bhog' ceremony (religious service) of the killed persons. The newspapers also raised their voice against this episode and for several days, this episode remained in the news headlines. But, the Govt. neither got any inquiry conducted into this incident nor any of the policemen involved was punished.

All of my family members and those of my parents' family were 'Amritdharis' (Baptised).

All of our relatives were terrorised due to the killing of six members of our family. In my parents' house only my sister-in-law and her son are alive. We sent Gurwinder Singh s/o Late Balbir Singh to a foreign country, due to fear, as only one male member was left alive in my parents' family.

After the killing of my husband and son, no male member is left in my family. I had four daughters. My in-laws did not give my husband's share of land to me. I am pulling on with the income from the land of my brother Surjit Singh Sandhu and my husband's pension.

My sister-in-law Jasvir Kaur is terrified due to this incident, till today. She does not wish to initiate any action against this incident."

**VFF/0630**

Wazir Singh 21 of Sidhwan Dona in Kapurthala. On 27-7-1989, Wazir Singh along with his cousin Dayal Singh s/o Malkit Singh went to the house of his aunt ('Maasi') w/o Jathedar Karnail Singh at village Sandhu Chatha. It was 1 P.M. They had hardly had their tea when police in civil clothes riding a Maruti Van came there. Ramu Cat (police tout) r/o village Bhangal Dona was also there with the police. They lifted Piara Singh (brother of Karnail Singh), Dayal Singh and Wazir Singh forcibly and while departing, they took away Karnail Singh's Jeep No. PB-080-3900 also along with them. Karnail Singh was not at home at that time.

"Late in the evening, Karnail Singh and myself (Hari Singh, father of Wazir Singh) went to C.I.A Staff Kapurthala, but, we were not allowed to meet them. According to Piara Singh, they were taken to C.I.A Staff Kapurthala. There, first, Piara Singh was interrogated. Thereafter, Wazir Singh was taken to the other room and after some time Dayal Singh was also taken to the other room. Wazir Singh's shrieks were heard by Piara Singh. It was clear that the police were torturing Wazir Singh. According to Piara Singh, thereafter, they were kept in separate rooms.

On the fourth day, Piara Singh was got released through the intervention of some influential persons. Piara Singh had been subjected to mild torture only. While releasing Piara Singh, the police officers namely DSP (D) Bachan Singh Randhawa, ASI Bachan Singh Buchar assured us that they would release the other boys also soon. The interveners told us that the other boys, especially Wazir Singh had been tortured very badly and as such they would be released only after few days. Swaran Singh Ghotna was the SSP Kapurthala at that time.

After releasing Piara Singh, the police released Dayal Singh also after few days. But, Wazir Singh was got admitted in Jawahar Hospital (near Jalaukhana), one week later. The family members could meet Wazir Singh at that time only. His condition was very critical. The police in civil clothes used to be present in the Hospital. On the third day after admission, Wazir Singh breathed his last in the Hospital. The police did not get the postmortem done. They handed over the body to us but the police accompanied us to the village and got the cremation done hurriedly.

The police terror was so much in those days that we did not even try to get the postmortem of the body done or take some other action. We were shadowed by the police at the Hospital all the time. We were not handed over the Hospital record also. It is quite possible that they might have not recorded Wazir Singh's admission at all at the Hospital.

I sent my other son Amrik Singh to Germany, due to fear. He has not returned home since then, due to fear. Dayal Singh s/o Malkit Singh also went away to some foreign country, later on."

**VFF/0631**

Joginder Singh 31 of Khassan, Bhullath in Kapurthala. According to his father Natha Singh Sandhu, "Joginder Singh was a truck driver and used to be away from home for days together. He had returned home on 27-28 July. On 1st August 1988 at about 10 P.M., all the family members including Joginder Singh were asleep in the courtyard of our house. Since there was no door in our house at that time, the police entered our house from both the sides. They woke up all the family members. At that time, Joginder Singh, Harjinder Singh (brother), Balwinder Singh (brother), Amarjit Singh (brother), Surinder Kaur (Bhabi), and children were present in the house.

The police party was led by Head Constable Jaswinder Singh of Bullath police station. There was 'Thanedar' (Sub-Inspector) also along with the police party of 15-20 policemen, but, I do not know his name. They said that they wanted to conduct a search of our house. They began to search the house. They searched everything including 'Petties' (Aluminium Boxes). Nothing incriminating was found from our house. No responsible person of the village was called at the time of search.

After the search was over, Head Constable Jaswinder Singh asked who was Joginder Singh from amongst us. I pointed towards my son and said that Joginder Singh was my son. All this while, Head Constable Jaswinder Singh kept standing with a revolver in his hand.

The police directed Joginder Singh to accompany them. On my asking the reason they said that they had to ask him some questions.

The police put Joginder Singh in their Mini Truck and went away. I immediately went to the house of the Sarpanch (head of village council) Darshan Singh. He was not available at home. Then I went to the house of Swaran Singh, then a Panch (member of village council) and now Sarpanch and narrated the whole incident to him. We started for the police station but came back from near the village School due to fear that the police may arrest us also during the night. We slept at home for the night.

On 2 August, I along with Swaran Singh, Pooran Singh, and Harjinder Singh (my son) reached Bhullath police station at 7/8 A.M. We met the SHO Harjit Singh Brar and enquired about Joginder Singh. The SHO flatly denied having picked up Joginder Singh. I told him that Head Constable Jaswinder Singh who had come along with the police party is known to me, but, the SHO did not listen to us at all. We came back.

That on the following day, the same persons along with some more people from our village met the SHO again. But he did not agree at all that they had picked up Joginder Singh.

We came to know about the arrest of Joginder Singh from the newspaper reports and Doordarshan news on 5 August. Same day we reached the District Courts as we were under the impression that the police would produce him before the Ilaqa Magistrate that day. But, he was not produced in any Court. We continued to enquire at various police stations about Joginder Singh, but, in vain. On 8 August, my lawyer Sh. Harjit Singh Sandhu submitted an application to the Court and prayed that a report may be called for from the police about the non-production of Joginder Singh in any Court so far. On 10 august, the SHO of Bhullath police station filed a report in the Court in which the police narrated their concocted story that the police were taking Joginder Singh for the recovery of arms and ammunition. The Jeep broke down on the bridge of the Bein river and all the policemen got down and started pushing the vehicle. Taking advantage of this, Joginder Singh jumped into the Bein along with the Constable to whose belt he had been strapped. However, the police succeeded in rescuing the Constable by pulling him by his hair, but, Joginder Singh got trapped in deep waters and thus he could not be rescued.

We suspect that Joginder Singh was tortured to death by the police in their illegal custody and later his dead body was thrown into the Bein (marshes)."

**VFF/0632**

Rajinder Singh alias Jinda 39 of Khassan, Bhullath in Kapurthala.

Rajinder Singh's brother Joginder Singh had been killed by the police after arresting him in August 1988. After that incident, the police had never arrested Rajinder Singh and no case was registered against him ever.

According to his father Natha Singh Sandhu, "about six months after Joginder Singh's incident, one day, Rajinder Singh along with another person from our village namely Sewa Singh had gone to Bullath. There, the SHO Harjit Singh Brar arrested both of them in the bazar. People from our village informed us about it. We went to the police station same day along with the Panchayat, but, the SHO did not allow us to meet Rajinder Singh. The SHO told me that the militants visited our house and that we wanted to get him (SHO) killed as we were angry over the death of my son Joginder Singh at the hands of the police. The SHO told me that they wanted to question my son about this matter. I continued to visit the police station along with the Panchayat for many days and after 9-10 days, the police released Rajinder Singh and Sewa Singh.

Thereafter, the police never arrested Rajinder Singh. However, they used to raid the house and return without making any arrests.

On 30 May 1990 at about 8 A.M., Rajinder Singh was working in his fields along with his brothers Balwinder Singh and Amarjit Singh. Some people in civil clothes came and took Rajinder Singh to one side and talked to him. Rajinder Singh told his brothers that he would be back soon and went away with those people, on foot.

At about 11/12 A.M., the police came to our house and informed me that my son and another person from our village were found dead on the bridge at Talwandi Mana. The police told me that my son and Sewa Singh had been killed by some militants. The police took me to the site of the incident on a scooter. Later, lot of people from our village reached the site of the incident on trollies.

The police put the bodies in the trollies and took them to Kapurthala for a postmortem. After the postmortem, the police handed over the bodies to us. We brought the bodies to the village and cremated them.

* After this incident, the police neither took any action nor conducted any investigation.
* For many years after this incident, till 1995-96, the police used to visit our house often but did not make any arrests.
* According to the police, Rajinder Singh had been killed by the militants but we were not paid the compensation normally paid to the families of those killed at the hands of the militants.
* We can say with full confidence as to who had killed Rajinder Singh."

## VFF/0633

Mehanga Singh 55 of Boparai, Bhullath in Kapurthala. The story, as narrated by Sarbjit Kaur, w/o the victim Mehanga Singh, to Amrik Singh Muktsar, in June 1999, is as follows:-

"On 9 July 1990 at about 2.30 P.M., my husband and my son went to my parents' house at village Littan, because we had received a message from my brother Surjit Singh that he needed our Three-Wheeler for ferrying doors and windows for his newy constructed house. My husband reached my parents' house which is situated outside village Littan, along with his Three-Wheeler. Hardly 10-15 minutes had passed that the sound of gun shots being fired outside was heard. My both the brothers used to live separately, their houses being separated by a wall. My husband and my son were sitting in the house of my elder brother (Balbir Singh).

Just then, Surjit Singh called out and said, "The police have surrounded the house. I am slipping away. You people also slip away if you can." But, my brother, my husband, my sister-in-law (brother's wife Jasvir Kaur), Gurwinder Singh (9 years) s/o Balbir Singh stayed put inside the house itself as firing was on, outside. My parents used to live with Surjit Singh in the house adjacent to that of Balbir Singh with a wall separating the courtyards.

Actually, on that day, an absconding militant Balwinder Singh of my parental village had come to my brother Surjit Singh. He was sitting on the first floor of Surjit Singh's house. The police had got the scent of it and that is why they had laid a seige to the house. Balwinder Singh fired from the first floor, killing a Sub-Inspector of police. Balwinder Singh also jumped out from the first floor, and got killed by police firing in the nearby fields. Surjit Singh suceeded in slipping away despite the police cordon and reached a nearby village Surkhan. The police followed him and killed him in a house, there.

The firing continued from 2.45 P.M. to 5.30 P.M. By the time the firing stopped, the SSP and a large police force had arrived on the spot.

At 5.30 P.M., the police entered our house and took out my father Darbara Singh, mother Gurmej Kaur, my husband Mehanga Singh, my son Sukhwinder Singh, my brother Balbir Singh, my sister-in-law Jasvir Kaur, Bachan Singh r/o Ramgarh, who used to till Surjit Singh's land on crop-sharing basis, and my nephew Gurwinder Singh (9 years). My sister-in-law dodged the police and saved her life by saying that she was the wife of Bachan Singh and that they used to till our land on crop-sharing basis. The police segregated Bachan Singh, Jasvir Kaur and Gurwinder Singh from others and made all others to stand in a line outside the house and shot them dead. The SSP H.S. Kahlon and several other police officers were present on this occasion. This incident was witnessed by my sister-in-law Jasvir Kaur, Bachan Singh, and my cousin (maternal uncle's son) Jagdish Singh r/o Bhullath. Jagdish Singh had saved his life by hiding in the Motor room (Tubewell) and telling the police that he was our servant who had come for transplanting paddy. Jagdish Singh was clean-shaven, so, the police did not suspect his statement.

I came to know about this incident at 7 P.M. However, my family members did not inform me about the death of my husband, brothers, parents, and son. They told me this much only that Surjit Singh had been wounded. I, along with my mother-in-law reached my parents' house at village Littan at 10 A.M. on 10 July. I came to know about the whole incident on reaching there. On 10 July, the police brought all the bodies (those of six family members and one that of Balwinder Singh) at 4 P.M. and got them cremated at the Village Cremation Ground under their supervision.

The police concocted a story that all these people had been killed in the encounter and got the same published in the newspapers. Whereas the fact is that the police killed six members of our family in revenge against the killing of one of their Sub-Inspectors at the hands of militant Balwinder Singh.

That all political parties of Punjab raised their voice against this episode. Representatives of all political parties of Punjab and prominent Akali leaders attended the 'Bhog' ceremony (religious service) of the killed persons. The newspapers also raised their voice against this episode and for several days, this episode remained in the news headlines. But, the Govt. neither got any inquiry conducted into this incident nor any of the policemen involved was punished.

All of my family members and those of my parents' family were 'Amritdharis' (Baptised).

All of our relatives were terrorised due to the killing of six members of our family. In my parents' house only my sister-in-law and her son are alive. We sent Gurwinder Singh s/o Late Balbir Singh to a foreign country, due to fear, as only one male member was left alive in my parents' family.

After the killing of my husband and son, no male member is left in my family. I had four daughters. My in-laws did not give my husband's share of land to me. I am pulling on with the income from the land of my brother Surjit Singh Sandhu and my husband's pension.

My sister-in-law Jasvir Kaur is terrified due to this incident, till today. She does not wish to initiate any action against this incident."

**VFF/0634**

Dhanna Singh 24 of Baria, Bhullath in Kapurthala. On 12-7-89, he was killed in an encounter with a Police party of Bhullath Police Station led by SHO of Police Station Bhullath and including one Head Constable, two Constables and one Driver, at Nangal Lubana.

**VFF/0635**

Virsa Singh 35 of Booh in Kapurthala. In the first week of October, Virsa Singh was brought by ASI Tirath Singh of Civil Lines P.S., on Police remand, from Jalandhar Jail.

On 10-10-92, there was a news item in the newspapers that Virsa Singh had been killed in an 'encounter'.

The following additional information about this incident has become available, after this case was investigated personally, by S. Amrik Singh Muktsar, towards the end of June, 1999 as well as from the Application dated 6/1/1992, submitted by Gurdeep Singh, elder brother of Virsa Singh, to the Additional Chief Judicial Magistrate, Kapurthala:-

That Virsa Singh was arrested on 2 January 1992 at about 11 AM, from his residence in the presence of village respectables. No recovery was effected from his house.

That on 3 Jan 92, the Panchayat of his village Booh met the DSP of C.I.A. Staff who did not give a satisfactory answer to the Panchayat and as such, the Panchayat returned to the village at 6 PM.

That on 6/1/92, Gurdeep Singh, elder brother of Virsa Singh sent telegrams to all the Punjab authorities at Chandigarh and also gave a written representation to the D.C. Kapurthala.

That the cases registered against Virsa Singh and two other persons namely Jaspal Singh s/o Harbans Singh r/o Mangupur (Sulatanpur) and Shingara Singh s/o Sadhu Singh r/o village Dandupur under P.S. Kotwali (Kapurthala), are as follows:-

1.  F.I.R. No. 103 dated 13-9-91 u/s 302/148/149 of I.P.C., 21/54/59 of Arms Act, 3/4/5 of T.D.A.(P) Act, registered at Kapurthala (Kotwali) P.S.

2.  F.I.R. No. 80 dated 1-9-91 u/s 302/309 IPC, 25/54/59 of Arms Act, 3/4/5 of T.D.A. (P) Act, registered at Sultanpur P.S.

3.  F.I.R. No. 98 dated 30-3-91 u/s 302/309/429/148/149 of IPC, 3/4 Arms Act, 3/4/5 of T.D.A. (P) Act, registered at Kapurthala (Kotwali) P.S.

This F.I.R. was in connection with a Bomb attack allegedly carried out at A.S.I. Tirth Singh. That is why he was brought on remand by the same ASI namely Tirth Singh and killed and later he was shown as having been killed in cross firing between militants and the Police.

4. F.I.R. No. 3 dated 7/1/92 u/s 309/34 IPC, 25/54/59 Arms act, 3/4/5 T.D.A. (P) Act, registered at Kapurthala (Kotwali) P.S.

That on 9-10-1992, ASI Tirth Singh took out Virsa Singh and two other youth namely Shingara Singh s/o Sadhu Singh r/o village Dandupur under P.S. Kotwali (Kapurthala), and Jaspal Singh s/o Harbans Singh r/o village Mangupur (Sultanpur), from Jalandhar jail, produced them in a Court, and obtained Police remand. Same day, he shot them dead in cold blood near village Chakko Ki under Police Station Dhilwan, and showed it as an incident of attack by militants on the police party which were taking these three persons for recovery of arms and in which these three persons were killed.

### VFF/0636

Sukhdev Singh alias Sukha 25 of Khassan, Bhullath in Kapurthala. In the words of his family, "In June 1990, one night, some plainclothesmen entered our house. At that time, his father Dalip Singh, sister Jaswinder Kaur, grandmother Jind Kaur were at home. They started beating Dalip Singh and questioned him about Sukhdev Singh. Dalip Singh said that he had gone out and they did not know about his whereabouts. On seeing her father being beaten up, Jaswinder Kaur started shouting. Those unidentified men shot Jaswinder Kaur dead. The family members are fully convinced that this was the handiwork of the police only.

On 12-7-90 at about 10/11 P.M., while Sukhdev Singh was sleeping in the room and all other family members were sleeping outside, the police entered the house by scaling the walls. The police party was led by SHO Pooran Singh. At that time, Dalip Singh (father), Jind Kaur (grandmother), Paramjit Kaur (wife), Rapinder Kaur (sister), Jatinder Kaur (sister), and the children were present in the house. SHO of Kapurthala (Sadar) police station asked about Sukhdev Singh and directed him to accompany them as they had to question him regarding something.

On the following day, his father Dalip Singh intimated the Sarpanch (head of village council) about this incident and along with the Panchayat (village council) went to Kapurthala (Sadar) police station. The SHO assured the Panchayat and family members that they would release Sukhdev Singh soon.

Thereafter, his father Dalip Singh along with the Panchayat met the SHO several times, but, the SHO did not listen to them at all.

On 26-7-90, his father Dalip Singh submitted written representations to the Governor Punjab, DGP, and Chief Justice of Punjab & Haryana High Court. This representation has been entered in the diary at No. 1169 on 28-7-90 by the Registrar (J) in the office of the Chief Justice of the High Court.

On 28-7-90, his father got a news item published about his disappearance in Ajit newspaper. In that he claimed that Sukhdev Singh had been tortured brutally and that his life may be in danger.

His father Dalip Singh continued meeting DSP Kapurthala, Kehar Singh, and SSP Kapurthala along with the panchayat. But, none of the officers disclosed anything about the whereabouts of Sukhdev Singh."

**VFF/0637**

Sewa Singh of Khassan, Bhullath in Kapurthala. In the words of his family, "On 30 May, 1990 at about 8 A.M., a policeman in civil clothes came to our house and took Sewa Singh away on his scooter. I had gone to Kapurthala on that day to get my eyes examined. I came to know there itself that my husband had been killed along with Rajinder Singh of our village on the bridge at Mana Talwandi and their bodies had been brought to Kapurthala hospital for postmortem. I along with my sister-in-law (husband's sister) Veer Kaur reached the hospital. Our village Panchayat and our relatives had already reached there. The police handed over the bodies to the Panchayat after getting the postmortem done. We brought the body of Sewa Singh to the village and cremated it.

We have not come to know till today as to who had killed my husband. We suspect that it was the handiwork of the police. The Govt. has not paid us any compensation so far. For about one and a half years, the police used to visit our house often and inquire about this incident. Thereafter, the police never came to our house."

**VFF/0638**

Pritam Singh 18 of Fattu Dhinga in Kapurthala. On 1-6-1984, Pritam Singh had gone to pay his obeisance at Sri Darbar Sahib (Golden Temple) Amritsar. It is suspected that he was killed by the para-military forces during Operation Blue Star from 4 to 6 June 1984.

**VFF/0639**

Sukhwinder Singh 22 of Boparai in Kapurthala. The story, as narrated by Sarbjit Kaur, w/o Mehanga Singh (Late), mother of the victim Sukhwinder Singh, to Amrik Singh Muktsar, in June 1999, is as follows:-

"On 9 July, 1990 at about 2.30 P.M., my husband Mehanga Singh and my son Sukhwinder Singh went to my parents' house at village

Littan, because we had received a message from my brother Surjit Singh that he needed our Three-Wheeler for ferrying doors and windows for his newy constructed house. My husband reached my parents' house which is situated outside village Littan, along with his Three-Wheeler. Hardly 10-15 minutes had passed that the sound of gun shots being fired outside was heard. My both the brothers used to live separately, their houses being separated by a wall. My husband and my son were sitting in the house of my elder brother (Balbir Singh).

Just then, Surjit Singh called out and said, "The police have surrounded the house. I am slipping away. You people also slip away if you can." But, my brother, my husband, my sister-in-law (brother's wife Jasvir Kaur), Gurwinder Singh (9 years) s/o Balbir Singh stayed put inside the house itself as firing was on, outside. My parents used to live with Surjit Singh in the house adjacent to that of Balbir Singh with a wall separating the courtyards.

Actually, on that day, an absconding militant Balwinder Singh of my parental village had come to my brother Surjit Singh. He was sitting on the first floor of Surjit Singh's house. The police had got the scent of it and that is why they had laid a seige to the house. Balwinder Singh fired from the first floor, killing a Sub-Inspector of police. Balwinder Singh also jumped out from the first floor, and got killed by police firing in the nearby fields. Surjit Singh suceeded in slipping away despite the police cordon and reached a nearby village Surkhan. The police followed him and killed him in a house, there.

The firing continued from 2.45 P.M. to 5.30 P.M. By the time the firing stopped, the SSP and a large police force had arrived on the spot.

At 5.30 P.M., the police entered our house and took out my father Darbara Singh, mother Gurmej Kaur, my husband Mehanga Singh, my son Sukhwinder Singh, my brother Balbir Singh, my sister-in-law Jasvir Kaur, Bachan Singh r/o Ramgarh, who used to till Surjit Singh's land on crop-sharing basis, and my nephew Gurwindder Singh (9 years). My sister-in-law dodged the police and saved her life by saying that she was the wife of Bachan Singh and that they used to till our land on crop-sharing basis. The police segregated Bachan Singh, Jasvir Kaur and Gurwinder Singh from others and made all others to stand in a line outside the house and shot them dead. The SSP H.S. Kahlon and several other police officers were present on this occasion. This incident was witnessed by my sister-in-law Jasvir Kaur, Bachan Singh, and my cousin (maternal uncle's son) Jagdish Singh r/o Bhullath. Jagdish Singh had saved his life by hiding in the Motor room (Tubewell) and telling the police that he was our servant who had come for transplanting paddy. Jagdish Singh was clean-shaven, so, the police did not suspect his statement.

I came to know about this incident at 7 P.M. However, my family members did not inform me about the death of my husband, brothers, parents, and son. They told me this much only that Surjit Singh had been wounded. I, along with my mother-in-law reached my parents' house at village Littan at 10 A.M. on 10 July. I came to know about the whole incident on reaching there. On 10 July, the police brought all the bodies (those of six family members and one that of Balwinder Singh) at 4 P.M. and got them cremated at the Village Cremation Ground under their supervision.

The police concocted a story that all these people had been killed in the encounter and got the same published in the newspapers. Whereas the fact is that the police killed six members of our family in revenge against the killing of one of their Sub-Inspectors at the hands of militant Balwinder Singh.

That all political parties of Punjab raised their voice against this episode. Representatives of all political parties of Punjab and prominent Akali leaders attended the 'Bhog' ceremony (religious service) of the killed persons. The newspapers also raised their voice against this episode and for several days, this episode remained in the news headlines. But, the Govt. neither got any inquiry conducted into this incident nor any of the policemen involved was punished.

All of my family members and those of my parents' family were 'Amritdharis' (Baptised).

All of our relatives were terrorised due to the killing of six members of our family. In my parents' house only my sister-in-law and her son are alive. We sent Gurwinder Singh s/o Late Balbir Singh to a foreign country, due to fear, as only one male member was left alive in my parents' family.

After the killing of my husband and son, no male member is left in my family. I had four daughters. My in-laws did not give my husband's share of land to me. I am pulling on with the income from the land of my brother Surjit Singh Sandhu and my husband's pension.

My sister-in-law Jasvir Kaur is terrified due to this incident, till today. She does not wish to initiate any action against this incident."

**VFF/0640**

Onkar Singh alias Kara 21 of Phagwara in Kapurthala. Onkar Singh had four brothers. Their family was associated with the Akali Dal since the beginning. Onkar Singh's uncle ('Taya') Kesar Singh and grand father also had been associated with the political activities of Akali Dal. Their family members had gone to jail during the Gurdwara Reform Movement along with the Akali 'Jathas' (Jatha means a squad or group). As such, Onkar Singh and his brothers also had Panthic (concerning Sikh affairs) inclinations. His elder brother Balwinder Singh only used to represent their family in the Akali Jathas during 'Dharam Yudh Morcha' (political agitation) launched by the Akalis in 1982. According to his brother Gurmeet Singh, first it was their grand father, then their uncle ('Taya') and later Balwinder Singh, who used to participate in the political activities of the Akali Dal. Due to these political activities of their family, this family became the focal point of suspicion of the Police after the Army attack on Sri Darbar Sahib in June 1984. That is why the Police used to pick up Balwinder Singh and his family members, often, on the basis of suspicion. In 1988, the Phagwara Police registered three cases against Balwinder Singh under the Arms Act and T.A.D.A. and sent him to Jail. He was released on bail in March 1989. Before the release of Balwinder Singh, Phagwara City Police had arrested his younger brother Onkar Singh, registered three cases against him and sent him to Jail. Onkar Singh got released on bail soon as he had to appear for his examination. Onkar Singh resumed his studies after his release. Even after his release, the Police used to pick up Onkar Singh as he was associated with the political activities of the Sikh Students Federation. Onkar Singh was the President of Guru Nanak College Sukhchiana Sahib unit of the Sikh Students Federation. The Police used to torture Onkar Singh every time he was picked up on the suspicion of his links with the militants. Whenever any militancy related incicdent used to take place in the area, the Police used to pick up Onkar Singh. In the meantime, Balwinder Singh started his own business of finance. The Police had stopped picking him up.

Due to repeated Police harassment, Onkar Singh deserted home and joined the ranks of the militants, once for all. After Onkar Singh absconded, the Police of Phagwara, Kapurthala (Sadar) and Jalandhar Police Stations began to arrest his family members. The Police used to pick up Onkar Singh's father, brothers, sisters and relatives, often. At times, the Police used to torture also his family members. In the meantime, the Police started picking up Balwinder Singh again. The cycle of this Police repression against his family continued from the time Onkar Singh deserted home in 1990 till the time he was shot dead at the hands of the Police.

On 7 July 1992 at about 9.30 A.M, Onkar Singh's elder brother Balwinder Singh had gone to his office near Chaura Khooh Mandir.

At about 10 A.M. plainclothes armed policemen came riding a Maruti Car. Balwinder Singh was alone in his office at that time. The above mentioned persons pushed Balwinder Singh and directed him to accompany them. Balwinder Singh protested and grappled with the said persons. This scene was witnessed by the shopkeepers in the neighbourhood of Balwinder Singh's office. Balwinder Singh was abducted by the above mentioned 4-5 persons riding a white Maruti Car. One of the boys from the Bazar came to Balwinder Singh's house and informed the family members about his abduction.

Later on, the family members met the Police officers at Phagwara, like SP Sanjeev Kalra, DSP Preetam Singh and SHO Devinder Sharma and tried to find out the whereabouts of Balwinder Singh. These officers told them that they had not arrested Balwinder Singh, however, they would try to find out as to which Police had arrested him. The family members along with prominent persons contacted the SSP Kapurthala, Shri Tiwari. He also told them that he would find out and let them know. A few days before and after the arrest of Balwinder Singh, the Phagwara Police had taken several youth of Phagwara city and neighbouring villages, into their custody. Among these arrested youth were Jaswinder Singh of village Palahi and Sandy of Phagwara who told the family members of Balwinder Singh that they had been detained in the custody of the Police at Phagwara and Kapurthala (Sadar) Police Stations along with Balwinder Singh. According to these youth, Balwinder Singh had been tortured brutally. Both the above mentioned youth told the family members that according to Balwinder Singh, he was got tortured during interrogation by the SSP, Shri Tiwari and SP Phagwara Sanjeev Kalra, only. After getting this information when the family members contacted SP Kalra and the SSP, both of whom flatly denied having Balwinder Singh in their custody.

About one month after the arrest of Balwinder Singh, one night, plainclothes policemen with masked faces raided his house and picked up his brother Gurmeet Singh, Charanjit Singh (brother), Gurdev Singh (sister's husband, resident of village Bada Aana), Harbhajan Singh (father) and detained them in the lock-up where they came to know after a few days that it was the Police Station Kapurthala (Sadar). These family members were detained at Kapurthala (Sadar) Police Station for about one month. There, several policemen whose names they don't know had told the family members that Balwinder Singh also had been detained in the same Police Station for quite some time. One month later, they were shifted to Kala Sangha Police Post from where Harbhajan Singh (father) and Gurdev Singh were released at the intervention of a Police agent. Gurmeet Singh and Charanjit Singh were also released from Kala Sangha Police Post, after a detention of 20-25 days. According to family members, they had paid Rs. 1,00,000/- to a Police agent for their release.

After their release, the family members asked Jaswinder Singh Palahi and Sandy whether they would depose in their favour in case they filed a case in the court about Balwinder Singh. But, these youth and their family members refused to do so due to the fear of the Police. As such, his family members were helpless and thus unable to take any action about Balwinder Singh. In the meantime, the Phagwara Police began to arrest the family members again and used to detain them in custody for days together.

On the night of 26 November 1992, Onkar Singh was killed in an encounter with the Police along with one of his accomplices namely Hazura Singh, near village Daroli Kalan in district Jalandhar. The family members came to know about this incident when the news item about the same was published in the newspapers on 28 November 1992. At that time, his father Harbhajan Singh and brother-in-law Gurdev Singh were already in Police custody at C.I.A Staff Jalandhar. The Police did not get the dead body of Onkar Singh identified from his family members. The Police released Harbhajan Singh and Gurdev Singh, about 3-4 days after the killing of Onkar Singh.

Even though, after the disappearance of Balwinder Singh and killing of Onkar Singh, the Police stopped picking up their family members, yet, the Police were still suspicious and used to visit their house, often. Whenever a SHO was posted newly at the local Police Station, he used to call the family members and note down the history of the family and names of the relatives. This routine continued till 1997 when DSP Phagwara had arrested Gurmeet Singh on the basis of suspicion and detained him in custody for 4 days. He was released at the intervention of a Human Rights Organization. According to Gurmeet Singh, the Police never visited their house thereafter.

* According to Gurmeet Singh, their mother Jeet Kaur suffered a tremendous mental shock due to the loss of her two young sons. She was not keeping well physically and expired about two years later due to this shock only. Their mother had reconciled herself to the death of Onkar Singh, but, the disappearance of Balwinder Singh shattered her completely. She used to wonder as to what had happened to Balwinder Singh, after all. She would always think of him, whether he was alive or not and if he may be alive, what may be his condition.

* According to Gurmeet Singh, due to the Police repression against their family, he had to abandon his studies. He could not pursue his study for M.A. after passing his B.A.

* For two years after the disappearance of Balwinder Singh, the family members could not look after his business due to which they suffered a colossal financial loss. The Police had arrested Balwinder Singh's business partner Sanjeev Kumar also, several times. As such, due to fear, he also attended to the business only after two years.

## VFF/0641

Balwinder Singh alias Binda 26 of Phagwara in Kapurthala. Balwinder Singh had four brothers. Their family was associated with the Akali Dal since the beginning. Balwinder Singh's uncle ('Taya') Kesar Singh and grand father also had been associated with the political activities of Akali Dal. Their family members had gone to jail during the Gurdwara Reform Movement along with the Akali 'Jathas' (Jatha means a squad or group). As such, Balwinder Singh and his brothers also had Panthic (concerning Sikh affairs) inclinations. Balwinder Singh only used to represent their family in the Akali Jathas during 'Dharam Yudh Morcha' (political agitation) launched by the Akalis in 1982. According to his younger brother Gurmeet Singh, first it was their grand father, then their uncle ('Taya') and later Balwinder Singh, who used to participate in the political activities of the Akali Dal. Due to these political activities of their family, this family became the focal point of suspicion of the Police after the Army attack on Sri Darbar Sahib in June 1984. That is why the Police used to pick up Balwinder Singh and his family members, often, on the basis of suspicion. In 1988, the Phagwara Police registered three cases against Balwinder Singh under the Arms Act and T.A.D.A. and sent him to Jail. He was released on bail in March 1989. Before the release of Balwinder Singh, Phagwara City Police had arrested his younger brother Onkar Singh, registered three cases against him and sent him to Jail. Onkar Singh got released on bail soon as he had to appear in the examination. Onkar Singh resumed his studies after his release. Even after his release, the Police used to pick up Onkar Singh as he was associated with the political activities of the Sikh Students Federation. Onkar Singh was the President of Guru Nanak College Sukhchiana Sahib unit of the Sikh Students Federation. The Police used to torture Onkar Singh every time he was picked up on the suspicion of his links with militants. Whenever any militancy related incicdent used to take place in the area, the Police used to pick up Onkar Singh. In the meantime, Balwinder Singh started his own business of finance. The Police had stopped picking him up.

Due to repeated Police harassment, Onkar Singh deserted home and joined the ranks of the militants, once for all. After Onkar Singh absconded, the Police of Phagwara, Kapurthala (Sadar) and Jalandhar Police Stations began to arrest his family members. The Police used to pick up Onkar Singh's father, brothers, sisters and relatives, often. At times, the Police used to torture also his family members. In the meantime, the Police started picking up Balwinder Singh again. The cycle of this Police repression against his family continued from the time Onkar Singh deserted home in 1990 till the time he was shot dead at the hands of the Police.

On 7 July 1992 at about 9.30 A.M, Balwinder Singh had gone to his office near Chaura Khooh Mandir. At about 10 A.M. plainclothes armed policemen came riding a Maruti Car. Balwinder Singh was alone in his office at that time. The above mentioned persons pushed Balwinder Singh and directed him to accompany them. Balwinder Singh protested and grappled with the said persons. This scene was witnessed by the shopkeepers in the neighbourhood of Balwinder Singh's office. Balwinder Singh was abducted by the above mentioned 4-5 persons riding a white Maruti Car. One of the boys from the Bazar came to Balwinder Singh's house and informed the family members about his abduction.

Later on, the family members met the Police officers at Phagwara, like SP Sanjeev Kalra, DSP Preetam Singh and SHO Devinder Sharma and tried to find out the whereabouts of Balwinder Singh. These officers told them that they had not arrested Balwinder Singh, however, they would try to find out as to which Police had arrested him. The family members along with prominent persons contacted the SSP Kapurthala, Shri Tiwari. He also told them that he would find out and let them know. A few days before and after the arrest of Balwinder Singh, the Phagwara Police had taken several youth of Phagwara city and neighbouring villages, into their custody. Among these arrested youth were Jaswinder Singh of village Palahi and Sandy of Phagwara who told the family members of Balwinder Singh that they had been detained in the custody of the Police at Phagwara and Kapurthala (Sadar) Police Stations along with Balwinder Singh. According to these youth, Balwinder Singh had been tortured brutally. Both the above mentioned youth told the family members that according to Balwinder Singh, he was got tortured during interrogation by the SSP, Shri Tiwari and SP Phagwara Sanjeev Kalra, only. After getting this information when the family members contacted SP Kalra and the SSP, both of them flatly denied having Balwinder Singh in their custody.

About one month after the arrest of Balwinder Singh, one night, plainclothes policemen with masked faces raided his house and picked up his brother Gurmeet Singh, Charanjit Singh (brother), Gurdev Singh (sister's husband, resident of village Bada Aana), Harbhajan Singh (father) and detained them in the lock-up where they came to know after a few days that it was the Police Station Kapurthala (Sadar). These family members were detained at Kapurthala (Sadar) Police Station for about one month. There, several policemen whose names they don't know had told the family members that Balwinder Singh also had been detained in the same Police Station for quite some time. One month later, they were shifted to Kala Sangha Police Post from where Harbhajan Singh (father) and Gurdev Singh were released at the intervention of a Police agent. Gurmeet Singh and Charanjit Singh were also released from Kala Sangha Police Post, after a detention of 20-25 days. According to family members, they had paid Rs. 1,00,000/- to a Police agent for their release.

After their release, the family members asked Jaswinder Singh Palahi and Sandy whether they would depose in their favour in case they filed a case in the court about Balwinder Singh. But, these youth and their family members refused to do so due to the fear of the Police. As such, his family members were helpless and thus unable to take any action about Balwinder Singh. In the meantime, the Phagwara Police began to arrest the family members again and used to detain them in custody for days together.

On the night of 26 November 1992, Onkar Singh was killed in an encounter with the Police along with one of his accomplices namely Hazura Singh, near village Daroli Kalan in district Jalandhar. The family members came to know about this incident when the news item about the same was published in the newspapers on 28 November 1992. At that time, his father Harbhajan Singh and brother-in-law Gurdev Singh were already in Police custody at C.I.A Staff Jalandhar. The Police did not get the dead body of Onkar Singh identified from his family members. The Police released Harbhajan Singh and Gurdev Singh, about 3-4 days after the killing of Onkar Singh.

Even though, after the disappearance of Balwinder Singh and killing of Onkar Singh, the Police stopped picking up their family members, yet, the Police were still suspicious and used to visit their house, often. Whenever a SHO was posted newly at the local Police Station, he used to call the family members and note down the history of the family and names of the relatives. This routine continued till 1997 when DSP Phagwara had arrested Gurmeet Singh on the basis of suspicion and detained him in custody for 4 days. He was released at the intervention of a Human Rights Organization. According to Gurmeet Singh, the Police never visited their house thereafter.

* According to Gurmeet Singh, their mother Jeet Kaur suffered a tremendous mental shock due to the loss of her two young sons. She was not keeping well physically and expired about two years later due to this shock only. Their mother had reconciled herself to the death of Onkar Singh, but, the disappearance of Balwinder Singh shattered her completely. She used to wonder as to what had happened to Balwinder Singh, after all. She would always think of him, whether he was alive or not and if he may be alive, what may be his condition.

* According to Gurmeet Singh, due to the Police repression against their family, he had to abandon his studies. He could not pursue his study for M.A. after passing his B.A.

* For two years after the disappearance of Balwinder Singh, the family members could not look after his business due to which they suffered a colossal financial loss. The Police had arrested Balwinder Singh's business partner Sanjeev Kumar also, several times. As such, due to fear, he also attended to the business only after two years.

**VFF/0642**

Gurmej Kaur 65 of Littan, Bhullath in Kapurthala. The story, as narrated by Sarbjit Kaur, d/o the victim Gurmej Kaur, to Amrik Singh Muktsar, in June 1999, is as follows:-

"On 9 July, 1990 at about 2.30 P.M., my husband Mehanga Singh and my son Sukhwinder Singh went to my parents' house at village Littan, because we had received a message from my brother Surjit Singh that he needed our Three-Wheeler for ferrying doors and windows for his newy constructed house. My husband reached my parents' house which is situated outside village Littan, along with his Three-Wheeler. Hardly 10-15 minutes had passed that the sound of gun shots being fired outside was heard. My both the brothers used to live separately, their houses being separated by a wall. My husband and my son were sitting in the house of my elder brother (Balbir Singh).

Just then, Surjit Singh called out and said, "The police have surrounded the house. I am slipping away. You people also slip away if you can." But, my brother, my husband, my sister-in-law (brother's wife Jasvir Kaur), Gurwinder Singh (9 years) s/o Balbir Singh stayed put inside the house itself as firing was on, outside. My parents used to live with Surjit Singh in the house adjacent to that of Balbir Singh with a wall separating the courtyards.

Actually, on that day, an absconding militant Balwinder Singh of my parental village had come to my brother Surjit Singh. He was sitting on the first floor of Surjit Singh's house. The police had got the scent of it and that is why they had laid a seige to the house. Balwinder Singh fired from the first floor, killing a Sub-Inspector of police. Balwinder Singh also jumped out from the first floor, and got killed by police firing in the nearby fields. Surjit Singh suceeded in slipping away despite the police cordon and reached a nearby village Surkhan. The police followed him and killed him in a house, there.

The firing continued from 2.45 P.M. to 5.30 P.M. By the time the firing stopped, the SSP and a large police force had arrived on the spot.

At 5.30 P.M., the police entered our house and took out my father Darbara Singh, mother Gurmej Kaur, my husband Mehanga Singh, my son Sukhwinder Singh, my brother Balbir Singh, my sister-in-law Jasvir Kaur, Bachan Singh r/o Ramgarh, who used to till Surjit Singh's land on crop-sharing basis, and my nephew Gurwindrer Singh (9 years). My sister-in-law dodged the police and saved her life by saying that she was the wife of Bachan Singh and that they used to till our land on crop-sharing basis. The police segregated Bachan Singh, Jasvir Kaur and Gurwinder Singh from others and made all others to stand in a line outside the house and shot them dead. The SSP H.S. Kahlon and several other police officers were present on this occasion. This incident was witnessed by my sister-in-law Jasvir Kaur, Bachan Singh, and my cousin (maternal uncle's son) Jagdish Singh r/o Bhullath. Jagdish Singh had saved his life by hiding in the Motor room (Tubewell) and telling the police that he was our servant who had come for transplanting paddy. Jagdish Singh was clean-shaven, so, the police did not suspect his statement.

I came to know about this incident at 7 P.M. However, my family members did not inform me about the death of my husband, brothers, parents, and son. They told me this much only that Surjit Singh had been wounded. I, along with my mother-in-law reached my parents' house at village Littan at 10 A.M. on 10 July. I came to know about the whole incident on reaching there. On 10 July, the police brought all the bodies (those of six family members and one that of Balwinder Singh) at 4 P.M. and got them cremated at the Village Cremation Ground under their supervision.

The police concocted a story that all these people had been killed in the encounter and got the same published in the newspapers. Whereas the fact is that the police killed six members of our family in revenge against the killing of one of their Sub-Inspectors at the hands of militant Balwinder Singh.

That all political parties of Punjab raised their voice against this episode. Representatives of all political parties of Punjab and prominent Akali leaders attended the 'Bhog' ceremony (religious service) of the killed persons. The newspapers also raised their voice against this episode and for several days, this episode remained in the news headlines. But, the Govt. neither got any inquiry conducted into this incident nor any of the policemen involved was punished.

All of my family members and those of my parents' family were 'Amritdharis' (Baptised).

All of our relatives were terrorised due to the killing of six members of our family. In my parents' house only my sister-in-law and her son are alive. We sent Gurwinder Singh s/o Late Balbir Singh to a foreign country, due to fear, as only one male member was left alive in my parents' family.

After the killing of my husband and son, no male member is left in my family. I had four daughters. My in-laws did not give my husband's share of land to me. I am pulling on with the income from the land of my brother Surjit Singh Sandhu and my husband's pension.

My sister-in-law Jasvir Kaur is terrified due to this incident, till today. She does not wish to initiate any action against this incident."

**VFF/0643**

Satnam Singh alias Satta 20 of Khukhrain in Kapurthala. On 17-9-91 at about 11 A.M., Satnam Singh was picked up along with two other village youth namely Lakhbir Singh s/o Sardul Singh, and Lakha Singh s/o Jarnail Singh from the house of Sarban Singh, a Mazhabi Sikh, by a police party of Kapurthala led by DSP Pritpal Singh. Many villagers were present there at that time. Satnam Singh had been called from his house by Lakha Singh s/o Jarnail Singh, about one hour prior to this incident. At the time of their arrest, Satnam Singh, Lakhbir Singh, Lakha Singh, and Sarban Singh were drinking liqour and eating eggs. We suspect that this action was masterminded by Lakha Singh s/o Jarnail Singh in connivance with the police, because, he was released after one month and he did not enter the village for many years.

**VFF/0644**

Jadwinder Singh alias Jali of Fattu Dhinga in Kapurthala. He was killed during Operation Blue Star on 6th June 1984.

**VFF/0645**

Resham Singh 35 Fattu Dhinga in Kapurthala. He was killed during Operation Blue Star at Sri Darbar Sahib Amritsar on 6 June 1984.

**VFF/0646**

Piara Singh 70 of Lakhan Khurd in Kapurthala. In the words of his son, "my brother Gurwinder Singh was an active worker of Sikh Students Federation and was studying at Doaba College Jalandhar. That is why the police used to raid our house for his arrest and often they used to arrest him and detain him in illegal custody. They used to release him on the responsibility of the panchayat (village council). Gurwinder Singh was active in Sikh Students Federation since 1986-87.

On 10 June 1988, a police party of Kapurthala (Sadar) police station led by SHO Dilbagh Singh and including ASI Jagtar Singh raided our house and asked for Raghbir Singh. But, Raghbir Singh was not at home. So they picked up myself and my brother Gurbachan Singh and took us away to the police station. They asked the family members to produce Raghbir Singh.

On 14-6-88, the village panchayat produced Raghbir Singh at the police station. The police tortured Raghbir Singh brutally in illegal custody for 20 days. Then they implicated him in a case u/s 216/212 IPC and 3/4/5 of TADA (P) Act vide FIR No. 50 of Kapurthala (Sadar) P.S. and sent him to jail.

On 27-2-1989, Designate Judge Kapurthala, Sh. Gurjit Singh Sandhu acquitted Raghbir Singh in the above case and he came home.

But, the police continued to raid our house even after his release. We sent Raghbir Singh to our relatives in Madhya Pradesh. There, he joined a Computer Course. The police raids continued and they continued to ask the family members to produce Raghbir Singh. Many times, the police of Kapurthala (Sadar) P.S. used to pick up our family members and torture them for days together in illegal custody.

On 24-5-1989, a police party of Kapurthala (Sadar) led by the SHO Pooran Singh raided our house and asked for my father, Jathedar Piara Singh. He was not at home. The police picked up my brother Gurbachan Singh, my uncle Amrik Singh and 13-14 other persons from our village and took them to the police station.

On 25-5-1989, Jathedar Piara Singh along with the panchayat members went to the P.S. (Sadar). The police made him to sit there and released all the arrested persons except Mewa Singh and my brother Gurbachan Singh.

8-9 days later, when Gurbachan Singh and Mewa Singh were released, they told us that Jathedar Piara Singh was tortured brutally by the police and that he died then and there. Gurbachan Singh and Mewa Singh saw him dead. In the meantime, the panchayat and family members had been meeting DSP Kehar Singh and SHO Pooran Singh regularly. Initially, the above mentioned officers continued to assure them that they would release Piara Singh. But, after the release of Mewa Singh and Gurbachan Singh, they began to say that they had released Piara Singh also and that they had asked Piara Singh to produce his son Raghbir Singh. Whereas it was a white lie. Thereafter, we have submitted written representatiions to Senior Officers. But nobody has listened to us so far.

Even after the disappearance of my father, the police used to raid our house and pick up our family members. Once, the police arrested Gurwinder Singh (Army Jawan) also. He was released at the intervention of Army Headquarters.

Ultimately, my brother Raghbir Singh went abroad in 1990-91 to escape police harassment and is living there only now-a-days. The police used to raid our house often till 1996-97. Now they have stopped it for the last one year and a half."

**VFF/0647**

Makhan Singh 33 of Sandhu Chatha in Kapurthala. In the words of his wife, "In 1986-87, my husband took up a job at Sangha Cold Store at Jalandhar. On 6 June, 1987, the police raided our house. My husband had gone to the Cold Store at that time. Same day, the police raided the Cold Store also at Jalandhar. But, they could not arrest my husband from there. Thereafter, my husband went underground. In the meantime, Jalandhar and Kapurthala (Sadar) police continued to raid our house.

The police used to pick me up often. Once, Major Singh, SHO of Kapurthala (Sadar) picked me up and detained me for abour seven days. Sometimes, C.I.A. Staff Jalandhar used to pick me up. At that time, I was carrying my younger child. SHO Major Singh tortured me also. In the meantime, my younger brother-in-law ('Devar') Karnail Singh, elder brother-in-law Subedar (retd.) Sarban Singh, Harbhajan Singh and Paramjit Singh, sons of Sarban Singh, my parents Swaran Singh and Tajinder Kaur, Devinderpal Singh (Pal) had been picked up by the Jalandhar police. Karnail Singh was tortured also, brutally. Subedar (retd.) Sarban Singh was detained illegally for about one month. This routine continued till the time my husband was arrested. We came to know about the arrest of my husband from a news report published in Ajit newspaper dated 13 August, 1988.

Same day, the CRPF raided our house. They picked me up and took me to the CRPF Camp at Jalandhar. There, they got my husband identified from me. My husband was lying on the floor. His condition seemed to be very critical. I was not allowed to go near him. Immediately after getting him identified they dropped me back at my village.

The news report (regarding his escape from police custody by jumping into the Satluj river) appeared in the Ajit newspaper dated 18 August, 1988.

After the publication of the news report on 18 August, 1988, we did not try to meet any police officer to know the fate of Makhan Singh because we could make out that the police had killed Makhan Singh and concocted a story (that he jumped into the Satluj river and escaped) and got the same published in the newspaper. That was the modus operandi of the police in those days.

One month after the publication of the news report, one day, 5-6 policemen in civil clothes came to my parents' house at Swaraj Ganj (near Lal Ratan). They enquired about me and told me that they wanted me to meet my husband Makhan Singh and asked me to accompany them. My parents were at home only at that time. Joginder Pal Pandey was there along with the police party at that time. They made me to sit in a vehicle and took me to the same place where I had identified my husband. When I reached the CRPF Camp, SP Joginder Pal Pandey was present there. He said, "Bibi (sister) we wanted to get him identified. Lest we kill an innocent person."

There, they let me meet my husband Makhan Singh in a room at first floor. He was alright at that time. I stayed with my husband that night in the same room. My husband said, "I am OK. I have full hope that I will survive. But you will not talk to anyone about this meeting. If you talk to anyone about this, they will kill me immediately."

On the following day, at 3/4 P.M., the CRPF personnel and my husband Makhan Singh came to drop me at home. In one vehicle, Joginder Pal Pandey was sitting on the front seat along with his driver and myself and my husband were sitting on the rear seat. Other CRPF personnel in uniform were following us in the other vehicle. They dropped me in a street near the Hotel Skylark and went away."

**VFF/0648**

Jeet Singh alias Jeeta of Sidhwan Dona in Kapurthala. He was abducted by about 10 persons from his farm house on 17-9-91 at 11 P.M.

This case was investigated personally by S. Amrik Singh Muktsar in June 1999. He interviewed Balbir Kaur, wife of the victim Jeet Singh. Given below are the details of the incident, as narrated to Amrik Singh

Muktsar, by Balbir Kaur w/o Jeet Singh. The true translation of the same is appended below:-

"I got married to Jeet Singh s/o Channan Singh in the year 1978. My husband was a farmer. He had two younger brothers namely Tarsem Singh and Sarban Singh. My husband has three sisters namely Gian Kaur, Simarjit Kaur, and Jeet Kaur. Gian Kaur had been married off before my marriage, whereas, Simarjit Kaur and Jeet Kaur were married off by Jeet Singh after our marriage. My father-in-law had expired long ago. As such, the whole family was dependent on the earnings of my husband only.

Younger brother of my husband namely Tarsem Singh who was studying at Randhir College at Kapurthala, had started taking part in the activities of Sikh Students Federation. That is why the Police used to pick him up often and he was tortured also by the Police once or twice. In 1985, Tarsem Singh absconded as he was fed up with Police harassment. The Police unleashed a reign of terror on his family after Tarsem Singh had absconded. The Police used to pick up our relatives apart from my husband Jeet Singh, brother-in-law ('Devar') Sarban Singh, and my mother-in-law Joginder Kaur, often, and take them to Sadar (Kapurthala) Police Station (P.S.) and C.I.A. Staff Kapurthala.

The Police picked up my husband about 8 times and many times they used to keep him in illegal custody for 2-3 months at a stretch and torture him. The Police used to torture my husband and my brother-in-law Sarban Singh and question them about my other brother-in-law Tarsem Singh. Our amily did not have any link whatsoever with my brother-in-law Tarsem Singh after he had absconded. But, the Police did not believe our words and they used to pick up our family members and relatives, repeatedly. The Police used to pick up aunts ('Bhua' & 'Maasi') and other relatives of my husband and used to keep them in illegal custody for days together.

My husband sent his brother Sarban Singh to Jordan (foreign country) in June 1991 due to the scare of the Police, so that at least some member of the family could escape the Police wrath.

Whenever the Police used to raid our house, they used to misbehave with other members of the family. Most of the time, ASI Tirth Singh and ASI Magat Rai only used to raid our house and pick up the family members. ASI Tirth had threatened us several times thus,"We will kill your whole family."

On 17-9-91 at about 11 PM, a police party of about 10 personnel led by ASI Mangat Rai and including Head Constable Manohar Singh, entered our house. There was no boundary wall around our house. All the family members i.e. myself (Balbir Kaur w/o Jeet Singh), my mother-in-law Joginder Kaur, my sister-in-law ('Devrani') Kulwant Kaur, and male members were asleep in the courtyard. The Police woke up my husband. On hearing the commotion, myself, my mother-in-law and my sister-in-law also woke up. The Police compelled my husband to accompany them and took him outside. I and my mother-in-law started shouting and followed the Police. But, the Police acted swiftly and put my husband forcibly into a vehicle which had been parked about 200 yards away on the road. All this while, they had been beating my husband.

The Police sped away in their vehicle before I and my mother-in-law could reach the road. I and my mother-in-law along with one of our close relatives namely Boota Singh s/o Gurbachan Singh (since deceased) went to the Police Post of our village and intimated them about this incident. They addressed my mother-in-law and said,"Mother, nothing can be done at this hour. You come and enquire in the morning." My mother-in-law was still standing at the Police Post when several Police vehicles sped past her. The incharge of the Police Post told my mother-in-law that the DSP Sahib had also come there.

Next day morning, we along with the Panchayat comprising my father Joginder Singh, Bukkan Singh Panch (since deceased), Budh Singh Sarpanch and other respectable persons went to Kapurthala (Sadar) Police Station and met the DSP and the SSP there. But, no Police Officer disclosed anything about the whereabouts of Jeet Singh. My family members and I myself continued to visit Kapurthala and other Police Stations but nothing was disclosed about the whereabouts of my husband.

In the beginning, ASI Mangat Rai and SSP Jasminder Singh continued to assure us that they would release him (Jeet Singh) if we produced Tarsem Singh in front of them. We approached Mangat Rai several times through some persons who were close to him (they would not depose). Once, he demanded Rs. 50,000/- We paid the money to the middlemen and told him that he could collect the money from them after he had released Jeet Singh. However, at last, Mangat Rai told that SSP Jasminder Singh had been transferred to Faridkot and he had taken Jeet Singh along with him there.

Thereafter, we continued to meet SSP S.K. Tiwari. He continued to say that our man was not with him and that we should find out from SSP Jasminder Singh only. We met the SSP at Faridkot along with Major Narinder Singh Jallo. He (SSP) asked us to see DSP Moga, Sh. Pritpal Singh. Same day, we went to Moga and met the DSP there. He said,"How do you hope to find your man after such a long time? You go and sit quietly at home."

My brother-in-law ('Devar') Tarsem Singh was killed in an encounter with the Police on 20 May 1992. We read about it in the newspapers. I hoped that the Police might release my husband now. However, even then the Kapurthala Police did not give any clue about the whereabouts of my husband. Till today, we don't know as to what had happened to my husband."

### VFF/0649

Jarnail Singh alias Jaila 36 of Fattu Dhinga in Kapurthala. He was killed by the Police in a fake encounter at the house of former Federation (AISSF) leader Balwinder Singh Khojkipur at village Khojkipur in police district Tarn Taran and Distt. Amritsar, on 21 May 1992. The police force was led by SSP Ajit Singh Sandhu and included SP(D) and an Inspector also.

### VFF/0650

Vasdev Sharma alias Pandit Ji 35 of Sultanpur Lodhi in Kapurthala. On 2-5-1990 at 10 A.M., Vasdev Sharma went from his house after informing his wife that he along with Avtar Singh s/o Bachan Singh r/o Vill. Kalru and Kulwant Singh @ Sukha, Travel Agent, was proceeding to Noormahal (Distt. Jalandhar) in his Ambassador Car No. DEB-1680 and that they would be back by evening. But, he did not return home that evening.

In the words of his father, "on 3-5-1990, we went to the house of Kulwant Singh at Sikhan Mohalla, Sultanpur. From there we took along Kulwant Singh's wife and went to the house of Avtar Singh at Vill. Kalru. Those who went to the house of Avtar Singh included Geeta Rani w/o Vasdev, Vasdev's father Pali Ram, and wife of Kulwant Singh. Avtar Singh's family members told them that Avtar Singh also had gone from home the day before but had not returned and that they themselves were worried.

Thereafter, we went to the Sultanpur police station and reported the matter to them. We asked them to register a FIR but they put us off saying that we should wait for one or two days. However, the police brought the wife of Kulwant Singh to the police station then and there. Naginder Singh Rana was the SHO of Sultanpur police station at that time. Kulwant Singh's wife also told them that she herself was worried that her husband had not returned home.

After lot of hectic efforts, the DDR regarding the disappearance of Vasdev Sharma was registered on 14-5-1990 at Sultanpur Lodhi police station.

According to the family members of Avtar Singh, these three persons had collected money from the house of Avtar Singh's aunt ('Maasi') at Vill. Dalla, near Noormahal and returned from there. Thereafter, their whereabouts are not known.

I, along with Sh. Ram Moorti Sharma (our brother-in-law—'Jeeja') and Geeta Rani wife of Vasdev Sharma, met the Governor of Punjab Sh. N.K. Mukherjee at Sultanpur Lodhi Civil Rest House. The Governor directed the Police officers to trace out Vasdev Sharma. We submitted a written representation also to the Governor in this connection.

A few days later, we went to the Kapurthala Sainik Rest House to meet the then External Affairs Minister Sh. I.K. Gujral. There the SSP H.S. Kahlon asked us the purpose of our visit. We told him about the disappearance of my brother. At this, the SSP told us not to see Mr. Gujral and that they would release my brother on the following morning. At that time, Geeta Rani wife of Vasdev Sharma and myself were present there. We had letter also from my wife's uncle namely Brahmdev Sharma who is a S.P. in Chandigarh Police, with us which the SSP Kahlon took from us and kept with him. The SSP asked us to see him at his office on the following morning.

On the following morning we met the SSP at his office at Kapurthala. He told us that our man was not in their custody.

In the meantime, the police of Kapurthala (Sadar) police station led by SHO Pooran Singh had shown Avtar Singh along with another militant Sukhwinder Singh r/o Vill. Dalla near Noormahal as having been killed in an encounter with the police. This was disclosed to us by the father of Avtar Singh when we met him. He said that his son had been killed by the police and asked us to find out about our boy.

Some time later, we met Sh. D.R. Bhatti, DIG Jalandhar Range. We narrated the whole story to him including the incident of killing of Avtar Singh in an encounter with the police and demanded that either Vasdev Sharma be released from police custody or his whereabouts be disclosed. The DIG told us that our Car was not involved in the encounter which took place near village Saidowal-Kammochahal. On the contrary, they were militants riding a Motor Cycle.

After few days, we were informed by some police sources unofficially that our man was no more. He had been killed."

**VFF/0651, VFF/0652, VFF/0653, VFF/0654, VFF/0655, VFF/0656**

Lakhwinder Singh, Ajit Singh, Swaran Singh, Mangal Singh, Gurmit Kaur and Kulwinder Singh of Bhudha Theh in Kapurthala. The details of this incident were given to Amrik Singh Muktsar by Sukhwinder Kaur w/o Swaran Singh s/o Labh Singh, Aunt ('Maami') of the victim Lakhwinder Singh, in an interview, in June 1999. The following relatives of the victim Lakhwinder Singh have also been disappeared along with him, by the police:-

1.   Ajit Singh (Father)
2.   Gurmit Kaur (Mother)
3.   Kulwinder Singh (brother)
4.   Swaran Singh (maternal uncle)
5.   Mangal Singh (cousin)

The following relatives of Lakhwinder Singh have been killed by the police in encounters:-

1.   Balwinder Singh Kalia (brother)
2.   Hardip Singh (maternal uncle)

The story as narrated by Sukhwinder Kaur is as follows:-

I got married to Swaran Singh s/o Labh Singh r/o Desal (Kapurthala) in 1964. In 1970, my husband purchased land in Lakhimpur (U.P. ). In the riots that broke out after Indira Gandhi's assassination in 1984, we suffered a lot economically and could save our lives with great difficulty. We came to my parents house at village Budha Theh in 1984 itself. My husband took up a job as a labourer in the factory at Hamira.

I have three sons and one daughter namely Balwant Singh (24-25 yrs), Lakhwinder Singh (21 yrs), Kuldip Singh (17 yrs), and Manjit Kaur (27 yrs & married). My husband had no connection whatsoever with any sort of political or unlawful activities.

Sisters of my husband namely Gurbachan Kaur and Gurmit Kaur were married to Inder Singh s/o Lehna Singh and Ajit Singh s/o Lehna Singh (real brothers) r/o Vill. Khanpur Bhukhe (Kapurthala), respectively. They had been married off before my marriage.

In 1991, my sister-in-law's (Nanad's) son Balwinder Singh s/o Ajit Singh joined the militant ranks. That is why the Kapurthala police used to pick up family members of Ajit Singh and compel them to produce their absconding son Balwinder Singh. Due to excessive police harassment, Ajit Singh along with his family went underground and started living incognito at Batala (Gurdaspur). The family of one of the brothers of Ajit Singh, late Inder Singh, was residing in Lakhimpur district of U.P. As Ajit Singh and his family had gone underground, the Kapurthala police used to pick up his relatives, often.

In 1992, one day, ASI Tirath Singh of C.I.A Kapurthala and incharge of Police Post Fattu Dhinga raided village Budha Theh and picked up my husband Swaran Singh. The same party of Kapurthala police picked up Ajit Singh's brother-in-law (wife's sister's husband) Gurbachan Singh r/o Chakko Ki (Kapurthala) also. Both of them were kept in illegal custody for 40 days. Thereafter they were got released with political influence and intervention of the Panchayat.

A few days later, a police party of Beas police station led by Balkar Singh, DSP of Baba Bakala picked up my husband Swaran Singh. The police kept him in their illegal custody for 14 days and released him thereafter on their own.

On 3-1-93 at 11 P.M., a police party headed by Bhupinder Singh, DSP of Goindwal and including Kashmira Singh, SHO of Verowal police station, and ASI Baldev Singh raided my and my father Anokh Singh's house at village Budha Theh. The whole family were asleep at that time. The police scaled the walls and entered the house. On that day, myself, my sons Balwant Singh, Lakhwinder Singh, Kuldip Singh and my daughter Manjit Kaur were present in the house. The police put me in the Mini Bus along with my children. I saw that already my father Anokh Singh, brother Inderjit Singh, my mother Gurcharan Kaur (aged 60 years), my sister-in-law (bhabi) Palwinder Kaur had been put by the police in the same Bus. As the police departed along with all of us, my father Anokh Singh asked the police to inform the Sarpanch of the village, but, the police did not agree. The police took all of us to police station Verowal at 12 O' clock. There, male and female members of the family were segregated and locked up in separate rooms.

On the following day at about 11 A.M., our village panchayat along with eminent persons of nearby villages, in many tractor trollies, reached Verowal police station. My brother Inderjit Singh was an employee of Electricty Board. So, many members of the Employees Union also had accompanied the Panchayat of our village to the Verowal police station. DSP Bhupinder Singh and SHO Kashmira Singh misbehaved with the Panchayat and refused to release us.

When we had reached Verowal police station, I noticed that our following relatives were already detained there:-

Ajit Singh and his wife Gurmit Kaur, Kulwinder Singh and Lakhwinder Singh, sons of Ajit Singh, Raj Kaur daughter of Ajit Singh w/o Gursharan Singh along with her 13 day old child, Simarjit Kaur daughter of Ajit Singh along with her 1 month old child, Rajwant Kaur (15 yrs) w/o Iqbal Singh r/o Vill. Bamuwal (sister-in-law of Balwinder Kalia's elder brother), and Mohinder Kaur (Raj Kaur's mother-in-law).

On 4-1-93 at 8 A.M. myself and Ajit Singh were separated from others and made to sit in a Mini Bus in which policemen were seated already. Then the police told us that we were to be taken to U.P. from where they were to arrest Balwinder Singh Kalia. Four other police Gypsies in which DSP Bhupinder Singh and DSP Gurmit Singh Randhawa were seated, accompanied the bus. SHO Kashmira Singh and ASI Baldev Singh were seated in the same bus.

On 5-1-93 the police party along with us reached village Rahi, Tehsil Muhammadi, Distt. Lakhimpur (U.P) at 2 P.M. My father-in-law Labh Singh and mother-in-law Kapoor Kaur used to live there. My husband Swaran Singh also was there on that day. The police arrested Swaran Singh then and there and thrashed him very badly in the village itself. They were asking him about Balwinder Singh Kalia. But, my husband Swaran Singh told them that he did not know anything about his whereabouts. The police made my husband, father-in-law, and mother-in-law also to sit in the bus and took us to police station Mehkal Ganj. My father-in-law and mother-in-law were released at the police station. Swaran Singh was made to sit in the bus again and thereafter all of us were taken to Village Chappar Thalla, Tehsil Muhammadi, police station Mehkal Ganj, Distt. Lakhimpur. Ajit Singh's brother Inder Singh's family used to live there. From there the police arrested family members of Late Inder Singh namely Mangal Singh (son), Gurbachan Kaur (wife), Geja (son), and Phino (daughter). They took all of us to police station Mehkal Ganj. There, the police released my father-in-law and mother-in-law, Geja, and Phino and departed with the rest of us.

On 6-1-93 at about 10 A.M., the police reached police station Verowal along with all of us. There Mangal Singh s/o Late Inder Singh, and my husband Swaran Singh were tortured brutally. For the fist two three days, the police beat up Lakhwinder Singh (15 yrs), and Kulwinder Singh (12 yrs) very badly with 'Pattas' (Leather Belts).

For the first ten days, they used to take away Swaran Singh and Mangal Singh and torture them brutally. During this period, our village Panchayat used to come to the Verowal police station. The police used to allow Sarpanch (head of village council) Gurbachan Singh and other eminent persons to meet us.

ON 6-1-93 morning, the police released my children Balwant Singh, Lakhwinder Singh, Kuldip Singh, and Manjit Kaur as also my mother Gurcharan Kaur, sister-in-law (bhabi) Palwinder Kaur at the instance of the village Panchayat. Same day evening, they released my father Anokh Singh and brother Inderjit Singh also. We came to know that the male members of the family were shifted to Bhikhiwind police station the same day.

We, the female members of the family were detained at Bhikhiwind police station for three months. We were detained in the building adjacent to the office of DSP Paramjit Singh. 10-15 other women belonging to the families of militants were also detained there. They used to release some of them and bring in some others. The police used to torture some of the women, brutally. There, one day, on the plea of Gurmit Kaur, the police brought her son Kulwinder Singh from Khemkaran police station and let her meet him. They took Kulwinder Singh back the same day evening. It was in July end.

On 1-8-93, a news item was published regarding the killing of Balwinder Singh Kalia in an encounter with the Faridkot police near Moga. This was disclosed to us by Lady Police Constables in whose custody we were detained.

Now, myself, my husband Swaran Singh, Ajit Singh and his whole family, Mangal Singh, Gurbachan Kaur w/o Late Inder Singh, Rajwant Kaur w/o Iqbal Singh r/o Bamuwal were left there in the lock-up. We were total 11 members apart from two infants (aged 11 days and one month).

We were detained at Verowal police station continuously for four months. Sometimes they used to take us to Khadur Sahib. During this period, neither they beat us nor we were interrogated. Our village Sarpanch Gurbachan Singh and Avtar Singh (Ex-Sarpanch) used to come and meet us. They used to assure us that they were trying to get us released.

Thereafter, one day, all of us and some other people who had been arrested from different police stations, were put in a four wheeler by the police and taken to Khalra police station. Fifteen minutes later, myself and all other women were sent to Bhikhiwind police station. Later on, on 2-8-93, Gurmit Kaur and Jagir Kaur r/o village Khojkipur ('Maasi Saas' of Kalia) were taken out at 8 P.M. and whisked away. Before that, one day, Balwinder Singh Kalia's wife Gurpreet Kaur and another girl (sister-in-law i.e. wife's sister of militant Harjit Singh Khojkipur) had escaped from the police custody.

On 3-8-93, the police told us that they were going to release us. We were produced before DSP Paramjit Singh. The DSP told us that we were going to be released and asked as to who was going to pay for our food. Then the DSP told me to go and arrange for the payment for food @ Rs 1100/- per woman i.e. total Rs 7,700/-. I was released from Bhikhiwind police station. I took a bus and reached my parents house after informing the in-laws of Raj Kaur. I informed my father and arranged the money.

On 4-8-93 morning, myself, my father Anokh Singh, Sarpanch Gurbachan Singh, Ex-Sarpanch Avtar Singh reached Bhikhiwind police station. We met DSP Paramjit Singh there who directed the Munshi to receive the payment for food from us and release the women. It is worth mentioning here that the police charged us for the food for seven women, but, did not release Gurmit Kaur and Jagir Kaur. I requested DSP Paramjit Singh to release my husband Swaran Singh also. The DSP said that as we had been released, similarly, Swaran Singh and other men also would be released soon and advised us not to worry. We came back home.

After our release, we continued to meet DSP Paramjit Singh at the Bhikhiwind police station and insisted that Swaran Singh, Ajit Singh, Kulwinder Singh, Lakhwinder Singh, and Mangal Singh be released. Initially, the DSP told us that they had been sent to U.P. to facilitate the arrest of militant Harjit Singh Khojkipur and that they would release them soon. But, one month later, DSP Paramjit Singh told us that our men had been sent to Verowal police station. We along with the Panchayat met DSP Bhupinder Singh (at Verowal police station). He denied and said that our men had not come back to him. We met DSP Paramjit Singh again. He said that none of our men were in his custody. He had released them and he did not know about their whereabouts. When we met him at another time, he also said that we should sit quietly at home. We were not going to get any of our men. We should accept it (as our fate) and sit quietly at home. We should thank God for those who had survived.

Thereafter, we filed a case in High Court. DSP Bhupinder Singh approached Inspector Angrez Singh son of Sarpanch Gurbachan Singh and asked them to urge us to withdraw the case. Sarpanch Gurbachan Singh and Angrez Singh asked us to withdraw the case. We could not refuse them as we were indebted to that family. Dr. Pishaura Singh Ajnala and DSP Bhupinder Singh met Anokh Singh also. Thus, we withdrew the case from the High Court.

My brother-in-law ('Devar') Hardip Singh s/o Labh Singh had been sent to Lucknow along with four others as the U.P. police had registered a case against them. It was in 1993. He had been apprehended in 1992. Fifteen days later, he was killed in an encounter with the police at village Kot under Beas police station. Only Hardip Singh had been killed in that encounter. The Beas police got his dead body identified by his brother Swaran Singh. Hardip Singh was cremated at Amritsar. The family members collected his ashes clandestinely from Durgiana Mandir (Temple).

While Ajit Singh and his wife Gurmit Kaur were in police custody, they were taken to Batala by DSP Bhupinder Singh and an amount of

Rs 1,40,000/- which they had in their account there, was withdrawn by DSP Bhupinder Singh. This was disclosed to me by Gurmit Kaur while we were in police custody.

On 28/29 December 1992, Ajit Singh, Gurmit Kaur, Kulwinder Singh, and Lakhwinder Singh had been arrested from their rented house at Batala (near railway station). The police had plundered the house and took away all household items. At that time only, the police could lay their hands on their pass books. This family was got arrested by the family members of militant Harjit Singh Khojkipur, because they knew the place of residence of these people. After arresting them, the police arrested Raj Kaur from Sham Nagar (near Majitha) and Simarjit Kaur from village Kulia (near Batala), on 2-1-93. Raj Kaur's mother-in-law also had been arrested.

Once, Nirmal Singh (son of Ajit Singh) also had been arrested by ASI Tirath Singh. He was tortured brutally in custody for two and a half months. He had been arrested from Batala while he was driving a truck. Nirmal Singh is married. He has gone underground. Nirmal Singh does not want to file a case due to fear.

Third brother of Ajit Singh was Mohinder Singh (handicapped) who has since expired. Fourth brother of Ajit Singh was a Nambardar. However, his family was not harassed by the police. He has also since expired.

### VFF/0657

Hardip Singh alias Deepa 35 of Bhudha Theh in Kapurthala. Hardip Singh was killed in an encounter with the police at village Kot, near Beas, in December 1992.

The following information which gives some more details about this incident, is available in Proforma No. 858, which pertains to the disappeared victim Gurmit Kaur, sister of Hardip Singh. This proforma as well as the following Six proformae are sent by the same person i.e. Sukhwinder Kaur w/o Swaran Singh s/o Labh Singh who is related to this as well as the following six victims. Sukhwinder Kaur is sister-in-law (Bhabi) of the victim Hardip Singh.

My brother-in-law ('Devar') Hardip Singh s/o Labh Singh had been sent to Lucknow along with four others as the U.P. police had registered a case against them. It was in 1993. He had been apprehended in 1992. Fifteen days later, he was killed in an encounter with the police at village Kot under Beas police station. Only Hardip Singh had been killed in that encounter. The Beas police got his dead body identified by his brother Swaran Singh. Hardip Singh was cremated at Amritsar.

The family members collected his ashes clandestinely from Durgiana Mandir (Temple).

**VFF/0658**

Pritam Singh 18 of Fattu Dhinga in Kapurthala. On 1-6-1984, Pritam Singh had gone to pay his obeisance at Sri Darbar Sahib (Golden Temple) Amritsar. It is suspected that he was killed by the para-military forces during Operation Blue Star from 4 to 6 June 1984.

**VFF/0659**

Anup Singh alias Baba 25 of Kassochahal in Kapurthala. In the words of his mother, "I had two sons namely Anup Singh (25 yrs) and Ravinder Singh (29 yrs). Anup Singh was a student of Randhir College, Kapurthala. There he began to take active part in the activities of Sikh Students Federation in 1985-86. Due to his activities in the Federation, SHO Pooran Singh of Kapurthala (Sadar) police station used to arrest him often. They used to detain him in custody for days together. Many times, he was implicated in cases by the police and sent to jail. He used to get released on bail. The police used to start raiding our house again for arresting him.

On 13-9-1989 at about 5.30 P.M., Head Constable Gurnam Singh and Constable Paramjit Singh, riding on a Motor Cycle No..........503 came to our house. At that time, my brother Sukhjinder Singh, my sister-in-law Lakhbir Kaur, my wife Daljit Kaur, and myself were present in the house. They told that the SSP had called Anup Singh for questioning and after that they would drop him back soon. They took away Anup Singh on their Motor Cycle.

Same day, myself and my brother Sukhjinder Singh went to the Sadar police station and met the SHO Pooran Singh. He said that Anup Singh was there only but only the SSP would release him.

On the following day, we along with eminent persons of the village met the SSP Swaran Singh Ghotna. He asked us to wait outside and talked to Pooran Singh. After some time, we again met the SSP, but, he did not listen to us at all and asked us to go back.

Thereafter, a call for a Bandh in Kapurthala City was given. Former Akali Minister Sukhjinder, Singh sat on hunger strike at Safed Gurdwara, for many days. A lot of hue and cry was raised about this arrest in the newspapers. However, the police did not divulge any information about this incident. We submitted written representations also to Senior Officers about this incident.

At that time, a police inquiry was got conducted into this incident but we did not get justice at all.

Thereafter, we filed a case in the High Court. The High Court marked an inquiry to DIG Jalandhar Range which was conducted in 1997. The police got the statements of many of their supporters made in their favour, but, the Sarpanches submitted affidavits in our favour."

### VFF/0660

Kashmir Singh 28 of house number 1, Ajit Nagar in Kapurthala. In the words of his father, "on 4-7-1992 at 10 A.M., two policemen namely Head Constable Jeet Singh, and Constable Manohar Lal of Kapurthala (Sadar) police station came to our house. Kashmir Singh also was at home at that time. They told that somebody had submitted a complaint against Kashmir Singh and that he was to be taken to Kapurthala (Sadar) police station for questioning in that connection. Despite our protests, they made Kashmir Singh to sit on the Motorcycle and told us to come to the police station. This incident was witnessed by the people standing at my neighbour's shop, also.

Immediately, I along with Jagir Singh s/o Karnail Singh, Balwinder Singh s/o Lal Singh, and some other persons went to the Sadar police station and met the Munshi (Clerk) there. He told that they did not know anything about him and asked us to come later and find out. While coming out of the gate, we met Head Constable Jeet Singh and Constable Manohar Lal. We asked them and they asked us to come at 4 P.M. and find out.

I reached Sadar police station at 4 P.M. along with the above mentioned respectable persons. Both the above mentioned policemen met me outside the police station. They demanded Rs. 50,000/- from me. I said O.K. But, instead of paying them the money we contacted the SSP Sh. N.K. Tiwari. He asked us to come on the following day and find out.

We went on the following day. Then again the SSP told us to come some other time. Like this, the SSP dodged us 2-3 times. When I met the SSP for the last time, he threatened me saying, "Shall we detain you also." I got frightened on hearing this and did not contact the SSP again. Like this, 7-8 days passed.

Thereafter, we submitted several written representations to Senior Officers but nobody listened to us."

### VFF/0661

Shingara Singh 38 of Booh, Fattu Dhinga in Kapurthala. He was killed during Operation Blue Star at Sri Darbar Sahib, Amritsar, on 6th June 1984.

### VFF/0662

Jagjit Singh alias Boola 22 of Booh, Fattu Dhinga in Kapurthala. He was killed during Operation Blue Star at Sri Darbar Sahib, Amritsar, on 6th June 1984.

**VFF/0663**

Mohan Singh 40 of Fattu Dhinga in Kapurthala. He was killed on 6th June 1984 at Sri Darbar Sahib, Amritsar, during Operation Blue Star.

**VFF/0664**

Kulwant Singh 22 of Booh, Fattu Dhinga in Kapurthala. According to his mother, "it happened about 5-6 years ago i.e. in 1992-93. Somebody told us that my son had been arrested by Phagwara Sadar Police. Sarpanch of our village had also told us that Phagwara Police had killed him, in an encounter. We met the SHO. He showed us his clothes and chappal(slippers)."

**VFF/0665**

Darbara Singh alias Bara 21 of Khukhrain in Kapurthala. In the words of his father, "on 17-9-91 at 8 A.M., Darbara Singh had gone to Kapurthala on his Scooter....... 4590 Bajaj Chetak Blue colour (which was registered at Kapurthala in his own name) for selling milk, as usual. Usually he used to come back home by 12 Noon and take the milk to Kapurthala again at 4 P.M. But, that day, he did not rteturn home even by 4 P.M.

I went to Kapurthala and enquired at the Dairy shop where he used to deliver the milk. They told me that he had got the cream extracted and went away. Then I enquired at the house of Bawa Singh where also he used to deliver the milk. He told me that as soon as my son had delivered the milk at his house, the police surrounded their house and questioned them about their relations with Darbara Singh. They told the police that he used to deliver the milk at their house and that apart from that they did not have anything to do with him. On hearing this from Bawa Singh, I suspected that the police had arrested my son. Another reason for my suspicion was that on the same day at 11 A.M., the police had arrested three other boys from our village. They were Satnam Singh s/o Baghel Singh, Lakhbir Singh s/o Sardul Singh, and Lakha Singh s/o Jarnail Singh. I returned to my village and informed my family members, the panchayat and other prominent citizens of the village about this incident. It was dark by now. So, we decided to find out the next day morning.

On the next day morning, I along with my son Atar Singh, wife Jagir Kaur, and next-of-kin of other boys reached C.I.A. Staff Kapurthala. But, neither we were allowed to meet any officer there nor anything was disclosed about the whereabouts of our sons. We got exhausted and came back home in the evening.

On the following day, we along with Jagir Singh Wadala (Akali leader) appeared before the SSP Jasminder Singh. There was an altercation between Jagir Singh Wadala and the SSP. As such, the SSP did not disclose anything about the whereabouts of our sons.

Next day again, I and my wife Jagir Kaur met the SSP Jasminder Singh. He told us that they would release our son on the third day. He said that they had been thrashed in excess. So, we should wait for one or two days.

I met the SSP again on the promised day. He said that he had made a promise to me by mistake and that actually they had not picked up my son at all. I got dejected and returned home.

In the meantime, I met DSP Pritpal Singh at his office at the C.I.A Staff Kapurthala. He flatly denied having picked up my son.

One and a half months after the incident, I along with my son Nirmal Singh, Sewa Singh (maternal grand father of Lakhbir Singh), Surjit Kaur (Satnam Singh's mother) went to Jalandhar and met the DIG Jalandhar Range Sh. Bhullar at his office. Just then DSP (who had replaced Pritpal Singh) incharge of Kapurthala C.I.A Staff also reached there. The DIG directed the DSP to release our sons. The DSP asked us to reach C.I.A. Kaputhala at 4 P.M. on the following day.

On the following day, all of us reached C.I.A Staff Kapurthala and met the DSP. He asked us to wait upto 5 P.M. saying that they would release our sons. At 6 P.M. we met the DSP again. He said that he had promised to release our sons in front of the DIG, by mistake. He further told us that he had enquired and found that our sons were not detained at any of the police stations of Kapurthala.

Next day we again met the DIG Jalandhar Range Sh. Bhullar who asked us to find out after a few days so that in the meantime he would make enquiries and find out.

But, so far, the whereabouts of our son are not known."

**VFF/0666**

Mangal Singh alias Manga 25 of Lakhan Ke Padde, Subhanpur in Kappurthala. In the words of his father, "after his release from jail, Mangal Singh started living at home. In the meantime, the police continued to make rounds of our house. On 15 August, 26 January or some other occasions, the police used to pick him up and release him after keeping him in custody for one or two days. After about one year, the Subhan Pur police arrested Mangal Singh. After keeping him in illegal custody for a few days, they registered three cases against him and sent him to Nabha jail. He got released on bail from there after 6-7 months.

After his release from jail, he took up a job with Pepsi Company at Husainpur. He used to live there itself and used to visit home at an interval of 10-12 days. By that time, Mangal Singh had been acquitted in all the cases against him except the one relating to Subhan Pur police station u/s 399/402 IPC. This case was sub-judice at Special Court at Kapurthala and Mangal Singh used to be present on all the hearings.

On 2 June 1992 at about 3 P.M., when Mangal Singh was working at the farm-house of Pepsi company at Husainpur, SHO Mangat Rai of Kapurthala (Sadar) P.S. raided the farm-house and picked up Mangal Singh. At that time, Balwinder Singh (Police Tout) r/o Sandal Jagir was also with the police party.

We received the news of Mangal Singh's arrest after five days, from Pritam Singh r/o village Surkhpur (Kapurthala) when he visited our house to convey this to us. Balkar Singh is an eyewitness to the arrest of Mangal Singh because he was also on duty at that time.

On the following day of receiving the news, I along with the village Panchayat met Balwinder Singh (Police Tout). He flatly denied. I along with the village Panchayat comprising of Sarpanch Mohinder Singh, Master Harbans Singh, Jagir Singh s/o Arjan Singh r/o Surkhpur and several others met SHO Mangat Rai several times and each time he made a false promise of releasing Mangal Singh. However, finally he denied having picked him up. He said he did not know and that he never picked him up. In the meantime, on 7-8-92, I submitted an application attested by the village Sarpanch, to the MLA (Member Legislative Assembly) of our area and Panchayat members met the MLA personally also. The MLA met the SSP in this connection.

I submitted applications to the SSP and Deputy Commissioner also. Mangal Singh's Lawyer S. Harjit Singh Sandhu submitted an application in the Special Court of Additional Sessions Judge Sh. A.K. Aggarwal where a case against Mangal Singh was sub-judice u/s 307 IPC of P.S. Subhan Pur, intimating the Court of Mangal Singh's arrest by SHO Mangat Rai of Kapurthala (Sadar) police station. This was done so that the Court may not issue arrest warrants against him due to his being absent during the hearing of the said case. Despite my repeateed visits to the offices of the Senior Officers, the whereabouts of Mangal Singh are not known, till today."

**VFF/0667**

Lakhbir Singh alias Lakha 30 of Khukhrain in Kapurthala. In the words of his his mother, "I got married to Sardul Singh s/o Pooran Singh r/o Patti in Distt. Amritsar, three years before Partition of India. Two children, one boy and a girl were born out of this wedlock. The boy is Lakhbir Singh.

5-7 years after our marriage, relations between me and my husband were strained. So, I came over to my father Sewa Singh's house along with my son Lakhbir Singh here in Village Khukhrain, Distt. Kapurthala. My daughter stayed with my husband. Later on, my husband married some other woman and since then I am living here in my father's house only.

My son Lakhbir Singh used to cultivate my father Sewa Singh's land and we were pulling on with the income from that. In the year 1990 (I don't remember the month) C.I.A Staff Kapurthala raided our house and enquired about Lakhbir Singh. But, Lakhbir Singh was not at home at that time. Lakhbir Singh got scared and went away to a relative's place at Bombay. He stayed there for six months. In the meantime, the police used to raid our house and ask us to produce Lakhbir Singh. Six months later, we called Lakhbir Singh back from Bombay and produced him at the C.I.A Staff Kapurthala through Chaudhary Pishaura Singh Advocate. The police questioned Lakhbir Singh and let him off the same day. Thereafter, the police never raided our house.

On 17-9-91, at about 10 A.M., Lakha Singh s/o Jarnail Singh came to our house and called Lakhbir Singh. They told us that they were going to the house of Sarban Singh (Mazhabi Sikh). At about 11 A.M., someone came to our house and informed us that the police had raided Sarban Singh's house and that my son also had been rounded up and they were taking him away. Myself and my father rushed to Sarban Singh's house. By that time, other villagers also had assembled there. The police had put my son Lakhbir Singh, Satnam Singh s/o Baghel Singh, and Lakha Singh s/o Jarnail Singh in their vehicle. The police party was led by DSP Pritpal Singh. Head Constable Chiman Lal was also there. Other policemen were not known to me. Just as we reached there, the police started their vehicle and went away.

After the police had gone, I came to know that all these three boys along with Sarban Singh were drinking Liqour and eating eggs. I also came to know that Satnam Singh also had been called from his house by Lakha Singh s/o Jarnail Singh. We got suspicious that my son and Satnam Singh had been got arrested by Lakha Singh s/o Jarnail Singh by enacting a drama.

Same day, my father Sewa Singh along with Surjit Kaur, mother of Satnam Singh, village panchayat (council) and other prominent persons of the village went to C.I.A Staff Kapurthala. But the police did not listen to them and all of them returned home."

**VFF/0668**

Inderjit Singh 23 of Dogranwala in Kapurthala. In the words of his father, "On 8 August 1992, Inderjit Singh went to the city for selling milk as usual. But he did not return home in the evening. I had gone out somewhere that day. On my return I came to know that Inderjit Singh had not returned home. Same night at 12 O'clock, Kapurthala (Kotwali) police raided our house and picked up myself, my sons Nirmal Singh, Jagir Singh , and my son-in-law Balwinder Singh and took all of us to police station Kapurthala (Kotwali). The Kotwali police informed us that my son Inderjit Singh had been killed in an encounter by the Kapurthala (Sadar) police. Two hours later, the Kotwali police dropped all of us at Sadar police station. There, the SHO Amrik Singh Chahal got my sons Nirmal Singh and Jagir Singh tortured. He said that we were in possession of robbed money and arms. But we denied the allegation.

On the following day, our village panchayat and eminent persons of several other villages met the Senior Officers. As a result, the police handed over his dead body to us for cremation and brought all of us to the cremation ground. The police released my son-in-law Balwinder Singh at the intervention of the panchayat and took all of us back to Sadar police station.

We were detained illegally at the Sadar police station for 13-14 days. Thereafter, myself and Nirmal Singh were released but Jagir Singh was released two days later. We were released due to the pressure by the panchayat. The police told us that we were detained in order to prevent us from raising our voice against the murder of Inderjit Singh.

After our release, we enquired from the people at the Taxi Stand. They told us that Inderjit Singh was abducted at 6 P.M. by the uniformed police from the Chungi near the Bus Stand. We also came to know that a few minutes before this incident, a boy had come and talked to Inderjit Singh. Later, the same boy came with the police and the police bundled Inderjit Singh into their vehicle.

We firmly believe that this action was the handiwork of some persons who are inimical towards our family. They are Ranjit Singh (former Sarpanch of our village) and Sucha Singh (Nambardar). We came to know from some reliable sources that they had paid Rs 90,000/- to the police to get Inderjit Singh killed. We also came to know that the boy who had talked to Inderjit Singh before he was abducted was Amrik Singh son of Sucha Singh.

The police extorted Rs 70,000/- for our release. This amount was paid by our relatives to ASI Mangat Rai for getting us released."

**VFF/0669**

Gurjant Singh alias Janta 20 of Jattan Wala in Zira. Mohinder Kaur, widow of Late S. Lal Singh, had four sons and one daughter. Gurjant Singh was Mohinder Kaur's youngest son. After passing his Matric exam. Gurjant Singh set up a Furniture shop at Mallanwala Town.

In August (Date not known), one day, Makhu police raided Mohinder Kaur's house and enquired about Gurjant Singh. But, Gurjant Singh was not at home at that time. The police directed Mohinder Kaur to produce her son at the Makhu police station. When Gurjant Singh came to know that the police were looking for him, he went underground. In the meantime, SHO Joginder Pal Sharma of Makhu police began to raid his house. The police picked up Ajmer Singh, brother of Gurjant Singh twice. They used to pressurise them to produce Gurjant Singh whereas the family members maintained that he had run away from home due to their (police) fear and that they did not know about his whereabouts. They used to keep him (Ajmer Singh) in their custody for several days.

During this period, once, the Ludhiana Police picked up Joga Singh, one of the brothers of Gurjant Singh, from his residence at Ludhiana City and detained him for 10 days. The police began to raid the houses of Mohinder Kaur's relatives also. Once, the Ludhiana police took Mohinder Kaur also along with Joga Singh in their custody.

The above mentioned members of his family were still in police custody when the Zira police arrested Gurjant Singh in October 1992 from the shop of his relative Baldev Singh resident of Vil Vakeel. Baldev Singh informed Gurjant Singh's brother Ajmer Singh about this incident, same day. On the following day, Ajmer Singh along with his maternal uncle Inder Singh, approached an Akali leader Harpal Singh Bhullar for pursuing the case of Gurjant Singh. But, Bhullar was not available at home. Then the family membrs along with the Panchayat and eminent persons of the village, met the SHO of Zira police station. The SHO admitted that Gurjant Singh was in their custody. However, he did not agree to release Gurjant Singh. According to Ajmer Singh, they negotiated with the SHO through a middle man. The SHO demanded Rs. 70,000/- but it was beyond their means to pay such a huge amount. Ajmer Singh and other family members used to go to the police station along with the Panchayat, daily.

On the fourth day of his arrest, when the family members along with the Panchayat went to Zira police station, they came to know that the police had killed Gurjant Singh the previous night in a false encounter at the bank of the canal at village Mallu Ke under P.S. Zira and that they had taken his body for cremation at cremation ground of Zira. The police had already cremated his body when the family members and the Panchayat reached the cremation ground. On the following day, family members and the Panchayat collected his ashes from the cremation ground.

* On the day following the "encounter", the police had picked up Inder Singh, maternal uncle of Gurjant Singh and got his dead body identified from him. Inder Singh was released after detaining him for three days.

* All the above information was given by Ajmer Singh, brother of Gurjant Singh. However, he did not rememeber the date of the arrest of Gurjant Singh and the name of the SHO of Zira P.S. May be, his maternal uncle or some other member of the family knows all this.

### VFF/0670

Sadhu Singh 37 of Phoolewala, Bagha Purana in Moga. On 18-6-87 at 11 A.M., he was picked up along with three other persons while he was working in his fields. The names of the other three persons picked up along with him are:-

1.  Kala Singh s/o Mall Singh
2.  Harbans Singh s/o Nirpal Singh
3.  Nirpal Singh Dhaliwal

However, the above named three persons were released later.

Note:-     As per his application (PCHR-0186) submitted to the People's Commission, the date of abduction has been mentioned as 18-7-87.

### VFF/0671

Chamkaur Singh alias Kauri 23 of Rode, Bagha Purana in Moga. On 10 April 1993, his mother Jagir Kaur and sister-in-law (Bhabi) Bhupinder Kaur were picked up alongwith two small children (aged 2 and 3 years) by C.I.A Staff Faridkot. They were beaten up and teeth of his mother were broken. On 19 April 1993 Chamkaur Singh appeared before DSP Harbans Singh through Havaldar Daljit Singh (of Badhni Kalan Police Post). On 18 April 1993, we were told by Daljit Singh that he (Chamkaur Singh) is going to surrender himself tomorrow. His mother met Chamkaur at the residence of Harbans Singh on 18 April 1993 and stayed there for the night. On 21 April 1993, he surrendered himself through DSP Harbans Singh and Havaldar Daljit Singh. His father was also brought there. On 21 April, both mother and father met Chamkaur at the residence of Harbans Singh. Therafter they met him at C.I.A Faridkot on 23 April 1993. After that, they used to meet him at C.I.A Staff Faridkot till 11 June 1993 when he was produced in Court.

On 12 June, he was again produced in the same court. On 13, 14, and 15 June they met him at Kotkapoora Sadar Police Station. After 15 June, they did not meet him. On 18 June 1993, a news item was published in newspapers that a militant namely Chamkaur Singh was killed/escaped when the Police was taking him for the recovery of arms and the Police party was ambushed by some militants.

### VFF/0672

Jang Singh 57 of Nathewala, Bagha Purana in Moga. Mukhtiar Kaur (widow of the victim Jang Singh) had three sons and one daughter. One of her sons, namely Varinder Singh was killed in an encounter with the Police and later on, the Police abducted her husband Jang Singh whose whereabouts are not known till today. Her daughter Sarbjit Kaur died due to illness.

Her eldest son Varinder Singh was active in the Sikh Students Federation since 1987. That is why the Police used to arrest him often. The Police had arrested him and registered cases against him on two different occasions. He was incarcerated in Faridkot Jail for about two years. The family members do not remember the dates of his detention in the Jail. After his release from Jail he stayed at home for 8-9 months. The Police had started harassing him again. They used to pick him up and torture him. As such, he deserted home and joined the ranks of the militants, once for all.

On 31-12-1990, Varinder Singh was killed in an encounter with the Police near VIllage Daulatpura Kalia Wala in district Ferozepur. The Police could not lay their hands on his dead body. His accomplices handed over his dead bpdy to his family members at his house on the following day. The family members cremated his dead body. The Police got a scent of it. As a consequence his family became a victim of Police wrath. The Police picked up his mother Mukhtiar Kaur, father Jang Singh and both the brothers and subjected them to brutal torture.

Mukhtiar kaur husband Jang Singh was a religious minded person. In those days, Jang Singh had joined the 'Panj Pyaras' and used to perform the duty of baptising ('Amrit Chhakana') the people. That is why Jang Singh also was a susepct in the eyes of the Police.

On 24-6-92, the Police had cordoned off village Pehla. The police identified Jang Singh particulary. Later, they made several rounds of the village in civil dress. Two policemen in civil dress came to his house and enquired about Jang Singh. Just then, Jang Singh was seen coming from the village side. Some other policemen who were waiting in a Maruti car followed Jang Singh in their car. They started pushing Jang Singh into their car. Jang Singh told his wife that the police were taking him away forcibly and that she should collect his purse and watch from him. On being asked as to where they were taking him, policemen replied that they would release him soon. There were Arms & Ammunition also inside the car. The car in question was seen speeding away towards Faridkot. The policemen who abducted Jang Singh were the body guards of the then SSP Faridkot, Jasminder Singh. One of them was later identified as Paramjit Singh by Mukhtiar Kaur. Paramjit Singh was seen in civil dress at the residence (Kothi) of SSP Faridkot (Jasminder Singh) by Mukhtiar Kaur when she had gone there to plead for the release of Jang Singh. At first, Paramjit Singh got nervous. Then he told Mukhtiar Kaur to see the SSP Faridkot. Initially, SSP Faridkot tried to put her off regarding Jang Singh, but later he said to Mukhtiar Kaur w/o Jang Singh,"O you, who offers milk to the offspring of Snakes, from where would you get your man (Jang Singh) now itself" i.e. in his opinion, Mukhtiar Kaur was a woman who offered milk to the little ones of Snakes thereby implying that she was nurturing those who were secessionists and thus enemies of Society. And that she did not deserve to get her man (husband Jang Singh) back. Since then, whereabouts of Jang Singh are not known.

### VFF/0673

Jagan Singh 40 of Talwandi Bhangarian in Moga. In the words of Amrit Kaur, wife of Jagan Singh, as narrated to Amrik Singh Muktsar in Punjabi. The true translation of the same is as follows:-

After the Army attack on Sri Darbar Sahib on 6 June, 1984, the B.S.F. (Border Security Force) and the Army surrounded our village on 7 June, 1984 in the morning. As the Army entered the village, some people pelted stones at them, in protest. The Army retaliated with firing and called for reinforcements. After surrounding the whole village, they collected all the male members of the village in an open space and they took me also there. While collecting the villagers, the Army beat them up severely with rifle butts and shoes. All the people were made to sit in the open till evening. In the evening the Army rounded up 16-17 persons and took them away. The Army authorities threatened me and asked me about the whereabouts of my husband Jagan Singh. I told them that he was at his brother's house at village Fatehgarh Bhatte. The Army took me in their vehicle to village Bhatte. Jagan Singh was sipping tea there. Hari Singh (brother), Soma (sister-in-law) and Lajwanti (mother) were also sitting there. They caught hold of Jagan Singh and tied his hands at his back. They pushed him in their vehicle at the rear side and made me to sit in the front side. I was pushed out of the vehicle at my village and they proceeded further. When the Army vehicle passed by the place where all the villagers had been assembled, the people saw that

Jagan Singh was lying on the floor of the vehicle and Army jawans were sitting over him. Surjan Singh, brother of Jagan Singh was also among the villagers who had been taken into custody by the Army. These 15-16 persons who had been taken into custody were detained for a day at local Army Headquarters at Khosa road and beaten up severely. On the following day, they were handed over to City Police and on the third day cases were registered against them and they were sent to jail.

Jagan Singh was detained separately from the other arrested persons. Next day, the Army authorities and the Police informed the villagers and the family members that Jagan Singh had died due to heart attack. The Army took me and Lajwanti (mother) in their vehicle and the villagers recahed local Army Headquarters at Khosa road in tractor trollies. The Officers told the prominent villagers viz. Gurnam Singh (Member Panchayat), Swaran Singh (Member Panchayat), Sukhdev Singh and Naib Singh etc. that if they intended to initiate any legal action then they won't hand over the dead body and if they won't initiate any legal action, then they could take the body. The family members agreed not to initiate any legal action. They obtained our signatures on blank papers. They handed over the body after obtaining the signatures of myself (wife), mother and father apart from those of Panchayat members. An Army vehicle accompanied the body. The body was in a very bad condition. There were injury marks all over his body. It seemed as if he had been dragged after tying him to something (vehicle etc.). The villagers and the family members did not give a bath also to the body as the Army authorities insisted on cremating the body at the earliest. After the cremation, the Army authorities went away. Thereafter also, the Army men continued to visit our house for many days. They used to threaten us but at the same time they used to sympathise with us saying that "We had killed him by mistake." The Army officers who used to visit our house in those days, assured me of help also. On one or two occasions the Army officers supplied ration items also for the household. However, thereafter, nobody has bothered about me.

I am a poor woman. We were totally dependent on my husband. After his death, I brought up my family by doing manual labour. I was not even issued with a death certificate in respect of my husband due to which I could not get family pension for five years. I succeeded in getting the family pension after struggling for 5-6 years.

**VFF/0674**

Ranjit Singh alias Joga 24 of Jogewal in Moga. Ranjit Singh had got himself baptised after 1984 and he used to take an active part in the ongoing political and religious movement in the Punjab. Due to his activities, the Police started raiding his house with a view to arrest him, in 1986. He went underground. In those days, he used to run a tyre repair shop at Ghall Kalan. As Ranjit Singh had gone underground, his family became a victim of Police wrath. The Moga (Sadar) Police arrested his father Dhanna Singh (since expired), Nirmal Singh, Preetam Singh and Baldev Singh, registered cases under TADA against them and sent them to jail. Often, the Police used to arrest other family members also and detain them in illegal custody for days together.

In 1990, the Faridkot Police arrested Ranjit Singh from Mari Mustafa. They detained him illegally for 10-12 days, registered several cases against him and sent him to jail. He was relaesed from jail in April-May 1993. In the beginning of July, he was arrested by Sadiq Police from his sister's house at village Dudd where he had gone to meet her.

According to his brother Preetam Singh, in July 1993, one evening, Ranjit Singh had gone on a scooter to meet his sister at village Dudd. He was stopped by Kirpal Singh, SHO of Police Station Sadiq at the Naka (Barrier) of village Dudd and arrested. However, the residents of village Dudd intervened immediately and the SHO released Ranjit Singh. But, on the following day morning, the Sadiq Police arrested Ranjit Singh from his sister's house. His family members tried their level best to get him released but they were helpless. They came to know that Ranjit Singh was in the custody of senior Police officers of Faridkot Police. So, they met SSP Tiwari and SP (Operations) Ania Gautam. But, the abovementioned Police officers denied his custody, flatly.

In the beginning of the month of July, Ranjit Singh was seen in custody at a secret interrogation centre of Faridkot Police (situated at the Headquarters of the CRPF), by Amrik Singh Muktsar who was also in the illegal custody of Faridkot Police. Ranjit Singh was detained at the abovementioned torture centre for about a week where SSP Tiwari, SP (Ops.) Ania Gautam and Bachan Singh Buchar of the C.I.A Staff used to interrogate him. One evening, the Police took out Ranjit Singh from the abovementioned torture centre. There was no news about him thereafter.

Ranjit Singh's brother Preetam Singh said that later on they had got information that the Police had killed Ranjit Singh in a fake encounter in Muktsar area and declared him as an unidentified (militant).

According to Preetam Singh, after the situation had improved, he filed a case in the Punjab and Haryana High Court, in 1996-97 about the disappearance of Ranjit Singh. His Advocate was Daljit Singh Rajput. However, the High Court dismissed their case. Preetam Singh said that their Advocate connived with the Police and did not pursue their case properly. He said that he did not have the case papers with him but he would try to get the papers from his Advocate and despatch the same to the Committee's office.

Note: In the abovementioned case, Paramjit Singh Brar was Advocate from the Police side. Harshinder Singh may be asked to procure the papers of the above case from Paramjit Singh Brar.

**VFF/0675**

Paramjit Singh alias Pamma 20 of Phoolewal in Moga. In 1986-87, some unidentified person had got puncture of his vehicle repaired from the shop of Paramjit Singh at Talwandi Sabo. The Police arrested him and questioned about that unknown person as to who he was. Paramjit expressed his ignorance as he did not know that person. He was detained at the Talwandi Sabo Police Station by SHO Dharma Singh for 28 days. After that, he was seen at Bathinda Jail by his mother and brother. Later, he was shown to have been killed in an encounter with the Police at village Maujian. A news item along with his photograph had appearaed in the newspapers.

**VFF/0676**

Prabhjit Singh alias Prabha 23 Phoolewal in Moga. In February 1992, at 7 A.M., he was going to take bath when he was called out by the Police from the bathroom and taken away. It was the Punjab Police with caps on their heads.

**VFF/0677**

Satwant Singh 35 of Sodhian Da Mohalla in Moga. Victim Satwant Singh's mother Resham Kaur, aged 65-70 years lives with her younger son Charanjit Singh at village Chugawan. She had four sons and two daughters. Satwant Singh was the eldest. Her husband Sunder Singh used to live at home after his retirement from service in Railway Police. He expired in 1991. At the time of his death, his son Satwant Singh had been lodged in Moga jail. Satwant Singh was active in Sikh Students Federation since 1984. According to his mother Resham Kaur, since 1984, he was arrested by the police numerous times and several cases had been registered against him. As Resham Kaur is illiterate, she cannot tell about the dates etc. when Satwant Singh was arrested or what all the cases were registered against him. She says that whenever Satwant Singh used to be not available at home, the police used to pick up his father and that they used to produce Satwant Singh before the police, later. The sequence of events, as narrated by her, is as given below:-

"On 25-9-93 (seventh year has begun since Satwant Singh disappeared. Hence the year 1993) at 5 AM, he (Satwant Singh) went out along with another youth of our village namely Hardeep Singh. While going he said, "I am going somewhere in connection with some job." He did not return home that night. On the next day morning I enquired at the house of Hardeep Singh. His father Bikkar Singh told that the police had arrested Hardeep Singh and Satwant Singh at a Naka (barrier) near village Rode. Bikkar Singh further told me that this information was given to him by the driver of the Maruti Van from which they were arrested. The driver had further told Bikkar Singh that both of them were lodged at C.I.A. (Criminal Investigation Agency) Staff Moga. I tried my best to locate him and visited police station Moga (City) twice but they did not give me any information at all. As I was a poor woman, nobody listened to me. I visited C.I.A. Staff also but there also nobody listened to me. On the contrary, Mehna police began raiding our house. They used to enquire about my son Satwant Singh. Fed up with the repeated police raids, one day I said to the police officer, "You only have disappeared my son and now you are harassing us. Better, you shoot me." After seeing this reaction of mine, the police stopped raiding our house.

"One month later, the family members of Hardeep Singh got him released from police station Nihalsingh Wala. He handed over Satwant Singh's watch, an underwear and three hundrred rupees to me and told that the same were given to him by the police. Hardeep Singh further told me that they had taken away Satwant Singh, after blindfolding him."

When the Investigation team led by me (Amrik Singh Muktsar) tried to find out more details about this (Satwant Singh's) arrest, she said, "Son, I am a poor woman. Who listened to me? Hardeep Singh was got released by the village Panchayat (Council). But nobody listened to this poor woman. Hardeep Singh also did not tell me properly as to what had happened to Satwant Singh." According to Resham Kaur, more details about this case can be had only from Hardeep Singh or the driver of the Maruti Van from which Satwant Singh, Hardeep Singh and the driver had been arrested. They only could give the names of the police officers. You ask them. Who would tell this poor woman." But, Hardeep Singh visits his village rarely only these days. As per the villagers, he is living at village Barbari. The driver's name is not known to Resham Kaur.

According to Resham Kaur, Hardeep Singh was a co-accused also along with Satwant Singh in a case. She told that after the disappearance of Satwant Singh, she told the Judge at Moga court that her son had been arrested by the police. At this, the Judge told her to go home. She does not remember as to in which court the said case was sub-judice and what was its current status.

**VFF/0678**

Manna Singh 24 of Nathewala, Bagha Purana in Moga. On 16 August 1992 at 11 A.M., Manna Singh was spraying (pesticide) in the fields of Boota Singh s/o Lakha Singh. Two persons on a scooter approached him and asked him to accompany them to see their fields as they also wanted to get the spraying done in their fields. At the Dhulkot bridge, they put him in a vehicle and drove away. One of the scooter borne persons was Bahla Singh r/o Booian Wala (Zira) Distt. Ferozepur and the other was unidentified. Bahla Singh is a Police 'Cat' who had spread terror in the area.

**VFF/0679**

Gurdeep Singh 40 of Saido Ke, Langar Patti, Nihal Singh Wala in Moga. Gurdeep Singh was an ordinary farmer and was engaged in agricultural farming. He had no link whatsoever with any sort of political or militant activities. His brother-in-law (wife's brother) Sher Singh resident of Gumti was a renowned militant. According to family members, they had no liaison with Sher Singh.

On 29-2-1992 at about 1 A.M., 6-7 Policemen entered inside his house. As the door had not been shut, the Policemen came straightaway inside. The Policemen woke up the family members and enquired about Gurdeep Singh. As Gurdeep Singh disclosed his identity, the Policemen directed him to come along with them. Gurdeep Singh's parents, wife and children were present in the house at that time. The abovementioned Policemen took away Gurdeep Singh along with them. The Police party neither disclosed the reason for the arrest of Gurdeep Singh nor did they disclose as to from which Police Station they had come.

On the following day morning, the family members informed the village Panchayat (Council) about this incident and along with eminent persons of the village enquired at Police Station Nihal Singh Wala where they were told that they had not arrested Gurdeep Singh and advised them to find out else where. According to the family members, they enquired several times about the whereabouts of Gurdeep Singh from all the Police Stations of Bathinda district apart from those of Faridkot district. They met senior Police officers several times but none of the officers admitted the custody of Gurdeep Singh. They continued to look for Gurdeep Singh at various Police Stations for one and a half years and as a result they were ruined economically. At last they got exhausted, reconciled themselves to their fate and sat quietly at home. Unable to bear the shock of the disappearance of Gurdeep Singh, his father died suddenly four months later. His mother was also shocked deeply due to this incident and fell sick. She expired in 1996.

Gurdeep Singh's wife said that so far they were not aware as to what happened to Gurdeep Singh, after all. The shadow of the terror of this incident is clearly visible on the face of his wife Nachhatter Kaur, even today. She was scared to provide information to the Investigation Team. She agreed to give details of this incident to the Investigation Team only on being asked repeatedly to do so by the eminent persons of the village. Even then, she refused to sign this proforma.

### VFF/0680

Jagroop Singh of Saido Ke Ram Ki Patti, Nihal Singh Wala in Moga. Victim Jagroop Singh's father Mahinder Singh, resident of village Saido Ke in district Moga, is a small farmer who owns one and a half acre land. He has three sons and five daughters. Jagroop Singh was his youngest son who had abandoned his studies after passing ninth standard and began to help his father in agricultural farming. His father told the Investigation Team that Jagroop Singh used to stay at home mostly and he was not an active worker of any political party. The family members told that he had gone from home 2-3 days prior to the publication of a news item in newspapers on 31 Asharh (Around 1st week of August) 1989 about his having been killed in an encounter with the Police along with two of his accomplices near village Lehar Khote. So far, they could not get any clue as to how this incident happened to Jagroop Singh. They do not know whether Jagroop Singh was arrested by the Police and then killed or it was a genuine Police encounter. On being asked by the Investigation Team about the militant activities of Jagroop Singh, the family members told that usually, Jagroop Singh used to stay at home only and they had no knowledge about his militant activities. They told the Investigation Team that once in 1988, he was arrested by the Police on the basis of suspicion from village Randhir Ke Khurd where he had gone to see one of his acquaintances. However, the Police released him after detaining him in their custody for 5-6 days as he was found to be innocent. Apart from that, no such incident had occured due to which they might have suspected that Jagroop Singh had any link with militant activities. So far, they could not know the truth behind the incident of killing of Jagroop Singh in an encounter with the Police.

### VFF/0681

Gurdeep Singh 35 of Patto Heer Singh, Nihal Singh Wala in Moga. Gurdeep Singh belonged to a Ramgarhia Sikh family. He had abandoned his studies while he was studying in class VIII and took up the job of a mason. He had married in 1982 and had two sons. He had got himself baptised in 1986. At that time, he used to live at village Dehar Ke (Jagraon) along with his family. There he came into contact with some such youth who were members of Sikh Students Federation. So, Nihal Singh Wala Police arrested him on the basis of suspicion and sent him to jail after registering cases against him. He got released on bail in 1988. Thereafter he remained politically active. The Police used to raid his house with a view to arrest him. As such, he stopped coming home. Thereafter, the Jagraon Police arrested him twice, registered several cases against him and sent him to jail. In 1991, he was acquitted in all the cases against him and he returned home. He stayed at home hardly for a month and went away again. The Police used to arrest his family members and torture them.

On 4-3-1992, a news item was published in the newspapers that a militant namely Gurdeep Singh was killed in an encounter with the Police near village Chaudhary Wala under Baghapurana Police Station along with one of his accomplices namely Jaswinder Singh resident of Rode.

The family members say that according to the people of nearby villages, both the abovementioned youth were surrounded by a large Police Force on a tip off and resorted to heavy firing due to which they were killed.

* Neither the Police handed over his dead body to his family members nor they got the same identified by them. His father Surjit Singh had been arrested by the Nihal Singh Wala Police, 15 days before the day of the encounter. He was released 2-3 days after the incident of the encounter. Even after killing Gurdeep Singh, the Police continued to harass his family members for another 2-3 years. The Nihal Singh Wala Police used to raid his house repeatedly for conducting a search of the house.

**VFF/0682**

Gurmeet Singh 30 of Bhagi Ke in Moga. Victim Gurmeet Singh's father Inder Singh Namberdar had three sons. Gurmeet Singh was the eldest. After passing his Matriculation, he joined (Punjab) Home Guards. However, he quit the job after about one year and got busy in agricultural farming. He was a Gursikh youth but not an "Amritdhari" (baptised). He never participated in any sort of political activities. Neither he had been arrested ever by the Police nor any case registered against him ever. His family members told that they did not have any knowledge of any such activities of Gurmeet Singh as would have aroused their suspicion about his links with the ongoing militant movement in the Punjab.

On 14-7-1992, Gurmeet Singh along with his wife and children had gone to his aunt's ('Bhua') house at village Ghunnas (Distt. Sangrur). On 19-7-1992, five armed men riding a red coloured Maruti car came to his house and enquired about Gurmeet Singh. According to his family members, they seemed to be Policemen. His family members told them that he had gone to Ghunnas. They directed Preetam Singh (younger brother of Gurmeet Singh) to accompany them. Those armed men made him to sit with them. They dropped two of their colleagues near the water works and directed them to keep a watch on Gurmeet Singh's house lest he may go away after reaching there. The remaining three reached Ghunnas along with Preetam Singh. At his aunt's house they came to know that Gurmeet Singh had gone to fetch fodder. Those persons directed (Preetam Singh) to accompany them to the fields. When they reached the fields, Gurmeet Singh was loading the fodder onto the bullock cart. The car borne persons directed him to come along with them. Gurmeet Singh enquired as to who they were. Instead of replying, they pushed him into the car forcibly and went away leaving Preetam Singh at the field itself.

Preetam Singh returned home immediately and intimated his family members about the whole incident. Immediately, his father Inder Singh Namberdar along with eminent persons of the village reached Police Station Nihal Singh Wala. However, they told that the men who had arrested him were not from their Police Station. Inder Singh lodged his complaint about the abduction of Gurmeet Singh at Nihal Singh Wala Police Station, then and there. On the following day, they enquired at Bagha Purana and Moga Police Stations also but nobody was ready to admit the arrest of Gurmeet Singh.

Inder Singh Namberdar told the Investigation Team that they met DSP Bagha Purana, DSP Moga and SSP Faridkot several times, but, these senior officers also did not disclose anything about Gurmeet Singh. He further told that in the beginning, SSP Faridkot, Jasminder Singh used to assure them that he would find out about Gurmeet Singh and let them know. But, later on, he denied flatly that Gurmeet Singh was in the custdoy of Faridkot Police. Inder Singh told that Gurmeet Singh's wife, Late Baljinder Kaur had personally met SSP Faridkot, Jasminder Singh several times. Inder Singh said that they ran from pillar to post for about two years while pursuing the case of Gurmeet Singh and they spent about 1.5 to 2 Lakhs Rupees also on the same but they did not get any clue about the whereabouts of Gurmeet Singh. This incident had a trermendous adverse impact on his wife Baljinder Kaur and she became a heart patient. Baljinder Kaur died of heart attack in 1997. At present, Gurmeet Singh's three children are being brought up by their grandfather Inder Singh.

### VFF/0683

Karnail Singh 70 of Budhsinghwala in Moga. In May 1984, the B.S.F. (Border Security Force) had laid seige to Gurdwara Bibi Kahn Kaur in Moga city which continued for a number of days. The Akali and Sikh Students Federation workers who had been trapped inside were fired at, killing nine persons on the spot. Karnail Singh was one of them. The bodies of Karnail Singh and others were not handed over to their respective families.

It was in those days that Gurjant Singh son of Nachhatter Singh and grandson (in relation) of Karnail Singh became politically active after the death of Karnail Singh at the hands of the B.S.F. and began living in the office of the Sikh Students Federation at Gurdwara Singh Sabha in Moga City along with other youth. In June 1984 during the Army attack on Sri Darbar Sahib at Amritsar and 38 other Gurdawaras, the Army arrested Gurjant Singh along with his other companions from Gurdwara Singh Sabha, Moga. The police implicated Gurjant Singh in many cases apart from booking him under N.S.A. and sent him to Ferozepur jail. Later on, he got released on bail.

In the meantime i.e. during the time Gurjant Singh was incarcerated in jail, Chand Singh (brother of Nachhatter Singh) remained fully active politically and the police used to arrest Chand Singh often, due to political reasons. However the police did not arrest any other member of the family during this time. Chand Singh was very religious minded and he had a thorough knowledge of Sikh tenets. He had received religious education from Sant Mian Singh Jheeri Wale Dera. Though Chand Singh was a farmer, yet, he often used to attend various functions for preaching Sikhism.

While Gurjant Singh was in jail, one of his cousins namely Jagga Singh s/o Major Singh s/o Mehar Singh also joined the militant ranks and he was absconding at the time of release of Gurjant Singh.

After the release of Gurjant Singh from jail, Bagha Purana police began raiding Nachhatter Singh's house for arresting Gurjant Singh. Once, the SHO (Station House Officer) of Bagha Purana police station Mr. Madan Lal Dhingra picked up Gurjant Singh and took him to Bagha Purana P.S. (Police Station). From there he was taken to Jaiton P.S. and then to Faridkot C.I.A. (Central Investigation Agency) Staff where he was detained illegally for 10 days. He was tortured brutally at Jaiton P.S. and CIA Staff Faridkot. He was got released from the CIA Staff by the family members and the Panchayat but on the next day itself, SHO of Bagha Purana P.S. raided his house. However, Gurjant Singh had not slept at his house that day. The police picked up Nachhatter Singh and detained him for 15 days. The police asked them to produce Gurjant Singh but Gurjant Singh had absconded once for all. When the family members talked to Gurjant Singh about producing himself before the police, he said, "These people (the police) will kill me. As such, I will not present myself before them now." The family members also felt that there was some logic in his argument, so, they also did not put much pressure on him to present himself before the police.

A few days after Gurjant Singh had absconded, his cousin Jagga Singh s/o Major Singh s/o Mehar Singh was arrested by the police. The Faridkot and Ferozepur police slapped several cases against him and sent him to Sangrur jail where he was detained for 3 years. In the meantime, the police arrested Gurjant Singh's brother Kulwant Singh, implicated him in several cases and sent him to Sangrur jail. Kulwant Singh had been tortured brutally by Faridkot police. As such he was in bad shape physically while in jail.

After Gurjant Singh had absconded in 1986, the police used to pick up his family members. They used to pick up his father Nachhatter Singh, brothers and uncle Chand Singh often and detain them illegally for days together. Once, the SHO of Bagha Purana police station Mr. Gurtej Singh picked up his mother Surjit Kaur also and released her on the following day.

In 1987, a person namely Jarnail Singh was murdered by someone. The police turned the needle of their suspicion towards Chand Singh and Gurjant Singh. keeping in view such an attitude of the police, Chand Singh also began to remain away from his house. As a result, the police began raidsing his house more frequently. In May 1987, under the leadership of Ray-Ribiero combine the police repression was intensified in Punjab and political workers were arrested in large numbers under TADA (Terrorist & Disruptive Activities (Prevention) Act). During this time, the SHO of Bagha Purana police station Mitt Singh (who was later killed by militants) arrested Gurjant Singh's father Nachhatter Singh and tortured him brutally for 10 days in illegal custody at Bagha Purana police station. Thereafter he implicated him in a case under TADA (that of giving shelter to militants) and sent him to Ferozepur jail. In the meantime, the police began to raid their house regularly. All the family members went underground. The police carried away all household goods including the main gate of the house. None of the family members returned home for complete three years and grass came up all over the house. No agricultural operations could be carried out for three years. Nobody dared to take their land on contract for cultivation due to the fear of the police.

In 1990, slowly, some members of Gurjant Singh's family began to return home and started cultivating their land. But, the fear of the police was still there and none of the male members used to sleep at home. While Gurjant Singh was absconding, the police arrested his sister Charanjit Kaur and brother-in-law (sister's husband) Sukhdev Singh Fauji resident of Kale Ke several times. The police tortured also Sukhdev Singh several times. Apart from that, the police used to pick up his other relatives also like aunts ('Maami', 'Bhua') and uncle ('Phuphar'). Not only that they used to pick up the relatives of their relatives also.

In 1987, while Gurjant Singh's father was in Ferozepur jail, the police arrested Chand Singh from village Ghall Kalan along with 4 other youth including Kuldip Singh r/o village Ghall Kalan from whose tubewell all the five were arrested. About 10 days after their arrest all of them were killed in an "encounter" with the police. At that time, all the family members and relatives were target of police wrath and all of them were homeless. Chand Singh's case could not be pursued. The family members had come to know about Chand Singh's arrest after 2-3 days. 10 days later they read the news in the newspapers about his having been killed in an "encounter" with the police.

In the maentime, Gurjant Singh's brother Kulwant Singh and cousin Jagga Singh were released from Sangrur jail. Even after his release, Kulwant Singh was picked up and tortured brutally by Bagha Purana police several times. Jagga Singh absconded from home 2-3 months after his release and ultimately he was killed in an encounter with the police at village Chhajanwali near Jagraon. During this period, Gurjant Singh's elder brother Jagroop Singh was also picked up several times and subjected to brutal torture by the police.

On 29 July 1992, Gurjant Singh was killed in an encounter with the police at the house of Kaur Singh in Model Town (Extension) at Ludhiana. However, his family remained the target of police wrath even thereafter. The police neither handed over the body of Gurjant Singh to the family members nor got it identified from them. The police put several restrictions on the family even at the time of his 'Bhog' (last rites) ceremony. Only his family memebrs were allowed to attend the same. Even after Gurjant Singh had been killed, Bagha Purana police continued to raid their house and they used to pick up Nachhatter Singh, Jagroop Singh, Kulwant Singh and Jaswant Singh, often. During this period the Bagha Purana police slapped a case under Arms Act against Jaswant Singh and sent him to jail. He was in jail for two months and thereafter he was released on bail.

In 1993, during the Panchayat elections in the Punjab, DSP (Deputy Superintendent of Police) Randhawa of Bagha Purana police arrested Binder Singh s/o Lal Singh, a Mazhabi Sikh and a worker of Jagroop Singh (Gurjant Singh's brother) and detained him for 15 days at the CIA Staff Bagha Purana. Thereafter, he implicated him in a case under the Arms Act and delivering provocative anti-national speeches and sent him to jail. He could be got released on bail only after one month. Now he has been acquitted in that case.

In April 1993, Havaldar (Head Constable) Jagraj Singh of Bagha Purana police along with some constables came in a Canter (four-wheeler), picked up Jaswant Singh on the way who was driving a Tractor and brought him to home to inform the family members that he was taking away Jaswant Singh to the police station as he had been summoned by the officers. After the arrest of Jaswant Singh, his father Nachhatter Singh along with the Sarpanch (Head of Village Council) of the village, Kirpal Singh reached police station Bagha Purana. They met the SHO Mr. Tehal Singh who said, "We will release him in the evening." Nachhatter Singh and the Sarpanch met Jaswant Singh in the police station. Jaswant Singh took off his watch and handed it over to Nachhatter Singh. Same day evening, Nachhater Singh was also picked up from his house by Bagha Purana police. Again the male members of the family began to remain away from home, due to fear. They sent respectable persons to the SHO several times. However, the SHO always used to say, "You don't talk to me about those people at all."

Nachhatter Singh was detained at different police stations and secret (torture) centres. During this period, he was subjected to inhuman torture several times in the presence of SSP (Senior Superintendent of Police) Tiwari, SP (Ops.) Shri Anil Gautam. Six months later, the Bagha Purana police dropped him at his house. At that time, his physical condition was very bad. He could recover only after medical treatment for several months. It was Head Constable Jugraj Singh who had come to drop Nachhatter Singh at home and he said, "You don't waste money in pursuing his case. Jaswant Singh is no more." The family members accepted it as the Will of God. Of course, they did not have any other alternative either.

In 1995, one day, Kulwant Singh who had started getting fits of insanity due to repeated police torture and whose health had deteriorated too much, breathed his last after a prolonged illness. According to family members the actual reason of Kulwant's death was the repeated police torture. Kulwant Singh was married and has a son namely Bhupinder Singh aged nine years. His wife's parents had got her remarried. Now Nachhatter Singh's elder son Jagroop Singh only is left in their family.

### VFF/0684

Mukand Singh 28 of Rode, bagha Purana in Moga. Victim Mukand Singh's father is a poor Dalit (one who belongs to oppressed class). He had ten children, five daughters and five sons. His two sons namely Charan Singh and Kewal Singh who are married live separately. His all the five daughters are married. Three of his sons namely Mukand Singh, Veeram Singh and Darshan Singh used to live with him. They were making both ends meet by doing manual labour and agricultural farming on contract basis. His family had come under the influence of religious discourses of Sant Jarnail Singh Bhindranwale and got themselves baptised ("Amritdhari") before 1984 itself. Jarnail Singh used to participate in the 'Akali Morchas' (peaceful agitations of Akali Dal—a political party) and whenever the Akali Dal used to give a call for any of their political programmes, he used to partcipate in it. Like his father, Mukand Singh also used to participate in the programmes of the Akali Dal, at times. The police used to view their family with suspicion due to their political activities. In June 1984, when the Army had attacked Sri Darbar Sahib at Amritsar along with 38 other Gurdwaras in Punjab, the Bagha Purana police had picked up Jarnail Singh on the basis of suspicion and detained him for few days.

In 1987, the Moga police arrested Mukand Singh from Moga City, registered several cases against him and sent him to Ferozepur Central Jail. He remained in jail for about 3 years. After his release, he was acquitted in the above mentioned cases. However, the family members don't remember as to for which offence, cases had been registered against him. Immediately after his release from jail, Mukand Singh got married to Jasvir Kaur. After his marriage, he used to live at home only. He was a News Agent for one of the Punjabi newspapers for Bagha Purana area and he used to sell the newspaper by going from door to door. Apart from that, he used to help the family in domestic jobs also.

According to his mother Dalip Kaur: "On 6-4-91 at about 6 PM, three armed youth in civil clothes entered our house and called out Mukand Singh by name. As Mukand Singh went near them, they caught hold of him and tied his hands at his back. I was at home at that time and I tried to restrain them, but, they threatened to kill me. After they had left along with Mukand Singh, I informed my husband and sons who had gone to work in the fields. Our family members went to the village in search of him in different directions.

"At about 8 PM, his father Jarnail Singh and brother Charan Singh who were in search of him saw Mukand Singh lying unconscious in the street near Bibi Wala Gurdwara. He was alive but his condition was very critical. They lifted him and brought him home. He breathed his last at home at about 9 PM as a result of physical torture. There were many injury marks on the body of Mukand Singh. Injury marks were there on his legs, arms and chest."

On 7-4-91 morning, the family members informed the police. The police got the post mortem conducted and a FIR No. 42 was registered at Bagha Purana police station u/s 302, 452, 34 IPC and 25,54,59 of Arms Act. The police declared it to be a case of inter-gang rivalry of the militants and no compensation or other relief was provided to the family as is normally given to the families of those killed by militants.

### VFF/0685

Sukhdev Singh alias Sukha 24 of Sangatpura in Moga. Sukhdev Singh had deserted home about three years prior to his arrest. The police had got him declared a proclaimed offender on the allegation of his involvement in militant activities. The police used to pick up his father Mohinder Singh, mother Surjit Kaur, relatives Gian Singh (maternal uncle), Deewan Singh (maternal uncle), Gajjan Singh (uncle— 'Massar') and Mann Singh (uncle—'Phuphar') repeatedly and torture them brutally. Due to this repeated torture, the whole family went underground and lived incognito at Amritsar for three years. There, they read in the newspapers that Sukhdev Singh had been arrested at Rishikesh. At the time of his arrest, his accomplice, a renowned militant namely Kuldip Singh Shekhupura was said to have consumed cyanide. The family memebrs have lost those newspapers in which this news item had been published. But, since then, the police have not disclosed as to what happened to Sukhdev Singh.

* According to his father Mohinder Singh, after Sukhdev Singh absconded, he (Mohinder Singh) was picked up by the police numerous times. Sometimes, the police used to detain him in custody for months together. At the time of Rumanian

Ambassador's abduction, 30 of their relatives had been arrested by Bagha Purana police and detained for one month.

* According to Mohinder Singh (father), the police have not left them alone yet. Often they come for inquiry. His children are not being issued with a passport. "If my son was a militant, they have eliminated him. Why the Government were bent upon ruining the future of my innocent children, now", he asks.

### VFF/0686

Veeran Singh 15 of Rode in Moga. Victim Veeram Singh's father Jarnail Singh is a poor Dalit (one who belongs to oppressed class). He had ten children, five daughters and five sons. His two sons namely Charan Singh and Kewal Singh who are married live separately. His all the five daughters are married. Three of his sons namely Mukand Singh, Veeram Singh and Darshan Singh used to live with him. They were making both ends meet by doing manual labour and agricultural farming on contract basis. His family had come under the influence of religious discourses of Sant Jarnail Singh Bhindranwale and got themselves baptised ("Amritdhari") before 1984 itself. Jarnail Singh used to participate in the 'Akali Morchas' (peaceful agitations of Akali Dal— a political party) and whenever the Akali Dal used to give a call for any of their political programmes, he used to partcipate in it.

A few days after the death of his brother Mukand Singh, who was killed at his village by three unidentified armed youth in civil clothes on 6-4-1991, the Bagha Purana police picked up Veeram Singh and tortured him brutally in illegal custody for one month and three weeks. During this period, he was detained at Bagha Purana, Moga and Mehna police stations. Two cases were registered against him. He got released on bail after 3-4 months. Barely two months later, on the third day after Diwali in 1993 at about 9 PM, the police entered their house after scaling the boundary wall while jarnail Singh, his wife Dalip Kaur and son Veeram Singh were asleep and knocked at the door. The police party of Bagha Purana was headed by the SHO and had a large number of policemen in it. Jarnail Singh and Dalip Kaur recognised Havaldar (Head Constable) Jugraj Singh and Havaldar Gurcharan Singh as they had picked up Veeram Singh earlier also.

On the following day, Jarnail Singh and Dalip Kaur along with Kaur Singh Sarpanch (Head of Village Council), Chowkidar (Watchman) Jeeta Singh and several other persons went to the police station. The SHO flatly denied having picked him up. However, he assured them that he would find out and in case any other police had arrested him he would get him released. Thereafter, the family members met DSP Randhawa, SHO and Havaldar Jugraj Singh several times personally as well as through eminent persons. Initially they continued to assure them that they would release him but after about 3 months, they flatly denied that Veeram Singh was in their custody. Even then, the family members continued to send eminent political persons like Capt. Harcharan Singh Rode, Kaur Singh Sarpanch and Jagdish Singh. But, the police neither released Veeram Singh nor they gave any information about him.

According to his mother Dalip Kaur: "The situation was very bad in those days. The police terror was at its peak. We poor people could not have done anything more than that also. I and my husband begged of the police officers of Bagha Purana and Moga, pleaded with them that we were poor people, but, nobody listened to us. We continued to look for Veeram Singh for 2-3 years but we did not get any clue about his whereabouts. In case the police have killed our son, then, at least they should let us know so that we may reconcile ourselves and sit quietly at home." She is under the impression that her son may still be alive. However she also says that she is losing hope now as so much time had elapsed.

* Dalip Kaur (mother of the victim) also said to the investigation team, "So many people come and write down (their tale of woe). Son, will there be any positive result or not?" But, even this investigation team (Amrik Singh Muktsar and others) had no answer to this query by his mother.

**VFF/0687**

Jaswant Singh alias Boongar 25 of Budhsinghwala in Moga. In April 1993, he was picked up by ASI Tehal Singh of Bagha Wala Police Station while he was going in his tractor trolley in the village. They brought him back to home the same day.

The following additional information related to this case has been collected by Amrik Singh Muktsar in November, 1999. The true translation of the same is appended below:-

Nachhatter Singh (victim Jaswant Singh's father) and Chand Singh sons of Late Kehar Singh were farmers and residing at village Budhsingh Wala. Nachhatter Singh had six children-four sons namely Jagroop Singh (36 years), Kulwant Singh (deceased), Gurjant Singh (deceased) and Jaswant Singh (disappeared). Chand Singh was unmarried and he used to live with his brother's family. Nachhatter Singh had two daughters namely Charanjit Kaur (married) and Gurdeep Kaur (expired). The uncle ('Chacha') of Nachhatter Singh and Chand Singh, S. Karnail

Singh (since deceased) also used to live at village Budhsingh Wala. His sons namely Gurcharan Singh and Visakha Singh had expired. Now only his grandsons live at village Budhsingh Wala. Karnail Singh was an "Amritdhari" (Baptised) Sikh. Apart from being religious minded he used to take active part in the political programmes of Shiromani Akali Dal. He had taken a very active part in the 'Dharam Yudh Morcha' (Religious War Front) launched by Shiromani Akali Dal in 1982. He was close to Sant Jarnail Singh Bhindranwale.

In May 1984, the B.S.F. (Border Security Force) had laid seige to Gurdwara Bibi Kahn Kaur in Moga city which continued for a number of days. The Akali and Sikh Students Federation workers who had been trapped inside were fired at, killing nine persons on the spot. Karnail Singh was one of them. The bodies of Karnail Singh and others were not handed over to their respective families.

It was in those days that Gurjant Singh son of Nachhatter Singh and grandson (in relation) of Karnail Singh became politically active after the death of Karnail Singh at the hands of the B.S.F. and began living in the office of the Sikh Students Federation at Gurdwara Singh Sabha in Moga City along with other youth. In June 1984 during the Army attack on Sri Darbar Sahib at Amritsar and 38 other Gurdwaras, the Army arrested Gurjant Singh along with his other companions from Gurdwara Singh Sabha, Moga. The police implicated Gurjant Singh in many cases apart from booking him under N.S.A. and sent him to Ferozepur jail. Later on, he got released on bail.

In the meantime i.e. during the time Gurjant Singh was incarcerated in jail, Chand Singh (brother of Nachhatter Singh) remained fully active politically and the police used to arrest Chand Singh often, due to political reasons. However the police did not arrest any other member of the family during this time. Chand Singh was very religious minded and he had a thorough knowledge of Sikh tenets. He had received religious education from Sant Mian Singh Jheeri Wale Dera. Though Chand Singh was a farmer, yet, he often used to attend various functions for preaching Sikhism.

While Gurjant Singh was in jail, one of his cousins namely Jagga Singh s/o Major Singh s/o Mehar Singh also joined the militant ranks and he was absconding at the time of release of Gurjant Singh.

After the release of Gurjant Singh from jail, Bagha Purana police began raiding Nachhatter Singh's house for arresting Gurjant Singh. Once, the SHO (Station House Officer) of Bagha Purana police station Mr. Madan Lal Dhingra picked up Gurjant Singh and took him to Bagha

Purana P.S. (Police Station). From there he was taken to Jaiton P.S. and then to Faridkot C.I.A. (Central Investigation Agency) Staff where he was detained illegally for 10 days. He was tortured brutally at Jaiton P.S. and CIA Staff Faridkot. He was got released from the CIA Staff by the family members and the Panchayat but on the next day itself, SHO of Bagha Purana P.S. raided his house. However, Gurjant Singh had not slept at his house that day. The police picked up Nachhatter Singh and detained him for 15 days. The police asked them to produce Gurjant Singh but Gurjant Singh had absconded once for all. When the family members talked to Gurjant Singh about producing himself before the police, he said, "These people (the police) will kill me. As such, I will not present myself before them now." The family members also felt that there was some logic in his argument, so, they also did not put much pressure on him to present himself before the police.

A few days after Gurjant Singh had absconded, his cousin Jagga Singh s/o Major Singh s/o Mehar Singh was arrested by the police. The Faridkot and Ferozepur police slapped several cases against him and sent him to Sangrur jail where he was detained for 3 years. In the meantime, the police arrested Gurjant Singh's brother Kulwant Singh, implicated him in several cases and sent him to Sangrur jail. Kulwant Singh had been tortured brutally by Faridkot police. As such he was in bad shape physically while in jail.

After Gurjant Singh had absconded in 1986, the police used to pick up his family members. They used to pick up his father Nachhatter Singh, brothers and uncle Chand Singh often and detain them illegally for days together. Once, the SHO of Bagha Purana police station Mr. Gurtej Singh picked up his mother Surjit Kaur also and released her on the following day.

In 1987, a person namely Jarnail Singh was murdered by someone. The police turned the needle of their suspicion towards Chand Singh and Gurjant Singh. keeping in view such an attitude of the police, Chand Singh also began to remain away from his house. As a result, the police began raidsing his house more frequently. In May 1987, under the leadership of Ray-Ribiero combine the police repression was intensified in Punjab and political workers were arrested in large numbers under TADA (Terrorist & Disruptive Activities (Prevention) Act). During this time, the SHO of Bagha Purana police station Mitt Singh (who was later killed by militants) arrested Gurjant Singh's father Nachhatter Singh and tortured him brutally for 10 days in illegal custody at Bagha Purana police station. Thereafter he implicated him in a case under TADA (that of giving shelter to militants) and sent him to Ferozepur jail. In the meantime, the police began to raid their house regularly. All the family members went underground. The police carried away all household goods including the main gate of the house. None of the family members returned home for complete three years and grass came up all over the house. No agricultural operations could be carried out for three years. Nobody dared to take their land on contract for cultivation due to the fear of the police.

In 1990, slowly, some members of Gurjant Singh's family began to return home and started cultivating their land. But, the fear of the police was still there and none of the male members used to sleep at home. While Gurjant Singh was absconding, the police arrested his sister Charanjit Kaur and brother-in-law (sister's husband) Sukhdev Singh Fauji resident of Kale Ke several times. The police tortured also Sukhdev Singh several times. Apart from that, the police used to pick up his other relatives also like aunts ('Maami', 'Bhua') and uncle ('Phuphar'). Not only that they used to pick up the relatives of their relatives also.

In 1987, while Gurjant Singh's father was in Ferozepur jail, the police arrested Chand Singh from village Ghall Kalan along with 4 other youth including Kuldip Singh r/o village Ghall Kalan from whose tubewell all the five were arrested. About 10 days after their arrest all of them were killed in an "encounter" with the police. At that time, all the family members and relatives were target of police wrath and all of them were homeless. Chand Singh's case could not be pursued. The family members had come to know about Chand Singh's arrest after 2-3 days. 10 days later they read the news in the newspapers about his having been killed in an "encounter" with the police.

In the meantime, Gurjant Singh's brother Kulwant Singh and cousin Jagga Singh were released from Sangrur jail. Even after his release, Kulwant Singh was picked up and tortured brutally by Bagha Purana police several times. Jagga Singh absconded from home 2-3 months after his release and ultimately he was killed in an encounter with the police at village Chhajanwali near Jagraon. During this period, Gurjant Singh's elder brother Jagroop Singh was also picked up several times and subjected to brutal torture by the police.

On 29 July 1992, Gurjant Singh was killed in an encounter with the police at the house of Kaur Singh in Model Town (Extension) at Ludhiana. However, his family remained the target of police wrath even thereafter. The police neither handed over the body of Gurjant Singh to the family members nor got it identified from them. The police put several restrictions on the family even at the time of his 'Bhog' (last rites) ceremony. Only his family memebrs were allowed to attend the same. Even after Gurjant Singh had been killed, Bagha Purana police continued to raid their house and they used to pick up Nachhatter Singh, Jagroop Singh, Kulwant Singh and Jaswant Singh, often. During this period the Bagha Purana police slapped a case under Arms Act against Jaswant Singh and sent him to jail. He was in jail for two months and thereafter he was released on bail.

In 1993, during the Panchayat elections in the Punjab, DSP (Deputy Superintendent of Police) Randhawa of Bagha Purana police arrested Binder Singh s/o Lal Singh, a Mazhabi Sikh and a worker of Jagroop Singh (Gurjant Singh's brother) and detained him for 15 days at the CIA Staff Bagha Purana. Thereafter, he implicated him in a case under the Arms Act and delivering provocative anti-national speeches and sent him to jail. He could be got released on bail only after one month. Now he has been acquitted in that case.

In April 1993, Havaldar (Head Constable) Jagraj Singh of Bagha Purana police along with some constables came in a Canter (four-wheeler), picked up Jaswant Singh on the way who was driving a Tractor and brought him to home to inform the family members that he was taking away Jaswant Singh to the police station as he had been summoned by the officers. After the arrest of Jaswant Singh, his father Nachhatter Singh along with the Sarpanch (Head of Village Council) of the village, Kirpal Singh reached police station Bagha Purana. They met the SHO Mr. Tehal Singh who said, "We will release him in the evening." Nachhatter Singh and the Sarpanch met Jaswant Singh in the police station. Jaswant Singh took off his watch and handed it over to Nachhatter Singh. Same day evening, Nachhater Singh was also picked up from his house by Bagha Purana police. Again the male members of the family began to remain away from home, due to fear. They sent respectable persons to the SHO several times. However, the SHO always used to say, "You don't talk to me about those people at all."

Nachhatter Singh was detained at different police stations and secret (torture) centres. During this period, he was subjected to inhuman torture several times in the presence of SSP (Senior Superintendent of Police) Tiwari, SP (Ops.) Shri Anil Gautam. Six months later, the Bagha Purana police dropped him at his house. At that time, his physical condition was very bad. He could recover only after medical treatment for several months. It was Head Constable Jugraj Singh who had come to drop Nachhatter Singh at home and he said, "You don't waste money in pursuing his case. Jaswant Singh is no more." The family members accepted it as the Will of God. Of course, they did not have any other alternative either.

In 1995, one day, Kulwant Singh who had started getting fits of insanity due to repeated police torture and whose health had deteriorated too much, breathed his last after a prolonged illness. According to family members the actual reason of Kulwant's death was the repeated police torture. Kulwant Singh was married and has a son namely Bhupinder Singh aged nine years. His wife's parents had got her remarried. Now Nachhatter Singh's elder son Jagroop Singh only is left in their family.

### VFF/0688

Sadhu Singh alias Naik Singh 23 of G T B Garh Rode in Moga. On 26-11-90 at 4.35 P.M., he was bringing the vehicle of Singh Sahib Bhai Jasbir Singh from Anandpur Sahib along with Jaswant Singh s/o Jagga Singh r/o Rode (Kothe). ASI Gurmel Singh had laid a Naka near Bughipura Chowk. The Police stopped their car and made Sadhu Singh to get down from it. The Police told Jaswant Singh to take the vehicle (Ambassador car No. PJO-656). Jaswant Singh came home and informed his family. Next day, his brother Gurcharan Singh, Preetam Singh Veroke, and Inderpal Singh, Chairman Market Committee, met the DSP Randhawa at C.I.A. Moga. He denied having arrested him. 4-5 days later, brother Gurcharan Singh along with former Chief Minister Harcharan Singh Brar, met SSP Faridkot, Swaran Singh Ghotna, at his residence. Brar Sahib came out after meeting the SSP and told that he had promised to release him after 4-5 days. After a few days, a 'Khula Darbar' was held by DC Faridkot at our village. His brother Gurcharan Singh raised the matter of his arrest and submitted an application also. The DC told that they would let us know something within 5-7 days. After 5-7 days, we received a letter from the DC. We went to his Office but nothing was intimated to us (regarding Sadhu Singh).

### VFF/0689

Varinder Singh 28 of Nathewala, Baghapurana in Moga. Mukhtiar Kaur (mother of the victim Varinder Singh) had three sons and one daughter. One of her sons, namely Varinder Singh was killed in an encounter with the Police and later on, the Police abducted her husband Jang Singh whose whereabouts are not known till today. Her daughter Sarbjit Kaur died due to illness.

Her eldest son Varinder Singh was active in the Sikh Students Federation since 1987. That is why the Police used to arrest him often. The Police had arrested him and registered cases against him on two different occasions. He was incarcerated in Faridkot Jail for about two years. The family members do not remember the dates of his detention in the Jail. After his release from Jail he stayed at home for 8-9 months. The Police had started harassing him again. They used to pick him up and torture him. As such, he deserted home and joined the ranks of the militants, once for all.

On 31-12-1990, Varinder Singh was killed in an encounter with the Police near VIllage Daulatpura Kalia Wala in district Ferozepur. The Police could not lay their hands on his dead body. His accomplices handed over his dead body to his family members at his house on the following day. The family members cremated his dead body. The Police got a scent of it. As a consequence his family became a victim of Police wrath. The Police picked up his mother Mukhtiar Kaur, father Jang Singh and both the brothers and subjected them to brutal torture.

### VFF/0690

Devinder Singh alias Johari 19 of Rajeana, Veera Patti in Moga. He was produced in front of SI Bachan Singh and SI Kashmira Singh at C.I.A Staff Faridkot. Prior to that, Mohinder Singh Thekedar (relative of SSP) r/o Handiaya alongwith Master Harpal Singh Rahi had met the SSP Jasminder Singh. He (SSP) told them to present their boy (Devinder Singh) at the C.I.A. He also promised to release him after questioning. Harpal Singh, Mahinder Singh, and Malkit Singh presented him (Devinder) at the C.I.A and came back home. We used to go to meet him, but were not allowed to meet him. On the fourth day, I (Malkit Singh) alongwith Mohinder Singh and Harpal Singh met SSP at his residence. The SSP said, "There is no danger to his life. We will release him in a week's time". After 8-10 days, Bachan Singh and Kashmir Singh from C.I.A Staff alongwith a police party came to our house and said, "Where is your boy?". We replied that we had left him at the C.I.A Staff. At this they said, "Your boy has run away". They started beating family members. They arrested Malkit Singh and brought him to Bagha Purana. They took him to all relatives' places. He was kept at the C.I.A Staff for 8-10 days after which he was released at the intervention of village Panchayat. After some time, we met the SSP again. He told us that our boy had been arrested again. We would release him. Nothing is known about his whereabouts since then. I suspect that the Police was pretending only as regards the escape of my son from their custody.

### VFF/0691

Gurcharan Singh alias Charna of Rode, Bagha Purana in Moga. He was picked up from his residence at 8 P.M. in a Gypsy by Police of Bagha Purana (Sadar) police station. We approached SHO Bagha Purana and DSP Moga but they denied having arrested him.

**VFF/0692**

Chamkaur Singh alias Babli 17 of Sangatpura in Moga. The details of this incident are contained in an Affidavit sworn by Roop Singh, father of victim Chamkaur Singh. The same is reproduced below:-

AFFIDAVIT

I, Roop Singh, son of Basant Singh son of Timra Singh, resident of village Sangat Pura, Tehsil Moga, Distt. Faridkot (now district Moga), do hereby solemnly affirm and declare as under:-

1. That my son, Chamkaur Singh, aged about 17 years, was kidnapped on 21-10-1992, at about 4.00 a.m., by Gurcharan Singh alias "Baba", Sub Inspector, then Station House Officer, Police Station Mehna, Tehsil Moga, in a white colour, Police Gypsy, which was then driven by Saudagar Singh, a Punjab Home Guard, who was also personal Body-guard of said Gurcharan Singh "Baba", and they are related to each other. I personally knew above-said Saudagar Singh, very well, because I performed/worked on contract as a labourer "Siri" in his village Ladhai Ke, with a farmer named Mithoo, and I had rather cordial relations with him. There were about six policemen with them.

2. That, firstly, the above-said party entered the house of my neighbour namely Binder Singh, and asked him whether he is Roop Singh, who told them directing them to my house. When they entered my house, first of all, I was awaken by a lean Head-constable and asked me whereabouts of my son. I told them that he is asleep in the 'Baithak' of our house (a small guest room). Then they went in the 'Baithak' where my wife's maternal aunt's son, was also there, who was awaken and asked,"if he was Chamkaur Singh, and seeing police, and being in confusion, suddenly the word "Yes" slipped from his mouth. Then from the next bed, Chamkaur Singh was awaken and asked as to who he was, then my above-said wife's cousin, named "Sira" from village Nathana, said that "he is Chamkaur Singh" — (pointing to my son). Then, the said Head Constable, took up a "Kahi" (Kassi) and beat my said relation with its handle, very severely, who expired about two years later, a natural death.

3. That, thereafter, the said Head Constable caught hold of my son from one arm and another constable caught from the other arm, and then above-said Gurcharan Singh "Baba"

ordered them to put my son Chamkaur Singh, in their Gypsy. And, when they were about to leave after putting my son Chamkaur Singh in their Gypsy, I asked the said Gurcharan Singh "Baba" as to from where this police is, and they (above-said Head Constable) replied that they are from Police Station Mehna, and they were taking my son Chamkaur Singh to Police Station Mehna.

4. That, on the morning/day break, I went to Sheera Singh, a farmer and owner of a van/plying as a taxi, with whom my son Chamkaur Singh had worked for sometime in his fields at his village Kotla Rai-ka, to take his help. I took Sheera Singh, above-said (a Zamidar), and Piara Singh, Mazhbi Singh— my distant relative from that village, who happened to be a supporter of Iqbal Singh, candidate for M.L.A., resident of Baghapurana, and then we went to above-said Iqbal Singh at Baghapurana in the van of Sheera Singh. Then we took Iqbal Singh with us to Police Station Mehna.

5. That we reached the Police Station Mehna at about 11 A.M. At the tea-Dhaba near the gate of Police Station Mehna, a police head constable met us. Above-said Iqbal Singh asked him—"Zora Singh, have you brought any boy from village Sangatpura, to which he replied 'No, I was on leave', and he shall confirm it for us. He asked another person, presumably policeman of P.S. Mehna, and then told us that they have not brought, and we were sent back from outside the gate of the police station.

6. That on 22-10-1992, I came to Faridkot and met Head Constable Sukhdev Singh, of our village, at Police Headquarter Office, upstairs of District Courts Buildings, Faridkot, who took me along on a scooter to P.S. Saddar, Faridkot, CIA Staff Faridkot and Police Station City, Faridkot, where it was confirmed that they have not brought my son Chamkaur Singh.

7. That after visiting Faridkot, I went to Goniana at about 4.00 P.M. on 22-10-1992, and reached house of Jalaur Singh, Sub-Inspector Police, who was then posted at P.S. Makhu, and whose wife happened to be my wife's cousin sister from their paternal families. Both of them were incidentally at their house. Jalaur Singh, gave me a letter in the name of Gurcharan Singh, SHO, Mehna, the so-called "Baba".

8. That on 23-10-1992, at about morning, I left Goniana for Bathinda and met Head Constable Roop Singh, C.I.D., Police, Bathinda, who is my maternal uncle's son. He also advised me that Bhallar Singh, their Inspector Police C.I.D., at Bathinda is from village Jitgill from where Gurcharan Singh "Baba" also belongs, and that I should first meet Gurcharan Singh "Baba" with that letter of Jalaur Singh, and if that does not work, then, he will take help of Bhallar Singh, Police Inspector. I returned home at village Sangatpura at about 2/2-30 P.M.

9. That on reaching my village Sangatpura, on 23-10-1992, I sent Preet Singh, my cousin brother and Baldev Singh, my sister's husband, to village Dayalpura Bhai-Ka, to meet Bikkar Singh, husband of my wife's sister, with the request that they should all go and meet Nindi, who is known to Bikkar Singh, and is a transporter and influential person, and they should confirm from Police Station Dayalpura Bhai-Ka, if my son is not transferred to that police station. Then I took a Jeep on hire and went to Iqbal Singh at Baghapurana, and taking Iqbal Singh along, I also reached P.S. Dayalpura Bhai-Ka. The S.H.O. Dayalpura Bhai-Ka told us that they did not go to Sangatpura village nor the boy—Chamkaur Singh has been transferred to their custody by any-one, and he offered the keys that we could see the rooms ourselves.

10. That on 24-10-1992, I visited my relations, etc. to collect money/few hundred rupees from each, making it about 4000/- rupees.

11. That on 25-10-1992, which was also Diwali day, I took along Preet Singh, my cousin brother, Jeet Singh, my brother, and Balbir Singh of v. Galoti and Harbans Singh, v.Manuke, both husbands of of my sisters, and we went to P.S. Mehna at about 10.00 a.m. We met Gurcharan Singh "Baba" who was present there and delivered to him the letter from Jalaur Singh, aforementioned. Then, he said that he had not gone to our village and he did not know about my son Chamkaur Singh. Then I told him that I have recognised you, and your face was partly covered with 'Black colour 'Loi' (Bhuri) below your nose level, but still I recognise you, and I now also further recognise this Saudagar Singh, Punjab Home Guard, standing here, who has also been previously well known to me rather having cordial relations with me, and you all were there

who have brought/kidnapped my son Chamkaur Singh from my house on 21-10-1992. Then we returned home at village Sangatpura.

12. That on 26-10-1992 I took van on hire, with its driver Sheera, alongwith my brother Jeet Singh, and Jugraj Singh from village Buraj Ladha Singh Wala, who happened to be 'Saddoo'—i.e. husband of sister of Jalaur Singh, aforementioned's wife, and also my relation, and we came to Goniana and met Jalaur Singh. Then Jalaur Singh told us that he would go to Gurcharan Singh "Baba", the next day, and he further assured us that since his letter has reached Gurcharan Singh "Baba", he would no-more harm Chamkaur Singh, any further.

13. That on 27-10-1992, I alongwith Pooran Singh, a zamidar of our village, (also called Pooran Singh Bhai-Ka (Mann), Sandhura Singh v. Nalkhote, my wife's aunt's husband and Balbir Singh and Harbans Singh, aforementioned husbands of my sisters, reached P.S. Mehna at about 9.00 a.m. and sat outside police station. At about 12-Noon, Jalaur Singh, aforementioned, reached at police station Mehna. He went inside the Police Station, and came back from inside the police station after about two hours, and told us that my son Chamkaur Singh is not there, but Chhinda son of Bhagat of village Kotla Rae-Ka is present in the Police Station Mehna, who they have brought day-before yesterday. I told then Jalaur Singh that my son is very well here. Then Jalaur Singh took me alone inside the police station and himself sat behind in a chair, while I was seated in front of Gurcharan Singh "Baba". Gurcharan Singh said that he did not go to our village, and I may be mistaken because sometimes faces are identical (identities are similar). I told him that this is not at all the case here, because I have recognised you, as well as the Head Constable here and also Saudagar Singh, your body-guard-cum-driver of Gypsy. And then Gurcharan Singh "Baba" said that he will trace/find out my son Chamkaur Singh and that I should contact him later. Then Jalaur Singh said that I should meet him a day-after the following ('parson'), whereupon, Gurcharan Singh said I should meet him after six days, and that I should meet him alone and nobody should accompany me to him.

14. That after six days, after having stayed inside my house, I reached P.S. Mehna at about 9.00 a.m. and the police on guard asked me to wait and they shall seek permission from Station

House Officer, Gurcharan Singh "Baba", and they went in, returned telling me that I should wait for about an hour, and I shall be called in by the S.H.O. later on. Then after about two hours waiting, I was called in at about 11.00 a.m. It was Sunday, around 2/3 Sept. 1992. Then he told me that Chamkaur Singh my son is in custody of another officer, and that we should give around rupees one lac and he will get my son released/freed. Then I asked him that I don't have any money because I am a labourer only and a daily wage earner, and he may challan my son. Then he further said that if challan is required, he don't have the boy, then.

15. That the following day, I went to Bathinda and brought Roop Singh Head Constable and Bhallar Singh, Inspector Police of Gurcharan Singh Baba's village, to P.S. Mehna, who contacted said Gurcharan Singh, and he told them that he has already conveyed to me that he is not having the boy with him, but if I meet him alone, he shall get the boy released from another person if I meet him alone. Both these officials, after conveying this to me, left Mehna P.S., in a Maruti van (Red colour), which I had hired for them from Bathinda, who dropped Bhallar Singh at v. Jitgill and took Roop Singh to leave at Bathinda.

16. That on the following day, I had gone to village Ladhai-Ke, at my 'Masi's' (mother's sister house), the aforementioned Saudagar Singh, Punjab Home Guard, who also belongs to village Ladhai-Ke, saw me in my relation's house and he called me to his own house at about 11.00 a.m. He then told me that, if I had not met him incidentally here, he was to come to my village Sangatpura to meet me. He then said that if I could manage to arrange about Rs. 60,000/- for them, your (my) son can be saved. I told him that I do not have any cash on me, and even nobody will purchase my house so quickly, but I have only two she-buffaloes, which my family can give. Then Saudagar Singh, Punjab Home-guard said that without cash "Kaam Mushkil Hai", work is difficult.

17. That, thereafter, I went to meet Gurmail Singh, Sarpanch, of village Maur-Nau-abad, residing at village Bhagta Bhai-Ka. That on the 3rd day of my going to him, he told me that I should meet him the following day. I took a Jeep on hire, from my village Sangatpura, with owner driver Iqbal Singh, and we took Gurmail Singh, Sarpanch, from Bhagta Bhai-

Ka, and went to village Jitgill and took Ajaib Singh from that village (village of also Gurcharan Dsingh 'Baba') and reached P.S. Mehna at about 12 Noon or 1.00 p.m. and met Gurcharan Singh S.H.O. and then he totally refused denying that he had not gone to village Sangatpura, and then we returned back.

18.    That after doing free labour for about three days at the house of Baldev Singh, Sarpanch of our village, I took him along to Gurcharan Singh 'Baba', to him also, he denied having gone to our village.

19.    That after another 5-6 days, I went taking along Baldev Singh Bhatti, M.L.A., along with his father-in-law Chand Singh, village Galoti, to Gurcharan Singh, but he again denied.

20.    That after about four months, I met Jaswant Singh, A.S.I. police, of v. Pipli and Lakhwinder Singh, Distt. Judge of v. Moranwali, both at a marriage at village Moranwali, and told them the above. Jaswant Singh met Gurcharan Singh 'Baba'. Gurcharan Singh 'Baba' told him that why he did not meet him earlier and that now the said boy had been killed by him. Then same thing was conveyed to me through relations of Jaswant Singh that Chamkaur Singh, my son, has been killed by Gurcharan Singh 'Baba' S.H.O. P.S. Mehna and final rites may be performed by me.

21.    That I heard speech of Sardar Simranjit Singh Mann, that such excesses by the police should be reported on an sworn affidavit and justice would be met, through the courts of law. But, being a very poor person, having no any money for engaging a counsel, I thought it all impossible. But, I have been now hopeful that justice is being met even to poor persons against criminal policemen by the Supreme court/law courts of India, as coming in newspapers, which was impossible previously, and as in the past, whosoever raised a voice or gave a vent of police misdeed was vanished for ever. I am prayfully hopeful that justice would be met to our marooned down-trodden family of Scheduled Caste (Mazhbi Sikh), and hence the whole tale of our woes about my minor son is vented through this affidavit.

22.    That as it has come through the press-media/newspapers, criminal policemen, who committed extra-judicial murders of persons, etc. reached higher horizons of promotions, and are now occupying higher positions, in police headquarters

of districts, etc. or even upwards. Many of those, though have been found guilty, of murders, etc. by the Apex Court and other courts, the State police authorities and the State of Punjab, have patronised and tended and attempted to support some such criminals at State level, which lends undoubted credence to the proof that some such extra-judicial murders by those criminal policemen, had the patronage, behest and backing of higher police echelon of the State headed by the State Police Chief of Punjab. Hence, it is prayed that orders be given only to the Central Bureau of Investigation to conduct investigation and submit their report to the Apex Court, as otherwise, if inquiry is ordered to be carried out by Punjab Police, it may result in liquidation of more innocent lives—of us, or involving in false cases, and will prove counter-productive, supporting police and suppression of innocent sufferers, and thus the criminals who have liquidated our minor son, Chamkaur Singh, for lust of money/promotion, would make mockery and laugh at us and make do further damage.

23. It is further prayed that this affidavit of mine be treated as an application for award of compensation and damages, etc. etc. as the Hon'ble courts/authorities may deem fit, as my family is poor and all indigent persons—myself (deponent—Roop Singh), Baldev Kaur, Joginder Singh, 14 years, Tarsem Singh, 12 years,—father, mother and minor brothers of deceased Chamkaur Singh, respectively, to whom our son Chamkaur Singh, was to support.

Dated:     12-11-1998

DEPONENT

Roop Singh s/o Basant Singh
r/o village Sangatpura, P.S. Mehna
Tehsil & Distt. Moga (Punjab).

I, Roop Singh, above-named deponent, do hereby further solemnly affirm and declare that the above statement of mine is true and correct to the best of my knowledge and belief and nothing has been concealed or mis-stated therein, and I have been explained its contents in Punjabi, the language I understand.

DEPONENT

At:Moga
Dated:     18 Nov 1998                    (Roop Singh—above named)

**VFF/0693**

Sewak Singh 26 of of Sangatpura in Moga. According to the wife of Sewak Singh, Karamjit Kaur:-

"In November 1991, a few days after Diwali, one night at 12 Midnight or 1 AM, we were asleep in one of the rooms of our house when we heard the sound of knocking at the door and that of opening the door. My husband Sewak Singh opened the door. A large number of policemen barged into the room. They asked the name of my husband and tied his hands at his back with a bedsheet lying in the house. In my presence itself, the police officer accompanying the police party enquired the address of an absconding militant of our village namely Sukhdev Singh. My husband told that he did not know anything about him. The police party asked him to accompany them. Neither they disclosed it themselves nor I dared to ask them as to from which police station they had come. I was too scared. I followed them for some distance outside the house. The police put my husband in the vehicle and took him away. Two vehicles had been parked near our house and three-four others had been parked on the road."

On the following day, Karamjit Kaur went to her brother-in-law (sister's husband) Roop Singh at village Bhai Roopa and narrated the whole incident to him. Roop Singh along with two other persons went to police station Bagha Purana. The Bagha Purana police told them that they had not arrested him. Next day, Preetam Singh, Gej Singh and Naib Singh (brother of Sewak Singh) went to police station Mehna. Head Constable Zora Singh told them that their boy had been taken away by C.I.A. Staff Ferozepur; so they should go and enquire there. On the following day, Karamjit Kaur along with Gej Singh went to C I A Staff Ferozepur but they did not get any information from there.

According to Karamjit Kaur (wife), "On the next day, Dr. Iqbal Singh, Major Singh r/o Sangatpur and Banta Singh r/o Sangatpur went to the C.I.A. Staff Ferozepur and talked to some officer there. They came out and told us that the life of Sewak Singh could be saved if we could pay Rs. 20,000/- to the police. According to them, the police would then send Sewak Singh to jail but his life would be saved. But, we could not arrange the money. The above mentioned three persons only used to go inside and talk to the police. We don't know with which officer they had struck the deal. All the above three persons have since expired."

*     We had been to C.I.A. Staff Ferozepur along with relatives, Panchayat and Janta Dal leader Iqbal Singh several times.
*     About 8 days after his arrest, a Home Guard Jawan took Rs.

150/- bribe from us and showed Sewak Singh inside the C.I.A. Staff from a distance to Gej Singh and Malkit Singh.

* Later on we along with the Panchayat, approached Inspector Daljit Singh several times. He declined the request of the Panchayat to release him and even hinted that they won't let him be alive. But, we don't know whether those Panchayat members would say so or not.

* Long after Sewak Singh's arrest, Ram Singh, SHO of Makhu police station had told Preetam Singh and another person hailing from village Langeane that Sewak Singh was killed in the "encounter" at Makhu in which a total of 19 militants had been killed. He had further told them that it was the handiwork of Inspector Daljit Singh and he had no hand in that. We can't say whether Preetam Singh would testify to it or not.

* When the investigation team (Amrik Singh Muktsar and other members) went to Sewak Singh's house, his wife called for Sewak Singh's cousin brother Gej Singh that he should come and give all the information to the investigation team. Gej Singh refused to come, due to fear. Then one of the members of the investigation team went to Gej Singh's house. On his persuation he agreed hesitantly to give all the details. However, time and again he asked whether any harm would come to them due to giving this information to us.

* According to Sewak Singh's wife Karamjit Kaur, so far, no police officer had told her clearly as to what happened to Sewak Singh. She had been meeting the then SHO of Bagha Purana police station Tehal Singh also. He used to say that he (Sewak Singh) was innocent and that he would get him released. But so far let alone release her husband, nobody had told her as to what happened to him. She said that she was a poor woman who was bringing up her children by doing manual labour. So far, nobody had bothered about her and she had not received any help either.

* Karamjit Kaur (wife) told the investigation team that let alone release her husband, on the contrary, for about 3-4 months, the Bagha Purana police continued to visit her house and ask her about the whereabouts of Sewak Singh.

* 6-7 months after the arrest of Sewak Singh, Tehal Singh, SHO of Bagha Purana police station picked up his brother-in-law (sister's husband) Roop Singh r/o Bhai Roopa and tortured

him brutally for 11 days in illegal custody. One of his legs got disabled due to the torture. Even today, he limps while walking.

* About one year prior to the arrest of Sewak Singh, one night, some armed persons (militants) had entered his house, pulled out his mother Amarjit Kaur and shot her dead outside in front of the house. Her all the four sons had received Rs. 1,00,000/- (One Lakh) as compensation for her death in that incident.

## VFF/0694

Mehar Singh 18 of Sangatpura in Moga. Victim Mehar Singh's father Preetam Singh who lost his eyesight about 25 years ago due to sickness, is a poor Dalit (oppressed class). He had three sons and one daughter. Mehar Singh was the eldest. He was mentally unsound and used to roam arond the village like a lunatic. After Preetam Singh lost his eyesight, the family used to pull on with the help of other people only. Daughter was the eldest. She used to support her family by doing manual labour before her marriage.

In 1992, three days before Lohri (a Punjabi festival) i.e. around 10 January, one night, the police surrounded the village. Mehar Singh used to go out to the fields early in the morning to ease himself. On that day also, as usual, he started from home for the fields to ease himself. The village Granthi (who recites Gurbani at the Gurdwara) saw him, paid him one rupee and persuaded him to go back because the Granthi apprehended danger to Mehar Singh's life in view of the siege laid to the village by the police. However Mehar Singh dodged him and went out of the village from the 'samadh' (tomb) side. It was 7 AM. A few minutes later the family members heard the sound of gun shots. A few minutes later, the police went from door to door and collected all the male members of the village in the village school. At that time the villagers saw the bullet riddled dead body of Mehar Singh lying in the Canter (Four wheeler). All the villagers told the police that he was a lunatic and asked them as to what had they done. Tehal Singh, SHO of Bagha Purana police station and DSP Randhawa were present on the occasion. The Sarpanch (Head of village Council) told these officers that they had killed a lunatic person unjustifiably. But, those officers, instead of listening to him said, "You will tell Pargat Singh Fauji (another absconding youth of the village) also to be a lunatic." The police carried away the body in their vehicle. The above mentioned officers told the Panchayat to reach Moga as the postmortem was to be got conducted. The Panchayat reached Moga. However the police did not reach there. The police brought the body themselves in the evening and cremated it themselves at 9 PM. The family members were allowed to attend the cremation.

The newspapers of the following day carried a news item which stated that a top militant namely Mehar Singh had been killed in an encounter at village Sangatpura. The photograph of his dead body with weapons kept by his side also appeared in the newspapers. The villagers were astonished to read this news items and wondered as to how the police claimed that they had killed a top militant after killing a mentally unsound youth. But, the family members and the village Panchayat could not do anything about it as the police terror was at its peak in those days.

The family members did not get any relief from the Government. On the contrary, once, his father Preetam Singh was called to the police station by Bagha Purana police and questioned about the particulars of all family relations. This inquiry was conducted presumably on suspicion basis as is normally done by the police with the family memebrs of other militants.

### VFF/0695

Gurjant Singh Budhsinghwala alias Janta 27 of Budhsinghwala in Moga. Nachhatter Singh (victim Gurjant Singh's father) and Chand Singh sons of Late Kehar Singh were farmers and residing at village Budhsingh Wala. Nachhatter Singh had six children-four sons namely Jagroop Singh (36 years), Kulwant Singh (deceased), Gurjant Singh (deceased) and Jaswant Singh (disappeared). Chand Singh was unmarried and he used to live with his brother's family. Nachhatter Singh had two daughters namely Charanjit Kaur (married) and Gurdeep Kaur (expired). The uncle ('Chacha') of Nachhatter Singh and Chand Singh, S. Karnail Singh (since deceased) also used to live at village Budhsingh Wala. His sons namely Gurcharan Singh and Visakha Singh had expired. Now only his grandsons live at village Budhsingh Wala. Karnail Singh was an "Amritdhari" (Baptised) Sikh. Apart from being religious minded he used to take active part in the political programmes of Shiromani Akali Dal. He had taken a very active part in the 'Dharam Yudh Morcha' (political agitation) launched by Shiromani Akali Dal in 1982. He was close to Sant Jarnail Singh Bhindranwale.

In May 1984, the B.S.F. (Border Security Force) had laid seige to Gurdwara Bibi Kahn Kaur in Moga city which continued for a number of days. The Akali and Sikh Students Federation workers who had been trapped inside were fired at, killing nine persons on the spot. Karnail Singh was one of them. The bodies of Karnail Singh and others were not handed over to their respective families.

It was in those days that Gurjant Singh son of Nachhatter Singh and grandson (in relation) of Karnail Singh became politically active after the death of Karnail Singh at the hands of the B.S.F. and began living in the office of the Sikh Students Federation at Gurdwara Singh Sabha in Moga City along with other youth. In June 1984 during the Army attack on Sri Darbar Sahib at Amritsar and 38 other Gurdawaras, the Army arrested Gurjant Singh along with his other companions from Gurdwara Singh Sabha, Moga. The police implicated Gurjant Singh in many cases apart from booking him under N.S.A. and sent him to Ferozepur jail. Later on, he got released on bail.

In the meantime i.e. during the time Gurjant Singh was incarcerated in jail, Chand Singh (brother of Nachhatter Singh) remained fully active politically and the police used to arrest Chand Singh often, due to political reasons. However the police did not arrest any other member of the family during this time. Chand Singh was very religious minded and he had a thorough knowledge of Sikh tenets. He had received religious education from Sant Mian Singh Jheeri Wale Dera. Though Chand Singh was a farmer, yet, he often used to attend various functions for preaching Sikhism.

While Gurjant Singh was in jail, one of his cousins namely Jagga Singh s/o Major Singh s/o Mehar Singh also joined the militant ranks and he was absconding at the time of release of Gurjant Singh.

After the release of Gurjant Singh from jail, Bagha Purana police began raiding Nachhatter Singh's house for arresting Gurjant Singh. Once, the SHO (Station House Officer) of Bagha Purana police station Mr. Madan Lal Dhingra picked up Gurjant Singh and took him to Bagha Purana P.S. (Police Station). From there he was taken to Jaiton P.S. and then to Faridkot C.I.A. (Central Investigation Agency) Staff where he was detained illegally for 10 days. He was tortured brutally at Jaiton P.S. and C.I.A Staff Faridkot. He was got released from the C.I.A Staff by the family members and the Panchayat but on the next day itself, SHO of Bagha Purana P.S. raided his house. However, Gurjant Singh had not slept at his house that day. The police picked up Nachhatter Singh and detained him for 15 days. The police asked them to produce Gurjant Singh but Gurjant Singh had absconded once for all. When the family members talked to Gurjant Singh about producing himself before the police, he said, "These people (the police) will kill me. As such, I will not present myself before them now." The family members also felt that there was some logic in his argument, so, they also did not put much pressure on him to present himself before the police.

A few days after Gurjant Singh had absconded, his cousin Jagga Singh s/o Major Singh s/o Mehar Singh was arrested by the police. The Faridkot and Ferozepur police slapped several cases against him and sent him to Sangrur jail where he was detained for 3 years. In the meantime, the police arrested Gurjant Singh's brother Kulwant Singh, implicated him in several cases and sent him to Sangrur jail. Kulwant Singh had been tortured brutally by Faridkot police. As such he was in bad shape physically while in jail.

After Gurjant Singh had absconded in 1986, the police used to pick up his family members. They used to pick up his father Nachhatter Singh, brothers and uncle Chand Singh often and detain them illegally for days together. Once, the SHO of Bagha Purana police station, Mr. Gurtej Singh, picked up his mother Surjit Kaur also and released her on the following day.

In 1987, a person namely Jarnail Singh was murdered by someone. The police turned the needle of their suspicion towards Chand Singh and Gurjant Singh. Keeping in view such an attitude of the police, Chand Singh also began to remain away from his house. As a result, the police began raiding his house more frequently. In May 1987, under the leadership of Ray-Ribiero combine the police repression was intensified in Punjab and political workers were arrested in large numbers under TADA (Terrorist & Disruptive Activities (Prevention) Act). During this time, the SHO of Bagha Purana police station Mitt Singh (who was later killed by militants) arrested Gurjant Singh's father Nachhatter Singh and tortured him brutally for 10 days in illegal custody at Bagha Purana police station. Thereafter he implicated him in a case under TADA (that of giving shelter to militants) and sent him to Ferozepur jail. In the meantime, the police began to raid their house regularly. All the family members went underground. The police carried away all household goods including the main gate of the house. None of the family members returned home for complete three years and grass came up all over the house. No agricultural operations could be carried out for three years. Nobody dared to take their land on contract for cultivation due to the fear of the police.

In 1990, slowly, some members of Gurjant Singh's family began to return home and started cultivating their land. But, the fear of the police was still there and none of the male members used to sleep at home. While Gurjant Singh was absconding, the police arrested his sister Charanjit Kaur and brother-in-law (sister's husband) Sukhdev Singh Fauji resident of Kale Ke several times. The police tortured also Sukhdev Singh several times. Apart from that, the police used to pick up his other relatives also like aunts ('Maami', 'Bhua') and uncle ('Phuphar'). Not only that they used to pick up the relatives of their relatives also.

In 1987, while Gurjant Singh's father was in Ferozepur jail, the police arrested Chand Singh from village Ghall Kalan along with 4 other youth including Kuldip Singh r/o village Ghall Kalan from whose tubewell all the five were arrested. About 10 days after their arrest all of them were killed in an "encounter" with the police. At that time, all the family members and relatives were target of police wrath and all of them were homeless. Chand Singh's case could not be pursued. The family members had come to know about Chand Singh's arrest after 2-3 days. 10 days later they read the news in the newspapers about his having been killed in an "encounter" with the police.

In the meantime, Gurjant Singh's brother Kulwant Singh and cousin Jagga Singh were released from Sangrur jail. Even after his release, Kulwant Singh was picked up and tortured brutally by Bagha Purana police several times. Jagga Singh absconded from home 2-3 months after his release and ultimately he was killed in an encounter with the police at village Chhajanwali near Jagraon. During this period, Gurjant Singh's elder brother Jagroop Singh was also picked up several times and subjected to brutal torture by the police.

On 29 July 1992, Gurjant Singh was killed in an encounter with the police at the house of Kaur Singh in Model Town (Extension) at Ludhiana. However, his family remained the target of police wrath even thereafter. The police neither handed over the body of Gurjant Singh to the family members nor got it identified from them. The police put several restrictions on the family even at the time of his 'Bhog' (last rites) ceremony. Only his family members were allowed to attend the same. Even after Gurjant Singh had been killed, Bagha Purana police continued to raid their house and they used to pick up Nachhatter Singh, Jagroop Singh, Kulwant Singh and Jaswant Singh, often. During this period the Bagha Purana police slapped a case under Arms Act against Jaswant Singh and sent him to jail. He was in jail for two months and thereafter he was released on bail.

In 1993, during the Panchayat elections in the Punjab, DSP (Deputy Superintendent of Police) Randhawa of Bagha Purana police arrested Binder Singh s/o Lal Singh, a Mazhabi Sikh and a worker of Jagroop Singh (Gurjant Singh's brother) and detained him for 15 days at the C.I.A Staff Bagha Purana. Thereafter, he implicated him in a case under the Arms Act and delivering provocative anti-national speeches and sent him to jail. He could be got released on bail only after one month. Now he has been acquitted in that case.

In April 1993, Havaldar (Head Constable) Jagraj Singh of Bagha Purana police along with some constables came in a Canter (four-wheeler), picked up Jaswant Singh on the way who was driving a Tractor and brought him to home to inform the family members that he was taking away Jaswant Singh to the police station as he had been summoned by the officers. After the arrest of Jaswant Singh, his father Nachhatter Singh along with the Sarpanch (Head of Village Council) of the village, Kirpal Singh reached police station Bagha Purana. They met the SHO Mr. Tehal Singh who said, "We will release him in the evening." Nachhatter Singh and the Sarpanch met Jaswant Singh in the police station. Jaswant Singh took off his watch and handed it over to Nachhatter Singh. Same day evening, Nachhater Singh was also picked up from his house by Bagha Purana police. Again the male members of the family began to remain away from home, due to fear. They sent respectable persons to the SHO several times. However, the SHO always used to say, "You don't talk to me about those people at all."

Nachhatter Singh was detained at different police stations and secret (torture) centres. During this period, he was subjected to inhuman torture several times in the presence of SSP (Senior Superintendent of Police) Tiwari, SP (Ops.) Shri Anil Gautam. Six months later, the Bagha Purana police dropped him at his house. At that time, his physical condition was very bad. He could recover only after medical treatment for several months. It was Head Constable Jugraj Singh who had come to drop Nachhatter Singh at home and he said, "You don't waste money in pursuing his case. Jaswant Singh is no more." The family members accepted it as the Will of God. Of course, they did not have any other alternative either.

In 1995, one day, Kulwant Singh who had started getting fits of insanity due to repeated police torture and whose health had deteriorated too much, breathed his last after a prolonged illness. According to family members the actual reason of Kulwant's death was the repeated police torture. Kulwant Singh was married and has a son namely Bhupinder Singh aged nine years. His wife's parents had got her remarried. Now Nachhatter Singh's elder son Jagroop Singh only is left in their family.

**VFF/0696**

Kamaljit Singh alias Mintu 21 of Budhsinghwala in Moga. Victim Kamaljit Singh's father Ajmer Singh is an Ex-Serviceman who had retired from the Army in 1985. He had three sons and two daughters. His second son Kamaljit Singh had studied upto Matric at the Govt. High School Bagha Purana and had failed in Matric exam in 1989. Thereafter he abandoned studies and started helping the family by doing manual labour.

In the beginning of July 1991, one day, SHO of Nihalsingh Wala raided his house and arrested Kamaljit Singh. He was detained illegally for 15 days. Thereafter they registered FIR No. 64 dated 15-7-91 against him u/s 25/54/59 of Arms Act, 3/4 of TADA (P) Act and FIR No. 62 dated 15-7-91 u/s 307/353/186/34 IPC and 25/54/59 of Arms Act, 5/6 of TADA (P) Act at police station Nihalsingh Wala and sent him to jail. He got released on bail after 5-6 months. In the meantime, Dharamkot police had also registered a case against Kamaljit Singh. After his release, Kamaljit Singh used to attend court regularly in connection with his cases. 2-3 months later, he was arrested again and implicated in cases by Bagha Purana and Jaiton police and sent to jail. He got released on bail in those cases also. After his release, Kamaljit stayed at home.

On 27-7-92 at about 8 PM, the police raided his house. On seeing the police, he ran away. The police party which was led by ASI Gurcharan Singh and Head Constable Jugraj Singh arrested Ajmer Singh (father), Rajinder Singh (brother) and Paramjit Singh (brother) and took them to Bagha Purana police station. There the SHO Tehal Singh told Ajmer Singh to produce his son before the police.

On 28-7-92, the village Sarpanch (Head of village Council) Kirpal Singh and other respectable persons went to the police station and talked to the SHO. The SHO released Ajmer Singh on the condition that he would trace out his son (Kamaljit) and produce him before the police by evening. The Panchayat also advised Ajmer Singh to produce Kamaljit Singh. In the evening, Ajmer Singh along with Kirpal Singh (Sarpanch), Chand Singh (Member Panchayat), Darshan Singh (Member Panchayat) and 10-15 other persons went to the police station Bagha Purana. The SHO was not present at that time. The above mentioned Panchayat members produced Kamaljit Singh before the Head Constable Jugraj Singh. Head Constable Jugraj Singh released Rajinder Singh and Paramjit Singh.

On 29-7-92 at 8 AM, Ajmer Singh went to the Bagha Purana police station. There he met Kamaljit Singh and served him tea also. Similarly on 30-7-92 also Ajmer Singh met Kamaljit Singh at the police station. On the following day (31-7-92), when Ajmer Singh went to the police station he was not allowed to enter the police station. After some time

Ajmer Singh met SHO Tehal Singh who told him that Head Constable Jugraj Singh would let him know about his son. But when Ajmer Singh met Jugraj Singh, he said, "I don't know. You ask the SHO about it." Ajmer Singh requested the Panchayat to pursue his case. Thereafter Ajmer Singh along with the panchayat met SHO Tehal Singh several times. Once or twice, the SHO made a false promise of releasing him but later on the SHO told the Panchayat clearly, "We have killed Kamaljit Singh."

According to Ajmer Singh: "When the police did not give any information even after several days, I submitted applications to Senior Officers the copies of which are attached herewith. Apart from that, I appeared in the courts on many scheduled dates of his (Kamaljit's) cases and submitted applications to various courts where Kamaljit's cases were sub-judice, through my counsel informing them that my son had been arrested by Bagha Purana police. Ultimately, various courts closed the cases saying that they would reopen them when the accused would be present in the court. But the court did not ask the police to produce Kamaljit Singh. In response to the applications which I had sent, I received acknowledgement from the Chief Minister's office only saying that my application had been forwarded to the Home Department.

"I was called twice by Bagha Purana police in connection with the inquiry of my son's case but I don"t know who had ordered the said inquiry. I had gone along with the Panchayat on both the occasions. First time, SHO Bagha Purana, Raj Singh had called me. I narrated the whole incident to him. The SHO obtained my signatures and those of Sarpanch Kirpal Singh on some papers. Six months later, I was called to the police station by ASI Gurmel Singh of Bagha Purana police station. He said, "You quietly sign on the blank papers." I signed, due to fear.

"Even now, I keep on sending applications to the Chief Minister, Agriculture Minister and Senior Officers. But nobody has bothered about me. I should have not signed the papers on both the occasions. But what could I do? The circumstances were such."

Ajmer Singh feels that had he not signed the papers, his son's case might have reached some logical conclusion.

Kamaljit Singh's disappearance has had a deep impact on the mind of his father Ajmer Singh.

**VFF/0697**

Jagga Singh alias Jagga 30 of Budhsinghwala in Moga. While Gurjant Singh, a cousin of Jagga Singh was in jail, Jagga Singh joined the militant ranks and he was absconding at the time of release of Gurjant Singh.

After the release of Gurjant Singh from jail, Bagha Purana police began raiding Nachhatter Singh's (Gurjant's father) house for arresting Gurjant Singh. Once, the SHO (Station House Officer) of Bagha Purana police station Mr. Madan Lal Dhingra picked up Gurjant Singh and took him to Bagha Purana P.S. (Police Station). From there he was taken to Jaiton P.S. and then to Faridkot C.I.A. (Central Investigation Agency) Staff where he was detained illegally for 10 days. He was tortured brutally at Jaiton P.S. and CIA Staff Faridkot. He was got released from the CIA Staff by the family members and the Panchayat but on the next day itself, SHO of Bagha Purana P.S. raided his house. However, Gurjant Singh had not slept at his house that day. The police picked up Nachhatter Singh and detained him for 15 days. The police asked them to produce Gurjant Singh but Gurjant Singh had absconded once for all. When the family members talked to Gurjant Singh about producing himself before the police, he said, "These people (the police) will kill me. As such, I will not present myself before them now." The family members also felt that there was some logic in his argument, so, they also did not put much pressure on him to present himself before the police.

A few days after Gurjant Singh had absconded, his cousin Jagga Singh was arrested by the police. The Faridkot and Ferozepur police slapped several cases against him and sent him to Sangrur jail where he was detained for 3 years. In the meantime, the police arrested Gurjant Singh's brother Kulwant Singh, implicated him in several cases and sent him to Sangrur jail. Kulwant Singh had been tortured brutally by Faridkot police. As such he was in bad shape physically while in jail.

After Gurjant Singh had absconded in 1986, the police used to pick up his family members. They used to pick up his father Nachhatter Singh, brothers and uncle Chand Singh often and detain them illegally for days together. Once, the SHO of Bagha Purana police station Mr. Gurtej Singh picked up his mother Surjit Kaur also and released her on the following day.

In 1987, a person namely Jarnail Singh was murdered by someone. The police turned the needle of their suspicion towards Chand Singh and Gurjant Singh. keeping in view such an attitude of the police, Chand Singh also began to remain away from his house. As a result, the police began raidsing his house more frequently. In May 1987, under the leadership of Ray-Ribiero combine the police repression was intensified in Punjab and political workers were arrested in large numbers under TADA (Terrorist & Disruptive Activities (Prevention)

Act). During this time, the SHO of Bagha Purana police station Mitt Singh (who was later killed by militants) arrested Gurjant Singh's father Nachhatter Singh and tortured him brutally for 10 days in illegal custody at Bagha Purana police station. Thereafter he implicated him in a case under TADA (that of giving shelter to militants) and sent him to Ferozepur jail. In the meantime, the police began to raid their house regularly. All the family members went underground. The police carried away all household goods including the main gate of the house. None of the family members returned home for complete three years and grass came up all over the house. No agricultural operations could be carried out for three years. Nobody dared to take their land on contract for cultivation due to the fear of the police.

In 1990, slowly, some members of Gurjant Singh's family began to return home and started cultivating their land. But, the fear of the police was still there and none of the male members used to sleep at home. While Gurjant Singh was absconding, the police arrested his sister Charanjit Kaur and brother-in-law (sister's husband) Sukhdev Singh Fauji resident of Kale Ke several times. The police tortured also Sukhdev Singh several times. Apart from that, the police used to pick up his other relatives also like aunts ('Maami', 'Bhua') and uncle ('Phuphar'). Not only that they used to pick up the relatives of their relatives also.

In 1987, while Gurjant Singh's father was in Ferozepur jail, the police arrested Chand Singh from village Ghall Kalan along with 4 other youth including Kuldip Singh r/o village Ghall Kalan from whose tubewell all the five were arrested. About 10 days after their arrest all of them were killed in an "encounter" with the police. At that time, all the family members and relatives were target of police wrath and all of them were homeless. Chand Singh's case could not be pursued. The family members had come to know about Chand Singh's arrest after 2-3 days. 10 days later they read the news in the newspapers about his having been killed in an "encounter" with the police.

In the meantime, Gurjant Singh's brother Kulwant Singh and cousin Jagga Singh were released from Sangrur jail. Even after his release, Kulwant Singh was picked up and tortured brutally by Bagha Purana police several times. Jagga Singh absconded from home 2-3 months after his release and ultimately he was killed in an encounter with the police at village Chhajanwali near Jagraon. During this period, Gurjant Singh's elder brother Jagroop Singh was also picked up several times and subjected to brutal torture by the police.

On 29 July 1992, Gurjant Singh was killed in an encounter with the police at the house of Kaur Singh in Model Town (Extension) at Ludhiana. However, his family remained the target of police wrath even thereafter. The police neither handed over the body of Gurjant Singh to the family members nor got it identified from them. The police put several restrictions on the family even at the time of his 'Bhog' (last rites) ceremony. Only his family memebrs were allowed to attend the same. Even after Gurjant Singh had been killed, Bagha Purana police continued to raid their house and they used to pick up Nachhatter Singh, Jagroop Singh, Kulwant Singh and Jaswant Singh, often. During this period the Bagha Purana police slapped a case under Arms Act against Jaswant Singh and sent him to jail. He was in jail for two months and thereafter he was released on bail.

In 1993, during the Panchayat elections in the Punjab, DSP (Deputy Superintendent of Police) Randhawa of Bagha Purana police arrested Binder Singh s/o Lal Singh, a Mazhabi Sikh and a worker of Jagroop Singh (Gurjant Singh's brother) and detained him for 15 days at the CIA Staff Bagha Purana. Thereafter, he implicated him in a case under the Arms Act and delivering provocative anti-national speeches and sent him to jail. He could be got released on bail only after one month. Now he has been acquitted in that case.

In April 1993, Havaldar (Head Constable) Jagraj Singh of Bagha Purana police along with some constables came in a Canter (four-wheeler), picked up Jaswant Singh on the way who was driving a Tractor and brought him to home to inform the family members that he was taking away Jaswant Singh to the police station as he had been summoned by the officers. After the arrest of Jaswant Singh, his father Nachhatter Singh along with the Sarpanch (Head of Village Council) of the village, Kirpal Singh reached police station Bagha Purana. They met the SHO Mr. Tehal Singh who said, "We will release him in the evening." Nachhatter Singh and the Sarpanch met Jaswant Singh in the police station. Jaswant Singh took off his watch and handed it over to Nachhatter Singh. Same day evening, Nachhater Singh was also picked up from his house by Bagha Purana police. Again the male members of the family began to remain away from home, due to fear. They sent respectable persons to the SHO several times. However, the SHO always used to say, "You don't talk to me about those people at all."

Nachhatter Singh was detained at different police stations and secret (torture) centres. During this period, he was subjected to inhuman torture several times in the presence of SSP (Senior Superintendent of Police) Tiwari, SP (Ops.) Shri Anil Gautam. Six months later, the Bagha

Purana police dropped him at his house. At that time, his physical condition was very bad. He could recover only after medical treatment for several months. It was Head Constable Jugraj Singh who had come to drop Nachhatter Singh at home and he said, "You don't waste money in pursuing his case. Jaswant Singh is no more." The family members accepted it as the Will of God. Of course, they did not have any other alternative either.

In 1995, one day, Kulwant Singh who had started getting fits of insanity due to repeated police torture and whose health had deteriorated too much, breathed his last after a prolonged illness. According to family members the actual reason of Kulwant's death was the repeated police torture. Kulwant Singh was married and has a son namely Bhupinder Singh aged nine years. His wife's parents had got her remarried. Now Nachhatter Singh's elder son Jagroop Singh only is left in their family.

**VFF/0698**

ChandSingh 45 of Budhsinghwala in Moga. Nachhatter Singh and Chand Singh sons of Late Kehar Singh were farmers and residing at village Budhsingh Wala. Nachhatter Singh had six children-four sons namely Jagroop Singh (36 years), Kulwant Singh (deceased), Gurjant Singh (deceased) and Jaswant Singh (disappeared). Chand Singh was unmarried and he used to live with his brother's family. Nachhatter Singh had two daughters namely Charanjit Kaur (married) and Gurdeep Kaur (expired). The uncle ('Chacha') of Nachhatter Singh and Chand Singh, S. Karnail Singh (since deceased) also used to live at village Budhsingh Wala. His sons namely Gurcharan Singh and Visakha Singh had expired. Now only his grandsons live at village Budhsingh Wala. Karnail Singh was an "Amritdhari" (Baptised) Sikh. Apart from being religious minded he used to take active part in the political programmes of Shiromani Akali Dal. He had taken a very active part in the 'Dharam Yudh Morcha' (political agitation) launched by Shiromani Akali Dal in 1982. He was close to Sant Jarnail Singh Bhindranwale.

In May 1984, the B.S.F. (Border Security Force) had laid seige to Gurdwara Bibi Kahn Kaur in Moga city which continued for a number of days. The Akali and Sikh Students Federation workers who had been trapped inside were fired at, killing nine persons on the spot. Karnail Singh was one of them. The bodies of Karnail Singh and others were not handed over to their respective families.

It was in those days that Gurjant Singh son of Nachhatter Singh and grandson (in relation) of Karnail Singh became politically active after the death of Karnail Singh at the hands of the B.S.F. and began living in the office of the Sikh Students Federation at Gurdwara Singh Sabha in Moga City along with other youth. In June 1984 during the Army attack on Sri Darbar Sahib at Amritsar and 38 other Gurdawaras, the Army arrested Gurjant Singh along with his other companions from Gurdwara Singh Sabha, Moga. The police implicated Gurjant Singh in many cases apart from booking him under N.S.A. and sent him to Ferozepur jail. Later on, he got released on bail.

In the meantime i.e. during the time Gurjant Singh was incarcerated in jail, Chand Singh (brother of Nachhatter Singh) remained fully active politically and the police used to arrest Chand Singh often, due to political reasons. However the police did not arrest any other member of the family during this time. Chand Singh was very religious minded and he had a thorough knowledge of Sikh tenets. He had received religious education from Sant Mian Singh Jheeri Wale Dera. Though Chand Singh was a farmer, yet, he often used to attend various functions for preaching Sikhism.

While Gurjant Singh was in jail, one of his cousins namely Jagga Singh s/o Major Singh s/o Mehar Singh also joined the militant ranks and he was absconding at the time of release of Gurjant Singh.

After the release of Gurjant Singh from jail, Bagha Purana police began raiding Nachhatter Singh's house for arresting Gurjant Singh. Once, the SHO (Station House Officer) of Bagha Purana police station Mr. Madan Lal Dhingra picked up Gurjant Singh and took him to Bagha Purana P.S. (Police Station). From there he was taken to Jaiton P.S. and then to Faridkot C.I.A. (Central Investigation Agency) Staff where he was detained illegally for 10 days. He was tortured brutally at Jaiton P.S. and CIA Staff Faridkot. He was got released from the CIA STaff by the family members and the Panchayat but on the next day itself, SHO of Bagha Purana P.S. raided his house. However, Gurjant Singh had not slept at his house that day. The police picked up Nachhatter Singh and detained him for 15 days. The police asked them to produce Gurjant Singh but Gurjant Singh had absconded once for all. When the family members talked to Gurjant Singh about producing himself before the police, he said, "These people (the police) will kill me. As such, I will not present myself before them now." The family members also felt that there was some logic in his argument, so, they also did not put much pressure on him to present himself before the police.

A few days after Gurjant Singh had absconded, his cousin Jagga Singh s/o Major Singh s/o Mehar Singh was arrested by the police. The Faridkot and Ferozepur police slapped several cases against him and sent him to Sangrur jail where he was detained for 3 years. In the meantime, the police arrested Gurjant Singh's brother Kulwant Singh, implicated him in several cases and sent him to Sangrur jail. Kulwant Singh had been tortured brutally by Faridkot police. As such he was in bad shape physically while in jail.

After Gurjant Singh had absconded in 1986, the police used to pick up his family members. They used to pick up his father Nachhatter Singh, brothers and uncle Chand Singh often and detain them illegally for days together. Once, the SHO of Bagha Purana police station Mr. Gurtej Singh picked up his mother Surjit Kaur also and released her on the following day.

In 1987, a person namely Jarnail Singh was murdered by someone. The police turned the needle of their suspicion towards Chand Singh and Gurjant Singh. keeping in view such an attitude of the police, Chand Singh also began to remain away from his house. As a result, the police began raidsing his house more frequently. In May 1987, under the leadership of Ray-Ribiero combine the police repression was intensified in Punjab and political workers were arrested in large numbers under TADA (Terrorist & Disruptive Activities (Prevention) Act). During this time, the SHO of Bagha Purana police station Mitt Singh (who was later killed by militants) arrested Gurjant Singh's father Nachhatter Singh and tortured him brutally for 10 days in illegal custody at Bagha Purana police station. Thereafter he implicated him in a case under TADA (that of giving shelter to militants) and sent him to Ferozepur jail. In the meantime, the police began to raid their house regularly. All the family members went underground. The police carried away all household goods including the main gate of the house. None of the family members returned home for complete three years and grass came up all over the house. No agricultural operations could be carried out for three years. Nobody dared to take their land on contract for cultivation due to the fear of the police.

In 1990, slowly, some members of Gurjant Singh's family began to return home and started cultivating their land. But, the fear of the police was still there and none of the male members used to sleep at home. While Gurjant Singh was absconding, the police arrested his sister Charanjit Kaur and brother-in-law (sister's husband) Sukhdev Singh Fauji resident of Kale Ke several times. The police tortured also Sukhdev Singh several times. Apart from that, the police used to pick up his other relatives also like aunts ('Maami', 'Bhua') and uncle ('Phuphar'). Not only that they used to pick up the relatives of their relatives also.

In 1987, while Gurjant Singh's father was in Ferozepur jail, the police arrested Chand Singh from village Ghall Kalan along with 4 other youth including Kuldip Singh r/o village Ghall Kalan from whose tubewell all the five were arrested. About 10 days after their arrest all of them were killed in an "encounter" with the police. At that time, all the family members and relatives were target of police wrath and all of them were homeless. Chand Singh's case could not be pursued. The family members had come to know about Chand Singh's arrest after 2-3 days. 10 days later they read the news in the newspapers about his having been killed in an "encounter" with the police.

In the maentime, Gurjant Singh's brother Kulwant Singh and cousin Jagga Singh were released from Sangrur jail. Even after his release, Kulwant Singh was picked up and tortured brutally by Bagha Purana police several times. Jagga Singh absconded from home 2-3 months after his release and ultimately he was killed in an encounter with the police at village Chhajanwali near Jagraon. During this period, Gurjant Singh's elder brother Jagroop Singh was also picked up several times and subjected to brutal torture by the police.

On 29 July 1992, Gurjant Singh was killed in an encounter with the police at the house of Kaur Singh in Model Town (Extension) at Ludhiana. However, his family remained the target of police wrath even thereafter. The police neither handed over the body of Gurjant Singh to the family members nor got it identified from them. The police put several restrictions on the family even at the time of his 'Bhog' (last rites) ceremony. Only his family memebrs were allowed to attend the same. Even after Gurjant Singh had been killed, Bagha Purana police continued to raid their house and they used to pick up Nachhatter Singh, Jagroop Singh, Kulwant Singh and Jaswant Singh, often. During this period the Bagha Purana police slapped a case under Arms Act against Jaswant Singh and sent him to jail. He was in jail for two months and thereafter he was released on bail.

In 1993, during the Panchayat elections in the Punjab, DSP (Deputy Superintendent of Police) Randhawa of Bagha Purana police arrested Binder Singh s/o Lal Singh, a Mazhabi Sikh and a worker of Jagroop Singh (Gurjant Singh's brother) and detained him for 15 days at the CIA Staff Bagha Purana. Thereafter, he implicated him in a case under the Arms Act and delivering provocative anti-national speeches and sent him to jail. He could be got released on bail only after one month. Now he has been acquitted in that case.

In April 1993, Havaldar (Head Constable) Jagraj Singh of Bagha Purana police along with some constables came in a Canter (four-wheeler), picked up Jaswant Singh on the way who was driving a Tractor and brought him to home to inform the family members that he was taking away Jaswant Singh to the police station as he had been summoned by the officers. After the arrest of Jaswant Singh, his father Nachhatter Singh along with the Sarpanch (Head of Village Council) of the village, Kirpal Singh reached police station Bagha Purana. They met the SHO Mr. Tehal Singh who said, "We will release him in the evening." Nachhatter Singh and the Sarpanch met Jaswant Singh in the police station. Jaswant Singh took off his watch and handed it over to Nachhatter Singh. Same day evening, Nachhater Singh was also picked up from his house by Bagha Purana police. Again the male members of the family began to remain away from home, due to fear. They sent respectable persons to the SHO several times. However, the SHO always used to say, "You don't talk to me about those people at all."

Nachhatter Singh was detained at different police stations and secret (torture) centres. During this period, he was subjected to inhuman torture several times in the presence of SSP (Senior Superintendent of Police) Tiwari, SP (Ops.) Shri Anil Gautam. Six months later, the Bagha Purana police dropped him at his house. At that time, his physical condition was very bad. He could recover only after medical treatment for several months. It was Head Constable Jugraj Singh who had come to drop Nachhatter Singh at home and he said, "You don't waste money in pursuing his case. Jaswant Singh is no more." The family members accepted it as the Will of God. Of course, they did not have any other alternative either.

In 1995, one day, Kulwant Singh who had started getting fits of insanity due to repeated police torture and whose health had deteriorated too much, breathed his last after a prolonged illness. According to family members the actual reason of Kulwant's death was the repeated police torture. Kulwant Singh was married and has a son namely Bhupinder Singh aged nine years. His wife's parents had got her remarried. Now Nachhatter Singh's elder son Jagroop Singh only is left in their family.

**VFF/0699**

Baldev Singh 55 of Burj Dhilwan in Mansa. On 4th October 1991 at about 7 A.M., a six member Police party from Police Station Sehna in Tehsil Barnala Distt. Sangrur led by SHO Hardeep Singh and including ASI Teja Singh, Havaldar Gurcharan Singh and three other members came in a blue Canter and picked up Baldev Singh in front of a large number of people without giving any reason and went away. The Police vehicle was followed by six people from the village in a Jeep. Out of the six people, three namely Ranjit Singh s/o Baldev Singh, Balaur Singh s/o Jangir Singh, and Mithu Singh s/o Jang Singh were taken aside by Police and asked to pay a sum of Rs. 50,000/- for the release of Baldev Singh. But the money could not be arranged. He was disappeared (enforced) on 6th October 1991. Till today, his whereabouts are not known since then.

**VFF/0700**

Charanjit Singh alias Channi of Talwandi Rai in Ludhiana. On 19 July 1982, Sant Jarnail Singh Bhindranwale started a "Morcha" (agitation) against the arrest of Federation leader Bhai Amrik Singh and a leader of Damdami Taksal namely Baba Dehra Singh. After the Morcha had begun, Charanjit Singh Channi (victim) went to Amritsar and started cooperating with Sant Jarnail Singh and Federation leadership. After 1983, he started living at Amritsar permanently. At the time of Army attack on Sri Darbar Sahib at Amritsar, Charanjit Singh Channi was inside Sri Darbar Sahib Compex itself. But, he along with some of his associates escaped from there.

In 1985, Charanjit Singh Channi also played a leading role along with other leaders in reactivating the Sikh Students Federation. As Charanjit Singh Channi had deserted home, the Police started harassing his family members. He had got married in 1981. His wife was a staff nurse. His wife and children also went underground in order to avoid the Police dragnet. The Police used to arrest his father often. False cases were also registered against his father by the Police.

Charanjit Singh Channi had achieved glorious heights in the militant movement and he was considered one of the top militant leaders in those days. He was understood to have played a key role in constituting the Panthic Committee (Sohan Singh). Keeping in view the important role being played by Charanjit Singh Channi in the militant movement, the Police were in hot pursuit for him.

On 2 June 1989, Charanjit Singh Channi had gone to meet an acquaintance, the owner of a scooter repair shop, at Phase VII of Mohali Town. The Police had already been tipped off about it. As Charanjit Singh Channi reached at the said shop, he got suspicious on seeing the Police present there and tried to escape by running away. But, the Police party had laid a tight trap. As he tried to run away, he was hit on his head by some of the Policemen with the butts of their rifles. As such, he was injured in his head and fell down. The Police party immediately caught hold of him, pushed him into their vehicle and sped away. The eyewitnesses had told the family members that the whole operation lasted hardly a few minutes. In those days, his wife also used to live at Mohali itself. She and some of his associates received the information about this incident immediately. Press Notes were issued to various newspapers about the arrest of Charanjit Singh Channi, as a precautionary measure.

Master Dev Raj Singh (father) and his elder son Lakhbir Singh (Channi's brother) were detained in Ludhiana jail under TADA at that time. As the news of Charanjit Singh Channi's arrest had spread and also as he was a youth who belonged to a family with political background, the Police did not keep him in their custody for long and cunningly killed him on the same day at night in a fake encounter on a river under Police Station Morinda (Distt. Ropar). The Police told that when the abovementioned militant was signalled to stop at a 'Naka' (barrier) he opened fire. The Police returned the fire and in the exchange of fire, the abovementioned militant was killed. The news of the killing of Charanjit Singh Channi was broadcast on the Radio and TV. On the basis of Channi having been killed, Advocate Gurcharan Singh Ghumman got Channi's father Master Dev Raj Singh bailed out immediately. Immediately after coming out on bail, on 3 June 1989 itself, Master Dev Raj Singh along with eminent political leaders met the Deputy Commissioner at Ropar. After talking to the SSP. the DC told that the Police had already cremated the dead body of Charanjit Singh Channi. His father Dev Raj Singh obtained a copy of the F.I.R. and postmortem and filed a case in the Court of the Magistrate at Ropar. The family had received a copy of the photograph of Charanjit Singh Channi's dead body through the Court only. In the photograph, blood was oozing out of Charanjit Singh Channi's head and rest of his body had been covered with a bed sheet. The family members wanted to pursue the case of extra-judicial killing of Charanjit Singh Channi after arresting him, but, the Lawyers, acquaintances and even the Magistrate in whose Court the case was sub judice advised them that keeping in view the prevailing circumstances, the case be got sealed and pursue it later at an appriopriate time. Master Dev Raj Singh said that till 1995, it was Police Raj only in Punjab. Thereafter he had tried to pursue the case again. But, his Lawyer Gurcharan Singh Ghumman had expired and the case file could not be traced out from his office.

Master Dev Raj Singh said that no doubt his son was a top militant leader, but, the story of his killing in an "encounter", concocted by the Police is a white lie. He was arrested by a Police party of Ropar Police, from near the Scooter Marker in Phase VII of Mohali in broad day light and killed later in a fake encounter under Morinda Police Station.

**VFF/0701**

Manjinder Singh 21 of Talwandi Rai in Ludhiana. Manjinder Singh had gone from home on 13 April, 1992. On 22-4-1992 at 10 A.M., a

Police party from Raikot Police Station came to his house. They told his family members that their son had been killed in an encounter with the Police at Nathana police Station. They further told that they had to take them to that place in order to get the dead body identified. His family members were astonished. According to them, their son was not involved in any sort of militant activities. He used to go for work daily. The Police party took Gurdeep Singh and four other persons along with them to Nathana. There, his father Gurdeep Singh identified his dead body. Bullet injury marks were there on his face. The Police cremated the dead body in the presence of his father at Bathinda. The Police released Gurdeep Singh from there. On the fourth day, the Jagraon Police arrested Gurdeep Singh and took him to C.I.A. Staff. They tortured him brutally. The Police alleged that the militants used to visit his house. He was detained for four days.

His father Gurdeep Singh told that they came to know later on that on 22-4-1992, Manjinder Singh was at Raikot itself and he had visited Raikot Police Station and C.I.A. Staff Jagraon also in connection with some personal job. As he had a dispute with his Bus Company, he had gone to the Police in that connection. According to his family members, they had absolutely no knowledge about any of his illegal activities. They said that they were surprised on hearing from the Police that Manjinder Singh had been killed in an encounter with the Police. They did not suspect that he was arrested and then killed in custody, either.

**VFF/0702**

Harjinder Pal Singh alias Jinder 21 of Bassian in Ludhiana. On 21 October, 1991, a Police party from Jagraon Police Station led by DSP Paramjit Singh Khehra raided his house. Harjinder Pal Singh had gone to the Gurdwara. The Police rounded up all the family members (men and women) and took them to the Village Police Post. They were detained there for one night and released on the following day morning at the intervention of the Panchayat (Council) and eminent persons of the Village. The Police used to pick up his family members regularly till the time Harjinder Pal Singh was killed.

On 29-4-1992, Harjinder Pal Singh was killed in an encounter with the Police at Village Rakba under Police Station Mullanpur. Another youth namely Pawandeep Singh resident of Kaonke Kalan was also killed in this encounter. The Police took his father from home for identification. His dead body was identified by his father and uncle ('Taya') at Police Station Jagraon. His dead body was cremated at Daresi Ground cremation ground at Ludhiana. The charges for the shroud and firewood for both the youth, Rs. 1500/-, were paid by above mentioned family (that of Harjinder Pal Singh). None of the family members of Pawandeep Singh had turned up.

### VFF/0703

Jagtar Singh alias Taar 31 of Patti Dana, Raikot in Ludhiana. Victim Jagtar Singh's father Gurcharan Singh, aged 70 years, is a Sikh farmer resident of village Jhoraran, Tehsil Raikot. Gurcharan Singh had four sons. It was Jagtar Singh only who used to look after the agricultural farming. Gurcharan Singh owns 9-10 acres of land. One of his sons who was in the Army ealier had joined the Police later and had met with an accident. He is handicapped now-a-days. Another son of Gurcharan Singh is serving in the Security Force known as Indo Tibetan Border Police.

Jagtar Singh had got married around 1982. It was he only who used to look after the household as two of his brothers were in service. He was an "Amritdhari" (baptised) Sikh youth having got himself baptised after 1984.

In December (date not known) 1992, one day, a Police party led by DSP Sodhi raided his house and enquired about Lakhwinder Singh (brother of Jagtar Singh) who was not at home. So, the Police picked up Jagtar Singh and his father Gurcharan Singh and took them to C.I.A Staff. For 2-3 days, the Police did not bother them. On the third day, DSP Sodhi tortured Jagtar Singh and Gurcharan Singh brutally. He said that the militants were visiting them and that they were in possession of their (militants') weapons. Jagtar Singh was tortured so brutally that he became unconscious. Few days later, Lakhwinder Singh presented himself before the Police. At the time of his release, Jagtar Singh was in very bad shape. He had injury marks on his thighs. His mental condition also was not OK. He had lost control over passing of stool and urine. His family members got him treated at Dayanand Hospital at Ludhiana for about 1 year. They took him to Rajindra Hospital also. They referred him back to Dayanand Hospital, Ludhiana. For a few days he remained admitted there. However, he never recovered and breathed his last on 12-12-1993. His family members said that the cause of his death was Police torture only.

* According to his father, Gurcharan Singh, meanwhile, the Police arrested him and Lakhwinder Singh, once each, on the basis of suspicion. However, they released them on their own, after few days.

### VFF/0704

Jarnail Singh alias Jaila 47 of Pheru Rai, Raikot in Ludhiana. Jarnail Singh had two brothers and one sister. He was the eldest and in his childhood itself, he had gone away to Baba Kundan Singh at Gurdwara Damdama Nanaksar Jhorara for receiving 'Gurmat Vidya' (knowledge about the teachings of the Gurus). He used to live there itself. There used to be constant tussle between different claimants in the Nanaksar Institution. There were three different claimants there. One group is led by Baba Kundan Singh, the second by Baba Narain Singh and the third by Baba Sadhu Singh. Jarnail Singh used to live with Baba Kundan Singh. Once, some unidentified persons fired at Baba Narain Singh. It was then that Jarnail Singh was arrested for the first time by Inspector Sant Kumar, SHO of Raikot Police Station and tortured brutally in illegal custody for 28-29 days. However, he was released as he was found to be innocent. Apart from that, at another time also Jarnail Singh was detained for a day by the Police on the basis of suspicion and tortured brutally. At the time of his release, he had to be helped to walk as he was unable to walk on his own. He was bed ridden for two months. He was again arrested from Jhorara along with two others namely Jaswant Singh and Balwinder Singh. Few respectables of village Jhorara intervened to seek his release. At the Police Station Raikot, SHO Randhir Singh told Jarnail Singh, in front of Hardev Singh (brother) that in case he got any two militants arrested by him (Randhir Singh) then he would release him, as he was due for promotion.

In January, 1993, one day, Raikot and Jagraon Police surrounded the village Pheru Rai and conducted a house to house search. On that day, the Police officers had asked the village Panchayat to produce Jarnail Singh before them. However, the Police did not say anything to his family members. On the fourth day, the village panchayat produced Jarnail Singh before DSP Raikot, Paramjit Singh Khehra. The DSP questioned him there itself in front of the Panchayat and sent him back with the direction that he mark his attendance at the DSP's office after every 10 days. Ten days later, for the second time, Jarnail Singh, along with the panchayat marked his attendance at DSP's office and came back.

Again, ten days later, on 21-2-1993, he along with Hardev Singh (brother), Major Singh, Ajaib Singh and Kartar Singh went to DSP Paramjit Singh Khehra at his office. The DSP made Jarnail Singh to sit near him and told (others) that they may come on the following day morning and take him back. His brother Hardev Singh immediately contacted a Police officer from his village namely SP Gurcharan Singh who was posted as SP (Vigilance) Patiala at that time, as he happened be present in the village on that day. Immediately, Gurcharan Singh came to Raikot Police Station along with Hardev Singh at about 5 P.M. However, the Police did not release Jarnail Singh, as the SHO Randhir Singh was not present in the Police Station. SP Gurcharan Singh left the Police Station leaving behind Hardev Singh with a direction to the Munshi to tell the SHO to send Jarnail Singh along with Hardev Singh. But, the SHO did not turn up till 8 P.M. During his stay for about three hours in the Police Station, Hardev Singh continued to chit chat with Jarnail Singh. At about 8 P.M., Policemen asked Hardev Singh to buy liquor for them with a view to send him out of the Police Station somehow. The Policemen closed the gate of the Police Station as soon as Hardev Singh came out from there.

Thereafter, his family members along with the Panchayat met SSP Harinder Singh Chahal and DSP Paramjit Singh Khehra several times, but, they did not oblige them. According to Hardev Singh, they used to go daily in a hired car to pursue his case and they became indebted but the Police did not release him.

Hardev Singh (brother) told that on 20-1-2000, he read a news item in Jagbani (a Punjabi daily newspaper published from Jalandhar) that the Punjab and Haryana High Court had ordered an inquiry by the CBI into the death of Kulwant Singh son of Kamikkar Singh resident of Chowki Mann, Tehsil Jagraon, Distt. Ludhiana. The newspaper had mentioned that the inquiry was being conducted by Inspector Bharat Bhushan of the CBI. Hardev Singh suspected that his brother Jarnail Singh had been shown as an unidentified militant among the five militants who, according to newspaper reports dated 9 October, 1993, had been shown as having been killed in an encounter with the Police. The Jagraon Police had shown 3 identified and 2 unidentified militants as having been killed in the said encounter near village Gagra.

* Hardev Singh met Inspector Bharat Bhushan at Chandigarh CBI office and requested him to look into the enforced disappearance of his brother Jarnail Singh, by the Police. Bharat Bhushan advised him to approach the Court as the CBI did not undertake investigation on its own. Hardev Singh told the Inspector that the Police had shown his brother as one of the militants among the five militants killed by them in an encounter near village Gagra. Fortunately, the case being investigated by Inspector Bharat Bhushan, that of Kulwant Singh (Chowki Mann) was related to the case of those five youth killed by the Police near village Gagra. As such, Bharat Bhushan accepted the application of Hardev Singh and began investigation into this case also. The CBI has visited him

(Hardev Singh) once in this connection. The investigation is in progress. At last, the efforts of Jarnail Singh's family bore fruit and investigation into their case had begun without their going to the Court.

### VFF/0705

Shamsher Singh alias Goli 20 of Raikot in Ludhiana. Victim Shamsher Singh's mother Chand Kaur had four sons and five daughters. Shamsher Singh was her youngest son. His father owned a "Lalaari" (Dyer) shop in Raikot city. He quit his studies and began to help his father in his profession. Towards the end of 1985, he went to Dubai (UAE), but came back after a year. After his return, he started attending the "Chunni" (Dupatta—made of fine cloth worn by Punjabi women on their head) shop at Raikot city which his father had set up for him.

In the third week of August 1987, the Sidhwan Bet Police raided Shamsher Singh's house. They enquired about Shamsher Singh but he was not at home. The Police party picked up his brother Gurjit Singh and took him along with them. A few days later, Sant Kumar, SHO of Raikot Police Station raided their house again and picked up his mother Chand Kaur, father Milkha Singh and brother Balbir Singh. The Police pressurised the family members to produce Shamsher Singh.

On 2 September 1987, Shamsher Singh reached his aunt's ("Maasi's") house at 5 A.M. The house was surrounded by the Police. On seeing the Police, family members, relatives and residents of the Mohalla (locality) gathered there. As the Police were trying to take him away, he insisted on bringing his mother there. His mother was brought there under Police escort. After Chand Kaur's (mother) arrival, he was handed over to the SHO Sant Kumar in the presence of large number of Mohalla residents and relatives, at 7 A.M. The Police assured them that they would not harm him at all and would release him after questioning.

However, on the intervening night of 4-5 September, 1987, the Police killed Shamsher Singh along with another youth namely Jatinder Singh Sohi in a fake encounter near village Malsheeha—Giddarvindi. The Police had claimed that both the abovementioned youth were coming on a scooter when they were signalled to stop. They opened fire on the Police party and in the retaliatory firing by the Police both of them were killed. Initially, the Police declared them as unidentified militants. But, Punjab Kesri (a Hindi daily newspaper published from Jalandhar) dated 8 September 1987 carried a news item in which Mr. Pandey, SSP Ludhiana had issued a statement that the militants killed in the encounter on 5 September 1987 had been identified as Jatinder Singh Sohi and Shamsher Singh Golu. The 'Jagbani' (a Punjabi daily newspaper published frpm Jalandhar) dated 20 September 1987, carried a news report giving details of the 'encounter'.

His family members came to know about his killing from the news report in the newspaper only. At that time, male members of the family were in Police custody. His father and one of the brothers were released on 6 September 1987 whereas another brother namely Gurjit Singh was released 15 days later after the family members had paid a bribe of Rs. 50,000/- to the SHO of Sidhwam Bet Police Station. The family members were afraid that the Police might kill Gurjit Singh also.

**VFF/0706**

Harbhajan Singh alias Bhajan 20 of Umarpur, Raikot in Ludhiana. Victim Harbhajan Singh's mother Gurdev Kaur had three sons. Harbhajan Singh has been killed at the hands of the Police. Her husband died due to the shock of his son's death. Her another son namely Makhan Singh had died as a result of electric shock. Her whole family are "Amritdhari" (baptised) and religious minded. They are well off economically.

Harbhajan Singh was a religious minded youth and he was influenced by the then ongoing militant and political movement in the Punjab. That is why the Police used to arrest him often. Cases were registered against him by the Police, 2-3 times. Whenever he used to come out on bail, the Police used to start harassing him again. On being harassed repeatedly by the Police, he deserted home in the beginning of 1991. As Harbhajan Singh had absconded, the Police started harassing his family members and relatives.

In November 1991, the Jagraon Police informed his family members that their son had been killed in an encounter with the Police near Muktsar. His father was taken to Police Station Muktsar and shown the photograph of his dead body. His father expired due to the shock of the death of his son, about 2 years later. His family members do not know whether the Police had arrested Harbhajan Singh and then killed him or he was killed in a genuine encounter.

**VFF/0707**

Harpal Singh Mann alias Pala 24 of Gharkhana, Samrala in Ludhiana. On 14-6-90, Harpal Singh Mann and his companion Baljit Singh Bhutto were going on a Scooter near Kotla Ajner. A Police party led by ASI Bhupinder Singh fired at Harpal Mann without warning, in broad daylight, in front of the Govt. High School. The bullet hit Harpal in the leg. The Police called for reinforcements from Khanna through wireless. DSP Param Raj Singh and SHO Rupinder Singh Bhullar reached the scene. They tortured Harpal brutally on the spot. Then he was taken to the Police Station. There they killed him and next day morning, his dead body was cremated at Khanna Cremation Ground by the Police. His ashes were handed over to his family.

### VFF/0708

Amarjit Singh of Gausla, Samrala in Ludhiana. On 20 May 1994, he was abducted by police in civil clothes and riding in a Maruti Van and a Maruti Car. It was witnessed by his colleagues (students). At 11 A.M., near Khanna Fatak, his mother Ajmer Kaur saw that Amarjit Singh is sitting in a Maruti Car. I went near the car. Amarjit signalled me from inside to go away from the scene. The police had got suspicious of me; so I walked away quickly. At about 12 noon, the police party came back, dug out something from a Motor, about 500 yards away from our field. This scene was witnessed by many people of the village. After the departure of this police party, i/c Barwali Police Chowki, Hakam Singh came to the village. He arrested Mann Singh, Nasib Singh (Fauji's brother), and Raj Singh s/o Swaran Singh. According to police post Barwali, ASI Hakam Singh was from Jagraon Police. At that time, Karnail Singh was the SHO at Jagraon Sadar. The encounter also had been staged jointly by the police of Sadar Jagraon and C.I.A Staff. Jagraon police had also told on 21st that he had been killed in an encounter. But we did not see his dead body. Only we saw the pyre after the body had been burnt.

### VFF/0709

Charan Singh 47 of Goslan, Samrala in Ludhiana. That on 17-5-94, at about 2.40 A.M., there was a knock on the door of the ComplainantÆs house. The Complainant woke up and saw the policemen on the rooftop of her house who directed her to open the door. On the opening of the door, the policemen barged into the house of the Complainant, the senior officer leading the police party who was later on identified as SSP Harinder Singh Chahal of Police Distt. Jagraon, asked about the ComplainantÆs husband Charan Singh. Hearing the reply of the Complainant that Charan Singh was sleeping inside, the police party accompanied the Complainant where Charan Singh was sleeping and he was woken up by the Complainant. They enquired about Amarjit Singh of the ComplainantÆs village from Charan Singh. The ComplainantÆs husband replied that he did not know anything about Amarjit Singh, still, the Police took away Charan Singh alongwith them. That when Nasib Singh, brother of Charan Singh tried to follow them, he was pushed back by the Police.

That on 19-5-94, a delegation comprising of Panchayat members and other respectables of the village which included the then Sarpanch

Malkeet Singh, Ex-Panch Sant Singh, Nambardar Shadi Singh, the then Panch Kashmira Singh, Mann Singh, and Nasib Singh, brother of Charan Singh met SHO of P.S. Sadar, Khanna, DSP Manmohan Singh, and SSP of Police Distt. Khanna, Ram Kishan Bedi. The SSP asked them to come over the next day. The Panchayat also met the SSP on 20-5-94 and 21-5-94. That when the Panchayat met the SSP on 21-5-94, Swaran Singh, brother of Charan Singh and Jagdish Singh, brother of the Complainant, were also in the delegation, the SSP told them that Charan Singh had been taken away by Jagraon Police. Thus, they should approach Jagraon Police.

That on evening of 20-5-94, Nasib Singh, brother of Charan Singh was picked up by ASI Hakim Singh in-charge Police Post Barwali who was later on released on 21-5-94. It was disclosed to Nasib Singh by the aforesaid ASI during his detention that Charan Singh had been picked up by Jagraon Police.

That on 20-5-94, a delegation comprising of Jagdish Singh r/o Vill. Ghulumajra, brother of the Complainant, Gurdial Singh, then Sarpanch of village Ghulumajra, met SSP Jagraon, but to no avail. Thereafter, the complainant and her family members had been consistently meeting SHO of P.S. Jagraon and SSP of Police Distt. Jagraon, but nothing was disclosed to them about the whereabouts of Charan Singh. In the meantime, SSP Jagraon, was transferred to Patiala. The village Panchayat and the brother of the Complainant also met him over there on 1-6-94 and 2-6-94. The SSP told them to meet one Inspector Puri of P.S. Sirhind.

Thereafter, the Complainant and her family members came to know that amongst the four militants killed in an encounter with the Police of P.S. Sadar Jagraon on 20-5-94 two were Charan Singh, the husband of the Complainant and Amarjit Singh s/o Balam Singh r/o village Goslan who was also picked up on 20-5-94 at 9 A.M. from Nabha City. But till date, no information has been given by the Police to the Complainant as whether her husband is alive or dead.

That after the disappearance of Complainant/Es husband, payment of pension was stopped. In that connection, the Complainant met the concerned authorities who asked the Complainant to produce some proof in the shape of a FIR or some other document in support of the contention of the Complainant so that the family pension could be sanctioned to the Complainant. The Complainant alongwith the Panchayat approached the Khanna Police, but they did not register a FIR against Police personnel. However, they agreed to register a FIR dated 6-7-95 showing that Charan Singh is missing since 17-5-94 when he had gone to the fields.

That the Police Officials of Police Distt. Jagraon are sending some persons to the Complainant and also seeking the services of Distt. Sainik Welfare Officer Ludhiana in order to dissuade her from pursuing further the matter of disappearance of Charan Singh. They have even offered a huge amount of money to the Complainant for entering into a compromise. The Deputy Director Sainik Welfare, Ludhiana wrote a letter dated 22-4-98, to the Complainant at the instance of SSP Jagraon, asking her to come over to his Office so that the matter may be settled once for all.

That the Complainant had been moving from pillar to post to locate the whereabouts of her husband namely Charan Singh but to no avail. That the Complainant is facing financial hardships after the death of her husband and the claim for compensation sent by the Complainant through the Dy. Director Sainik Welfare Ludhiana, to the Distt. Grievances Officer, Ludhiana bears testimony to this fact.

### VFF/0710

Manjinder Singh 22 of Binjal, Raikot in Ludhiana. Victim Manjinder Singh's father Master Gurbakhsh Singh, resident of village Binjal, belongs to an educated farmer family. His wife Shamsher Kaur was also a teacher. They had three sons and have one daughter. Manjinder Singh was their 2nd son and he was an outstanding football player. He was recruited in the Police from the Sports quota only. He had passed his 10+1 at that time. He used to be posted to a Police Station rarely only. Most of the time, he used to be busy in his sports training camps. He used to come home on leave, sometimes. Manjinder Singh was a thorough gentle man and a Gursikh youth. He had got himself baptised after joining the Police.

On 16 November 1991, for the first time, the Jagraon Police riding a large number of vehicles raided the house of Master Gurbakhsh Singh. The Police party was led by Inspector Manmohan Singh of Jagraon (Sadar) Police. The Police entered the house by scaling the wall, at 11 P.M. The Police enquired about Manjinder Singh. master Gurbakhsh Singh replied that he was on duty. The Police party took away Master Gurbakhsh Singh to the Police Station Jagraon (Sadar) and on the following day, they took away his younger son Sukhjit Singh to the Police Station (Sadar), Jagraon. Sukhjit Singh was tortured also by the Police. They (the Police) asked them about Manjinder Singh, but, Master Gurbakhsh Singh and Sukhjit Singh told that he used to be on duty only and that they did not know anything more about his whereabouts. After few days, the Police released Master Gurbakhsh Singh and three days later, Sukhjit Singh was released.

On 27 December 1991, DSP Raikot, Mr. Shiv Kumar and ASI Dilawar Singh picked up Master Gurbakhsh Singh from his residence. He was detained at the Raikot Police Station for three days and released thereafter. He was picked up again on 31 December (1991) and tortured brutally. He was released a few days later at the intervention of eminent persons. From January 1992 onwards, Master Gurbakhsh Singh was detained at Raikot Police Station continuously for several months. In between, he was released for a few days only. During the month of August, SHO Bharat Kumar used to send Master Gurbakhsh Singh to school from the Police Station itself. On 26 August (1992), SHO Darshan Singh tortured Master Gurbakhsh Singh brutally. Whenever a new DSP or SHO used to be posted in, the Police wrath against their family used to increase. According to Master Gurbakhsh Singh, at last, he was released on 29 November 1992. Till that time, Master Gurbakhsh Singh had spent about 7 months in the illegal custody of Raikot Police. He showed a copy of the attendance register of his school to the Investigation Team as a proof of the same. At the time of his release, the SSP Swaran Singh Ghotna himself came to Raikot Police Station and told Master Gurbakhsh Singh that his son Manjinder Sibngh had been killed in an encounter with the Police on 19 November 1992 at 9:30 P.M. near village Hasanpur under Police Station Dakha in Jagraon Police district. Manjinder Singh was said to be a top militant of Khalistan Liberation Force.

Master Gurbakhsh Singh told that after his release, even though, he did not get any clue about Manjinder Singh's killing in an encounter, yet, from the attitude of the Police, it seemed that the story of his killing in an encounter was false. On 12 January 1993, an ASI of Patiala Police came to their house with a summon and told that theirt son was absent from duty since October 1991. Master Gurbakhsh Singh told the said ASI that he was telling that Harjinder Singh was a deserter whereas SSP Jagraon had claimed that Manjinder Singh had been killed in an encounter with the Police on 19 November 1992. To this, the ASI had no answer and went away after handing over the summon.

According to Master Gurbakhsh Singh, thereafter, whenever the Police used to visit his house he used to get annoyed with the Police and used to tell them that on the one hand they had killed his son and on the other they were humiliating him by raiding his house. He told the Investigation Team that he was sure that the Police had killed his son after arresting him. However, he did not collect more facts about it as he had no intention to file a case. The reason being that both he and his wife were Government employees and they were afraid that if they filed a case, the Police would harass them. Master Gurbakhsh Singh was most annoyed with the Akali Government that those people who talked about the atrocities committed by the Congress regime and the Police Raj, never bothered about their plight.

**VFF/0711**

Jagdev Singh 19 of Seeloani, Raikot in Ludhiana. Bhag Singh Dhariwal (victim Jagdev Singh's father) is a small farmer, resident of village Seeloani. He had three daughters and a son. His son Jagdev Singh started helping his father in agricultural farming after passing class VI. Jagdev Singh was clean shaven and a Kabbadi player. According to his family members, Jagdev Singh never participated in any sort of militant or political activities. Neither any case had ever been registered against him nor was he arrested anytime on the basis of suspicion.

On 11 February, 1993 at about 5 A.M., the Police entered Bhag Singh's house by breaking open the gate of the house. The Police party directed Jagdev Singh to come along with them and beat him up at the gate of the house. The same Police party had picked up the Sarpanch (Head of Village Council) Harbhajan Singh also. The Police took them to Police Station Mehna (Distt. Moga). For three consecutive days, his father Bhag Singh along with members of the village Panchayat (Council) enquired at the Police Stations of Jagraon, Raikot and surrounding places, but, did not get any information. On 14-2-1993, the family members of the Sarpanch got him released from Mehna Police Station. from him only, they came to know that Jagdev Singh had been detained at Mehna Police Station. On getting this information, his father Bhag Singh along with members of the Panchayat reached Mehna Police Station on the following day. However, they were not allowed to go inside, but, came to know from the Constables unofficially that Jagdev Singh was indeed inside the Police Station. Bhag Singh used to go to Mehna daily. He used to take along one Comrade also, from village Ajitewal. The said Comrade came out and told Bhag Singh that the Police had demanded Rs. 1,00.000/- (One Lakh only) for releasing Jagdev Singh. Bhag Singh told that as he was a poor man he could not afford to pay such a huge amount to the Police. For many days, they (Mehna Police) used to say also that the SHO had gone to U.P. for arresting some persons and that they would release him (Jagdev Singh) on the return of the SHO. Bhag Singh does not remember the name of the said SHO now.

On 8-3-1993, the Jagraon Police raided their house and picked up Jagdev Singh's father Bhag Singh, Nasib Kaur (mother), Karamjit Kaur (sister), Avnit Kaur (sister) and took them to the C.I.A. Staff. There, the SSP Harinder Singh Chahal and other Police officers recorded their statements. On 10-3-1993, the Police released Nasib Kaur, Karamjit Kaur and Avnit Kaur and directed them to produce Chhinder Kaur (elder sister of Jagdev Singh). The Panchayat produced Chhinder Kaur on 10-3-1993. During their custody, the Police arranged a meeting of Jagdev Singh with Karamjit Kaur (sister) and Nasib Kaur (mother). Jagdev Singh was in a very bad shape due to Police beating and was too scared. He cried and said, "Mummy, these people will kill us." The Police tortured Jagdev Singh brutally in front of Nasib Kaur and Karamjit Kaur also. He was crying and saying, "Get me released."

The Police arranged a meeting between Chhinder Kaur, who had been produced on 10-3-1993 and Jagdev Singh at the C.I.A Staff. Jagdev Singh said, "Sister, in case any of the weapons of the militants is there in our house, hand the same over to the Police. Our lives will be saved." But, Chhinder Kaur told that the militants had indeed visited their house but they had not kept any of their items (weapons etc.) in their house. On 14-3-1993, the Police released Bhag Singh and Chhinder Kaur. At that time, they were not aware as to where the Police had detained Jagdev Singh. During his detention, Bhag Singh had injured his head by banging it agaisnt the wall.

According to Bhag Singh, for the next 2-3 months, he continued to visit the Police Station along with different people and approach the senior officers but he was not told anything about the whereabouts of his son. He mortgaged one acre of his land. At last, he got exhausted and sat quietly at home. Some people came and told him that the Police had killed Jagdev Singh and declared him as unidentified. But, he did not get any proof to believe it, he said.

* Later on, SSP Chahal and Incharge of C.I.A Staff had told family members of Jagdev Singh that he had been taken away from them by Mehna Police.

**VFF/0712**

Kuldeep Singh alias Gogi 21 of Cheemna, Jagroan in Ludhiana. Bhajan Singh (victim Kuldeep Singh's father) is an Ex-Serviceman and he had seven sons. Kuldeep Singh was his third son. After passing his Matriculation, Kuldeep Singh started learning an electrician's job at Jagraon and side by side he used to help his father in agricultural farming. He was a Gursikh and a religious minded youth. His father told that he was not aware of his (Kuldeep's) links with any of the militant groups. Bhajan Singh had joined the Telephone Department after his retirement from the Army.

Bhajan Singh told that in July 1991, Kuldeep Singh stopped coming home. 10 days after Kuldeep Singh had gone away from home without any intimation, C.I.A. Staff Jagraon raided his house and picked up Bhajan Singh. Bhajan Singh said that till the time Kuldeep Singh was killed, the Police used to raid their house daily in a routine manner and used to take him (Bhajan Singh) and Gulzar Singh (uncle—'Taya' of Kulddeep Singh) to the C.I.A Staff. Sometimes, Chowki Mann Police used to raid their house while at other times, Sidhwan Bet Police used to raid their house. The Panchayat (village council) used to get them released. They used to arrest them again a few days later. Bhajan Singh and Gulzar Singh used to be tortured by the Police using third degree methods.

On 26-6-1992, the Jagraon Police picked up Bhajan Singh and Gulzar Singh and took them to C.I.A Staff. First, they took them to the cremation ground where they got the dead body of Kuldeep Singh identified by them. According to Bhajan Singh, the dead body of another youth also was lying there about whom they did not know anything. After getting the dead body identified, they took them to the C.I.A Staff where they were tortured brutally. Gulzar Singh was got released after 15 days whereas Bhajan Singh was released by the Police after 25-26 days only, thanks to the tireless efforts made by his family members. Bhajan Singh and Gulzar Singh were tortured on the orders of the SSP Swaran Singh Ghotna and they were released also at his orders only.

Bhajan Singh told that even after Kuldeep Singh had been killed, the Sidhwan Bet Police picked him up twice and tortured him brutally. The SHO (whose name he did not remember) alleged that Kuldeep Singh had left behind money with him. This routine continued upto six months after the death of Kuldeep Singh. The Police did not allow the family members to perform Kuldeep Singh's last rites even. As per newspaper reports, Kuldeep Singh was associated with the militant outfit known as Khalistan Commando Force (Wassan Singh Group).

### VFF/0713

Major Singh 42 of Burj Kalra, Jagraon in Ludhiana. On 3 May, 1993 at about 11 P.M., the Police entered Major Singh's house while all the family members were asleep. At that time, Major Singh, his wife and children, Amarjit Singh (nephew—sister's son), Mohinder Kaur (mother), Jagtar Singh (wife's brother), Balbir Singh (wife's brother) were present in the house. The Police party directed all the four male members to accomapny them. The Police party had come in three vehicles which they had parked far away. His mother and wife informed the eminent persons of the Village immediately. Three four persons followed the Police vehicles in a car. The Police vehicles entered Nihal Singh Wala Police Station. The Villagers returned to the Village. On the following day, eminent persons visited the Police Station. The Police allowed them to meet the detained persons and assured them of their early release. All the four of them had been tortured by the Police.

On the third day, the SHO accepted a bribe of Rs. 50,000/- and released Jagtar Singh and Balbir Singh. On the fourth day, when his mother Mohinder Kaur and eminent persons of his Village met Major Singh at the Police Station they saw that one of his legs had been fractured due to Police torture. He informed them that he had been got tortured by SP (D) Shiv Kumar. His family members continued to meet him for 13 days continuously. During this period, the SHO had extorted another one and a half Lakh Rupees from his family members for the release of Major Singh. On the fourteenth day, when the family members and the eminent persons visited the Police Station to meet Major Singh, neither the Police allowed them to meet him nor told them anything about his whereabouts. All this while, the family members were never allowed to meet Amarjit Singh.

In the meantime, the SHO incharge of Hathur Police Post (Chowki), Ajaib Singh, started raiding his (Major Singh's) house daily. Other members of the family went underground, due to fear. The SHO of Hathur Police Post carried away all the household goods. The Police forced the family members to park one of the Trucks of Major Singh at Nihal Singh Wala Police Station. Meanwhile, relatives and friends of Major Singh continued to pursue his case in order to get him released. But they were helpless. The Police were not disclosing anything about the whereabouts of Major Singh and Amarjit Singh. The family members had gone underground due to the fear of the Police.

In the meantime, one day, a Police party visited his Village and told that his mother and the Village Panchayat had been called by SSP Tiwari to his office. Initially the members of the panchayat got scared. However, the Police visisted them a second time and assured them that they won't be harmed in any way. His mother Mohinder Kaur along with the Panchayat met SSP Tiwari at Faridkot after about three months of the arrest of Major Singh and Amarjit Singh. The SSP returned the amount of one and a half Lakh Rupees to his mother in front of the Panchayat. Then only it was known that the SSP had suspended the SHO of Nihal Singh Wala Police Station, Rachhpal Singh on the charge of bribery and arrested him. The panchayat asked the SSP about Major Singh Sarpanch and apprised him that the work of the Panchayat had come to a standstill. The SSP advised them to elect somebody as a Sarpanch temporarily for two months. Later on, the SSP used to put off the members of the Panchayat by saying that they should approach the SSP of their own Police District, that is, SSP Jagraon, in this conection.

\*      According to the family members, a few days after the arrest of Major Singh, the Faridkot Police had got a news item published in the newspapers that a militant namely Major Singh had been killed in an encounter with the Police near Village Beer Sikhan Wala. The said news item carried the details of the escape of a militant from Police custody, also.

As the Police did not disclose anything about his whereabouts, the family members filed a case in the Supreme Court. The Supreme Court marked an inquiry to District Judge, Chandigarh. According to his mother Mohinder Kaur, their lawyer was Ranjan Lakhanpal and that all the witnesses had deposed properly as advised by the lawyer. However, the lawyer did not get them any positive results, she said. They do not know what order was passed in the case. In the meantime, SHO Rachhpal Singh offered money to the family for reaching a compromise but they rejected the same. The documents pertaining to this case are not available with the family members but the same are available with the family members of Amarjit Singh at Mahal Kalan.

His mother Mohinder Kaur also said, "We were named as witnesses in the bribery case which the Police had registered against SHO Rachhpal Singh. He begged of us and made numerous rounds of our house. Ultimately he succeeded in getting our signatures on Court papers in his favour. I was not in favour of this, but, my son's brother-in-law Jagtar Singh got influenced by SHO Rachhpal Singh or may be he had got scared. As it was Jagtar Singh only who used to look after my household after the death of my son, I came under his influence and signed on the dotted line."

Note:      The legal status lof the case and the order(s) passed by the Court can be known only after inspection of the case documents. They might have lost the case due to technical reason as they had already deposed in favour of SHO Rachhpal Singh in the bribery case.

## VFF/0714

Bachan Singh 43 of Dalla, Jagraon in Ludhiana. On 22-12-92 at 4 P.M., 4 Policemen in civil dress came in a white Van. They pushed Dr. Bachan Singh and his wife Satpal Kaur forcibly into the Van and took them away. There was a Naka on the bridge of the Canal. Along with them, they were taken towards Malla. Satpal Kaur was dropped at a distance of 4 Kms. Police Naka was organised by SI Bhag Singh Leehan and Joginder Singh Kothe Sherjung of Police Distt. Jagraon (in civil dress). I know them very well. Dr. Bachan Singh and his wife Satpal Kaur were picked up by Ajmer Singh, incharge Chowki Chuharchakk under police station Mehna and he joined Joginder Singh Kothe Sherjung and SI Bhag Singh. He took them towards Malla. He was asking for an AK-47.

### VFF/0715

Sukhdev Singh alias Sukhi 35 of Umarpur, Raikot in Ludhiana. After passing his Matriculation, Sukhdev Singh joined the Army in 1977. He got married in 1982. In 1992, he came on discharge from the Army and was getting pension. He stayed at home for 6-7 months and he was busy in the construction of his house during this period. Once, in July-August 1993, Raikot Police raided his house with a view to arrest Sukhdev Singh. He got scared and went away to Hazur Sahib (Nanded in Maharashtra) along with his wife and child. There, he beagn to perform 'Sewa' (voluntary service) at the 'Dera' (religious establishment) of Baba Nidhan Singh. Two younger brothers of Sukhdev Singh were in foreign countries and they wished that Sukhdev Singh also should join them there. In those days, Sukhdev Singh was making preparations to go abroad. He was living at Hazur Sahib as he was scared of the Police.

But, one day in November (date not known) 1993 at 11 P.M., some Policemen in uniform and some others in civil clothes entered the room and arrested Sukhdev Singh. The Management of the Dera contacted the local Police but they did not disclose anything and told them that he had been arrested and taken away by Baroda Police. Later, it became known that they were from Jagraon Police. On the fourth day, his wife informed her in-laws about this incident. His wife Jasvir Kaur said that she did not know any of the Policemen. Sukhdev Singh's parents and in-laws ran from pillar to post and tried their level best to get him released, but, the Police did not disclose anything about his whereabouts.

One day, in December 1993, the newspapers carried a news report stating that a militant namely Sukhdev Singh had been killed along with another militant in an encounter with the Police near village Rasulpur Jandi under Sidhwan Bet Police Station.

    \*    The family members said that the newspaper in which the news report about the Police encounter had been published was not available with them at home. It was lying at a relative's house. They told that they would send the same by post. His wife Jasvir Kaur did not remember the date of his arrest.

However, she said that it was about 20 days before the Police encounter. It is said that he was killed by the Jagraon Police in a fake encounter in the month of December 1993.

\*     Jasvir Kaur further told that the Police had definite information. They did not ask his name even at the time of his arrest. They had said, "Sister! we will release him just now, after questioning him."

### VFF/0716

Harjinder Singh alias Khaddu 14 of Manuke, Jagraon in Ludhiana. On 4-5-93 evening, Harjinder Singh was returning home after watering his 'Barseem' fields from the Deharke side. On the way, he was abducted by a Police party led by Inspector Joginder Singh of C.I.A Staff Hathur and accompanied by Ajaib Singh, SHO of Police Chowki Hathur. According to the family, "We approached SSP Harinder Singh Chahal through Darshan Singh Brar MLA, Retd. DSP Mahinderpal Singh Kokari, Lucky Chahal's father, Congress leader Santokh Singh Aliwal; but could not get any clue about the whereabouts of Harjinder Singh. Only once, Mohinderpal Singh Kokari told us that our boy was with C.I.A. Jagraon."

### VFF/0717

Gurdev Singh 44 of Kaonke Kalan, Jagraon in Ludhiana. On 20 December, 1992, at 4 A.M., a police party consisting of 10-15 policemen came and told that they intend to arrest the Jathedar and take him along with them. On that night, newly born child of my daughter Paramjit Kaur, had died. We told the policemen that a child's death had occured in the family and that they were talking of arresting and taking him away. The Police Officer told that they would consult with their superior Officer and release him. The police took him along. The police released him in the afternoon. On 21st (December'92), Jathedar went to his daughter's in-laws at Ahmedgarh and we all came back on 22nd. On 25th December (1992) at 5.30 A.M., the Police party in a Gypsy and led by Inspector Gurmeet Singh came home. We told them that he had gone to the local Gurdwara. The police went to the Gurdwara and told that they had come to arrest and take him along. At this, Singh Sahib (Gurdev Singh) told that let the discourse come to a close. At the 'Samapati' (close) of the discourse, he told that he would go home and then accompany them. Singh Sahib came home, followed by the whole Sangat. At home, he took his bath and then the police party took him along to Sadar Police Station Jagraon. His younger son Hari Singh, and Mohinder Singh went to the Police Station with food but were turned away by the police. I came to know about this on my return in the evening. I prepared the food and went to the Police Station to serve it to him at 6 P.M. I met SHO Harbans Singh and informed him the purpose of my visit. He told that you hand over the food to us and we will give it to him. Then we met Jathedar Gurcharan Singh Jagraon, who is known to us. He told that, you go second time and that they would oblige you. But they (Police) refused the second time also.

**VFF/0718**

Randhir Singh alias Dhira 40 of Dangian, Jagraon in Ludhiana. On 13-2-94 at 8 A.M., he was produced in front of ASI Gurmit Singh at Police Post (Chowki) Kaonke Kalan. Jagdishar Singh (Sarpanch), Pishaura Singh (Panch) both from Dangian village last saw him at Police Chowki Kaonke Kala on 13th Feb 1994 at 4 PM.

**VFF/0719**

Avtar Singh 27 of Fatehgarh Sivian in Ludhiana. Avtar Singh was an "Amritdhari" (baptised) Sikh youth. His elder brother Punjab Singh was a top militant of Khalistan Liberation Force. That is why the Police used to pick up Avtar Singh and other members of his family. The Police used to torture the family members brutally. In 1989, the Police of Sidhwan Bet Police Station picked up Avtar Singh, his brothers Desraj Singh and Makhan Singh. They tortured them in illegal custody for several days and later registered cases against them under TADA and sent them to jail. All the three of them were acquitted in those cases in 1991 and they came back home. However, the Police used to pick them up again and used to torture them brutally. Most of the time, they used to be tortured by Balbir Chand Tiwari, Incharge of C.I.A Staff Ludhiana, Inspector Manmohan Singh of C.I.A Staff Ludhiana, SHO Sidhwan Bet Surjit Singh and DSP Jagraon, Harbhagwan Singh Sodhi. The above mentioned Police officers used to pick up Avtar Singh and his brothers repeatedly. Apart from that, the relatives of Avtar Singh and female members of his family also used to be picked up by the Police, often and detain them in illegal custody for several days. Whenever any militancy related incident used to occur, his family used to become the target of Police wrath.

On 2-9-91 Avtar Singh's brother Punjab Singh was killed along with another youth in an encounter with the Police near Sangeet Cinema at Ludhiana. However, even then the Police did not stop harassing his family. Often, the Police of Sidhwan Bet, C.I.A Staff Jagraon and C.I.A Staff Ludhiana used to raid their house. Whosoever male member used to be available at home, the Police used to pick him up and detain him in illegal custody for several days. After killing Punjab Singh, the Police accused his brothers of helping the militants. Mostly the focus of Police suspicion was Avtar Singh only. In 1992, the Police started harassing his family members too much. DSP Jagraon Harbhagwan Singh Sodhi pressurised the family members to produce Avtar Singh before the Police as they wanted to question him about something. Fed up with daily raids by the Police, his family members decided to produce Avtar Singh before the Police through some eminent persons.

The family members produced Avtar Singh before DSP Jagraon, Harbhagwan Singh Sodhi through a guarantor namely Inspector Ram Singh who hailed from the same Village and was close to the family of Avtar Singh. At that time, several other eminent persons of the Village were also present there. DSP Harbhagwan Singh assured them that he would release him after interrogation in a few days time.

About 8-10 days later, a news item appeared in the newspapers that six militants had been killed (on 18 August, 1992), in an encounter with the Police near Village Kular under Police Station Sudhar. The name of Avtar Singh also figured in the list of the militants shown to have been killed in an encounter with the Police apart from that of another youth of Vilage Fatehgarh Sivian namely Teja Singh son of Basant Singh who also had been produced before the Jagraon Police by his family members a few days ago. After the publication of the said news item, his family members talked to Inspector Ram Singh of their Village through whom they had produced him before the Police. Inspector Ram Singh enquired from DSP Harbhagawan Singh Sodhi who told him that Avtar Singh was involved in many incidents by militants and as such they (the Police) had killed him. Inspector Ram Singh conveyed this information to his family members. In those days, the family of Avtar Singh was the victim of Police terror. So, on hearing such a reply from the Police, they had no option except to keep quiet. According to his family members, they had decided to produce Avtar Singh before the Police in an attempt to save his life. Little did they know that this step of theirs itself would become the cause of his death. On being asked by the Investigation Team as to why did they not initiate any leagl action against the extra-judicial killing of Avtar Singh by the Police, his brother Desraj Singh told the Investigation Team that even after killing Avtar Singh in a fake encounter, the Police did not leave them alone and that all the brothers started living away from home. Desraj Singh said, "I myself came to live at my house only after five years. We could not even think of any action against the Police in such an environment."

**VFF/0720**

Bhagwan Singh of Hinsowal, Jagraon in Ludhiana. On 25 May 1993 at about 11 A.M., he was abducted by a police party in civil clothes from near a Cinema and a PCO at Mullanpur Mandi. Bhagwan Singh was kept at Police Station Dakha Mandi Mullanpur. After repeated requests by Comrade Rachhpal Singh of Ludhiana and Sardara Singh of village Hinsowal, DSP Pritpal Singh, then posted at Dakha P.S., assured them that he would be released on 5 June 1993. But instead of releasing him, the police got a news item published in newspapers on 5 June 1993, that Bhagwan Singh had been killed in an 'encounter' with the police.

**VFF/0721**

Harnek Singh alias Neka 30 of Malha, Jagraon in Ludhiana. In the words of Amarjit Kaur, wife of Harnek Singh, as narrated to Amrik Singh Muktsar:-

"On 16.6.1993 at about 5.30 A.M., the Police entered our house by scaling the boundary wall. Harnek Singh, myself, his father Gurnam Singh were asleep inside the house. The Police woke us up and asked Harnek Singh to accompany them as they wanted to enquire about somebody's house from him. The Police party led by SHO Ajmer Singh had come from Police Station Mehna. The Police took away Harnek Singh in a Gypsy and they had a Canter (four wheeler) also with them. They asked us not to worry as they wanted to ask him about somebody's house only. However, the family members understood that the Police were making a lame excuse. As such, the family members along with the Panchayat (Village Council) reached Mehna Police Station at 10/11 A.M. But, the SHO denied his custody. We along with the eminent persons and the Panchayat continued to meet SHO Ajmer Singh for 10 consecutive days and he denied his custody each time. However, on the 11th day, he admitted and demanded Rs. 50,000/- (Fifty Thousand only) for the release of Harnek Singh. On the same night, the family members approached SSP Chahal at Jagraon as he was close to his (Harnek's) family. On the folowing day, when the family members along with the money went to see the SHO, he said that he did not have Harnek Singh in his custody. Probably he got annoyed with us due to our approach to the SSP Jagraon."

    \*    The family members continued to approach senior officers in this connection for several months but nobody gave them any clue regarding his whereabouts. so far, the family members do not know as to what happened to Harnek Singh, after all.

Note:    Harnerk Singh's young wife lives alone at her house in the village. She has got only 2 bighas of land and makes both ends meet by selling milk. Her in-laws (elder and younger brothers-in-law) also do not help her at all.

\*      After this incident, the Police used to raid their house often. At times, they used to pick up his father and take him to the Police Station. However, they have not visited her house since the last 2-3 years.

## VFF/0722

Bhabhinder Singh of Kamalpura, Jagraon in Ludhiana. He arrived at Ludhiana Railway Station on 6 June 1984 on leave from the Army and deposited his luggage in the cloak room. After that, his whereabouts are not known.

## VFF/0723

Gurdial Singh 33 of Bassian, Jagraon in Ludhiana. Victim Gurdial Singh's father Surjit Singh has a younger brother namely Gurdev Singh. Surjit Singh's parents had expired in 1985. He is in touch with Damdami Taksal since the age of 18 years. He had got married to Surjit Kaur daughter of Kundha Singh, resident of Bhai Ka Chowk in district Sangrur. In 1953, he came in contact with Baba Gurbachan Singh, Chief of Damdami Taksal. Since then, he is an "Amritdhari" (baptised) Sikh. He received religious education at the Taksal and became a preacher. He used to stay at the Taksal for several months and he used to look after his family affairs also. As the children grew up, his sons Gurdial Singh and Preetam Singh took over the responsibility of agricultural farming.

By virtue of his association with Damdami Taksal, Surjit Singh took an active part in the Punjabi Suba agitation and he was jailed for 5 months and lodged in Ambala jail. He courted arrest alongwith a 'jatha' (group) of agitators during the "Dharam Yudh Morcha" (political agitation) and he remained in jal for 3 months. On 6 June 1984, when the Army attacked Sri Darbar Sahib at Amritsar and 38 other Gurdwaras, Surjit Singh had gone to village Eesru (near Khanna) for "Amrit Parchar" (religious discourses). The Army surrounded him alongwith his complete jatha and arrested all of them. A case was registered against them and they were sent to Ludhiana jail. He got released from there on bail, after 15 days.

In the meantime, the Police raided his house and arrested his younger son Preetam Singh and sent him to Ludhiana jail from where he was released on bail, one month later.

Thereafter, the Punjab Police included the above mentioned family in the list of "suspected" persons. The Police used to raid their house, often, on the basis of suspicion. Often, whosoever, whether Gurdial Singh or Surjit Singh, used to be available at home, the Police used to pick him up. The Police used to release them at the intervention of the village Panchayat (Council) only.

In February 1993, Jagraon Police raided their house and enquired about Gurdial Singh. He was not available at home at that time as he had gone to perform the duty of a "Paathi" (one who recites Gurbani from Guru Granth Sahib) at somebody's house where "Akhand Paath" (non-stop recitation of Gurbani from Guru Granth Sahib) function had been organised. The Police picked up Gurdial Singh's uncle ('chacha') Gurdev Singh and took him away along with them. When Gurdial Singh came to know about it, he slipped away from home, due to the fear of the Police. Meanwhile, the Jagraon Police started raiding the houses of Gurdial Singh's relatives with a view to arrest him. A Police party of Jagraon Police even went to the Headquarters of Damdami Taksal at Chowk Mehta with a view to arrest the parents of Gurdial Singh. The said Police party had earlier picked up the relatives, female as well as male, of the above mentioned family and taken them along with them. The Police sent these arrested relatives inside the Damdami Taksal Gurdwara and called Surjit Kaur, mother of Gurdial Singh, ouside and were about to arrest her and take her alongwith them when Baba Thakur Singh intervened. The Police had to leave her behind. But, while departing, the Police directed the family members to produce Surjit Singh, father of Gurdial Singh before them.

Thereafter, Surjit Singh met the SSP Jagraon, Harinder Singh Chahal, through some politician. Gajjan Singh, another leader of Damdami Taksal, was also with him. The SSP advised Surjit Singh to produce Gurdial Singh before them. He told him that Gurdial Singh was in possession of some of the weapons of the militants which he must hand over to the Police. The SSP assured Surjit Singh that they will not harm Gurdial Singh at all. Even they would not register any case against him, the SSP had said. Before this meeting, the Police had released all of their relatives on the condition that they would look for Gurdial Singh and produce him before them. Those relatives had been detained at the village Police Post itself. While releasing them, the Police had threatened them that in case they did not produce Gurdial Singh before them immediately, they would be arrested again. Those arrested included Gurdev Singh, Gurdev Singh Bhai Ka Chakk (Sangrur) (maternal uncle of Gurdial Singh), Gurdev Kaur (maternal aunt of Gurdial Singh), Zaila Singh, Hari Singh s/o Inder Singh, resident of Bassian (relative) and another uncle ('Maasar') of Gurdial Singh.

The family sucumbed to Police pressure and repression and they decided to produce Gurdial Singh before the Police. Another reason for this decision was that the SSP had assured that they would release Gurdial Singh after interrogation. As such, through the Sarpanch of a neighbouring village Sivia, namely Avjinder Singh, who was close to the Police, they produced Gurdial Singh before the SSP Harinder Singh Chahal at Jagraon who assured them that he would be released a few days later, after interrogation.

A week after Gurdial Singh was produced before them the Jagraon Police got a news item published in the newspapers that Gurdial Singh had escaped from their custody. Even though the family members suspected that the Police had killed Gurdial Singh, because in those days it was the common modus operandi of the Police to concoct such stories of escape from custody in order to save their skin from the clutches of law, yet, the family members continued running from pillar to post to find out the truth as to what exactly had happened to Gurdial Singh. But, even then the Police did not tell them the truth. However, on the basis of unofficial information received by them from the SSP and other sources in the Jagraon Police, they had to accept that Gurdial Singh was no more. But, so far the family members do not have any information as to in what manner the Jagraon Police killed Gurdial Singh and where did they cremate his body.

Before this incident, Surjit Singh had got one of his daughters namely Raminder Kaur, married off in America and he had sent his younger son Preetam Singh also to America. Preetam Singh is, now-a-days, an American citizen.

### VFF/0724

Harchand Singh alias Chand 35 of Chowki Mann, Jagraon in Ludhiana. Harchand Singh and Sukhdev Singh were real brothers and residents of village Chowki Mann in district Ludhiana. In all, they were four brothers. Their father had expired in 1991 and their other two brothers namely Iqbal Singh and Kunda Singh used to live separately. Harchand Singh was married to Kulwant Kaur and has two children namely Jaspreet Singh (16 years) and Harinderpal Singh (19 years). In the beginning, Harchand Singh and Sukhdev Singh had joined the Army. But, Harchand Singh quit the service after 7 years and Sukhdev Singh after 1 year. At present, they were engaged in agricultural and dairy farming. Harchand Singh was a 'Kesadhari' (one who grows hair) and Sukhdev Singh was clean shaven. According to their family members, both the brothers did not have any sort of political affiliations whatsoever. Neither any of them had ever been arrested on the basis of suspicion nor any case was ever registered against any of them during the zenith of militancy in the Punjab. Both the brothers were leading a normal life.

On 29 September 1993 at about 11 P.M. while Harchand Singh, his wife Kulwant Kaur and their children, Sukhdev Singh, Bhagwant Kaur (mother), Sukhjinder Kaur (sister, who is married at village Bhanur, but, had come to her parents' house that day) were asleep in their house, there was a knock on the door. Kulwant Kaur asked as to who was at the door. The reply came from outside that they were Policemen and directed them to open the door. Kulwant Kaur opened the door. A large number of Policemen entered the house and directed Kulwant Kaur to put on all the lights in the house. They asked her about Harchand Singh. Kulwant Kaur told that he was sleeping on the roof. Some of the Policemen went on the roof and brought Harchand Singh down and directed him to come along with them. On being asked by Kulwant Kaur the reason, the Policemen replied that they should not worry and that they would release him very soon. Kulwant Kaur informed their neighbour Rajinder Singh who in turn rang up the Sarpanch (head of village Council). The Sarpanch told that they would initiate some action in the morning.

Half an hour later, the Police came again. They asked Kulwant Kaur as to whose house was adjacent to that of theirs. Kulwant Kaur replied that it was their own house only. Sukhdev Singh was asleep in the said house. The Police took Sukhdev Singh also along with them. The Police party conducted a search of the house, also. On the following day, Kulwant Kaur informed the Sarpanch and other eminent persons of the village about the arrest of Harchand Singh and Sukhdev Singh. According to Kulwant Kaur, the Sarpanch (head of village Council) and the Panchayat (village Council) assured them that they would find out. But, till 30-9-1993 evening, the Panchayat did not tell the family members as to what action they had taken.

The newspapers of 1-10-1993 carried a news item that three militants had been killed in an encounter with the Jagraon Police near village Chowki Mann on the path leading to village Sohian. The news item gave the details of the killing of Harchand Singh and Sukhdev Singh in the said encounter. After reading the news item, Iqbal Singh, elder brother of Harchand Singh and Sukhdev Singh along with his neighbour Iqbal singh went to Jagraon. He tried to find out about this incident from an acquaintance who was posted in the security of the SSP, but, he did not tell them anything due to fear and advised him to enquire at the hospital from the persons who carried out the postmortem. Iqbal Singh went to the hospital and inquired from a class IV employee about the identification of the youth who had been killed in an encounter on 30-9-1993 and who were brought to the hospital for postmortem. From the information he received, it was clear to Iqbal Singh that out of the three youth whom the Police had shown as having been killed in the encounter on 30-9-1993, two were his brothers Harchand Singh and Sukhdev Singh. After getting this information, Iqbal Singh returned home and told the whole thing to his family members. The family members sat in mourning. Some time later, a DSP of the Jagraon Police along with Policemen came in civil dress. On seeing the family members sitting in mourning, he asked them as to why they were sitting in mourning and whether any of their kin had died. The family members kept quiet due to fear. The DSP inquired about the mother of Harchand Singh and Sukhdev Singh and took Bhagwant Kaur along with them in the vehicle.

After making efforts for two days and with the help of some eminent politicians, the family members got Bhagwant Kaur released from the custody of C.I.A. Staff Jagraon. Bhagwant Kaur told her family members that the Police had directed her not to raise their voice against the killing of her sons, not to talk to anyone about it and not to initiate any action against the Police. They threatened her that if they did, then the consequences would be disastrous. The family members got frightened to such an extent that they did not even perform the last rites of Harchand Singh and Sukhdev Singh.

Kulwant Kaur further told that her mother-in-law expired after four months of this incident. Both her elder brothers-in-law used to live separately. As such she called her mother Dalip Kaur to live with her. However, she also expired two years later. The family members are terrified of the Police, till today. They said that keeping in view what they had experienced, they could not even think of filing any case against the Police. Kulwant Kaur said that even though they were still terrified of the Police, yet, in their heart of hearts, they longed for getting justice. But, so far, nobody has come out in their support for getting justice done to them.

### VFF/0725

Gulzar Singh alias Gudu 26 of Manj Phaguwal in Ludhiana. On 4 March 1988, he was picked up from Patiala, Mall Road, near the College Gate. He was killed on 14 March 1988. The dead body had been kept at Sirhind Bassi police station. The respectables of the Village and brother of the deceased followed the police party. The cremation was carried out at Cremation Ground Bassi Pathana in front of the next-of-kin. His ashes were collected by his next-of-kin and immersed at Kiratpur Sahib. The Police Officer responsible for his death is Inspector Surjit Singh Grewal.

**VFF/0726**

Tara Singh Sandhu of Manj Phaguwal in Ludhiana. On 13 July 1987 at about 12 Noon, he was abducted by Manjit Singh, SHO Sadar Ludhiana along with 6 other policemen and taken to Ludhiana Sadar police station. Respectable persons of the Village and the area continued to visit Ludhiana Sadar P.S. and approached the SHO and the SSP but they were disappointed. He was not released.

**VFF/0727**

Atamjit Singh Mavi alias Goldy 18 of 9/19, PAU Ludhiana 141004. On 05-2-91, Atamjit Singh had gone to his college as usual. He was picked up on the way by C.I.A. Staff Ludhiana and since then, his whereabouts are not known. The personnel responsible are :-

1.   DSP Shiv Kumar, C.I.A. Staff Ludhiana
2.   Inspector Manmohan Singh, C.I.A. Staff Ludhiana
     The incident is described in more detail in a letter written on 16-2-1991, by Sh. Hari Singh Brar, President of Punjab Agricultural University Teachers Association, to the Prime Minister of India. The relevant portion of the same is reproduced below:-
3.   The facts of the case are as follows:-
     On February 5, Atamjit Singh aged 19 was abducted along with his friend Mohan Singh, by a police team led by DSP Shiv Kumar Sharma and C I A Inspector Manmohan Singh in broad day light from Bhai Bala Chowk, Ludhiana in full view of public. Both the boys were put into a private Matador (DL 3 C 3066) and taken to CRPF Interrogation Centre, Dugri. Their bicycle was left by the police at a nearby Dhaba ( a roadside eating place) and was picked up later in the afternoon by a C I A Constable.
4.   From Dugri, the victims were taken to Khanna Sadar Police Station where they were asked to change their clothes. It was from there that they were taken to Nasrali, the site of the alleged encounter where they were murdered in cold blood under the supervision of DSP Shiv Kumar. In order to suppress the identity of the victims, not only had their clothes been changed before the killing but the photographs of their dead bodies were also tampered with after the crime.
4.   The Ludhiana Police has all along been maintaining a criminal silence over this heinous crime. Even, the Punjab Governor, Mr. O.P. Malhotra went to the extent of publically denying that the boys had ever been picked up by the Ludhiana Police.

As per the murder at Nasrali, the Police came out with its own version. The F.I.R No. 26 of 6.2.91 lodged at Sadar Police Station claims that two unidentified militants had been killed in an encounter with two police parties led by Inspectors Manmohan Singh and Sant Kumar. Needless to say that this version is totally false and fabricated.

5.    The investigation both by our Association and Punjab Human Rights Organisation confirm the veracity of the above facts. The Ludhiana SSP Mr. Sharma, has, in the meantime, pulled up some of the eye witnesses who narrated the facts to our investigation team. They have been threatened with dire consequences if they divulge anything.

**VFF/0728**

Sudama Singh 19 Dheri, Jodhewal Basti in Ludhiana. He was killed in an encounter with the Police on 02/5/89 according to the Police. The Police Officers involved are SSP Sh. A.P. Pandey and an Inspector of Punjab Police.

**VFF/0729**

Sukhdev Singh alias Sukhi 26 of Chowki Mann, Patti Dhaliwal in Ludhiana. On 29-9-93 at 10 P.M., a Police party from Police Post, Chowki Mann led by SHO Gurmeet Singh Pinki raided the house of Sukhdev Singh and picked him up. During the same night, on 30/09/93 at 4 A.M., near the village itself, the Police enacted a drama of an encounter and shot him dead.

The following additional information about this case has been extracted from Proforma No. CCDP/01028 pertaining to Harchand Singh, real brother of the victim Sukhdev Singh, who also was abducted and shot dead along with him. The case of Harchand Singh was investigated by Amrik Singh Muktsar, in June 2000. The true translation of the said additional information is appended below:-

Sukhdev Singh and Harchand Singh were real brothers and residents of village Chowki Mann in district Ludhiana. In all, they were four brothers. Their father had expired in 1991 and their other two brothers namely Iqbal Singh and Kunda Singh used to live separately. Harchand Singh was married to Kulwant Kaur and has two children namely Jaspreet Singh (16 years) and Harinderpal Singh (19 years). In the beginning, Harchand Singh and Sukhdev Singh had joined the Army. But, Harchand Singh quit the service after 7 years and Sukhdev Singh after 1 year. At present, they were engaged in agricultural and dairy farming. Harchand Singh was a 'Kesadhari' (one who grows hair) and Sukhdev Singh was clean shaven. According to their family members, both the brothers did not have any sort of political affiliations whatsoever. Neither any of them had ever been arrested on the basis of suspicion nor any case was ever registered against any of them during the zenith of militancy in the Punjab. Both the brothers were leading a normal life.

On 29 September 1993 at about 11 P.M. while Harchand Singh, his wife Kulwant Kaur and their children, Sukhdev Singh, Bhagwant Kaur (mother), Sukhjinder Kaur (sister, who is married at village Bhanur, but, had come to her parents' house that day) were asleep in their house, there was a knock on the door. Kulwant Kaur asked as to who was at the door. The reply came from outside that they were Policemen and directed them to open the door. Kulwant Kaur opened the door. A large number of Policemen entered the house and directed Kulwant Kaur to put on all the lights in the house. They asked her about Harchand Singh. Kulwant Kaur told that he was sleeping on the roof. Some of the Policemen went on the roof and brought Harchand Singh down and directed him to come along with them. On being asked by Kulwant Kaur the reason, the Policemen replied that they should not worry and that they would release him very soon. Kulwant Kaur informed their neighbour Rajinder Singh who in turn rang up the Sarpanch (head of village Council). The Sarpanch told that they would initiate some action in the morning.

Half an hour later, the Police came again. They asked Kulwant Kaur as to whose house was adjacent to that of theirs. Kulwant Kaur replied that it was their own house only. Sukhdev Singh was asleep in the said house. The Police took Sukhdev Singh also along with them. The Police party conducted a search of the house, also. On the following day, Kulwant Kaur informed the Sarpanch and other eminent persons of the village about the arrest of Harchand Singh and Sukhdev Singh. According to Kulwant Kaur, the Sarpanch (head of village Council) and the Panchayat (village Council) assured them that they would find out. But, till 30-9-1993 evening, the Panchayat did not tell the family members as to what action they had taken.

The newspapers of 1-10-1993 carried a news item that three militants had been killed in an encounter with the Jagraon Police near village Chowki Mann on the path leading to village Sohian. The news item gave the details of the killing of Harchand Singh and Sukhdev Singh in the said encounter. After reading the news item, Iqbal Singh, elder brother of Harchand Singh and Sukhdev Singh along with his neighbour Iqbal singh went to Jagraon. He tried to find out about this incident from an acquaintance who was posted in the security of the SSP, but, he did not tell them anything due to fear and advised him to enquire at the hospital from the persons who carried out the postmortem. Iqbal Singh went to the hospital and inquired from a class IV employee about the identification of the youth who had been killed in an encounter on 30-9-1993 and who were brought to the hospital for postmortem. From the information he received, it was clear to Iqbal Singh that out of the three youth whom the Police had shown as having been killed in the encounter on 30-9-1993, two were his brothers Harchand Singh and Sukhdev Singh. After getting this information, Iqbal Singh returned home and told the whole thing to his family members. The family members sat in mourning. Some time later, a DSP of the Jagraon Police along with Policemen came in civil dress. On seeing the family members sitting in mourning, he asked them as to why they were sitting in mourning and whether any of their kin had died. The family members kept quiet due to fear. The DSP inquired about the mother of Harchand Singh and Sukhdev Singh and took Bhagwant Kaur along with them in the vehicle.

After making efforts for two days and with the help of some eminent politicians, the family members got Bhagwant Kaur released from the custody of C.I.A. Staff Jagraon. Bhagwant Kaur told her family members that the Police had directed her not to raise their voice against the killing of her sons, not to talk to anyone about it and not to initiate any action against the Police. They threatened her that if they did, then the consequences would be disastrous. The family members got frightened to such an extent that they did not even perform the last rites of Harchand Singh and Sukhdev Singh.

Kulwant Kaur further told that her mother-in-law expired after four months of this incident. Both her elder brothers-in-law used to live separately. As such she called her mother Dalip Kaur to live with her. However, she also expired two years later. The family members are terrified of the Police, till today. They said that keeping in view what they had experienced, they could not even think of filing any case against the Police. Kulwant Kaur said that even though they were still terrified of the Police, yet, in their heart of hearts, they longed for getting justice. But, so far, nobody has come out in their support for getting justice done to them.

**VFF/0730**

Manjinderpal Singh alias Nanna 23 of Leelan Megh Singh, Jagraon in Ludhiana. He was an 'Amritdhari' (Baptised) Sikh since the age of 5-6 years. He was wearing Cream Shirt, Checked Brown and Black Pant, Punjabi Jooti in his feet, and black turban on his head. He was wearing

Sri Sahib under his shirt. He was abducted by the Police party. As I raised a hue and cry, Hartej Singh Sekhon whom the policemen called Sekhon Sahib, pushed me to the ground, and took him towards Jagraon in an Allwyn of red colour. There were several other Gypsies also along with them. They tortured him to death in custody, shown him as having been killed in an 'encounter', cremated his dead body as unclaimed on the third day and intimated us thereafter only. My child had set up a Dairy Farm consisting of twenty 'Vilayati' (imported) Cows by raising a loan from the Bank. He used to cultivate his land himself and Tractor also he had purchased on loan only.

On 12-7-93 at about 11 P.M. a Police party led by Shiv Kumar, SP (D) of Jagraon knocked at our door. As the door was opened, the uniformed policemen barged in. They abducted Manjinderpal Singh. Hartej Singh Sekhon told the Constables to take him along as he had carried out a Bomb Blast. We raised a lot of hue and cry. We told them that he had a Dairy Farm consisting of twenty imported Cows and three four Buffaloes and that he had no spare time as he was too busy in his occupation. He is a lone worker and that he used to cultivate his land also himself. His brother was serving in the Army as a 2nd Lieut. They did not listen to us at all. They pushed me to the ground, put the child in a Matador and went towards Jagraon. He died as a result of torture. On 15-7-93 at night, they showed him as a militant having been killed in an 'encounter' and cremated his dead body as an unclaimed one.

**VFF/0731**

Gurwinder Singh alias Gobinda 29 of 2846 Moti Nagar, Ludhiana. On 18 September 1993, at about 2.30 P.M., police of Focal Point Ludhiana led by Inspector Paramjit Singh and including Munshi Balwinder Singh, and 4-5 Commandoes raided his house and picked up Gurwinder Singh and his younger brother Daler Singh. After 2 days, his brother Daler Singh was released at the intervention of responsible persons of the Mohalla. Daler Singh and Gurwinder Singh were taken to different rooms on arrival at the P.S. In the evening, Gurwinder Singh was tortured brutally. The Police were asking him to disclose where he had kept the AK-47. Daler Singh witnessed the torture of Gurwinder Singh. While releasing Daler Singh, SHO Paramjit Singh told that he would release Gurwinder Singh also after 2-4 days.

**VFF/0732**

Kuldeep Singh Gill 19 of Gill near Chabutra in Ludhiana. On 13-6-92 at 6 A.M., Kuldeep Singh was abducted from his aunt's (Massi's) house at village Pakhowal in Ludhiana District. Police had raided the houses of all our relatives simultaneously and they abducted Kuldeep

Singh from Pakhowal. The police party was led by DSP Shiv Kumar and it inculded Inspector Manmohan Singh and they belonged to C.I.A Ludhiana. The incident was witnessed by Harbans Kaur (Mother) and Gurdial Kaur (Aunt).

**VFF/0733**

Kulwant Singh alias Gun 25 of Chowki Mann, Jagraon in Ludhiana. Victim Kulwant Singh's mother Preetam Kaur aged 68 years is a resident of village Chowki Mann. Her husband Kamikkar Singh is an aged and somewhat mentally handicapped person. Preetam Kaur had one son namely Kulwant Singh (victim) and she has two daughters. After studying upto Middle, Kulwant Singh took up a job on a truck, first as a cleaner and later as a driver. His family owned just one and a half acres of land and the family used to make both ends meet with Kulwant Singh's earnings. During this period, he got his two younger sisters married off. At the time he used to work as a driver, once he had come home and was chopping the fodder with a "Toka" (fodder chopping) machine. His right hand got entangled in the 'Toka' machine and it was chopped off. As such, Kulwant Singh quit driver's job and returned home. He began to help his father in agricultural farming and used to feed his family by selling the milk of boffaloes which he had reared at his house.

Preetam Kaur told that her son was a thorough gentleman and he was not associated with the then ongoing militant movement in the Punjab. She said that the whole village appreciated his gentleness. According to her, on 29-9-1993 night, she, her husband Kamikkar Singh were sleeping in the courtyard of the house, Kulwant Singh was sleeping on the roof and Manjit Kaur was sleeping in the room. First of all, the Police party woke up Preetam Kaur and asked as to whose house it was. She replied that it was Kamikkar Singh's house. Then the Policemen asked as to who all were members of the family. At this, Preetam Kaur pointed towards her husband and daughter and said that those were all the members of the family. According to Preetam Kaur, for once the Policemen went back but half an hour later a large number of Policemen came to her house and directed her to accompany them as she had been called by the "Sardar" (SSP). The Police took Preetam Kaur and Kamikkar Singh to the village Police Post, forcibly. A lot of hue and cry had been raised at the Police Post. The Police were torturing Harchand Singh son of Nachhatter Singh. They had placed a stick over his private parts and were pressing the same with the stick. He was screaming.

Just after some time, some Policemen entered the Police Post with her son Kulwant Singh in their custody. Immediately, two of the

Policemen put Preetam Kaur and Kamikkar Singh in their vehicle and took them to Jagraon. According to Preetam Kaur, lot of other women also had been detained there. There, she was separated from her husband Kamikkar Singh. Preetam Kaur's condition became critical. On the third day she was shifted to a house where she was given medical treatment for three days. Thereafter, she along with other detained people from her village was locked up in a room near the SSP's office in the Police lines.

According to Preetam Kaur, a few days later, her husband, her son and other men and women of her village who were detained there, were shifted to Lohat Baddi Police Post. However, she was kept at Jagraon itself. She thinks that may be due to her ill health she was kept at Jagraon itself. Preetam kaur said that on 7 October 1993 at 8 P.M., Kulwant Singh, Ranjit Singh s/o Gurdev Singh, Gurdeep Singh and Ujagar Singh resident of Binjal were taken out of the Jagraon Police Lines in front of them. According to Preetam Kaur, her son said, "Mother! we take leave of you." She raised a hue and cry, but the Police shut the door of her room and threatened her to keep quiet. At that time, she herself, her husband, Gurdev Singh, Surjan Singh, Bachint Singh and several others had been detained there itself. All the others were released but she was detained for one month and a half. The Police forced her to cook food daily. One day, she happened to be alone in the Police Station. She went on the roof and sent a message with two boys of her village whom she had recognised. Then only she was got releasecd by the village Panchayat (Council).

According to Preetam Kaur, she came to know on her return home, that the Police had killed Kulwant Singh along with four other youth in a fake encounter near village Gagre. The Police had concocted the story that a Police party were taking Ranjit Singh, Gurdeep Singh and Ujagar Singh for the recovery of weapons when they were attacked by two unidentified militants lying in ambush. In the return firing by the Police, all the three arrested militants and both the attackers were killed. The family members believe that out of the two unidentified militants killed, one was Kulwant Singh only. All her household items were taken away by the Police while they were under detention.

* Preetam Kaur's elder brother-in-law ("Jeth") Bachint Singh and his son Jasvir Singh Rana were arrested by the Jagraon Police two three days after their arrest. Bachint Singh was released later along with Kamikkar Singh and Gurdev Singh, but, nothing is known about the whereabouts of Jasvir Singh Rana, so far. According to Preetam Kaur, the Police had killed

Jasvir Singh Rana also. Jasvir Singh Rana had been seen by other detained people of village Chowki Mann, in a critical condition. According to the people who were released later, Jasvir Singh Rana had died in Police custody itself. He was also the only son of his parents. His mother had expired already. According to Preetam Kaur, her brother-in-law Bachint Singh does not wish to initiate any action against the Police about the killing of his son by them.

* Preetam Kaur said that at the time of her release, the officers of the Jagraon Police had assured her that her son was alive and that they would releasse him. According to her, she believed them as Kulwant Singh's name had not been mentioned in the list of those five youth killed in the encounter. After her release, she ran from pillar to post. Gurmeet Singh Pinki (a Police "Cat" and Incharge of Police Post Chowki Mann) even took Rs. 14,000/- from her and assured her that he would show her son to her. Once, Gurmeet Singh Pinki told that Kulwant Singh would be produced in a Court at Jagraon that day. However, he was never produced there. The youth who had been brought from Nabha jail and produced there told her that there was no youth in the Nabha jail by the name of Kulwant Singh. According to Preetam Kaur, DSP Ashok Puri, Gurmeet Singh Pinki (Cat) and several other Policemen continued to make false promises to her for several years that her son was alive.

* According to Preetam Kaur, ultimately, she appeared before the Chief Minister Parkash Singh Badal along with her application. The Chief Minister marked her application to the SSP Jagraon. She said that she had demanded to know that she must be told whether her son was dead or alive. When she appeared before the SSP Jagraon he sent her to DSP Ashok Puri. After hearing her, the DSP called for Gurmeet Singh Pinki ("Cat"—incharge of Police Post Chowki Mann). Pinki returned Rs. 13,000/- to her out of Rs. 14,000/- which she had paid him. He told her that he had produced her son before the SSP, Harinder Singh Chahal and thereafter he did not know anything about him. He advised her to find out from SSP Chahal. DSP Ashok Puri told Preetam Kaur, "Mother! they are unnecessary keeping you in the dark. The Police have killed your son." On being counselled by the DSP, she accepted that Kulwant Singh had indeed been killed by the Police.

\*     Thereafter, Preetam Kaur, through one of her relatives, filed a case about the disappearance of Kulwant Singh, in the Punjab & Haryana High Court through Advocate Daljit Singh Rajput, in 1998. The High Court ordered an inquiry into this case by the C.B.I, vide their order dated 3-12-1999. The said inquiry is in progress.

\*     After the High Court had ordered an inquiry, several Police officers approached Preetam Kaur at different times to withdraw her case and offered inducements as well as issued threats to her. These Police officers included DSP Raghbir Singh, DSP Ashok Puri and some others. They threatened her to withdraw her case or else the Police might harm them. The Police officer who had threatened Preetam Kaur had said that he was a DSP but had not disclosed his name. But, DSP Raghbir Singh and DSP Ashok Puri had offered her inducemnets only.

**VFF/0734**

Girdeep Singh alias Deep 35 of Chowki Mann, Jagraon in Ludhiana. Gurdeep Singh, aged about 35 years was a resident of village Chowki Mann and he belonged to a Sikh family. His father had expired and one of his brothers used to live in Holland. When Gurdeep Singh failed in his Middle examination, his family members sent him to his uncle at Hyderabad who owned Transport business there. In 1979, he got married to Baljit Kaur. By then, he owned a truck of his own. He used to come home only when he used to get some cargo to be transported to Punjab, in his truck. Most of the time, he used to be out of home. He was a clean shaven youth and he had no link whatsoever with any sort of political activities. Neither he had been ever arrested nor any case registered against him ever throughout the period of militancy in the Punjab.

In September 1993, Gurdeep Singh had come from Hyderabad to Punjab along with his truck. His mother Gurdev Kaur had planned to visit her daughter in Holland. As such, Gurdeep Singh decided to stay at home for a few days. On 29-9-1993 at about 11 P.M., a large Police force entered his house by scaling the walls and woke up the family members who were asleep. At that time, Gurdeep Singh, Baljit Kaur (wife), Kartar Kaur (grand mother), Jagmohan Singh (son) and other children were present in the house. The Police party arrested Gurdeep Singh, Baljit Kaur and Jagmohan Singh, put all of them in a vehicle and took them to the village Police Post. Gurmeet Singh Pinki (Police Cat) incharge of Police Post Chowki Mann was also accompanying the Police party. SSP Harinder Singh Chahal and SP (D) Shiv Kumar also arrived at the Police

Post. Gurdeep Singh and Baljit Kaur were tortured brutally at the Police Post. The Police alleged that the militants were visiting their house. As such, they must get them arrested and they must disclose where the militants had hidden their arms and ammunition. On the following day, a Police party took Gurdeep Singh and Jagmohan Singh to C.I.A. Staff Jagraon whereas Baljit Kaur was detained at Police Post Chowki Mann itself for two three days. On the fourth day, a Police party took Baljit Kaur to Police Post Lohat Baddi. There, she was detained along with Gurdeep Singh (husband), Kulwant Singh s/o Kamikkar Singh, Kamikkar Singh, Preetam Kaur (mother of Kulwant Singh), Ujagar Singh s/o Jarnail Singh resident of Binjal, Harnek Singh resident of Chowki Mann and Surjan Singh resident of Chowki Mann. All of them were detained there for one night and day and on the second night brought back to Jagraon. At Jagraon, Gurdeep Singh, Kulwant Singh, Ranjit Singh and Ujagar Singh were locked up in one room whereas their next-of-kin were locked up in a separate room. On 6 October 1993, Baljit Kaur and her son Jagmohan Singh were released, thanks to the continuous efforts made by their relatives.

Baljit Kaur was informed by the persons who were released after she had been released, namely Gurdev Singh (Kulwant Singh's father), Kamikkar Singh and Bachint Singh (Kamikkar Singh's brother) that the Police had taken out all the four youth namely Kulwant Singh, Gurdeep Singh, Ranjit Singh and Ujagar Singh from the lock up on 7 October 1993 evening. Later on, the news report of their having been killed was published in the newspapers of 9 October 1993 that 5 militants had been killed in an "encounter" with the Police near Jagraon. The names of Gurdeep Singh, Ranjit Singh and Ujagar Singh had been mentioned in the said news item. The Police had claimed that they were taking three arrested militants for the recovery of arms and ammunition when they were attacked by two militants. In the retaliatory firing by the Police, three arrested militants and two attackers were killed. The Police had claimed that the two attackers could not be identified. But, the villagers knew that out of the two allegedly unidentified militants one was Kulwant Singh s/o Kamikkar Singh. However, the identity of the fifth killed militant was not known to the above mentioned families.

Baljit Kaur said that like other families, she was also threatened by Gurmeet Singh Pinki and senior officers of Jagraon Police that they should neither perform "Bhog" (last rites) of their killed relatives nor raise their voice against the Police in this matter. She told that they performed the "Bhog" of Gurdeep Singh after three years, due to fear.

Baljit Kaur further told that the parents of Kulwant Singh, another youth of her village who also had been killed along with Gurdeep Singh in the said fake encounter, filed a case in the Punjab & Haryana High Court through Advocate Daljit Singh Rajput. The High Court ordered an inquiry by the CBI in his case. The CBI team have visited Baljit Kaur also twice and recorded her statement.

### VFF/0735

Harjinder Singh alias Pappu 30 of Galib Kalan, Jagraon in Ludhiana. On 7th Vaisakh (around 20th April) at 3 A.M., Harjinder Singh and his wife were asleep in their house. Some Policemen scaled the walls of the house and entered it. They woke up the family members who were asleep. First of all, they woke up his wife Mukhtiar Kaur and asked her as to who was Harjinder Singh Pappu. She pointed towards her husband who was sleeping. The Policemen woke up Harjinder Singh Pappu and started abusing him. The house was thoroughly searched. The Police had surrounded the house from all sides. Nothing incriminating was found from the house. The Police party departed along with Harjinder Singh.

Same day, the same Police party had arrested another youth also from the village namely Billu s/o Gurdial Singh. At dawn, Mukhtiar Kaur intimated the village Sarpanch (head of village council) Uddam Singh. He said that they would go to the Police Station after some time and find out. Thereafter, she sent a message to her paternal village Heran and in-laws village Galib Kalan. Her father-in-law Surjit Singh along with Sardara Singh and village Sarpanch Jeeta Singh reached Jagraon Police Station to find out about this incident. The Police rebuked the Panchayat (village council) and turned them out.

Seven days after his arrest, a news item appeared in the newspapers that a militant namely Harjinder Singh Pappu had been killed in an encounter with the Police near village Sohian (near bridge on the Sem drain). The Police neither got the body identified nor they handed over the same to the next-of-kin. Mukhtiar Kaur said that they tried their level best to get him released but they were helpless. Being poor, they reconciled to their fate and sat quietly at home.

    *    Mukhtiar Kaur told the Investigation Team that after about one year of this incident, a youth from village Daiya in district Moga came to her and told that he had been detained along with Harjinder Singh Pappu at Jagraon (Sadar) in those days. He further told her that Harjinder Singh had died as a result of Police torture in the Police Station itself in front of him. The said youth had been released by the Police later.

## VFF/0736

Harbhajan Singh alias Bhajan 31 of Ramgarh Bhullar, Jagraon in Ludhiana. Harbhajan Singh s/o Surjit Singh, was a resident of village Ramgarh Bhullar and an "Amritdhari" (baptised) Sikh. They were three brothers and two sisters. His father Surjit Singh was a retired A.S.I. of Police. Shortly after passing his Matriculation, Harbhajan Singh had gone to Dubai (UAE) and stayed there for two years. On his return, initially he worked as a driver and later he purchased a three wheeler (Auto Rickshaw) of his own. Harbhajan Singh was a religious minded person of firm determination. The Army attack on Sri Darbar Sahib in June 1984 proved to be a turning point in his life. He was among the "Jatha" (a group of people) who had tried to proceed to Amritsar on hearing about the news of the attack on Sri Darbar Sahib. Thereafter, the Police began to look at him with suspicion. The Police used to pick him up often on the basis of suspicion. In 1987, once, C.I.A. Staff Jagraon tortured him brutally in their custody. Joginder Singh was the DSP there at that time. Later on, Sidhwan Bet Police registered a case against him and sent him to Nabha jail. He was in jail for about two to two and a half years. After his release from jail, the Police began to arrest him again. Ultimately, he got fed up with Police harassment and deserted home. The Police began to raid his house. Harbhajan Singh had got married in 1987 before he went to jail.

On 12 April 1991, Harbhajan Singh was sitting in the house of his in-laws at village Sidhwan Kalan. The Police surrounded the house. Harbhajan Singh committed suicide by consuming cyanide. The Police had handed over his dead body to the family members after getting the postmortem done. The cremation was carried out at his native village, Ramgarh Bhullar. His father Surjit Singh had expired on 12 April, 1990. Surjit Singh, who was a former Policeman, was very much upset due to being arrested by the Police time and again. As such, he became a drunkard and this habit of drinking only became a cause of his death.

Harbhajan Singh's uncle ('Taya') Jagjit Singh told that they got Harbhajan Singh's wife Kuldip Kaur remarried to his younger brother Baldev Singh. Now-a-days, they are living at Nawanshahr. Harbhajan Singh's elder brother Gurdarshan Singh had expired in an accident at Saudi Arabia. Gurdarshan Singh was also married and has two children. His wife is also living with her parents. Harbhajan Singh's mother Jaswant Kaur expired in 1998 due to illness.

## VFF/0737

Gian Singh alias Darshan Singh 40 of Sohian, Jagraon in Ludhiana. In the month of Gian Singh had gone to village Boparai Kalan to participate in the 'Kar Sewa' which was in progress on the under construction building of the Gurdawara Sahib there. On when the lintering of the roof of the Gurdwara Sahib was in progress, the Sudhar Police surrounded the Gurdwara Sahib as the Police had received information that a militant namely Sahib Singh Chandi was staying inside the building of the Gurdwara Sahib. On seeing that he had been surrounded by the Police, the militant who was staying inside opened fire. There was a stampede. All those who were present in the Gurdwara ran away. Gian Singh also ran away, due to fear. Gian Singh ran for about two kilometers through the fields and reached near the Jassowal road. As an encounter had ensued, the Police had cordoned off the area from all the four sides. Gian Singh was still running when a Police party led by DSP Harnek Singh arrived on the scene from the Jassowal road side. The Police directed Gian Singh to raise his hands. The farmers working in their fields nearby told that Gian Singh was advancing towards the Police as directed by them with his hands raised. But, the Police opened fire killing him on the spot.

The family members of Gian Singh came to know about this incident the same day itself as some of the teachers of Sohian school were residents of Boparai Kalan. This incident had occured at 11 A.M. and the news about it reached the village (Sohian) at about 1:30 P.M. Gian Singh's brother Malkeet Singh and another person namely Malkeet Singh reached Boparai Kalan and met the President of the Gurdwara Committee there. He testified to this incident and told them that the Police had taken Gian Singh's dead body to Sudhar Police Station. Malkeet Singh reached Sudhar police Station along with his companion. The Sudhar Police made them to sit there itself. Some time later, DSP Harnek Singh arrived there. He abused Malkeet Singh and alleged that his brother was a militant. But, Malkeet Singh told him that Gian Singh had no link whatsoever with the militants and that he had gone there for performing 'Kar Sewa' only at the Gurdwara Sahib. When the Police showed the dead body to him, Malkeet Singh identified it. Another dead body was also there which was that of militant Sahib Singh Chandi. The Police brought Malkeet Singh and both the dead bodies to Jagraon. They got the postmortem conducted and took the bodies to the cremation ground. By that time, several people from the village had reached Jagraon. The Police got the cremation done in their presence. The Police did not agree to hand over the dead body to the next-of-kin. The SDM also refused to hand over the dead body.

On the following day, the Police got a news item published in the newspapers that two dreaded militants had been killed in an encounter with the Police near village Boparai Kalan. The family members said that Gian Singh was not at all connected with militancy in any way. The people of Boparai Kalan who are eyewitnesses, testified that the Police had fired at Gian Singh and killed him without any reason. The Police could have arrested Gian Singh. Had the Police arrested him he would have been proved to be innocent. Instead of admitting their mistake, the Police unleashed a propaganda that Gian Singh was a dreaded militant which is a white lie. The people of the whole area knew that Gian Singh had no link whatsoever with any sort of political or militant activities.

Malkeet Singh (brother) further told that the Police terror was at its zenith in those days. As they are poor, they accepted it as the Will of God and sat quietly at home. The family members claimed that even today if an independent inquirty is conducted into this incident, the Police would be found guilty.

### VFF/0738

Nahar Singh 52 of Malak, Jagraon in Ludhiana. On 29 April 1991 at 10 P.M., when all the family members were asleep, someone knocked at the door of Sarpanch Nahar Singh. He opened the door and saw that some armed men in civil clothes were at the door. The persons standing outside claimed to be militants and told Nahar Singh to guide them to the houses of those people who had partaken of the "Amrit" (i.e. had got themselves baptised) but had broken the vows. At that time, Nahar Singh's wife Mohinder Kaur and Jeet Singh (elder brother) were also there in the house. The armed men were three in number and they were accompanied by another resident of the village namely Kulwant Singh s/o Jagir Singh. It was Kulwant Singh only who had knocked at the door of Nahar Singh and Nahar Singh had opened the door at the instance of Kulwant Singh only. But, the armed men made Kulwant Singh to stand at a distance and did not allow him to talk to Nahar Singh at all. The abovementioned men took Nahar Singh to the back side of the house and his wife Mohinder Kaur was not aware as to about what they talked to him there. Kulwant Singh continued to sit far away on one side. Kulwant Singh's legs had been incapacitated as a result of Police thrashing. Those armed men had brought him there on a bicycle.

Nahar Singh's wife Mohinder Kaur told that after two hours, Nahar Singh came inside the house to fetch his watch. At that time the armed men questioned Mohinder Kaur about some other persons of the village. They questioned her mainly about those persons who were associated with the militant movement either directly or indirectly. As Nahar Singh came out after collecting his watch, those armed men told that they wanted Nahar Singh to guide them to the houses of certain persons and that they would send him back shortly. They took Kulwant Singh on a bicycle and Nahar Singh on foot along with them to the house of Kapur Singh. Kapur Singh had constructed a Gurdwara at a little distance away from his house. The armed men called out Kapur Singh who was saying his prayers at that time. They threatened the other members of the family not to shout, otherwise they would kill them. A short while later, they shot all three of them dead in the Bagh (garden) situated in between Kapur Singh's house and the Gurdwara. According to Kapur Singh's family members, before killing them, those armed men had asked the inmates of the house to bring water and had offered the same to these three. Nahar Singh had a heated argument also with those armed men that why were they going to kill a handicapped person like Kulwant Singh and a religious person like Kapur Singh and if at all they wanted to kill someone they may kill him only. But, they did not listen to him. At about 1.15 A.M., those armed men shot Nahar Singh, Kapur Singh and Kulwant Singh dead on the spot. The villagers heard the sound of gunshots at about 1.15 A.M.

The villagers and family members of Nahar Singh were so scared that nobody dared to go to the site of the incident. At about 4 A.M. the villagers gathered and went to the site. They saw that the dead bodies of Nahar Singh, Kulwant Singh and Kapur Sinbgh were lying there. Mohinder Kaur told that she was apprehensive about some mishap since the time those armed men had taken away Nahar Singh from home. But, nobody was ready to accompany her to go and find out.

The family members of Nahar Singh told that a few days before this incident, on 13 April 1991, the militants had shot dead two persons of the village namely Bant Singh and Piara Singh near the Gurdwara in broad day light in front of several villagers. The militants had targetted Bant Singh only but Piara Singh came in the firing range while trying to save him. Bant Singh's cousin was a Policeman. The militants alleged that Bant Singh was a Police informer. In those days, It was a hot topic of discussion among the residents of the village and the area that Nahar Singh, Kulwant Singh and Kapur Singh were killed to avenge the kiling of Bant Singh. The people talked openly that the Police had carried out this operation in the guise of militants. As per a news report, the militants had owned the responsibility for the killing of Kulwant Singh, Nahar Singh and Kapur Singh. Howevere, in those days several militants had visited the local Gurdwara and assured the villagers that the militants had not done it. A few days later, the militants gunned down Bant Singh's relative who was a Policeman, at Patiala. The people said that this action was carried out by the militants in order to avenge the killing of Nahar Singh, Kulwant Singh and Kapur Singh at the hands of the Police. After talking to the family members, the Investigation Team gathered this impression only that the family members were fully convinced that the killing of Nahar Singh, Kulwant Singh and Kapur Sibngh was the handiwork of the Police only. But, since the family members of Nahar Singh, Kulwant Singh and Kapur Singh had filed a case now before the Deputy Commissioner, Ludhiana for claiming the compensation normally paid to the families of the persons killed at the hands of the militants, they did not wish to talk about it openly. However, the Investigation Team was told by several other residents of the village this only that it was the handiwork of the Police.

The Investiagtioin Team examined the copies of the threatening letters received by the family members of Nahar Singh, allegedly from the militants. But, it was clearly evident by looking at them that they were not from the militants. The case filed by the family members of Nahar Singh, Kulwant Singh and Kapur Singh before the Deputy Commissioner for claiming the compensation normally paid to the families of those killed at the hands of the militants is based on the statement issued by the militants in the newspapers owning the responsibility for the killing of Nahar Singh, Kulwant Singh and Kapur Singh and the threatening letters received by the family members of Nahar Singh. Three and a half years have elapsed since the said case was filed. In the beginning, the hitch in getting the compensation was that the Police had shown it as a case of inter-gang rivalry of the militants in the FIR registered by them in connection with this incident. But, now, with their influence, they have got a fresh FIR registered wherein it has been recorded that all these three persons had been killed at the hands of the militants. Now the family members are hopeful of receiving the compensation from the Government. As such, all the three abovementioned families do not wish to speak openly about the killing of Nahar Singh, Kulwant Singh and Kapur Singh at the hands of the Police. It is evident from their economic constraints also that these families want to give priority to their economics only. The Investigation Team questioned Sukhwinder Kaur, the daughter of Nahar Singh that if they had suspected that the Police and the family members of a Policeman of their village were behind the killing of her father then why did they not press their allegation and fight a legal battle. She replied, "Who will do us justice and did they listen to anybody earlier?". By filing this case (for compensation), we would get some financial help at least. Sukhwinder Kaur said, "We could not understand as to who in fact was responsible for this incident." However, the Investigation Team have reached the final conclusion that the Police was behind this incident. The people of the village and the area, to whom the Investigation Team talked about this topic, have corroborated it.

### VFF/0739

Jarnail Singh 45 of Rasulpur, Jagraon in Ludhiana. It was 14 May, 1993. Jarnail Singh and his wife were asleep in their house. Two of his sons namely Kewal Singh and Sukhmandar Singh had been picked up by Nathana Police (District Bathinda) on 13 May, 1993. On 14 May, 1993 at about 9 P.M., the Police scaled the walls and climbed on to the roof top. They caught hold of Jarnail Singh and started beating him. They brought him down from the roof and continued beating him. They searched the house. His wife got scared and jumped onto her neighbour's house. The family members suspect that the Police thrashed Jarnail Singh so brutally at his house itself that he might have died there itself or he might have been injured seriously. Jarnail Singh's party Kirti Kisan Union raised their voice against his arrest, staged dharnas and issued press statements. His family members pursued his case persistently. They along with eminent persons and the Panchayat continued to meet senior officers of Police District Jagraon. But, the Police did not disclose anything about the whereabouts of Jarnail Singh.

Note: At the time of his arrest, Avtar Singh Tari son of Lal Singh was also present on the scene and he witnessed this incident. When the family members filed a case in the High Court, the Police threatened them and tortured Avtar Singh brutally after taking him into their custody.

Note: Jarnail Singh is related to Prabhsharan Deep Singh. Harshinder Singh may find out about the Advocate and the status of the case from Prabhsharan Deep Singh.

### VFF/0740

Manjit Singh alias Billa 27 of Cheema, Jagraon in Ludhiana. On 20-4-1993, at village Uppal Bhoopa under Phillaur Police Station, he was surrounded by the Police and attained martyrdom after a fierce encounter. He was eating food in somebody's house when he was surrounded by the Police. After fighting for some time, Manjit Singh came out of the house so that the inmates of the house may not be harmed due to the Police firing. After coming out, he tried to escape by running away but he was shot dead by the Police. The family members read the news report in the newspaper of 21-4-1992 and reached Phillaur Police Station immediately. His dead body was lying at Phillaur Police Station at that time. His mother Joginder Kaur identified the dead body. She demanded the dead body. At this, the Police made a false promise of handing over the body but immediately took the body to Phillaur cremation ground clandestinely and cremated it. His mother and the members of the Panchayat (village Council) reached the crematiion ground while the cremation was in progress. Joginder Kaur (mother) told that she had visited the site of the encounter and verified the incident. According to the family members, it was a genuine encounter.

### VFF/0741

Jagroop Singh 32 of Malha, Jagraon in Ludhiana. Jagroop Singh was taken into custody for the last time by the Jagraon Police. He was tortured brutally in illegal custody for 10-15 days. The village Panchayat had got him released. He fell sick immediately on arrival at home. Puss had formed in his stomach. He used to cry with pain. Harnek Singh was the SSP of Jagraon Police district at that time. He (Jagroop Singh) was under treatment for about three years. He was unable to do any work. He remained under treatment at Patiala but did not recover. Ultimately, he died in 1996.

According to the family members, the cause of his death was the sickness only, caused by Police torture. His mother told that he had received internal injuries as a result of Police torture. They did not spare any effort to get him treated but his health deteriorated day by day. During that period of three years, till the time of his death, he was incapable of doing any physical work.

### VFF/0742

Atma Singh 22 of Malha, Bukkan Patti, Jagraon in Ludhiana. On 4-5-1993 at 1 A.M. a Police party led by S.I. Gurcharan Singh of Mehna Police Station and S.I. Darshan Singh of Badni Kalan Police Station accompanied by a truck load of CRPF personnel raided our house. They conducted a search of the house but nothing incriminating was recovered. They tortured Atma Singh brutally, in front of the whole family. Atma Singh asked for water but the Police did not allow us to give it to him. Thereafter, the Police pushed all other family members inside the house and locked them up there. They took away Atma Singh.

On the following day, the village Panchayat (Council) went to the Police Station Mehna. SHO Gurcharan Singh abused the Panchayat profusely and made them to stand in the sun. That is why nobody dared to pursue the case of Atma Singh, thereafter.

4-5 days later, the Police came in a vehicle and enquired about the whereabouts of Atma Singh. His mother replied that they only had arrested and taken him away. Actually, Atma Singh was seated in the Police vehicle itself. He was in a very bad shape. They conducted a search of the house, but nothing incriminating was found. All the Policemen were in uniform except one who was in civil dress.

Even after the disappearance of Atma Singh, the Police continued to raid our house. 15-20 days later, they picked up Atma Singh's father Inder Singh and took him to Hathur Chowki (Police Post). They pressurised him to produce his other sons namely Jagroop Singh and Harbhajan Singh. He was got released from there three days later, by the Panchayat.

**VFF/0743**

Ajmer Singh 35 of Rasulpur Malla, Jagraon in Ludhiana. "On 15-10-1991, the Police had surrounded the village Rasulpur and the neighbouring village Chakkar. The Police came to our house at 5.30 A.M. There was no boundary wall around the house. The Police enquired about Ajmer Singh. As Ajmer Singh identified himself, they immediately tied his hands at his back with his own 'Patka' (a small cloth worn on the head). The Police told that the militants had kept their arms and ammunition with him. On Ajmer Singh's refusal, the Police started beating him with sticks. They pushed him into the room and started torturing him. I was in the courtyard. I could hear his shrieks outside. The thrashing continued for six hours. The Police beat up Jagtar Singh (our son aged 9 years) also mercilessly. They asked him as to whether the militants were visiting their house or not. After the thrashing, the Police brought two vehicles inside the house. They directed me and the children to go away and not to look that side. The Police directed me to turn my face towards the other side. The Police took away Ajmer Singh. I cannot say as to what his condition was at that time. The Police left at about 12 Noon. Some of the villagers went to my parents' village and informed them about this incident. Nobody tried to pursue his case due to Police terror. On the next day, my brothers met the senior officers of Ludhiana Police. However, they denied the arrest of Ajmer Singh."

The newspapers of 17-10-1991 carried a news item that a militant namely Ajmer Singh had escaped from Police custody. This news item was got published by the Faridkot Police. However, Ajmer Singh's address etc. was not given. The family members continued to meet senior officers of Ludhiana, Moga, Faridkot and Jagraon Police districts. The eminent persons and political leaders also recommended their case. But, Police did not disclose anything about his whereabouts. Unofficially, some of the Police officers used to give this much information alright that Ajmer Singh had died at his house itself due to Police thrashing. In the beginning, the officers of Ludhiana Police had been assuring the family about his release also.

Note:　　At that time, the Chief of Faridkot Police was SSP Swaran Singh Ghotna and that of Jagraon Police, SP Harnek Singh.

According to Gurjit Kaur, the Police force was very large and that she did not know who were all the officers with the Police party. The case was pursued by her brothers. As such, they only could give detailed information about this case. At present, Gurjit Kaur lives at village Rasulpur itself along with her two children and mother. The shadow of Police terror over the family is clearly visible. They talked to the Investigation Team after a lot of hesitation. They said that the information given by them may not become a cause of some trouble for them.

### VFF/0744

Yugwinder Singh alias Binder 27 of Hathur, Jagraon in Ludhiana. After his primary education, Yugwinder Singh had gone away to Nanaksar Religious Institution at Kaler where he used to perform 'Sewa' (voluntary service) for about 18-19 years. In 1987, his parents got him married and he started living at home. He was a religious minded youth but he was not involved in any sort of political activities. After his return home, he ran a shop for some time and later on he took up a job as a car driver at Moga. His wife and children also used to live at Moga along with him. Yugwinder Singh used to live separately from his parents as he was not in good terms with them. As such, he used to contact his family very rarely only.

In the first week of March, 1993, Bhadaur Police of Police District Sangrur raided his house and enquired about Yugwinder Singh. His father Balwant Singh was at home who informed the Police that he lived at Moga and that he was not aware of his residential address at Moga. The Police party took away Balwant Singh to Bhadaur Police Station. After detaining him there for three days, they sent him to Police Post Gehal (Sangrur). The Police tortured Balwant Singh brutally. At that time, Shamsher Singh was the SHO of Police Station Bhadaur and ASI Nachhatter Singh was the incharge of Police Post. On 10 March, when Balwant Singh's wife Kartar Kaur went to C.I.A. Staff Handiaya to enquire about Balwant Singh, the Police detained her also at the Police Station. The incharge of C.I.A. Staff Handiaya was Inspector Sant Kumar and the DSP was Harbhajan Singh Sandhu. After the arrest of Balwant Singh, the Bhadaur Police had carried away all the household goods from his house. DSP Harbhajan Singh got Kartar Kaur also tortured brutally. Kartar Kaur was released on 17 March. In the meantime, the Police arrested several relatives of the abovementioned family. While releasing Kartar Kaur, the Police had directed her to find out about the whereabouts of Yugwinder Singh and appear before them again on 20

March with this information. When Kartar Kaur went to C.I.A. Staff Handiaya on 20 March, she was met by Inspector Sant Kumar there who told her that they had arrested her son Yugwinder Singh from Moga and asked her to go back.

In the meantime, Kartar Kaur came to know that the Police had picked up Yugwinder Singh along with his wife and two children from his residence at Moga. However, she did not have any details about it. Her husband Balwant Singh was in Police custody. All the household items had been taken away by the Police. Kartar Kaur went underground.

After keeping him in illegal custody for about one month, Balwant Singh was released from Gehal Police Post. According to Balwant Singh, he was also informed by the Chowki incharge ASI Nachhatter Singh that his son had been arrested from Moga. After the release of Balwant Singh, the family members came to know that the Police had released Kulwinder Kaur, wife of Yugwinder Singh and his children and that she had gone away to her parents' house at village Aulakh. Kartar Kaur met Kulwinder Kaur at Aulakh who told her that on 19-3-1993 at about 8 A.M., a Police party led by DSP Harbhajan Singh, Inspector Shamsher Singh, SHO of Bahdaur P.S., and SHO of Tappa P.S. had picked up Yugwinder Singh, herself (Kulwinder Kaur) and their two children aged 6 years and 2 years. Kulwinder Kaur was pregnant at that time. The Police got her admitted to a hospital at Bhadaur. According to Kulwinder Kaur, after all of them were taken to Police Station Bhadaur, the Police tortured Yugwinder Singh brutally in front of her and the same day they took him away from her. Kulwinder Kaur also was detained illegally along with her children for about one month where she gave birth to a boy. But, she did not get any information about Yugwinder Singh, thereafter. She told that the Police had carried away all the household goods from their house at Moga also.

For a long time, the family members along with eminent persons and relatives, continued to meet DSP Harbhajan Singh, SHO Shamsher Singh and Inspector Sant Kumar. For a number of days, the abovementioned officers continued to assure them that Yugwinder Singh would be released. However, later on, the Bhadaur Police started telling that they had already released Yugwinder Singh. But, DSP Harbhajan Singh had told Kartar Kaur that Yugwinder Singh was in the custody of senior officers at that time and that nothing was in his control now. According to Kartar Kaur, they ran from pillar to post for several months and continued to meet senior officers. But, they did not oblige them at all. Even household items which included one scooter also, were not returned. Balwant Singh (father) met SSP Barnala also. But, he also did not disclose anything about Yugwinder Singh.

* His mother Kartar Kaur told that even today they were hopeful that their son might be alive. They have not been given any information about him.

* Kulwinder Kaur's (wife of Yuygwinder Singh) parents waited for three years. Ultimately, they got her married again. She has taken her children also along with her.

### VFF/0745

Rajinder Singh alias Raja 45 of Chakkar, Jagraon in Ludhiana. In October (month of Ashwin according to Indian Calendar), 1993, one day, the Police knocked at his door at about 3.15 A.M. Rajinder Singh himself opened the door. The Policemen asked as to who was Raja to which Rajinder Singh replied that he only was Raja. 4-5 Policemen of the Police party who had entered the house directed Rajinder Singh to accompany them. His wife and one of his sons were present in the house at that time. On the same day, the Police had arrested Mohan Singh s/o Ganda Singh also from the same village. However, he was released later on. The Police took him (Rajinder Singh) to C.I.A. Staff Jagraon. However, his wife does know the names of the Police officials. At that time, Harinder Singh Chahal was the SSP Jagraon and Shiv Kumar was the SP (D) Jagraon. The family members continued to meet the SSP and SP (D) along with relatives and eminent persons, but, the Police did not admit that they had picked up Rajinder Singh.

### VFF/0746

Kaour Singh 91 of Malak, Jagraon in Ludhiana. On 30 April 1991 at about 1 A.M., 4-5 armed men accompanied by Sarpanch (head of village Council) Nahar Singh and another resident of the village namely Kulwant Singh came to the Dera (religious establishment) of Bhai Kapur Singh. At that time, Jagtar Singh s/o Harbans Singh also was sleeping there near Bhai Kapur Singh who was still awake. Nahar Singh told Jagtar Singh that those "Singhs" (the abovementioneed armed men) had been sent by Bhai Gurdev Singh Kaonke (former Jathedar of Sri Akal Takht). Jagtar Singh went inside and informed Baba Kapur Singh that Singhs had come. Baba Kapur Singh came out and offered prasad to those armed men. The armed men expressed their desire of talking to him at a little distance away from the Dera, but, he insisted on talking to them there itself. However, they insisted on going to the 'Bambi' (Tubewell) which is at a distance of 70-80 yards. Jagtar Singh who is an eyewitness saw that for some time those armed men kept talking to these three persons. After some time, they called for him and asked him to bring water which was drunk by Nahar Singh and Kulwant Singh. While Jagtar Singh was serving water, the armed men directed him to go and shut the door of the Gurdwara. Jagtar Singh had come a few steps only towards the Gurdwara when he heard the sound of gunshots. Jagtar Singh got frightened and went inside the Gurdwara.

Jagtar Singh's house is at a little distance away from the Dera. Those armed men had passed through his house on their way to the Dera along with Nahar Singh, Kulwant Singh and another resident of the village namely Kulwant Singh s/o Lal Singh (Driver) who had been forced by those armed men to accompany them on bicycle to the Dera of Bhai Kapur Singh. At that time Jagtar Singh's father Harbans Singh had woken up, but, one of those armed men had threatened him and directed him to sleep quietly. Some time later, Harbans Singh also heard the sound of gunshots. But, nobody was willing to come out and see as to what had happened, due to fear. About 15-20 minutes later, Jagtar Singh went to his house and informed his father that those armed men had shot Baba Kapur Singh, Nahar Singh and Kulwant Singh, dead. Some time later, the family members of Nahar Singh and Kulwant Singh also arrived on the scene. At about 5 A.M., the Jagraon Police were informed and they arrived at about 6:30 A.M. In the morning it became known that earlier, those armed men had abducted Avtar Singh s/o Bhag Singh also from his house and directed him to guide them to the house of Bant Singh (former Sarpanch). But, Avtar Singh had refused saying that he did not wish to go to his house. Avtar Singh told that the armed men had made him to sit in the fields for quite some time and before shooting Nahar Singh, Kulwant Singh and Kapur Singh, they had directed him and Kulwant Singh s/o Lal Singh (Driver) to run away from there. He further told that after they had covered some distance running, they heard the sound of gunshots. In the morning, they came to know that the abovementioned armed men had shot Nahar Singh (Sarpanch), Kulwant Singh s/o Jagir Singh and Bhai Kapur Singh, dead. The Police also recorded Avtar Singh's statement. The Police had registered a FIR No. 66 u/s 302/34 IPC and 25/54/59 of Arms Act in connection with this case at Jagraon Police Station wherein they had shown it as a case of inter-gang rivalry of militants. A few days later, a news item appeared in the newspapers wherein the responsibility for this incident was owned by a militant namely Sukhwinder Singh Pappu of Khalistan Commando Force (Wassan Singh Group). However, just after few days of the publication of the said news item, a denial of the news about owning the responsibility was published. The family members of Nahar Singh as well as those of Bhai Kapur Singh wonder as to what the militants stood to gain by killing a Gurmukh, Sant and social worker like Bhai Kapur Singh. The family members told that Sarpanch Nahar Singh had very cordial relations with Baba Kapur Singh. Both Nahar Singh and Kulwant Singh were considered to be supporters of militant movement and both of them were close to Baba Kapur Singh. Bant Singh, who had been killed at the hands of the militants on 13 April 1991, was not on good terms with Baba Kapur Singh, Nahar Singh and Kulwant Singh. One of the nephews of Bant Singh namely Harnek Singh s/o Preetam Singh was a Head Constable in the Police and was posted at Patiala at that time. Harnek Singh was also killed by the militants a few days later. The villagers suspected that all these three incidents are inter-related. The villagers believe that the Police in the guise of militants had killed Nahar Singh, Kulwant Singh and Baba Kapur Singh to avenge the killing of Bant Singh. And the militants had killed Head Constable Harnek Singh in retaliation. But, the people told that even though they are not in possession of any evidence to corroborate their belief, yet, the circumstantial evidence points in that direction only. The people seemed to be talking in hushed tones, even today.

The house of Harbans Singh, a nephew of Baba Kapur Singh, is situated adjacent to the field where Baba Kapur Singh used to reside. The sons of Harbans Singh only used to look after Baba Kapur Singh. Harbans Singh told that the family members of Sarpanch Nahar Singh have filed a case before the Deputy Commissioner, Ludhiana to claim the compensation granted to the heirs of persons killed at the hands of the militants, but, they are not a party to it. He expressed the apprehension that the real grandson of Baba Ji might have become a party in this case. According to the information he had received, even though the said case had been filed by the family members of Nahar Singh only but the family members of Kulwant Singh also had become a party to it.

The family members of Harbans Singh said that they believed firmly that it was the handiwork of the Police. As such, they did not think it appropriate to claim the compensation paid to the families of persons killed at the hands of the militants. They further told that Baba Kapur Singh did not maintain any link with his family (grandsson), so much so that his grandson never came to see Baba Ji. And that now, due to greed (of money), he had become a party in this case.

    \*   When Baba Kapur Singh had gone to the house of Bant Singh to mourn his death at the hands of the militants, his brother Preetam Singh (father of Head Constable Harnek Singh had said, "You have come to offer condolences after getting him killed yourself." At that time, Harmel Singh s/o Harbans Singh also was with Baba Kapur Singh.

## VFF/0747

Dilbhag Singh alias Bgha 22 of Rasulpur Jandi, Jagraon in Ludhiana. Victim Dilbagh Singh's mother Baljit Kaur, aged 66 years, widow of Joginder Singh, is a resident of Rasulpur (Jandi), Police Station Sidhwan Bet, Distt. Ludhiana. Her family owned two and a half acres of land which has been completely sold out for pursuing the case of her son. Her son Dilbagh Singh Bagha has been killed at the hands of the Police. Due to Police repression against their family for several years, the wife of his elder brother Gurdial Singh, got scared and had gone to her parents' house. Her son (grandson of Baljit Kaur) is living with Baljit Kaur. Baljit Kaur's elder son also does not stay at home due to fear as he also had been tortured by the Police several times. The Police used to pick up their relatives also. The Police had started harassing their family in 1987.

His mother Baljit Kaur claimed that Dilbagh Singh had been arrested on 24-5-1989 by the Police in wounded condition from Vishwakarma Chowk at Ludhiana before he was killed by them. This fact was disclosed to her by the companions of Dilbagh Singh at her house. However, all of them have also been killed at the hands of the Police. Later on, the Police had concocted a story that he had been killed in an encounter with them in front of Sahni Tyres at Ludhiana. She has claimed that he was tortured brutally by the Police before he was killed by them.

The economic condition of his mother is miserable. Her land and residential plot have been sold out. Now she is living in a small house.

## VFF/0748

Sukhwinderpal Singh alias Kaka 26 of Dakha in Ludhiana. Victim Sukhwinderpal Singh's mother Amrit Kaur, widow of Teja Singh, is a resident of village Dakha. Sukhwinderpal Singh was her youngest child and the only son. She has four daughters. Their family land holding is very small. After passing his Matriculation, Sukhwinderpal Singh took up a private job. He used to change jobs often. He was an "Amritdhari" (baptised) Sikh youth. But, he had never been arrested by the Police earlier, not even on the basis of suspicion.

In 1991, six days before Dushehra, at about 6 or 7 P.M., the Police raided his house. Sukhwinderpal Singh and his mother Amrit Kaur were at home. SHO Joginder Singh, SI Darshan Singh and Munshi

Dharampal were with the Police party. They asked Sukhwinderpal Singh his name and said, "Are you called 'Kaka' also?" There were 6-7 other Policemen also in the Police party. On being asked the reason for his arrest, the Police began to threaten the family members. They took away Sukhwinderpal Singh to their vehicle parked at a little distance away and made him to sit in it. Another resident of the same village namely Harnek Singh was also seated in the Police vehicle. The family members approached the Sarpanch (head of village Council) and other eminent persons of the village. Sarpanch Gurdev Singh and other members of the Panchayat (village Council) met the SHO who promised to relesase him after interrogation. The Sarpanch and the Panchayat members met Sukhwinder Singh in the Police Station. He had been tortured and was locked up in the lock-up.

On the third day of the arrest of Sukhwinderpal Singh, the Mullanpur Police arrested another youth of his village namely Navtej Singh Harry s/o Giani Harcharan Singh. Apart from that, another two youth of the same village had been arrested by the Mullanpur Police. The then Sarpanch of the village, Gurdev Singh told the Investigation Team that they had been visiting Mullanpur Police Station for the release of these four youth and the SHO had been assuring them of their release.

Amrit Kaur told that on the Dushehra day or on the following day, a news report was published in the newspapers that two unidentified youth were coming from the side of bridge of village Changra. The Police 'naka' (barrier) party tried to stop them but they opened fire. Both of them were killed in the encounter which ensued. Before the publication of the said news report and on the day of the "encounter" itself, the people of the village had come to know that the Police had killed Sukhwinderpal Singh and Navtej Singh in a fake encounter. The panchayat approached the Police for obtaining the dead bodies but the Police did not hand over the bodies. The Police did not allow even their ashes to be collected. Now-a-days, Amrit Kaur lives alone. Her daughters have been married off. The economic condition of the family is not good.

**VFF/0749**

Gurcharan Singh 29 of Sheikh Daulat, Jagraon in Ludhiana. Victim Gurcharan Singh's mother Kartar Kaur, widow of Bachan Singh, had two sons and she has four daughters. Her husband had expired while the children were still young. All her daughters have been married off. Gurcharan Singh was her younger son. His share of land was just two acres only. As such, he used to work as a truck driver and he used to come home rarely only. He had got married in 1990 and in 1992, a son was born out of the wedlock. His family members were not aware of his links with the militants. He was an "Amritdhari" (baptised) Sikh and all his family members are also "Amritdharis".

In July 1992, his family members received information that Gurcharan Singh had been arrested by the Police. DSP Paramraj Singh Umranangal of Fatehgarh Sahib Police had arrested him at Bhopal and brought him to Punjab. His family members came to know that another youth namely Bhola, resident of Paut (Ropar), was also arrested along with Gurcharan Singh and brought to Punjab. In October 1992, a news item appeared in the newspapers that Gurcharan Singh had escaped from the custody of Fatehgarh Sahib Police. As soon as his family members came to know about his arrest they went to Fatehgarh Sahib and enquired there. But, they did not disclose anything. His family members went to Bhopal also where his arrest from a hotel was confirmed. Eyewitnesses told them that Gurcharan Singh was inside his truck which he had parked near the 'Dhaba' (a roadside eating place) and Bhola was lying on a cot on the ground. The Police party pounced on them. Bhola tried to consume cyanide but the Police took it out from his mouth. The family members do not know as to what happened to Bhola but about Gurcharan Singh the Fatehgarh Sahib Police concocted a story of his escape from their custody. After the publication of the news item, Fatehgarh Sahib Police visited Gurcharan Singh's house once or twice and met the village Sarpanch also. They also told that Gurcharan Singh had escaped from their custody. But, the family members maintain that after killing Gurcharan Singh, the Police had concocted this story.

**VFF/0750**

Balwinder Singh alias Kaka 27 Sheikh Daulat, Jagraon in Ludhiana. Victim Balwinder Singh's mother Nasib Kaur widow of Zora Singh is a resident of village Sheikh Daulat. She had three sons and two daughters. Her second son Balwinder Singh was a farmer earlier but in 1987, he learnt the job of a truck driver and took up a job as a driver. Balwinder Singh was clean shaven and he did not have any link whatsoever with any sort of militant activities. He used to return home after several days and used to go back on duty after staying for a day or two.

Nasib Kaur told that on 22.6.92, a news report was published in the newspapers that five militants had been killed in an encounter at Ludhiana and the name of her son Balwinder Singh was also there among the killed militants. She further told that the name of their relative and a resident of their village Baldev Singh s/o Jaswant Singh was also there in the list of militants killed in the said encounter. Baldev Singh was involved in militant activities. But, they were astonished to hear that her son also had links with the militants, she said. Her son was doing his job and he used to come home often. The Police also had never visited her house. She told that may be Balwinder Singh had developed contacts with Baldev Singh.

According to Kulwinder Singh (Balwinder's brother), his brother used to drive the gas tanker of Kapur & Co. of Ludhiana. After the publication of the news item about the killing of Balwinder Singh, he had inquired and he came to know that Balwinder Singh had quit his job about two months earlier. Balwinder Singh had been arrested by the Hoshiarpur Police, on 19 June 1992 from Harjit Garage at Ludhiana while he was getting a truck repaired. Kulwinder Singh told that after attending Balwinder Singh's 'Bhog' (last rites ceremony) he had gone to Ludhiana and found out from Harjit Garage that Balwinder Singh had been arrested on 19 June 1992 at about 2 P.M. At the time of his arrest another boy was seated in the Police vehicle who identified him to the Police and the Police arrested him. The eyewitnesses told that Balwinder Singh abused the said boy at the time of his arrest. The owners of Harjit Garage also vouched for Balwinder Singh, but, the Police took out some arms and ammunition from his truck and showed the same to the Garage owners and said that he was a militant. The Police showed Balwinder Singh as having been killed in an encounter with them along with four other militants at a 'Naka' (barrier) on Tajpur Road at Ludhiana on 20-6-1992 at 2:35 A.M. and claimed it as a big achievement. The truck which was shown as being used by the militants was actually taken away from Balwinder Singh from Hatjit Garage at Ludhiana by Hoshiarpur Police. In the said news report, DIG Chander Shekhar had claimed this success as a jojnt operation carried out by the Hoshiarpur and Ludhiana Police.

Kulwinder Singh told that even today if the Government may order an independent inquiry into this incident then several persons associated with transport business at Ludhiana would come forward to depose about the arrest of Balwinder Singh by the Police. He further told that his brother might have been associated with militants but the story of the encounter was a white lie.

\* The evidence that Balwinder Singh had been arrested goes to show that the encounter shown to have taken place at a Naka on 20-6-92 at 2:35 A.M. was a fake one and the militants were already in the custody of the Police. It was claimed that in this encounter, five militants including Devinderr Singh Paut (Ropar), Surmukh Singh Reechha resident of Garanga (Ropar), Baldev Singh resident of Sheikh Daulat (Ludhiana) and Balwinder Singh Kaka were killed.

**VFF/0751**

Baljit Singh alias Itta 18 of Roomi, Jagraon in Ludhiana. According to Amolak Singh and Gurdev Kaur, father and mother respectively of the victim Baljit Singh, their sons were busy in their respective jobs. It was around 13-14 August, 1992 that the Police had arrested Ranjit Singh Comrade, his wife Harbhajan Kaur, Surjit Singh and Bara Singh (Mazhabi Sikh) all residents of our village at different times. Harbhajan Kaur had been arrested by a Police party a day earlier. Around that time itself, one day, at 7 A.M., a Police party from Jagraon Police Station came to our house. The Officer who was leading the Police party said, "Militants are visiting your house. Hand over the arms and ammunition." The Police beat up Amolak Singh (father) who was present at home, mercilessly. The Police party picked up Amolak Singh and Lakhbir Singh (brother of Baljit Singh) and took them along to the C.I.A Staff Jagraon. The Police inquired about Joginder Singh and Baljit Singh from Amolak Singh. Joginder Singh was present in the village itself at that time but Baljit Singh was out of station where he had gone to ply his Tempo. Joginder Singh did not come home due to fear. After the Police had gone, Joginder Singh met his mother for the last time. Since then his whereabouts are not known. Thereafter, Baljit Singh also did not return home, due to fear.

Amolak Singh and Lakhbir Singh were detained in custody for one month. Amolak Singh was released after 10 days. 15 days later, the Police brought Lakhbir Singh along, to his house. They told that the dead body of Baljit Singh had been recovered from the road leading to Cheema and the same was to be identified. The Police party took Amolak Singh along with them. However, they did not get any dead body identified. They detained Amolak Singh and Lakhbir Singh in illegal custody for 15 days and relesased both of them, thereafter.

According to the family members, the Police had told them that Baljit Singh had been killed by the militants. However, they did not believe the Police version, they said. So far, they do not know as to what happened to Baljit Singh and Joginder Singh, after all. They could not say anything with confidence as to what happened to Baljit Singh and Joginder Singh. It was still a mystery for them.

      \*    As both Amolak Singh (father) and Gurdev Kaur (mother) are illiterate and scared, they were unable to provide any

more information than this. This much information also was
extracted by the Investigatiion Team after a lot of efforts.

**VFF/0752**

Sukhdarshan Singh alias Sukha 22 of Gure, Jagraon in Ludhiana.
The details of this incident, as narrated to the Investigation Team by
the family members, are as follows:-

On 29 December, 1992 at about 5 P.M. a Police party led by
Inspector Bhag Singh of C.I.A Staff Jagraon came to their house (to arrest
Sukhdarshan Singh). Inspector Ajit Singh was also there along with the
Police party. On being asked by Gurcharan Singh s/o Harnasm Singh as
to what the matter was, Ajit Singh told that they should come to Chowki
Mann Police Post and they (Police) would talk to them there. His mother
and sister were present in the house at the time of Sukhdarshan Singh's
arrest. Immediately after the Police had left, Karnail Singh (uncle – 'Taya'),
Kartar Singh (Ex-Sarpanch), Harbant Singh (uncle – 'Chacha' – Member
Panchayat), Manjit Singh (Policeman) and Ranjit Singh reached Police
Post Chowki Mann. SSP Swaran Singh Ghotna and DSP Harbhagwan
Singh Sodhi were also present there. The abovementioned persons asked
the reason for the arrest of Sukhdarshan Singh. At this, DSP Sodhi and
the abovementioned officers started beating Karnail Singh and other
persons. By that time, Gurcharan Singh and Harcharan Singh Mann
also reached Chowki Mann Police Post. However, they came back from
there as they came to know that the Police were beating the people who
had reached there earlier to them for pursuing the case of Sukhdarshan
Singh. Immediately thereafter, the Police took away Sukhdarshan Singh
and those five persons to C.I.A Staff Jagraon. On raeching there, DSP
Sodhi got Sukhdarshan Singh tortured brutally for two hours under his
supervision. He fell unconscious while being tortured. All those five
persons witnessed Sukhdarshan Singh being tortured.

The family members and their acquaintances approached some
eminent persons and through them they approached the SSP Swaran
Singh Ghotna. The SSP told that they could take those five persons
back but Sukhdarshan Singh was not to be released yet. All those five
persons were released then and there at 8 A.M. Those persons disclosed
that Sukhdarshan Singh had been tortured brutally. On the third day,
on 31 December at about 1 P.M. the Police released Sukhdarshan Singh
under constant pressure from eminent persons. At that time he was in a
very bad shape and could not walk. He was helped to sit in the car. First,
they got medicines for him from Jagraon and brought him to the village.
He was in great pain throughout the night. On 1st January morning,
the family members took him to Dr. Harish Kumar at Mullanpur. He

remained admitted to his clinic for the whole day and was brought back home at night. At night again, Sukhdarshan Singh was in great pain. In the morning, the family members shifted him quickly again to Dr. Harish Kumar's clinic at Mullanpur. He remained there throughout the day but as his condition worsened at night the family members shifted him to Dayanand Hospital. His conditiion improved there and he started talking also. However his condition deteriorated suddenly again and he breathed his last on 5th January. The family members got the post mortem conducted on his dead body.

  * In those days, the atmosphere was one of Police terror. So the family members took it as the Will of God and sat quietly at home. In 1996 as the Akali Dal had won the parliamentary elections, there was a change in the environment. The family members consulted the Member of Parliament of their area, Amrik Singh and on his advice they filed a case in the High Court through Advocate Baltej Singh Sidhu. The decision is reserved in the said case.

### VFF/0753

Teja Singh alias Giani 40 of Fatehgarh Sivian in Ludhiana. On 2-8-1992 at about 4 P.M., we had produced him in front of Deputy Kamaljit Singh and Harbhagwan Singh Sodhi. They told us that they wanted to interrogate him and won't harm him. Also they told that we could take him back on the following day. Following police personnel are involved:-

1. Deputy Kamaljit Singh
2. Deputy Harbhagwan Singh
3. Inspector Randhir Singh
4. Charanjit Singh—Doaba
5. Bhag Singh—Leehan
6. Darshan Singh—Sudhar
7. Swaran Singh Ghotna

The following information about this case is based on investigation carried out by Amrik Singh Muktsar, in June, 2000. The true translation of the same is appended below:-

On 31 July 1992, DSP Harbhagwan Singh Sodhi raided Teja Singh's house. He was not at home. The Police arrested Charanjit Kaur (wife) and Major Singh (brother) and brought them to the C.I.A. Staff. The Police party had beaten up Charanjit Kaur at her home itself, severely. On 2 August 1992, the village Panchayat produced Teja Singh before DSP Harbhagwan Singh Sodhi at CIA Staff Jagraon. The Police released Charanjit Kaur and Major Singh. At the time of her release, Charanjit

Kaur demanded her ear rings and watch. The Policemen asked her to collect the same on the following day.

On 3 August 1992, Charanjit Kaur went to CIA Staff Jagraon for collecting her ear rings etc. Teja Singh saw her and called for her. She went near him. At that time no senior officer was present there. The junior employee, a Constable allowed them to talk to each other. Teja Singh told Charanjit Kaur that on the day he was produced before the Police, he was got tortured brutally by DSP Harbhagwan Singh Sodhi and DSP Kanwaljit Singh. Thereafter, he was shifted to the SSP's office at Civil Lines where the SSP Swaran Singh Ghotna got him tortured brutally. There were blood stains on Teja Singh's shirt. On being asked, he told that he was hit with a Lathi (stick) there. He further told that Avtar Singh s/o Telu singh resident of Fatehgarh Sivian also was detained there along with him and that he too had been got tortured brutally.

Charanjit Kaur said that her husband was killed along with four other youth on 18 August 1992 near village Kular under Police Station Sudhar.

Charanjit Kaur told that even after killing her husband the Police did not leave them alone. She was arrested and taken to CIA Staff where SSP Harinder Singh Chahal got her tortured brutally. The Police asked her to get the militants arrested. She was released on the third day. She further told that there were many other women also detained there, some of them for a month. But, her family members had pursued her case and got her released. She was tortured by male Policemen only and they used all those methods on her which they used against men. Even today, it sends shivers down her spine when she thinks of that Police torture, she said. The Police continued to raid her house so that the family members may not raise their voice against them. According to Charanjit Kaur, Inspector Bhag Singh had once visited her house and threatened to kill her son.

**VFF/0754**
Mandeep Singh alias Bittu 22 of Halwara, Jagraon in Ludhiana. Thinking that Gurdeep Singh can manage the fodder stall alone, he had gone to Barnala to meet one of his acquaintances for discussing his plans for starting a business of manufacturing Aluminium Boxes at Barnala, on 8-7-1990. On 9-7-90, a police party in plain clothes brought him to their fodder stall at Sangrur and enquired about Gurdeep Singh who had gone to see a movie. They picked up Gurdeep Singh from the cinema hall and took Mandeep Singh also along and went away. So far, their whereabouts are not known. We don't know the name of any of the policemen. But, once, we received a letter written by Gurdeep Singh

that both of them (Gurdeep Singh and Mandeep Singh) are lodged at Sangrur Jail. On the third day after getting the letter, I went to Sangrur Jail and enquired about them but nobody told me anything. At last, after a long time, I came to know that another boy from our village namely Preet is also lodged at Sangrur Jail. I handed over the letter to him and asked him to find out, but, he also could not find out anything. Ultimately, after running from pillar to post in various police stations, I received a photostat copy from a policeman at police station Pakhowal, which contained the details about Gurdeep Singh having been killed in an 'encounter' with the Police. But this document also did not mention anything about Mandeep Singh.

**VFF/0755**

Gurdeep Singh Bola alias Bola 25 of Halwara, Jagraon in Ludhiana. On 9 July 1990 after 6 P.M., he had gone to see a movie along with his cousin (Bhua's son) with whom he used to live and two other friends. At night, he was picked up by plainclothesmen. The family says "we know this much only that he was picked up from a Cinema Hall. We don't know the name of anybody."

**VFF/0756**

Rajinder Singh alias Jinder 23 of Fatehgarh Sivian, Jagraon in Ludhiana. Rajinder Singh was an "Amritdhari" (baptised) Sikh youth. After passing his 10+2 exam, he learnt the trade of Lathe Operator for about two years and thereafter joined Onkar as a Foreman at Ludhiana. He used to reside at the shop itself at Ludhiana. Sometimes he used to go to his aunt's ('Bhua') house at village Bulara. He used to visit his house after 15-20 days. He was a religious minded youth. His brother Bhupinder Singh told that it never came to their notice that Rajinder Singh had any link with the then ongoing militant movement in the Punjab. He further told that all those youth who were friends of Rajinder Singh had been arrested by the Police on the allegation of having links with the militants. In view of the deteriorating situation in the village, the family members sent Rajinder Singh to a relative's place (cousin sister—Bhua's daughter) at Indore. It was in 1990. Bhupinder Singh said that their uncle ('Chacha') Avtar Singh was the Sarpanch (Head of village Council) and an eminent person of the area. SP Harnek Singh of Jagraon Police told him (Avtar Singh) that they had received information that his nephew Rajinder Singh had links with the militants. As such they should produce Rajinder Singh before him. His (Bhupinder Singh's) family members along with Amrik Singh, resident of Kishanpura and a relative of SP Harnek Singh, produced Rajinder Singh before SP Harnek Singh.

Rajinder Singh was detained at the C.I.A. Staff for 15 days and released thereafter. SP Harnek Singh directed him to mark his presence at the Police Station every week. For four months, Rajinder Singh used to mark his presence at the CIA Staff every week, regularly. They used to send him back after marking his attendance. During this period, SP Harnek Singh continued to extort money (bribe) from his family. He extorted two buffaloes also from his family. During the same period, SP Harnek Singh's relative Amrik Singh, resident of Kishanpura, solemnised the engagement of his daughter with Rajinder Singh. Bhupinder Singh told that now the family members were convinced that the Police would not harm Rajinder Singh.

In December 1992, an incident occured in which the militants had taken out some members of a particular community from a bus near Sidhwan Kalan and shot them dead. On that day, SP Harnek Singh had sent a message and directed them to produce Rajinder Singh before him. On the third day after this incident, Avtar Singh Sarpanch along with Amrik Singh Kishanpura and Jaspal Singh Killi Chahal ('Phuphar') produced Rajinder Singh before SP Harnek Singh. A few days later, when the family members along with Amrik Singh met SP Harnek Singh, he was evasive. Sometimes he would say that he had been taken away from him by the SSP Swaran Singh Ghotna and at other times he used to say that Inspector Darshan Singh of Dehlon Police Station had taken him away. In short, SP Harnek Singh did not disclose the reality about Rajinder Singh. He (SP Harnek Singh) used to say alright that Rajinder Singh was an innocent youth. Some time later, Amrik Singh Kishanpura told his family members that SP Harnek Singh had demanded two Lakh rupees for showing Rajinder Singh to the family members. But, the family members insisted that the SP should first show the boy to them, then only they would make the payment. But, SP Harnek Singh did not even show Rajinder Singh to his family members. Unofficially, some Policemen of Police Station Jagraon informed Sarpanch Avtar Singh that the Police had killed Rajinder Singh. As such, his family members were not willing to fall into the trap of Amrik Singh. Later on, they came to know also that in fact Amrik Singh was a Police Tout only and his job was to work as a middleman between the Police and the public.

However, some time later, the family members got this information also that Rajinder Singh was seen with SP Harnek Singh at Mullanpur. His family members continued to enquire at various Police Station, but, they did not get any information about him. For two three years they hoped that Rajinder Singh may be alive. Thereafter they lost that hope also. Many times they received information that Rajinder Singh was detained at so and so Police Station but when they used to go and enquire there, nobody admitted that he was there.

Amrik Singh Kishanpura used to take small amounts of money from them, often. The family spent about two Lakhs rupees in bits and pieces. Bhupinder Singh told that they would have paid two Lakhs rupees also, had somebody not told them that their boy had been killed and that they would be deceived.

**VFF/0757**

Baldev Singh alias Khalsa of Sheikh Daulat, Jagraon in Ludhiana. Baldev Singh was born in 1965. He had three brothers and three sisters. He studied upto B.A. and then went to Dubai foreign country). There, he came in contact with Singh Sahib Bhai Jasvir Singh Rode and got himself baptised. He was very firm in his religious views. He returned from Dubai in 1990. However, his family members told that they were not aware that he had returned from Dubai. In fact, he had come into contact with a militant group. However, his family members did not have any knowledge about it. They read a news item in the newspapers in 1991 that Baldev Singh had been appointed area commander of Bhindranwala Tigers Force. The family shifted to Calcutta, due to fear. They had a transport business at Bombay. As the Police came to know that their son was a militant they began to raid their house. But, none of the family members were present in the house. The Police carried away all the household items. They arrested their relatives. Baldev Singh's brothers-in-law (husbands of sisters) were tortured brutally. The Police went all the way to Calcutta also to arrest his family members but did not succeed in their mission.

On 22 June 1992, his family members read a news report in the newspapers at Calcutta that Baldev Singh had been killed at the hands of the Police on 20-6-92 at Ludhiana along with one of his relatives namely Balwinder Singh Kaka and three other militants. On the fourth or fifth day after reading the news, the family members reached the village. By that time, the ashes of Baldev Singh and Balwinder Singh had been already immersed. Senior Akali leaders had joined the procession of the ashes of these militants and three truck loads of the people from their village had also accompanied the ashes.

The family members were informed by the people of Ludhiana district that all those five militants had been killed by the Police after arresting them. This episode remained a hot topic for discussion in the newspapers for several days. These militants belonged to Bhindranwala Tigers Force. Just a few days earlier, the Police had arrested the Chief of this group namely Rachhpal Singh Chhandra and the Vice-Chief namely

Jagdish Singh Deesha and had killed them also in a fake encounter. It was said that the members of this militant group had been arrested while they were holding a meeting and the Police had showed them as having been killed in separate encounters. The family members said that as they were victims of Police terror, they did not go to Ludhiana for collecting information about this incident, but, there was no doubt that the Police had arrested Baldev Singh and his associates and then killed them. Balwinder Singh Kaka who was also killed along with Baldev Singh was also a resident of village Sheikh Daulat and was related to Baldev Singh in that he was the uncle ('Chacha') of Baldev Singh.

**VFF/0758**

Varinder Singh Dakha 22 of Dakha, Jagraon in Ludhiana. Varinder Singh Dakha was also one of those youth whose life was transformed suddenly after the Army attack on Sri Darbar Sahib at Amritsar. He was a student and had taken admission in College in BA-I in those days. In December 1984, some slogans were written on the walls of their village which concerned the Sikh Students Federation. The Police registered a case under section 124 of the IPC against Varinder Singh Dakha and some other youth of the village and started conducting the raids. Varinder Singh's uncle ('chacha') Jathedar Gurdev Singh was the Sarpanch of the village (head of village council) and a prominent political leader of the area. His uncle approached the senior officers and got the case dropped, after an inquiry.

A few months later, somebody shot at and injured a Nirankari of village Dakha. The Mullanpur Police arrested a youth of Dakha village namely Patwant Singh on the basis of suspicion. The Police claimed that he had confessed before the Police that he along with Varinder Singh had written the slogans on the walls of the village in the month of December. The SHO of Mullanpur Police Station, Didar Singh, registered a case against 3-4 youth of the village including Varinder Singh and started conducting raids. In those days, Varinder Singh was writing his exam of BA-I. The family members advised Varinder Singh to go underground so that he could appear for his exam. But, on 25 May 1985, Varinder Singh did not return home. The Police began to harass his family members. Cases under sections 212, 216 (sheltering militants) were registered against his father and uncle. The Police used to raid their house often. This process continued till the time of Varinder Singh's arrest.

On 1 July 1987, Varinder Singh was arrested by Ludhiana Police after he was identified by one of his associates namely Gurnam Singh

Mehmoodpura, from near the bus stand of Nakodar town in Jalandhar district. The Police concocted a story that they had arrested him from village Mandiani on 4 July 1987 and the news about it was published in the newspapers on 5 July 1987. The family members immediately started pursuing his case from legal angle with the help of their advocates. They filed a petition in the Punjab & Haryana High Court also wherein they had expressed an appehension about the danger to the life of Varinder Singh from the Police. The Ludhiana Police registered several cases against Varinder Singh and he was sent to Ludhiana jail on the orders of the Court. In the meantime, the Patiala Police also tried to obtain his Police remand in a case but the advocates of Varinder Singh demanded an identification parade and consequently the Court sent him again to Ludhiana jail under judicial custody. Meanwhile, his family members came to know that once again the Patiala Police were trying to obtain Varinder Singh's Police remand. In view of the danger to the life of Varinder Singh, his family members had filed a petition in the Punjab & Haryana High Court. In their reply to the said petition, the Police had filed an affidavit that they had no such intention.

On 25 July 1987, the Patiala Police obtained a production warrant from a Patiala Court and took away Varinder Singh from Ludhiana jail. His family members received the information about it immediately. His uncle Gurdev Singh along with their advocate Arshi reached Patiala immediately. The Police produced Varinder Singh in the Court of SDM and requested his Police remand in the same case for which Varinder Singh was already in judicial custody and for which the Court had refused Police remand earlier. His advocates opposed the Police remand by raising legal objections and also expressed their apprehension about the danger to his life. But, the Court granted 10 days Police remand. At the expiry of the Police remand, the Police produced Varinder Singh before a Magistrate clandestinely at a Rest House. However, his family members and advocates got a scent of it and they also reached there. The Police requested for further remand. The Court extended his Police remand upto 8 September 1987. On 8 September 1987, Varinder Singh was produced by Surjit Singh Grewal, SHO of Patiala (Kotwali) Police Station in the Court at Patiala. On that occasion, Varinder Singh expressed his apprehension to his uncle that the Police intended to kill him. On that day, the Court extended his remand by another three days.

Varinder Singh's uncle Gurdev Singh told that in view of the apprehension expressed by Varinder Singh, they along with former member of Parliament Late S. Basant Singh Khalsa, met the DIG Patiala range, Mahal Singh Bhullar, on 9 September 1987 and told him everything. He gave an assurance that nothing of that sort would happen. His uncle Gurdev Singh and several other family members stayed put at Patiala for pursuing his case. On 10 September 1987 morning, the family members who were pursuing his case received information from their sources that the Police had taken out Varinder Singh from the Kotwali Police Station and taken him away somewhere. They got suspicious. His uncle Gurdev Singh tried to contact the senior officers, but, none of the senior Police or Civil officers were available on that day.

On 11 September 1987 also the family members continued to pursue his case. However, nothing could be known about the whereabouts of Varinder Singh. Same night, a news was broadcasrt on the Radio that the Patiala Police were taking a militant namely Varinder Singh for the recovery of weapons. On the bridge at the Sirhind canal under Fatehgarh Police Station, two Police vehicles had been parked. Those people signalled the Police party to stop. When the Police party stopped, those armed men directed them to hand over Varinder Singh to them and took away Varinder Singh forcibly from the Police party. The Police party tried to vchase them but the culprits sped away. The Patiala (Kotwali) Police had got a FIR also recorded at Fatehgarh Sahib Police Station in connection with this incident. The copy of the said FIR had been obtained by the family members. Varinder Singh's uncle Gurdev Singh told that this drama was enacted by the Police in order to eliminate Varinder Singh. Was it possible to abduct someone from the custody of such a large Police force, he asked. Jathedar Gurdev Singh further told that on the one hand the Police killed Varinder Singh and on the other, they continued to harass them intentionally, by inquiring about Varinder Singh, for several years. He said that the Police continued to harass the family members upto 1991. He further told that due to Police harassment only, they did not try to initiate any legal action against the extra-judicial killing of Varinder Singh.

Note: We (the Investigation Team) could not obtain the file containing the copy of the FIR regarding Varinder Singh's escape and the documrents pertaining to the case filed by his family members in the High Court. The concerned Advocate told that the file had been lost.

**VFF/0759**

Navtej Singh alias Harry of Dakha, Jagraon in Ludhiana. Navtej Singh Harry was arrested by the Mullanpur Dakha Police, three days after the arrest of another youth of his Mohalla (locality) namely

Sukhwinderpal Singh. Apart from them, the Police had arrested two other youth also of their village in those days on the allegation of having links with the militants. The then Sarpanch (head of village Panchayat (Council)), Gurdev Singh and other eminent persons of the village had been visiting Mullanpur Police Station to pursue the case of these four youth of their village and seek their release from Police custody. The SHO had assured them that they would be released after interrogation. But, out of these four, Sukhwinderpal Singh and Navtej Singh Harry were killed by the Police in a fake encounter near bridge of village Changra, on the Dushehra day or the day following Dushehra. The above information about Navtej Singh has been given to the Investigatioin Team by the mother of Sukhwinderpal Singh and the then Sarpanch of the village namely Gurdev Singh Dakha. Navtej Singh's father Giani Harcharan Singh lives abroad now-a-days and none of his family members resides in the village.

**VFF/0760**

Jagjit Singh of Dakha, Jagraon in Ludhiana. Victim Jangjit Singh's mother Surjit Kaur, widow of Dharam Singh, had three sons and three daughters. Jangjit Singh was her youngest child. After passing his 10+1 exam, Jangjit Singh began learning the job of an electrician.

Jangjit Singh had got himself baptised after June 1984 and he had become religious minded. He used to take interest in the political struggle also which had begun after June 1984. A youth of his village namely Varinder Singh Dakha was already active in the Sikh Students Federation. Jangit Singh had links with him also. He had been arrested by the Police numerous times on the basis of suspicion and he was tortured also on the basis of his alleged links with militants. Once, the Police had registered a case also against him under TADA and he was detained in jail for six months. After his release from jail, the Police started harassing him again. He deserted home in 1989-90, due to repeated Police harassment. The Police started harassing his family members.

On 25 June 1991, Jangjit Singh along with one of his associates namely Jagroop Singh Kalakh resident of village Kalakh Majra under Dehlon Police Station was surrounded by the Police at village Dhunga under Police Station Amargarh in district Sangrur. Later on, it was known that the house owner in whose house Jangit Singh and his accomplice had taken shelter, had tipped off the Police. The Police surrounded the house and killed both the militants. The news about this encounter was publsihed in the newspapers on 27 June 1991. However, the residents of village Dakha had come to know on the day following the encounter itself that Jangjit Singh had been killed in an encounter at village Dhunga under Amargarh Police Station. According to the people, the said encounter lasted several hours and the Police had set the abovementioned house on fire by throwing a bomb.

**VFF/0761**

Tarlok Singh Khalsa alias Avtar Singh 35 of Rurka Kalan in Ludhiana. On 27 June 1990, he disappeared from near the Govt. Higher Secondary School Dakha. His whereabouts are not known since then.

**VFF/0762**

Hardeep Singh of Balaspur, Payal in Ludhiana. He was picked up by the Police from Doraha. According to the family, "a lady who was employed in the Police sent a message to our home that our boy was at Sadar Police Station, Ludhiana. But that lady did not disclose her name. We met the Chief Minister of Punjab, Beant Singh, who hails from our village, several times, but no information was given to us."

**VFF/0763**

Kulwant Singh alias Kanti 28 of Balaspur, Payal in Ludhiana. On 12-2-92 at 8 A.M., he was picked up from the bus stand Balaspur in front of the general public, for interrogation. It was disclosed by the police that they were from C.I.A Staff Ludhiana.

**VFF/0764**

Sarbjit Singh alias Sarbi 22 of Raikot, Jagraon in Ludhiana. On 11 May 1988, he committed suicide by consuming cyanide after he was surrounded by the Police at village Anandgarh Kotla in district Bathinda. On 18 May 1988, the Police came to his house and the Balianwala Police showed them the photograph at Raikot Police Station and got him identified. The Police told that the said youth was killed in an encounter on 11 May 1988.

**VFF/0765**

Jagraj Singh alias Jagga 18 of Raikot, Jagraon in Ludhiana. Jagraj Singh was the youngest son of Hari Singh among his three sons. He had desrted home in August 1987. He was arrested 19 months later in 1989 and was detained in Patiala jail. After his release, he again joined the ranks of the militants. On 15 May 1990, he was killed in an encounter with the Police in the area of Jagraon Police Station.

**VFF/0766**

Ujagar Singh 38 of Binjal, Raikot in Ludhiana. Ujagar Singh aged 38 years was an "Amritdhari" (baptised) Sikh youth, resident of village Binjal. He was married and had two children from the wedlock. His family owned very little land and he used to repair engines. His family members told that the relatives of two of the renowned militants of their area namely Jatinder Singh Sohian and Ajmer Singh Lodhiwal lived at a nearby village namely Umarpura. In 1987, Ujagar Singh came into contact with these youth. As he was sympathetic towards the militant movement, he began to cooperate with the militant youth. The Police got the information about it. The SHO of Raikot Police Station, Sant Kumar, arrested him, registered several cases against him and sent him to jail. He came out on bail after remaining in the jail for several months. Then it became a routine. The Police used to arrest him often. Cases were registered against him several times. Whenever he used to come out on bail, the Police used to arrest him. He had come out of the jail on bail for the last time in 1992.

On 22-23 September 1993, one or two days before the Chhapaar 'Mela' (fair) at 8 A.M., two three Policemen came to his house from Police Station Raikot and directed the family members to send Ujagar Singh to the Police Station as he had been called by the SHO Sahib. At that time, Ujagar Singh was not at home. As he returned home, the family members conveyed the message. He went away from home at about 4-5 P.M. saying that he was going to the Police Station. He did not return home that evening. On the following day, his father Karnail Singh, along with 4-5 others went to the Raikot Police Station and met the SHO (name not known) there who assured them that they would release him on the next morning. Karnail Singh (father) and the Panchayat members met Ujagar Singh in the Police Station. Till that time, neither he had been interrogated nor had he been tortured. On the following day, the Panchayat went again. But, no responsible Police officer was available at the Police Station.

According to his father Karnail Singh, on the third day, a Police party which included Inspector Bhag Singh (since deceased) incharge of Police Post Lohat Baddi brought Ujagar Singh to his house at about 2 P.M. The family members were not allowed to go near him. The Police gave the impression that they had come to recover something on the basis of the information provided by Ujagar Singh. Karnail Singh said that for a few days they continued to enquire about Ujagar Singh at the Raikot Police Station. But, the the SHO did not even meet them. They are poor people. They had pursued the case of Ujagar Singh for six years continuously and now they were exhausted. They were not capable of pursuing it any longer. As such, they had accepted it as the Will of God and reconciled themselves to the situation.

The newspapers of 9 October 1993 caried a news item that five militants had been killed in an encounter near village Gagre near Jagraon. Ujagar Singh's name also was there among them. Accordibng to Karnail Singh, in those days, the Police did not hand over the dead bodies of the killed youth and used to misbehave with the people who used to pursue the case of such youth. As such, they did not try to pursue his case even after reading the news item.

According to Karnail Singh, a few months later, he got his daughter-in-law married to Sukhdev Singh. However, a few months later, Sukhdev Singh also died suddenly. Shortly afterwards, Ujagar Singh's wife married a youth of their vilage itself. Binder Kaur took both her children also along with her.

Now Karnail Singh has come to know that the CBI is inquiring into the case of the youth killed in the Police encounter at Gagre. Also, he has come to know that Binder Kaur had already approached the CBI. Karnail Singh told that it was beyond him to pursue his case. So, if Binder Kaur is pursuing his case then let her do it. If the CBI would approach him in connection with the investigation of this case then they would tell everything to them.

    *    Ujagar Singh was seen (in Police custody) by several residents of village Chowki Mann who had been detained at CIA Staff and Police Lines at Jagraon. Ujagar Singh's name has been mentioned in the cases of Ranjit Singh s/o Gurdev Singh, Gurdeep Singh s/o Gurmel Singh and Kulwant Singh s/o Kamikkar Singh. The abovementioned three youth also were killed along with Ujagar Singh in the Police encounter near villlage Gagre. The family members of these three youth who were in the custody of Jagraon Police at that time, had seen Ujagar Singh for the last time on 7 October 1993 at about 7 P.M. when the Police had taken out all the abovementioned four youth from there. It is pertinent to mention here that on the same night at bout 10 P.M. i.e. on 7 October 1993 all these four youth along with another person were killed in a fake encounter near village Gagre near Sem bridge. The CBI have started inquiring into this case on the orders of the High Court as the family members of Kulwant Singh s/o Kamikkar Singh had filed a case in the High Court.

**VFF/0767**

Tarlochan Singh 25 of Ghuman, Raikot in Ludhiana. According to statements given to the Civil Lines Police Patiala by other inmates of Doctors' Hostel Rajindra Hospital Patiala, Dr Tarlochan Singh got ready at 7.30 A.M. on 18-1-91 and went for duty as usual. But he did not return from duty that day. We were informed about disappearance of Dr Tarlochan Singh by the Medical Suerintendent Rajindra Hospital Patiala on 5-2-91, 15 days after he had been found missing. The Police has not taken any action so far. That is why we suspect Police hand in his disappearnce.

**VFF/0768**

Som Nath 22 of Binjal, Raikot in Ludhiana. Som Nath belonged to a Hindu Arora family who resided at village Binjal under Raikot Police Station. His father Kashmiri Lal owned a grocery shop in the village. Kashmiri Lal had five sons and two daughters, Som Nath being his youngest child. After passing his Middle exam, Som Nath began learning truck driving. After he was fully trained as a truck driver after a training of 2-3 years, his parents purchased a truck for him in partnership with somebody and he started plying the same. Later on, his partner withdrew his share of the capital and Som Nath started plying the truck on his own. Som Nath used to ply the truck and he used to visit his home only when he used to get some cargo to be transported to Punjab. Som Nath was not associated with any type of illegal activities whatsoever.

Som Nath's elder brother Bharat Bhushan alias Hardeep Singh had got himself baptised in 1986 and he had links with those youth who were associated with the militant movement. Bharat Bhushan had been arested by the Jagraon Police on the allegation of having links with the militants, several cases were registereed against him and he was sent to jail. Bharat Bhushan had come out on bail in 1988. But, Inspector Sant Kumar of Raikot Police used to pick him up often. He had been marking his attendance also at the Police Station for quite some time. But, Som Nath, who was his younger brother, had never been arrested by the Police. However, Som Nath also was "Kesadhari" (one who does not shorn his hair) youth.

Som Nath had come home on 9 October 1993 along with his truck. On 10 October at about 3 A.M., a Police party of C.I.A Staff Handiaya led by Inspector Sant Kumar raided his house. At that time, all the members of the family including his parents, brothers Ramesh Kumar, Hardeep Singh and Bihari Lal were present in the house. The Police party enquired about Som Nath. The family members told that he was asleep in the truck. The Police party woke up Som Nath from the truck and made him to sit in their vehicle. They took him away along with his truck. At that time the family members did not know as to from where the Police party had come. They enquired at Jagraon and met the DIG at Ludhiana. The DIG assured the Panchayat that they would find out and let them know. In the meantime the family members suspected that Som Nath might have been picked up by the Handiaya Police. They enquired at Handiaya and met the senior officers of Barnala Police like

SSP and DSP Harbhajan Singh. However, none of the officers admitted the custody of Som Nath.

On 29 October 1993, a news item was published in Ajj Di Awaz (a Punjabi daily newspapers published from Jalandhar) and other newspapers that a truck borne militant had been killed while his accomplice escaped, near Barnala. This news item was published at the instance of SSP Barnala, Mr. Jagdish Kumar that a truck borne militant had been killed while another had escaped in an encounter with a Police party led by DSP Harbhajan Singh. This encounter was shown to have taken place near village Kattu-Walia. However, the registration number of the truck was different. The registration number of Som Nath's truck was PUJ 9390. Still, the family members suspected that the killed militant could be Som Nath.

After the publicatiion of the said news item, the family members approached a distant relative namely Shri Mohinder Mohan Punchhi, a Supreme Court Judge. He brought this cae to the notice of senior Police officers. At this, the Barnala Police left the truck of Som Nath near the Sem drain near village Pholan. Somebody informed the family members about it. The family members informed the Jagraon Police. However, the Police did not accompany them and they brought the truck back. The truck was not in a running condition and all the costly items had been removed from it.

A few days after the abduction of Som Nath, the Police had picked up another youth also of their village namely Balwinder Singh s/o Dev Singh and had taken him also to C.I.A Staff Handiaya. Binder (Balwinder Singh) used to work as a conductor on the truck of Som Nath. Later on, the Police had released Binder after accepting a bribe. A case was registered against him and he was sent to jail. The Police had brought Binder in front of Som Nath at the C.I.A Staff Handiaya.

Som Nath's family submitted applications against the injustice done to them to the senior officers, Chief Minister of Punjab and Governor of Punjab. In response to their application, an inquiry also had been ordered by the Chief Minister, at that time. The family members submitted their statements also to the senior officers at Ludhiana, but, nothing came out of it. The family members told that they ran from pillar to post for a long time. But, the Police did not tell them as to what the fault of Som Nath was and what happened to him, after all.

**VFF/0769**

Charanjit Singh alias Channi of Talwandi Rai, Raikot in Ludhiana. On 19 July 1982, Sant Jarnail Singh Bhindranwale started a "Morcha" (agitation) against the arrest of Federation leader Bhai Amrik Singh and a leader of Damdami Taksal namely Baba Dehra Singh. After the Morcha had begun, Charanjit Singh Channi (victim) went to Amritsar and started cooperating with Sant Jarnail Singh and Federation leadership. After 1983, he started living at Amritsar permanently. At the time of Army attack on Sri Darbar Sahib at Amritsar, Charanjit Singh Channi was inside Sri Darbar Sahib Compex itself. But, he along with some of his associates escaped from there.

In 1985, Charanjit Singh Channi also played a leading role along with other leaders in reactivating the Sikh Students Federation. As Charanjit Singh Channi had deserted home, the Police started harassing his family members. He had got married in 1981. His wife was a staff nurse. His wife and children also went underground in order to avoid the Police dragnet. The Police used to arrest his father often. False cases were also registered against his father by the Police.

Charanjit Singh Channi had achieved glorious heights in the militant movement and he was considered one of the top militant leaders in those days. He was understood to have played a key role in constituting the Panthic Committee (Sohan Singh). Keeping in view the important role being played by Charanjit Singh Channi in the militant movement, the Police were in hot pursuit for him.

On 2 June 1989, Charanjit Singh Channi had gone to meet an acquaintance, the owner of a scooter repair shop, at Phase VII of Mohali Town. The Police had already been tipped off about it. As Charanjit Singh Channi reached at the said shop, he got suspicious on seeing the Police present there and tried to escape by running away. But, the Police party had laid a tight trap. As he tried to run away, he was hit on his head by some of the Policemen with the butts of their rifles. As such, he was injured in his head and fell down. The Police party immediately caught hold of him, pushed him into their vehicle and sped away. The eyewitnesses had told the family members that the whole operation lasted hardly a few minutes. In those days, his wife also used to live at Mohali itself. She and some of his associates received the information about this incident immediately. Press Notes were issued to various newspapers about the arrest of Charanjit Singh Channi, as a precautionary measure.

Master Dev Raj Singh (father) and his elder son Lakhbir Singh (Channi's brother) were detained in Ludhiana jail under TADA at that time. As the news of Charanjit Singh Channi's arrest had spread and also as he was a youth who belonged to a family with political background, the Police did not keep him in their custody for long and cunningly killed him on the same day at night in a fake encounter on a river under Police Station Morinda (Distt. Ropar). The Police told that when the abovementioned militant was signalled to stop at a 'Naka' (barrier) he opened fire. The Police returned the fire and in the exchange of fire, the abovementioned militant was killed. The news of the killing of Charanjit Singh Channi was broadcast on the Radio and TV. On the basis of Channi having been killed, Advocate Gurcharan Singh Ghumman got Channi's father Master Dev Raj Singh bailed out immediately. Immediately after coming out on bail, on 3 June 1989 itself, Master Dev Raj Singh along with eminent political leaders met the Deputy Commissioner at Ropar. After talking to the SSP, the DC told that the Police had already cremated the dead body of Charanjit Singh Channi. His father Dev Raj Singh obtained a copy of the F.I.R. and postmortem and filed a case in the Court of the Magistrate at Ropar. The family had received a copy of the photograph of Charanjit Singh Channi's dead body through the Court only. In the photograph, blood was oozing out of Charanjit Singh Channi's head and rest of his body had been covered with a bed sheet. The family members wanted to pursue the case of extra-judicial killing of Charanjit Singh Channi after arresting him, but, the Lawyers, acquaintances and even the Magistrate in whose Court the case was sub judice advised them that keeping in view the prevailing circumstances, the case be got sealed and pursue it later at an appriopriate time. Master Dev Raj Singh said that till 1995, it was Police Raj only in Punjab. Thereafter he had tried to pursue the case again. But, his Lawyer Gurcharan Singh Ghumman had expired and the case file could not be traced out from his office.

Master Dev Raj Singh said that no doubt his son was a top militant leader, but, the story of his killing in an "encounter", concocted by the Police is a white lie. He was arrested by a Police party of Ropar Police, from near the Scooter Marker in Phase VII of Mohali in broad day light and killed later in a fake encounter under Morinda Police Station.

**VFF/0770**

Nasib Kaur 48 of Thuliwal, Barnala in Sangrur. She alighted from a bus at the Khiali bus stand alongwith her husband and another person namely Jangan Singh of Jhordan. All the three were taken in custody by a police party headed by DSP Pawar of Barnala Police.

**VFF/0771**

Randhir Singh alias Raju 17 of Amargarh in Sangrur. Randhir Singh was picked up from his residence at 5 A.M. on 24-3-93 by a police party led by DSP Samana, Varinder Pal Singh and including SHO of Amargarh

P.S., Gurmel Singh. It was not disclosed where they were taking him and in connection with which case.

**VFF/0772**

Amrik Singh of Amargarh in Sangrur. On 1-10-92 at 6.30 P.M., he was coming from Patiala to Amargarh in a bus when he was abducted by a police party of 4-5 men in civil clothes, headed by Gurmel Singh SHO Amargarh and including Bir Atma Ram SHO Sadar P.S. Nabha. We came to know about this incident at 7.30 P.M. At 9 P.M. same night, we met Bir Atma Ram, SHO Nabha (Sadar). He expressed ignorance about this incident.

On 2-10-92, we again met Bir Atma Ram, SHO Nabha (Sadar). He told that there is a possibility of Amrik Singh having been picked up by C.I.A. Staff Patiala. Then we met Satpal Singh, incharge of C.I.A. Staff Patiala (Mai Ki Saran). But, no clue could be found regarding the whereabouts of Amrik Singh.

On 3-10-92, we met Bir Atma Ram, SHO Nabha (Sadar). He said,"Don't worry, your son is with the Police only. You come tomorrow and take him back." Apart from myself, Mukhtiar Singh retired SP of Nabha, Iqbal Singh Khanna, and Manpal Singh Raipur were present there when he uttered these words.

On 4-10-92, we met DSP Gurmeet Singh at Nabha. He asked the SHO about the boy. The SHO denied any knowledge about the whereabouts of the boy. On being reminded about his words of the previous day, he denied having spoken those words also. We enquired at other police stations around Nabha, like Bhawanigarh, Chheenta etc, but no clue was found anywhere.

On 5-10-92, a delegation of the Panchayat of Amargarh met the SHO and DSP of Nabha again. But, to no avail. When requested to register the FIR, SHO Nabha evaded doing so till the evening. Ultimately, in the evening, SHO Nabha registered a DDR No. 21 dated 5-10-92, with great hesitation.

On 6-10-92, we met the then Taxation and Excise Minister, Punjab, Sh. Shamsher Singh Doolo. He gave a letter addressed to SSP Sangrur Narinder Pal Singh. We met the SSP with that letter. He enquired from all police stations in Sangrur District on the Wireless, but no clue was found.

On 7-10-92, we met Karam Singh, the then Minister for Industry, Punjab. He gave a letter addressed to SSP Patiala, Sh. Suresh Arora. We went to the SSP's Office at Patiala with that letter. The SSP was not present, but, the SP (D) was present there. He enquired over the

Wireless from all police stations in Patiala District, but no clue was found.

On 10-10-92, Chief Minister of Punjab, Sh. Beant Singh had come to Khanna to attend a wedding. We along with Amrik Singh, Sarpanch of village Rauni (Ludhiana) met him and narrated the incident to him. He put the application in his pocket and asked us to meet him at Chandigarh.

On 12-10-92, we met Sh. Beant Singh, Chief Minister Punjab at Chandigarh. He directed his political advisor Gurmeet Singh to inquire into the matter. We met Gurmeet Singh after 3-4 days. He said that there was no information about Amrik Singh.

On 13-10-92, registered written representations were sent to DGP Punjab, Governor Punjab, Chief Minister Punjab, and SSP Patiala. Representatives of various newspapers also came to our home and enquired about this incident. A news item about his disappearance was published in various newspapers.

On 15-10-92, a delegation of the village Panchayat met the IG Punjab Sh. Sube Singh. But, after 3-4 days, he also sent a mesage that no information was available regarding the whereabouts of Amrik Singh.

On 16-10-92, a delegation of the village Panchayat met the SSP Patiala, Sh. Suresh Arora. He told that we had come late; thereby implying that the boy had been arrested by the Police, but had now disappeared. Same day, a delegation of Shere Punjab Club Amargarh met the MLA of the area, Sh. Dhanwant Singh (Dhuri). The MLA rang up DIG Sh. Rajan Gupta. The DIG replied that Amrik Singh had indeed been arrested and had been kept underground in a Cellar along with some other boys. He said that they would release them after a few days. 4-5 days later, the MLA again rang up the DIG. Then he denied his earlier statement saying that he had mistaken some other boy for Amrik Singh.

On 21-10-92, DIG Patiala came to village Amargarh to listen to the people's complaints against Police excesses. First of all, the Panchayat of village Amargarh put forth the serious complaint of the disappearance of Amrik Singh. They also told the DIG that in case the boy may be at fault i.e. he may be a militant, then he may be shot dead in front of all of them. But, if he may be innocent, then why was he picked up without informing about his crime to his parents.

4-5 days later, we again met the DIG. He expressed his ignorance again. Thereafter, for two three months, residents of the village, freinds, relatives and other sympathisers made every effort to locate him. Whosoever had an approach in any police station, he enquired from there, but, all in vain.

So far, we do not know as to what his fault was. Whether he had any connection with any militant Organisation. Or which Police had arrested him, where he was taken and what they did to him. It is still a mystery.

### VFF/0773

Jaswinder Singh alias Kala 19 of Rajo Majra, Dhuri in Sangrur. Sukhdev Singh (victim Jaswinder Singh's father) who has become a mental wreck, as two of his sons have been killed at the hands of the Police, had five sons and two daughters. His eldest son is a farmer and two younger ones are serving in the Army. The youngest one namely Jaswinder Singh had studied upto primary level only and thereafter he had started helping his father and brother in agricultural farming. Sukhdev Singh is an old Akali worker and an "Amritdhari" (Baptised) Sikh. His father Jagdeep Singh had taken part in the Gurdwara Reform Movement.

Sukhdev Singh's youngest son (victim Jaswinder Singh) was an "Amritdhari" (Baptised) Sikh youth. In 1990, he was arrested by the Dhuri Police and sent to jail at Sangrur. The Police of different Police Stations had registered several cases against Jaswinder Singh. About one year later, the militants kidnapped one of the nephews of a Congress leader and in return for his release they got Jaswinder Singh and some other militants released. Thereafter, Jaswinder Singh did not return home. In the month of Baisakh (Apr-May) 1991, he was killed by the Sangrur Police at Village Chooga under Malerkotla Police Station, after a fierce encounter.

During the period Jaswinder Singh was absconding, the Police used to pick up his father and brothers and detain them in illegal custody. This process continued even after Jaswinder Singh had been killed in an encounter with the Police. In August-September 1991, the Moonak Police raided the house of Nirmal Singh Kanda (brother of Jaswinder Singh) in order to arrest him. However, Kanda was not available at home. A few days later, the family members produced him before the Sangrur Police through one of their relatives. Nirmal Singh was detained for 15 days at the Kotwali Police Station at Sangrur and released thereafter. Thereafter, Nirmal Singh used to stay at home only. But, the Police of Sanaur, Dhuri and Sangrur (Sadar) Police Stations used to raid his house often and pick up Nirmal Singh. However, the Panchayat used to get him released after a few days.

On 2-2-1993 at 9 P.M., the Police of C.I.A. Staff Sangrur (Bahadur Singh Wala) raided his (Nirmal Singh's) house. Shamsher Singh, SHO of Dhuri Police Station also was there alongwith the Police party. At that time all the family members including his father Sukhdev Singh, Surjit Kaur (mother) and Balwinder Singh (brother) were present in the house. The Police enquired about Nirmal Singh, made him to sit in the vehcile and took him away. On being asked by his family members the reason for his arrest, they said,"You come to Sangrur in the morning."

On the following day, family members alongwith the Panchayat went to the C.I.A. Staff Bahadur Singh Wala. The Police said that DSP Sahib was not available and asked them to come on the following day. The Panchayat and family members continued to go to the Police Station for several days but the Police continued to dodge them by making vague and false statements.

On 10 February 1993, SSP Sangrur, Jasminder Singh got a news item published in the newspapers that the Police had arrested a militant namely Nirmal Singh Kanda, who was wanted by the Police in connection with several cases. The family members came to know that the Police had produced him in a Court and obtained Police remand for three days. He was to be produced in the Court again on 13-2-1993. On 13-2-1993, his family members, Sukhdev Singh (father), Balwinder Singh (brother), relatives and other important persons reached the Court and waited. However, the Police did not produce him in the Court. Finally, at 5 P.M., the Magistrate issued a copy of a F.I.R. No. 31 dated 12-2-1993 registered at Dhuri Police Station u/s 301/34/224/225 IPC, 25/54/59 of Arms Act and 3,4 and 5 of TDA (P) Act. According to the said FIR, a Police party of Dhuri Police Station were taking Nirmal Singh for the recovery of arms when they were attacked by some unidentified militants lying in ambush near Village Meemsa. Nirmal Singh escaped taking advantage of the fog and an unidentified militant was killed in the encounter which ensued. The family members and the villagers understood that the Police had killed Nirmal Singh and concocted a dramatic story (of escape and encounter). According to Balwinder Singh (brother), though, according to the F.I.R. the Police had shown Nirmal Singh as having escaped from their custody, yet, in those days, it was common for the Police to concoct such stories in order to cover up their misdeeds. Balwinder Singh further told that on the day when the Police produced Nirmal Singh in the Court for the first time and obtained a remand, he was unable to walk, according to eyewitnesses. The Police had lifted him physically and brought him down from the vehicle. His hands had been covered and it seemed that there were injuries on his hands. Balwinder Singh told that they accepted it as the Will of God and performed his 'Bhog' (religious last rites).

### VFF/0774

Harnam Singh alias Kala of Haji Gate in Bathinda. On 16-12-91 at 5 A.M., Police raided our house. They asked the son of the landlord to call us. At his call, we opened our door. The Police party enquired whether Amrik Singh Kauli frequented our place or not. We replied in the negative. The Police asked my husband Harnam Singh and my mother-in-law Bachan Kaur to accomapny them. My mother-in-law was dropped at some distance. The whereabouts of my husband and Paramjit Singh are not known till today.

### VFF/0775

Kuldeep Singh of Dansinghwala in Bathinda. On 30-1-93 at 8 A.M., a Police party led by ASI Surjit Singh came to our house in a Canter vehicle driven by Constable Beant Singh r/o Vill. Balahar Mehma and enquired about Kuldeep Singh. He was placing the fodder in the bin for the cattle at that time. ASI Surjit Singh caught hold of his neck and made him to sit in the Canter and took him away. He never came back after that.

### VFF/0776

Gurtej Singh alias Bhola of Ghuman Kalan, Maur Mandi in Bathinda. On 11-7-92 at 6 P.M, a Police party led by Sub Inspector Gurjit Singh of Bathinda Sadar police station, picked up my son Gurtej Singh from our residence at Pratap Nagar, Bathinda. Since then his whereabouts are not known.

### VFF/0777

Jagjit Singh of Kesar Singh Wala, Phool in Bathinda. On 25-2-92 at 8 A.M., Jagjit Singh had gone to Moga City, but, never returned.

### VFF/0778

Balwant Singh 50 of Dialpur, Rampura Phool in Bathinda. Balwant Singh aged 50 years belonged to an educated family. Balwant Singh was employed as a Section Officer in the Audit Department at Faridkot. His wife Upkar Kaur was employed as a Supervisor in the Rural Development Department. Their elder son Devinder Pal Singh had obtained a degree in Mechanical Engineering from Ludhiana and had done a job also for some time after getting his degree. Balwant Singh or his family were not directly involved in any sort of militant activities. They did not know either whether their son Devinder Pal Singh had any link with the militant activities or not.

On 13-12-1991, for the first time, a party of Chandigarh police led by DSP Baldev Singh Saini raided his house and picked up Balwant Singh.

After picking up Balwant Singh the same police party went to Rampura (village) and picked up the father-in-law of Prof. Devinder Pal Singh namely Kultar Singh. Before that, the Chandigarh police had picked up Balwant Singh's brother-in-law (wife's sister's husband') (name not known but he is missing) and his son from Mohali and at their instance only they had conducted a raid at village Dialpura. The other members of his family did not pursue his case at Chandigarh lest the police should arrest them also.

A week later, the Chandigarh police led by an Inspector again raided village Dialpura. At that time Balwant Singh was also along with the police in their custody. His condition was very bad due to police beating. The police picked up Mukhtiar Singh (nephew—'Bhatija'), Joginder Singh (nephew—'Bhanja') and Mohinder Singh (nephew—'Bhatija') and took them to Chandigarh. Immediately on arrival at Chandigarh, all the four of them were tortured brutally from 4 PM to 11 PM at one of the police stations there. They were asking them about Prof. Devinder Pal Singh. The police subjected them to Roller treatment (rolling iron rollers on thighs and legs with policemen sitting on the rollers on both sides), and beat them up with rubber belts. According to Mukhtiar Singh, there were many wounds on the body of Balwant Singh as a result of this torture.

On the following day, all the four of them were taken to C.I.A. Staff Chandigarh where SSP Saini got them tortured brutally in his presence from 3 PM to 7 PM. The police were asking them about Prof. Devinder Pal Singh. According to Mukhtiar Singh, the father-in-law of Prof. Devinder Pal Singh namely Kultar Singh had been released due to political approach before their arrest itself. Balwant Singh, Mukhtiar Singh and Joginder Singh were detained together at Sector 11 police station at Chandigarh. On the third day of his arrest, Mohinder Singh was released at the instance of Akali leader Captain Kanwaljit Singh.

On the next day evening, a police party took away Balwant Singh from amongst those three. And one hour later, the police party put Mukhtiar Singh and Joginder Singh in a vehicle and took them to Mani Majra police station. Both of them were detained at Mani Majra police station for eight days. On the eighth day, Joginder Singh's physical and mental condition deteriorated suddenly. Therefore, they released both of them on the ninth day.

After their release, Balwinder Singh (nephew—'Bhanja'), Gurbachan Singh (nephew—'Bhatija') and Jathedar Mohan Singh r/o Phool made about four trips to Chandigarh for pursuing the case of Balwant Singh. Once, 4-5 members of the village Panchayat also accompanied them.

During this period they met SSP Saini and DSP Randhawa. During the first meeting, the SSP told that they would release Balwant Singh and he asked them to meet DSP Randhawa. Thereafter, family members met DSP Randhawa at CIA Staff Chandigarh twice about the release of Balwant Singh, but, he used to put them off by making false promises. During the fourth trip, Darshan Singh (nephew—'Bhatija'), and Balwinder Singh (nephew—'Bhanja') took along with them Sarpanch Lal Singh, Member Panchayat Tarlok Singh and Member Panchayat Harbhajan Singh and met DSP Randhawa. The DSP swore by God in front of the Panchayat and told that he had already released Balwant Singh and advised them to look for him at his relatives' places. But, the family members and the Panchayat got suspicious that the police might have killed Balwant Singh.

In the meantime, Dialpura police and that of CIA Staff Bathinda used to raid his (Balwant Singh's) house regularly. The police picked up his family members numerous times and used to detain them in their illegal custody for months together. This process continued till the time Prof. Devinder Pal Singh was arrested from Germany. He was brought back from Germany by Delhi police. For about two years, the police did not allow family members of Balwant Singh to cultivate their 12 acres land. The house remained locked. Balwant Singh's younger son Tajinder Pal Singh and wife Upkar Kaur also used to live in hiding. The police used to enquire about them also. Only due to the fear of the police, Tajinder Pal Singh, Upkar Kaur and Manpreet Kaur (wife of Prof. Devinder Pal Singh) went away to America.

At the time when Prof. Devinder Pal Singh was brought from Germany to Delhi, the Bathinda police had arrested Balwinder Singh (nephew—'Bhatija' of Balwant Singh) and brought him to Delhi. Balwinder Singh was kept at Delhi for about eight days. However, Prof. Devinder Pal Singh was not brought before him there. On the eighth day, the Bathinda police brought Balwinder Singh to his vilage and released him. Prof. Devinder Pal Singh remained with the Delhi police on remand for a long time. Then he remained on remand with the police of various districts of Punjab and Chandigarh. Thereafter he was sent back to Tihar Jail. At present Prof. Devinder Pal Singh is deatined at Tihar jail. He has been acquitted in several cases. Now only one case is pending against him at Delhi. So far, the family members do not know about the whereabouts of Balwant Singh. They continued to visit Chandigarh for several months after his arrest, but, they did not get any information about the whereabouts of Balwant Singh.

**VFF/0779**

Nehru Singh 17 of Dansingh Wala in Bathinda. On 30-1-93 at 8 A.M., he was picked up from the house of Landlord Ajmer Singh s/o Atar Singh, for whom he used to work. The Panchayat went to the Police Station. They were also beaten up. Ajmer Singh was also insulted. Since then whereabouts of Nehru Singh are not known. The Police personnel involved are :-

1.    Nek Singh, SHO Jaiton
2.    Ranjit Singh Sotha, i/c Police Chowki Baja.

**VFF/0780**

Kamaljit Singh of Ghaniye Ke Bangar, Batala in Gurdaspur. On 19 April 1993, he was made to get down from the pillion seat of the scooter driven by Head Constable (HC) Jagdish Singh near the University at Amritsar.

As per the application (PCHR/425) submitted to the People's Commission by his mother Gurbachan Kaur, Kamaljit Singh was arrested by the Police on 19 April, 1993, from the gate of Khalsa College at Amritsar. He was tortured brutally by the Police and on 25 April, 1993, he was killed by Jalandhar Police, in a fake encounter near village Cheema under Kartarpur Police Station. She has further alleged in her application that Head Constable Jagdish Singh had played a crucial role in getting him eliminated.

**VFF/0781**

Hardeep Singh 24 of Parowal, Batala in Gurdaspur. Details of occurance are not given in this Proforma. The following is the true translation of the information extracted from the photostat copy of the F.I.R attached herewith:-

That on 1-6-86, Hardeep Singh had gone to his maternal village Putli to the house of Bachan Singh. On 3-6-86, from village Kotla Gujjaran, he reached village Wadala under P.S. Majitha, on a Tractor Trolley along with Tota Singh, resident of Kotla Gujjaran. But, he did not return home. It became known that he was spotted at village Wadala on 4-6-86 where he was picked up by a patrolling party of CRPF and taken to Police Station Majitha. One Amarvir Singh s/o Balvir Singh of our village (Parowal) had seen him sitting in a Jeep outside the Police Station Majitha. We enquired at Police Station Majitha where they expressed ignorance about Hardeep Singh and said that the CRPF might have taken him back. As such, we enquired from CRPF Headquarters at Dana Mandi (Grain Market) Majitha. They told us that Hardeep Singh had been released. Till today, we have been enquiring from CRPF Majitha, but they have not given any satisfactory reply.

**VFF/0782**

Surinderpal Singh 40 of Dhudhipura, Batala in Gurdaspur. Surinder Pal Singh along with Satwant Singh were picked up by Mr. G.G.A. Sharma, Commandant 25 Battalion CRPF Punjab and his men on 3 February 1988 at 8 A.M. from the bus stand Naushehra while they were going on duty to Batala. One Banta Singh s/o Mota Singh was present at the place of occurance when the two were picked up by the Police. When the family members came to know about it, his brother Hardeep Singh rushed to Dhariwal police station and made a report about the picking up of his brother Surinder Pal Singh by the CRPF. The Police authorities refused to register any FIR about the incident.

Then his brother sent a number of telegrams and also made written representations to the concerned officials. He met the DGP Punjab Police and submitted a written representation requesting him to get his brother released from the illegal custody of the Punjab Police. Mr. Ribeiro, the then DGP assured him that his brother would be released soon. In fact, the then SSP Gurdaspur Mr. J.P. Virdi sent a wireless message that two persons namely Satwant Singh and Surinder Pal Singh had been rounded up by the CRPF and anybody wants them may take them.

That afterr waiting for some time, when his brother did not come back, Hardeep Singh again approached DGP Punjab who in turn ordered an enquiry into the matter and deputed Mr. Umrao Singh, SP (Crime) to enquire into the matter. One Mr. Mohinder Singh visited their house also. The outcome of that enquiry is not known till today.

That then Hardeep Singh met Mr. Chaman Lal, the then DIG of Border Security Force. He gave him a patient hearing and wrote a forwarding letter to the then advisor to the Governor of Punjab to help him.

That then he approached the Central Government and met a number of Ministers to get his brother released. The then Environment Minister was kind enough to write a D.O. letter to the then Governor of Punjab to get the detenues released.

That then he wrote a letter to the National Human Rights Commission to enquire into the whereabouts of his brother. In response to that letter, an enquiry was ordered by NHRC and one Jaswinder Singh of NHRC visited their village and made enquiries about his brother. But, he did not hear anything from the NHRC for quite some time. Then he wrote a letter again to the Chairman of NHRC to send the enquiry report to him. But, so far, there is no reply from the NHRC.

That till date, the whereabouts of my husband Surinder Pal Singh are not known.

**VFF/0783**
Sukhwinder Kaur 20 of Kala Afghana, Batala in Gurdaspur.
Sukhwinder Kaur had gone along with her husband and three month
old child to Avtar Singh Tari (Cat) at village Khudda, to find out the
whereabouts of Sukhpal Singh, a cousin (Bhua's son) of her husband,
but, did not return home.

**VFF/0784**
Channan Singh 18 of Bhole Ke, Batala in Gurdaspur. On 1 April
1988, he was arrested from Amritsar. On 4 April 1988, he was brought
to the Canal at Bhaume Wadala and shot dead. It was claimed by Police
to be an 'encounter'.

**VFF/0785**
Sukhwant Singh 25 of Marhian Wala, Batala in Gurdaspur.
Sukhwant Singh was arrested from village Majhi in Nabha area and later
shot dead in a fake encounter near village Kakrala. The family members
came to know about his death after 10 days only. His mother recognised
his clothes.

**VFF/0786**
Boota Singh alias Boota 45 Ghaniye Ke Bangar, Batala in
Gurdaspur. On 14 February 1992, Boota Singh was returning along with
his colleagues, after unloading his truck at Phillaur. The Police had laid
a Naka on the way near the police station Goraya. They were arrested
by the police at the Naka. The Police Officers involved are:-
Inspector Jatinder Pal
SHO Surjit Singh Ghora

**VFF/0787**
Gurdial Singh alias Tota 23 of Nawan Pind, Bhagowal in Gurdaspur.
On 23-4-88, he was made to get down from the Bus of the Janta
Transport, in which he was travelling, by a uniformed Police party, put
in a Gypsy and taken away.

**VFF/0788**
Tejinderpal Singh 18 of Satkoha, Batala in Gurdaspur. Tejinderpal
Singh had come home from Ludhiana on 24 April, 1991. At about 4 P.M.,
same day, he went to the tubewell at his farm to give food and tea to the
farm workers who were working there. Some police informer, who was
inimical towards the family of Tejinderpal Singh, tipped the Police that
a militant namely Tejinderpal Singh had come from Ludhiana to his
home in the village Satkoha. A Police party led by ASI Basant Singh and
including four or five Constables of Police Post Satkoha, came to his
tubewell. ASI Basant Singh addressed Tejinderpal Singh and said,"Kaka,
tere nal kutchh gal karni hai, ithhe aa (Boy, come here, I want to talk

to you)." At first, a farm worker namely Bitta came forward, but, ASI Basant Singh told him that he wanted the other boy i.e. Tejinderpal Singh. Tejinderpal Singh went to him. ASI Basant Singh told him that they would take him to the Police Post. Tejinder asked the ASI the reason for taking him to the Police Post and said that he would not come with them until they disclosed the reason for taking him along. At this, ASI Basant Singh slapped him on his face. Tejinder lost his temper and started abusing the ASI. The Police lifted Tejinderpal Singh forcibly and took him to the Police Post Satkoha.

Our farm worker Bitta came running to our house and informed us that the Police had taken away Tejinderpal Singh. I, along with the Sarpanch Jaswant Singh, my brother Sardool Singh, Panch Jaswant Singh and other elders went to the Police Post. There, one Constable told us that he had been taken to Dhariwal Police Station. Then we went to Dhariwal Police Station and reached there at about 6 P.M. I asked the SHO Makhan Singh as to what the fault of my son was. He asked me to come in the morning and then he would talk to me. However, he allowed me to meet my son and offer him some food and tea. My son was sitting alone in the room when I met him and served him food and tea, in the presence of all the persons accompanying me. He told me that the ASI had slapped him without any reason and thus provoked him and that he had abused the ASI. However, Tejinder did not express any sort of apprehension as he did not suspect anything.

Next day (25 April 1991) morning, I along with my brother and Sarpanch Jaswant Singh and Panch Jaswant Singh went to the Dhariwal Police Station. But, SHO Makhan Singh was not present there. His orderlies informed us that the SHO had gone out. The Munshi allowed me to meet my son. I met Tejinder and served him food and tea. My son told me that he had been beaten up very badly, the last night, under the supervision of the SHO Makhan Singh. He showed me the injuries on his body. He had injuries on his chest and legs. His legs had been pulled apart and also given roller treatment. Blue marks were visible on his legs. They were asking him for information about some terrorists of our village. He told them that he did not know anything as he was studying away from the village, at Ludhiana. The injuries on his body were of a grave nature. There must have been some internal injuries also. He also told me that unless he was rescued soon, they would kill him. At about 3 P.M., I went to Gurdaspur to meet a political leader Sewa Singh Sekhon (now a Minister in the Akali Govt.) I met him at the district courts and narrated him the whole story. Even though, he was busy in his election work, yet he accompanied me to the office of DSP (HQ) Gurdev Singh.

Sewa Singh was made to deposit his revolver at the counter before he was allowd to go inside. I met DSP Gurdev Singh at about 4 P.M. who said that there was no such case in his knowledge. He asked us to enquire in the morning next day so that he would make enquiries in the meantime. Sewa Singh went away for his election work and I came back to Dhariwal Police Station. The SHO Makhan Singh had not turned up yet. I waited there till 7 P.M., and came back to my house.

Next day (26 April 1991) morning, when we went to Dhariwal Police Station we were not allowed to enter inside. I pleaded for a meeting with the SHO Makhan Singh, but, in vain. Then I sent somebody inside secretly to find out the condition of my son. He came and informed me that Tejinderpal Singh was not inside the Police Station. Thereafter, I went to Gurdaspur. There I met the DSP Gurdev Singh at about twelve noon along with Sewa Singh, my relatives, and village elders. He asked me to go back to Dhariwal and promised to come himself there and find out from the SHO. I came back to Dhariwal where someone told me that my son had been killed already.

Immediately, I went to Gurdaspur Civil Hospital where the Police used to send bodies for postmortem. After some inquiries, I was able to meet Dr. Kartar Singh Babbar, who had conducted the postmortem. He described the body brought by Dhariwal Police as that of a young boy who had not grown the beard yet. He also told me that an Identity Card had been found on his person which bore his name Tejinder Singh Kalon, Guru Nanak Polytechnic Engineering College, Ludhiana. It was now clear that my son was dead. The Police had taken away the clothes and the Identity Card. I went to the district courts where many people had gathered and told them what had happened. It was 26 April 1991 at 1 P.M. that a large number of people mainly the Akalis who had come to file their nomination papers to the district courts accompanied me in a procession to the cremation grounds. There were only two or three policemen present at the cremation grounds who ran away on seeing the crowd approaching. The man on duty at the cremation ground told us that Dhariwal Police had come with the body of a young man whose pyre was still burning.

The Police had registered a F.I.R. in which they said that the Police had set up a Check Post in the night. The Police force was led by DSP Gurdev Singh and SHO Makhan Singh was also there. An encounter took place between the militants and the Police in which the firing continued for a long time and many trucks were destroyed. After the encounter, the area was searched and one dead body was found.

After the cremation, I sent written representations to the DGP, the Chief Minister, the Governor, and the DC. There was no response from any one of them. Two weeks after the incident, I met SSP Goyal for the first time through Harbhajan Singh Ghumman, ex-MLA. He did not listen to me and misbehaved with me. I told him that my son was a regular student at Guru Nanak Polytechnic College, Ludhiana. I challenged him to go and verify his antecedents from there. I further told him that no inquiry had ever been conducted against him and no F.I.R. had been registered against him anytime in the district or anywhere else in Punjab. Then how come, overnight he was declared to be a terrorist. I told the SSP that the truth was that my son had been picked up at the instigation of an informer who had some enmity with our family. My son was tortured to death. According to the inside information, Makhan Singh even called for a doctor in an attempt to revive him. But his condition did not improve. Makhan Singh then decided to eliminate him in a faked encounter. But, the SSP accused me of lying and supported his policemen. Just like the terrorists had formed gangs and supported each other, so also the Police had formed gangs and supported each other. The SSP said that I would suffer more if I talked like this.

Two years later, the Police started harassing my elder son. There was a fight in our village. Someone instigated Makhan Singh, who was by now a DSP and posted at Gurdaspur, to catch my other son also. He sent his police although he had nothing to do with our area, which is under the jurisdiction of Dhariwal Police Station. They came and picked up my son. The same night at twelve o'clock I went and met the SSP, Mr. Mohammad Mustafa. He immediately asked Makhan Singh for an explanation and thus, Makhan Singh's hands were tied. Even then he detained my son for two days, and tried to extort fifty thousand rupees as ransom. He had picked up my son on 25th January 1993, or 1994. On 26th January, which is the Republic day, he asked for the ransom. The deal was settled for twenty thoudsand rupees. On 27th, I gave him the money and he released my son. I reported this to the SSP who called him up for an explanation and also made Makhan Singh return the money to me. Makhan Singh was transferred.

That I have not filed any petition in any court. I had already lost my son. Makhan Singh tried to eliminate my second son also. I was fortunate in having been able to save his life, thanks to the good offices of SSP Mustafa. But, Punjab was still under the Police Rule and no one dared to speak against the Police. No Government listened to us. No Court listened to us.

**VFF/0789**
Gurmej Singh Geja 45 of Marhian Wala, Batala in Gurdaspur. On 03 June 1984, he had gone to Sri Darbar Sahib for paying his obeisance. He used to live at Sri Darbar Sahib only due to the repeated harassment at the hands of the police.

**VFF/0790**
Rajbir Singh alias Raju 20 of Zafarwal in Gurdaspur. On 27-4-89, he was killed in a fake encounter with the police. A news item appearaed in the newspapers on 28-4-89. In Ajit dated 28-4-89, his name was erroneously mentioned as Ranjit Singh.

**VFF/0791**
Gurmeet Singh of Tugalwala in Gurdaspur. On 07-2-84 at 7 P.M., he had gone to meet the Granthi at Gurdwara (Thakarwal). On 08-2-84 at 5 A.M. He was killed in a false encounter by a police party led by SHO Jagroop Singh (who was HC at that time). The police themselves cremated the dead body after post mortem.

**VFF/0792**
Gurmukh Singh 32 Zafarwal in Gurdaspur. Despite enquiries made from family members and villagers, exact date of his death could not be ascertained. It was the month of 'Bhadon', about 13 years ago when he was killed by the Police in a fake encounter. The economic condition of the family is pathetic.

**VFF/0793**
Baljit Singh alias 16 of Jagrian in Gurdaspur. On 4-1-92, he was killed by the Police in a false encounter at village Bahian, Tehsil & Distt. Gurdaspur.

**VFF/0794**
Ravinder Singh alias Laadi of Dugalwal in Gurdaspur. On 12 July 1991, he had gone along with his wife, to Achal Sahib at Batala to see 'Masya' fair. At 4 P.M., he was arrested by Batala City Police. His wife who was alongwith him had gone to the house of her 'Nanad' (Ravinder's Sister's house) and he had come to the market to buy fruits when he was nabbed. The then DSP R.P. Singh was inimical towards Ravinder Singh. He got him arrested through an Inspector. When he did not return, his wife came and informed us at home. We went to City Batala Police Station but, they did not give us any clue. One Constable told us that they had killed him.

**VFF/0795**
Narinder Singh alias Bittu 24 of Batala in Gurdaspur. On 12-08-89, at about 12 Noon, he was sitting in the courtyard of his house and reading a newspaper under a Mullberry tree. It was a Saturday and Power

Shutdown was there. That is why he was sitting under a Mullberry tree and reading. Only my younger daughter Raminder was at home on that day. I and his mother had gone for duty in the school. His brother had gone for duty at the Sugar Mill Batala. His other sister had gone to college. At about 12 Noon, a police party led by ASI Rachhpal Singh Bajwa came to our house and abducted Bittu. The Police did not listen to the residents of the Mohalla. At 8 P.M., I met Rachhpal Singh along with one of my colleagues, who had been his class fellow. He assured us that there is nothing to worry and that they were picking up all the boys named 'Bittu' as a precautionary measure only, due to 15th August. They would be released later. But, ultimately, they killed him in a false encounter.

**VFF/0796**

Baldev Singh alias Debu 36 of Bhamri, Batala in Gurdaspur. On 12-11-91, evening, he was picked up from his residence by Baldev Singh, SHO Sri Hargobindpur.

**VFF/0797**

Surjit Singh alias Bittu 18 Bhamri, Batala in Gurdaspur. He was picked up from Sultanwind from the place of his maternal uncle and in front of him. His maternal uncle also was killed.

**VFF/0798**

Balwant Singh alias Balla 35 Dhapei, Batala in Gurdaspur. As mentioned elsewhere in this form, on 26-2-91 in the afternoon, he was shot dead by the Police in a false encounter near his house in front of his wife. The police personnel involved are as follows:-

1.  Rajbir, Inspector, SHO, police station Sri Hargobindpur.
2.  Gurnam Singh, ASI, P.S. Sri Hargobindpur.
3.  Dilbag Singh, ASI, P.S. Sri Hargobindpur.
4.  An aged SI whose name is not known.

**VFF/0799**

Punjab Singh 25 of Dhapei, Batala in Gurdaspur. On 3-12-91 at about 5 P.M., Baldev Singh, then SHO of Sri Hargobindpur police station, along with his 7-8 Gunmen raided our house, put my son Punjab Singh in a vehicle and took him away in front of me and my husband Mann Singh. While departing he told us to come to Sri Hargobindpur and find out.

That on 4-12-91, my husband Mann Singh along with respectable persons of the vilage including Jagir Singh s/o Teja Singh, and Baldev Singh s/o Gurditta Singh went to Sri Hargobindpur police station and assured SHO Baldev Singh about Punjab Singh being absolutely innocent. The SHO made an excuse that he would conslut his Superior Officers and then release Punjab Singh.

However, when we went to the P.S. on 9-12-91, SHO Baldev Singh told us that Punjab Singh had escaped from Police custody. We continued to enquire about him, but could not get any clue regarding his whereabouts. My husband Mann Singh and Baldev Singh s/o Gurditta Singh continued to enquire about him at Sri Hargobindpur P.S. from time to time.

On 11-12-91 at about 6 A.M., SHO Baldev Singh along with other policemen shot dead Punjab Singh and 5 other youth, in a false encounter, on a Kutcha footpath at Village Dhade Mahesh under Police Station Ghuman. However, we came to know about this fact only in April 1996 when it was disclosed by Baldev Singh s/o Gurditta Singh and Jagir Singh s/o Teja Singh, both residents of our village, that they had heard the sound of gunshots and also witnessed this incident. They told that they did not open their mouth so far due to the fear of the Police.

**VFF/0800**

Satnam Singh alias Satta 28 of Dhapei, Batala in Gurdaspur. On 26 February 1991, Qadian Police raided our house in broad day light. Our house is situated outside the village on the Canal side in our fields. The Police picked up my son Satnam Singh and a labourer Balwant Singh whom Satnam had hired that day for planting the nursery of Onions in our fields. They tied their hands to their backs. The Police already had another unidentified youth in their custody whose hands were also tied to his back. All the three of them were kicked with Boots and Rifle Butts and were taken to one side by the Police saying that we should not have any hope of their coming back. Myself and my daughter-in-law pleaded a lot with the Police to release them but they beat us up badly. Even then I followed them upto some distance, but had to stop on being manhandled a lot. A little further at a distance of about 150-200 yards from my house, near a Sugarcane field, the Police shot all three of them in cold blood in front of me, my daughter-in-law and many other persons working in nearby fields. Neither anybody was allowed to go near the dead bodies nor they were handed over to us. Then they called police reinforcements and carried away the dead bodies.

The names of police personnel involved are given as under:-
1. Rajbir, Inspector, SHO, P.S. Qadian
2. Gurnam Singh, ASI, P.S. Qadian
3. Dilbag Singh, ASI, P.S. Qadian
4. An aged S.I. whose name is not known

**VFF/0801**

Joginder Singh alias Panju 35 of Kalanaur, Batala in Gurdaspur. No details are given, except the alias (Bai) of a police officer.

This proforma was updated on 20.5.2002 on the basis of another proforma received about this case. The true translation of the same is appended below:

He was arrested by SHO Jarnail Singh, on 10.3.94. On 12.3.94, a drama of a false encounter was enacted and he was sent to jail.

**VFF/0802**

Punjab Singh 15 of Khujala, Batala in Gurdaspur. This incident has been decribed in detail in a petition by Bachan Singh son of Harnam Singh, Jat, resident of Khujala, Tehsil Batala, dated 22 august, 1991. The petition was sent to the DC Gurdaspur, SSP Batala, DGP Punjab, Home Minister, PM, and the President. The true translation of the same is appended below:-

"It is prayed that on 13 August 1991, the encounter that was shown to have taken place under police station Hargovindpur, village Khujala, was actually an incident of police brutalities. The police went to the house of Sucha Singh at village Thande which comes under police station Sri Hargovindpur, Distt. Gurdaspur at ten in the morning. Sucha Singh offered them water and tea, and asked them to sit down. Policemen told him that we will not drink any water here. We will drink water later. They asked him to pluck a lot of lemons from the trees in his land. They told him that the big boss—badde sahib—was going to come, and had called for him. Sucha Singh wanted to know why he had been called. But the policemen asked him not to worry about anything and told him that they had to go to Bachan Singh's house in village Khujala. Sucha Singh plucked about one kilogram of lemons. But the policemen asked him not to be stingy and to pluck up more lemons since they were going to pay him the price. They forced him to pluck about ten kilos of lemons. After that they asked him to go ahead of them with the bagfull of lemons. Sucha Singh's house is next to a canal. They walked for one and a half miles towards Khujala and stopped by a canal at Dapayi (a small hamlet). There they asked Sucha Singh to show them Bachan Singh's house. Sucha Singh said that Khujala was a big village and that he did not know Bachan Singh's house because he was from a different village. Hearing this, they started beating Sucha Singh. Many people saw him getting beaten. They crossed the canal and around 11 a.m. reached the house of Bachan Singh son of Harnam Singh, village Khujala, police station Sri Hargovindpur, Distt. Gurdaspur. That is about two kilometers from Sucha Singh's house. Reaching the house, they asked for Bachan Singh. Bachan Singh's wife Jasbir Kaur said that she and her daughter Rano, who is ill, had just returned home after purchasing some medicines from Qadian. As Bachan Singh was running a high temperature, they had left him behind with the doctor. He would come back when his fever comes down. Hearing this, the policemen started abusing her in filthy language. They searched the house. They also beat up Sucha Singh in front of Bachan Singh's house. One constable took the bag of lemons away from him, and put it in the courtyard of Bachan Singh's house. At that time, only Jasbir Kaur, her unmarried daughter Miko (Amrik Kaur) and her married daughter (Rano) were alone in the house. They had just reached the house from Qadian. Rano is married to an Army man who is away on the duty. She had been ill for a long time and therefore had come to her mother to be looked after. Search yielded nothing incriminating. But Inspector Baldev Singh asked Jasbir Kaur about her son Punjab Singh who had gone to irrigate the fields. Jasbir Kaur asked Miko to go and call her brother. But some constable followed her to the field where Punjab Singh was. Seeing him, Inspector asked him to come to him—"Kaka, idhar aa!—I have to ask you about an address." Punjab Singh came to him. Inspector asked him something to which Punjab Singh gave a reply. Thereafter, the Inspector and the other policemen started beating him. Miko could not bear to watch her brother thus getting thrashed and she fell down on him. Policemen also abused her and beat her up. Jasbir Kaur also came running there. The Inspector caught hold of her hair and pulled her down on the ground, beat her up and humiliated her. He abused the women in filthiest language. We cannot repeat them. Jasbir Kaur asked the Inspector to tell her what was their fault, why they were being beaten and abused. The Inspector said that he had information that she had been feeding the terrorists. "I will not let you go. I will kill you all", he said. The policemen caught hold of Punjab Singh and went to his uncle Sewa Singh's house that was nearby also in the fields. The two houses are divided by the distance of four killas—char killas! Punjab Singh caught hold of his sister Miko and started crying: "Bahan mainnu chhudalo, ye Bibi mainu chhudalo. Minnu inane mardena hai." Meanwhile, a lot of other policemen also arrived there. The policemen made an announcement that all neighbours should get inside their homes, close the doors and not come out. Whosoever steps out would be shot, they announced. All the seven-eight households in the neighbourhood obeyed the orders. The policemen took out their wireless sets, and started relaying messages in loud voices to the effect that they had been surrounded by terrorists. They asked for reinforcements to reach the village Khujala near Bachan Singh's house. They kept up this drama for about one hour. All the people in the village were able to listen to all this. Around 12 noon, several police and BSF vehicles arrived there. They surrounded Sewa Singh's house from all the sides. Some policemen climbed the roof of the house, and then the firing commenced. People were watching all this concealed in their homes. All the firing was going on from the sugarcabne fields near Bachan Singh's house. Sugarcane was not yet ripe. After firing intermittently for half an hour, the police force went up to the sugarcane fields. They all started shouting that three terrorists had been killed. The people had been watching all the drama. The police said that the terrorists who had been hiding in the sugarcane fields had been killed. The people asked who were the terrorists, and where were they lying dead. The policemen said that they were lying dead near the sugarcane fields. When big officers arrive, then we would know who they were. The firing stopped. Some policemen entered the house and ordered the family to prepare fresh lemon water for all the policemen. The people in that house said that they had no sugar. The policemen then shouted if they did not even have salt. The family got scared and taking all the lemons which Sucha Singh had brought made the fresh lemon drink for all the policemen. Even the policemen who had been surrounding Bachan Singh's house, went down to drink fresh lemon water. Several buckets of lemon drink was consumed by all. Then they asked Jasbir Kaur to make nice tea for them. Also to take out nice cups. We would save your son by recommending his case to senior officers. Otherwise, your son too would be killed along with the terrorists. When Rano and Miko also came there, one constable swore that their brother was alright. Jasbir Kaur made a large pot of tea for them. One head constable stood by her in the kitchen to watch her prepare the tea. When she finished making the tea, they locked up Jasbir Kaur, Miko and Rano inside. The policemen said that the big boss—vadda sahib—was coming. Jasbir Kaur started crying that she should be allowed to see the big officer so that she might request him to save her only son's life. The policmen said that they had orders not to allow anyone out of the houses, that it was the question of their jobs. Again, there was a firing outside. This time, Punjab Singh and Sucha Singh had been shot dead on an elevated part of the land outside Sewa Singh's house. The entire episode of this stage-managed encounter kiling was witnessed by Sewa Singh's wife (vaddi?) who was locked up in her house. Sucha Singh and Punjab Singh were shot on a patch of fodder crop (chari?), which is four killas away from the sugarcane fields in which the terrorists had been killed. After this, there was no more firing. The policemen dragged three dead bodies to the courtyard of Bachan Singh's house and then loaded them in a vehicle. No one said anything about Sucha Singh and Punjab Singh. One officer opened the door of Jasbir's house. At this she started wailing about her only son who was barely fifteen years old, and was completely innocent. He told her that he would be released after some inquiries. He pretended that Punjab Singh was still alive. But Sewa Singh's wife said that both Sucha Singh and Punjab singh had been shot in front of her. For the next three four days, we went from police station to police station along with several village elders to find Punjab Singh. But no one told us anything about Punjab Singh. Unofficially, some policemen told the village elders that both had been killed along with the terrorists. Some policemen came to the house on 14 August 1991 and warned that whoever talked about Sucha Singh and Punjab Singh would also be killed. Some policemen abused the Inspector who was responsible for these murders. On 14 august 1991, the Ajit newspaper reported that Jaswant Singh Ahluwalia and Sukhjit Singh Bijli had been identified among the terrorists killed in the armed encounter. But the Punjabi Tribune of 15 August 91 identified the five dead terrorists as the following: :Batala— Yesterday, the police from this district identified the five terrorists killed in an encounter that took place under police station Qadian near village Nakkmokal in the following fashion: Jaswant Singh Ahluwalia, Paramjit Singh Pappu, Sucha Singh and Pappu. All these are from Khujala under Sri Hargovindpur police station. The fifth terrorist has been idenrtified as Mangat Singh from village Dhand. The truth is that there is no one called Mangat Singh from village Dhand. Sucha Singh is from that village and he was brought from his village to this place of the encounter. The Tribune said that three terrorists and two who give them shelter have been killed. But, in the Ajit newspaper of 21 August 1991, a statement from the militants has said that Jaswant Singh Ahluwalia was alright—Chadh di kala vich hai! The people have become completely confused by these contardictory reports as to what may be the truth. It is also not known whether Punjab Singh is still in the police custody or whether he has been killed. Why do not the police officilas release his name, if he is in the custody? Or, even if he has been killed in the so called encounter......What was the idea of bringing Sucha Singh from two kilomwetres to this place only to be killed? He could also have been killed in his own house. He was made to pluck ten kilos of lemons, and to carry the bag on his head for more than two kilometeres where he was killed. Why was he killed? What ws his crime? He was a very truthful, gentle and a hardworking person. Punjab Singh was only a fifteen years old lad, completely innocent. What is the objective of killing so young a lad who had nothing to do with terrorist activities. Bachan Singh is a sixty years old man, and Punjab Singh was his only son. The people want that this case should be investigated by some senior officer who may be fair and that on the establishment of the truth, the guilty may be punished....

This action has prdouced an atmosphere of terror in the area. They are afraid of speaking the truth. They fear that whosoever speaks the truth would be labelled as terrorist or harbourers and would be killed. The people do not care how the security forces deal with the problem of terrorism, but the common people who have nothing to do with the terrorism are subject to grave atrocities. Innocent people are getting killed. The Government seems to trust as true whatever the policemen report. But, the policemen are the children of the same soil, and they also engage in falsehood. When the people complain of atrocities, the Government should carry out independent investigations. people need to be reassured that they can speak the truth without fearing death as the inevitable consequence. It is known that masquerading as terrorists they come to the houses to demand shelter and food. In the day time, they come back in their uniforms to harass and to extort money. It is the duty of the Government to protect the people, and to pay attention to their genuine complaints. When people get justice, they would automatically begin to support the Government. We do not say that all policemen are bad. But, those who are bad, are ruling the roost. They must be punished. Otherwise, only the rule of the jungle would prevail. people of the village have no idea who were the terrorists killed in the encounter; from where they had come. No one was told the truth. The truth is that the killed people were not from the village. They had not come from any house in the village. They had either been hiding in the sugarcane field, or the police had brought them there. The truth is known only to the policemen who carried out the operation. We suspect that the encounter was the result of a conspiracy involving the policemen from the top to the bottom of the heirarchy. People want justice. Atrocities (dhakkeshahi!) must cease. There must be a thorough inquiry into this brutal incident, and justice must be done to the anguished family members of the victims. "

**VFF/0803**

Jagjit Singh 22 Khajiala, Batala in Gurdaspur. On 23rd April, 1988 morning, Jagjit Singh started from home for Amritsar by bus for purchasing newsprint, stationary, and other things for our printing press. A carpenter who has a shop at Ghuman in front of our printing press was sitting two seats next to Jagjit Singh. The bus was stopped and all the passengers were searched one by one and allowed to board the bus again. Jagjit Singh was also searched. Nothing incriminating was found on his person. He was signalled to go into the bus, but, immediately called back by the inspecting officer and asked to get into the CRPF bus. Obviously, some police informer, so called "Cat" must have been there with the search team who must have got my son picked up. The CRPF vehicle belonged to Mal Mandi Interrogation Centre.

When Jagjit Singh did not return home till late in the evening, I went to the printing press assuming that he might be sleeping there having returned from Amritsar very late. He was not there. The next day also he did not return. Then I went to Amritsar. There I found out from our stationary shop that he had gone back after making all the purchases. He had left Amritsar on 23rd soon after 1 p.m. I came back. My son had no terrorist involvement and had no police record. I was confident that even if the police had picked him up on suspicion, he would soon be released after some questioning.

But, on the third day, when there still was no news of my son, I became nervous and went back to Amritsar. I went to the SSP Amritsar and told him my story. I told him about our printing press and that Jagjit Singh who had gone to Amritsar to purchase printing paper had not returned. He might have got detained somehwere as there was no news of him. I requested him to find out and to intervene to get my son released if he would be found in any police station or place of detention under his jurisdiction. He then called the wireless operator and asked him to send the wireless message to all the police stations and police posts to look for Jagjit Singh, son of so and so, resident of such and such village. And if he would be found anywhere, to, immediately contact the SSP. I was very happy to see that he was such a nice officer, so conscientious and acting so promptly on my complaint. I was now relieved of my anxiety that some brute of a policeman might not bump him off only to get a reward or to get a promotion. That is what many had started to do. Seven eight minutes later, the SSP got the confirmation that he was nowhere. The SSP then said that it was possible that my son might be at the Mal Mandi Interrogation Centre which is controlled by the CRPF. The CRPF people never take the Amritsar police into confidence, and also do not respond to interventions from them.

Now, I was again very worried and went to the Mal Mandi Interrogation Centre a number of times. They never let me come close. Even as I would get down from the bus on the road and begin to move towards the gate, the Sentries would begin to shout threateningly, "Get back. Get back. Get back—peechhe ho jao, peechhe ho jao, peechhe ho jao." No one listened to me. I was not even allowed to go near the Mal Mandi Interrogation Centre. Three times I went there. Nothing worked, so I returned home.

Two days later, I appeared before the D.I.G. Virk. I hoped that he would listen to me and help. Before going to him, I had gone to Ghuman Police Post and met ASI Sucha Singh. I told him that my son was missing for so many days and requested him to lodge a complaint. I further requested him to try to get some information and help me in tracing him. Sucha Singh said, "What is there to lodge a complaint about. Nothing would be gained by that. You should go to the Police Post of Chowk Mehta. Go there and ask. Some policemen from there have told me that there was a boy there who looked like your son, and was wearing these clothes." He even mentioned the tailor's label on his shirt. The label was of a tailor from Ghuman. "Go there and find out whether the person is your own son." He was talking in ominously roundabout way. It was immediately clear to me that he knew everything. Immediately, I went to Chowk Mehta. There was no SHO there, not even an Assistant Sub-Inspector. Only one Head Constable was there. I enquired from him but he did not know my son's name. I then gave him a physical description. The Head Constable said, "Yes, there was boy of that description there. But, his clothes are here. He was killed and cremated at the Durgiana Mandir Cremation Grounds. You can go there and find out. If you want to see the clothes, I would show them to you." I wanted to see the clothes. The Head Constable brought a bundle that was wrapped in a khaki turban. The turban was that of a policeman. I thought this cannot be my son's. But when I opened the knot and saw the clothes, they were my son's. The same pant. The same shirt. The same underwear. The same waist (belt). All clothes were his. The turban was not his. Clearly, someone had pinched it since he had a new turban, replacing the old turban in its stead. His shoes and watch were missing. The wallot and the money were also gone. I asked the Head Constable to tell me what happened to my son. He claimed to know nothing except that the CRPF men had brought him there, and had also taken him out. The next morning, they came back to return these clothes as the case was from our area. The Head Constable asked me to go to Durgiana Mandkir Cremation Grounds and try to find out more details.

I went to the Durgiana Mandir Cremation Grounds. I told them about my son, and asked for ashes from his cremation. They laughed and asked, "Do you want to collect your son's ashes, or do you also want your own ashes?—Unki jo ashthiyan hain wo chahiye, ya apni bhi leni hain" I said I had come to collect my son's mortal remains if he had been cremated there. I pleaded, "Please, help me!" They said, "Don't come here. If you come here again, we would also cremate you." I had to come back.

Soon afterwards, I was again taken to the BIKO Interroagtion Centre. There I was told never to talk about the disappearance of my son Jagjit Singh. The officer there said, "Your son who worked in the printing press. who disappeared—you better never talk about him to anyone. It would not be good if you go on saying that he was innocent and became a victim of highhandedness. "If you would propagate this, you would go the same way as your son has gone, " he warned me.

### VFF/0804

Hargovinder Singh 28 of Kala Bala, Batala in Gurdaspur. On 6 February 1993 at 5 or 6 P.M., four or five officers of Indora Police Station of the Himachal police in uniforms came to the house. I and all my children were at home. The policemen were being led by SHO Mahinder Singh. They simply caught hold of Hargovinder Singh and took him away in their jeep, Gypsy. First they took him to Indora Police Station. There, his custody was transferred to Pathankot Police. I did not go to Indora Police Station to meet him as I was afraid and worried about my children. They had to be looked after. I was afraid of the consequences if the Police took me also in custody. However, one Police Constable took pity at my plight and found out after six seven days, that he had been handed over to Pathankot Police.

His family members also could not take any steps to secure his release, as they were very poor. Also, they were under much pressure. Later, Punjab Kesri, a Hindi daily newspaper published from Jalandhar, dated 26 February 1993, carried a news report which stated that he was killed when the police party which was taking him for the recovery of weapons was attacked by some militants. The report did not identify the Police officers who were carrying him when the incident supposedly happened. But, later, Rajinder Singh Manhar, Sarpanch of village Chak Manahsa which is situated at the border in Punjab, found out that Pradeep Kumar Malik, SHO of Pathankot Police Station and DSP Gurpal Singh Bakshi had killed him. The Police did not return the body to the family. We do not know how and where he was cremated.

### VFF/0805

Bhupinder Singh alias Bhinda 28 of Balpurian in Gurdaspur. On 8-4-92, he had gone to work at the house of Joginder Singh at Village Boli Inderjit. He was abducted from there by the Police.

**VFF/0806**

Jasbir Singh of Madra, Batala in Gurdaspur. Jasbir Singh was abducted on 18-3-91, by a police party of Gurdaspur police district, led by ASP Gurmel Singh. SHO of Dhariwal police station Makhan Singh was also there. The police took Jasbir Singh along with Amandip Singh son of Balraj Singh to his house at village Madra for conducting a search of his house for weapons. Only his sister-in-law (Bhabi) Jagdish Kaur wife of his elder brother Balbir Singh was there in the house at that time. The police ordered her to go out of the house. She was reluctant to go out of the house as she feared that they might take away some valuables from the house. And she was right. Indeed, the policemen stole gold jewellery, a Lady's wrist watch and six thousand rupees cash from the house. They did not find any weapons or other objectionable item in the house. Thereafter, the police took away these two boys to Dhariwal police station. There, Balraj Singh, father of Amandip Singh saw some other boys who had been detained by the police. They were—Hardev Singh alias Pahalwan of Panjgraeen village, a boy called Dimple resident of Kazampur village, another unidentified boy from Soniya village of Amritsar district.

A Hindi daily newspaper Punjab Kesri dated 20 March 1991 carried a news item which stated that according to SSP Gurdaspur Sh. S.K. Goyal, three militants were killed in an encounter with a combined patrol party of Punjab police and BSF, when they attacked the patrol party near village Sabkoda, and the security forces encircled the area and returned the fire. They have been identified as Jagbir Singh Chata, Hardev Singh alias Pahalwan, Satnam Singh of Chaiyan village. One sten gun, one 7.62 bolt action rifle, four hand grenades, and a lot of cartridges were recovered from the site of the encounter. The killed militants were involved in bombing the BSF patrol vehicles in the police district of Batala and in twenty murders. They were connected to Bhindranwale Tigers Force...........

I returned home three days later. I did not initiate any action as I did not see any point in doing so.

**VFF/0807**

Piara Singh 32 of Tibbar of Gurdaspur. On 21-7-90, the Police killed him in a false encounter at Mahi Chak Chowki, Kathua border, Jammu.

**VFF/0808**

Surjan Singh 39 of Tibbar of Gurdaspur. On 4-1-92, he was killed in an encounter with the Police at Village Bahian, Tehsil & Distt. Gurdaspur.

**VFF/0809**

Manjit Singh 29 of Alawal Pur in Gurdaspur. That on 27/28 December 1983 Manjit Singh was arrested for the first time in Jammu, by the Jammu police and was involved in 3/4 cases. On his release from Jammu Jail in 1985 he was handed over to C.I.A Staff Gurdaspur on the basis of production warrants. The said police implicated him in a case of Bank dacoity and he was in Gurdaspur Jail for about 3 months. Thereafter, the process of his being legally and illegally detained by the police of different police stations of Gurdaspur District continued till he finally disappeared on 19.3.91

During his period in Jail, he was brutally tortured. In 1983 he was an active member of the AISSF, but later on joined Shiromani Akali Dal (Mann) and just before his disappearance was the Vice President of District unit of Akali Dal (Mann). He also took active part in canvassing support for the party candidate in November 1989 elections

That in the afternoon of 19.3.91 when Manjit had gone to Sadar Bazar of Gurdaspur to make some purchases he was picked up by the then S.P (D) Balbir Bawa along with his police party. When the police Gypsy carrying Manjit Singh passed in front of the gate of Govt. Secondary School, where his father Balbir Singh, was a teacher and also the hostel superintendent, Jarnail Singh another teacher standing near the gate spotted him in the Gypsy. Manjit Singh shouted at Jarnail Singh to inform his father that he had been picked up by the police party led by the then S.P (D) Balbir Bawa. Jarnail Singh immediately went inside the school and informed Balbir Singh about the occurrance.

Immediately thereafter, Balbir Singh gathered his several other colleagues and took a delegation including Jarnail Singh, Pal Singh, Karan Singh and others. They approached the SHO of P.S. Gurdaspur (Sadar). The said SHO told them that Manjit Singh was in the custody of S.P. (D) Balbir Bawa and would be released after interrogation and they need not worry.

On the third day from detention, a delegation comprising the aforementioned met S.P (D) Balbir Bawa who also gave them the assurance to release Manjit Singh after interrogation. Balbir Singh kept on conssitently approaching the then SHO P.S.Sadar Gurdaspur and S.P.(D) Gurdaspur Balbir Bawa, who initially kept on giving false promises to release him and then later on flatly refused having taken him into custody. Till date nothing is known about the whereabouts of Manjit Singh as to whether he is alive (still in detention of police) or dead.

That it may be mentioned, the family members of Manjit Singh including his brothers and father were also illegally detained several times by the police. The illegal detention, which according to family was due to Manjit Singh's active political life, hampered their cultivation of crops and caused an economic setback. Moreover, the family even had to pay ransom to the police to secure the release of Manjit Singh and in this process had to sell off their house and residential plots situated in their village, thus suffering a colossal financial loss.

Manjit Singh's wife Lakhbir Kaur is mentally unstable and lives in a state of constant terror.

### VFF/0810

Balkar Singh alias Kala 38 of Ratta Khera, Zira in Ferozepur. In the last week of June 1993 (date not known), Gurdev Singh, SHO of Police Station Sarhali Kalan, raided village Rani Walah and arrested Shinda Singh s/o Bachan Singh, Desa Singh s/o Amar Singh, Sukhdev Singh s/o Piara Singh, Balkar Singh Bobby s/o Joginder Singh Thekedar (all SPOs in Punjab Police), Daljit Singh s/o Piara Singh and Balkar Singh Kala s/o Shingara Singh. The Police party had arrested Shinda Singh, Desa Singh, Sukhdev Singh and Balkar Singh Bobby at 7 AM from the house of Thekedar (contractor) Joginder Singh. All these four youth were SPOs and body guards of Thekedar Joginder Singh. Thekedar Joginder Singh was on the hit list of the militants. It was he only who had got these four youth enrolled as SPOs 3-4 years ago. Out of these four youth, Balkar Singh Bobby was the son of Thekedar Joginder Singh himself. At the time of raid, the Police party arrested Daljit Singh (Lance Naik in 13 Sikh Light Infantry of Indian Army) s/o Piara Singh also, who was on leave and who happened to visit Thekedar Joginder Singh's house, coincidentally. All these four youth had been arrested on the suspicion that they had committed a theft at a nearby village namely Sangatpura.

The same Police party raided the house of Balkar Singh Kala s/o Shingara Singh also on the same day, with a view to arrest him. However, Balkar Singh was not at home. As such, thev Police picked up his mother Taro and his wife Shinder Kaur, along with her children, and took them away. On the follwoing day, he (Balkar Singh Kala) was produced brefore the Sarhali Kalan Police through Thekedar Joginder Singh at village Rani Walah itself.

Daljit Singh (Fauji) s/o Piara Singh had been released in the evening, on the (same) day they were arrested (in the morning). According to Daljit Singh (Fauji), all of them were taken by the Police to Police Station Sarhali Kalan and immedaietly after their arrival there, the SHO got Shinda Singh, Sukhdev Singh and Desa Singh tortured brutally under his personal supervision. Iron rollers were rolled over their thighs. On the day of arrest itself, the Police had brought Shinda Singh, Sukhdev Singh and Desa Singh to their respective houses. The Police party lifted two suits and one hundred rupees from the house of Sukhdev Singh, the gold necklace of his wife from the house of Shinda Singh and some cash from the house of Desa Singh. According to the family members and other villagers, the condition of all the three of them was very critical. All the three of them were brought down by the Police from the vehicle turn by turn and taken to their respective houses.

Balkar Singh Kala s/o Shingara Singh also was brought by Sarhali Kalan Police to his house on the same day as he was produced before them, after he had been interrogated by them. His house was searched. At that time, his condition was very critical and he was unable to walk. In the meantime, Thekedar Joginder Singh continued to assure the families that he was pursuing their cases and that he would get the arrested boys released soon. On the third day of his arrest, Thekedar Joginder Singh's son Balkar Singh Bobby was indeed released by the Police.

5-6 days after these arrests had taken place, a news item appeared in the newspapers which stated that the SPOs namely Shinda Singh, Desa Singh and Sukhdev Singh had deserted their place of duty along with their weapons and wireless sets. The families of these three got worried greatly on reading this news item as the said boys were in the custdoy of the Police whereas the Police had claimed that the above mentioned SPOs had absconded from their place of duty.

The family memebrs went to Police Station Sarhali, but they were not allowed to enter the Police Station. They used to sit outside the Police Station and return (in the evening). On 13-14 July 1993, a news item was published in the newspapers that Shinda Singh, Desa Singh, Balkar Singh Kala and Mangal Singh s/o Karnail Singh, resident of Karmoowala were killed in an "encounter" with a Police party of Sarhali Kalan Police Station near village Kaure Wadhaun. According to the people (who lived) at the site of the incident, the Police had shown this incident as having taken place at 5-6 AM. Two of these four killed youth, namely Shinda Singh and Desa Singh had been declared by the Police as having absconded from their place of duty and Balkar Singh Kala and Mangal Singh were already in the custody of the Police.

Even the bodies of all these youth were not handed over to their next-of-kin. the families were not even informed by the Police. The families did not themselves also approach the Police, due to fear. So much so that the families did not perform their "Bhog" (last rites) even.

After the publication of the news item about the killing of Shinda Singh and Balkar Singh Kala, in an encounter with the Police, the family members of Sukhdev Singh s/o Piara Singh approached Sarhali Kalan Police several times. But either they used to be not allowed to enter the Police Station or the Police did not tell them anything about Sukhdev Singh. However, the family members of Sukhdev Singh came to know that he had been detained at Police Station Verowal. But they did not go to Police Station Verowal, due to fear.

On 29.7.1993, a news item was published in the newspapers that a militant namely Sukhdev Singh, along with another unidentified militant, had been killed in an encounter with the Verowal Police near village Fazilka. According to the family members of Sukhdev Singh, on enquiry, they came to know that the Police had cremated the bodies of Sukhdev Singh and the other youth at Tarn Taran cremation ground on 28.7.1993 itself. As such, they did not approach the Verowal Police. The Police did not inform the family on their own, either about the killing of Sukhdev Singh or about his cremation

The family members of all these youth said that they are poor people. The Police terror was at its peak in those days. Therefore, they did not initiate any action against this injustice meted out to them by the Police.

In 1996-97, as the Supreme Court ordered an inquiry by the CBI in the case of unclaimed and unidentified bodies, Ninder kaur w/o Shinda Singh also submitted an application to the CBI at Amritsar for an inquiry into the death of her husband. The CBI had inquired into this case. The CBI officers had been visiting the family continuously for 2-3 years and they had recorded the statements of all the witnesses. Now, for the last about one and a half years, no CBI officer had visited them. The family members don't know whether the CBI had filed the charge sheet in the CBI Court at Patiala or not.

These families told that during the course of CBI inquiry, the accused Police officers, through some persons, had offered them an amount of one and a half lakh rupees each for reaching a compromise with them. But these families had rejected their offers. So much so that the Police of Police Post Chola Sahib also had been approaching the said families for a compromise.

### VFF/0811

Mukhtiar Singh alias Mukha 30 of Aale Wala, Zira in Ferozepur. On 27.12.1991, at about 10 AM, Mukhtiar Singh and one of his accomplices, namely Boota Singh, resident of Bundala, district Ferozepur, were sitting at a farmhouse near village Sabhran when they were surrounded by Patti Police and security forces. The family members said that they did not know as to whether both these youth were arrested and killed or they were shot dead from a distance itself. Because, after they had surrounded them, the security forces did not allow anybody to come near (to the site of the incident). The Police seige continued for 3-4 hours. Thick fog was there on that day. The people did hear the sound of gunshots, but nothing was visible from a distance. The site of the incident was about three Kms away from Mukhtiar Singh's house. His family came to know about this incident on the same day, but owing to presence of the Police at the site of the incident, till evening, the family members did not go there, due to the fear of the Police. On the following day, morning, they (the family members) reached the site of the incident and made enquiries. Thereafter, they reached the cremation ground at Patti where the Police were getting the post-mortem done. The Police did not hand over his body to his next-of-kin. However, they were allowed to be present at the time of the cremation.

**VFF/0812**

Swaran Singh of Talwandi in Ferozepur. On 30 July 1991 at about 7 PM, a Police party of Amritsar (Sadar) Police Station, led by SHO Tejinder Singh, along with CRPF personnel, raided the house of an Akali leader, Kirpal Singh Randhawa, at 36, Kabir Park, Amritsar. At that time, apart from the family of Kirpal Singh Randhawa, Daljit Singh s/o Saudagar Singh, resident of Chhapa and Swaran Singh s/o Lal Singh, resident of Talwandi (Ferozepur) were also staying at the said house. Daljit Singh and Swaran Singh were drying their hair after taking bath. Immediately after entering the house, the Police arrested both the youth, Daljit Singh and Swaran Singh. The Police arrested house owner Kirpal Singh Randhawa also and took him along with them. The family of Kirpal Singh Randhawa sent telegrams to higher authorities about his arrest on the same day.

On 3 August 1991, a statement by Justice (retd.) Ajit Singh Bains, a human rights leader, was published in the newspapers regarding the arrest of Daljit Singh. From 30th July itself, Police had been posted at the house of Kirpal Singh Randhawa from where the arrests had been made. On 3rd August (1991), a Police party led by Inspector Tejinder Singh and DSP Gurdev Singh, brought Daljit Singh and Swaran Singh, again to the house of Kirpal Singh Randhawa. Immediately after entering the house, the Police directed the wife of Kirpal Singh Randhawa, Lakhiwnder Kaur, to go out of the house as they wanted to conduct a search. According to Lakhwinder Kaur, the condition of Daljit Singh and Swaran Singh was very critical. Both the youth had been held by two policemen each. According to her, both the youth were not wearing anything except an underwear each.

Two minutes after making the family members to go out of the house, the Police started shouting that the boys had consumed poison. The Police reversed the vehicle and broughgt it inside the house. Both the youth were lifted and put in the vehicle. When Lakhwinder Kaur entered her house after the Police had taken out their vehicle, a foul smell of some chemical substance was emanating from the drawing room. The policemen told Lakhwinder Kaur to wash the floor of the drawing room with water so that the smell of the chemical may be eliminated. The Police threw glasses etc. used by them to force both the youth to drink some chemical, into the pond opposite to the said house. In view of this evidence, the Police statement that both the youth had consumed cyanide, is proved false. Further it was established during our investigartion that both the youth were in Police custody since 30 July and that they were brought to the house of Kirpal Singh Randhawa, on 3 Aufgust. At that time, they were not wearing anything except an underwear each. Then from where did they get the cyanide?

After forcing both these youth to drink some poisonous substance, the Police got a news item published in the newspapers, as follows: "Two militants, belonging to K.C.F., namely Bhai Swaran Singh and Bhai Daljit Singh, committed suicide by consuming cyanide, after they had been arrested in the area under Police Station, Amritsar (Sadar). According to the information received, Bhai Swaran Singh and Bhai Daljit Singh had been arrested by the Police, this morning. After preliminary interrogation, while they were being taken to a house at Kabir Nagar (near Khalsa College), both of them swallowed cyanide capsules which they had hidden in their clothes. Both of them died on the way to hospital.

According to Akali leader, Kirpal Singh Randhawa, after arresting Daljit Singh, Swaran Singh and himself, from his the house, all the three of them were taken to Police Station Amritsar (Sadar) where all three of them were subjected to inhuman, brutal, torture. So much so that their bodies were injured by poking with a poker and the nails of their toes were pulled outwards. On 3 August 1991, the Police showed Daljit Singh and Swaran Singh as having committed suicide by consuming cyanide and a case was registered against Kirpal Singh Randhawa and he was produced in a court on 8 August, 1991.

### VFF/0813 and VFF/0814

Amrik Singh 26 and Jaspal Singh alias Jassa of Killi Bodlan, Makhu in Ferozepur. Baaj Singh, aged 60 years, resident of village Killi Bodlan is a small farmer. He had two sons namely Amrik Singh and Jaspal Singh and one daughter namely Simarjit Kaur. Now-a-days, Baaj Singh and his wife Sukhwinder Kaur are living with her daughter and her husband at their house as both of their sons have fallen victim to the barbaric attitude of the Police during the turmoil in Punjab.

Both sons of Baaj Singh, after completing their education, began to train themselves in the trade of Motor Mechanic. After the training, both Amrik Singh and Jaspal Singh set up separate Motor Repair shops at Makhu City. In 1989, Jaspal Singh started participating in militant activities and closed down his shop. In the meantime, Makhu police and C.I.A Staff Ferozepur began to raid their house. Many times, the police used to pick up Baaj Singh and release him after keeping him in custody for few days. Once, the Makhu police had picked up Amrik Singh also but released him when the village Panchayat vouched for him.

### VFF/0815

Harnek Singh alias Neka 21 of Kaurotana, Zira in Ferozepur. After Harnek Singh had absconded, the police used to pick up his family members viz. Atma Singh (brother) and Jhanda Singh (father), detain them in illegal custody for days together and torture them brutally. The police used to ask the family members about Harnek Singh. This routine of police torture continued for 8-9 months till the time Harnek Singh was not killed in an encounter with the police along with two of his companions at village Ball, Dhariwal in district Gurdaspur. The family members were informed about this incident a few days after the said encounter by a companion of Harnek Singh. Family members of Harnek Singh showed the newspaper in which the photograph of his dead body had been published to the policemen posted at their village Police Post. Then only the police left them alone. Thereafter even though the police used to visit their house for one or two years, yet, they did not pick up any of the family members.

### VFF/0816

Chand Singh 35 of Korotona Fatehgarh, Zira in Ferozepur. Surjit Kaur aged 80 years is a resident of village Korotana Fatehgarh. Her husband had expired about 35-40 years ago when her children were young. She had two sons and four daughters. The marriage of eldest daughter was solemnised by Pratap Singh (Surjit Kaur's husband) himself. After his death the responsibility of the household fell on the shoulders of Chand Singh. When he grew up, he arranged the marriages of all his three remaining sisters. Younger son of Surjit Kaur namely Ranjit Singh has also expired seven months ago due to sickness. Now-a-days she is living with her daughter-in-law and one grand son and one grand daughter.

Chand Singh was neither an "Amritdhari" (Baptised) Sikh nor he had any political affiliations whatsoever. After 1984, Dharamkot police had picked him up several times on the basis of suspicion of having links with militants. Each time, the police used to detain him in illegal custody for days together and at times used to torture him also. The Village panchayat and a Congress leader namely Late Shri Sarban Singh used to get him released. No case was ever registered against Chand Singh.

According to Surjit Kaur, a few days before Deepawali in 1991 (according to Indian Calendar in the month of Ashwin and corresponding Christian era months of August-September), one day at about 8.30 PM, she along with Chand Singh and a servant namely Mohinder Singh were present in the house and Chand Singh was getting ready to go to bed. Just then a Gypsy halted on the road in front of their house and focussed its headlights at their house. Their house was lit and Nachhatter Singh, SHO of Dharamkot police station along with several other policemen entered their house. The SHO asked Chand Singh to come along with them. Chand Singh asked for his stick from the servant as he had met with an accident a few days ago. The police took away Chand Singh in the Gypsy parked outside.

On the following morning, Gurmeet Singh (cousin brother) along with one or two other persons went to the Dharamkot police station. But, the SHO denied flatly that he had picked up Chand Singh and brought him there. According to Surjit Kaur, her younger son Ranjit Singh along with relatives and Chand Singh's friends met SHO Nachhatter Singh and Senior Officers repeatedly but nobody gave them any clue about the whereabouts of Chand Singh. Surjit Kaur said, "We moved from pillar to post even upto Chandigarh, arranged for recommendations but could not get any information about his whereabouts. What should I tell you, son (Amrik Singh Muktsar—Investigator) who are all the people we met. One who could tell you about all this (her younger son Ranjit Singh) is also no more."

According to Surjit Kaur, for many years they hoped that Chand Singh might be alive with the police because the police had not declared him killed anywhere. But, she has lost hope now as she cannot do anything now. She said, "I had another son who also has been snatched by God this year. Now God alone will do justice to me. You (Amrik Singh Muktsar) have come, may God bless you. They must have killed my son. If only I get justice in my lifetime."

**VFF/0817**

Kulbir Singh of Jatana in Ropar. A report about his missing appeared in the newspaper on August 31, 1991.

**VFF/0818**

Gursewak Singh alias Babbu 28 of Kotla Nihang in Ropar. On 17-8-95, two policemen in civil dress came to our house on scooter No. PB-27-4959 and told Gursewak Singh to accompany them as he had been called by DSP Kulshinder Singh who wanted to ask him some questions. They had tea and left the place alongwith Gursewak Singh. Gursewak's freind Sohan Singh Soni and his mother were present at that time. I came home in the evening and came to know about this incident. I alongwith the Panchayat and some other respectables reached Sadar P.S. Ropar. SHO Arvinderbir Singh told me that they had not arrested any person by such a name. Then we went to Police Station Ropar (City). There SHO Sohan Lal Sandhu told that they had not called Gursewak Singh there.

On 18-8-95, Surinder Singh s/o Nasib Singh, an employee of Punjab State Electricity Board and a freind of Gursewak came to our house and told me that Gursewak had rung him up and told him to meet him at Gurdwara Amb Sahib at Mohali on 19-8-95 at 10 A.M.

On 19-8-95, I reached Gurdwara Amb Sahib at Mohali alone. A policeman in civil clothes brought Gursewak there on scooter. His condition was horrible. He had been tortured brutally. He was bleeding near the head and was unable to stand on his legs. There was a bench near the outer gate. I helped him to sit down on that and asked him a number of questions in the same breath. "What had happened? How you happened to be in such a horrible condition? Where were you taken from home? " He replied that he was taken to P.S. Sadar Ropar from home and from there put in a vehicle and taken to Phase VIII P.S. Mohali. From there, they took him to an unknown place, blindfolded. There, in the presence of SSP Jasminder Singh, he was tortured brutally in three shifts. Then I asked him as to what they (Police) say now. He said that they were going to take him to Mohali Phase VIII Police Station for recording his statement. They had said that they would release him after that. He also told me that he was not involved in any unlawful activity. The police had some misconceptions about him. He asked me to go home. I rang up Ropar from Mohali and told those people that I had found Gursewak and they should come to P.S. Phase VIII Mohali alongwith the Panchayat. From Ropar Avtar Singh, Bhag Singh and 4-5 other Panchayat members came to Phase VIII Mohali P.S. We enquired from the staff there. They told that Gursewak Singh was not there with them. Then we enquired from other police Stations of Mohali. Everywhere the reply was that Gursewak was not there with them. We came back home.

On 22-8-95, Ratan Singh, Chairman Zila Parishad rang up SSP Ropar and Bibi Daljit Kaur member Zila Parishad and S. Bhag Singh met the SSP Ropar, Jasminder Singh. He said that he would depute a DSP who would look into the whole matter. I met SP (O) Basra also in this connection.

On 24-8-95, a Police party in two vehicles led by DSP Kulshinder Singh and alongwith SHO Arvinderbir Singh came to our house and wanted to search the house including the upper storey of the house. I asked them to wait so that I could call the panchayat. I called the panchayat and Sarpanch Sukhwinder Singh, Panchayat member Bhoop Singh, Jarnail Singh and Bibi Daljit Kaur member Zila Parishad came. And the house was searched in the presence of all these persons. Nothing objectionable was found. The police party left the place. After that, we kept in touch with DSP, SP (O), SSP Jasminder Singh, but we were not told anything about Gursewak Singh. We have received a letter from DC Ropar dated 19-7-96 in which he has informed us that our son was wanted by Ropar Police in case No. 95 and that he had been declared absconding. This is a white lie.

**VFF/0819**
Jaswinder Singh alias Kala 24 of Bhauwal in Ropar.

**VFF/0820**
Manjit Singh of #273, Phase VII, Mohali in Ropar. Manjit Singh was picked up on 16-1-88 by a Police party of 25-30 men from Patiala led by DSP Surjit Singh Grewal. Some of them were in uniform and some others were in civil clothes.

**VFF/0821**
Amarjit Singh 36 of Gagon, Bhaku Majra in Ropar. On 29-12-92 he had gone from home at about 7 A.M. to Chamkaur Sahib. He was to drive the bus bound for Nangal from there. The bus was to pass through Gagon village. Harinder Singh Fauji, younger brother of Amarjit Singh, who was going back after leave, was to travel to Ropar in the same bus. He signalled the bus to stop in front of his house at Gagon, but Amarjit Singh did not stop the bus. At that time, a Maruti Van was following the bus. The bus halted at Talapur bus stand (near Gurdwara Tibbi Sahib) on the requset of the father of one of the drivers of Punjab Roadways, because he wanted to hand over the leave application of his son. As the bus halted, immediately two persons in civil clothes who had been travelling in the bus from Chamkaur Sahib, went upto

Amarjit Singh and asked him his name. Just then, two men alighted from the Maruti Car which was following, and came there. They asked him to get down from the bus. Amarjit Singh asked the reason. At this, two men who were inside, pushed him and threw him out of the bus. Then they put him in the car and went away. The bus passengers and Conductor Gurmeet Singh r/o village Manauli (near Chamkaur Sahib) tried to know the reason for his abduction from his abductors, but they started to abuse all of them. The Conductor sent a message through some persons of our village about this incident and he himself went to Nangal Depot to inform his colleagues. The bus continued to be parked at Talapur bus stand for three days. Next day, the Village Panchayat consisting of Gurmel Singh (Panch), Kashmira Singh (Sarpanch), and other respectable persons met SHO Harpal Singh at police station Chamkaur Sahib. He registered a F.I.R based on the statement of the Conductor Gurmeet Singh.

**VFF/0822**

Sukhdev Singh alias Sukha 47 of #108, Phase IV, Mohali in Ropar. According to Kamaljit Kaur, wife of the victim Sukhdev Singh alias Sukha:-

On 3 June 1984, Sukhdev Singh had gone to Gurdwara Kafalgarh Sahib at Chamkaur Sahib in connection with the meeting called regarding the 'Kar Sewa'. But due to the imposition of the curfew and the encirclement of the Gurdwara by the Army, he could not come out. He was arrested from there on 6 June 1984 along with 30-40 others and he remained detained for about 3 months under NSA before it was quashed. Kamaljit Kaur says that as per her information, Sukhdev was the first person against whom NSA was withdrawn/quashed in Punjab. After his release he shifted to Mohali from Chamkaur Sahib and started participating actively in the Sikh politics. He remained associated with Babbar Akali Dal in the beginning and later on with Akali Dal (Mann). He was again arrested by the Police and booked in some case and remained detained for over a month before he was released on bail.

In the month of March 1988, the Police wanted to frame him up in a case of recovery of arms and ammunition from the fields adjoining his petrol pump. This made the family to flee from the house and remain underground for over a month. It was only after Sukhdev surrendered before the Police that the family were able to return to their house. He remained in jail for 3-4 months in this case before being released on bail. He was later acquitted. Thereafter, the Police kept on regularly raiding his house. It was again in May, 1990 that the Chandigarh Police conducted a raid on his house at Mohali and enquired about him from

Kamaljit. But Sukhdev Singh was away to Chamkaur Sahib. Thus, the Police went away. The Police party was led by DSP Surjit Singh and DSP Abrol. At that time, the SSP of Chandigarh was Sumedh Saini. The Police party again turned up 5 days later. The time was 10 PM. Again finding Sukhdev missing from his house, they took along with them his wife Kamaljit. She was not allowed to inform her neighbours or relatives even. Their behvaiour towards her was quite harsh. The Police party was led by the same officials. The people from the neighbourhood approached the SSP, the same very night, but he refused to release Kamaljit Kaur. Next day, she was booked in a case u/s 302, 153, 124 and sent to jail. She remained in jail for about a month before being released on bail. She was finally acquitted in the year 1995. It was in August that Sukhdev surrendered before the Police and remained in jail for 4-5 months in the aforesaid case. During Police remand he was tortured brutally. At the time of his arrest he was the General secretary of Babbar Akali Dal. He was tortured so brutally in Police custody that his back bone problem, for which he had been operated upon sometime ago, got aggravated.

Thereafter, the cycle of Police raids over their house continued and he was called to the Police Station several times but not detained for the night.

Finally, it was on 18 March 1993, that the then SHO of Sohana Police Station, Ramesh Chander rang him up at 11 AM and asked him to come over to the Police Station as he wanted to talk on some issue regarding the petrol pump. Ramesh Chander was quite close to Sukhdev Singh and it was due to this faith that Sukhdev Singh went to meet him at the Police Station. Sukhdev Singh went to the Police Station along with one Jaspal Singh of village Raipur who happened to be in their house at that time. At about 2 PM, Jaspal came back from the P.S. and informed Kamaljit that Sukhdev had been made to sit in the Police Station by SHO Ramesh Chander who had told Sukhdev that the SSP wanted to see him. The same very moment, Kamaljit went to Chamkaur Sahib and informed Surjit Singh, younger brother of Sukhdev Singh about this incident. She, along with Surjit came back to Mohali the very same day. Surjit went to the Police Station and met Sukhdev and the SHO Ramesh Chander who assured him that he would be released in a day or two. Surjit used to visit the Police Station daily and SHO Ramesh Chander used to give him the same assurance each time. He also used to meet Sukhdev Singh every day and serve him meals. He also used to give him his medicines and clothes for changing. This went on till 29 March 1993 when SHO Ramesh Chander informed Surjit that Sukhdev had been shifted to C.I.A Staff Ropar. At the CIA Staff Ropar, Surjit was not allowed to meet Sukhdev. In the meantime, the family members approached the then SSP Ropar, Mr. Sanjiv Gupta through Shamsher Singh Rai, the then MLA Chamkaur Sahib who assured Mr. Rai that he would be released soon.

On 29 April 1993, Sukhdev Singh was again transferred to P.S. Sohana. On 30 April 1993, SHO Ramesh Chander visited their house and asked for medicines and clothes for Sukhdev Singh from Kamaljit which she gave him. Surjit continued to meet Sukhdev at P.S. Sohana and also at the CRPF Post at Industrial Arae in Phase VII of Mohali throughout the months of May and June 1993.

On 1st July 1993, Jagtar Singh took over as SHO at Sohana and Ramesh Chander was transferred to Kurali. On 3 or 4 July 1993, Surjit was informed by SHO Jagtar that Sukhdev had been shifted to CIA Staff Ropar. Thereafter, none of the family members was allowed to meet Sukhdev. However, one Malkeet Singh of Village Panjola met Sukhdev Singh at the CIA Staff Ropar on 5 July 1993 as he also was detained along with him there. According to Malkeet Singh, Sukhdev Singh was taken out of the CIA Staff Ropar at night time on 5 July 1993. Thereafter, the family members of Sukhdev Singh had been meeting the SSP Ropar, Mr. Sanjiv Gupta through Shamsher Singh Rai and the SSP had been assuring Mr. Rai that they would release him after some time. The same was the refrain of Ramesh Chander. They had been giving the same assurance for more than two months. It was after a long wait on the basis of assurances being given by the Police officials that the family was constrained to file a petition in the High Court. The Police officers had been repeatedly approaching the family to withdraw the petition giving them a false assurance that he was still alive and would be released soon.

Kamaljit stated that the whole family remains mentally upset after the loss of the sole breadwinner and male member of the family. She remains under acute depression constantly thinking about the future of her grown up daughters in the absence of her husband. Moreover, the loss suffered by the family due to the winding up of the transport business and the fall in the levels of the monthly income and the increase in the expenses with the growing up of the children is also a cause for constant mental worry for Kamaljit since his disappearance.

**VFF/0823**

Kulwinder Singh alias Kid 20 of #259, Phase IV, Mohali in Ropar. Victim Kulwinder Singh's father Tarlochan Singh hails originally from village Chhajumajra in Tehsil Kharar of Ropar district. He passed his B.A.

from DAV College, Chandigarh. After passing his B.Ed exam in 1966, he joined as a Social Studies Teacher at Khalsa High School at Ropar. He served at various Khalsa Schools in Ropar district. He was promoted as a Headmaster in 1978 and as a Principal in 1983. On 12 May 1997, he retired as Principal from Khalsa Senior secondary School, Kurali.

Kulwinder Singh, the only son of his parents, was an "Amritdhari" (baptised) Sikh youth. He had taken "Amrit" from Sant Jarnail Singh Bhindranwale in 1979. He joined AISSF (All India Sikh Students Federation) before 1984 while he was studying in the school at Mohali and started actively participating in Federation's activities. For the first time at about 9 PM, a Police party from Phase I Mohali Police Station raided Tarlochan Singh's house on 9 May, 1985. The Police party was led by Inspector Jagdish Singh. On not finding Kulwinder in the house, they took both Tarlochan Singh and Nachhatter Kaur to the Police Station. Family members of about eleven families were also brought to the Police Station and detained along with them. On the following day, Nachhatter Kaur was released at about 11 AM as she was not feeling well. On 11-5-85, Tarlochan Singh, along with one Gopal Singh Baidwan, father of Upkar Singh, resident of Manakmajra, class fellow of Kid, were trabsferred to Police Station Kharar. Inspector Jaspal Singh Dhanoa was SHO of P.S. Kharar. On 11-5-85, when Kid and Upkar Singh were produced at P.S. before SHO Jaspal Singh, Tarlochan Singh was released. When Tarlochan Singh went to the P.S. Kharar on the following day, i.e. 12/5/85, he was told that Kid was not in their custody. Thereafter, Tarlochan Singh started a search for his son in the various Police Stations of the Ropar district, which proved futile. It was only on 15/5/85 that he came to know from newspaper reports that Kid had been arrested along with four others after an encounter and one of their accomplices had escaped. Tarlochan Singh stated that the youth shown to have escaped during an encounter was actually killed by the Police. He was also picked up from his house and killed. He belonged to village Boothgarh near Morinda, but he did not know his name. They were booked in a case and sent to Patiala jail. At that time, SSP Ropar was Izhar Alam. On 31/5/85, Kid was also booked in one case by the Chandigarh Police of P.S. Sector 39 in a car snatching case. The car was recovered by the Chandigarh Police from outside Bassi theatre at Mohali and not from the possession of the accused. Tarlochan Singh was present during their appearance at the Chandigarh Court where Kid disclosed to him that he along with the others were brutally tortured using third degree methods at P.S. Morinda. He was also tortured during remand at P.S. Sector 39, Chandigarh in a brutal manner. On 6/6/85, Tarlochan Singh, along with representatives of 90 Panchayats and 30 School Principals of Ropar district, met the Deputy Commissioner, Ropar and gave him a written representation. The DC called SSP Izhar Alam to his office. On being cornered by the people about the encounter, he had to admit that it was a false encounter, but he also stated that the Government had instructed them to take the youth of this age group who are said to be members of the Federation, into custody and detain them for six months. Thus, he was forced by the people to commit that he would withdraw the case. On 12/8/85, the case registered at P.S. Morinda, was withdrawn by the Police. In a few days time, after the withdrawl of the Punjab case, Kid was released on bail in Chandigarh case. His co-accused were acquitted in this case by the end of the year 1985 or in the beginning of 1986. It is pertinent to mention here that Kid at the time of the registration of the case, was below 16 years of age and the case qua him was transferred to the Juvenile Court and decided by it. According to Tarlochan Singh, the case made by the Police failed in the Court qua his co-accused as the owner of the car was unable to identify Kid and his co-accused in the Court as those involved in the snatching. On the case being transferred to the Juvenile Court, the proceedings against him were launched in the said Court. The Mohali Police did not stop conducting raids against him in his house at Mohali. In order to avoid harassment and torture at the hands of the Police, he started living away from his house and also stopped attending the Court at Chandigarh. This cycle of Police raids continued till he was arrested on 13th April, 1987 at Chamkaur Sahib from village Salabatpur Kheri by P.S. Chamkaur Sahib Police, along with four others again in a case of armed encounter. He was also involved in one more case by Nawanshahar Police. In total, he was involved in around 25 cases after his arrest. During the remand he was brutally tortured. These cases pertained to various districts of Punjab. After undergoing Police remand in various cases he was sent to judicial lock-up at Nabha. He was acquitted in all the cases registered against him and came out of the jail in the month of October, 1988.

Thereafter, he was again unable to stay at home as the cycle of frequent Police raids continued unabated. In the meantime, he got married and started living in a separate undisclosed place along with his wife Ravinder Kaur. Lastly, it was on February 22, 1989 that Tarlochan Singh met Kid when he produced him before SSP Ropar, Mr. Chandrashekhar. The SSP had given him an assurance that if Tarlochan Singh arranged a meeting with him, he will not be harmed. The SSP backtracked on the plegde given by him when Kid was produced in his office on 22.2.89, but was unable to take him in custody as a large crowd of about 1000 people had gone along with them. Initially, the SSP had assured Tarlochan that he would try to prevail upon Kid during his meeting with him and that he would be able to persuade him to start his life afresh peacefully, since he had got married recently. Tarlochan Singh stated that on seeing Kid in his office, the attitude and behaviour of the SSP changed completely. However, the Police could not take him in their custody on that day. Consequently, Kid was again forced to leave home and live at an undisclosed place. This time, even his parents did not know as to where he lived.

It was on 22 July, 1989 (Saturday) that Tarlochan Singh received a phone call at the School at Kharar, where he was a Principal, The anonymous caller informed him that H.No. 1752, Phase-V, had been cordoned off by the Police in plainclothes since 9.30 AM. Mr. Tarlochan Singh said that he had received this call by virtue of his being an active member of a Committee formed to highlight and protest the Police excesses in Kharar area. He added that his active involvement in this task had also brought him into direct confrontation with the Police a number of times. The Committee was so active during those days that it used to meet daily at 2 PM at Kharar. One Hakikat Singh of village Deh Kalan was the chairman and apart from him, other members were Jathedar Ajmer Singh Kumbra, Harpreet Singh Bhagomajra, Shamsher Singh Desumajra, Inderjit Singh Waraich, Mohali. Tarlochan Singh passed on the information received by him to the other members and they decided to proceed to Mohali in a Jeep. They left Kharar in the Jeep and reached the PTL Chowk at Mohali where they parked their Jeep at the Tempo stand. From there they proceeded to the place mentioned by the caller, on foot. They enquired from somebody about the location of the house and turned as directed by that person and entered the street in which the said house was situated. Just then, from a distance of about 30 yards, they saw Kulwinder Singh Kid along with another youth entering the said house. They also saw 3 vehicles parked in the street, one of them being a Gypsy. They witnessed Kulwinder Singh opening the wire-net door of the house while the other youth kept standing in the courtyard of the house. In a spur of a moment, they saw 7-8 men in plainclothes come out from the garage of the house and pounce upon Kid. They overpowered him and threw him onto the ground and covered him with a blanket. The other youth, who had stood in the courtyard, tried to escape by jumping over the wall of the house. But, he was shot at by some persons stationed on the rooftop and killed him on the spot. These people heard three gunshots being fired. Kid was first taken into the garage where Dr. Amarjit Kaur, the land lady, had been detained since morning by these policemen in plainclothes. Then he was bundled into the white/cream coloured Gypsy and all the three vehicles sped away except 3 or 4 of the plainclothesmen who had been left behind to guard the dead body of the slain youth. The Police did not allow anybody to come near the site of the incident. This incident was also witnessed by a number of people who were peeping through their windows. All the above mentioned Committee members then decided to proceed to the Police Station Phase-I. But, they were not allowed to enter inside the Police Station. They tried their level best to meet the Police officers, but in vain. After waiting for 2-3 hours there, Tarlochan Singh decided to go to Chandigarh with a view to post the telegrams. He posted telegrams to Chief Justice of Punjab & Haryana High Court, Governor, Punjab, SSP, Ropar, DGP, Punjab, on the same day in the evening. Then he went to the office of newspaper Punjabi Tribune where he was informed that the Police had issued a press statement wherein they had stated that one Palwinder Singh Pola had been killed in an encounter with the Police while Kulwinder Singh Kid had escaped. Tarlochan Singh gave his version of the story to the news persons which was published in the said newspaper on the following day. This incident was reported by another Punjabi daily also, namely "Ajit". He had posted the telegrams on 22.7.89. Later on, he was informed by Kulwant Singh (Advocate, since deceased) and Dr. Cheema, lady doctor who had conducted the post mortem, that two unidentified youth were killed in an encounter on the intervening night of 23/24 July, 1989 near Tangori and that one of them resembled the identity of Kid. The other killed youth hailed from village Boothgarh. This encounter was said to have taken place under the jurisdiction of Police Station Sohana. Inspector Birbal Dass was the SHO of P.S. Sohana at that time. The dead bodies were not handed over to the families. Even an attempt by Justice Ajit Singh Bains to claim the body proved futile. The Police had maintained throughout that both the killed youth were unidentified and that Kid was not one of them. However, the family members were able to claim the ashes and immerse them. They approached the then SSP Ropar, to know the truth about Kid. The SSP maintained Kid was not in their custody and that he had escaped. It was then that on 22.8.89 that he gave a detailed/speaking representation to the President of India. When nothing came out, he filed a Petition in the High Court through Balwant Singh Guiliani in the first week of September.

Enquiry was marked to CJM Ropar on 9.6.1990, by Justice R.S. Mongia.

S. Tarlochan singh stated that no doubt, the parents who loose their sons in the prime of their youth, have to undergo mental depression and suffering. But, the realisation and thought that theirs is not the only son and they are not alone in their suffering, kept them going and comforts them. Moreover, the thought of their so having laid down his life for a good cause also keeps them away from going into low spirits and avoid any sort of mental depression.

**VFF/0824**

Gurjit Singh alias Guri 24 of Rahi Basti, Nanaksar, Barnala in Sangrur. On 15/8/92 at 7.45 P.M., he was picked up from his residence at H.No. 106, 13B, Mohalla Rahi Basti, Near S.D. College, Railway Fatak by a police party led by DSP Surinderpal Singh Parmar and his gunmen, and SI Ashutosh, SHO City Barnala.

**VFF/0825**

Buta Singh alias Jasbant Singh of Moom, Barnala in Sangrur.

**VFF/0826**

Lehmbar Singh 27 of Khaddi Khurd, Handiaya, Barnala in Sangrur. On 18-1-93, Lehmbar Singh had come to his Village Khuddi Khurd to cast his vote. At about 11.30 P.M. he was abducted from there by a Police party led by SSP Ishwar Chander Sharma. Other Police Officers in the police party were Inspector Sant Kumar from C.I.A. Staff Handiaya, and DSP (D) Barnala, Surinderpal Singh Parmar.

**VFF/0827**

Chamkaur Singh 30 of Naraingarh Sohian, Barnala in Sangrur. On 1-12-93, he was produced in front of Inspector Sant Kumar at C.I.A. Staff Handiaya. We came to know about his death from a news item published in the Punjabi daily Ajit dated 15-12-93.

**VFF/0828**

Sukhdev Singh alias Sewa Singh 35 of Baba Bhan Singh Kothe, Barnala in Sangrur. He was picked up from his residence at night between 12 and 1.30 A.M. by a Police party from Bhadaur about whom nothing is known except that they were uniformed. Nobody could be recognised due to darkness. Some of them were wearing caps. All of them were carrying Rifles.

**VFF/0829**

Mithu Singh of Kot Dunna, Barnala in Sangrur. On 3-9-91 at 5 A.M., he was picked up from his residence by a police party of 11 policemen from police station Joga, Distt. Mansa led by SHO Budh Singh who came in a vehicle. They beat up Mithu Singh, pushed him into the vehicle and took him away. His whereabouts are not known, till today.

**VFF/0830**

Jasvir Singh alias Seera of Khuddi Kurd, Barnala in Sangrur. He had come from Calcutta with his truck loaded with goods to be delivered at Moga. He disappearaed on the way. Now only it has become known that his truck No. DIG 6263 is parked at C.I.A. Staff Faridkot. Its number plate has been changed. As such, we suspect that the Police killed him in a false encounter at Moga.

**VFF/0831**

Jasvir Singh alias Seera of Khaddi Khurd, Barnala in Sangrur. He had come from Calcutta with his truck loaded with goods to be delivered at Moga. He disappearaed on the way. Now only it has become known that his truck No. DIG 6263 is parked at C.I.A. Staff Faridkot. Its number plate has been changed. As such, we suspect that the Police killed him in a false encounter at Moga.

**VFF/0832**

Mukund Singh 60 of Dhaula, Barnala in Sangrur. On 12-12-1991 at 6 A.M., Mukand Singh was abducted from his residence by four armed policemen in civil clothes in a white Maruti Van. Mukand Singh opened the door in response to their call. They put him forcibly in the van and took him along with them. Mukand Singh was the real Maternal Uncle of Militant Jasvir Singh Bhagi Bandar (Bathinda). On 11-12-1991, a news item was published in the newspapers that Jasvir Singh and his associates had killed three relatives of a policeman at Village Bhamme (under P.S. Jhunir in Distt. Bathinda). Mukand Singh was abducted due to a feeling of revenge for that incident. Thus, the policeman whose relatives were killed by Militants, the Bathinda police, especially the police of Jhunir are responsible for his disappearance.

**VFF/0833**

Amarjit Singh alias Pala 23 of Mehal Kalan, Barnala in Sangrur. Amarjit used to live with his maternal uncle Major Singh Sarpanch r/o village Burj Kalara, because, Major Singh needed his help in his work. On 3-5-93 at 11 P.M., a Police party from P.S. Nihal Singh Wala (Faridkot) led by SHO Rachhpal Singh raided the house of Major Singh. Two of the brothers-in-law of Major Singh namely Balbir Singh and Jagtar Singh were also there as they had come to assist Major Singh in transporting the fodder ('Toori'). They were sleeping after finishing their days work when the police picked up all the four of them i.e. Major Singh, Balbir Singh, Jagtar Singh, and Amarjit Singh.

**VFF/0834**

Darshan Singh alias Darshi 21 of Sehke, Malerkotla in Sangrur. On 5 October 1992, he had gone to Gurdwara Rara Sahib. The Police killed him on the way near village Chemo under Malaud Police Station in Ludhiana District. We got his ashes only from the Cremation Ground, Ludhiana after we identified him from the photographs shown to us by the police.

### VFF/0835

Tarlochan Singh alias Tochi of Sehke, Malerkotla in Sangrur. He was produced by us before SSP Bedi Sahib at Khanna on 10-2-93. Khanna Police slapped a case of assault against him and sent him to Nabha Jail. He was taken out on remand from there by a police party from Malerkotla Police Station led by DSP Brar. Next day, the police party of DSP Sukhdev Singh Brar and SHO Bikram Singh declared him to be an absconder. Since then, the whereabouts of our child are not known to us.

### VFF/0836

Maghar Singh alias Sukhdev Singh 25 of Ladewal, Malerkotla in Sangrur. On 24-8-1991 at 10 A.M., he was picked up from his residence by a Police party from Malaud police post led by ASI Darshan Singh incharge of Malaud police post under Dehlon police station in police district Jagraon. Names of other 5-6 policemen who were accompanying ASI Darshan Singh are not known.

### VFF/0837

Kulwant Singh 28 of Sehke, Malerkotla in Sangrur. In April/May 1993, ASI Balbir Chand, incharge of Manvi police post, raided his house. Kulwant Singh was not at home. He was at the University. So, the Police picked up his father Bahadur Singh, mother, sisters Jaswinder Kaur and Bhupinder Kaur, both residents of Manvi along with their husbands Jagdev Singh and Sajjan Singh and children. They were detained illegally for one week at police post Manvi. His cousins (Bhua's sons) namely Baldev Singh, Hari Singh, Gurmel Singh, and Bhupinder Singh and both of their sisters r/o Vill. Dialpur Chhanna were also picked up and taken to Amargarh police station by SHO, Inspector Gurmel Singh. They were detained illegally at Amargarh P.S. for one week. They were released only after Kulwant Singh had been produced before SSP Jasminder Singh. Kulwant Singh was detained illegally for 10-15 days. SSP Jasminder Singh tortured him brutally, personally, during this time. The Police wanted that he should get some of the militants active in the area, arrested. Finally, the SSP released him on the condition that he would get some of the militants arrested. He also instructed him to report to SP Malerkotla Pritpal Singh Virk every fortnight. He and his brother Hardev Singh Ex-Sarpanch continued to report to SP regularly every fortnight. On 16 January 1994, a police party from

Malerkotla came to my (Hardev Singh's) house and left a mesage with
my wife that Kulwinder Singh should be produced in front of the SSP
Jasminder Singh at Sangrur. It was about 5 P.M. Kulwant Singh was
called from Sudhar where he was studying for his B.Ed. Next day i.e.
on 17 January 1994 morning, I, along with Narpinder Singh Sekhon, and
Kulwant Singh reached SSP Jasminder Singh's office at 11 A.M. Karnail
Singh of village Sohian was also there along with us. SSP asked them to
produce Kulwant Singh in front of SP Pritpal Singh Virk at Malerkotla.
We came to SP Virk at Malerkotla same day. At that time, apart from
the abovementioned persons, we were accompanied by Paramjit Singh
Shergill, Secretary, Bar Association, Balwinder Singh, President Bar
Association, and another Secretary of Bar Association Mr. Puri, Jasbir
Singh Advocate, and other Advocates. We reached there at 3 P.M. The
SSP told that he wanted to investigate whether Kulwant Singh was
indeed a student of the University or not. He said that he would a send
a police team with us to the University so that it could be verified. He
asked us to come back to him on 20 January 1994. After that, I, along
with Advocate Narpinder Singh Sekhon, Commission Agent Naseem
Ahmad of Malerkotla, and Kulwant Singh reached SP Malerkotla's
office. We met SP Virk at 9 A.M. He made us to wait upto 11 A.M. and
then asked me to get a vehicle. I hired a red coloured Maruti Van. Then
the SP directed his reader Satnam Singh to go along with us to the
University at Patiala and find out whether Kulwant Singh was studying
there or not. Security staff of the SP noted down the number of our
Van when we departed from there. When asked about it, the reader
replied that it was a formality of their department. At the University, the
reader kept standing with us outside the Examination Branch for 15-20
minutes. He never tried to make any enquiries at the University despite
being insisted to do so by us and Kulwant Singh. After some time, he
looked at his watch and asked us to hurry up as he had to go back. While
on our way back, near Village Rakhra, 10-15 uniformed policemen were
waiting in two vehicles, one a white Maruti Van and the other a blue
Tempo (open top). We halted at their signal. They segregated Kulwant
from us after getting him identified by the reader and put him in the
Tempo. They segregated all of us. The ASI (Satnam Singh) remained
with us intentionally and did not go along with the police party. Within
seconds, the police sped away along with Kulwant. Before going away,
the police party locked our Van and took the keys along with them.
We reached Nabha on a three wheeler. Same day, Advocate Narpinder
Singh and Commission Agent Naseem Ahmad met the SP at Patiala and
protested. The SP said that they had picked up Kulwant Singh without

his knowledge. When asked to release Kulwant, he promised to get him released and asked them to come on the third day. On the third day, Advocate (Narpinder Singh) went alone to the SP who told him that Kulwant had confessed to having met militant Manjinder Singh Issi. He further told him that he would get him released and asked him to come after a week. On 23 January, Narpinder, Bahadur Singh (father), Hari Singh brother-in-law (wife's brother) of Kulwant Singh, met the SSP Jasminder Singh. He also agreed to get Kulwant released and asked them to come after one week. We have been meeting SP and SSP regularly, but so far, nothing has been disclosed about the whereabouts of Kulwant Singh. We even approached Amrinder Singh through Avtar Singh Sandhu Muktsar in the month of April/May. Amrinder Singh promised to talk to KPS Gill. But nothing materialised despite Amrinder Singh approaching KPS Gill.

**VFF/0838**

Hardeep Singh alias Neeta 19 of Hamidi, Barnala in Sangrur. This Proforma was updated on 08 September 2000, on the basis of information collected by Amrik Singh Muktsar in August 2000, when he visited the house of the victim Hardeep Singh s/o Zora Singh at Village Hamidi, Tehsil Barnala, District Sangrur. The true translation of the same is appended below:

Victim Hardeep Singh's father Zora Singh is a poor farmer. However, before the rise of militancy in Punjab, he was a well-to-do farmer who owned 10 acres of land. The wave of militancy in Punjab has claimed his only son Hardeep Singh as well as all of his property. Hardeep Singh was his eldest child among three daughters and one son. Hardeep Singh abandoned his studies while he was studying in class XI and got busy in trying to secure his future in different vocations. Once, in 1992, the Sherpur Police had arrested him on the basis of suspicion. He was tortured for 10-15 days in illegal custody and released thereafter as nothing was proved against him. Later on, he joined Punjab Home Guards and he was posted at Police Lines Sangrur.

On 2-2-1993 at 10 or 11 P.M., Dhuri Police raided Zora Singh's house and enquired about Hardeep Singh. The family members told that he had joined the Police and he was posted at Police Lines Sangrur at that time. The Police party asked Zora Singh and Harbans Singh to accompany them upto the village. As they reached near the Police vehicle which had been parked at some distance away, the Police directed Zora Singh and Harbans Singh to sit inside the vehicle. His (Zora Singh's) father-in-law was already seated in the Police vehicle. After making them to sit in the vehicle, one of the Policemen sent a message through wireless to somebody that they did not find Hardeep Singh at home but they had arrested his father and uncle ('chacha'). He sought further directions as to whether they should bring these people there or not. They received a reply that Hardeep Singh had been arrested from his place of duty at Sangrur and that they should release these people. The Police told Zora Singh and Harbans Singh to go away as they were no longer needed. Zora Singh told that SHO Shamsher Singh who accompanied the Police party did not show that they had come to arrest Hardeep Singh. However, Zora Singh got suspicious that threy must have come to arrest Hardeep Singh only. On their way back, the Police party dropped Gurdial Singh at his village Pendani Kalan and told him that his grandson ('Dohta') Hardeep Singh had met with an accident and that he may come to Sangrur on the following day and find out. On the following day in the morning, Gurdial Singh went to Sangrur where Hardeep Singh's colleagues told him that the Dhuri Police had arrested him at 11 P.M. last night. Gurdial Singh informed Zora Singh immediately about this incident.

On the following day, the family members alongwith Village Panchayat (Council) and that of Village Pendani Kalan and other eminent persons of both the villages, met the SHO Shamsher Singh at Dhuri Police Station. He flatly denied the arrest of Hardeep Singh and advised them to enquire at Sangrur or other Police Stations. For several days, the family members of Hardeep Singh enquired at different Police Stations but they did not get any clue about his whereabouts from anywhere. In the meantime, they met SP (H) Baldev Singh, DSP Sherpur and several other senior Police officers but nobody gave them any information about his whereabouts.

On 24-2-1993, a news item was published in the newspapers that a militant namely Hardeep Singh had escaped from the custody of Dhuri Police. According to the story put out by the Police, they were escorting a militant namely Hardeep Singh for the recovery of arms when the Police party was attacked by the militants lying in ambush. Taking advantage of this, Hardeep Singh escaped from Police custody. However, an unidentified militant was killed.

Hardeep Singh's family members including his uncle ('chacha') Malkeet Singh Nambardar enquired at Dhuri Court and found out that a F.I.R. No. 40 dated 21-2-1993 u/s Sections 25/54/59 of Arms Act had been registered against Hardeep Singh at Dhuri Police Station in which they had shown that he had been arrested by them from Village Kanjhla and 5 cartridges had been recovered from his possession. The

Police had produced Hardeep Singh in a Court at Dhuri and obtained a remand for three days.

The family members suspected that the Police version was false and that the unidentified militant who had been killed by the Police must be Hardeep Singh only. But, they did not have any proof of the same. A few days later, Malkeet Singh Nambardar and Harbhajan Singh member Panchayat met SSP Jasminder Singh at Sangrur and requested him to disclose as to whether Hardeep Singh was still alive or he had been killed. The SSP's reply was that Hardeep Singh had killed the family of a Policeman at Village Bugra and that they very well knew what they (the Police) did in retaliation to such an action. He advised them to perform his 'Bhog' (religious last rites) quietly. The members of the Panchayat demanded the clothes of Hardeep Singh but the SSP refused. In the Police records, Hardeep Singh is still an absconcder. Even today, the Police enact the drama of enquiring about Hardeep Singh from his family members in order to prove the truthfulness of their story. The Police visit his house often.

### VFF/0839

Gurwinder Singh alias Binder 19 of Kumbharwal, Dhuri in Sangrur. On 10-9-1992, he was taken away by DSP Hardeep Singh, and SHO Bakhshish Singh and other members of the police party of Sherpur police station. Jarnail, Sarpanch of Gumti was also there along with them. His maternal house was at village Tibba. Jarnail Singh, Sarpanch of Gumti told us that he would keep him with him and that he was responsible and we should not worry at all.

This proforma was updated on 18th August, 2000, on the basis of information collected by Amrik Singh Muktsar during Jul-Aug, 2000, when he visited the victim Gurwinder Singh's village Kumbarwal for an on-the-spot investigation. The true translation of the updated version is appended below:-

Jathedar Kaur Singh (father of the victim Gurwinder Singh) was an 'Amritdhari' (baptised) Sikh and his whole family was very steadfast in their religion. He was a supporter of the political movement which supported the militant movement which had begun in the Punjab after June, 1984. In those days, the management of the Gurdwara of their village Kumbharwal was in the hands of Nihang Sikhs who used to drink liquor in the Gurdwara and show disrespect to Sri Guru Granth Sahib. The Nihangs used to gulp down the income from 80 bighas of land which belonged to the Gurdwara. Jathedar Kaur Singh, being religious-minded, was unable to tolerate the disrespect shown to Sri Guru Granth Sahib. He motivated the people of the village and with their help started the construction of a new building for the Gurdwara. A Committee was elected by the people from among themselves for managing the affairs of the Gurdwara. The Police used to support the Nihangs against the villagers as their Chief, Santokh Singh, was a Government supporter. The SHOs (Station House Officers) who were posted at Sherpur Police Station at different times, had threatened Jathedar Kaur Singh not to interfere in the affairs of the Gurdwara as otherwise his family would have to face dire consequences. The Nihang Sikhs used to give false information to the Police that Kaur Singh had links with the militants. The Police used to arrest Kaur Singh often, on the allegation that he had links with the militants. They used to torture him for days together in their illegal custody. Due to repeated harassment at the hands of the Police, Kaur Singh deserted home. The Police started harassing his family members. All his family members locked-up their house and went underground. His wife Bhupinder Kaur left one of his sons namely Gurwinder Singh at the house of one of their relatives at Malerkotla where he began to learn the job of an Assistant to a Doctor. She sent her another son out of Punjab to her brother-in-law's (sister's husband's) place. Her youngest child used to stay with her and they used to stay at the houses of their acquaintances in different villages. In the meantime Kaur Singh joined the ranks of the militants once for all and the Police began arresting his relatives. Meanwhile his son Gurwinder Singh also had joined the ranks of the militants once for all. However the family members were not aware of that development. As two members of his family were absconding, the Police started harassing his relatives, too much. The Police used to arrest Randhir Singh s/o Thakar Singh, resident of Manaki, a brother-in-law of Kaur Singh (wife's sister's husband) and Gurdeep Singh (wife's brother) resident of Tibba, often and used to turture them brutally. In May-June 1992, Bhupinder Kaur (w/o Kaur Singh) alongwith her brother Gurdeep Singh was arrested by a Police party of Dehlon Police Station from Malerkotla where they had gone for purchasing clothes. They were taken to Dehlon Police Station where the SHO Darshan Singh tortured Bhupinder Kaur and Gurdeep Singh brutally. Male Policemen used to strip Bhupinder Kaur naked and subject her to brutal and inhuman torture. This torture was inhuman to such an extent that petrol was poured into her anus, her private parts were pulled by the SHO Darshan Singh. She was beaten up with Lathis (batons) and rollers were rolled over her thighs and legs. Gurdeep Singh also was tortured so brutally that one of his legs became disbaled. It was restored somewhat after several months of treatment. Even today, he cannot bend his leg. Both of them—brother and sister—were got released by the militants in exchange for the release of a relative of a Congress MLA (Member Legislative Assembly) whom they had kidnapped earlier.

On 19-9-1992, Gurwinder Singh was killed in an encounter with the Police alongwith two of his associates namely Sukhdev Singh resident of village Badbad and Gurcharan Singh Bhola resident of village Bahadurpur at village Gumti of Sangrur district when they were surrounded by the Police. Gurwinder Singh's 'Bhog' (last rites) was scheduled to be held on 28-9-1992. The newspapers of that date carried a news item that Gurwinder Singh's father Kaur Singh had been killed in an encounter with the Police alongwith two of his associates namely Nirmal Singh Mandvi and Gurmel Singh Jagga resident of village Kumbharwal, near villages Mastuana and Hindra. The Police did not hand over the dead bodies of Gurwinder Singh and Jathedar Kaur Singh. The village panchayat and a large number of people who had gone to collect the dead body of Gurwinder Singh were lathi-charged and tortured by the Police at Barnala. So much so that the Police took 15-20 persons into their custody and detained them till the time the 'Bhog' of Gurwinder Singh was not over. Several people received injuries during this beating by the Police which was ordered by DSP Hardeep Singh Bhau. Thanks to Police terror, the family members did not return home for seven years and they could not cultivate their land during all these seven years. Their house had been demolished by the Police. All the household goods as well as the bricks of the house were carried away by the Police. Even the whereabouts of their livestock like buffaloes and cows could not be known. The financial loss is estimated at Rs. 1,50,000/- worth of household items plus loss due to non-cultivation of land for seven years at the rate of Rs. 50,000/- per year which comes to a total of Rs. 3,50,000/-

**VFF/0840**

Deputy Singh Dhillon alias Dhillon 50 of Sangrur. On 16-10-93, he was picked up from Patiala Gate, Sangrur, in front of State Bank, by 4 police personnel, one of them being ASI Bachittar Singh, C.I.A Staff. Vehicle No. was CHW 72 and it was being run as a Taxi at Bhawanigarh.

**VFF/0841**

Yadwinder Singh alias Pinka 23 of Bhawanigarh in Sangrur. He was abducted by SHO Bhawanigarh, Surinderpal Sodha and his staff on 23-8-91 from Bhawanigarh.

**VFF/0842**

Saudagar Singh 24 of Bakhtari in Sangrur. On 20 December 1992 at 7 A.M., a Police party consisting of 15-18 men in a Gypsy and a closed vehicle and led by DSP Pritpal Singh Virk surrounded our house. They searched our house but nothing objectionable was found. Still they picked up Sudagar Singh and his elder brother Bahadar Singh alongwith two 315 Bore licenced Rifles and Cartridges. On 23-12-92, both of them were brought by police to the house and house was searched again for Nazar Singh.

### VFF/0843

Gurjant Singh alias Janta 30 of Dhadogal, Dhuri in Sangrur. The details are given in the extra sheets attached with this form, which are as follows:-

On 28-2-93 at 4 A.M., Sub Inspector and ASI Teja Singh came to our house along with a police party. But not finding him (Gurjant Singh) at home, they took his father Joginder Singh along and put him in the lock up at Police Station Dhuri. They told that they would release him after we produced Gurjant Singh.

On 3-3-93, we, along with the Panchayat and respectable persons of the village produced Gurjant at P.S. Dhuri. After that, the Dhuri Police did not tell us anything. They told that nothing was in their hands. We should contact Senior Officers. Later, we continued to meet Pritpal Singh Virk, DSP Sangrur and Jasminder Singh, SSP Sangrur through Panchayat and Political leaders. They told that they would release him only after they were satisfied. If he might have committed a crime, then we should give up any hope in respect of him and if he had not committed any crime, then they would release him. They inflicted inhuman torture on him for one month at C.I.A. Ladda Kothi (Bahadar Singh Wala) and C.I.A. Bhawanigarh, due to which he lost his memory and became unfit to move about. At last, in order to hide their (black) deeds, the Police Officers implicated him in a case and sent him to Patiala Central Jail. Case No. 85 dt. 24-10-92 u/s 302 IPC and 25/54/59 under (Arms) Act was registered at Police Station Bhawanigarh and on 6-4-93, he was sent to Central Jail Patiala.

He was produced in front of the Judge at Sangrur again on 19-4-93. On 28-4-93, he was brought from Central Jail Patiala by a police party consisting of Inspector Tarsem Singh of C.I.A. Barnala, ASI Darshan Singh, HC Iqbal Singh No. 158, Constable Sukhdev Singh No. 283, Constable Gursewak Singh No. 128, Constable Surjit Singh No. 328, Constable Banwari Lal No. 336 in a bullet proof vehicle No. PB13/7741 and produced in the Court of Judge J.S. Kular at Barnala, in pursuance of FIR No. 168 dt. 1-9-91 u/s 302/148/149 IPC and u/s 25 Arms Act and a remand was obtained. When we went to see him in jail, we were told that he had been taken by C.I.A. Barnala police.

Then, along with some persons, we met the C.I.A. Incharge Sant Kumar who demanded Rs. 1,00,000/- from us. But, being poor, we could not arrange the money. Again we met Sant Kumar at C.I.A. and SP Parmar. He replied that in case we had brought the money then they would slap some case against him and send him to Jail; otherwise we should have no hope (to see him alive) for him. But when the money was not paid to him, next day he told us that Gurjant Singh had escaped from their custody. And that in case we found him, we should produce him, otherwise we would also meet the same fate.

As per our information, the Police were taking Gurjant Singh for the recovery of AK-47. On the bridge of the Canal at Village Kot Dunna, he felt pain. He broke the belt of Constable Surjit Singh No. 328 and ran upstream towards the track of Village Pandher. On 29-4-93, C.I.A. Incharge Sant Kumar and Surjit Singh, Chowki Incharge Kot Dunna, got a case No. 35 and a Report No. 38 registered at P.S. Dhanaula u/s 224 IPC. Later, we continued to search for him. The Police authorities only looted us instead of helping us. And they continued to threaten us that in case we did not sit quietly at home, then we would be treated in same manner as that of Gurjant Singh. We sat quietly at home due to fear of the Police. Even then, the Police continued to harass us.

After a few months, Amargarh Police picked up my elder daughter-in-law Charanjit Kaur w/o Harpal. She was released the next day with a threat to us that in case we initiated any legal action, our family would face dire consequences. After about one year, Cats (uniformed police) of C.I.A. Malerkotla, picked up my younger son Gurjit Singh. He was tortured for one week and let off with threats. Like this, the Police continued to visit our house and harass us. Later, in June 1994, Gurbhajan Singh, Incharge of Dhuri P.S., came to my house, insulted me and beat me up saying that they (Police) would deal with our family in the same manner as they did with Gurjant Singh. When the Police terror subsided, we filed a writ in the High Court at Chandigarh, through Advocate Ranjan Lakhanpal. So, the details given above are absolutely correct and based on facts. We have full faith in you that you would definitely help us in this difficult time and get us justice.

### VFF/0844

Jagdeep Singh alias Changiara 16 of Rao Majra, Dhuri in Sangrur. This Proforma was updated on 07 September 2000, on the basis of information gathered by Amrik Singh Muktsar in August 2000, when he visited the house of victim Jagdeep Singh s/o Late Kishan Singh at Village Rajo Majra, Tehsil Dhuri, District Sangrur, for an on-the-spot investigation. The true translation of the same is appended below:

Jagdeep Singh was the last son of such a family who had been victim of nature's wrath. His parents and brother had expired and he lived with his aunt ('Maasi') Mohinder Kaur, widow of Jeon Singh. The abovementioned family were Ramdasia Sikhs. Jagdeep Singh's father Kishan Singh was an ex-serviceman who had got a job at Bank after his retirement. After the sudden death of his father, his mother Ranjit Kaur was given a job in the Bank. However, soon thereafter, his mother also expired due to illness caused by the shock of the death of her elder son Gurdeep Singh who had committed suicide. Jagdeep Singh's mother and aunt ('Maasi') were married in the same family, to real brothers. Mohinder Kaur's husband Jeon Singh had expired. His aunt began to bring him up. At the time of his mother's death, Jagdeep Singh was studying in class IX and he psssed his Matriculation, later on. He hoped that he would get a job in the Bank in his father's place. He was preparing the documents for that purpose. Meanwhile, he developed contacts with some of the supporters of militancy, also. he had got himself baptised also.

In the beginning of February, plainclothes Polcemen visited his house and enquired about Jagdeep Singh. He was not at home. As such, his aunt ('Maasi') Mohinder Kaur told that he came to her house rarely only, now-a-days. On the following day, as Jagdeep Singh came home, his aunt informed him about the Police visit. He went away from the village. The Police raided Mohinder Kaur's house again on the same day at night. In view of the attitude of the Police, Jagdeep Singh, on his own, requested his aunt to make arrangements to produce him before the Police.

On 5-2-1993, Jagdeep Singh was produced before Shamsher Singh, SHO of Dhuri Police Station, by Raj Singh MLA (Member Legislative Assembly), Mohinder Kaur (aunt), Shamsher Singh (maternal uncle), Jagir Singh (Panch—member of Village Council) and Mukhtiar Singh (Panch). The SHO told that in case he was found rto be innocent, they would release him after a day's custody. On the third day, Mohinder Kaur alongwith one of her relatives went to Dhuri Police Station. They told that they had handed over Jagdeep Singh to C.I.A. Staff (Sangrur) at Bahadur Singh Wala. Mohinder Kaur approached Raj Singh MLA who assured her that he would try to get him released. But, as Jagdeep Singh was not released even after the expiry of several days, Mohinder Kaur approached Raj Singh MLA again. He demanded Rs. 40,000/- from her to be paid, ostensibly, to the Police. However, he could not get Jagdeep Singh released. Two months passed and the family members lost all hope pf Jagdeep Singh being alive even. One day, Sukhwinder

Singh, the Village Nambardar told them that the Police had produced Jagdeep Singh in a Court at Dhuri and sent him to jail at Sangrur and that they could go and meet him there. On the following day, his family members met him at Sangrur jail. He was to be produced in a Court at Sangrur on 27-4-1993. Mohinder Kaur reached the Court with a view to meet Jagdeep Singh. However, the Police did not bring Jagdeep Singh there. On the third day, they enquired at Sangrur jail and they came to know that Samana (Patiala) Police had taken him on remand from there. The family members went to Police Station Samana where the Police told them that they had not brought him there. Thereafter, the family members did not get any clue about the whereabouts of Jagdeep Singh. His aunt Mohinder Kaur told that thereupon, they reconciled themselves to their fate and sat quietly at home.

### VFF/0845

Chamkaur Singh alias Kora 21 of Rao Majra, Dhuri in Sangrur. On 20-10-91 at 4 A.M., he was abducted by Barnala Police in a police vehicle.

Police Officers responsible are:-
1. Bakhshish Singh, SHO P.S. Barnala
2. Joginder Singh Kutiwal, DSP
And other members of the police party.

### VFF/0846

Siukhdeep Singh 24 of Rao Majra, Dhuri in Sangrur. This Proforma was updated on 07 September 2000, on the basis of information gathered by Amrik Singh Muktsar in August 2000, when he visited the house of victim Sukhdeep Singh s/o Darshan Singh, Village Rajo Majra, Tehsil Dhuri, District Sangrur, for an on-the-spot investigation. The true translation of the same is appended below:

Sukhdeep Singh, aged 24 years, resident of Village Rajo Majra, was a religious minded and an "Amritdhari" (baptised) Sikh youth. He was associated with Baba Chand Singh Rajo Majra and most of the time he used to be busy in organizing religious functions alongwith Baba Ji. He was sympathetic towards the militant movement then going on in the Punjab and he used to attend 'Bhog' (religious last rites) ceremonies of militant youth killed at the hands of the Police. He was very enthusiastic and sentimental youth whose blood used to boil at the sight of oppression let loose by the Police on the youth. Ultimately, he was carried away by emotions, deserted home in 1990 and joined the ranks of the militants, once for all. After Sukhdeep Singh had absconded, the Police began to harass his family members. The Police used to pick up his father Darshan Singh, Hardeep Singh (brother), Gurmel Singh (brother) and relatives, often and torture them in illegal custody for days together. This process continued till the time Sukhdeep Singh was killed in an encounter with the Police and even thereafter for a long time.

On 7-8-1992, Sukhdeep Singh was killed in an encounter with the Police at Village Pedani Kalan, alongwith two of his associates namely Bhupinder Singh Eisee and Balbir Singh Guara. However, the Police continued raiding their house on the basis of suspicion, even thereafter.

In January 1994, Sukhdeep Singh's brother Hardeep Singh joined the Punjab Police. He was allotted Sangrur district and he began his training at Police Training Centre near Bhawanigarh. There, he was recognised by some such Police officers who used to raid their house at the time Sukhdeep Singh was absconding or who used to pick him (Hardeep Singh) up during their raids at their house. One day, Hardeep Singh was on guard duty at the Armoury. Sub Inspector (S.I.) Sadara Singh remarked in Punjabi, "Dudh di rakhi billa kinhe khara keeta hai." i.e. who had detailed a cat to guard the milk. Hardeep Singh discussed about the Police attitude with his family members alright, but he continued with his training.

In the last week of February, one day, Hardeep Singh returned home and said,"I have been thrown out of the Police job saying that my brother was a militant." Same day, Hardeep Singh, alongwith the Village Panchayat went to Sangrur with a view to meet SSP Sangrur. But, they could not meet the SSP as he had gone out for some work and they returned home. While he had gone to Sangrur, a Police Constable had visited his house and delivered a message that the officers had asked Hardeep Singh to return and resume his training. His family members informed him about this on his return. On the following day, he went and resumed his training. That day and night and another day passed. On the second day night the Dhuri Police raided his house and searched it. His brother Gurmel Singh asked them as to what the matter was. At this, the Policemen replied that nothing in partticular and asked them to sleep peacefully. Saying this, the Police party departed. On the next day, Gurmel Singh went to (Police) Training Centre near Bhawanigarh to meet his brother Hardeep Singh. He enquired from the Incharge S.I. sardara Singh as to why the Police had raided their house on the previous night. Sardara Singh said,"Your brother Hardeep Singh has run away from duty alongwith his rifle." Gurmel Singh came back immediately. He was afraid that some harm may not come to Hardeep Singh.

On the following day, Darshan Singh (father) alongwith the Panchayat (Village Council) and an Akali leader Gobind Singh Kanjhla met the SSP Jasminder Singh at Sangrur. He told that no such incident had come to his notice and advised them to see him on the following day morning so that by that time he would find out. On the next day again, all the abovementioned persons met the SSP who said that Hardeep Singh had indeed run away alongwith his rifle. He advised them to produce the boy and promised that no action would be taken against him. The family members suspected the bonafides of the Police. However, they continued to pursue his case. But, even after running from pillar to post they could not get any information as to what happened to Hardeep Singh. His family members are sure that the Police must have killed Hardeep Singh.

**VFF/0847**

Sukhwinder Singh Bhatti alias Bhatti Sahib of Badbar, Barnala in Sangrur. 4 Kms away from Vill. Badbar, there is a Police Naka. The boundary of Sangrur police district ends at police Naka Kunran and that of Barnala police district starts. On 12 May 1994 at 4.40 P.M., he was made to get off from a bus belonging to Barnala Depot (obviously of Punjab Roadways) No. 95/9PB.11C (Driver Malwinder Singh S/89, Conductor Preetam Singh S293), on the side of Badbar from the Naka, by a police party in civil clothes. The reason for his abduction is not known. The Police Officers of that time, responsible for this incident are:-

SSP Jaswinder Singh — Sangrur
SP Pritpal Singh Virk — Malerkotla (One of the abductors)
SHO Rajinder Singh Sohal — Mansa (One of the abductors)
DSP Surjit Singh Commando — (One of the abductors)
SHO Rajbir Singh — perhaps then posted at Dhuri

**VFF/0848**

Gurjit Singh alias Guri 24 of Rahi Basti, Nanaksar, Barnala in Sangrur. On 15/8/92 at 7.45 P.M., he was picked up from his residence at H.No. 106, 13B, Mohalla Rahi Basti, Near S.D. College, Railway Fatak by a police party led by DSP Surinderpal Singh Parmar and his gunmen, and SI Ashutosh, SHO City Barnala.

**VFF/0849**

Jagseer Singh alias Kaka 20 of Surjitpura, Barnala in Sangrur. On 17-4-91, he was abducted from his residence by Police. After that we met him once only. Then, I, along with the Sarpanch and other members of the panchayat saw his post mortem being conducted at Barnala on 10 Dec 91. The Police have looted us (by extorting money). Whenever we talk of filing a case, the Police starts harassing our whole family. The Police Officers responsible for his abduction and extra-judicial killing are:-

1.    Rabbi, ASi
2.    Jaspal, SHO
3.    Sardul Singh, DSP

And other members of the police party. In all, 15 men were there.

This proforma was updated on 18th August, 2000 on the basis of additional information collected by Amrik Singh Muktsar during Jul-Aug, 2000, when he visited the victim Jagseer Singh's village Kothe Surjitpura, Tehsil Barnala and district Sangrur, for an on-the-spot investigation. The true translation of the updated version is appended below:-

In April 1991, the Police of Barnala (Sadar) Police Station raided his house at the time when Phoola Singh Sanghera (Barnala), a renowned militant, had taken shelter in his house. On seeing the Police, Phoola Singh tried to escape through the rear door. But the Police had surrounded the house from all sides. As such, Phoola Singh committed suicide by consuming cyanide. Jagseer Singh ran away from home as he was scared of the Police. The Police began harassing his family members. A case was registered against his father Arjan Singh and he was sent to jail where he was detained for three and a half months. Apart from that, his brother Malkeet Singh was picked up by the Police and detained in their illegal custody for a month.

On 15-10-1991, his family members received information that the youth killed by the Police near village Deewana was Jagseer Singh. As such, his father Arjan Singh reached Civil Hospital Barnala where thre Bhadaur Police had brought the body for a post mortem. Arjan Singh identified the body of Jagseer Singh. The village Panchayat also reached the place and demanded the dead body. But the Police did not hand over the body and did not allow them to collect his ashes even. The Police had declared Jagseer Singh to be an unidentified militant in the newspapers even though his father Arjan Singh had identified the body at the Civil Hospital at the time of post mortem. According to the family members, this attitude of the Police was illegal as well as suspect. Hwever, the family members do not know as to what had happened to Jagseer Singh; whether he was arrested and killed or he was killed in an encounter with the Police as claimed by the Police. Later on, they heard several rumours.

### VFF/0850

Manohar Singh alias Manhori 27 of Mehal Khurd, Barnala in Sangrur. On 30 June, 1991, Mehal Kalan Police raided their house and arrested Manohar Singh's father Gurdev Singh and brother Gurcharan Singh. The Police told the family members that their son Manohar

Singh had been killed at the hands of the Raikot Police near village Jauhal. Gurcharan Singh (brother) was detained at Mehal Kalan Police Station and tortured brutally. and his father was taken to Raikot Police Station. However, the Police did not get the dead body of Mmanohar Singh identified either from his father Gurdev Singh or from his brother Gurcharan Singh.

His father Gurdev Singh told that they did not know how much truth there was in the Police claim about Manohar Singh having been killed in an encounter with the Police. If his son was a militant, how come the Police never came earlier to his house in order to arrest him, he asked. The family members asserted that Manohar Singh was a promising boy and he was busy in his studies only.

**VFF/0851**

Sarbat Singh alias Laadi 21 of Kattu, Barnala in Sangrur. As Sarbat Singh absconded, the Dhanaula Police started raiding his house and they used to pick up his family memebrs, mostly his father Amar Singh. At that time, Amar Singh was a member of the village Panchayat (Council). Once, SHO of Dhanaula Police Station picked up Amar Singh and tortured him so brutally that the village Panchayat (Council) had to carry him home on a cot, after getting him released.

On 16 January, 1992 at 10 A.M., a Police party of Dhanaula Police Station led by the SHO arrested Sarbat Singh at a distance of 1 Km from Barnala from a bus which was on its way to Moga from Barnala. Zora Singh, resident of village Kattu who was travelling to Pakho Qaidian in the same bus, witnessed the arrest of Sarbat Singh. Zora Singh and Channan Singh, both residents of village Kattu, informed his family members promptly about this incident. The village Panchayat (Council), immediately went to Dhanaula Police Station. But, the Police did not admit having arrested him. Same day at night, Sarbat Singh alongwith another youth namely Kesar Singh resident of village Chhajli, was killed by the Police in a fake encounter on the drain at Dhanaula. Kesar Singh had been arrested from his house at village Chhajli on 16th January evening. It is believed that the Police subjected both the youth to brutal torture before kiling them in a fake encounter during the same night.

**VFF/0852**

Jarnail Singh alias Giani 55 of Wajid Ke Khurd, Barnala in Sangrur. Jarnail Singh was a Granthi (Sikh Cleric) of the village Gurdwara. Before that, he was in the service of the Agriculture Department of Himachal Pradesh Government which he had quit. His whole family were 'Amritdhari' (Baptised) Sikhs. Once, Shamsher Singh, SHO of Barnala (Sadar) Police Station picked up Giani Jarnail Singh. The village

Panchayat and other eminent persons of the village got him released. By virtue of his being a Granthi, the village panchayat used to pursue his case promptly.

On 15th August, 1992 at 11 P.M., a Police party of Barnala (Sadar) Police Station led by the SHO Shamsher Singh, raided the village Gurdwara and arrested Giani Jarnail Singh in the presence of his wife and children. On being asked by Giani Jarnail Singh, the reason for his arrest the SHO replied that he would let him know the reason also and directed him to just come alongwith them. To a query by his wife Swaran Kaur, they told that they were taking him to Barnala Police Station. But, on the following day, when the eminent persons of the village went to Barnala Police Station, the Police flatly denied having arrested him and brought him there. The family members and the village Panchayat approached the Police Officers repeatedly for 2-3 years for the release of Jarnail Singh, but, nothing was disclosed about his whereabouts. They enquired at almost every Police Station but nothing was disclosed about the whereabouts of Jarnail Singh.

About 20-22 days after the arrest of Jarnail Singh, the Police surrounded Jarnail Singh's son Didar Singh, who had absconded earlier and joined the militants' ranks, at the kutcha track near village Sahora and shot him dead. Ram Piari (Jarnail Singh's mother), unable to bear the shock of her son Jarnail Singh's disappearance and the death of her grandson Didar Singh, breathed her last, one month later. Meanwhile, the village Panchayat continued to approach the Police Officers, in search of Jarnail Singh. After a period of 6-7 months, as the whereabouts of Jarnail Singh were still not known, his wife Swaran Kaur also, unable to bear the shock, breathed her last. The village Panchayat begged of the Police Officers to release Jarnail Singh, pleading that six children would become orphans. However, the Police Officers continued to deny the arrest of Jarnail Singh, flatly. Under such circumstances, his children used to beg for food in the village. With the passage of time, as the elder son Manjit Singh matured, the villagers appointed him Granthi. With the money earned by him, Manjit Singh established his brothers in different vocations. Thus, now only, the family members are on their own. When the Investigation Team visited their house, Manjit Singh was scared of giving any information. He said that they had already suffered too much. They might get into trouble again. After repeated assurances only, Manjit Singh agreed to give this information. However, he flatly refused to sign the information given by him in this proforma. The villagers told the Investigation Team that this family had undergone tremendous suffering. Now only, with the help of villagers, the destitute children have become capable of fending for themselves. The responsibility of the whole family is now on the shoulders of Manjit Singh, aged 24 years. On being asked repeatedly by the Investigation Team whether he wanted to get justice about the atrocities committed against his family, he replied that they longed to get justice alright, but at the same time they did not want to initiate any action against the Police, as they were scared of the Police.

### VFF/0853

Darshan Singh 30 of Kutba, Barnala in Sangrur. Victim Darshan Singh's father Sadhu Singh, resident of village Kutba, Tehsil Barnala, District Sangrur is a well-to-do man. He owns 20-25 acres of land. He had two sons namely Darshan Singh and Manjinder Singh. Darshan Singh was a religious minded and 'Amritdhari' (Baptised) Sikh youth. According to his family members and other villagers, Darshan Singh was steadfast in the folowing the principles of Sikh religion and a sentimental person. He was an active political worker of Akali Dal (Mann) group at the village level. He had courted arrest also during the 'Dharam Yudh' (political agitation) launched by the Akali Dal in 1982. Once, the Police of Chhapa Police Post had tried to arrest Darshan Singh on the basis of suspicion, but the village Panchayat had vouched for him and saved him. His family members told that some people of their own village who were inimical towards the family, used to give false information about Darshan Singh, to the Police. A Police Constable also who belonged to the same village, was inimical towards Darshan Singh.

His (Darshan Singh's) family members and other villagers told that once the abovementioned Constable Kulwant Singh abused militants at a meeting of villagers and Darshan Singh had restrained him from doing so. A few days later, the abovementioned Constable was attacked by some armed men. However, the Constable escaped unhurt. The said Constable suspected Darshan Singh to be behind this incident. Darshan Singh's family members told that undoubtedly, Darshan Singh supported the ongoing militant movement in the Punjab, wholeheartedly, but, he was not directly involved in any sort of militant activities. He used to cultivate his own land as well as others' land, on contract basis.

On 30 August 1992 at 7.30 or 8 P.M., a youth in civil clothes came and told Darshan Singh that "Singhs" (Militants) had called him. At that time Darshan Singh was sitting in a neighbouring (uncle's) house. He put on his clothes and went away with the said youth. His family members waited for him to return throughout the night, but he did not return. Two hours after Darshan Singh's departure, the abovementioned Constable youth of his village came alongwith 2-3 other Policemen and knocked at the door of Darshan Singh's uncle ('Chacha') Chamkaur Singh and asked him to bring 4-5 cups of tea to the village bus stand. Chamkaur Singh got scared. Neither he delivered the tea as asked to nor he informed Darshan Singh's family members about it. On the following day also, Darshan Singh did not return. Though his family members were scared, yet, they did not raise any hue and cry about this incident. They were under this impression also that Darshan Singh might have gone away with the militants. As such, they did not disclose this to anybody other than their trusted people only. They did not inform the Police either. On the intervening night of 2-3 September, 1992 at midnight 12 O'Clock, the villagers heard the sound of gun shots. In the morning, the villagers saw some blood as well as a Pyjama and Chappals on the bridge of a canal at a distance of one and a half Km from the village. The villagers guessed that somebody had been murdered and his dead body had been thrown into the canal. However, the family members (of Darshan Singh) did not suspect any foul play and did not visit the site of the incident also. Darshan Singh did not return home even on 3rd September, 1992. On 4th September, his younger brother alongwith another youth went to the bridge on the canal to see the Pyjama and Chappals. He recognised those items as those of Darshan Singh. His family members told that even though this incident had occured on the intervening night of 2-3 September, yet, the Police had not initiated any action in this matter so far. After his Pyjama and Chapplas had been identified, the family members and other villagers started looking for the dead body of Darshan Singh. The body could not be found on 4th September. However, it was found on 5th September at village Tolewal. The Police neither registered any F.I.R. about this incident nor got the postmortem done. The body had decomposed and the Police instead of taking any legal action, said that Darshan Singh was an associate of the militants. His family members were certain that Constable Kulwant Singh of their village had trapped Darshan Singh and got him abducted. Kulwant Singh was posted at Malerkotla at that time. The injury marks on the body of Darshan Singh showed that he had been subjected to inhuman torture before he was killed. His family members said that the incharge of Police Post Chhapa also had reached the spot at the time when the body was found. However, he also, instead of taking any legal action, advised the family members and other villagers to cremate the body. Even though the family members now feel that they had committed a blunder by not getting a postmortem done, yet, they said that it was the duty of the Police to complete all the legal formalities. The incharge of Chhapa Police Post wrote that Darshan Singh had links with the militants and got the same signed by Darshan Singh's father. Sadhu Singh, Darshan Singh's father signed the same, due to the fear of the Police. His father Sadhu Singh is of the firm belief that the killing of Darshan Singh was the handiwork of the Police only and that the Constable of their village also had a hand in it. The above information was given to the Investigation Team by Sadhu Singh, father of Darshan Singh in the presence of eminent persons of the village.

### VFF/0854

Sukhpal Singh Babbar 26 of # B-XII 458, Tagore Street, Barnala in Sangrur. On 12 February 1988, the Police raided his house. Then only, his parents came to know that their son had some sort of link with the movement going on in the Punjab. Just a few days earlier only, his parents had arranged a rented house for him so that he may realise his responsibility towards his family by living separately and desisit from other (unlawful) activities. They told the Police that they did not know as to where he lived at that time. The Police went away but returned a short while later. They enquired about Sukhpal Singh's father. Sukhpal's mother called his father. The Police party took Balwant Singh along to his (Sukhpal Singh's) in-laws' place. From there, they took his brother-in-law (wife's brother) along and raided Sukhpal Singh's residence. Sukhpal Singh was not at home. However, they found him on the way and made him to sit in their jeep. The Police released his brother-in-law and Balwant Singh. The Police implicated him in a case of conspiracy in the murder of RSS workers at Barnala. He was released on bail after one year. A few months after his release, he was arrested again, a case was registered against him and he was sent to jail. Four months later, in the year 1990, he was released on bail. Sometime later, the Mehal Kalan Police picked him up, detained him in their illegal custody for three months and tortured him brutally. He was released on the recommendation of the Panchayat (village Council) and other eminent persons. He stayed at home for about a month. The Police continued to raid his house. Thereafter, he deserted home and joined the ranks of the militants, once for all. Even though the Police used to raid his house, yet, they never arrested any of his family members.

On 10-5-1991, in the fields between villages Jaimalsingh Wala and Raiwala, he was surrounded by the Police. An encounter ensued and he was killed in the said encounter. Thre Police had to hand over his dead body to his family members due to tremendous public pressure. According to his father, thousands of people had attended his funeral and 'Bhog' (religious last rites) which is a proof of his popularity.

Now-a-days, Balwant Singh, aged 70 years, lives at Barnala city alongwith his wife. Earlier, he used to work as a mason but, now-a-days, he cannot do any work due to ill health. His elder son lives separately. Neither this aged couple has any source of income, nor any organisation has come forward to help them. Sukhpal Singh's father is sore about this fact. He told that in the hey day of militancy, all the leaders used to visit them but, as the influence of militant movement declined, nobody bothered about them.

**VFF/0855**

Labh Singh 18 of Thikriwal, Barnala in Sangrur. Victim Labh Singh's father Jugraj Singh is an active Akali worker. He was jailed thrice during the 'Dharam Yudh Morcha' (political agitation) launched by the Akali Dal. He was in jail for a total period of two and a half years. Jugraj Singh is a medium farmer and apart from his 8 acres of land he cultivates other people's land also, on contract basis. He had two sons and one daughter. His eldest son Labh Singh was studying in class 10+1 in the Govt. Higher Secondary School, Thikriwal. Militancy was at its zenith in the Punjab in those days. By virtue of his father Jugraj Singh being an Akali suporter, Labh Singh was also greatly influenced by the political and militant movement going on in the Punjab. Labh Singh had been baptised in his childhood itself and he was a religious-minded youth. According to Labh Singh's mother, in the month of Chet (March-April) in 1991, Labh Singh was arrested by Barnala (City) Police under the charge of his links with militants. Some other boys of his village also were arrested by the Police during this period. All of them were charged with giving shelter to militants and sent to jail. Labh Singh was bailed out after two and a half months. Thereafter, he could not resume his studies and he got busy in agricultural farming at home.

According to his mother Dalip Kaur, Labh Singh used to stay at home itself but he used to go out also. However, they were not aware of any of his (unlawful) activities, if any, she said, as according to her, young boys never used to take their parents into confidence about their activities. In the beginning of the month of Sawan (July) 1991, Labh Singh went to village Dhilwan to attend the marriage of his cousin brother. From there, he went away somewhere without the knowledge of his family members. His mother told that in those days, family members of some boys namely Bunty, Teja Singh and Bhola Singh, all residents of Bajwa Patti in Barnala City came to their house and told that their son Labh Singh was seen by them in the custody of the Police party which had raided their respective houses and it was Labh Singh only who had got their sons arrested. Those people had seen Labh Singh sitting in the Police vehicle at the time their houses at Barnala were raided by the Badhni Kalan Police with a view to arreast the said boys. However, those people did not disclose as to from where the Police party had come. As such, after getting this news, the family members enquired about Labh Singh at various Police Stations. They even availed the services of DSP Karnail Singh who was a relative of Darbara Singh s/o Channan Singh of their village and was posted at Anmritsar at that time. He enquired at all the Police Stations of district Anmritsar but nothing could be known about the whereabouts of Labh Singh. While on his way back from Amritsar, as the bus halted at Badhni Kalan bus stop, Jugraj Singh noticed that next-of-kin of those boys of Barnala who had been got arrested by Labh Singh, were standing near the Police Station Badhni Kalan. On seeing them, Jugraj Singh, Major Singh s/o Zail Singh and Darbara Singh got down from the bus. Darbara Singh stayed at the bus stand itself. Jugraj Singh and Major Singh met Kartar Singh Joshila and other eminent persons standing alongwith him. They told them that his (Jugraj Singh's) son was also there inside the Police Station. They further told him that they had got Bunty, Bhola Singh and Teja Singh released and advised him to pursue the case of his son. Both Jugraj Singh and Major Singh went inside the Police Station and met the SHO Kuldeep Singh. They told him that they were next-of-kin of Labh Singh and requested him to let them meet Labh Singh. The SHO started abusing Jugraj Singh and Major Singh and directed them to get out of the Police Station. While coming out of the SHO's room, Jugraj Singh and Major Singh saw Labh Singh who was lying in a verandha of the Police Station. He had been hand-cuffed and his legs had been shackled. His condition seemed to be critical. Outside the Police Station, they talked to a private doctor and came to know that he had just returned after giving an injectiion to Labh Singh whose condition was critical. Jugraj Singh, Major Singh and Darbara Singh returned to their village and on the following day, they alongwith eminent persons of the village and other villagers in two trucks, reached Badhni Kalan. According to Jugraj Singh, they came to know outside the Police Station itself that the Badhni Kalan Police had killed two militants near a drain near village Kaonke Kalan. He further told that they suspected that the Police might have killed Labh Singh also. The leading members of the Panchayat (village Council) met the SHO who denied flatly having ever arrested Labh Singh. On being confronted by Jugraj Singh that he had personally seen Labh Singh at the Police Station and that the boys who were released by him had also told him that they had seen Labh Singh in the custody of the Badhni Kalan Police. At this, the SHO said, "It is upto me. I won't tell you anything." Saying this, he directed the Panchayat to get out of the Police Station. According to Jugraj Singh, the behaviour of the SHO towards the public was very rude. In front of them, a bus driver sounded the horn in front of the Police Station. At this, the SHO stopped the bus there for half an hour alongwith all the passengers. The Panchayat of Thikriwal are eyewitness to this incident. Seeing no way out, the panchayat returned to the village. On the following day, the news item about the "encounter" at Kaonke Kalan was published in the newspapers. However, the names of the killed militants had not been published. According to Jugraj Singh, even though they suspected that Labh Singh must have been killed in the said "encounter" itself, yet, in the absence of any proof, they were not ready to believe that such a tragedy had struck them.

Thereafter, Jugraj Singh alone went to Civil Hospital at Moga city and met the doctors there. The doctors told him that numerous bodies were brought there for postmortem and as such they were unable to tell him anything. They advised him to enquire at the cremation ground. Jugraj Singh enquired from the employees at the cremation ground as to whether they had cremated a boy with the name of Labh Singh. If yes, then they should hand over his ashes to him. They pointed towards several cloth pouches lying there and told him that the Police brought numerous bodies for cremation there. They told him to collect whatever pouch of ashes he wished to take. Jugraj Singh returned disappointed. According to Jugraj Singh, he did not have any proof of Labh Singh's death. In the meantime, the Court where a case against Labh Singh was sub-judice, issued warrants against him and the person who had stood surety for him as Labh Singh had not appeared in the Court on the scheduled date. Therefore, Jugraj Singh went again to Badhni Kalan Police Station. There, junior Policemen told him that the SHO had been transferred. He requested those junior Policemen to hand over some proof of his son's death in case he had been killed so that he may produce the same in the Court. They advised him to come and meet the new SHO on the following day. On the following day again, Jugraj Singh went to Badhni Kalan and apprised the SHO of his predicament. The SHO whom Jugraj Singh had met at his residence, listened to him and advised him to go to the Police Station saying that he also would be reaching there shortly. At his office, the SHO called Jugraj Singh into his room and offered him a seat. The SHO gave in writing about Labh Singh having been killed. While the SHO was looking for stamp inside the drawer of his table, he had kept the items in the drawer on the table. Among those items, there were photographs of several boys who had been killed. Jugraj Singh picked up the photograph of the dead body of his son and put it into his pockert as the SHO was looking the other way. Jugraj Singh produced the certificate issued by the SHO in the Court at Sangrur. But, he did not keep any photo copy of the same with him.

Jugraj Singh told that gradually, it became known that the Police had arrested Labh Singh and another youth namely Partap Singh, resident of district Amritsar, near village Luhara when they had picked up a row with a bus conductor. Jugraj Singh verified this fact at Luhara where he came to know that in those days, it was a hot topic of discussion among the residents of the area that the Police had made two youth to get down from a bus at the bus stand near the Police Post. According to Labh Singh's mother, Labh Singh was killed on 17th Sawan (1 August) 1991 and he had been arrested 5-6 days earlier. The family members don't remember the date of his arrest. However, his mother told that it was 17th day of Sawan (Indian Calendar) and 1st day of the month (according to Christian Era). But, she did not remember the name of the month of the C.E.

During the course of the interview, the Investigation Team realised that this incident had a deep adverse impact on the mind of Labh Singh's father Jugraj Singh. He has started drinking liquor also. The Investigation Team had to ask him repeatedly for the details of this incident, which consumed a lot of time.

### VFF/0856

Mohinderpal Singh alias Bhola 28 of Sanghera, Barnala in Sangrur. One family were close to Mohinderpal Singh's family and they also had returned from Burma. One of the sons of that family, namely Phoola Singh, resident of Barnala, was a renowned militant. As Phoola Singh was an absconder, he often used to take shelter at Mohinderpal Singh's house. The Police got a scent of this. The Barnala Police picked him up twice and tortured him brutally. Bhola Singh deserted home due to the fear of Police beating and joined the ranks of the militants, once for all. The Police began harassing his family members. All the family members deserted home due to fear and did not return home for three years.

In December, 1992, Barnala (City) Police showed the photograph of the dead body of a youth, to the village Sarpanch and asked him to identify him. The Sarpanch identified it (as that of Mohinderpal Singh's dead body). By and by, his family members also came to know about it. His militant colleagues had inserted an advertisement also in Ajit and other newspapers about his 'Bhog' (last rites) ceremony. The family members told that as they came to know that Mohinderpal Singh had been killed by the Police, they returned home. But, still, the Police used to visit their house and enquire about Mohinderpal Singh. At this, they used to show them the advertisement inserted by the militants in various newspapers about the 'Bhog' of Mohinderpal Singh. According to his family members, the Sangrur and Barnala Police had in their possession the photographs of the dead body of Mohinderpal Singh which they used to get identified from the arrested persons. Inspite of that, the Police continued to make enquiries about him from his family members. His family members said that the Police had not told them so far as to what happened to Mohinderpal Singh, after all. They further told that the Police never showed them any photograph. However, they (the Police) had shown the photograph of his dead body to the village Sarpanch and several other people and got the same identified from them. They said that such a behaviour by the Police, aroused their suspicion that the Police were trying to cover up some of their misdeeds. They further told that till today they had not come to know as to what happened to Mohinderpal Singh, after all.

**VFF/0857**

Didar Singh alias Dari 25 of Wajid Ke Khurd, Barnala in Sangrur. Didar Singh was the eldest among seven brothers and sisters. His father was a Granthi (Sikh Cleric) of the village Gurdwara. Before that, his father was in the service of the Agriculture Department of Himachal Pradesh Government which he had quit. Didar Singh abandoned his studies while he was styding in seventh standard and started learning the trade of tailor. After a training of four years at Barnala, he opened a tailoring shop at his village. Didar Singh was an 'Amritdhari' (Baptised) Sikh youth. His father was a Granthi and his whole family were 'Amritdhari' (Baptised) Sikhs. In 1991, one day, when Didar Singh was going to deliver the invitation for marriage party to someone on behalf of a client, the Police of his village Police Post (under Bhadaur Police Station) arrested him merely on the basis of suspicion and thrashed him severely. 4-5 days later, the village Panchayat (Council) got him released. Thereafter, the Barnala Police started raiding his house for his arrest. Due to repearted Police raids, Didar Singh went underground. Gradually, he developed contacts with the militants. After Didar Singh absconded, the Police started raiding his house. Once, Shamsher Singh, SHO of Barnala (Sadar) Police Station picked up Didar Singh's father Giani Jarnail Singh. The village Panchayat and other eminent persons of the village got him released. By virtue of his being a Granthi, the village panchayat used to pursue his (Jarnail Singh's) case promptly. Didar Singh's brothers were young, yet.

On 15th August, 1992 at 11 P.M., a Police party of Barnala (Sadar) Police Station led by the SHO Shamsher Singh, raided the village Gurdwara and arrested Giani Jarnail Singh (Didar Singh's father) in the presence of his wife and children. On being asked by Giani Jarnail Singh, the reason for his arrest the SHO replied that he would let him know the reason also and directed him to just come alongwith them. To a query by his wife Swaran Kaur, they told that they were taking him to Barnala Police Station. But, on the following day, when the eminent persons of the village went to Barnala Police Station, the Police flatly denied having arrested him and brought him there. The family members and the village Panchayat approached the Police Officers repeatedly for 2-3 years for the release of Jarnail Singh, but, nothing was disclosed about his whereabouts. They enquired at almost every Police Station but nothing was disclosed about the whereabouts of Jarnail Singh.

About 20-22 days after the arrest of Jarnail Singh, the Police surrounded Didar Singh at the kutcha track near village Sahora and shot him dead. Ram Piari, unable to bear the shock of her son Jarnail Singh's disappearance and the death of her grandson Didar Singh, breathed her last, one month later. Meanwhile, the village Panchayat continued to approach the Police Officers, in search of Jarnail Singh. After a period of 6-7 months, as the whereabouts of Jarnail Singh were still not known, his wife Swaran Kaur also, unable to bear the shock, breathed her last. The village Panchayat begged of the Police Officers to release Jarnail Singh, pleading that six children would become orphans. However, the Police Officers continued to deny the arrest of Jarnail Singh, flatly. Under such circumstances, his children used to beg for food in the village. With the passage of time, as the elder son Manjit Singh matured, the villagers appointed him Granthi. With the money earned by him, Manjit Singh established his brothers in different vocations. Thus, now only, the family members are on their own. When the Investigation Team visited their house, Manjit Singh was scared of giving any information. He said that they had already suffered too much. They might get into trouble again. After repeated assurances only, Manjit Singh agreed to give this information. However, he flatly refused to sign the information given by him in this proforma. The villagers told the Investigation Team that this family had undergone tremendous suffering. Now only, with the help of villagers, the destitute children have become capable of fending for themselves. The responsibility of the whole family is now on the shoulders of Manjit Singh, aged 24 years. On being asked repeatedly by the Investigation Team whether he wanted to get justice about the atrocities committed against his family, he replied that they longed to get justice alright, but at the same time they did not want to initiate any action against the Police, as they were scared of the Police.

**VFF/0858**

Dayadeepak Singh 21 of Mehraj Bhaini, Barnala in Sangrur. Victim Dayadeepak Singh's father Gurdev Singh, aged 55 years, was a small farmer. He had three daughters and two sons. His elder son, Dyayadeepak Singh had taken admission in Akal Degree College at Mastuana after passing his Matriculation. There he started taking active part in the activities of Sikh Students Federation. Dayadeepak Singh was arrested by the Police during the repression let loose by the Police in Punjab after the imposition of President's Rule in May 1987. Several cases were registered against him and he was sent to jail where he was detained for one to one and a half years. After his release from jail, the Police started harassing him again. Ultimately, he got fed up with Police harassment and absconded. He had stayed at home also for about one and a half to two years after his release from jail. When he used to stay at home, the Police used to arrest him often and beat him up. After Dayadeepak had absconded, the Police used to pick up his father.

On 13 or 14 May at 5 A.M., the Police knocked at the door of Gurdev Singh. He opened the door. They asked him whether he only was Gudev Singh to which he replied in the affirmative. The Police made him to sit in their vehicle and drove away. His wife Surjit Kaur followed him upto the door but the Police drove away quickly. Surjit Kaur did not remember the date. She told that a militant namely Sukhpal Singh had been killed on 10-5-1991. Gurdev Singh was among the persons who had collected the ashes of the said militant. Thereafrter, on the third day morning, he was lifted away. According to the family members, they enquired at Police Post Badbar and Dhanaula Police Station, on the same day. But, the Police did not make any commitment. As Gurdev Singh was not released for several days, the people of his village and those of the neighbouring villages organised a Dharna at Badbar (Police Post). The SHO of Dhanaula Police Station came there, promised to release Gurdev Singh and appealed to the people to lift the Dharna. Preetam Singh (Gurdev Singh's brother) told that he alongwith eminent persons met SP Sangrur, Mr. Poohli and he assured the delegation that Gurdev Singh would be released. He asked them to bring new clothes even, for Gurdev Singh as well as the money to pay for his food. Later on, when Preetam Singh met the SP, he asked him to hand over the clothes (of Gurdev Singh) to him. At this, Preetam Singh and Panchayat members told him to produce the old clothes of Gurdev Singh first so that they would be sure that indeed he was in their custody and then only they would hand over the new clothes to him. At this, hot words were exchanged between the SP and the Panchayat members. Gian Singh resident of Qila Hakeema also had accompanied Preetam Singh. It was he only who had a heated argument with the SP. The family members of Gurdev Singh told that they approached each and every officer at each and every Police Station of Barnala and Sangrur Police Districts but the Police did not give any information about the whereabouts of Gurdev Singh.

Dayadeepak Singh was killed in an encounter with the Police, on 19 Sawan (August) 1991, near village Bhamma Bandi. Another youth of village Bhaini Mehraj namely Harbans Singh Fauji s/o Bakhshish Singh was also killed in the said encounter. The bodies of both these youth were not handed over to their next-of-kin. The people of the area came to know about this encounter soon and they assembled at the site of the incident in large numbers.

This (Dayadeepak Singh's) family are so terrified of the Police that the Investigation Team had to counsel them for a long time for getting this information. Gurdev Singh's wife Surjit Kaur is most affected by this terror (of the Police).

**VFF/0859**

Jagwinder Singh alias Jagga 17 of Sandhu Kalan, Barnala in Sangrur. Victim Jagwinder Singh's mother Karamjit Kaur had two sons and one daughter. Her husband Karnail Singh had expired in 1985. Her family owned 3 acres of land and she used to augment the family income by stitching clothes. Her elder son Jagwinder Singh used to stay and study at his maternal uncle's house at village Marhi. Jagwinder Singh was an "Amritdhari" (Baptised) Sikh youth and he was influenced by the current militant and political movement in Punjab in those days. After getting himself baptised, Jagwinder Singh had started participating in the activities of Sikh Students Federation.

In 1988, the Bagha Purana police raided his house but Jagwinder Singh was not at home at that time. The police directed his maternal uncle Chand Singh to produce him at the Bagha Purana police station on the following morning. On the following day, Chand Singh took Jagwinder Singh along with him and produced him before the SHO of Bagha Purana police station, Kashmira Singh. The police detained him for three days and tortured him also. Three days later, the police implicated him in a case under the Arms Act. In the FIR of this case, Jagwinder Singh had been shown arrested along with three other youth at a Naka near village Vehoke, whereas he had been produced before the police. He remained in jail at moga and Central Jail Ferozepur for about one year and thereafter came out on bail.

After his release, his maternal uncle Chand Singh sent him to a workshop at Moga for training. Jagwinder Singh used to got o Moga daily in the morning and return home in the evening. This routine continued for 15-20 days. On 15-2-91 he went to Moga as usual but did not return home in the evening. Next day, his maternal uncle looked for him but could not locate him. On 18-2-91, ASI Kuldeep Singh of Samalsar Chowki (post) raided his house and enquired about Jagwinder Singh. Chand Singh said, "He had gone to Moga two days ago and has not returned home. We are worried." The police arrested Chand Singh and took him to Samalsar Chowki. He was released on 19-2-91 at the interventiion of one of his relatives (police officer) with a direction from the SHO to trace out Jagwinder Singh and produce him before the police.

On 20-2-91 a staff member of Bagha Purana police station told Chand Singh that his nephew had been killed at village Nangal under P.S. Nihalsingh Wala. Same day evening, Chand Singh along with the Panchayat reached police station Nihal Singh Wala but by that time the police had cremated his body already.

On 21-2-91, the newspapers carried a news item that two militants namely Jagwinder Singh resident of Sandhu Kalan and another unidentified had been killed in inter-gang rivalry.

*    Chand Singh suspects that the police killed Jagwinder Singh after arresting him. According to him, since his (Chand Singh's) maternal uncle is a DSP in Punjab Police and he had intervened on their behalf, the police did not show Jagwinder Singh as having been killed in an "encounter" but showed him as having been killed in inter-gang rivalry.

**VFF/0860**

Bhola Singh 35 of Raisar Patiala, Barnala in Sangrur. Bhola Singh was an 'Amritdhari' (Baptised) Sikh youth and belonged to a poor farmer family. He used to feed his family by selling milk. He had two children. In 1992, the Police of C.I.A. Staff Handiaya arrested him, registered a case under the Arms Act against him and sent him to jail. He got released on bail. He resumed his work at home. According to his mother Bachan Kaur, two boys of their village namely Jagga Singh and Bikkar Singh were arrested by the Police, a few days before Diwali in the year 1992. She said that they were not aware whether those boys named Bhola Singh or not but the Police came to their house. Bhola Singh was not at home. They asked him to stay away from home. They sent him to the house of an eminent leader of their village namely Harjit Singh as they planned to produce him before the Police later through him (Harjit

Singh). They came to know about Bhola Singh's arrest, one day before Diwali day, in 1992, as a rumour had spread in the village that he had been arrested by a Police party of C.I.A. Staff from the neighbouring village of Mallian. Bhola Singh's brother Surjit Singh alongwith Harjit Singh went to C.I.A. Staff. Harjit Singh went inside and met the Police Officers. He told Surjit Singh on coming out that the Police had told him that they would release Bhola Singh after interrogation. The family members continued to approach various eminent persons with a view to get Bhola Singh released. They did not approach the Police directly. They used to approach eminent political leaders only.

According to his mother Bachan Kaur, on the day following the Diwali, a Police party brought Bhola Singh to their farmhouse. They searched the house and broke open the door of Bhola Singh's room. His father Sher Singh and mother Bachan Kaur were present in the house at that time. Bhola Singh was sitting in the Police vehicle outside.

On the following day, a Police party brought Bhola Singh to Harjit Singh's house. He had been covered with a blanket at that time. However, Harjit Singh was not at home at that time. A constable held Bhola Singh's hand and took him into the courtyard of Harjit Singh's house. Bhola Singh enquired from Harjit Singh's son about the whereabpouts of Harjit Singh. At this, the child replied, "Uncle, daddy has gone to Barnala for pursuing your case only." The Police party took Bhola Singh back in their vehicle. The family members tried their level best (to get him released) but nobody listened to them. 15-20 days later, a news item appeared in the newspapers that a militant namely Bhola Singh had escaped from Police custody.

According to his family members, this was a drama enacted by the Police. Whereas the fact was that either the Police had killed him or they had made him a "Cat" for the purpose of arresting other militants and had hidden him somewhere. His mother Bachan Kaur told that a few months later, some Policemen came and pasted a Court Notice outside their house and told them verbally that their son had escaped from Police custody and that in case he returned home they should intimate them. The family members alleged that in those days it was routine for the Police to enact such dramas. Sometimes they (the Police) used to show the arrested youth as having escaped from their custody and at other times, they used to show them as having been killed in the cross firing between the Police and the militants. Actually, it used to be a white lie. His mother Bachan Kaur told amid sobs that it was blatant highhandedness (of the Police).

**VFF/0861**

Major Singh 38 of Sehajra, Barnala in Sangrur. Lachhmi Devi (victim Major Singh's mother) was earlier married to Pirthi Chand, resident of village Sehajra in district Sangrur. She had two sons and one daughter out of this wedlock. After the death of Pirthi Chand, Lachhmi Devi married his friend Lachhman Singh, resident of Valtoha in district Amritsar. She had two sons out of this wedlock, namely Gurmukh Singh (since expired) and Major Singh. Major Singh was a religious minded youth and used to reside at Valtoha. After the eruption of Sikh—Nirankari controversy in Punjab, Major Singh came closer to Sant Jarnail Singh Bhindranwale.

After the death of Major Singh's mother, his father Lachhman Singh ousted his (Major Singh's) step-brother Amarjit Singh from his house at Valtoha. Amarjit Singh, now a destitute, sought refuge in the Damdami Taksal. There, Sant Gurcharan Singh Bhindra lent him his support and also he got his (Amarjit's) share of land at village Sehajra restored to him. After Amarjit Singh had settled down at village Sehajra, Major Singh used to visit him sometimes, as in the meantime Major Singh's father Lachhman Singh had expired.

During the year 1982, Major Singh was arrested by the Police on the allegation of the murder of a Nirankari at Amargarh (District Sangrur). Several cases were registered against him and he was sent to jail. He was incarcerated in Amritsar jail till the year 1991 and was released in Feb-Mar, 1991. During this period, he was detained in different jails and tried in different cases. Major Singh contested the elections of May 1991 as an independent candidate from Barnala Assembly constituency. But the elections were cancelled and the Police started harassing him again. Major Singh went underground, due to Police raids. The Police started harassing his family members. Once, the Jagraon Police picked up his brother Amarjit Singh, his wife and his children and took them to Jagraon. The Jagraon Police tortured his brother Amarjit Singh and his sister-in-law (Amarjit's wife) brutally. They asked them about the whereabouts of Major Singh. As the Panchayat (village Council) used to get them released from one Police Station, the Police of another Police Station used to raid their house. The Police continued to harass the family members of Major Singh for full three years till the time Major Singh was arrested. His family members used to stay away from home, often.

On 18th August, 1994, night, Major Singh was arrested by a Police party of C.I.A. Staff Handiaya led by Inspector Sant Kumar, from the house of an Akali leader Sohan Singh Sandhu at Barnala (Sandhu Patti). Later on, it became known that Major Singh had approached a senior

Akali leader for surrendering himself before the Police and had stayed for the night at the house of Sohan Singh who was close to the said Akali leader. Major Singh's family members told that God only knows whether the said Akali leader informed the Police and got Major Singh arrested or it was somebody else who had tipped the Police. The Police had arrested Sohan Singh also alongwith Major Singh. The family members disclosed that on the night when Major Singh was arrested from Barnala, a large Police force had serached their house and those of their neighbours. The Police had arrested Sukhchain Singh and the village Chowkidar also from their village but they released them at the next village. Apart from that, the Police had raided several other villages and enquired about Major Singh. The family members said that from all this, it was evident that the Police had got the information that Major Singh had arrived in the Barnala area. The family members came to know about Major Singh's arrest from a resident of their village namerly Sukhchain Singh s/o Hakam Singh, whom they suspected of conspiracy in the matter of Major Singh's arrest. Sukhchain Singh was Major Singh's friend also. One day, under the influence of liquor he blurted out that Major Singh had been detained at C.I.A. Staff Handiaya. They said that they did not pursue his case due to fear. However, they were sure now that Major Singh had been trapped and arrested under a conspiracy. They further alleged that the case of illegal arms against Sohan Singh was also a drama only so that nobody would suspect that Major Singh had been got arrested by somebody. The SSP and other senior officers of Barnala Police district were a part of this conspiracy, the family members said.

Major Singh was killed (in a fake encounter) by the Police at village Moom under Mehal Kalan Police Station on the intervening night of 20-21 September, 1994. His family members said that they did not pursue his case due to fear. They told that Sohan Singh, from whose house Major Singh had been arrested, would not depose in this case as he, according to them, was also a part of the conspiracy for getting him arrested. They further told that they were themselves victims of Police repression, what to talk of pursuing the case of Major Singh's extra-judicial killing. Even today, they shudder to think of that period, they said.

**VFF/0862**

Jarnail Singh alias Chowkidar 60 of Tibba, Dhuri in Sangrur. Jarnail Singh was a poor Dalit resident of Village Gandewal, PO. Tibba, Tehsil Dhuri, District Sangrur. He was the Village Chowkidar and used to make both ends meet by manual labour. He had three daughters and four sons. His eldest son Achhra Singh used to work with a landlord on a crop sharing basis.

In the month of 'Sawan' (Jul-Aug) in the year 1992, a murder took place at Village Gandewal. It was suspected to be the handiwork of the militants. The Police suspected that Achhra Singh also had a hand in the said murder. The Police raided Achhra Singh's house with a view to arrest him but he ran away from home, due to fear. The Police began picking up his father Jarnail Singh and other relatives. The family members used to stay away from home due to the fear of the Police. The Police used to pick up Jarnail Singh but they used to release him soon. In those days, father-in-law of Achhra Singh's sister Jinder Kaur who was married at Barnala, namely Bhan Singh, was picked up by the Police due to Achhra Singh (being a militant). Her mother-in-law quarrelled with her and alleged that they were suffering due to her (Jinder Kaur's) family's misdeeds. Why does your father not present himself before the Police, she asked her. Jinder Kaur was fed up with her mother-in-law's taunts and she went to the house of her aunt (Bhua) Charno at Village Wajid Ke Khurd as her parents were staying there due to the fear of the Police. She informed her father about the arrest of her father-in-law and her mother-in-law's complaint. Jarnail Singh listened to his daughter and said," OK. I am going to Sherpur Police Station. I will try to get your father-in-law released by the Police by producing myself before them." Saying this, he went away. As he alighted from the bus at Sherpur bus stand and started walking towards the Police Station, he saw that his brother-in-law ("Sadhu") Sajjan Singh also was walking towards the Police Station. Sajjan Singh told him that the Police had arrested his son Gurjant Singh and brought him there. He further told him that he was going to meet BSP leader and MLA Raj Singh Kheri. Jarnail Singh told Sajjan Singh to bring Raj Singh and that he was going to the Police Station.

The Police released Jinder Kaur's father-in-law Bhan Singh immediately after Jarnail Singh presented himself before them. His family members told that firstly they had deserted home due to the fear of the Police and secondly they were not much worried about Jarnail Singh, as, by virtue of being a Chowkidar, the Police did not torture him and often they used to release him on their own. A few days after Jarnail Singh had presented himself at the Police Station, the news item about the killing of Achhra Singh in an encounter with the Police was published in the newspapers. A Havaldar (Head Constable) of Samrala Police had visited their house and informed them that they may collect the ashes of their son from Samrala Police Station. As Jarnail Singh did not return home for a few days, his family members enquired at Sherpur Police Station. They replied that he had gone away from there, that is, they had already released him. The family members met SHO Sherpur and DSP Sherpur several times to know about the whereabouts of Jarnail Singh, but each time they gave only one stock reply that they had released him.

    *    On being asked by the Investigation Team about her reaction to the killing of Achhra Singh in an encounter, Basant Kaur said, "What can we say about this?" She told that in those days, often, the Police used to arrest the youth and kill them. Later on, they used to concoct the story of an encounter.

### VFF/0863

Chand Singh alias Baba 40 of Longowal in Sangrur. On 28-6-1992, the Sangrur Police in large numbers, had picked up a youth of Longowal (Dullat Patti) namely Darshan Singh s/o Tarlok Singh. On 29-6-1992, Baba Chand Singh had gone alongwith Darshan Singh's father Tarlok Singh to the Police Station Longowal, to enquire from the SHO Tarlochan Singh about Darshan Singh. On 30-6-1992, Baba Chand Singh received a phone call from SHO Tarlochan Singh who said, "Baba Ji, I wanted to have your 'Darshan' (i..e I wanted to meet you). Are you available at the Gurdwara itself today." Baba Chand Singh replied that he himself would come to the Police Station if he wanted him for some job. But the SHO told that they would come and see him there only.

On the same day (30-6-1992) at about 11 P.M., 5-7 persons in civil clothes came to the Gurdwara. Baba Chand Singh was taking rest at his residence adjacent to the Gurdwara. Plainclothes Policemen entered Baba's room and directed him to come alongwith them. One of the Sewadars namely Gurjant Singh resisted them but they pushed him and threw him away on the ground.

The Policemen pushed Baba Chand Singh, who was wearing underwear and Banian (Vest) only, forcibly into their Maruti Van and took him away. Even the Sewadars (devout volunteers) who were reciting Gurbani in the main building of the Gurdwara did not come to know about this incident. The Dera is situated at a little distance away from the Village. The Sewadars informed the important persons of the Village about this incident in the morning only, due to fear.

The Villagers were still terrorised due to an incident which had occured on 28-6-1992 in which a large Police force riding in 10-15 vehicles had raided the Village on 28-6-1992 and arrested a youth of the Village. Secondly, there were no next-of-kin of Baba Chand Singh. As such, nobody from the Village pursued his case with the Police. Some of the villagers told the Investigation Team that a faction in the Village had opposed the appointment of Baba Chand Singh as the Mahant of the abovementioned Gurdwara. It was due to this factionalism that nobody pursued his case. On being questioned by the Investigation Team as to why at all was Baba Chand Singh abducted by the Police, the villagers and present Sewadars told that Baba Chand Singh had links with the militants. The militants, on their way, used to stay or have their meals at the Gurdwara. Apart from this, it was revealed that a few days before this incident, the militants had kidnapped a child of a Police officer and demanded the release of some of their associates in return for the safety of the said child. Some of the villagers told that Baba Chand Singh had acted as an intermediary also in this episode and the Police were forced to release some of the renowned militants. As such, since then, the Police considered Baba Chand Singh to be a supporter of the militants. The villagers suspect that this may also be one of the reasons for the disappearance of Baba Chand Singh.

**VFF/0864**

Karnail Singh alias Kaila 35 of Dhilwan, Tappa in Sangrur. Karnail Singh was an 'Amritdhari' (Baptised) Sikh youth and a married man who had two children. He was a farmer only. He was influenced by the militant movement going on in Punjab and he joined the ranks of the militants in 1989, once for all. For about six months, the Police were in the dark about his activities. But, thereafter, the Tappa Police, especially the Police party led by DSP Harnek Singh Sekhon started raiding his house. The Police used to pick up his brother Jarnail Singh, often and the village panchayat (council) used to get him released. Sometimes, the Police of other Police Stations also used to raid his house and pick up his brother.

On 2-11-1992 at 9 P.M. a Police party of Tappa Police Station raided his house and directed Jarnail Singh to accompany them. Jarnail Singh told that he would produce himself at the Police Station in the morning alongwith the Panchayat. At this, the Police party told that the Sarpanch (Head of village Council) and the Panchayat were already present at the Tappa Police Station. The Police party took Jarnail Singh to the Police Station. Sarpanch Karnail Singh was sitting there at that time. The SHO (Station House Officer) told that a militant had been killed and they wanted to get him identified lest he may be his brother. A Police party took Jarnail Singh and the village Sarpanch to Bhucho Mandi Police Post. A dead body was lying there in the verandah which Jarnail Singh identified as that of his brother Karnail Singh. The Police got some papers regarding this identification signed by the Sarpanch and Jarnail Singh and asked them to go away. Jarnail Singh protested and told them that how could he go back without performing the last rites of his brother. At this, the Police asked him to come in the morning. However, they put a condition that they would allow him to attend the funeral only if he did not bring more than five persons alongwith him. On the following day, Jarnail Singh alongwith 6-7 members of the panchayat reached Bhucho Mandi at 10 A.M. The Police took the body to Bathinda for a post mortem. The panchayat followed the Police in their own vehicle. After the post mortem, the Police took the body to the cremation ground. There, his brother and 5-7 members of the Panchayat carried out the cremation in the presence of the Police. Acording to Jarnail Singh, they noticed only one bullet injury mark on the right side of Karnail Singh's rib cage while they were giving a bath to the body. According to the Police, the encounter in which Karnail Singh had been killed, lasted for nine hours.

### VFF/0865

Bhola Singh 25 of Kattu, Dhanaula in Sangrur. In the month of Jeth (Indian Calendar month corresponding to May-June of Christian Calendar) in the year 1992, his family members read a news item which was published in all the newspapers, about Bhola Singh having been killed in an encounter with the Police at village Rashin in Ludhiana district. However, his family members did not remember the exact date. According to his mother Tej Kaur, it was the month of Jeth in the year 1992. After Bhola Singh had absconded, the Police used to pick up his father Bogha Singh, often and detain him in their illegal custody for days together. After the publication of the news item, neither his family members visited the site of the incident nor they pursued his case further. They told that they were not aware as to what actually happened and that they had no alternative other than believing the Police version. The Police neither informed the family members about this incident nor got the dead body identified by them.

### VFF/0866

Amrik Singh alias Mangu 32 of Ghanauri Kalan, Dhuri in Sangrur. Petition by his wife is appended below.

1.   That my husband Sh. Amrik Singh @ Mangu s/o Bhan Singh was abducted from his shop on 31-8-92 at 6/7 P.M. by a Police party from P.S. Dhuri led by SHO Darshan Singh.

2.   That my brother-in-law ('Devar') Darshan Singh s/o Bhan Singh had recognised SHO Darshan Singh fully. I and my brother-in-law pleaded a lot with SHO Darshan Singh, that Mangu never went out any where anytime and that he should

be spared. But they did not listen to us, pushed him into a car and went away.

3. That after that also, the Police came to our house several times and enquired about younger brothers of my husband. We also went to P.S. Dhuri and tried to find out about my husband, but we did not get any information.

4. That my father had submitted representations regarding this to SSP Sangrur and Punjab Police Chief, Sh. K.P.S. Gill. At this, I was called by Sherpur Police. However, they did not tell us anything about Mangu @ Amrik Singh and obtained my and those of my family members signatures/thumb impressions.

5. That once I had met Advocate Ravinder Singh Bains also. He also obtained my signatures/thumb impressions. But he has neither given me any paper nor told me anything, so far.

6. That the Police had obtained my signatures on the abovementioned papers saying that "We would trace out your husband soon. You need not have any fear."

**VFF/0867**

Amrik Singh of Amargarh, Malerkotla in Sangrur. On 1-10-92 at 6.30 P.M., he was coming from Patiala to Amargarh in a bus when he was abducted by a police party of 4-5 men in civil clothes, headed by Gurmel Singh SHO Amargarh and including Bir Atma Ram SHO Sadar P.S. Nabha. We came to know about this incident at 7.30 P.M. At 9 P.M. same night, we met Bir Atma Ram, SHO Nabha (Sadar). He expressed ignorance about this incident.

On 2-10-92, we again met Bir Atma Ram, SHO Nabha (Sadar). He told that there is a possibility of Amrik Singh having been picked up by C.I.A. Staff Patiala. Then we met Satpal Singh, incharge of C.I.A. Staff Patiala (Mai Ki Saran). But, no clue could be found regarding the whereabouts of Amrik Singh.

On 3-10-92, we met Bir Atma Ram, SHO Nabha (Sadar). He said,"Don't worry, your son is with the Police only. You come tomorrow and take him back." Apart from myself, Mukhtiar Singh retired SP of Nabha, Iqbal Singh Khanna, and Manpal Singh Raipur were present there when he uttered these words.

On 4-10-92, we met DSP Gurmeet Singh at Nabha. He asked the SHO about the boy. The SHO denied any knowledge about the whereabouts of the boy. On being reminded about his words of the previous day, he denied having spoken those words also. We enquired at other police stations around Nabha, like Bhawanigarh, Chheenta etc, but no clue was found anywhere.

On 5-10-92, a delegation of the Panchayat of Amargarh met the SHO and DSP of Nabha again. But, to no avail. When requested to register the FIR, SHO Nabha evaded doing so till the evening. Ultimately, in the evening, SHO Nabha registered a DDR No. 21 dated 5-10-92, with great hesitation.

On 6-10-92, we met the then Taxation and Excise Minister, Punjab, Sh. Shamsher Singh Doolo. He gave a letter addressed to SSP Sangrur Narinder Pal Singh. We met the SSP with that letter. He enquired from all police stations in Sangrur District on the Wireless, but no clue was found.

On 7-10-92, we met Karam Singh, the then Minister for Industry, Punjab. He gave a letter addressed to SSP Patiala, Sh. Suresh Arora. We went to the SSP's Office at Patiala with that letter. The SSP was not present, but, the SP (D) was present there. He enquired over the Wireless from all police stations in Patiala District, but no clue was found.

On 10-10-92, Chief Minister of Punjab, Sh. Beant Singh had come to Khanna to attend a wedding. We along with Amrik Singh, Sarpanch of village Rauni (Ludhiana) met him and narrated the incident to him. He put the application in his pocket and asked us to meet him at Chandigarh.

On 12-10-92, we met Sh. Beant Singh, Chief Minister Punjab at Chandigarh. He directed his political advisor Gurmeet Singh to inquire into the matter. We met Gurmeet Singh after 3-4 days. He said that there was no information about Amrik Singh.

On 13-10-92, registered written representations were sent to DGP Punjab, Governor Punjab, Chief Minister Punjab, and SSP Patiala. Representatives of various newspapers also came to our home and enquired about this incident. A news item about his disappearance was published in various newspapers.

On 15-10-92, a delegation of the village Panchayat met the IG Punjab Sh. Sube Singh. But, after 3-4 days, he also sent a message that no information was available regarding the whereabouts of Amrik Singh.

On 16-10-92, a delegation of the village Panchayat met the SSP Patiala, Sh. Suresh Arora. He told that we had come late; thereby implying that the boy had been arrested by the Police, but had now disappeared. Same day, a delegation of Shere Punjab Club Amargarh met the MLA of the area, Sh. Dhanwant Singh (Dhuri). The MLA rang up DIG Sh. Rajan Gupta. The DIG replied that Amrik Singh had indeed been arrested and had been kept underground in a Cellar along with some other boys. He said that they would release them after a few days. 4-5 days later, the MLA again rang up the DIG. Then he denied his earlier statement saying that he had mistaken some other boy for Amrik Singh.

On 21-10-92, DIG Patiala came to village Amargarh to listen to the people's complaints against Police excesses. First of all, the Panchayat of village Amargarh put forth the serious complaint of the disappearance of Amrik Singh. They also told the DIG that in case the boy may be at fault i.e. he may be a militant, then he may be shot dead in front of all of them. But, if he may be innocent, then why was he picked up without informing about his crime to his parents.

4-5 days later, we again met the DIG. He expressed his ignorance again. Thereafter, for two three months, residents of the village, freinds, relatives and other sympathisers made every effort to locate him. Whosoever had an approach in any police station, he enquired from there, but, all in vain.

So far, we do not know as to what his fault was. Whether he had any connection with any militant Organisation. Or which Police had arrested him, where he was taken and what they did to him. It is still a mystery.

### VFF/0868

Randhir Singh alias Raju of Amargarh, Dhuri in Sangrur. Randhir Singh was picked up from his residence at 5 A.M. on 24-3-93 by a police party led by DSP Samana, Varinder Pal Singh and including SHO of Amargarh P.S., Gurmel Singh. It was not disclosed where they were taking him and in connection with which case.

### VFF/0869

Achhra alias 19 of Tibba, Dhuri in Sangrur. Achhra Singh was an illiterate and "Amritdhari" (Baptised) Sikh youth. He used to work with a Village landlord on crop sharing basis. He was absconding for about a month and thereafter, in the month of 'Bhadon' (Aug-Sep, but the year is not known) a news item about his having been killed at the hands of the Samrala Police, was published in the newspapers.

The family members of Achhra Singh don't know as to what happened to Achhra Singh. Whether he was arrested and killed in a fake encounter or he was killed in a genuine encounter with the Police as alleged by them. The family members asked that if at all Achhra Singh was killed in an encounter with the Police, how did they identify him. Because, the area falling under Samrala Police Station is far away from their Village. They suspect that he was arrested and after interrogation, he was killed in a fake encounter. That is how they must have come to know about his name and that of his Village. However, they (family members) do not have any proof of the same.

**VFF/0870**

Harpal Singh 30 of Alal, Mollowal, Dhuri in Sangrur. Harpal Singh belonged to a middle class farmer family of Village Alal in district Sangrur. He had one brother. Their father had expired when they were young. As such, Harpal Singh could not study at all. He was a farmer. He had got married in 1980. In 1982, he got interested in the "Dharam Yuddh Morcha" (Political agitation) launched by the Akali Dal (a political party) in Punjab. He was a religious minded and sentimental youth. In his opinion, the Sikhs as a community were being discriminated against, politically. He had been going to Amritsar alongwith the 'Jathas' (groups of political activists) to participate in the "Dharam Yuddh Morcha". However, he had never been arrested by the Police.

After the Army attack on Sri Darbar Sahib in 1984, Harpal Singh used to attend the political and religious functions. He used to attend the "Bhog" (religious last rites) ceremonies of the youth killed at the hands of the Police, also. However, he had not formally joined any political party. He used to be saddened and enraged at the sight of youth being killed at the hands of the Police, daily. According to his wife Gurjit Kaur, gradually, Harpal Singh's interest in his work decreased. On 1 January 1991, he went away alongwith another youth. On being asked by his wife as to where he was going he had replied that he was going to Hazur Sahib and that he would be back in a month's time. But, Harpal Singh did not return home. Two months after he had left home, the Police started raiding his house in search of him. The family members said that he had not intimated them as to where he was going to. The Police used to pick up his brother Harbhajan Singh, his father-in-law Bhag Singh (since expired), his brother-in-laws and other relatives, detain them in illegal custody for days together and then release them. Once, Harbhajan Singh and Bhag Singh were detained illegally at Khemkaran (District Amritsar) for a period of five months. They were picked up by the local Police only, but later on, they were sent to Khemkaran. Their family members thought that the Police must have killed them. But they were released five months later at the intervention of some politicians.

On 6-7-1992, the Sherpur Police visited his house and directed Harbhajan Singh (Harpal Singh's brother) to accompany them to U.P. as they wanted him to identify Harpal Singh who had been killed at the hands of the U.P. Police. The family members did not send harbhajan Singh alongwith the Police. However, on 7-7-1992, Harpal Singh's brother-in-law (wife's brother) Ajit Singh went alongwith the Police to Palia Police Station in U.P. The Police had already cremated the dead body before they reached there. The Police told that Harpal Singh and Gurjant Singh, resident of Village Chagli, alongwith two of their associates had been killed in an encounter with the Police of Police Station Palia, Police Post Chandan and Police Station Sampooran Nagar. According to the news item published in the newspapers, all the abovementioned youth had been killed in an encounter with the Police parties of these three Police Stations led by their respective SHOs under the overall command of DSP R.K. Chaturvedi. The Police handed over the ashes of Harpal Singh and Gurjant Singh to their next-of-kin and got them identified also from them by showing them the photographs of their dead bodies.

After Harpal Singh had been killed, the Police of Sherpur and Malerkotla began raiding his house with a view to arrest his wife Gurjit Kaur. Gurjit Kaur remained away from home for 2-3 months. Ultimately, her relatives approached DSP Malerkotla and produced her before him. He recorded her statement and set her free.

    *     Gurjit Kaur told that they did not know whether the U.P. Police had arrested her husband and other youth killed alongwith him and then killed them or they were killed in a genuine encounter. Gurjit Kaur told that when her brother Ajit Singh was taken to U.P. for identifying his body and to collect his ashes, he was informed by the people of the area that the news item about the said encounter, which was got published by the Police, was false. The people told that Harpal Singh, Gurjant Singh and two other youth were arrested after the Police had surrounded a bus. Some people told that those youth had committed suicide by consuming cyanide. But, the Police concocted a story of an encounter, later on. Gurjit Kaur said, "God only knows the truth!"

**VFF/0871**

Gulab Singh alias Gulaba 35 of Mullowal, Dhuri of Sangrur. Sajjan Singh (victim Gulab Singh's father) is an old man of 80 years, resident of Village Mullowal in District Sangrur. His son Gulab Singh, after passing his Matriculation examination, joined a two year Diploma course for Religious Preacher at the Missionary College, Damdama Sahib. Thereafter, Gulab Singh started working as a Granthi (one who recites Gurbani). This was his only source of livelihood. He was a religious minded peerson and a thorough gentleman. He often used to visit various Gurdwaras and attend various religious functions. His family members pressed him hard for getting married but he did not agree at all. His father Sajjan Singh told that his son had no link whatsoever with any sort of political or militant activities. His father emphasised that his son had no link whatsoever with militancy. According to Sajjan Singh, he was a gentle and shy youth.

Sajjan Singh told that about 10-12 years ago, three days before Baisakhi, he (Gulab Singh) had gone away from home saying that he was going to the Baisakhi fair at Damdama Sahib Talwandi Sabo. But, there was no trace of him after that. As the Investigation Team urged Sajjan Singh to recollect the year in which Gulab Singh had gone away from home, he told that it was three days before Baisakhi in the year when President of Shiromani Akali Dal, Sant Harchand Singh Longowal was killed at the hands of the militants. Harchand Singh Longowal was killed by the militants on 20 August 1985. If Sajjan Singh had recollected the year of this incident correctly, then Gulab Singh must have gone away from home on 10 April, 1985. According to Sajjan Singh, thereafter they did not get any information about his whereabouts. He further told that once the Sherpur Police had picked up his younger son and directed him to produce Gulab Singh. But they told the Police that they did not know about his whereabouts. Then the Police released his son.

According to Sajjan Singh, they did not know anything more than this as to what happened to Gulab Singh, after all. Neither the Police have told them anything so far. However, thereafter, the Police also never visited their house. But, he believes that Gulab Singh had been killed by the Police only.

**VFF/0872**

Avtar Singh alias Tari 28 of Mander Dona, Sandhu Chatha in Kapurthala. The case of Avtar Singh Mander is linked to that of Jagwinder Singh Happy, an Advocate (Attorney) of Kapurthala. The proof of the arrest of Avtar Singh Mander has come to the fore in a report of the CBI inquiry into the case of Happy.

**VFF/0873**

Gurcharan Singh alias Charna of Rode in Moga. He was picked up from his residence at 8 P.M. in a Gypsy by Police of Bagha Purana (Sadar) police station.

**VFF/0874**

Jaswant Singh alias Boongar 25 of Budhsinghwala, Baghapurana in Moga. In April 1993, he was picked up by ASI Tehal Singh of Bagha Wala Police Station while he was going in his tractor trolley in the village. They brought him back to home the same day.

The following additional information related to this case has been collected by Amrik Singh Muktsar in November, 1999. The true translation of the same is appended below:-

Nachhatter Singh (victim Jaswant Singh's father) and Chand Singh sons of Late Kehar Singh were farmers and residing at village Budhsingh Wala. Nachhatter Singh had six children-four sons namely Jagroop Singh (36 years), Kulwant Singh (deceased), Gurjant Singh (deceased) and Jaswant Singh (disappeared). Chand Singh was unmarried and he used to live with his brother's family. Nachhatter Singh had two daughters namely Charanjit Kaur (married) and Gurdeep Kaur (expired). The uncle ('Chacha') of Nachhatter Singh and Chand Singh, S. Karnail Singh (since deceased) also used to live at village Budhsingh Wala. His sons namely Gurcharan Singh and Visakha Singh had expired. Now only his grandsons live at village Budhsingh Wala. Karnail Singh was an "Amritdhari" (Baptised) Sikh. Apart from being religious minded he used to take active part in the political programmes of Shiromani Akali Dal. He had taken a very active part in the 'Dharam Yudh Morcha' (Religious War Front) launched by Shiromani Akali Dal in 1982. He was close to Sant Jarnail Singh Bhindranwale.

In May 1984, the B.S.F. (Border Security Force) had laid seige to Gurdwara Bibi Kahn Kaur in Moga city which continued for a number of days. The Akali and Sikh Students Federation workers who had been trapped inside were fired at, killing nine persons on the spot. Karnail Singh was one of them. The bodies of Karnail Singh and others were not handed over to their respective families.

It was in those days that Gurjant Singh son of Nachhatter Singh and grandson (in relation) of Karnail Singh became politically active after the death of Karnail Singh at the hands of the B.S.F. and began living in the office of the Sikh Students Federation at Gurdwara Singh Sabha in Moga City along with other youth. In June 1984 during the Army attack on Sri Darbar Sahib at Amritsar and 38 other Gurdwaras, the Army arrested Gurjant Singh along with his other companions from Gurdwara Singh Sabha, Moga. The police implicated Gurjant Singh in many cases apart from booking him under N.S.A. and sent him to Ferozepur jail. Later on, he got released on bail.

In the meantime i.e. during the time Gurjant Singh was incarcerated in jail, Chand Singh (brother of Nachhatter Singh) remained fully active politically and the police used to arrest Chand Singh often, due to political reasons. However the police did not arrest any other member of the family during this time. Chand Singh was very religious minded and he had a thorough knowledge of Sikh tenets. He had received religious education from Sant Mian Singh Jheeri Wale Dera. Though Chand Singh was a farmer, yet, he often used to attend various functions for preaching Sikhism.

While Gurjant Singh was in jail, one of his cousins namely Jagga Singh s/o Major Singh s/o Mehar Singh also joined the militant ranks and he was absconding at the time of release of Gurjant Singh.

After the release of Gurjant Singh from jail, Bagha Purana police began raiding Nachhatter Singh's house for arresting Gurjant Singh. Once, the SHO (Station House Officer) of Bagha Purana police station Mr. Madan Lal Dhingra picked up Gurjant Singh and took him to Bagha Purana P.S. (Police Station). From there he was taken to Jaiton P.S. and then to Faridkot C.I.A. (Central Investigation Agency) Staff where he was detained illegally for 10 days. He was tortured brutally at Jaiton P.S. and CIA Staff Faridkot. He was got released from the CIA Staff by the family members and the Panchayat but on the next day itself, SHO of Bagha Purana P.S. raided his house. However, Gurjant Singh had not slept at his house that day. The police picked up Nachhatter Singh and detained him for 15 days. The police asked them to produce Gurjant Singh but Gurjant Singh had absconded once for all. When the family members talked to Gurjant Singh about producing himself before the police, he said, "These people (the police) will kill me. As such, I will not present myself before them now." The family members also felt that there was some logic in his argument, so, they also did not put much pressure on him to present himself before the police.

A few days after Gurjant Singh had absconded, his cousin Jagga Singh s/o Major Singh s/o Mehar Singh was arrested by the police. The Faridkot and Ferozepur police slapped several cases against him and sent him to Sangrur jail where he was detained for 3 years. In the meantime, the police arrested Gurjant Singh's brother Kulwant Singh, implicated him in several cases and sent him to Sangrur jail. Kulwant Singh had been tortured brutally by Faridkot police. As such he was in bad shape physically while in jail.

After Gurjant Singh had absconded in 1986, the police used to pick up his family members. They used to pick up his father Nachhatter Singh, brothers and uncle Chand Singh often and detain them illegally for days together. Once, the SHO of Bagha Purana police station Mr. Gurtej Singh picked up his mother Surjit Kaur also and released her on the following day.

In 1987, a person namely Jarnail Singh was murdered by someone. The police turned the needle of their suspicion towards Chand Singh and Gurjant Singh. keeping in view such an attitude of the police,

Chand Singh also began to remain away from his house. As a result, the police began raidsing his house more frequently. In May 1987, under the leadership of Ray-Ribiero combine the police repression was intensified in Punjab and political workers were arrested in large numbers under TADA (Terrorist & Disruptive Activities (Prevention) Act). During this time, the SHO of Bagha Purana police station Mitt Singh (who was later killed by militants) arrested Gurjant Singh's father Nachhatter Singh and tortured him brutally for 10 days in illegal custody at Bagha Purana police station. Thereafter he implicated him in a case under TADA (that of giving shelter to militants) and sent him to Ferozepur jail. In the meantime, the police began to raid their house regularly. All the family members went underground. The police carried away all household goods including the main gate of the house. None of the family members returned home for complete three years and grass came up all over the house. No agricultural operations could be carried out for three years. Nobody dared to take their land on contract for cultivation due to the fear of the police.

In 1990, slowly, some members of Gurjant Singh's family began to return home and started cultivating their land. But, the fear of the police was still there and none of the male members used to sleep at home. While Gurjant Singh was absconding, the police arrested his sister Charanjit Kaur and brother-in-law (sister's husband) Sukhdev Singh Fauji resident of Kale Ke several times. The police tortured also Sukhdev Singh several times. Apart from that, the police used to pick up his other relatives also like aunts ('Maami', 'Bhua') and uncle ('Phuphar'). Not only that they used to pick up the relatives of their relatives also.

In 1987, while Gurjant Singh's father was in Ferozepur jail, the police arrested Chand Singh from village Ghall Kalan along with 4 other youth including Kuldip Singh r/o village Ghall Kalan from whose tubewell all the five were arrested. About 10 days after their arrest all of them were killed in an "encounter" with the police. At that time, all the family members and relatives were target of police wrath and all of them were homeless. Chand Singh's case could not be pursued. The family members had come to know about Chand Singh's arrest after 2-3 days. 10 days later they read the news in the newspapers about his having been killed in an "encounter" with the police.

In the meantime, Gurjant Singh's brother Kulwant Singh and cousin Jagga Singh were released from Sangrur jail. Even after his release, Kulwant Singh was picked up and tortured brutally by Bagha Purana police several times. Jagga Singh absconded from home 2-3 months after his release and ultimately he was killed in an encounter with the police at village Chhajanwali near Jagraon. During this period, Gurjant Singh's elder brother Jagroop Singh was also picked up several times and subjected to brutal torture by the police.

On 29 July 1992, Gurjant Singh was killed in an encounter with the police at the house of Kaur Singh in Model Town (Extension) at Ludhiana. However, his family remained the target of police wrath even thereafter. The police neither handed over the body of Gurjant Singh to the family members nor got it identified from them. The police put several restrictions on the family even at the time of his 'Bhog' (last rites) ceremony. Only his family memebrs were allowed to attend the same. Even after Gurjant Singh had been killed, Bagha Purana police continued to raid their house and they used to pick up Nachhatter Singh, Jagroop Singh, Kulwant Singh and Jaswant Singh, often. During this period the Bagha Purana police slapped a case under Arms Act against Jaswant Singh and sent him to jail. He was in jail for two months and thereafter he was released on bail.

In 1993, during the Panchayat elections in the Punjab, DSP (Deputy Superintendent of Police) Randhawa of Bagha Purana police arrested Binder Singh s/o Lal Singh, a Mazhabi Sikh and a worker of Jagroop Singh (Gurjant Singh's brother) and detained him for 15 days at the CIA Staff Bagha Purana. Thereafter, he implicated him in a case under the Arms Act and delivering provocative anti-national speeches and sent him to jail. He could be got released on bail only after one month. Now he has been acquitted in that case.

In April 1993, Havaldar (Head Constable) Jagraj Singh of Bagha Purana police along with some constables came in a Canter (four-wheeler), picked up Jaswant Singh on the way who was driving a Tractor and brought him to home to inform the family members that he was taking away Jaswant Singh to the police station as he had been summoned by the officers. After the arrest of Jaswant Singh, his father Nachhatter Singh along with the Sarpanch (Head of Village Council) of the village, Kirpal Singh reached police station Bagha Purana. They met the SHO Mr. Tehal Singh who said, "We will release him in the evening." Nachhatter Singh and the Sarpanch met Jaswant Singh in the police station. Jaswant Singh took off his watch and handed it over to Nachhatter Singh. Same day evening, Nachhater Singh was also picked up from his house by Bagha Purana police. Again the male members of the family began to remain away from home, due to fear. They sent respectable persons to the SHO several times. However, the SHO always used to say, "You don't talk to me about those people at all."

Nachhatter Singh was detained at different police stations and secret (torture) centres. During this period, he was subjected to inhuman torture several times in the presence of SSP (Senior Superintendent of Police) Tiwari, SP (Ops.) Shri Anil Gautam. Six months later, the Bagha Purana police dropped him at his house. At that time, his physical condition was very bad. He could recover only after medical treatment for several months. It was Head Constable Jugraj Singh who had come to drop Nachhatter Singh at home and he said, "You don't waste money in pursuing his case. Jaswant Singh is no more." The family members accepted it as the Will of God. Of course, they did not have any other alternative either.

In 1995, one day, Kulwant Singh who had started getting fits of insanity due to repeated police torture and whose health had deteriorated too much, breathed his last after a prolonged illness. According to family members the actual reason of Kulwant's death was the repeated police torture. Kulwant Singh was married and has a son namely Bhupinder Singh aged nine years. His wife's parents had got her remarried. Now Nachhatter Singh's elder son Jagroop Singh only is left in their family.

### VFF/0875

Sadhu Singh alias Naik Singh 23 of G T B Garh Rode, Baghapurana in Moga. On 26-11-90 at 4.35 P.M., he was bringing the vehicle of Singh Sahib Bhai Jasbir Singh from Anandpur Sahib along with Jaswant Singh s/o Jagga Singh r/o Rode (Kothe). ASI Gurmel Singh had laid a Naka near Bughipura Chowk. The Police stopped their car and made Sadhu Singh to get down from it. The Police told Jaswant Singh to take the vehicle (Ambassador car No. PJO-656). Jaswant Singh came home and informed his family. Next day, his brother Gurcharan Singh, Preetam Singh Veroke, and Inderpal Singh, Chairman Market Committee, met the DSP Randhawa at C.I.A. Moga. He denied having arrested him. 4-5 days later, brother Gurcharan Singh along with former Chief Minister Harcharan Singh Brar, met SSP Faridkot, Swaran Singh Ghotna, at his residence. Brar Sahib came out after meeting the SSP and told that he had promised to release him after 4-5 days. After a few days, a 'Khula Darbar' was held by DC Faridkot at our village. His brother Gurcharan Singh raised the matter of his arrest and submitted an application also. The DC told that they would let us know something within 5-7 days. After 5-7 days, we received a letter from the DC. We went to his Office but nothing was intimated to us (regarding Sadhu Singh).

**VFF/0876**

Varinder Singh 28 of Nathewala, Baghapurana in Moga. Mukhtiar Kaur (mother of the victim Varinder Singh) had three sons and one daughter. One of her sons, namely Varinder Singh was killed in an encounter with the Police and later on, the Police abducted her husband Jang Singh whose whereabouts are not known till today. Her daughter Sarbjit Kaur died due to illness.

Her eldest son Varinder Singh was active in the Sikh Students Federation since 1987. That is why the Police used to arrest him often. The Police had arrested him and registered cases against him on two different occasions. He was incarcerated in Faridkot Jail for about two years. The family members do not remember the dates of his detention in the Jail. After his release from Jail he stayed at home for 8-9 months. The Police had started harassing him again. They used to pick him up and torture him. As such, he deserted home and joined the ranks of the militants, once for all.

On 31-12-1990, Varinder Singh was killed in an encounter with the Police near VIllage Daulatpura Kalia Wala in district Ferozepur. The Police could not lay their hands on his dead body. His accomplices handed over his dead body to his family members at his house on the following day. The family members cremated his dead body. The Police got a scent of it. As a consequence his family became a victim of Police wrath. The Police picked up his mother Mukhtiar Kaur, father Jang Singh and both the brothers and subjected them to brutal torture.

**VFF/0877**

Chand Singh 45 of Budhsinghwala in Moga. Nachhatter Singh and Chand Singh sons of Late Kehar Singh were farmers and residing at village Budhsingh Wala. Nachhatter Singh had six children-four sons namely Jagroop Singh (36 years), Kulwant Singh (deceased), Gurjant Singh (deceased) and Jaswant Singh (disappeared). Chand Singh was unmarried and he used to live with his brother's family. Nachhatter Singh had two daughters namely Charanjit Kaur (married) and Gurdeep Kaur (expired). The uncle ('Chacha') of Nachhatter Singh and Chand Singh, S. Karnail Singh (since deceased) also used to live at village Budhsingh Wala. His sons namely Gurcharan Singh and Visakha Singh had expired. Now only his grandsons live at village Budhsingh Wala. Karnail Singh was an "Amritdhari" (Baptised) Sikh. Apart from being religious minded he used to take active part in the political programmes of Shiromani Akali Dal. He had taken a very active part in the 'Dharam Yudh Morcha' (political agitation) launched by Shiromani Akali Dal in 1982. He was close to Sant Jarnail Singh Bhindranwale.

In May 1984, the B.S.F. (Border Security Force) had laid seige to Gurdwara Bibi Kahn Kaur in Moga city which continued for a number of days. The Akali and Sikh Students Federation workers who had been trapped inside were fired at, killing nine persons on the spot. Karnail Singh was one of them. The bodies of Karnail Singh and others were not handed over to their respective families.

It was in those days that Gurjant Singh son of Nachhatter Singh and grandson (in relation) of Karnail Singh became politically active after the death of Karnail Singh at the hands of the B.S.F. and began living in the office of the Sikh Students Federation at Gurdwara Singh Sabha in Moga City along with other youth. In June 1984 during the Army attack on Sri Darbar Sahib at Amritsar and 38 other Gurdawaras, the Army arrested Gurjant Singh along with his other companions from Gurdwara Singh Sabha, Moga. The police implicated Gurjant Singh in many cases apart from booking him under N.S.A. and sent him to Ferozepur jail. Later on, he got released on bail.

In the meantime i.e. during the time Gurjant Singh was incarcerated in jail, Chand Singh (brother of Nachhatter Singh) remained fully active politically and the police used to arrest Chand Singh often, due to political reasons. However the police did not arrest any other member of the family during this time. Chand Singh was very religious minded and he had a thorough knowledge of Sikh tenets. He had received religious education from Sant Mian Singh Jheeri Wale Dera. Though Chand Singh was a farmer, yet, he often used to attend various functions for preaching Sikhism.

While Gurjant Singh was in jail, one of his cousins namely Jagga Singh s/o Major Singh s/o Mehar Singh also joined the militant ranks and he was absconding at the time of release of Gurjant Singh.

After the release of Gurjant Singh from jail, Bagha Purana police began raiding Nachhatter Singh's house for arresting Gurjant Singh. Once, the SHO (Station House Officer) of Bagha Purana police station Mr. Madan Lal Dhingra picked up Gurjant Singh and took him to Bagha Purana P.S. (Police Station). From there he was taken to Jaiton P.S. and then to Faridkot C.I.A. (Central Investigation Agency) Staff where he was detained illegally for 10 days. He was tortured brutally at Jaiton P.S. and CIA Staff Faridkot. He was got released from the CIA STaff by the family members and the Panchayat but on the next day itself, SHO of Bagha Purana P.S. raided his house. However, Gurjant Singh had not slept at his house that day. The police picked up Nachhatter Singh and detained him for 15 days. The police asked them to produce Gurjant Singh but Gurjant Singh had absconded once for all. When the family members talked to Gurjant Singh about producing himself before the police, he said, "These people (the police) will kill me. As such, I will not present myself before them now." The family members also felt that there was some logic in his argument, so, they also did not put much pressure on him to present himself before the police.

A few days after Gurjant Singh had absconded, his cousin Jagga Singh s/o Major Singh s/o Mehar Singh was arrested by the police. The Faridkot and Ferozepur police slapped several cases against him and sent him to Sangrur jail where he was detained for 3 years. In the meantime, the police arrested Gurjant Singh's brother Kulwant Singh, implicated him in several cases and sent him to Sangrur jail. Kulwant Singh had been tortured brutally by Faridkot police. As such he was in bad shape physically while in jail.

After Gurjant Singh had absconded in 1986, the police used to pick up his family members. They used to pick up his father Nachhatter Singh, brothers and uncle Chand Singh often and detain them illegally for days together. Once, the SHO of Bagha Purana police station Mr. Gurtej Singh picked up his mother Surjit Kaur also and released her on the following day.

In 1987, a person namely Jarnail Singh was murdered by someone. The police turned the needle of their suspicion towards Chand Singh and Gurjant Singh. keeping in view such an attitude of the police, Chand Singh also began to remain away from his house. As a result, the police began raidsing his house more frequently. In May 1987, under the leadership of Ray-Ribiero combine the police repression was intensified in Punjab and political workers were arrested in large numbers under TADA (Terrorist & Disruptive Activities (Prevention) Act). During this time, the SHO of Bagha Purana police station Mitt Singh (who was later killed by militants) arrested Gurjant Singh's father Nachhatter Singh and tortured him brutally for 10 days in illegal custody at Bagha Purana police station. Thereafter he implicated him in a case under TADA (that of giving shelter to militants) and sent him to Ferozepur jail. In the meantime, the police began to raid their house regularly. All the family members went underground. The police carried away all household goods including the main gate of the house. None of the family members returned home for complete three years and grass came up all over the house. No agricultural operations could be carried out for three years. Nobody dared to take their land on contract for cultivation due to the fear of the police.

In 1990, slowly, some members of Gurjant Singh's family began to return home and started cultivating their land. But, the fear of the police was still there and none of the male members used to sleep at home. While Gurjant Singh was absconding, the police arrested his sister Charanjit Kaur and brother-in-law (sister's husband) Sukhdev Singh Fauji resident of Kale Ke several times. The police tortured also Sukhdev Singh several times. Apart from that, the police used to pick up his other relatives also like aunts ('Maami', 'Bhua') and uncle ('Phuphar'). Not only that they used to pick up the relatives of their relatives also.

In 1987, while Gurjant Singh's father was in Ferozepur jail, the police arrested Chand Singh from village Ghall Kalan along with 4 other youth including Kuldip Singh r/o village Ghall Kalan from whose tubewell all the five were arrested. About 10 days after their arrest all of them were killed in an "encounter" with the police. At that time, all the family members and relatives were target of police wrath and all of them were homeless. Chand Singh's case could not be pursued. The family members had come to know about Chand Singh's arrest after 2-3 days. 10 days later they read the news in the newspapers about his having been killed in an "encounter" with the police.

In the maentime, Gurjant Singh's brother Kulwant Singh and cousin Jagga Singh were released from Sangrur jail. Even after his release, Kulwant Singh was picked up and tortured brutally by Bagha Purana police several times. Jagga Singh absconded from home 2-3 months after his release and ultimately he was killed in an encounter with the police at village Chhajanwali near Jagraon. During this period, Gurjant Singh's elder brother Jagroop Singh was also picked up several times and subjected to brutal torture by the police.

On 29 July 1992, Gurjant Singh was killed in an encounter with the police at the house of Kaur Singh in Model Town (Extension) at Ludhiana. However, his family remained the target of police wrath even thereafter. The police neither handed over the body of Gurjant Singh to the family members nor got it identified from them. The police put several restrictions on the family even at the time of his 'Bhog' (last rites) ceremony. Only his family memebrs were allowed to attend the same. Even after Gurjant Singh had been killed, Bagha Purana police continued to raid their house and they used to pick up Nachhatter Singh, Jagroop Singh, Kulwant Singh and Jaswant Singh, often. During this period the Bagha Purana police slapped a case under Arms Act against Jaswant Singh and sent him to jail. He was in jail for two months and thereafter he was released on bail.

In 1993, during the Panchayat elections in the Punjab, DSP (Deputy Superintendent of Police) Randhawa of Bagha Purana police arrested

Binder Singh s/o Lal Singh, a Mazhabi Sikh and a worker of Jagroop Singh (Gurjant Singh's brother) and detained him for 15 days at the CIA Staff Bagha Purana. Thereafter, he implicated him in a case under the Arms Act and delivering provocative anti-national speeches and sent him to jail. He could be got released on bail only after one month. Now he has been acquitted in that case.

In April 1993, Havaldar (Head Constable) Jagraj Singh of Bagha Purana police along with some constables came in a Canter (four-wheeler), picked up Jaswant Singh on the way who was driving a Tractor and brought him to home to inform the family members that he was taking away Jaswant Singh to the police station as he had been summoned by the officers. After the arrest of Jaswant Singh, his father Nachhatter Singh along with the Sarpanch (Head of Village Council) of the village, Kirpal Singh reached police station Bagha Purana. They met the SHO Mr. Tehal Singh who said, "We will release him in the evening." Nachhatter Singh and the Sarpanch met Jaswant Singh in the police station. Jaswant Singh took off his watch and handed it over to Nachhatter Singh. Same day evening, Nachhater Singh was also picked up from his house by Bagha Purana police. Again the male members of the family began to remain away from home, due to fear. They sent respectable persons to the SHO several times. However, the SHO always used to say, "You don't talk to me about those people at all."

Nachhatter Singh was detained at different police stations and secret (torture) centres. During this period, he was subjected to inhuman torture several times in the presence of SSP (Senior Superintendent of Police) Tiwari, SP (Ops.) Shri Anil Gautam. Six months later, the Bagha Purana police dropped him at his house. At that time, his physical condition was very bad. He could recover only after medical treatment for several months. It was Head Constable Jugraj Singh who had come to drop Nachhatter Singh at home and he said, "You don't waste money in pursuing his case. Jaswant Singh is no more." The family members accepted it as the Will of God. Of course, they did not have any other alternative either.

In 1995, one day, Kulwant Singh who had started getting fits of insanity due to repeated police torture and whose health had deteriorated too much, breathed his last after a prolonged illness. According to family members the actual reason of Kulwant's death was the repeated police torture. Kulwant Singh was married and has a son namely Bhupinder Singh aged nine years. His wife's parents had got her remarried. Now Nachhatter Singh's elder son Jagroop Singh only is left in their family.

### VFF/0878

Sukhdev Singh alias Sukha 24 of Sangatpura, Baghapurana in Moga. Sukhdev Singh had deserted home about three years prior to his arrest. The police had got him declared a proclaimed offender on the allegation of his involvement in militant activities. The police used to pick up his father Mohinder Singh, mother Surjit Kaur, relatives Gian Singh (maternal uncle), Deewan Singh (maternal uncle), Gajjan Singh (uncle—'Massar') and Mann Singh (uncle—'Phuphar') repeatedly and torture them brutally. Due to this repeated torture, the whole family went underground and lived incognito at Amritsar for three years. There, they read in the newspapers that Sukhdev Singh had been arrested at Rishikesh. At the time of his arrest, his accomplice, a renowned militant namely Kuldip Singh Shekhupura was said to have consumed cyanide. The family memebrs have lost those newspapers in which this news item had been published. But, since then, the police have not disclosed as to what happened to Sukhdev Singh.

* According to his father Mohinder Singh, after Sukhdev Singh absconded, he (Mohinder Singh) was picked up by the police numerous times. Sometimes, the police used to detain him in custody for months together. At the time of Rumanian Ambassador's abduction, 30 of their relatives had been arrested by Bagha Purana police and detained for one month.

* According to Mohinder Singh (father), the police have not left them alone yet. Often they come for inquiry. His children are not being issued with a passport. "If my son was a militant, they have eliminated him. Why the Government were bent upon ruining the future of my innocent children, now", he asks.

### VFF/0879

Sewak Singh 26 of Sangatpura, Baghapurana in Moga. According to the wife of Sewak Singh, Karamjit Kaur:-

"In November 1991, a few days after Diwali, one night at 12 Midnight or 1 AM, we were asleep in one of the rooms of our house when we heard the sound of knocking at the door and that of opening the door. My husband Sewak Singh opened the door. A large number of policemen barged into the room. They asked the name of my husband and tied his hands at his back with a bedsheet lying in the house. In my presence itself, the police officer accompanying the police party enquired the address of an absconding militant of our village namely Sukhdev Singh. My husband told that he did not know anything about him. The police party asked him to accompany them. Neither they disclosed it themselves nor I dared to ask them as to from which police station they had come. I was too scared. I followed them for some distance outside the house. The police put my husband in the vehicle and took him away. Two vehicles had been parked near our house and three-four others had been parked on the road."

On the following day, Karamjit Kaur went to her brother-in-law (sister's husband) Roop Singh at village Bhai Roopa and narrated the whole incident to him. Roop Singh along with two other persons went to police station Bagha Purana. The Bagha Purana police told them that they had not arrested him. Next day, Preetam Singh, Gej Singh and Naib Singh (brother of Sewak Singh) went to police station Mehna. Head Constable Zora Singh told them that their boy had been taken away by C.I.A. Staff Ferozepur; so they should go and enquire there. On the following day, Karamjit Kaur along with Gej Singh went to C I A Staff Ferozepur but they did not get any information from there.

According to Karamjit Kaur (wife), "On the next day, Dr. Iqbal Singh, Major Singh r/o Sangatpur and Banta Singh r/o Sangatpur went to the C.I.A. Staff Ferozepur and talked to some officer there. They came out and told us that the life of Sewak Singh could be saved if we could pay Rs. 20,000/- to the police. According to them, the police would then send Sewak Singh to jail but his life would be saved. But, we could not arrange the money. The above mentioned three persons only used to go inside and talk to the police. We don't know with which officer they had struck the deal. All the above three persons have since expired."

*    We had been to C.I.A. Staff Ferozepur along with relatives, Panchayat and Janta Dal leader Iqbal Singh several times.

*    About 8 days after his arrest, a Home Guard Jawan took Rs. 150/- bribe from us and showed Sewak Singh inside the C.I.A. Staff from a distance to Gej Singh and Malkit Singh.

*    Later on we along with the Panchayat, approached Inspector Daljit Singh several times. He declined the request of the Panchayat to release him and even hinted that they won't let him be alive. But, we don't know whether those Panchayat members would say so or not.

*    Long after Sewak Singh's arrest, Ram Singh, SHO of Makhu police station had told Preetam Singh and another person hailing from village Langeane that Sewak Singh was killed in the "encounter" at Makhu in which a total of 19 militants had been killed. He had further told them that it was the handiwork of Inspector Daljit Singh and he had no hand in

that. We can't say whether Preetam Singh would testify to it or not.

* When the investigation team (Amrik Singh Muktsar and other members) went to Sewak Singh's house, his wife called for Sewak Singh's cousin brother Gej Singh that he should come and give all the information to the investigation team. Gej Singh refused to come, due to fear. Then one of the members of the investigation team went to Gej Singh's house. On his persuasion he agreed hesitantly to give all the details. However, time and again he asked whether any harm would come to them due to giving this information to us.

* According to Sewak Singh's wife Karamjit Kaur, so far, no police officer had told her clearly as to what happened to Sewak Singh. She had been meeting the then SHO of Bagha Purana police station Tehal Singh also. He used to say that he (Sewak Singh) was innocent and that he would get him released. But so far let alone release her husband, nobody had told her as to what happened to him. She said that she was a poor woman who was bringing up her children by doing manual labour. So far, nobody had bothered about her and she had not received any help either.

* Karamjit Kaur (wife) told the investigation team that let alone release her husband, on the contrary, for about 3-4 months, the Bagha Purana police continued to visit her house and ask her about the whereabouts of Sewak Singh.

* 6-7 months after the arrest of Sewak Singh, Tehal Singh, SHO of Bagha Purana police station picked up his brother-in-law (sister's husband) Roop Singh r/o Bhai Roopa and tortured him brutally for 11 days in illegal custody. One of his legs got disabled due to the torture. Even today, he limps while walking.

* About one year prior to the arrest of Sewak Singh, one night, some armed persons (militants) had entered his house, pulled out his mother Amarjit Kaur and shot her dead outside in front of the house. Her all the four sons had received Rs. 1,00,000/- (One Lakh) as compensation for her death in that incident.

### VFF/0880

Gurjant Singh Budhwingh Wala alias Janta 27 of Budhsinghwala in Moga. Nachhatter Singh (victim Gurjant Singh's father) and Chand Singh sons of Late Kehar Singh were farmers and residing at village Budhsingh Wala. Nachhatter Singh had six children-four sons namely Jagroop Singh (36 years), Kulwant Singh (deceased), Gurjant Singh (deceased) and Jaswant Singh (disappeared). Chand Singh was unmarried and he used to live with his brother's family. Nachhatter Singh had two daughters namely Charanjit Kaur (married) and Gurdeep Kaur (expired). The uncle ('Chacha') of Nachhatter Singh and Chand Singh, S. Karnail Singh (since deceased) also used to live at village Budhsingh Wala. His sons namely Gurcharan Singh and Visakha Singh had expired. Now only his grandsons live at village Budhsingh Wala. Karnail Singh was an "Amritdhari" (Baptised) Sikh. Apart from being religious minded he used to take active part in the political programmes of Shiromani Akali Dal. He had taken a very active part in the 'Dharam Yudh Morcha' (political agitation) launched by Shiromani Akali Dal in 1982. He was close to Sant Jarnail Singh Bhindranwale.

In May 1984, the B.S.F. (Border Security Force) had laid seige to Gurdwara Bibi Kahn Kaur in Moga city which continued for a number of days. The Akali and Sikh Students Federation workers who had been trapped inside were fired at, killing nine persons on the spot. Karnail Singh was one of them. The bodies of Karnail Singh and others were not handed over to their respective families.

It was in those days that Gurjant Singh son of Nachhatter Singh and grandson (in relation) of Karnail Singh became politically active after the death of Karnail Singh at the hands of the B.S.F. and began living in the office of the Sikh Students Federation at Gurdwara Singh Sabha in Moga City along with other youth. In June 1984 during the Army attack on Sri Darbar Sahib at Amritsar and 38 other Gurdawaras, the Army arrested Gurjant Singh along with his other companions from Gurdwara Singh Sabha, Moga. The police implicated Gurjant Singh in many cases apart from booking him under N.S.A. and sent him to Ferozepur jail. Later on, he got released on bail.

In the meantime i.e. during the time Gurjant Singh was incarcerated in jail, Chand Singh (brother of Nachhatter Singh) remained fully active politically and the police used to arrest Chand Singh often, due to political reasons. However the police did not arrest any other member of the family during this time. Chand Singh was very religious minded and he had a thorough knowledge of Sikh tenets. He had received religious education from Sant Mian Singh Jheeri Wale Dera. Though Chand Singh was a farmer, yet, he often used to attend various functions for preaching Sikhism.

While Gurjant Singh was in jail, one of his cousins namely Jagga Singh s/o Major Singh s/o Mehar Singh also joined the militant ranks and he was absconding at the time of release of Gurjant Singh.

After the release of Gurjant Singh from jail, Bagha Purana police began raiding Nachhatter Singh's house for arresting Gurjant Singh. Once, the SHO (Station House Officer) of Bagha Purana police station Mr. Madan Lal Dhingra picked up Gurjant Singh and took him to Bagha Purana P.S. (Police Station). From there he was taken to Jaiton P.S. and then to Faridkot C.I.A. (Central Investigation Agency) Staff where he was detained illegally for 10 days. He was tortured brutally at Jaiton P.S. and C.I.A Staff Faridkot. He was got released from the C.I.A Staff by the family members and the Panchayat but on the next day itself, SHO of Bagha Purana P.S. raided his house. However, Gurjant Singh had not slept at his house that day. The police picked up Nachhatter Singh and detained him for 15 days. The police asked them to produce Gurjant Singh but Gurjant Singh had absconded once for all. When the family members talked to Gurjant Singh about producing himself before the police, he said, "These people (the police) will kill me. As such, I will not present myself before them now." The family members also felt that there was some logic in his argument, so, they also did not put much pressure on him to present himself before the police.

A few days after Gurjant Singh had absconded, his cousin Jagga Singh s/o Major Singh s/o Mehar Singh was arrested by the police. The Faridkot and Ferozepur police slapped several cases against him and sent him to Sangrur jail where he was detained for 3 years. In the meantime, the police arrested Gurjant Singh's brother Kulwant Singh, implicated him in several cases and sent him to Sangrur jail. Kulwant Singh had been tortured brutally by Faridkot police. As such he was in bad shape physically while in jail.

After Gurjant Singh had absconded in 1986, the police used to pick up his family members. They used to pick up his father Nachhatter Singh, brothers and uncle Chand Singh often and detain them illegally for days together. Once, the SHO of Bagha Purana police station, Mr. Gurtej Singh, picked up his mother Surjit Kaur also and released her on the following day.

In 1987, a person namely Jarnail Singh was murdered by someone. The police turned the needle of their suspicion towards Chand Singh and Gurjant Singh. Keeping in view such an attitude of the police, Chand Singh also began to remain away from his house. As a result, the police began raidsing his house more frequently. In May 1987, under the leadership of Ray-Ribiero combine the police repression was intensified in Punjab and political workers were arrested in large numbers under TADA (Terrorist & Disruptive Activities (Prevention) Act). During this time, the SHO of Bagha Purana police station Mitt Singh (who was later killed by militants) arrested Gurjant Singh's father Nachhatter Singh and tortured him brutally for 10 days in illegal custody at Bagha Purana police station. Thereafter he implicated him in a case under TADA (that of giving shelter to militants) and sent him to Ferozepur jail. In the meantime, the police began to raid their house regularly. All the family members went underground. The police carried away all household goods including the main gate of the house. None of the family members returned home for complete three years and grass came up all over the house. No agricultural operations could be carried out for three years. Nobody dared to take their land on contract for cultivation due to the fear of the police.

In 1990, slowly, some members of Gurjant Singh's family began to return home and started cultivating their land. But, the fear of the police was still there and none of the male members used to sleep at home. While Gurjant Singh was absconding, the police arrested his sister Charanjit Kaur and brother-in-law (sister's husband) Sukhdev Singh Fauji resident of Kale Ke several times. The police tortured also Sukhdev Singh several times. Apart from that, the police used to pick up his other relatives also like aunts ('Maami', 'Bhua') and uncle ('Phuphar'). Not only that they used to pick up the relatives of their relatives also.

In 1987, while Gurjant Singh's father was in Ferozepur jail, the police arrested Chand Singh from village Ghall Kalan along with 4 other youth including Kuldip Singh r/o village Ghall Kalan from whose tubewell all the five were arrested. About 10 days after their arrest all of them were killed in an "encounter" with the police. At that time, all the family members and relatives were target of police wrath and all of them were homeless. Chand Singh's case could not be pursued. The family members had come to know about Chand Singh's arrest after 2-3 days. 10 days later they read the news in the newspapers about his having been killed in an "encounter" with the police.

In the maentime, Gurjant Singh's brother Kulwant Singh and cousin Jagga Singh were released from Sangrur jail. Even after his release, Kulwant Singh was picked up and tortured brutally by Bagha Purana police several times. Jagga Singh absconded from home 2-3 months after his release and ultimately he was killed in an encounter with the police at village Chhajanwali near Jagraon. During this period, Gurjant Singh's elder brother Jagroop Singh was also picked up several times and subjected to brutal torture by the police.

On 29 July 1992, Gurjant Singh was killed in an encounter with the police at the house of Kaur Singh in Model Town (Extension) at Ludhiana. However, his family remained the target of police wrath even thereafter. The police neither handed over the body of Gurjant Singh to the family members nor got it identified from them. The police put several restrictions on the family even at the time of his 'Bhog' (last rites) ceremony. Only his family memebrs were allowed to attend the same. Even after Gurjant Singh had been killed, Bagha Purana police continued to raid their house and they used to pick up Nachhatter Singh, Jagroop Singh, Kulwant Singh and Jaswant Singh, often. During this period the Bagha Purana police slapped a case under Arms Act against Jaswant Singh and sent him to jail. He was in jail for two months and thereafter he was released on bail.

In 1993, during the Panchayat elections in the Punjab, DSP (Deputy Superintendent of Police) Randhawa of Bagha Purana police arrested Binder Singh s/o Lal Singh, a Mazhabi Sikh and a worker of Jagroop Singh (Gurjant Singh's brother) and detained him for 15 days at the C.I.A Staff Bagha Purana. Thereafter, he implicated him in a case under the Arms Act and delivering provocative anti-national speeches and sent him to jail. He could be got released on bail only after one month. Now he has been acquitted in that case.

In April 1993, Havaldar (Head Constable) Jagraj Singh of Bagha Purana police along with some constables came in a Canter (four-wheeler), picked up Jaswant Singh on the way who was driving a Tractor and brought him to home to inform the family members that he was taking away Jaswant Singh to the police station as he had been summoned by the officers. After the arrest of Jaswant Singh, his father Nachhatter Singh along with the Sarpanch (Head of Village Council) of the village, Kirpal Singh reached police station Bagha Purana. They met the SHO Mr. Tehal Singh who said, "We will release him in the evening." Nachhatter Singh and the Sarpanch met Jaswant Singh in the police station. Jaswant Singh took off his watch and handed it over to Nachhatter Singh. Same day evening, Nachhater Singh was also picked up from his house by Bagha Purana police. Again the male members of the family began to remain away from home, due to fear. They sent respectable persons to the SHO several times. However, the SHO always used to say, "You don't talk to me about those people at all."

Nachhatter Singh was detained at different police stations and secret (torture) centres. During this period, he was subjected to inhuman torture several times in the presence of SSP (Senior Superintendent of Police) Tiwari, SP (Ops.) Shri Anil Gautam. Six months later, the Bagha

Purana police dropped him at his house. At that time, his physical condition was very bad. He could recover only after medical treatment for several months. It was Head Constable Jugraj Singh who had come to drop Nachhatter Singh at home and he said, "You don't waste money in pursuing his case. Jaswant Singh is no more." The family members accepted it as the Will of God. Of course, they did not have any other alternative either.

In 1995, one day, Kulwant Singh who had started getting fits of insanity due to repeated police torture and whose health had deteriorated too much, breathed his last after a prolonged illness. According to family members the actual reason of Kulwant's death was the repeated police torture. Kulwant Singh was married and has a son namely Bhupinder Singh aged nine years. His wife's parents had got her remarried. Now Nachhatter Singh's elder son Jagroop Singh only is left in their family.

### VFF/0881

Kamaljit Singh alias Mintu 21 of Budhsinghwala in Moga. Victim Kamaljit Singh's father Ajmer Singh is an Ex-Serviceman who had retired from the Army in 1985. He had three sons and two daughters. His second son Kamaljit Singh had studied upto Matric at the Govt. High School Bagha Purana and had failed in Matric exam in 1989. Thereafter he abandoned studies and started helping the family by doing manual labour.

In the beginning of July 1991, one day, SHO of Nihalsingh Wala raided his house and arrested Kamaljit Singh. He was detained illegally for 15 days. Thereafter they registered FIR No. 64 dated 15-7-91 against him u/s 25/54/59 of Arms Act, 3/4 of TADA (P) Act and FIR No. 62 dated 15-7-91 u/s 307/353/186/34 IPC and 25/54/59 of Arms Act, 5/6 of TADA (P) Act at police station Nihalsingh Wala and sent him to jail. He got released on bail after 5-6 months. In the meantime, Dharamkot police had also registered a case against Kamaljit Singh. After his release, Kamaljit Singh used to attend court regularly in connection with his cases. 2-3 months later, he was arrested again and implicated in cases by Bagha Purana and Jaiton police and sent to jail. He got released on bail in those cases also. After his release, Kamaljit stayed at home.

On 27-7-92 at about 8 PM, the police raided his house. On seeing the police, he ran away. The police party which was led by ASI Gurcharan Singh and Head Constable Jugraj Singh arrested Ajmer Singh (father), Rajinder Singh (brother) and Paramjit Singh (brother) and took them to Bagha Purana police station. There the SHO Tehal Singh told Ajmer Singh to produce his son before the police.

On 28-7-92, the village Sarpanch (Head of village Council) Kirpal Singh and other respectable persons went to the police station and talked to the SHO. The SHO released Ajmer Singh on the condition that he would trace out his son (Kamaljit) and produce him before the police by evening. The Panchayat also advised Ajmer Singh to produce Kamaljit Singh. In the evening, Ajmer Singh along with Kirpal Singh (Sarpanch), Chand Singh (Member Panchayat), Darshan Singh (Member Panchayat) and 10-15 other persons went to the police station Bagha Purana. The SHO was not present at that time. The above mentioned Panchayat members produced Kamaljit Singh before the Head Constable Jugraj Singh. Head Constable Jugraj Singh released Rajinder Singh and Paramjit Singh.

On 29-7-92 at 8 AM, Ajmer Singh went to the Bagha Purana police station. There he met Kamaljit Singh and served him tea also. Similarly on 30-7-92 also Ajmer Singh met Kamaljit Singh at the police station. On the following day (31-7-92), when Ajmer Singh went to the police station he was not allowed to enter the police station. After some time Ajmer Singh met SHO Tehal Singh who told him that Head Constable Jugraj Singh would let him know about his son. But when Ajmer Singh met Jugraj Singh, he said, "I don't know. You ask the SHO about it." Ajmer Singh requested the Panchayat to pursue his case. Thereafter Ajmer Singh along with the panchayat met SHO Tehal Singh several times. Once or twice, the SHO made a false promise of releasing him but later on the SHO told the Panchayat clearly, "We have killed Kamaljit Singh."

According to Ajmer Singh: "When the police did not give any information even after several days, I submitted applications to Senior Officers the copies of which are attached herewith. Apart from that, I appeared in the courts on many scheduled dates of his (Kamaljit's) cases and submitted applications to various courts where Kamaljit's cases were sub-judice, through my counsel informing them that my son had been arrested by Bagha Purana police. Ultimately, various courts closed the cases saying that they would reopen them when the accused would be present in the court. But the court did not ask the police to produce Kamaljit Singh. In response to the applications which I had sent, I received acknowledgement from the Chief Minister's office only saying that my application had been forwarded to the Home Department.

"I was called twice by Bagha Purana police in connection with the inquiry of my son's case but I don"t know who had ordered the said inquiry. I had gone along with the Panchayat on both the occasions. First time, SHO Bagha Purana, Raj Singh had called me. I narrated the whole incident to him. The SHO obtained my signatures and those of Sarpanch Kirpal Singh on some papers. Six months later, I was called to the police station by ASI Gurmel Singh of Bagha Purana police station. He said, "You quietly sign on the blank papers." I signed, due to fear.

"Even now, I keep on sending applications to the Chief Minister, Agriculture Minister and Senior Officers. But nobody has bothered about me. I should have not signed the papers on both the occasions. But what could I do? The circumstances were such."

Ajmer Singh feels that had he not signed the papers, his son's case might have reached some logical conclusion.

Kamaljit Singh's disappearance has had a deep impact on the mind of his father Ajmer Singh.

**VFF/0882**

Mehar Singh 18 of Sangatpura in Moga. Victim Mehar Singh's father Preetam Singh who lost his eyesight about 25 years ago due to sickness, is a poor Dalit (oppressed class). He had three sons and one daughter. Mehar Singh was the eldest. He was mentally unsound and used to roam arond the village like a lunatic. After Preetam Singh lost his eyesight, the family used to pull on with the help of other people only. Daughter was the eldest. She used to support her family by doing manual labour before her marriage.

In 1992, three days before Lohri (a Punjabi festival) i.e. around 10 January, one night, the police surrounded the village. Mehar Singh used to go out to the fields early in the morning to ease himself. On that day also, as usual, he started from home for the fields to ease himself. The village Granthi (who recites Gurbani at the Gurdwara) saw him, paid him one rupee and persuaded him to go back because the Granthi apprehended danger to Mehar Singh's life in view of the siege laid to the village by the police. However Mehar Singh dodged him and went out of the village from the 'samadh' (tomb) side. It was 7 AM. A few minutes later the family members heard the sound of gun shots. A few minutes later, the police went from door to door and collected all the male members of the village in the village school. At that time the villagers saw the bullet riddled dead body of Mehar Singh lying in the Canter (Four wheeler). All the villagers told the police that he was a lunatic and asked them as to what had they done. Tehal Singh, SHO of Bagha Purana police station and DSP Randhawa were present on the occasion. The Sarpanch (Head of village Council) told these officers that they had killed a lunatic person unjustifiably. But, those officers, instead of listening to him said, "You will tell Pargat Singh Fauji (another absconding youth of the village) also to be a lunatic." The police carried away the body in their vehicle. The above mentioned officers told the Panchayat to reach Moga as the postmortem was to be got conducted. The Panchayat reached Moga. However the police did not reach there. The police brought the body themselves in the evening and cremated it themselves at 9 PM. The family members were allowed to attend the cremation.

The newspapers of the following day carried a news item which stated that a top militant namely Mehar Singh had been killed in an encounter at village Sangatpura. The photograph of his dead body with weapons kept by his side also appeared in the newspapers. The villagers were astonished to read this news items and wondered as to how the police claimed that they had killed a top militant after killing a mentally unsound youth. But, the family members and the village Panchayat could not do anything about it as the police terror was at its peak in those days.

The family members did not get any relief from the Government. On the contrary, once, his father Preetam Singh was called to the police station by Bagha Purana police and questioned about the particulars of all family relations. This inquiry was conducted presumably on suspicion basis as is normally done by the police with the family memebrs of other militants.

### VFF/0883

Veeram Singh 15 of Rode in Moga. Victim Veeram Singh's father Jarnail Singh is a poor Dalit (one who belongs to oppressed class). He had ten children, five daughters and five sons. His two sons namely Charan Singh and Kewal Singh who are married live separately. His all the five daughters are married. Three of his sons namely Mukand Singh, Veeram Singh and Darshan Singh used to live with him. They were making both ends meet by doing manual labour and agricultural farming on contract basis. His family had come under the influence of religious discourses of Sant Jarnail Singh Bhindranwale and got themselves baptised ("Amritdhari") before 1984 itself. Jarnail Singh used to participate in the 'Akali Morchas' (peaceful agitations of Akali Dal— a political party) and whenever the Akali Dal used to give a call for any of their political programmes, he used to partcipate in it.

A few days after the death of his brother Mukand Singh, who was killed at his village by three unidentified armed youth in civil clothes on 6-4-1991, the Bagha Purana police picked up Veeram Singh and tortured him brutally in illegal custody for one month and three weeks. During this period, he was detained at Bagha Purana, Moga and Mehna police stations. Two cases were registered against him. He got released on bail after 3-4 months. Barely two months later, on the third day after Diwali in 1993 at about 9 PM, the police entered their house after scaling the boundary wall while Jarnail Singh, his wife Dalip Kaur and son Veeram Singh were asleep and knocked at the door. The police party of Bagha Purana was headed by the SHO and had a large number of policemen in it. Jarnail Singh and Dalip Kaur recognised Havaldar (Head Constable) Jugraj Singh and Havaldar Gurcharan Singh as they had picked up Veeram Singh earlier also.

On the following day, Jarnail Singh and Dalip Kaur along with Kaur Singh Sarpanch (Head of Village Council), Chowkidar (Watchman) Jeeta Singh and several other persons went to the police station. The SHO flatly denied having picked him up. However, he assured them that he would find out and in case any other police had arrested him he would get him released. Thereafter, the family members met DSP Randhawa, SHO and Havaldar Jugraj Singh several times personally as well as through eminent persons. Initially they continued to assure them that they would release him but after about 3 months, they flatly denied that Veeram Singh was in their custody. Even then, the family members continued to send eminent political persons like Capt. Harcharan Singh Rode, Kaur Singh Sarpanch and Jagdish Singh. But, the police neither released Veeram Singh nor they gave any information about him.

According to his mother Dalip Kaur: "The situation was very bad in those days. The police terror was at its peak. We poor people could not have done anything more than that also. I and my husband begged of the police officers of Bagha Purana and Moga, pleaded with them that we were poor people, but, nobody listened to us. We continued to look for Veeram Singh for 2-3 years but we did not get any clue about his whereabouts. In case the police have killed our son, then, at least they should let us know so that we may reconcile ourselves and sit quietly at home." She is under the impression that her son may still be alive. However she also says that she is losing hope now as so much time had elapsed.

    \*    Dalip Kaur (mother of the victim) also said to the investigation team, "So many people come and write down (their tale of woe). Son, will there be any positive result or not?" But, even this investigation team (Amrik Singh Muktsar and others) had no answer to this query by his mother.

**VFF/0884**

Jagga Singh alias Jagga 30 of Budhsinghwala in Moga. While Gurjant Singh, a cousin of Jagga Singh was in jail, Jagga Singh joined the militant ranks and he was absconding at the time of release of Gurjant Singh.

After the release of Gurjant Singh from jail, Bagha Purana police began raiding Nachhatter Singh's (Gurjant's father) house for arresting Gurjant Singh. Once, the SHO (Station House Officer) of Bagha Purana police station Mr. Madan Lal Dhingra picked up Gurjant Singh and took him to Bagha Purana P.S. (Police Station). From there he was taken to Jaiton P.S. and then to Faridkot C.I.A. (Central Investigation Agency) Staff where he was detained illegally for 10 days. He was tortured brutally at Jaiton P.S. and CIA Staff Faridkot. He was got released from the CIA Staff by the family members and the Panchayat but on the next day itself, SHO of Bagha Purana P.S. raided his house. However, Gurjant Singh had not slept at his house that day. The police picked up Nachhatter Singh and detained him for 15 days. The police asked them to produce Gurjant Singh but Gurjant Singh had absconded once for all. When the family members talked to Gurjant Singh about producing himself before the police, he said, "These people (the police) will kill me. As such, I will not present myself before them now." The family members also felt that there was some logic in his argument, so, they also did not put much pressure on him to present himself before the police.

A few days after Gurjant Singh had absconded, his cousin Jagga Singh was arrested by the police. The Faridkot and Ferozepur police slapped several cases against him and sent him to Sangrur jail where he was detained for 3 years. In the meantime, the police arrested Gurjant Singh's brother Kulwant Singh, implicated him in several cases and sent him to Sangrur jail. Kulwant Singh had been tortured brutally by Faridkot police. As such he was in bad shape physically while in jail.

After Gurjant Singh had absconded in 1986, the police used to pick up his family members. They used to pick up his father Nachhatter Singh, brothers and uncle Chand Singh often and detain them illegally for days together. Once, the SHO of Bagha Purana police station Mr. Gurtej Singh picked up his mother Surjit Kaur also and released her on the following day.

In 1987, a person namely Jarnail Singh was murdered by someone. The police turned the needle of their suspicion towards Chand Singh and Gurjant Singh. keeping in view such an attitude of the police, Chand Singh also began to remain away from his house. As a result, the police began raidsing his house more frequently. In May 1987, under the leadership of Ray-Ribiero combine the police repression was intensified in Punjab and political workers were arrested in large numbers under TADA (Terrorist & Disruptive Activities (Prevention)

Act). During this time, the SHO of Bagha Purana police station Mitt Singh (who was later killed by militants) arrested Gurjant Singh's father Nachhatter Singh and tortured him brutally for 10 days in illegal custody at Bagha Purana police station. Thereafter he implicated him in a case under TADA (that of giving shelter to militants) and sent him to Ferozepur jail. In the meantime, the police began to raid their house regularly. All the family members went underground. The police carried away all household goods including the main gate of the house. None of the family members returned home for complete three years and grass came up all over the house. No agricultural operations could be carried out for three years. Nobody dared to take their land on contract for cultivation due to the fear of the police.

In 1990, slowly, some members of Gurjant Singh's family began to return home and started cultivating their land. But, the fear of the police was still there and none of the male members used to sleep at home. While Gurjant Singh was absconding, the police arrested his sister Charanjit Kaur and brother-in-law (sister's husband) Sukhdev Singh Fauji resident of Kale Ke several times. The police tortured also Sukhdev Singh several times. Apart from that, the police used to pick up his other relatives also like aunts ('Maami', 'Bhua') and uncle ('Phuphar'). Not only that they used to pick up the relatives of their relatives also.

In 1987, while Gurjant Singh's father was in Ferozepur jail, the police arrested Chand Singh from village Ghall Kalan along with 4 other youth including Kuldip Singh r/o village Ghall Kalan from whose tubewell all the five were arrested. About 10 days after their arrest all of them were killed in an "encounter" with the police. At that time, all the family members and relatives were target of police wrath and all of them were homeless. Chand Singh's case could not be pursued. The family members had come to know about Chand Singh's arrest after 2-3 days. 10 days later they read the news in the newspapers about his having been killed in an "encounter" with the police.

In the meantime, Gurjant Singh's brother Kulwant Singh and cousin Jagga Singh were released from Sangrur jail. Even after his release, Kulwant Singh was picked up and tortured brutally by Bagha Purana police several times. Jagga Singh absconded from home 2-3 months after his release and ultimately he was killed in an encounter with the police at village Chhajanwali near Jagraon. During this period, Gurjant Singh's elder brother Jagroop Singh was also picked up several times and subjected to brutal torture by the police.

On 29 July 1992, Gurjant Singh was killed in an encounter with the police at the house of Kaur Singh in Model Town (Extension) at Ludhiana. However, his family remained the target of police wrath even thereafter. The police neither handed over the body of Gurjant Singh to the family members nor got it identified from them. The police put several restrictions on the family even at the time of his 'Bhog' (last rites) ceremony. Only his family memebrs were allowed to attend the same. Even after Gurjant Singh had been killed, Bagha Purana police continued to raid their house and they used to pick up Nachhatter Singh, Jagroop Singh, Kulwant Singh and Jaswant Singh, often. During this period the Bagha Purana police slapped a case under Arms Act against Jaswant Singh and sent him to jail. He was in jail for two months and thereafter he was released on bail.

In 1993, during the Panchayat elections in the Punjab, DSP (Deputy Superintendent of Police) Randhawa of Bagha Purana police arrested Binder Singh s/o Lal Singh, a Mazhabi Sikh and a worker of Jagroop Singh (Gurjant Singh's brother) and detained him for 15 days at the CIA Staff Bagha Purana. Thereafter, he implicated him in a case under the Arms Act and delivering provocative anti-national speeches and sent him to jail. He could be got released on bail only after one month. Now he has been acquitted in that case.

In April 1993, Havaldar (Head Constable) Jagraj Singh of Bagha Purana police along with some constables came in a Canter (four-wheeler), picked up Jaswant Singh on the way who was driving a Tractor and brought him to home to inform the family members that he was taking away Jaswant Singh to the police station as he had been summoned by the officers. After the arrest of Jaswant Singh, his father Nachhatter Singh along with the Sarpanch (Head of Village Council) of the village, Kirpal Singh reached police station Bagha Purana. They met the SHO Mr. Tehal Singh who said, "We will release him in the evening." Nachhatter Singh and the Sarpanch met Jaswant Singh in the police station. Jaswant Singh took off his watch and handed it over to Nachhatter Singh. Same day evening, Nachhater Singh was also picked up from his house by Bagha Purana police. Again the male members of the family began to remain away from home, due to fear. They sent respectable persons to the SHO several times. However, the SHO always used to say, "You don't talk to me about those people at all."

Nachhatter Singh was detained at different police stations and secret (torture) centres. During this period, he was subjected to inhuman torture several times in the presence of SSP (Senior Superintendent of Police) Tiwari, SP (Ops.) Shri Anil Gautam. Six months later, the Bagha

Purana police dropped him at his house. At that time, his physical condition was very bad. He could recover only after medical treatment for several months. It was Head Constable Jugraj Singh who had come to drop Nachhatter Singh at home and he said, "You don't waste money in pursuing his case. Jaswant Singh is no more." The family members accepted it as the Will of God. Of course, they did not have any other alternative either.

In 1995, one day, Kulwant Singh who had started getting fits of insanity due to repeated police torture and whose health had deteriorated too much, breathed his last after a prolonged illness. According to family members the actual reason of Kulwant's death was the repeated police torture. Kulwant Singh was married and has a son namely Bhupinder Singh aged nine years. His wife's parents had got her remarried. Now Nachhatter Singh's elder son Jagroop Singh only is left in their family.

**VFF/0885**

Chamkaur Singh alias Babli 17 of Sangatpura in Moga. The details of this incident are contained in an Affidavit sworn by Roop Singh, father of victim Chamkaur Singh. The same is reproduced below:-

AFFIDAVIT

I, Roop Singh, son of Basant Singh son of Timra Singh, resident of village Sangat Pura, Tehsil Moga, Distt. Faridkot (now district Moga), do hereby solemnly affirm and declare as under:-

1.   That my son, Chamkaur Singh, aged about 17 years, was kidnapped on 21-10-1992, at about 4.00 a.m., by Gurcharan Singh alias "Baba", Sub Inspector, then Station House Officer, Police Station Mehna, Tehsil Moga, in a white colour, Police Gypsy, which was then driven by Saudagar Singh, a Punjab Home Guard, who was also personal Body-guard of said Gurcharan Singh "Baba", and they are related to each other. I personally knew above-said Saudagar Singh, very well, because I performed/worked on contract as a labourer "Siri" in his village Ladhai Ke, with a farmer named Mithoo, and I had rather cordial relations with him. There were about six policemen with them.

2.   That, firstly, the above-said party entered the house of my neighbour namely Binder Singh, and asked him whether he is Roop Singh, who told them directing them to my house. When they entered my house, first of all, I was awaken by a lean Head-constable and asked me whereabouts of my son. I told them that he is asleep in the 'Baithak' of our house (a

small guest room). Then they went in the 'Baithak' where my wife's maternal aunt's son, was also there, who was awaken and asked,"if he was Chamkaur Singh, and seeing police, and being in confusion, suddenly the word "Yes" slipped from his mouth. Then from the next bed, Chamkaur Singh was awaken and asked as to who he was, then my above-said wife's cousin, named "Sira" from village Nathana, said that "he is Chamkaur Singh" — (pointing to my son). Then, the said Head Constable, took up a "Kahi" (Kassi) and beat my said relation with its handle, very severely, who expired about two years later, a natural death.

3. That, thereafter, the said Head Constable caught hold of my son from one arm and another constable caught from the other arm, and then above-said Gurcharan Singh "Baba" ordered them to put my son Chamkaur Singh, in their Gypsy. And, when they were about to leave after putting my son Chamkaur Singh in their Gypsy, I asked the said Gurcharan Singh "Baba" as to from where this police is, and they (above-said Head Constable) replied that they are from Police Station Mehna, and they were taking my son Chamkaur Singh to Police Station Mehna.

4. That, on the morning/day break, I went to Sheera Singh, a farmer and owner of a van/plying as a taxi, with whom my son Chamkaur Singh had worked for sometime in his fields at his village Kotla Rai-ka, to take his help. I took Sheera Singh, above-said (a Zamidar), and Piara Singh, Mazhbi Singh — my distant relative from that village, who happened to be a supporter of Iqbal Singh, candidate for M.L.A., resident of Baghapurana, and then we went to above-said Iqbal Singh at Baghapurana in the van of Sheera Singh. Then we took Iqbal Singh with us to Police Station Mehna.

5. That we reached the Police Station Mehna at about 11 A.M. At the tea-Dhaba near the gate of Police Station Mehna, a police head constable met us. Above-said Iqbal Singh asked him — "Zora Singh, have you brought any boy from village Sangatpura, to which he replied 'No, I was on leave', and he shall confirm it for us. He asked another person, presumably policeman of P.S. Mehna, and then told us that they have not brought, and we were sent back from outside the gate of the police station.

6. That on 22-10-1992, I came to Faridkot and met Head Constable Sukhdev Singh, of our village, at Police Headquarter Office, upstairs of District Courts Buildings, Faridkot, who took me along on a scooter to P.S. Saddar, Faridkot, CIA Staff Faridkot and Police Station City, Faridkot, where it was confirmed that they have not brought my son Chamkaur Singh.

7. That after visiting Faridkot, I went to Goniana at about 4.00 P.M. on 22-10-1992, and reached house of Jalaur Singh, Sub-Inspector Police, who was then posted at P.S. Makhu, and whose wife happened to be my wife's cousin sister from their paternal families. Both of them were incidentally at their house. Jalaur Singh, gave me a letter in the name of Gurcharan Singh, SHO, Mehna, the so-called "Baba".

8. That on 23-10-1992, at about morning, I left Goniana for Bathinda and met Head Constable Roop Singh, C.I.D., Police, Bathinda, who is my maternal uncle's son. He also advised me that Bhallar Singh, their Inspector Police C.I.D., at Bathinda is from village Jitgill from where Gurcharan Singh "Baba" also belongs, and that I should first meet Gurcharan Singh "Baba" with that letter of Jalaur Singh, and if that does not work, then, he will take help of Bhallar Singh, Police Inspector. I returned home at village Sangatpura at about 2/2-30 P.M.

9. That on reaching my village Sangatpura, on 23-10-1992, I sent Preet Singh, my cousin brother and Baldev Singh, my sister's husband, to village Dayalpura Bhai-Ka, to meet Bikkar Singh, husband of my wife's sister, with the request that they should all go and meet Nindi, who is known to Bikkar Singh, and is a transporter and influential person, and they should confirm from Police Station Dayalpura Bhai-Ka, if my son is not transferred to that police station. Then I took a Jeep on hire and went to Iqbal Singh at Baghapurana, and taking Iqbal Singh along, I also reached P.S. Dayalpura Bhai-Ka. The S.H.O. Dayalpura Bhai-Ka told us that they did not go to Sangatpura village nor the boy—Chamkaur Singh has been transferred to their custody by any-one, and he offered the keys that we could see the rooms ourselves.

10. That on 24-10-1992, I visited my relations, etc. to collect money/few hundred rupees from each, making it about 4000/- rupees.

11. That on 25-10-1992, which was also Diwali day, I took along Preet Singh, my cousin brother, Jeet Singh, my brother,

and Balbir Singh of v. Galoti and Harbans Singh, v.Manuke, both husbands of of my sisters, and we went to P.S. Mehna at about 10.00 a.m. We met Gurcharan Singh "Baba" who was present there and delivered to him the letter from Jalaur Singh, aforementioned. Then, he said that he had not gone to our village and he did not know about my son Chamkaur Singh. Then I told him that I have recognised you, and your face was partly covered with 'Black colour 'Loi' (Bhuri) below your nose level, but still I recognise you, and I now also further recognise this Saudagar Singh, Punjab Home Guard, standing here, who has also been previously well known to me rather having cordial relations with me, and you all were there who have brought/kidnapped my son Chamkaur Singh from my house on 21-10-1992. Then we returned home at village Sangatpura.

12.  That on 26-10-1992 I took van on hire, with its driver Sheera, alongwith my brother Jeet Singh, and Jugraj Singh from village Buraj Ladha Singh Wala, who happened to be 'Saddoo'—i.e. husband of sister of Jalaur Singh, aforementioned's wife, and also my relation, and we came to Goniana and met Jalaur Singh. Then Jalaur Singh told us that he would go to Gurcharan Singh "Baba", the next day, and he further assured us that since his letter has reached Gurcharan Singh "Baba", he would no-more harm Chamkaur Singh, any further.

13.  That on 27-10-1992, I alongwith Pooran Singh, a zamidar of our village, (also called Pooran Singh Bhai-Ka (Mann), Sandhura Singh v. Nalkhote, my wife's aunt's husband and Balbir Singh and Harbans Singh, aforementioned husbands of my sisters, reached P.S. Mehna at about 9.00 a.m. and sat outside police station. At about 12-Noon, Jalaur Singh, aforementioned, reached at police station Mehna. He went inside the Police Station, and came back from inside the police station after about two hours, and told us that my son Chamkaur Singh is not there, but Chhinda son of Bhagat of village Kotla Rae-Ka is present in the Police Station Mehna, who they have brought day-before yesterday. I told then Jalaur Singh that my son is very well here. Then Jalaur Singh took me alone inside the police station and himself sat behind in a chair, while I was seated in front of Gurcharan Singh "Baba". Gurcharan Singh said that he did not go to our village, and I may be mistaken because sometimes faces are identical (identities are similar).

I told him that this is not at all the case here, because I have recognised you, as well as the Head Constable here and also Saudagar Singh, your body-guard-cum-driver of Gypsy. And then Gurcharan Singh "Baba" said that he will trace/find out my son Chamkaur Singh and that I should contact him later. Then Jalaur Singh said that I should meet him a day-after the following ('parson'), whereupon, Gurcharan Singh said I should meet him after six days, and that I should meet him alone and nobody should accompany me to him.

14. That after six days, after having stayed inside my house, I reached P.S. Mehna at about 9.00 a.m. and the police on guard asked me to wait and they shall seek permission from Station House Officer, Gurcharan Singh "Baba", and they went in, returned telling me that I should wait for about an hour, and I shall be called in by the S.H.O. later on. Then after about two hours waiting, I was called in at about 11.00 a.m. It was Sunday, around 2/3 Sept. 1992. Then he told me that Chamkaur Singh my son is in custody of another officer, and that we should give around rupees one lac and he will get my son released/freed. Then I asked him that I don't have any money because I am a labourer only and a daily wage earner, and he may challan my son. Then he further said that if challan is required, he don't have the boy, then.

15. That the following day, I went to Bathinda and brought Roop Singh Head Constable and Bhallar Singh, Inspector Police of Gurcharan Singh Baba's village, to P.S. Mehna, who contacted said Gurcharan Singh, and he told them that he has already conveyed to me that he is not having the boy with him, but if I meet him alone, he shall get the boy released from another person if I meet him alone. Both these officials, after conveying this to me, left Mehna P.S., in a Maruti van (Red colour), which I had hired for them from Bathinda, who dropped Bhallar Singh at v. Jitgill and took Roop Singh to leave at Bathinda.

16. That on the following day, I had gone to village Ladhai-Ke, at my 'Masi's' (mother's sister house), the aforementioned Saudagar Singh, Punjab Home Guard, who also belongs to village Ladhai-Ke, saw me in my relation's house and he called me to his own house at about 11.00 a.m. He then told me that, if I had not met him incidentally here, he was to come to my village Sangatpura to meet me. He then said that if I could manage to arrange about Rs. 60,000/- for them, your (my)

son can be saved. I told him that I do not have any cash on me, and even nobody will purchase my house so quickly, but I have only two she-buffaloes, which my family can give. Then Saudagar Singh, Punjab Home-guard said that without cash "Kaam Mushkil Hai", work is difficult.

17. That, thereafter, I went to meet Gurmail Singh, Sarpanch, of village Maur-Nau-abad, residing at village Bhagta Bhai-Ka. That on the 3rd day of my going to him, he told me that I should meet him the following day. I took a Jeep on hire, from my village Sangatpura, with owner driver Iqbal Singh, and we took Gurmail Singh, Sarpanch, from Bhagta Bhai-Ka, and went to village Jitgill and took Ajaib Singh from that village (village of also Gurcharan Dsingh 'Baba') and reached P.S. Mehna at about 12 Noon or 1.00 p.m. and met Gurcharan Singh S.H.O. and then he totally refused denying that he had not gone to village Sangatpura, and then we returned back.

18. That after doing free labour for about three days at the house of Baldev Singh, Sarpanch of our village, I took him along to Gurcharan Singh 'Baba', to him also, he denied having gone to our village.

19. That after another 5-6 days, I went taking along Baldev Singh Bhatti, M.L.A., along with his father-in-law Chand Singh, village Galoti, to Gurcharan Singh, but he again denied.

20. That after about four months, I met Jaswant Singh, A.S.I. police, of v. Pipli and Lakhwinder Singh, Distt. Judge of v. Moranwali, both at a marriage at village Moranwali, and told them the above. Jaswant Singh met Gurcharan Singh 'Baba'. Gurcharan Singh 'Baba' told him that why he did not meet him earlier and that now the said boy had been killed by him. Then same thing was conveyed to me through relations of Jaswant Singh that Chamkaur Singh, my son, has been killed by Gurcharan Singh 'Baba' S.H.O. P.S. Mehna and final rites may be performed by me.

21. That I heard speech of Sardar Simranjit Singh Mann, that such excesses by the police should be reported on an sworn affidavit and justice would be met, through the courts of law. But, being a very poor person, having no any money for engaging a counsel, I thought it all impossible. But, I have been now hopeful that justice is being met even to poor persons against criminal policemen by the Supreme court/law courts of India, as coming in newspapers, which was impossible previously,

and as in the past, whosoever raised a voice or gave a vent of police misdeed was vanished for ever. I am prayfully hopeful that justice would be met to our marooned down-trodden family of Scheduled Caste (Mazhbi Sikh), and hence the whole tale of our woes about my minor son is vented through this affidavit.

22. That as it has come through the press-media/newspapers, criminal policemen, who committed extra-judicial murders of persons, etc. reached higher horizons of promotions, and are now occupying higher positions, in police headquarters of districts, etc. or even upwards. Many of those, though have been found guilty, of murders, etc. by the Apex Court and other courts, the State police authorities and the State of Punjab, have patronised and tended and attempted to support some such criminals at State level, which lends undoubted credence to the proof that some such extra-judicial murders by those criminal policemen, had the patronage, behest and backing of higher police echelon of the State headed by the State Police Chief of Punjab. Hence, it is prayed that orders be given only to the Central Bureau of Investigation to conduct investigation and submit their report to the Apex Court, as otherwise, if inquiry is ordered to be carried out by Punjab Police, it may result in liquidation of more innocent lives—of us, or involving in false cases, and will prove counter-productive, supporting police and suppression of innocent sufferers, and thus the criminals who have liquidated our minor son, Chamkaur Singh, for lust of money/promotion, would make mockery and laugh at us and make do further damage.

23. It is further prayed that this affidavit of mine be treated as an application for award of compensation and damages, etc. etc. as the Hon'ble courts/authorities may deem fit, as my family is poor and all indigent persons—myself (deponent—Roop Singh), Baldev Kaur, Joginder Singh, 14 years, Tarsem Singh, 12 years,—father, mother and minor brothers of deceased Chamkaur Singh, respectively, to whom our son Chamkaur Singh, was to support.

Dated:    12-11-1998

                                                        DEPONENT

Roop Singh s/o Basant Singh
r/o village Sangatpura, P.S. Mehna

Tehsil & Distt. Moga (Punjab).

I, Roop Singh, above-named deponent, do hereby further solemnly affirm and declare that the above statement of mine is true and correct to the best of my knowledge and belief and nothing has been concealed or mis-stated therein, and I have been explained its contents in Punjabi, the language I understand.

DEPONENT

:Moga

Dated:      18 Nov 1998                    (Roop Singh—above named)

**VFF/0886**

Suba Singh alias Amarjit Singh 38 of Sukhna Ablu, Giddarbaha in Moga. Suba Singh had joined the Army Medical Corps after passing his Matriculation. In 1977-78, Suba Singh quit the Army service and came home. Suba Singh had got married in 1976. After leaving the Army, Suba Singh set up a shop at village Dadda and started practising medicine. After the Army attack on Darbar Sahib in 1984, Suba Singh became religious minded and he got himself and his whole family baptised ("Amritdhari"). Suba Singh's wife was employed at the time of her marriage itself.

Being religious minded, Suba Singh used to participate in religious functions enthusiastically. No case had ever been registered against Suba Singh.

It was Novemebr 1991. A boy from our village namely Surjan Singh s/o................ (who had a farm in Rajasthan) was arrested by Rajasthan police. Suba Singh had family relations with the family of Surjan Singh. On 22 Novemebr 1991, Suba Singh had gone from home to Rai Singh Nagar (Distt. Ganganagar, Rajasthan) for pursuing the case of Surjan Singh. On 25 November 1991 while Suba Singh was on his way back home, he was arrested by Rajasthan police at Rai Singh Nagar Bus Stand. 3-4 days later, as his family members came to know about his arrest, his father Inder Singh along with other relatives, went to Rai Singh Nagar. There they came to know that the Rajasthan police had registered a case against Suba Singh and sent him to Ganganagar jail. His family members met him also twice in Ganganagar jail.

On 1 January 1992 in the evening, we received a message that the Kot Bhai police had brought Suba Singh on police remand from Ganganagar jail and that they had obtained a police remand from the court of Magistrate at Giddarbaha. Three other men namely Surjan Singh r/o Sukhna Ablu, Malkit Singh r/o Dan Singh Wala (Distt. Bathinda) and another youth also were brought on remand from Ganganagar jail alongwith Suba Singh. On the night of 1 January 1992, a police party of Kot Bhai P.S. led by SHO Bhupinder Singh raided our village and picked up myself (Mohinder Kaur—Wife) and the mother of a youth Sukhmandar Singh of our village and took us to Kot Bhai police station. They detained us for the night there and released us in the morning. The family members and prominent persons of the village tried to meet Suba Singh during his police remand, but, were not allowed to do so by the police. The family members were scared lest the police should kill Suba Singh.

On 6th or 7th January (I don't remember the date) a news item was published in the newspapers which stated that a police party escorting four militants was attacked by the militants and in the encounter which ensued, three militants namely Surjan singh, Malkit Singh and another (whose name I don't remember) were killed while another militant namely Suba Singh escaped from police custody.

Later on, the family members were told unofficially by some policemen and some other people who had been in police custody at that time, that on the night of the above mentioned encounter, the police never took out Suba Singh from the lock-up. For some time, the family members hoped that Suba singh may be still in police custody. But, the police did not disclose anything about it. They maintained that he had escaped from their custody.

We can't say for sure as to what happened to Suba Singh, after all. However we are damn sure that the claim of the police that Suba Singh had escaped from their custody is a bundle of lies.

Had I not been saddled with the responsibility of looking after my children and had there not been terror of the police, I would have definitely struggled to get justice for this incident involving my husband. I am scared that if I initiate any action, it may generate a backlash for my children. I am not afraid of any danger to my own life, but I am scared of any incident which might involve my children.

My family is getting two square meals a day and my children are being brought up; thanks to my job. Otherwise we would have been in dire straits.

We had seen a ray of hope (of getting justice) at the time of formatiion of Akali Govt in Punjab but now that hope had been shattered.

After this incident involving my husband, till date, the police have visited our house several times. Each time they note down the complete family history. This process is continuing even today due to which my family is terrorised. My children are always in a state of mental tension. Despite my best efforts I have not been able to get rid my children of this mental tension.

**VFF/0887**

Balraj Singh alias Baja 23 of Thandewala in Muktsar. S. Bohar Singh had two sons namely Balraj Singh and Gurbaj Singh. Balraj Singh was his elder son. Balraj Singh studied upto sixth standard and thereafter he began to assist his father in agricultural farming. Balraj Singh was a hard working and religious minded youth. In 1992, the police of Sadar (Muktsar) police station picked up Balraj Singh for the first time on the basis of suspicion and tortured him brutally for 2-3 days in illegal custody. The village Panchayat and prominent political leaders intervened and got Balraj Singh released from police custody. But, the condition of Balraj Singh was pathetic at that time due to police beating and he was unable to walk for many days. S.I. Bhupinder Singh was the incharge of Sadar (Muktsar) police station at that time.

In the beginning of month of 'Jeth' (around 15th May) 1993, Gurdarshan Singh, SHO of Sadar (Muktsar) police station raided our house. Balraj Singh was not at home on that day. The police party picked up Balraj Singh's grand mother (aged 80 years) and his wife Jaswinder Kaur and took them away and directed the family members to produce Balraj Singh. The women were released after two days. However, the police raids continued. The family members began to stay away from home due to fear of the police. Scared of this action of the police, the family members planned to produce Balraj Singh (in front of the police) through some responsible political leader because in those days, the police often used to pick up the youth from home and kill them in fake encounters. Family members approached various political leaders in this connection. But, due to the situation being bad, no politician was ready to take the responsibility. In the meantime the police used to raid the house of another youth also of our village namely Gurjant Singh s/o Ishar Singh and ask the family members to produce him. Apart from that, the police of Sadar police station had arrested Gulzar Singh of the same village who was the District President of the Sikh Students Federation.

On 10th 'Jeth' (around 25th May) 1993, Balraj Singh's father Bohar Singh and family members of Gurjant Singh alongwith prominent persons of the village handed over Balraj Singh and Gurjant Singh to Gurdarshan Singh, SHO of Sadar (Muktsar) police station at about 9 A.M. The SHO assured these people that they would release them after few days of interrogation.

That 3-4 days later, when the family members of Balraj Singh approached Sadar police to know the fate of Balraj Singh, they were not allowed to enter the police station and were told that they had been sent to C.I.A Staff Faridkot. The family members did not dare to approach Faridkot C.I.A due to terror of the police. They waited in the hope that the police would release them on their own.

The newspapers of 6th 'Harh' (around 20th June) 1993 carried a news item which stated that three militants had been killed in an "encounter" with the police near village Jhuraran near Malout. One was identified as Mandar Singh resident of Bhuttiwala and other two had been declared as "unidentified". The family members and the villagers got suspicious on reading this news items that the "unidentified" youth were Balraj Singh and Gurjant Singh only. Because the family members knew that Mandar Singh also had been produced at Sadar police station through an Akali leader from his family namely Diyal Singh Sandhu. But, Diyal Singh had not accepted the responsibility of producing Balraj Singh and Gurjant Singh saying that it was beyond his control. Mandar Singh had been produced about 5-6 days earlier to Balraj Singh and Gurjant Singh.

On the day following the publication of this news item, a police party raided our house, searched it and went back. Thereafter, the police never visited our house.

That officially, the police never intimated the family members as to what happened to Balraj Singh, after all. However, the family members are damn sure that out of the three youth killed in the so called encounter at village Jhuraran, one was Balraj Singh. As such, family members accepted it as the Will of God and kept quiet.

That 3-4 days after the publication of the said news item, the police released the Federation leader Gulzar Singh of the same village who told the family that Balraj Singh and Gurjant Singh were detained at C.I.A Staff Faridkot for 15 days along with him. And that one day at 10 P.M. the police took both of them out from there. At that time, Comrade Rajinder Raja and Balwinder Singh resident of Boora Gujjar also had been detained at the C.I.A Staff. Inspector Kashmira Singh was the incharge of C.I.A Staff at that time. However, interrogation used to be carried out under the supervision of SSP Tiwari and SP (Operations). Balraj Singh and Gurjant Singh had been subjected to inhuman torture. This fact was disclosed to the family members by youth who were released from the Faridkot C.I.A Staff.

The family did not take any action against this illegal action of the police due to the terror of the police. Even today, the family is scared that if they initiated any action, the police might harm them.

**VFF/0888**

Surjan Singh 40 of Sukhna Ablu in Muktsar. Surjan Singh was brought by Kot Bhai police on police remand from Ganganagar

(Rajasthan) jail in October 1991. He was killed by the police of Kot Bhai police station on 6-1-1992.

### VFF/0889
Sahib Singh alias Punjab Singh 17 of Sangan in Kaithal. On 6-6-84, he attained martyrdom during the attack on Harmandir Sahib by the Indian Army.

### VFF/0890
Hardev Singh son of Sulakhan Singh 21 years old of Panj Garaian, Batala in Gurdaspur. He was disappeared on 18th March 1991.

VFF/0891　　61Hardial Singh of Kotli Surat Malian in Gurdaspur was disappeared on March 4, 1990.

VFF/0892　　Kashmir Singh 25 of Ransike Talla, Dera Baba Nanak in Gurdaspur. He was killed on April 8, 1992.

VFF/0893　　Santokh Singh 26 of Ransike Talla, Dera Baba Nanak in Gurdaspur. He was killed on December 12, 1993.

VFF/0894　　Sulakhan Singh 50 of Panj Garaian, Batala in Gurdaspur. He was killed on May 29, 1991.

VFF/0895　　Nishan Singh Kanwar 23 of Ransike Talla, Dera Baba Nanak in Gurdaspur. He was killed on September 12, 1992.

VFF/0896　　Satnam Singh of Ransike Talla, Dera Baba Nanak in Gurdaspur. He was killed in 1991.

VFF/0897　　Dalbir Singh 20 of Jiwan Nangal, Shikharmachian in Gurdaspur was killed on September 7, 1992.

VFF/0898　　Sukhdev Singh of Panj Garaian, Batala in Gurdaspur. He was disappeared on May 29, 1991.

VFF/0899　　Kulwant Singh of Butter Kalan in Gurdaspur was killed in 1993.

**VFF/0900** Gurdev Singh of Panj Garaian, Batala in Gurdaspur. He was disappeared on November 13, 1991.

VFF/0901　　Harwant Singh of Rasulpur in Gurdaspur was killed in August 1990.

VFF/0902　　Sukhwinder Singh 33 of Nagera Dhadiala in Batala, Gurdaspur was killed on May 18, 1991.

VFF/0903　　Sukhwinder Singh 27 of Najuara Dhadiala in Batala, Gurdaspur was killed on January 26, 1991.

VFF/0904　　Lakha Singh of Malakpur in Batala, Gurdaspur was killed on May 15, 1998.

VFF/0905　　Baljit Kaur of Malakpur in Batala, Gurdaspur was killed in January 1991.

VFF/0906　　Gurdial Singh of Kalian, Batala in Gurdaspur was killed in December 1991.

VFF/0907          Ranjit Singh of Dialgarh, Batala in Gurdaspur was killed on January 15, 1997.

VFF/0908          Parmjeet Singh Billu 20 of Najuara Dhadiala in Batala, Gurdaspur was killed in 1990.

VFF/0909          Pall Singh 30 of Najuara Dhadiala in Batala, Gurdaspur was killed and disappeared. The family does not know when and how was he killed.

**VFF/0910**          Malkiat Singh 31 of Najuara Dhadiala in Batala, Gurdaspur was killed in 1990.

VFF/0911          Baljit Singh 40 of Jiwan Nangal, Shikharmachian in Gurdaspur was killed on May 14, 1989.

VFF/0912          Mohinder Singh of Malakpur in Gurdaspur was killed on January 1, 1991.

VFF/0913          Sukhwinder Singh of Malakpur in Gurdaspur was killed on May 16, 1998.

VFF/0914          Santokh Singh of Kullian, Windala Granthian in Gurdaspur was killed by the police but the family has no information as to when and how.

VFF/0915          Rajinderpal Singh of Kullian, Windala Granthian in Gurdaspur was killed by the police but the family has no information as to when and how.

VFF/0916          Sarabjit Singh of Dehar Fattopur in Dera Baba Nanak in Gurdaspur was killed in 1990.

VFF/0917          Lovejit Singh of Sikdar Masian, Dihaanpur in Gurdapsur was killed by the police but the family has no information as to when and how.

VFF/0918          Jaswinder Singh of Athwal, Dehar Fattopur in Dera Baba Nanak in Gurdaspur was killed by the police but the family has no information as to when and how.

VFF/0919          Harjinder Singh of Butter Kalan in Gurdaspur was killed on January 16, 1990.

**VFF/0920** Baljeet Kaur of Malkpur in Gurdaspur was killed bu police in January 1991.

VFF/0921          Ranjit Singh of Dialgarh, Batala in Gurdaspur was killed on January 15, 1997.

VFF/0922          Dalbir Singh of Jiwan Nangal in Gurdaspur was killed on September 7, 1992.

VFF/0923          Kulwinder Singh of Mastkot in Gurdaspur was killed on June 22, 1991.

VFF/0924          Kanwaljit Singh of Sarwali in Gurdapsur was killed on May 12, 1989.

VFF/0925        Baljit Singh of Jiwan Nangal in Gurdaspur was killed by the police but the family has no information.

VFF/0926        Bachan Singh of Jiwan Nangal in Gurdaspur was killed by the police but the family has no information.

# Appendix I

**Akali Dal:** The main political party professing to be the political representatives of the Sikhs.

**Akhand Pathi:** Priest who recites Gurbani.

**Akhand Paths:** continuous recitation of Gurbani (Verses from Sri Guru Granth Sahib).

**Amritdharis:** Baptised Sikhs. Amritdhari (or baptized Sikhs) are not to cut their hair, consume any alcohol or drugs, and not to eat meat. Sikhs are to meditate on One God only and never to do idol worship. The Amrit bearer has five symbols or articles of faith, which he or she is always to keep with them. These five symbols are Hair (covered), Comb, Steel bracelet, under shorts and a small sword. The sword is emblem of courage and self-defense. It symbolizes dignity and self-reliance, the capacity and readiness to always defend the weak and the oppressed. It helps sustain one's martial spirit and the determination to sacrifice oneself in order to defend the truth, Sikh moral values and suppress the oppression. When all other means of self-protection fail, the Sikh can use his sword to protect himself. A Sikh will never use his sword to attack anyone.

**APO:** Army Post Office.

**Bhog:** The culmination of the Akhand Path which is performed as a closing of the recitation of the Guru Granth Sahib.

**Brahmin:** Highest caste in the Hindus. They are preachers by profession.

**CBI:** Central Bureau of Investigation a premier institution of the Central Government on the lines of the FBI.

**Chowki:** Police post.

**CIA Staff:** Central Investigating Staff, a unit of Panjab Police that interrogated the criminals and all those who came under its suspicion.

**D:** The abbreviation D when used after a Police rank means Detective.

**Dharma Bhain:** An adopted sister.

**FIR:** First Information Report which is submitted as an application against any crime. It is the preliminary step of filing a case in the police station.

**Gatra Kirpan:** A miniature sword worn by baptised Sikhs across their shoulders with the help of a cloth belt called Gatra.

**Istagasa:** A habeas Corpus.

**Sikh:** A caste in Sikhs referring to a farmer.

**Jutti:** Panjabi shoes.

**Kharku:** A term in vernacular meaning a militant and it was often used for the boys involved in militant activity during that period.

**Kurta:** Shirt or upper top worn over Indian Pyajamas.

**Langar:** Sikh Community Kitchen where everyone partakes of the meals irrespective of the caste or class.

**Maruti:** A Car Brand in India.

**Mazhabi Sikh**: A caste in Sikhs referring to menial labour. Professions that are "described" as castes like "Ramgarhia for Carpenter", "Jutt for Farmer", "Mazhabi for Worker" "Luhar for Ironsmith", etc, etc, are not castes when followed by Sikhs. These are their ancestral professions.

**Nambardar:** Headman.

**Ops:** The abbreviation Ops when used after a police rank means Operations.

**Panchayat:** An elected village council with constitutional rights in the Indian democratic system.

**Ramgarhia:** A caste representing carpenters by profession.

**Sadar:** Terminology used to denote a zone of Police division within a district and a town.

**Sevadar:** Voluntary helper in the Gurudwaras.

# APPENDIX II

**INDIAN POLICE TERMINOLOGY ACCORDING TO HIERARCHY**

Recruitment to the Police is made at 4 levels—viz., the Constables, Sub Inspectors (SI), Deputy Superintendent of Police (DSP) and Assistant Superintendent of Police (ASP)

**Constable**: are the junior most police officers generally posted in police stations and chowkis i.e. police check posts.
**Head Constable:** are promoted through a test conducted at the state level. The officers are posted the same way a constable.
**Assistant Sub Inspector:** are promoted or recruited direct through a test conducted at the state level. They undergo a six month training at Panjab Police Academy Phillaur.
**Sub Inspector:** are promoted from the ASI. They undergo a six month training at Panjab Police Academy Phillaur.
**Inspector:** are promoted from the SI. They undergo a six month training at Panjab Police Academy Phillaur.
**Deputy Superintendent of Police:** are promoted or recruited direct through a test conducted at the state level by the Panjab Civil Services Board. They undergo one year's training at Panjab Police Academy Phillaur.
**Superintendent of Police:** are promoted or recruited direct through a test conducted at the national level by the Indian Civil Services Board.

**The subsequent positions are achieved through promotion based on merit and length of service.**

**Senior Superintendent of Police:**
**Deputy Inspector General of Police:**
**Inspector General of Police:**
**Director General of Police:**

# Bibliography

Dhillon, Gurdarshan Singh. "11pp." 27 April 2006. www.globalsikhstudies.net/articles/isc2k/Gurdarshan%20Singh%20Dhillon%201.doc

Torture  http://www.amnesty.ca/resource_centre/news/view.php?load=arcview&article=332&c=Resource+Centre+News

Tools of Torture
http://www.commondreams.org/headlines03/1203-05.htm

International Justice
http://www.amnestyusa.org/international_justice/index.do

Prevention of Torture and Other Cruel, Inhuman or Degrading Treatment or Punishment by Agents of the State
http://www.amnestyusa.org/stoptorture/document.do?id=B10C72B4FFC25C7180256FEA00424B4F

Denounce Torture: Get Involved!
http://www.amnestyusa.org/stoptorture/index.do

Punjab police yet to act against its encounter specialist
http://www.hindu.com/2006/10/16/stories/2006101603890500.htm

India: Human Rights Developments
http://www.hrw.org/reports/1992/WR92/ASW-07.htm

Convention Against Torture And Other Cruel, Inhuman Or Degrading Treatment Or Punishment
http://www.hrweb.org/legal/cat.html

UN Convention (I) for the Amelioration of the Condition of the
Wounded and Sick in Armed Forces in the Field
http://www.hrweb.org/legal/geneva1.html

Code Of Criminal Procedure
http://www.indialawinfo.com/bareacts/crpc.html

Special Rapporteur on torture and other cruel, inhuman or degrading
treatment or punishment.
http://www.ohchr.org/english/issues/torture/rapporteur/

Convention against Torture and Other Cruel, Inhuman or Degrading
Treatment or Punishment
http://www.ohchr.org/english/law/cat.htm

Optional Protocol to the Convention against Torture and Oher Cruel,
Inhuman or Degrading Treatment or Punishment
http://www.ohchr.org/english/law/cat-one.htm

Panjab Police Code
http://www.punjabpolice.gov.pk/user_files/File/code_of_criminal_
procedure_1898.pdf

The Rome Statute
http://www.un.org/law/icc/index.html

The Convention on the Elimination of All Forms of Discrimination
against Women
http://www.un.org/womenwatch/daw/cedaw/

Geneva Convention relative to the Treatment of Prisoners of War
http://www.unhchr.ch/html/menu3/b/91.htm

Geneva Convention relative to the Protection of Civilian Persons in
Time of War
http://www.unhchr.ch/html/menu3/b/92.htm

Protocol Additional to the Geneva Conventions of 12 August 1949, and
relating to the Protection of Victims of International Armed Conflicts
(Protocol 1)
http://www.unhchr.ch/html/menu3/b/93.htm

Protocol Additional to the Geneva Conventions of 12 August 1949, and Relating to the Protection of Victims of Non-International Armed Conflicts (Protocol II)
http://www.unhchr.ch/html/menu3/b/94.htm

International Covenant on Civil and Political Rights
http://www.unhchr.ch/html/menu3/b/a_ccpr.htm

International Covenant on Economic, Social and Cultural Rights
http://www.unhchr.ch/html/menu3/b/a_cescr.htm

Convention on the Rights of the Child
http://www.unhchr.ch/html/menu3/b/k2crc.htm

Convention relating to the Status of Refugees
http://www.unhchr.ch/html/menu3/b/o_c_ref.htm

Geneva Convention for the Amelioration of the Condition of Wounded, Sick and Shipwrecked Members of Armed Forces at Sea
http://www.unhchr.ch/html/menu3/b/q_genev2.htm

Books:
Michel Foucault. *Discipline and Punish: The Birth of the Prison*. trans. Alan Sheridan, London: Penguin, 1991.
Crossette Barbara. *India: Facing the Twentieth-First Century*. Bloomington: Indiana University Press, 1993.
Geelani Bismillah Geelani. *Manufacturing Terrorism: Kashmiri Encounters with Media and the Law*. New Delhi: Promilla and Co. Publishers, 2006.
Dhillon G S. *India Commits Suicide*. Chandigarh: Singh and Singh Publishers, 2004.
Hayner Priscilla B. *Unspeakable Truths: Facing the Challenge of Truth Commissions*. New York: Routledge, 2002.

# ENDNOTES

1   Paramjeet Kaur Khalra, Personal interview, 11/04/2006
2   Ibid
3   Ibid
4   Personal interview, 20/05/06
5   Amar Singh, Person interview, 20/05/06
6   Station House Officer, the title given to the officer in charge of a police station.
7   Village council often made up of elders
8   Deputy Superintendent of Police
9   Gurdev Kaur, Op Cit.
10  Gurdev Kaur, Op Cit.
11  Ibid
12  Paramjeet Kaur, Op Cit.
13  Ibid
14  Ibid
15  Ibid
16  Ibid
17  **The instr**uctions were issued through an army circular known as "Baat Cheet", A publication of the Department of Defense, Government of India, Serial Number 153, July 1984; reproduced in "Surya" a Monthly magazine of October 1984, page 6 and it read as under :- "Some of our innocent countrymen were administered oath in the name of religion to support extremists and actively participate in the act of terrorism. These people wear a miniature kirpan round their neck and are called *Amritdhari* .... Any knowledge of the *'Amritdharis'*, who are dangerous people and pledged to commit murders, arson and acts of terrorism, should immediately be brought to the notice of the authorities. These people may appear harmless from outside but they are basically committed to terrorism. In the interest of all of us their identity and whereabouts must always be disclosed."

Dr Ranbir Singh Sandhu. *Struggle for Justice: Speeches and Conversations of Sant Jarnail Singh Bhindranwale.* Ohio: Sikh Educational and Religious Foundation, 1999. Email: butalia.1@osu.edu *also available at* www.sikhgenocide.org

18  As per the official version given by the government in its white paper the army raided 38 Gurudwaras ,where as unoffical versions claim the figure to be 72. A total strength of eleven infantry divisions, roughly two lakh strength, apart from thousands of paramilitaries, were deployed in Panjab to flush out the so-called terrorists and to seal the Pakistan border. According to the Government version, 38 Gurudwara including the Golden Temple complex, were to be dealt with, but in actual fact 72 Gurudwara were attacked. For the Amritsar operation, one division, roughly 18,000 personnel, was earmarked to deal with 40 terrorists on the Government wanted list a figure given out by the Home Minister, Government of India, in the Parliament a few days prior to the attack. Even Rajiv Gandhi had said that Sant Bhindranwale, whose name was, most probably, included in the list of 40, was a religious leader and not a terrorist. Hardit Singh. "The Amritsar Tragedy", *Abstracts of Sikh Studies.* July 1984. 1380, Sector 33-C, Chandigarh 160 047 also available at www.sikh-history.com.

19  Official figures of Delhi killings were 2733, whereas unofficial figures reveal 4000 killings. www.carnage84.com

20  **SUPREME COURT OF INDIA**
Before :- Kuldip Singh & S. Saghir Ahmed, JJ.
Writ Petition (Criminal) No. 497 of 1995. D/d. 15.11.1995.
15.11.1995.
Mrs. **Paramjit Kaur** - Petitioner Versus **State** of **Panjab** - Respondents

21  http://nhrc.nic.in/

22  Ibid

23  http://nhrc.nic.in/

24  Section 36 of the Act relates to "Matters not subject to jurisdiction of the Commission" and its section (2) reads as follows "The Commission or the State Commission shall not inquire into any matter after the expiry of one year from the date on which the act constituting violation of human rights is alleged to have been committed." http://nhrc.nic.in/hract.htm

25  http://nhrc.nic.in/

26  Ibid

27 http://nhrc.nic.in/
28 Priscilla B. Hayner, "Introduction," *Unspeakable Truths: Facing the Challenge of Truth Commissions,* New York; Routledge, 2002, p. 6
29 Priscilla B. Hayner, p.11.
30 http://www.usip.org/library/tc/doc/reports/el_salvador/tc_es_03151993_intro.html
31 http://www.usip.org/library/tc/doc/reports/chile/chile_1993_pt1_ch1.html#A
32 National Intelligence Directorate. http://www.usip.org/library/tc/doc/reports/chile/chile_1993_acronyms.html
33 National Center for Information http://www.usip.org/library/tc/doc/reports/chile/chile_1993_acronyms.html
34 http://www.usip.org/library/tc/doc/reports/chile/chile_1993_pt4_ch1.html
35 http://www.usip.org/library/tc/doc/reports/chile/chile_1993_pt4_ch3.html
36 http://hrw.org/english/docs/2000/12/01/chile634.htm
37 http://www.pbs.org/newshour/bb/latin_america/july-dec97/argentina_10-16.html
38 http://en.wikipedia.org/wiki/Proceso_de_Reorganizaci%C3%B3n_Nacional
39 http://www.derechos.org/koaga/iii/1/cuya.html#arg
40 http://www.yendor.com/vanished/madres.html
41 Priscilla B. Hayner, p.34.
42 Priscilla B. Hayner p. 38.
43 http://www.usip.org/library/tc/doc/reports/el_salvador/tc_es_03151993_intro.html
44 http://www.usip.org/library/tc/doc/reports/el_salvador/tc_es_03151993_casesA.html
45 http://www.usip.org/library/tc/doc/reports/el_salvador/tc_es_03151993_chron1.html
46 http://www.usip.org/library/tc/doc/reports/el_salvador/tc_es_03151993_V.html
47 http://www.greensborotrc.org/mandate.doc (last visited 11/20/06)
48 http://www.greensborotrc.org/exec_summary.pdf (last visited 11/20/06)
49 http://www.greensborotrc.org/exec_summary.pdf (last visited 11/20/06)
50 http://www.greensborotrc.org/exec_summary.pdf Last visited on 11/21/2006
51 http://nhrc.nic.in/Panjab.htm Last visited on 11/21/2006

52   http://www.greensborotrc.org/exec_summary.pdf

53   Priscilla B. Hayner. P 45.

54   http://www.usip.org/library/pa/guatemala/guat_940623.html   Last
     visited on 11/21/2006

55   Priscilla B. Hayner. P. 47.

56   Priscilla B. Hayner. P. 47.

57   http://shr.aaas.org/guatemala/ceh/report/english/conc1.html   Last
     visited on 11/21/2006

58   http://shr.aaas.org/guatemala/ceh/report/english/conc2.html   Last
     visited on 11/21/2006

59   http://shr.aaas.org/guatemala/ceh/report/english/conc2.html   Last
     visited on 11/21/2006

60   http://nhrc.nic.in/ Last visited on 11/21/2006

1654059

Made in the USA